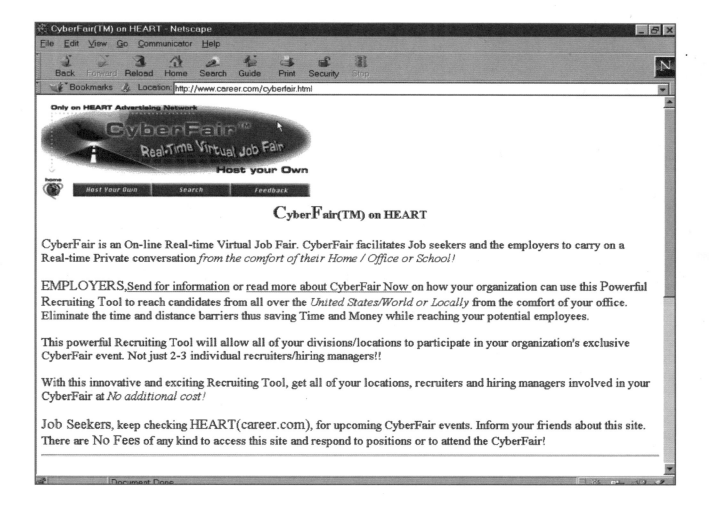

In addition to the HR Web Wisdom links, you'll find other useful material on the Mondy Web site including Internet exercises, regular updates to chapter material, and more.
Visit the site at: **www.prenhall.com/mondy**

SEVENTH EDITION

HUMAN RESOURCE MANAGEMENT

SEVENTH EDITION

HUMAN RESOURCE MANAGEMENT

R. WAYNE MONDY, SPHR
McNeese State University

ROBERT M. NOE, SPHR
Texas A&M University-Commerce

SHANE R. PREMEAUX
McNeese State University

Prentice Hall, Upper Saddle River, NJ 07458

Senior Editor:	Stephanie Johnson
Editorial Assistant:	Hersch Doby
Editor-in-Chief:	Natalie Anderson
Marketing Manager:	Tamara Wederbrand
Senior Production Editor:	Judith Leale
Managing Editor:	Dee Josephson
Manufacturing Buyer:	Ken Clinton
Manufacturing Supervisor:	Arnold Vila
Manufacturing Manager:	Vincent Scelta
Designer:	Cheryl Asherman
Design Manager:	Patricia Smythe
Interior Design:	Lee Goldstein
Cover Design:	Cheryl Asherman
Illustrator (Interior):	ElectraGraphics
Cover Illustration:	©Barton Stabler/SIS
Composition:	Progressive Information Technologies

Copyright © 1999, 1996 by Prentice Hall, Inc.

A Simon & Schuster Company

Upper Saddle River, New Jersey 07458

Library of Congress Cataloging-in-Publication Data

Mondy, R. Wayne
    Human resource management / R. Wayne Mondy, Robert M. Noe, Shane
R. Premeaux. — 7th ed.
      p.   cm.
    Includes bibliographical references and index.
    ISBN 0-13-922782-2
    1. Personnel management—United States. 2. Personnel management.
I. Noe, Robert M. II. Premeaux, Shane R.   . III. Title.
HF5549.2.U5M66 1998
658.3—dc21   98-12218
                                     CIP

Prentice-Hall International (UK) Limited, London
Prentice-Hall of Australia Pty. Limited, Sydney
Prentice-Hall Canada, Inc., Toronto
Prentice-Hall Hispanoamericana, S.A., Mexico
Prentice Hall of India Private Limited, New Delhi
Prentice-Hall of Japan, Inc., Tokyo
Simon & Schuster Asia Pte. Ltd., Singapore
Editora Prentice-Hall do Brasil, Ltda., Rio de Janeiro

Printed in the United States of America

10 9 8 7 6 5 4 3 2 1

To my daughters and new granddaughter
Alyson Lynn, Marianne Elizabeth, Madison Jon

RWM

To my grandchildren
Michael, Lillie, Robert, Vaughan, and Anna

RMN

To my daughter
Paige Elizabeth (PEP)

SRP

Brief Contents

Contents

Special Features

HR TRENDS AND INNOVATIONS

These features focus on the many changes that are currently occurring in the field of HRM.

HRM IN ACTION

These exercises permit students to make decisions regarding real situations that occur in the business world.

A GLOBAL PERSPECTIVE

These sections focus on new major global topics.

HRM INCIDENTS

These are short cases that highlight the material covered in each chapter.

Preface

The world of human resource management has experienced major changes since the sixth edition of this book was published. The impact of global competition and rapid technological advances has accelerated trends such as shared service centers, outsourcing, and just-in-time training. All business areas, including human resources, are being restructured in many organizations. Some observers have predicted that these changes will diminish the importance of human resource management. A more prevalent view of human resources, and one held by the authors, is that they are an organization's primary competitive edge. The management of human resources has been a major issue in organizations, and managers of human resources are evolving into the role of strategic partners with top management.

As we enter the next millennium, the seventh edition of *Human Resource Management* provides a realistic approach to the human resource management field. Even though the book is essentially pragmatic, it is balanced throughout by current human resource management theories and concepts. The interrelationships among the various human resource functions is a theme that runs throughout the book. Each of the functions is described from the standpoint of its relationship to the strategic needs of organizations. This book is written primarily for students who are being exposed to human resource management for the first time. It puts them in touch with the real world through the use of numerous illustrations and company material showing how human resource management is practiced in today's foremost organizations.

FEATURES OF THIS BOOK

We have included a number of features to promote the readability and understanding of important human resource management concepts.

- A model (see Figure 2-1) has been developed that provides a vehicle for relating all human resource management topics. We believe the overview provided will serve as an excellent teaching device.

- A caselet (short case study) involving human resource management is provided at the beginning of each chapter to set the tone for a discussion of the major topics included in the chapter.

- A brief exercise called "HRM In Action" is included in the body of each chapter. These exercises are designed to permit students to make decisions regarding real-world situations that could occur in the business world. A debriefing guide is provided for the instructor in the *Instructor's Resource Manual*. Fifty percent of the incidents are new to this edition.

- *NEW "A Global Perspective"* Because of the impact of the global environment on human resource management, new major global topics have been added to each chapter under the heading of "A Global Perspective."

- *NEW "HR Trends and Innovations"* New to the seventh edition of *Human Resource Management* is a section in each chapter entitled "HR Trends and Innovations." This section was added to portray the current trends in Human Resource Management.

- *NEW "Exploring with 'HR Web Wisdom'"* New to the seventh edition of *Human Resource Management* are three recommended Web sites per chapter entitled "HR Web Wisdom." These Web sites relate to topics highlighted in each chapter. One of the sites in each chapter refers to the Society of Human Resource Management home page. The corresponding Web address for each "HR Web Wisdom" is located in the Prentice Hall Web site at <http://www.prenhall.com/mondy>. The Internet and the World Wide Web are dynamic and ever evolving structures, and therefore users of these and other HR related Web sites should frequently contact our Prentice Hall Web site where changes, improvements, and new resources are provided.

- *NEW Showtime Integrative Video Case* A new feature to this edition is an eight-part integrative video case featuring an in-depth look at the HR practices at Showtime Networks Inc., the premium cable movie channel. This continuing video case provides students with the opportunity to apply information from the text to an actual business and allows students to view this same company from several different perspectives.

- *NEW Learning Objectives and Summary are tied together.* The summary at the end of the chapter is tied to the objectives at the beginning of the chapter.

- In addition to the integrative Showtime video case, this edition also offers selections from the ABC News video library.

- Two HRM Incidents are provided at the end of each chapter. These short cases highlight material covered in the chapter. Fifty percent of these incidents are new to this edition.

- A discussion of the *Human Resources Management Simulation* by Smith and Golden is provided in each chapter. These simulations give students the opportunity to practice managing an organization's human resources function. With a simulation, students have the opportunity to make decisions, see the effects of those decisions, and then try again, if necessary. Players get *hands-on* experience with manipulating key human resources variables in a dynamic setting. The player's manual for this simulation (ISBN: 0-13-556425-5) may be purchased separately or can be shrink-wrapped with this text.

- A comprehensive exercise called "Developing HRM Skills: An Experiential Exercise" is provided at the end of each chapter. These exercises provide for considerable class participation and group involvement. A comprehensive debriefing guide is provided for the instructor in the *Instructor's Resource Manual*.

- Actual company examples and material are used throughout the book to illustrate how a concept is actually used in organizations. A minimum of five company examples are included in each chapter.

- Objectives are listed at the beginning of each chapter to highlight the general purpose and key concepts of the chapter.

- Review questions appear at the end of each chapter to test the student's understanding of the material.

- Key terms are listed at the beginning of each chapter. In addition, a key term is presented in bold print the first time it is defined or described in the chapter.

- The relevance of the text is ensured through the use of current references.

- Finally, a glossary of all key terms appears at the end of the book.

IMPROVEMENTS TO THE SEVENTH EDITION

The previous editions of this book enjoyed considerable success. Many of our adopters provided us with suggestions for improving the seventh edition. All topics have been updated to provide the most recent coverage available, and the following are topics that have been added to this edition.

CHAPTER 1: HUMAN RESOURCE MANAGEMENT:
AN OVERVIEW
New sections include "HR Restructuring Trends," "Adjusting to HR Restructuring Trends—Who Performs the Human Resource Management Tasks?" "HR as a Strategic Partner," "Human Resource Management and the Small Business Manager," "Technology Impact," and "A New and Evolving HR Organization for Large-Size Firms."

CHAPTER 2: THE ENVIRONMENT OF HUMAN RESOURCE
MANAGEMENT
New sections include "Single Parents and Working Mothers," "Dual-Career Couples," "Educational Level of Employees," "Corporate Culture," "Factors That Influence Corporate Culture," and "Changing the Corporate Culture."

CHAPTER 3: EQUAL EMPLOYMENT OPPORTUNITY AND
AFFIRMATIVE ACTION
New sections include "Illegal Immigration Reform and Immigrant Responsibility Act," "Equal Employment Overseas," "*O'Connor v Consolidated Coin Caterers Corp.*" and "Employment Standards to Avoid."

CHAPTER 4: JOB ANALYSIS
New sections include "The Expanded Job Description," "Timeliness of Job Analysis," and "Design Approaches: Fad or Fashion."

CHAPTER 5: STRATEGIC HUMAN RESOURCE PLANNING
New sections include "HR and Strategic Planning," "The Levels of Strategic Planning," "The Strategic Planning and Implementation Process," "Strategy Implementation," "Succession Planning," and "Succession Development."

CHAPTER 6: RECRUITMENT
New sections include "Outsourcing," "Innovative Methods of Recruitment," "Internet Recruitment," "Virtual Job Fairs," "Recruitment for Diversity," and "Utilization of Minorities, Women, and Individuals with Disabilities."

CHAPTER 7: SELECTION
New sections include "Behavior Description Interviewing" and "Legal Implications of Interviewing." Other new topics are "Genetic Testing," "Video-taped Interviews," and "Computer Interviews." Also included in this chapter is a discussion of the need to consider organizational fit in the selection decision and software programs that permit automated resumé handling.

CHAPTER 8: TRAINING AND DEVELOPMENT
New sections include "Training in the Information Age," "Cyberlearning," "Virtual Reality," "The Internet, Intranets, and Just-in-Time Training," "Corporate Universities," "Return on Investment (ROI) for Evaluating T&D," and "Benchmarking for Evaluating T&D."

CHAPTER 9: CAREER PLANNING AND DEVELOPMENT
New sections include "The Evolution of Work Impacting Career Planning and Development," "Impacting HR Developmental Practices," "Job Revitalization and Career Enhancement," "Developing Unique Segments of the Workforce," "Developing Generation X Employees," and "Developing the New Factory Workers."

CHAPTER 10: PERFORMANCE APPRAISAL
New sections include "What to Evaluate" and "Customer Appraisal of Performance." Expanded coverage is given to 360 Degree Feedback and PC software to assist in writing performance appraisals.

CHAPTER 11: COMPENSATION
New topics include a discussion of variable pay (lump sum bonuses) as opposed to merit pay. New sections are "Broadbanding" and "Workplace Flexibility" (with expanded treatment of flextime, compressed workweek, job sharing, flexible compensation plans, telecommuting and modified retirement).

CHAPTER 12: BENEFITS AND OTHER COMPENSATION ISSUES
New topics include "Team Based Compensation Plans," "The Health Insurance Portability and Accountability Act of 1996," and "Severance Pay." Other new topics are "Well Pay," "Exclusive Provider Organizations (EPO)," and "Relocation Benefits and Financial Services." Expanded coverage is provided for Family and Medical Leave Act of 1993 (FMLA) and defined contribution plans [401(k) plans]. Numerous citations of the 1997 SHRM benefits survey are included.

CHAPTER 13: A SAFE AND HEALTHY WORK ENVIRONMENT
New sections include "Safety and Health Trends," "Ergonomics," "Workplace and Domestic Violence," and "The Northwestern Mutual Life Insurance Company's Program." A new section on sabbatical leaves is included, and the topic "Smoking in the Workplace" is expanded.

CHAPTER 14: THE EVOLUTION OF LABOR UNIONS
New sections include "The Labor Movement into the Year 2000," and "Teams and Organized Labor." Also included in this chapter is a discussion of an open-door policy, grievance procedures, the ombudsperson, the state of certification elections, strikes, the diminishing strength of unions, and a discussion of Executive Order 12954, which bans the hiring of permanent strike replacements by certain federal contractors.

CHAPTER 15: LABOR MANAGEMENT RELATIONS
New sections include "The Future of Worker-Management Relations" and "Labor Management Relations and Individual Bargaining." Also included new in this chapter is a discussion of the ramifications of union-management cooperation prohibited by the National Labor Relations Act of 1935, the growing incidents of plant-closure threats by nearly half of managers facing union elections, the impact of such threats on labor loses, the AFL-CIO's bargaining push on work-family issues, scarcity of pay increases in key economic sectors, the growing importance of mediation skills to executives, alternative dispute resolution, the impact of activism and union focus, and the reality of NAFTA being used as a union-busting weapon.

CHAPTER 16: INTERNAL EMPLOYEE RELATIONS
New sections on "Evaluating the Human Resource Management Function" and "Alternative Dispute Resolution (ADR)" are included. There is also new material on the termination of executives and outplacement.

CHAPTER 17: GLOBAL HUMAN RESOURCE MANAGEMENT
This entirely new chapter includes the following sections: "The Evolution of Global Business," "The Evolution of Global Human Resource Management," "Global Human Resource Management Functions," "Possible Barriers to Effective Global Human Resource Management," "Equal Employment Opportunity and Global HR," "Eight Keys to Global HR Management of Expatriates," and "Keeping up Globally with HR."

ACKNOWLEDGMENTS

The assistance and encouragement of many people is normally required in the writing of any book. This is especially true in the writing of the seventh edition of *Human Resource Management*. Although it would be virtually impossible to list each person who assisted in this project, certain people must be credited because of the magnitude of their contribution. We especially appreciate the efforts of the professionals who reviewed this edition: James A. Browne, University of Southern California; Paul A. Fadil, Valdosta State University; Claudia Salvano, Valencia (FL) Community College; Jim Wanek, University of Minnesota; and Steven Werner, University of Houston.

We would also like to thank Marthanne Lamansky, Anita Platt, Kendra Ingram and Sue Weatherbee, all very competent and professional individuals, who were always available to ensure that our deadlines were met. As with the previous editions, the support and encouragement of many practicing HRM professionals has made this book possible.

SEVENTH EDITION

HUMAN RESOURCE MANAGEMENT

INTRODUCTION

1
Human Resource Management: An Overview

CHAPTER OBJECTIVES

1. Identify the human resource management functions.
2. Explain how organizations are adjusting to human resource restructuring trends.
3. Explain the need for human resources to be a strategic partner.
4. Describe human resource management and the small business manager.
5. Distinguish among executives, generalists, and specialists.
6. Describe the changes that occur in the human resource function as a firm grows larger and more complex.
7. Explain the nature of professionalization of human resources and the direction it has taken.
8. Define *ethics* and relate ethics to human resource management.

*A*s Samuel Curtis, vice president of strategic human resources for Automotive Elements & Design (AED), headquartered in New Jersey, walked to his office after the executive meeting, he realized that his job would be even busier than usual during the next nine months. AED produces automotive trim and interior components for luxury automobiles. The company had recently signed an exclusive 10-year contract with a luxury sport-utility manufacturer. Because of the just-in-time requirements of the manufacturer and the frequent interactions necessary between the manufacturer's design people and AED's design people, AED must locate a new design and production facility in Vance, Alabama. Samuel and other members of the executive committee analyzed various alternative plans for the expansion of the current New Jersey plant to avoid building an additional production and design facility. The luxury sport-utility manufacturer's requirements, however, made the development of a new facility in Vance the only viable alternative. In a year when the plant is completed, 300 new employees must be available and trained in the advanced methods utilized at the new high-tech design and production facility in Vance. In addition, 70 employees at the New Jersey facility will be transferred to Vance, necessitating their retraining. Samuel is responsible for ensuring that qualified new workers are hired and trained and that the transferred workers are retrained and are effectively integrated into the new workforce.

Carl Edwards is the supervisor of 10 Baby Giant convenience stores in Sacramento, California. Because the Baby Giant chain is relatively small (only 40 stores), it has no human resource department. Each supervisor is in charge of all employment activities for his or her store. Carl must ensure that only the best people are recruited for positions as store managers, and then he must properly train these individuals. If one of the managers fails to report for an assigned shift and Carl cannot find a replacement, he is expected to work the shift. On one recent Friday afternoon, Carl was hurriedly attempting to locate a replacement because a store manager had quit without giving notice.

*S*amuel and Carl have one thing in common; they are deeply involved with some of the challenges and problems related to human resource management. Managers of human resources must constantly deal with the often volatile and unpredictable human element that makes working in this field very challenging. Managing people in organizations is becoming more complex than ever before because of rapidly changing and increasingly complicated work environments.

In the first part of this chapter, we discuss the human resource management functions. Next, we address the issues of adapting to human resource restructuring trends, the human resource manager as a strategic partner, and human resource management in the small business environment. Then we review the impact of technology. The distinction among human resource executives, generalists, and specialists and the human resource function in organizations of different sizes are addressed next. Finally, we discuss professionalism and ethics in this dynamic discipline and describe the scope of the book.

Human Resource Management Functions

Human resource management (HRM):
The utilization of a firm's human resources to achieve organizational objectives.

Human resource management (HRM) is the utilization of human resources to achieve organizational objectives. Consequently, all managers at every level must concern themselves with human resource management. Basically, managers get things done through the efforts of others; this requires effective human resource management.

Today's human resource problems and opportunities are enormous and appear to be expanding. Individuals dealing with human resource matters face a multitude of challenges, ranging from a constantly changing workforce to the ever-present scores of government regulations and a major technological revolution. Samuel Curtis of AED must ensure that the new workforce is capable of being productive in the new high-tech facility in Vance, Alabama. Furthermore, global competition has caused organizations both large and small to be more conscious of cost and productivity. Because of the critical nature of human resource issues, these matters are receiving major attention from upper management.

People who are engaged in the management of human resources develop and work through an integrated human resource management system. As Figure 1-1 shows, five functional areas are associated with effective human resource management: human resource planning, recruitment, and selection; human resource development; compensation and benefits; safety and health; and employee and labor relations. A major study conducted for the Society for Human Resource Management confirmed that these areas, along with management practices, constitute the field of human resource management. These functional areas mirror the human resource certification examination format, which is shown in the appendix to this chapter. Regardless of the size of the firm, performance in these human resource areas has a tremendous impact on growth, market/book value, and productivity.[1] We discuss these functions next.

Global competition has caused organizations both large and small to be more cost and productivity conscious.

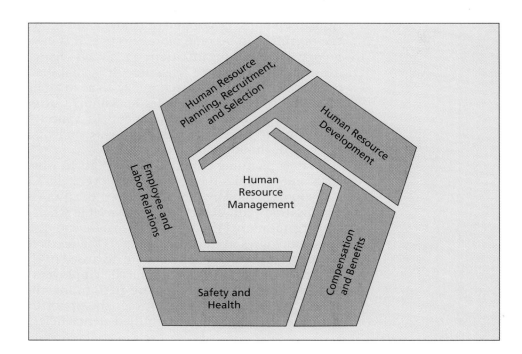

Figure 1-1
The Human Resource Management System

HUMAN RESOURCE PLANNING, RECRUITMENT, AND SELECTION

An organization must have qualified individuals in specific jobs at specific places and times to accomplish its goals. Obtaining such people involves human resource planning, recruitment, and selection. Firms must ensure that their workforces are productive both today and in the foreseeable future. Basically, selecting the most effective human resources will ultimately mean the difference between success and failure.[2] This is certainly the case with AED in Vance, Alabama.

Human resource planning (HRP) is the process of systematically reviewing human resource requirements to ensure that the required numbers of employees, with the required skills, are available when needed. Job analysis is an essential part of human resource planning and the topic of chapter 4. Job analysis is the systematic process of determining the skills, duties, and knowledge required for performing jobs in an organization. It is a pervasive human resource technique that basically provides a summary of a job's duties and responsibilities, the job's relationship to other jobs, the knowledge and skills it requires, and the working conditions under which the job is performed. Recruitment is the process of attracting qualified individuals and encouraging them to apply for work with the organization. Selection is the process through which the organization chooses, from a group of applicants, those individuals best suited both for open positions and for the company. Successful accomplishment of these three tasks is vital if the organization is to accomplish its mission effectively. Chapters 5, 6, and 7 are devoted to these topics.

HUMAN RESOURCE DEVELOPMENT

Human Resource Development (HRD) helps individuals, groups, and the entire organization become more effective. It is essential because people, technology, jobs, and organizations are always changing. Technology is advancing at a staggering pace. Therefore, it is vital that employees be trained and developed to utilize this technology so as to attain the highest levels of productivity[3] (the topic of chapter 8). Samuel Curtis of AED must prepare 370 employees for their new assignments in Vance, Alabama. The training and development process should begin when individuals join the firm and continue throughout their careers.

Career planning is an ongoing process in which an individual sets career goals and identifies the means to achieve them. Career development is a formal approach used by the organization to ensure that people with the proper qualifications and experience are available when needed. Individual careers and organizational needs are not separate and distinct. Organizations should assist employees in career planning so the needs of both can be satisfied. Career planning and development are discussed in chapter 9.

Through performance appraisal, employees and teams are evaluated to determine how well they are performing their assigned tasks. Performance appraisal affords employees the opportunity to capitalize on their strengths and overcome identified deficiencies, thereby becoming more satisfied and productive employees. Performance appraisal is discussed in chapter 10.

Throughout this text, but especially in the training and development chapters, we use the term *operative employees*. **Operative employees** are all the workers in an organization except managers and professionals, such as engineers, accountants, or professional secretaries. Steel workers, truck drivers, and waiters are examples of operative employees.

Operative employees:
All workers in a firm except managers and professionals such as engineers, accountants, or professional secretaries.

COMPENSATION AND BENEFITS

The question of what constitutes a fair day's pay has plagued management, unions, and workers for a long time. A well-thought-out compensation system provides employees with adequate and equitable rewards for their contributions to meeting organizational goals. As used in this book, the term *compensation* includes all rewards that individuals receive as a result of their employment. The reward may be one or a combination of the following:

- *Pay*: The money that a person receives for performing a job
- *Benefits*: Additional financial rewards, other than base pay, such as paid vacations, sick leave, holidays, and medical insurance
- *Nonfinancial rewards*: Nonmonetary rewards, such as enjoyment of the work performed or a pleasant working environment

Although compensation includes all these rewards, the increasing importance of incentives and benefits warrants separate treatment. Regarding incentives, many companies are cautiously experimenting with various incentive programs, in which small reductions in the increase in a worker's base pay are accompanied by large potential incentives based on team or area performance above an established norm. Companies like MBNA Corporation and IBM have had surprisingly good results with incentive programs, which may expand dramatically in the future.[4] We discuss compensation in chapter 11 and address benefits and other compensation issues in chapter 12.

SAFETY AND HEALTH

Safety involves protecting employees from injuries caused by work-related accidents. Health refers to the employees' freedom from illness and their general physical and mental well-being. These aspects of the job are important because employees who work in a safe environment and enjoy good health are more likely to be productive and yield long-term benefits to the organization. For this reason, progressive managers have long advocated and implemented adequate safety and health programs. Because the Vance plant will be a state-of-the-art facility, safety and health issues are likely to be more than adequately addressed there. Today, because of federal and state legislation, which reflects societal concerns, most organizations have become attentive to their employees' safety and health.[5] Chapter 13 explores the topics of safety and health.

EMPLOYEE AND LABOR RELATIONS

Since 1983, union membership has fallen nearly 8 percent, to only 14.5 percent of the workforce—the lowest level since the Great Depression. Subtracting government employees, unions represent 10 percent of the private industry workforce, a figure that by 2000 could plunge to 4 or 5 percent.[6] Even so, a business firm is required by law to recognize a union and bargain with it in good faith if the firm's employees want the union to represent them. In the past, this relationship was an accepted way of life for many employers. According to a survey of labor-management relations, however, preventing the spread of unionism and developing effective employee relations systems are now more important to some managers than achieving sound collective bargaining results.[7] Chapters 14, 15, and 16 address employee and labor relations issues.

HUMAN RESOURCE RESEARCH

Although human resource research is not listed as a separate function, it pervades all HRM functional areas and the researcher's laboratory is the entire work environment. For instance, a study related to recruitment may suggest the type of worker most likely to succeed in that particular firm. Research on job safety may identify the causes of certain work-related accidents.

The reasons for problems such as excessive absenteeism or too many grievances may not be readily apparent. When such problems occur, human resource research can shed light on their causes. Human resource research is clearly an important key to developing the most productive and satisfied workforce possible.

INTERRELATIONSHIPS OF HRM FUNCTIONS

All HRM functional areas are highly interrelated. Management must recognize that decisions in one area will affect other areas. For instance, a firm that emphasizes recruiting top quality candidates but neglects to provide satisfactory compensation is wasting time, effort, and money. In addition, a firm's compensation system will be inadequate unless employees are provided a safe and healthy work environment. The interrelationships among the five HRM functional areas shown in Figure 1-1 will become more obvious as we address each topic throughout the book.

HR Restructuring Trends

The previously mentioned five HR functions must be accomplished if satisfactory productivity levels are to be ensured. However, a number of firms are changing the way these tasks are performed. For example, some companies are restructuring HR for reasons such as time pressures, financial considerations, and market pressures.[8] This restructuring often results in a shift in who performs each function. Organizations still perform the majority of a firm's HR functions inside the firm, but as internal operations are reexamined, questions are being raised: Can some HR tasks be performed more efficiently by line managers or outside vendors? Can some HR tasks be automated or eliminated altogether?[9]

One study, conducted by Mercer Management Consulting, suggested that the role of HR departments was changing in a dramatic way. Responses from the 17 firms included in the study indicated a shift in the roles of their HR departments in achieving the companies' corporate strategies. Such moves had cut their overall HR management costs.[10] One fact that is apparent is that all functions within today's organizations are being scrutinized for cost cutting, and HR is no exception. However, according to Eric Greenberg, director of research at the American Management Association (AMA), even more important than cost cutting in HR is the timely delivery of HR services. Basically, for HR time is money.[11]

The Mercer study also revealed three common threads that form a new organizational model for HR. First, strategic recentralization emphasizes that companywide direction for HR strategy should be set at corporate headquarters. Companies such as the software developer Oracle is now providing a more centralized, formalized HR function. Second, there is more focus on cost reductions, and therefore, routine administrative tasks are being consolidated. At IBM, a centralized service group designs HR programs for all its U.S. units and also provides direct support to managers and employees through an 800 number. Third, delivery of many HR functions has shifted to line managers. For instance, General Electric has reduced the size of its HR area and now holds line managers accountable for leading and developing their people.[12] Although such trends appear to exist in some firms, they do not currently represent the norm.

TRENDS & INNOVATIONS

THE SARATOGA STUDY

A study produced by the Saratoga Institute for the American Management Association entitled "Restructuring the Human Resources Department" was published in 1997. Although the results represent only 26 companies, a few of the projections from the study are of interest:

- The traditional responsibilities of human resources are changing. Only 30 percent of the participants retained the standard HR functions.
- Thirty-two percent of participants reported having a corporate university.
- Only 27 percent reported retaining the training area as is.
- There is a trend to increase the number of total employees serviced by each HR employee.
- The benefits area is being outsourced or moved to employee response centers or transaction centers.
- The staffing function is being delegated to line managers.[13]

Adjusting to HR Restructuring Trends— Who Performs the Human Resource Management Tasks?

All units must operate under a strict budget in this competitive global environment and HR is no exception. Because of time and budgetary constraints, some company and HR executives have had to make difficult decisions regarding how traditional HR tasks are accomplished. Naturally, the basic HR functional areas previously discussed must be performed, but the person(s) or units accomplishing these functions are being altered. As discussed in the following sections, the traditional human resource manager continues to be in place in most organizations, but some organizations are also using shared service centers, outsourcing, and line managers to assist in the delivery of human resources to accomplish organizational objectives more efficiently. Additionally, some HR departments are getting smaller because certain functions are now being accomplished by others. This shift permits HR managers to focus on more strategic and mission-oriented activities.

THE HUMAN RESOURCE MANAGER

Human resource managers: Individuals who normally act in an advisory (or staff) capacity when working with other (line) managers regarding human resource matters.

A **human resource manager** is an individual who normally acts in an *advisory* or *staff* capacity, working with other managers to help them deal with human resource matters. One general trend is that HR personnel are servicing an increasing number of employees. A study of 26 HR departments revealed that five years ago the average was one HR person servicing 60 employees; today the average is one to 90 employees. Respondents in the survey expect this ratio to expand further to one to 100.[14] During the past three decades, the HR department basically performed the five functional areas internally.[15] Although this continues to be the model in most companies, certain changes are occurring. Often large HR departments were created with the central figure being the HR manager or executive. The human resource manager is primarily responsible for coordinating the management of human resources to help the organization achieve its goals. As vice president of human resources, Samuel Curtis is in charge of selecting and recruiting 300 new employees in addition to facilitating the transfer of 70 employees from the New Jersey facility. There is a shared responsibility between line managers and human resource professionals. The distinction between human resource management and the human resource manager is clearly illustrated by the following account:

> Bill Brown, the production supervisor for Ajax Manufacturing, has just learned that one of his machine operators has resigned. He immediately calls Sandra Williams, the human resource manager, and says, "Sandra, I just had a Class A machine operator quit down here. Can you find some qualified people for me to interview?" "Sure Bill," Sandra replies. "I'll send two or three down to you within the week, and you can select the one that best fits your needs."

In this instance, both Bill and Sandra are concerned with accomplishing organizational goals, but from different perspectives. Sandra, as a human resource manager, identifies applicants who meet the criteria specified by Bill. Bill, however, will make the final decision as to who is hired because he is responsible for the machine operator's performance. His primary responsibility is production; hers is human resources. As a human resource manager, Sandra must constantly deal with the many problems related to human resources that Bill and the other managers face. Her job is to help them meet the human resource needs of the entire organization. In some firms, her function is also referred to as personnel, employee relations, or industrial relations.

SHARED SERVICE CENTERS

Shared service centers (SSC): A central place where routine, transaction-based activities that are dispersed throughout the organization are consolidated.

A concept that is receiving increased consideration in the area of human resource management is the **shared service center (SSC)**. These centers take routine, transaction-based activities that are dispersed throughout the organization and consolidate them in one place.[16] A major advantage of this concept is that HR managers can assume a more strategic role as they are freed from the more routine tasks. For example, a company with 20 strategic business units could consolidate routine HR tasks and perform them in one location. The increased volume makes the tasks more suitable for automation, which in turn would result in the need for fewer HR personnel. For instance, Amoco estimates that the use of shared service centers combined with selective outsourcing of some functions achieved $400 million in annual savings for the company.[17]

Exploring with HR Web Wisdom

New to the seventh edition of *Human Resource Management* is "HR Web Wisdom," which has Internet sources for three topics in each chapter. To ensure that the sources for each topic can be updated to provide the most current information, the Internet addresses for each are posted on the Prentice Hall Web site at <http://www.prenhall.com/mondy>. One of the sites in each chapter relates to the home page of the Society for Human Resource Management.

HR Web Wisdom

http://www.prenhall.com/mondy
OUTSOURCING
Outsourcing solutions in human resources are reviewed.

OUTSOURCING FIRMS

Outsourcing: The process of transferring responsibility for an area of service and its objectives to an external provider.

Outsourcing is the process of transferring responsibility for an area of service and its objectives to an external provider.[18] In the 1997 Saratoga Institute report, all 26 participating HR departments were planning to or had already outsourced some HR functions. The main reason for this movement was to reduce transaction time, but other benefits include cost reductions and quality improvements.[19] Companies found that administrative, repetitive tasks are often performed in a more cost-effective manner by external sources.[20]

A 1996 survey of 619 companies showed that 57 percent of the companies outsourced temporary staffing, 32 percent outsourced training, 26.2 percent outsourced recruiting, and 21.8 percent outsourced benefits administration.[21] With outsourcing, a function such as training would be assigned to a firm outside the organization. Training tasks such as registration, scheduling, marketing, logistics, facilities management, instructor selection, course selection and development, and course evaluation would be outsourced. As one might expect, the key to outsourcing success is to determine which functions to outsource, the extent to which the function should be outsourced, and which ones to keep in-house.[22]

LINE MANAGERS

Line managers, by the nature of their jobs, are involved with human resources. Carl Edwards, the convenience store supervisor in Sacramento, California, fully understands the challenges a line manager faces with human resources because he will have to work Friday night if he cannot find a replacement. As reported in the Saratoga study, line managers in certain firms are being used more to deliver HR services. Remember that General Electric reduced the size of the HR area and now holds line managers accountable for leading and developing their people.[23] When implemented, this change reduces the size of the HR department.

HRM IN ACTION
HOW HUMAN RESOURCE MANAGEMENT IS PRACTICED

At the front of each chapter are one or two lead cases that focus on the chapter material. These lead cases are integrated into the material at least five times per chapter. Sections entitled "HRM in Action" and "HRM Incidents" are included in all chapters. These sections permit you to make decisions about situations that could occur in the real world. They are designed to put you on the spot and let you think through how you would react in typical human resource management situations. "Developing HRM Skills," an experiential exercise, permits students to see how they would react in simulated *real-life* situations. Each exercise enables you to analyze how well you will deal with the subject matter.

HR as a Strategic Partner

The role of HR is changing with the globalization of business that began in earnest in the late 1980s. The increasing recognition of HR as a legitimate business unit has made it highly strategic in nature and more critical to achieving corporate objectives. To succeed, HR executives must "understand the complex organizational design and be able to determine the capabilities of the company's workforce, both today and in the future."[24] HR involvement in strategy is necessary to ensure that human resources support the firm's mission.

The HR executive should be a partner to the chief executive officer (CEO) on the deployment of human resources, and therefore should be accountable for making today's decisions to position the company's future workforce. Members of management from the CEO on down are responsible for implementing the strategic plan.[25] As previously mentioned, a trend may be developing whereby more companies will be outsourcing some HR tasks, placing other functions with shared service centers, or assigning the function to line managers. As the more routine and mundane task are removed from the responsibility of HR manager, these individuals are able to focus their attention on issues of greater strategic importance to the organization. The human resource executive will increasingly become a strategic business partner and decision maker.[26] This trend was emphasized by J. W. Marriott, Jr., chairman of the board and president of Marriott International, when he stated, "Human resources is at the core of our business. Because of the importance of human resources, the senior vice president of human resources reports to me, is on my executive committee and is a corporate officer."[27]

Even titles of HR executives are being changed to reflect this new partnership. Peggy Tate is now vice president of human resources strategy for DFS Group Limited, having added the word *strategy* to her title. She states, "I have to be very closely linked to what senior management is thinking in terms of where the business is heading. I have to think about how to recruit the right people and train them; how to reward them; how to hold on to them."[28] The current functions of many chief human resource managers is epitomized by a banking executive who states, "I am now a strategic partner with line management and participate in business decisions which bring human resources perspectives to the general management of the company."[29]

The future appears bright for HR managers willing to forge a strategic partnership with other business units. If these managers are to become strategic partners in their organizations, they must run their departments according to the same rigid criteria that apply to other units. They must be able to use data available in their unit to forecast outcomes and become real partners with upper management. HR units must be able to show how they add value to the company.[30]

Table 1-1, which lists some of the *OUTs* and *INs* of human resources, provides a brief insight into why the profession itself is in a great deal of flux.[31] Although several trends are appearing, the only certainty is that the job of human resource professionals is continuously evolving. Yesterday's solutions may not be sufficient for tomorrow's challenges.

TABLE 1-1

Some Outs and Ins of HR: A List of Trends That Will Affect How Work Is Done in the Future

OUT:	Job titles and labels such as "employee," "manager," "staff," and "professional"
IN:	Everyone a business person, an "owner" of a complete business process, president of his or her job
OUT:	Chain-of-command, reporting relationships, department, function, turf, sign-off, work as imposed-from-above tasks
IN:	Self-management, responsiveness, proactivity, initiative, collaboration, egalitarianism, self-reliance, standards of excellence, personal responsibility, work as collection of self-initiated projects and teams
OUT:	Stability, order, predictability, structure, better-safe-than-sorry
IN:	Flux, disorder, ambiguity, risk, better sorry-than-safe
OUT:	Good citizenship—show up, be a good soldier, stay 9-to-5 in cubicle, don't make waves, wait for someone else to decide your fate, work in same organization for 30 years, retire with gold watch
IN:	Make a difference—add value, challenge the process, work four hours or 18 hours per day, accept the job site as wherever the action is, learn from mistakes, develop career mobility and fluidity, work your tail off and be intensely loyal to Company X for one year or 10 years, and then move on to Company Y, a better, more marketable person

Source: Adapted from Oren Harari, "Back to the Future of Work," *Management Review* 82 (September 1993): 35.

HRM IN ACTION
A DYING JOB?

"Mr. Klass, I am really concerned with the outsourcing of training and benefits administration. It appears that my authority base is being depleted, and unless I am in charge of training it can't be done correctly. How can someone else provide the training services we need? Only we know what we need?"

"Johnny, I understand that you are apprehensive about change, but you will decide what type of training is needed and will select who provides the training. Also, I understand there are several excellent training providers in the area. Another thing, Johnny, you are going to become my strategic partner just like the vice presidents of production, finance, and marketing/sales. Your authority will expand, you will have input into the actual direction of the company in the future."

"I appreciate the pep talk, Mr. Klass, but as the importance and scope of what I *actually do* diminishes, so will my authority and my ability to develop human resources properly."

How should Mr. Klass respond?

Human Resource Management and the Small Business Manager

In the United States today, 90 percent of all U.S. businesses have fewer than 20 employees. Further, small businesses create two out of three new net jobs and provide 60 percent of all private sector jobs.[32] Every year, approximately 400,000 such businesses are established.[33] Since 1988, companies employing fewer than 100 workers have accounted for over 90 percent of all job growth.[34]

There is no commonly agreed-on definition of what constitutes a small business. The Small Business Act of 1953 defines a small business as one that is independently owned and operated and not dominant in its field. Basically, a small business is one in which the owner-operator knows personally the key personnel. In most small businesses, this key group would ordinarily not exceed 12 to 15 people. Regardless of the specific definition of a small business, this category certainly makes up the overwhelming majority of business establishments in this country.

Small businesses are ideal for implementing human resource initiatives because of their lack of bureaucracy and their ability to involve all individuals in the process of the business. Some aspects of the human resource function may actually be more significant in smaller firms than in larger ones. For instance, if the owner of a small business hires her first and only full-time salesperson, and this individual promptly alienates the firm's customers, the business might actually fail. Also, with regard to laws, no firm is too small to ignore the laws relating to human resource issues. The violation of some employment laws or acts carries heavy financial penalties whether the firm has one, 15, 50, or 500 employees.

As shown in chapter 3, small businesses are impacted substantially by federal, state, and local laws. In fact, the laws are structured in a manner that may have an uneven effect on small businesses. Small businesses typically do not have a formal HR unit; therefore, line managers have to be aware of the many pitfalls associated with these laws. For instance, a business with four or more employees is covered under the Immigration Reform and Control Act. Under the Civil Rights Act, a company with 15 or more workers is covered, and the Americans with Disabilities Act applies to a company with 20 or more workers. Probably no company with fewer than 20 workers will have a formal human resource activity; consequently, line managers will be required to ensure adherence to the law.

Impact of Technology

The world has never before seen technological changes appear as rapidly as they are presently occurring in the computer and telecommunications industries. One estimate is that technological changes are coming so fast that a person may have to change his or her entire skill repertoire three or four times in a career.[35] The advances being made affect every area of a business including human resource management. For example, technology makes it feasible to provide *just-in-time training* for employees and the delivery of other HR services regardless of where employees are located or when they need them. This capability can potentially affect virtually every major HR task. The impact of technology on these practices is noted throughout the book.

Human Resource Executives, Generalists, and Specialists

Executive: A top-level manager who reports directly to a corporation's chief executive officer or the head of a major division.

Generalist: A person who performs tasks in a wide variety of human resource-related areas.

Specialist: An individual who may be a human resource executive, a human resource manager, or a nonmanager and who is typically concerned with only one of the five functional areas of human resource management.

Various classifications occur within the human resource profession and you need to recognize and understand them. Among these are human resource executives, generalists, and specialists. An **executive** is a top-level manager who reports directly to the corporation's chief executive officer (CEO) or to the head of a major division. A **generalist**, who is often an executive, performs tasks in various human resource–related areas. The generalist is involved in several or all of the five human resource management functions. A change is taking place in some companies. They are assigning a human resource generalist to each line organization and maintaining a smaller core of centralized staff. These individuals then serve the specific HR needs of the department.[36] A **specialist** may be a human resource executive, manager, or nonmanager who is typically concerned with only one of the five functional areas of human resource management. Figure 1-2 helps clarify these distinctions.

The vice president of industrial relations shown in Figure 1-2 specializes primarily in union-related matters. This person is both an executive and a

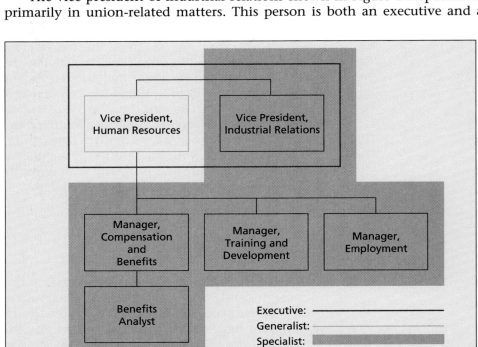

FIGURE 1-2
Human Resource Executives, Generalists, and Specialists

specialist. The human resource vice president is both an executive and a generalist, having responsibility for a wide variety of functions. The manager of compensation and benefits is a specialist, as is the benefits analyst. Whereas an executive is identified by position level in the organization, generalists and specialists are distinguished by the breadth of responsibility of their positions.

In today's HR environment, a trend is developing for human resource professionals to be more generalists than specialists. The change does not suggest that this professional become a jack of all trades and master of none. The generalist is expected to be capable of working knowledgeably with all aspects of HR. In addition, the HR professional should be familiar with tasks that have been outsourced or placed with shared service centers.

The Human Resource Functions in Organizations of Various Sizes

As firms grow and become more complex, the human resource function also becomes more complex and its function achieves greater importance. The basic purpose of human resource management remains the same; the change is in the approach used to accomplish its objectives.

Small businesses seldom have a formal human resource unit and HRM specialists, as Figure 1-3 shows. Rather, other managers handle human resource functions. The focus of their activities is generally on hiring and retaining capable employees.

To illustrate that some aspects of the human resource function may be more significant in smaller firms than in larger ones, a serious mistake in hiring an employee may cause the smaller business to fail. In a larger firm, such an error would be much less harmful. As a firm grows, a separate staff function may be required to coordinate human resource activities. In a larger firm, the person chosen to fill this role will be expected to handle most of the human resource activities, as Figure 1-4 implies. For a medium-size firm, there is little specialization. A secretary may be available to handle correspondence, but the human resource manager is essentially the entire department.

Figure 1-3
The Human Resource Function in a Small Business

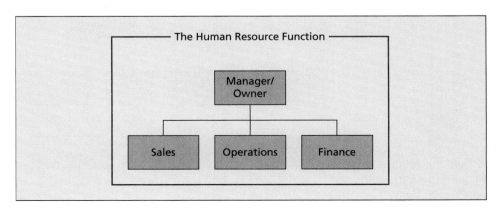

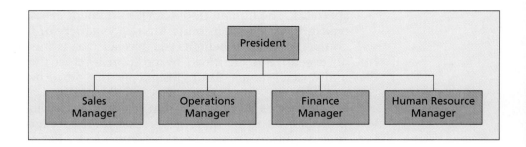

Figure 1-4
The Human Resource
Function in a Medium-
Size Business

When the firm's human resource function becomes too complex for one person, separate sections are often created and placed under a human resource manager. These sections will typically perform tasks involving employment, training and development, compensation and benefits, safety and health, and labor relations, as depicted in Figure 1-5. Each human resource function may have a supervisor and staff reporting to the human resource manager. The HR manager works closely with top management in formulating corporate policy. This arrangement is the traditional HR model.

The HR organizational structure of large-size firms changes as firms outsource, use shared service centers, and evolve in other ways to make HR more strategic. Regardless of an organization's design, the five human resource functions must still be accomplished. The organizational mission and corporate culture have a major impact in determining an appropriate HR organization. For example, the company depicted in Figure 1-6 has outsourced the training and development function and placed the benefits function with a shared service center. Safety and health have been removed from HR and because of their importance in this particular firm report directly to the chief executive officer. Other HR tasks remain under the control of the HR manager.

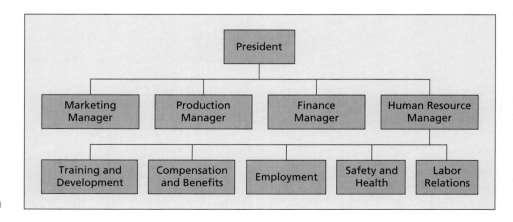

Figure 1-5
The Human Resource
Functions in a Large Firm

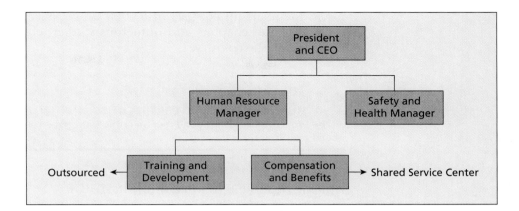

Figure 1-6
An Example of a New and Evolving HR Organization for Large Firms

Professionalization of Human Resource Management

Profession: A vocation whose practitioners share and use a common body of knowledge and recognize a procedure for certifying the practitioners.

A **profession** is characterized by the existence of a common body of knowledge and a procedure for certifying members of the profession. Performance standards are established by members of the profession (self-regulation) rather than by outsiders. Most professions also have effective representative organizations that permit members to exchange ideas of mutual concern. These characteristics apply to the field of human resources, and several well-known organizations serve the profession. Among the more prominent are the Society for Human Resource Management (SHRM), the Human Resource Certification Institute (HRCI), the American Society for Training and Development (ASTD), the American Compensation Association (ACA), the National Human Resources Association (NHRA), and the International Personnel Management Association (IPMA).

HR Web Wisdom

http://www.prenhall.com/mondy

SHRM–HR LINKS
To facilitate HR excellence, the Society for Human Resource Management has a series of Web Hot Links to topics of particular interest to HR professionals and students.

SOCIETY FOR HUMAN RESOURCE MANAGEMENT

The largest national professional organization for individuals involved in all areas of human resource management is the Society for Human Resource Management (SHRM). The name reflects the increasingly important role that human resource management plays in the overall bottom line of organizations. The basic goals of the society include defining, maintaining, and improving standards of excellence in the practice of human resource management. Membership consists of 63,000 individuals; there are currently more than 433 local chapters and numerous student chapters on university campuses across the country.[37]

> *HR Web Wisdom*
>
> **http://www.prenhall.com/mondy**
>
> **HUMAN RESOURCE CERTIFICATION INSTITUTE (HRCI)**
> The Professional Certification Program in HR Management is for individuals seeking to expand their formal HR training.

HUMAN RESOURCE CERTIFICATION INSTITUTE

One of the more significant developments in the field of HRM has been the establishment of the Human Resource Certification Institute (HRCI), an affiliate of SHRM.[38] Founded in 1976, the goal of the institute is to recognize human resource professionals through a certification program.[39] This program encourages human resource professionals to update their knowledge and skills continuously. Certification indicates that they have mastered a validated common body of knowledge (see appendix on page 31.) A number of years ago, Wiley Beavers, a former national president of SHRM, stated that human resource certification would

■ Allow students to focus on career directions earlier in their education
■ Provide sound guidelines for young practitioners in important HR areas
■ Encourage senior practitioners to update their knowledge

AMERICAN SOCIETY FOR TRAINING AND DEVELOPMENT

Founded in 1944, the American Society for Training and Development (ASTD) has grown to become the largest specialized professional organization in human resources. Its membership exceeds 55,000, and it has more than 155 local chapters.[40] The membership consists of individuals who are concerned specifically with training and development. The society publishes a monthly journal, *Training and Development*, to encourage its members to remain current in the field.

AMERICAN COMPENSATION ASSOCIATION

The American Compensation Association (ACA) was founded in 1955 and currently has a membership of more than 20,000.[41] The ACA consists of managerial and human resource professionals who are responsible for the establishment, execution, administration, or application of compensation practices and policies in their organizations. The association's quarterly journal, which contains information related to compensation issues, is the *ACA Journal*.

NATIONAL HUMAN RESOURCES ASSOCIATION

Founded in 1950, the National Human Resources Association (NHRA), formerly the International Association for Personnel Women (IAPW), was established to expand and improve the professionalism of women in human resource management. Its membership consists of human resource executives in business, industry, education, and government. The NHRA has approximately 1,500 members.[42]

INTERNATIONAL PERSONNEL MANAGEMENT ASSOCIATION

The International Personnel Management Association (IPMA) was founded in 1973 and currently has more than 6,500 members. This organization seeks to improve human resource practices by providing testing services, an advisory service, conferences, professional development programs, research, and publications. It sponsors seminars and workshops on various phases of public human resource administration. The organization's journal, *Public Personnel Management*, is published quarterly for those involved in human resource administration in public agencies.[43]

Ethics and Human Resource Management

Ethics: The discipline dealing with what is good and bad, or right and wrong, or with moral duty and obligation.

Professionalization of human resource management created the need for a uniform code of ethics. Today, more and more companies are concerned with values and ethics.[44] **Ethics** is the discipline dealing with what is good and bad, or right and wrong, or with moral duty and obligation. According to one survey, more companies than ever in the United States are stressing ethical conduct in business. A major reason for this change is that employees are better educated and well-versed in the realities of the workplace.[45] Apparently, the attitude has changed from "Should we be doing something in business ethics?" to "What should we be doing in business ethics?"[46] Every day, individuals who work in human resources must make decisions that have ethical implications. Ethical dilemmas, such as whether a manager should recommend against hiring a woman applicant strictly because she will be working exclusively with men, occur somewhat frequently and need to be addressed correctly. These issues must be dealt with on the basis of what is ethically correct, not just what will benefit the organization most in the short run.

According to Louis V. Larimer, president of the Larimer Center for Ethical Leadership Inc., HR professionals must take responsibility for the design and implementation of ethics programs. Their first and foremost challenge is to educate and influence the organization's CEO to make ethics a priority. Progressive HR professionals must be the constant voice that calls for ethical commitment, vision, behavior, achievement, and courage. Larimer recommends that HR be the keeper of the corporate conscience, thereby reminding the organization of the need to err on the side of goodness.[47]

There are many kinds of ethical codes, and most professions have their own. An example is SHRM's Code of Ethics shown in Figure 1-7. A growing number of firms are establishing ethical codes and communicating these codes to all employees.[48] Few of the numerous codes that exist in our society conflict in principle. They vary primarily in the extent to which they are applied under particular circumstances. It is vitally important that those who work with human resource management understand which practices are unacceptable and ensure that organizational members behave ethically in dealing with others.

A GLOBAL PERSPECTIVE

Attention HR, We Are Going Global!

In today's economic environment, companies are realizing that they must deal with global competition. To grow, they must expand overseas, a move that can greatly complicate the job of human resource management. The decision to enter foreign markets has profound implications for human

As a member of the Society for Human Resource Management, I pledge myself to:

■ Maintain the highest standards of professional and personal conduct.

■ Strive for personal growth in the field of human resource management.

■ Support the Society's goals and objectives for developing the human resource management profession.

■ Encourage my employer to make the fair and equitable treatment of all employees a primary concern.

■ Strive to make my employer profitable both in monetary terms and through the support and encouragement of effective employment practices.

■ Instill in the employees and the public a sense of confidence about the conduct and intentions of my employer.

■ Maintain loyalty to my employer and pursue its objectives in the ways that are consistent with the public interest.

■ Uphold all laws and regulations relating to my employer's activities.

■ Refrain from using my official positions, either regular or volunteer, to secure special privilege, gain or benefit for myself.

■ Maintain the confidentiality of privileged information.

■ Improve public understanding of the role of human resource management.

This Code of Ethics for members of the Society for Human Resource Management has been adopted to promote and maintain the highest standards of personal conduct and professional standards among its members. Adherence to this code is required for membership in the Society and serves to assure public confidence in the integrity and service of human resource management professionals.

Figure 1-7
SHRM Code of Ethics

Source: Reprinted from *Who's Who in HR 1992 Directory*, 4. Copyright 1992, The Society for Human Resource Management, Alexandria, Virginia.

resource functions requiring domestic practices to evolve in line with global HR requirements. Assigning and managing human resources outside the United States is a complex and sometimes overwhelming task. Understanding the organization's global business plan is essential. To administer global human resource functions properly and successfully, HR executives must have a thorough knowledge of the ongoing international operations of the company, the business and economic situation in each of the countries where the company operates, and the types of skills required of employees for international assignments.[49]

One viable alternative for an organization experiencing globalization is to outsource some of the international human resource functions. Traditionally, global organizations have turned to outsourcing only to handle income tax compliance and relocation matters. In the current era of increased activity and decreased resources, the expanded use of outsourcing may occur. Unfortunately, in most countries it is difficult to find outsourcing firms with the expertise necessary to handle the complex problems associated with a global operation. Also, the U.S. parent corporation usually wants to maintain ties and a certain degree of control over global operations and HR is often an essential connection.[50]

Melissa DeCrane of the Corporate Resources Group believes that international expertise is a very real asset for human resources people because every company is challenged by the global marketplace.[51] Effectively dealing with global human resources issues is essential for success in the global marketplace. Chapter 17 is devoted to global HRM.

Scope of This Book

Effective human resource management is crucial to the success of every organization. To be effective, managers must understand and competently practice human resource management. We designed this human resource management book to give you the following:

- An insight into the evolving role of human resource management in today's organizations and the impact of technology and global competition
- An understanding of human resource planning, recruitment, and selection
- An awareness of the importance of training and development
- An appreciation of how compensation and benefits programs are formulated and administered
- An understanding of safety and health factors as they affect the firm's profitability
- An opportunity to view employee and labor relations from both unionized and union-free standpoints
- An appreciation of the global dimension of human resource management

I. Introduction
Chapter 1: Human Resource Management: An Overview

II. The Environment of HRM, Legal Aspects of HRM, and Job Analysis
Chapter 2: The Environment of Human Resource Management
Chapter 3: Equal Employment Opportunity and Affirmative Action
Chapter 4: Job Analysis

III. Human Resource Planning, Recruitment, and Selection
Chapter 5: Strategic Human Resource Planning
Chapter 6: Recruitment
Chapter 7: Selection

IV. Human Resource Development
Chapter 8: Training and Development
Chapter 9: Career Planning and Development
Chapter 10: Performance Appraisal

V. Compensation and Benefits
Chapter 11: Compensation
Chapter 12: Benefits and Other Compensation Issues

VI. Safety and Health
Chapter 13: A Safe and Healthy Work Environment

VII. Employee and Labor Relations
Chapter 14: The Evolution of Labor Unions
Chapter 15: Labor Management Relations
Chapter 16: Internal Employee Relations

VIII. Operating in a Global Environment
Chapter 17: Global Human Resource Management

Figure 1-8
Organization of This Book

Students often question whether the content of a book corresponds to the realities of the business world. In writing and revising this book, we have drawn heavily on the comments, observations, and experiences of human resource practitioners as well as our own extensive research efforts. We cite the human resource practices of leading business organizations to illustrate how theory can be applied in the real world. Our intent is to enable you to experience human resource management in action.

This book is organized under eight parts, as shown in Figure 1-8; combined, they provide a comprehensive view of human resource management. As you read the book, we hope you will be stimulated to increase your knowledge of this rapidly changing, expanding, and challenging field.

SUMMARY

1. *Identify the human resource management functions.*
   The human resource management functions include human resource planning, recruitment, and selection; human resource development; compensation and benefits; safety and health; and employee and labor relations.

2. *Explain how organizations are adjusting to human resource restructuring trends.*
   Shared service centers take routine, transaction-based activities that are

dispersed throughout the organization and consolidate them in one place. Outsourcing is the process of transferring responsibility for an area of service and its objectives to an external provider. Line managers in certain firms are being used more frequently than before to deliver HR services.

3. *Explain the need for human resources to be a strategic partner.*
The growing recognition of HR as a legitimate business unit has made it highly strategic in nature and increasingly critical to achieving corporate objectives. HR involvement in strategy is necessary to ensure that these functions support the firm's mission.

4. *Describe human resource management and the small business manager.*
Some aspects of the human resource function may actually be more significant in smaller firms than in larger ones. Small businesses are impacted substantially by federal, state, and local laws. The laws are structured in a manner that may have an uneven effect on small businesses. Small businesses typically do not have a formal HR unit and line managers must be aware of the many pitfalls associated with these laws.

5. *Distinguish among executives, generalists, and specialists.*
Executives are top-level managers who report directly to the corporation's chief executive officer or the head of a major division. Generalists, who are often executives, are persons who perform tasks in a wide variety of human resource–related areas. The generalist is involved in several or all of the human resource management functions. A specialist may be either a human resource executive, manager, or nonmanager who is typically concerned with only one of the functional areas of human resource management.

6. *Describe the changes that occur in the human resource function as a firm grows larger and more complex.*
As firms grow and become more complex, the human resource function also becomes more complex and intricate. The basic functions remain essentially the same, but the company changes the approach it uses to accomplish its objectives.

7. *Explain the nature of professionalization of human resources and the direction it has taken.*
A profession is characterized by the existence of a common body of knowledge, and a procedure for certifying practitioners of this knowledge. Performance standards are established by members of the profession (self-regulation) rather than by outsiders. Most professions also have effective representative organizations that permit members to exchange ideas of mutual concern. These characteristics apply to the field of human resources, and several well-known organizations serve the profession.

8. *Define* ethics *and relate ethics to human resource management.*
Ethics is the discipline dealing with what is good and bad, or right and wrong, or with moral duty and obligation. With the professionalization of human resource management, a need arises for the development of a uniform code of ethics. Individuals working with human resources must make ethical (or unethical) decisions every day.

QUESTIONS FOR REVIEW

1. What human resource management functions must be performed regardless of the organization's size?
2. What are the current restructuring trends in human resource management?
3. What adjustments are necessary to deal with HR restructuring trends?
4. How should HR act as a strategic partner?
5. How is the small business manager impacted by HR management?
6. By definition and example, distinguish among human resource executives, generalists, and specialists.
7. How does the implementation of human resource functions change as a firm grows? Briefly describe each stage of development.
8. Define profession. Do you believe the field of human resource management is a profession? Explain your answer.
9. Define ethics. Why is ethics important to the field of human resource management?

DEVELOPING HRM SKILLS

AN EXPERIENTIAL EXERCISE

In many organizations, managers work with both individuals and groups. Cooperation is essential if human resource tasks are to be accomplished effectively. The Blue-Green exercise provides students with the opportunity to experience some of the interrelationships that occur in a structured setting, such as an organization or work group.

The Blue-Green exercise is one of the best to use when working with a relatively large group. In fact, it is not recommended for groups of fewer than 12 people. It has been used successfully with groups as large as 40. This exercise works equally well with groups who have been working together for some time and with heterogeneous groups whose members barely know one another.

Those who participate in this exercise usually find it quite enlightening. The total group will be divided into four subgroups as nearly equal in size as possible. These subgroups will be called teams and designated as Team A-1, Team A-2, Team B-1, and Team B-2. Your instructor will provide the participants with additional information necessary to participate. Enjoy the classic Blue-Green exercise.

 *Take It to the Net*

We invite you to visit the Mondy home page on the Prentice Hall Web site at:

http://www.prenhall.com/mondy

for updated information, Web-based exercises, and links to other HR-related sites.

HRM SIMULATION

*A*vailable for use with your text is the *Human Resource Management Simulation* by Jerald R. Smith and Peggy A. Golden. In this simulation you will be acting as the human resource director (or a general manager) of a moderate-size organization, making the types of decisions required of a modern human resource department. The simulation gives life to the text material. You will not only read about the decisions that managers make, but you will also make those decisions.

You will be organized into teams and implement your recommendations in an ongoing simulation. There is no single winning strategy! Instead, there are many successful strategies depending on the specific plans your team makes and the diligence with which you implement them. You will make decisions in the following four categories: overall strategy, human resource operating decisions, financial matters, and behavioral decisions. Have fun!

HRM INCIDENT

1

The Hiring of a Friend's Daughter

*M*arcie Sweeney had recently graduated from college with a degree in general business. Marcie was quite bright, although her grades did not reflect this. She had thoroughly enjoyed school—dating, tennis, swimming, and similar stimulating academic events. When she graduated from the university, she had not found a job. Her dad was extremely upset when he discovered this, and he took it on himself to see that Marcie became employed.

Her father, Allen Sweeney, was executive vice president of a medium-size manufacturing firm. One of the people he contacted in seeking employment for Marcie was Bill Garbo, the president of another firm in the area. Mr. Sweeney purchased many of his firm's supplies from Garbo's company. On telling Bill his problem, Allen was told to send Marcie to Bill's office for an interview. Marcie went, as instructed by her father, and before she left Bill's firm, she was surprised to learn that she had a job in the accounting department. Marcie may have been lazy but she certainly was not stupid. She realized that Bill had hired her because he hoped that his action would lead to future business from her father's company. Although Marcie's work was not challenging, it paid better than the other jobs in the accounting department.

It did not take long for the employees in the department to discover the reason she had been hired—Marcie told them. When a difficult job was assigned to Marcie, she normally got one of the other employees to do it, implying that Mr. Garbo would be pleased with that person if he or she helped her out. She developed a pattern of coming in late, taking long lunch breaks, and leaving early. When the department manager attempted to reprimand her for this unorthodox behavior, Marcie would bring up the close relationship her father had with the president of the firm. The department manager was at his limit when he asked for your help.

Questions
1. From an ethical standpoint, how would you evaluate the merits of Mr. Garbo's employing Marcie? Discuss.
2. Now that she is employed, what course would you follow to address her on-the-job behavior?
3. Do you feel that a firm should have policies regarding practices such as hiring people like Marcie? Discuss.

HRM INCIDENT

2

What Should I Outsource?

*E*dward Loomis is the new human resource manager of Developmental Technologies, Inc., which was once the research and development division of a large, long distance phone service provider. Developmental Technologies, Inc. became a separate business entity so the long distance provider could prepare for the competitive changes resulting from the telecommunication bill that deregulated communication services. Edward was the assistant to the vice president of HR for the long distance carrier before the reorganization, so he believed he was well prepared to deal with his new responsibilities as manager. However, the new company does not have the unlimited resources of the older one; therefore, reducing operating costs is a necessity. Although Edward was not totally enthusiastic about the idea, outsourcing of certain HR functions appeared to be a solution. Even though Edward had no previous experience with outsourcing, he believed it would be one way of relieving the burden on his rather small staff. Just as he was to meet with potential outsourcing providers, his boss called to set up a meeting to discuss his role as a strategic partner in upper-level planning. This was the first Edward had heard of being a strategic partner and he was both apprehensive and somewhat excited about the opportunity to influence the future direction of Developmental Technologies. Evidently, there would now be a new way of doing things.

Questions
1. What human resource management tasks might Edward outsource? Explain your answer.
2. What should be Edward's role as a strategic partner?

Notes

1. Susan S. Barnes, "Even Small Firms Need Focus on Human Resource Issues," *Wichita Business Journal* (March 14, 1997): 13.
2. James L. Wilkerson, "The Future Is Virtual HR," *HR Focus* 74 (March 1997): 15.
3. Donald V. Brookes, "HR in the '90s: From Tacticians to Strategists," *HR Focus* 71 (September 1994): 12.
4. Donald J. McNerney, "Spreading the Wealth," *HR Focus* 74 (March 1997): 1, 4–5.
5. The key law in the area of health and safety is the Occupational Safety and Health Act of 1970. This act is discussed in chapter 13.

6. Aaron Bernstein, "Why America Needs Unions But Not the Kind It Has Now," *Business Week* (May 23, 1994): 70; and Bill Vlasic and Aaron Bernstein, "Workplace: Unions: Sweeney's Blitz," *Business Week* (February 2, 1997): 56.

7. Alexander B. Trowbridge, "A Management Look at Labor Relations," in *Unions in Transition* (San Francisco: ICS Press, 1988): 414.

8. *Restructuring the Human Resources Department*, a report by Saratoga Institute, sponsored by American Management Association, 1997.

9. Donald J. McNerney, "Career Development: As HR Changes, so Do HR Career Paths," *HR Focus* 73 (February 1996): 1.

10. James Down, "Human Resources Takes a Strategic Role," *Executive Forum* (March 1997): 1.

11. Donald McNerney, "Outsourcing of HR Continues," *HR Focus* 74 (March 1997): 2.

12. Down, "Human Resources Takes a Strategic Role."

13. *Restructuring the Human Resources Department.*

14. Ibid.

15. Reyer A. Swaak, "Are We Saying Good-bye to HR?" *Compensation & Benefits Review* 28 (September/October 1996): 32.

16. Donna Keith and Rebecca Hirschfield, "The Benefits of Sharing," *HR Focus* 73 (September 1996): 15.

17. Ibid.

18. Janet Garry-McLaughlin DeRose, "Outsourcing through Partnerships," *Outsourcing through Partnerships* 49 (October 1995): 51.

19. McNerney, "Outsourcing of HR Continues."

20. *Restructuring the Human Resources Department.*

21. McNerney, "Outsourcing of HR Continues."

22. John B. Wyatt, "Customer-Driven HR," *HR Focus* 74 (February 1997): 3.

23. Down "Human Resources Takes a Strategic Role."

24. Ibid.

25. Brookes, "HR in the '90s: From Tacticians to Strategists."

26. Ibid., 54–62.

27. Charlene Marmer Solomon and Brenda Paik Sunoo, "What Image Do You Project," *Workforce* 76 (January 1997): 140.

28. McNerney, "Career Development: As HR Changes, so Do HR Career Paths."

29. Ibid.

30. Elizabeth Sheley, "Share Your Worth," *HRMagazine* 41 (June 1996): 86.

31. Charlene Marmer Solomon, "Managing the HR Career of the 90's," *Personnel Journal* 73 (June 1994): 62–64.

32. Jack Faris, "Small Business Works for America," *Enterprise/Salt Lake City* 26 (June 1997): 18.

33. Gene Koretz, "A Surprising Finding on New-Business Mortality Rates," *Business Week* (June 14, 1993): 22.

34. Louis S. Richman, "Jobs That Are Growing and Slowing," *Fortune* 128 (July 12, 1993): 52–53.

35. David Snyder, "The Revolution in the Workplace: What's Happening to Our Jobs?" *Futurist* 30 (March 1996): 8.

36. Down, "Human Resources Takes a Strategic Role."

37. Sandra Jaszczak and Tara E. Sheets (eds.), *Encyclopedia of Associations*, 32nd ed., vol. 1: National Organizations of the United States, part 1 (Detroit: Gale Research Company, 1997): 274.

38. Juanita F. Perry, "Accredited Professionals Are Better Prepared," *Personnel Administrator* 30 (December 1985): 48.

39. Details of the HRCI are shown in the appendix to this chapter.

40. Jaszczak and Sheets, *Encyclopedia of Associations*, 782.

41. Ibid., 120.

42. Ibid., 274.

43. Ibid., 122.

44. Elizabeth Bankowski, "Ethics Must Come from the Top Down," *Compensation and Benefits Review* 29 (March/April 1997): 25–26.

45. Alan Weiss, "Seven Reasons to Examine Workplace Ethics," *HRMagazine* 36 (March 1992): 71.

46. Bill Leonard, "Business Ethics Touch HR Issues, Survey Finds," *HR News* 10 (June 1991): 13.

47. Louis V. Larimer, "Reflections on Ethics and Integrity," *HR Focus* 74 (April 1997): 5.

48. Patricia Buhler, "How Can We Encourage Ethical Behavior?" *Supervision* 52 (January 1991): 3.

49. David E. Molnar and G. Michael Loewe, "Global Assignments: Seven Keys to International HR Management," *HR Focus* 74 (May 1997): 11.

50. Ibid.

51. Stephenie Overman, "Is HR a Weak Link in the Global Chain?" *HR Magazine* 38 (June, 1994): 67–68.

Appendix

Professional Certification

The Human Resource Certification Institute (HRCI) is an affiliate of the Society for Human Resource Management. Since its inception in 1976, the HRCI has granted certification to many human resource professionals. The number of certified individuals will likely increase substantially as the benefits of certification become more apparent.

The Human Resource Certification Institute program provides for two levels of certification: Professional in Human Resources (PHR), and Senior Professional in Human Resources (SPHR). These two levels recognize degrees of expertise and responsibility.

ELIGIBILITY

The HRCI grants certification after an applicant has:

1. verified current professional exempt-level experience in the HR field as either a practitioner, educator, researcher or consultant, and

2. passed a comprehensive written examination to demonstrate mastery of knowledge.

To earn the basic generalist designation, Professional in Human Resources (PHR), an individual must have:

1. four years of professional HR exempt-level experience *or* either two years professional HR exempt-level experience and a bachelor's degree *or* one year professional HR exempt-level experience and a graduate degree. Degrees must be earned from a higher education institution accredited by a generally recognized college or university accrediting association.

2. passed a comprehensive examination.

NOTE: Students are allowed to take the PHR examination within one year of graduation even if they do not have the required experience. If they pass the exam, they receive notification of the results. They then have four years in which to complete the experience requirements for certification. They receive the PHR certification when they submit evidence of meeting the work experience requirements.

To earn the senior generalist designation, Senior Professional in Human Resources (SPHR), an individual must have:

1. eight years of professional HR exempt-level experience *or* six years professional HR exempt-level experience and a bachelor's degree *or* five years professional HR exempt-level experience and a graduate degree. Degrees must be earned from a higher education institution accredited by a generally recognized college or university accrediting association.

2. passed a comprehensive examination.

DEFINITIONS

The credentialing program established and administered by the HRCI is intended for those professionals who are currently working in the field. While the work need not always be exclusively in the HR field, it is expected that work in the field be the dominating thrust. Therefore, the following general definitions apply:

Practitioner: One whose duties are those normally found in the typical HR/Personnel activity.

Educator: One whose principal area of instruction is in the HR/Personnel field in an accreditated institution of higher education.

Researcher: One whose research activities are restricted primarily to the HR/Personnel field.

Consultant: One whose consulting activities are predominantly in the HR/Personnel field.

The HRCI defines professional HR exempt-level experience as "work that would meet the test for 'exempt' as defined by the Fair Labor Standards Act and its amendments."

EXAM COMPOSITION

Functional Areas

1. Selection and placement

2. Training and development

3. Compensation and benefits

4. Health, safety, and security

5. Employee and labor relations

6. Management practices

The content of HRCI's comprehensive examinations is divided up (by percentage) as follows:

Functional Content Area	PHR Level	SPHR Level
Selection and placement	20%	15%
Training and development	12%	12%
Compensation and benefits	21%	18%
Employee and labor relations	18%	19%
Health, safety, and security	7%	7%
Management practices	22%	29%

In addition:

■ Both exams have a four-hour time limit.

- Both exams have 250 multiple-choice questions with each question having four possible answers.
- Passing or failing is based on the examinee's scaled score for the total test. A scaled score of at least 500 is needed to pass.
- Questions unanswered are counted as incorrect.

Recertification. Certification is earned by individuals who demonstrate their mastery of the defined body of knowledge. The human resources field, however, is not static. Rapid changes require new and more sophisticated knowledge and behaviors by human resource professionals who wish to grow and develop with their field. Recertification is a method that certified individuals can use to demonstrate their accomplishments in keeping abreast of these changes and to update their knowledge in the field.

Recertification is required within three years of certification. Each subsequent recertification period is also for three years. There are two ways to become recertified. Testing is one method. The other method involves continuing one's educational and professional experience.

Certification examinations are given on the first Saturday of each May and December at designated test sites. Applications must be submitted at least ten weeks in advance of the examination date. For additional certification information, contact the Human Resource Certification Institute, 1800 Duke Street, Alexandria, VA 22314 (703) 548-3440. Fax: (703) 836-0367; TDD (703) 548-6999; E-mail:hrci@shrm.orgHRCIhomepage:http://www.shrm.org/hrci

PART TWO

THE ENVIRONMENT OF HRM, LEGAL ASPECTS OF HRM, AND JOB ANALYSIS

2

The Environment of Human Resource Management

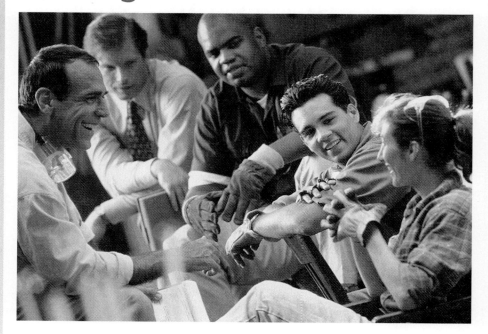

CHAPTER OBJECTIVES

1. Identify the environmental factors that affect human resource management.
2. Distinguish between a proactive and a reactive response to the external environment.
3. Define diversity and identify the diverse workforce that management now confronts.
4. Explain the importance of small business in today's work environment.
5. Define *corporate culture*.
6. Identify factors that influence corporate culture.

As Wayne Simmons, vice president of human resources for Lone Star Manufacturing, returned to his office from the weekly executive staff meeting, he was visibly disturbed. Lone Star, a producer of high-quality telecommunications equipment, is headquartered in Longview, Texas, and has manufacturing plants throughout Texas, Louisiana, and Oklahoma. Wayne had just heard a rumor that an overseas firm had developed a new manufacturing process that had the potential to cut costs substantially. Should this report prove true, customers might switch to the cheaper product. The three plants in the Longline Division that produce similar products would then be in serious trouble. The Longline Division had been expanding rapidly, but Wayne knew that demand for Lone Star's products was far from automatic. If the new technology was superior, he also knew Lone Star might have to cut back production severely or even close the three plants in the Longline Division. These plants are located in areas that are already experiencing high unemployment because of the depressed price of crude oil. Plant closings would have a devastating effect on the economies of their respective communities. A few workers could be transferred to other locations, but most would have to be laid off. Thus, Wayne is now keenly aware of ways in which the external environment can have an impact on the operations of Lone Star Manufacturing.

*I*n this chapter, we first identify the environmental factors that affect human resource management. Then we describe the means by which specific external environmental factors can influence human resource management and distinguish between a proactive and reactive response to the external environment. Next, we describe the diverse workforce that management now confronts and explain the importance of small business in today's work environment. Then we discuss corporate culture, describe factors that influence it, and address changing corporate culture.

Environmental Factors Affecting Human Resource Management

Many interrelated factors affect human resource management (HRM). Such factors are part of either the firm's external environment or its internal environment (see Figure 2-1). The firm often has little, if any, control over how the external environment affects management of its human resources. These factors impinge on the organization from outside its boundaries. Moreover, important factors within the firm itself, such as corporate culture, also have an impact on how the firm manages its human resources.

Certain interrelationships tend to complicate the management of human resources. For instance, human resource professionals constantly work with people who represent all organizational levels and functional areas. Therefore, they must recognize the different perspectives these individuals bring to human resource management if the professionals are to perform their tasks properly.

Understanding the many interrelationships implied in Figure 2-1 is essential for the human resource professional to help other managers resolve issues and problems. For instance, a production manager may want to give a substantial pay raise to a particular employee. The human resource manager may know that this employee does an exceptional job; he or she should also be aware that granting the raise may affect pay practices in the production department and set a precedent for the entire firm. The human resource manager may have to explain to the production manager that such an action is not an isolated decision. They may have to consider alternative means of rewarding the employee for superior performance, without upsetting the organization's reward system. One solution may be for the human resource manager to point to a higher paying position the employee is qualified to fill.

Whatever the case, the implications of a particular act must be considered in light of its potential impact on a department and the entire organization. Those involved in human resource management must realize the overwhelming importance of the big picture, rather than concentrating on a narrow phase of the company's operation. The basic HRM tasks remain essentially the same regardless of the source of the impact. However, the manner in which those tasks are accomplished may be altered substantially by factors in the external environment. Wayne Simmons is

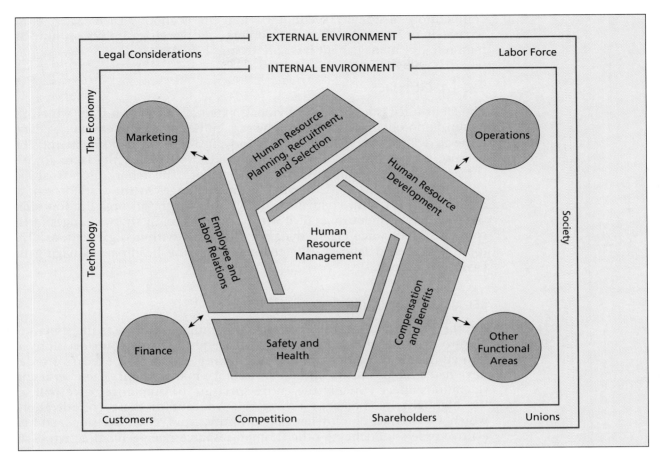

Figure 2-1
The Environments of Human Resource Management

fully aware of the external environment, particularly the overall impact of new technology on the organization as well as the communities in the Longline Division.

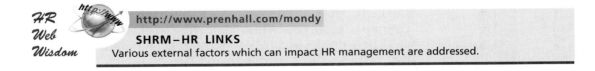

HR Web Wisdom

http://www.prenhall.com/mondy

SHRM—HR LINKS
Various external factors which can impact HR management are addressed.

The External Environment

External environment:
The factors that affect a firm's human resources from outside the organization's boundaries.

Factors that affect a firm's human resources from outside its boundaries make up the **external environment**. As illustrated in Figure 2-1, external factors include the labor force, legal considerations, society, unions, shareholders, competition, customers, technology, and the economy. Each factor, either separately or in combination with others, can place constraints on how human resource management tasks are accomplished.

THE LABOR FORCE

The labor force is a pool of individuals external to the firm from which the organization obtains its workers. The capabilities of a firm's employees determine to a large extent how well the organization can perform its mission. Because new employees are hired from outside the firm, the labor force is considered an external environmental factor. The labor force is always changing, and these shifts inevitably cause changes in the workforce of an organization. In turn, changes in individuals within an organization affect the way management must deal with its workforce. In short, changes in the country's labor force create dynamic situations within organizations. This topic is discussed later in this chapter under the heading "Managing the Diverse Workforce."

LEGAL CONSIDERATIONS

Another significant external force affecting human resource management relates to federal, state, and local legislation and the many court decisions interpreting this legislation. In addition, many presidential executive orders have had a major impact on human resource management. These legal considerations affect virtually the entire spectrum of human resource policies. We highlight in chapter 3 the most significant of these considerations, which affect equal employment opportunity. Laws, court decisions, and executive orders influencing other human resource management activities are described in the appropriate chapters.

SOCIETY

Society may also exert pressure on human resource management. The public is no longer content to accept without question the actions of business. Individuals and special interest groups have found that they can effect change through their voices, votes, and other actions. The influence of activists is obvious in the large number of regulatory laws that have been passed since the early 1960s. To remain acceptable to the general public, a firm must accomplish its purpose while complying with societal norms.

Social responsibility:
The implied, enforced, or felt obligation of managers, acting in their official capacities, to serve or protect the interests of groups other than themselves.

The attitudes and beliefs of the general public can affect the firm's behavior, because those attitudes and beliefs often directly affect profitability. When a corporation behaves as if it has a conscience, it is said to be socially responsible. **Social responsibility** is an implied, enforced, or felt obligation of managers, acting in their official capacities, to serve or protect the interests of groups other than themselves. Many companies develop patterns of concern for moral and social issues. Wayne Simmons was aware and apparently concerned about the impact that possible closure of the three plants in the Longline Division would have on their respective communities.

Companies can show social concern through their policy statements, their practices, and leadership over time. Open-door policies, grievance procedures, and employee benefit programs often stem as much from a desire to do what is right as from a concern for productivity and avoidance of strife.[1]

You may well ask, "Why should a business be concerned with the welfare of society? Its goal is to make a profit and grow." Obviously, a business must make a profit over the long run if it is to survive, but you should also remember another basic point: If a firm does not satisfy society's needs, it will ultimately cease to exist. A firm operates by public consent to satisfy society's requirements. The organization is a member of the community in which it operates. Just as citizens work to improve the quality of life in their community, the organization should also respect and work with the other members of its community. For instance, a high unemployment rate among a certain minority group may exist within the firm's service area. A philosophy of hiring workers who are capable of being trained in addition to applicants who are already qualified may help to reduce unemployment for that minority group. In the long run, this philosophy will certainly enhance the firm's image and may actually improve its profitability.

In recent years, companies have been struggling with how they will compete in the new global environment. They are constantly looking for new ideas that will make them more efficient. In view of this new environment, some are questioning whether efficiency and social responsibility can be married.[2] For example, IBM once had the reputation of never laying off workers. This reputation was shattered when many workers were laid off in the early 1990s. In view of these layoffs, it would be reasonable to question whether IBM can afford to do many of the things that gained it the reputation of being socially responsible. Resource utilization may need to be thoroughly analyzed to determine whether a certain *socially responsible* action actually assists the firm in remaining competitive in this ever-expanding global environment. Only time will tell how the concept of social responsibility fares in this new environment.

UNIONS

Union: A group of employees who have joined together for the purpose of dealing collectively with their employer.

Wage levels, benefits, and working conditions for millions of employees now reflect decisions made jointly by unions and management. A **union** is a group of employees who have joined together for the purpose of dealing with their employer. Unions are treated as an environmental factor because, essentially, they become a third party when they bargain with the company. In a unionized organization, the union rather than the individual employee negotiates an agreement with management.

Although unions remain a powerful force, union membership as a percentage of the nonagricultural workforce slipped from 33 percent in 1955 to 14.5 percent in 1996.[3] When government employees are subtracted, unions represent 10 percent of the private industry workforce.[4] This trend is expected to continue, and as the power and influence of unions wanes, the emphasis will likely shift further to a human resource system that deals directly with the individual worker and his or her needs.

SHAREHOLDERS

Shareholders: The owners of a corporation.

The owners of a corporation are called **shareholders**. Because shareholders, or stockholders, have invested money in the firm, they may at times challenge programs considered by management to be beneficial to the organization. Managers may be forced to justify the merits of a particular program in terms of how it will affect future projects, costs, revenues, and profits. For instance, $50,000 spent on implementing a management development program may require more justification than stating, "Managers should become more open and adaptive to the needs of employees." Shareholders are concerned with how such expenditure decisions will increase revenues or decrease costs. Management must be prepared to explain the merits of a particular program in terms of its economic costs and benefits.

Stockholders are wielding increasing influence. There are frequent stockholder lawsuits against managers and directors, claiming they failed to look out for stockholder interests. For instance, when Medco merged with Merck, unhappy shareholders filed five suits alleging that the Merck deal was designed to enrich top executives at other shareholders' expense.[5]

COMPETITION

A firm may face intense competition in both its product and labor markets. Unless an organization is in the unusual position of monopolizing the market it serves, other firms will be producing similar products or services. A firm must maintain a supply of competent employees if it is to succeed, grow, and prosper. At the same time, other organizations are striving for that same objective. A firm's major task is to ensure that it obtains and retains a sufficient number of employees in various career fields to allow the firm to compete effectively. A bidding war often results when competitors attempt to fill certain critical positions in their firms. Because of the strategic nature of their needs, firms are sometimes forced to resort to unusual means to recruit and retain such employees. The poster shown in Figure 2-2 exemplifies the extreme approaches some organizations have used to recruit qualified workers. Because of the low unemployment rate and the demand for skilled workers in mid-1997, some firms were paying bonuses of 25 percent to 30 percent of a person's annual salary to influence individuals to change companies.[6]

CUSTOMERS

The people who actually use a firm's goods and services are also part of its external environment. Because sales are crucial to the firm's survival, management has the task of ensuring that its employment practices do not antagonize the customers it serves. Customers constantly demand high-quality products and after-purchase service. Therefore, a firm's workforce should be capable of providing quality goods and services. Sales are often lost or gained because of variances in product quality and follow-up service. These conditions relate directly to the skills, qualifications, and motivations of the organization's employees.

Figure 2-2
A Recruitment Poster

TECHNOLOGY

The rate of technological change is accelerating, and as a result, few firms operate today as they did even a decade ago. Wayne Simmons is well aware of the impact of technology on the workforce, realizing that technological disadvantage will possibly result in plant closures. Of major concern to those dealing with human resource management is the effect technological changes have had and will have on businesses. During the next decade, one of the most challenging aspects of human resource management will be training and developing employees to keep up with rapidly advancing technology. Products that were not envisioned only a few years ago are now being mass produced, substantially enlarging the tasks of all managers. New skills are typically not in large supply; recruiting qualified individuals in areas that demand them is often difficult.

As technological changes occur, certain skills are no longer required. This situation necessitates some retraining of the current workforce. Between 1990 and 1993, the need for computer literacy for managers and other professionals rose 35 percent, according to *Managing Today's Workplace*—a report from the Olsten Forum for Information Management of the Olsten Corporation. Today, more than 70 percent of management positions require computer-literacy skills.[7]

The trend toward a service economy also affects the type and amount of technology needed. While the number of manufacturing jobs has been decreasing, the number of service industry jobs has dramatically increased. By some estimates, approximately 80 percent of the jobs in the United States are now in service-related industries.[8]

THE ECONOMY

The economy of the nation, on the whole and in its various segments, is a major environmental factor affecting human resource management. As a generalization, when the economy is booming, recruiting qualified workers is more difficult than in less prosperous times. This was the case in mid-1997 when the national unemployment rate was below 5 percent. Some companies had to use bonuses to entice needed employees. On the other hand, when a downturn is experienced, more applicants are typically available.

To complicate this situation even further, one segment of the country may be experiencing a downturn, another a slow recovery, and another a boom. Such was the situation in the early 1990s. Some of the northeast states were facing a downturn; Houston, Texas, was gradually recovering; and Salt Lake City, Utah, was booming.[9]

The External Environment: Proactive versus Reactive

Proactive response: Taking action in anticipation of environmental changes.

Reactive response: Simply reacting to environmental changes after they occur.

Managers approach changes in the external environment proactively or reactively. A **proactive** response involves taking action in anticipation of environmental changes. A **reactive** response involves simply responding to environmental changes after they occur. For example, while the Americans with Disabilities Act (ADA) of 1990 was weaving its way through Congress, some companies had already implemented its anticipated provisions. Managers of these companies were being proactive. Those who waited until the law went into effect even to plan the required changes were being reactive.

Organizations exhibit varying degrees of proactive and reactive behavior. When the Occupational Health and Safety Act (OSHA) was enacted, some firms did only what the letter of the law required. Others went far beyond that and allocated significant resources to create a safe and healthful environment for employees. The response to Title VII of the Civil Rights Act of 1964 provides another example. Prior to passage of that law, many firms were inactive with regard to equal employment opportunity. However, many of these same companies later became aggressive in promoting equal opportunity. Convinced that the national agenda was to eliminate discrimination in employment based on race, color, sex, religion, or national origin, they went beyond the explicit requirements of the law. Those dealing with human resource management have discovered a proactive attitude leads to performance improvement and reduces the level of damaging discrimination suits.[10]

A firm may be either reactive or proactive in any matter, legal or otherwise. For example, reactive managers may demonstrate concern for employee welfare only after a union organizing attempt starts. Proactive managers try to spot early signs of discontent and correct the causes of that discontent before matters get out of hand. Proactive managers prevent customer complaints rather than handle them. In the markets they serve, proactive managers tend to set the prices competitors must match. They install scrubbers on exhaust stacks before environmental groups begin picketing the plant and before federal regulators file suit. In all matters, proactive managers initiate rather than react. When an unanticipated environmental change occurs, proactive managers go beyond what the change forces them to do.

HR
Web
Wisdom

http://www.prenhall.com/mondy

DIVERSITY AND COMPETITIVE ADVANTAGE
Diversity management presents new challenges that, if handled effectively, can enhance competitiveness.

Managing the Diverse Workforce

From McDonald's to Holiday Inn, AT&T to Levi Strauss, managers are learning not only to understand their *kaleidoscopic workforce* but also to manage diverse environments effectively. Diversity management presents new challenges in the workplace. Not only are more businesses expanding their operations overseas, but many workers in the United States are working alongside individuals whose cultures differ substantially from their own, and more ethnic minorities are entering the workforce. Managers must be knowledgeable about common group characteristics to manage diversity effectively. **Diversity** refers to any perceived difference among people: age, functional specialty, profession, sexual orientation, geographic origin, lifestyle, tenure with the organization, or position.[11] R. Roosevelt Thomas Jr., president of the American Institute for Managing Diversity, clarified certain misconceptions about diversity in corporate America when he said, "People vary along an infinite number of possibilities." He continued, "They vary according to race and gender, but they also vary according to age, sexual orientation and when they joined the company. Some workers are union members; some are not. Some are exempt; some are nonexempt." The variety is endless. "Your definition has to be sufficiently broad to encompass everyone," advised Thomas.[12]

In 1997, the U.S. labor force was 121.8 million people with a national unemployment rate of only 4.8 percent.[13] Size alone, however, does not tell

Diversity: Any perceived difference among people: age, functional specialty, profession, sexual orientation, geographic origin, lifestyle, tenure with the organization, or position.

Managers are learning how to manage effectively in a diverse environment.

the whole story. The labor force now includes more women and older people than ever before. Employees with disabilities are being included in increasing numbers. Many immigrants from developing areas, especially Southeast Asia and Latin America, are joining the labor force.

TRENDS & INNOVATIONS

DIVERSITY IN THE WORKPLACE

The issue of diversity is one reality of being globally competitive. Today it would seem socially irresponsible to proclaim in an advertising brochure that "none but white women and girls are employed," but in 1908 that is just what was included in a Levi Strauss brochure. Today, Levi Strauss has taken the moral high ground in terms of being socially responsible by developing a diverse workforce. The firm appears to be exceptional in this area and is currently recognized as "one of the most ethnically and culturally diverse companies in the United States, if not the world." Approximately 56 percent of the 23,000 people in the U.S. workforce belonged to minority groups. Fourteen percent of Levi Strauss's top managers are nonwhite and 30 percent are female. In another step up the social responsibility ladder, Levi Strauss is doing its best to eliminate the "glass ceiling" that may have prevented some qualified minorities and women from being promoted into the company's top ranks. Promoting diversity makes good business sense for Levi Strauss and has allowed the company to design and develop merchandise for diverse markets that it may not have understood or appreciated in the past. Levi Strauss credits the Dockers line of casual pants, now worth more than $1 billion a year, to Argentine employees. Both diversity and social responsibility are often costly and time-consuming, but Levi Strauss chief executive officer Robert B. Haas believes that harnessing diversity will continue to benefit the company well into the future. According to Levi Strauss executives, "Standing firm . . . sends an important message to employees of all races and lifestyles."[14]

The challenge for managers in the coming decades will be to recognize that people with common, but different characteristics from the mainstream, often think differently, act differently, learn differently, and communicate differently. Because every person, culture, and business situation is unique, there are no simple rules for managing diversity, but diversity experts say that employees need to develop patience, open-mindedness, acceptance, and cultural awareness. Only by such measures can productivity be maximized.[15]

SINGLE PARENTS AND WORKING MOTHERS

The number of nontraditional, single-parent households in the United States is growing. Because more than half of all marriages today end in divorce, this trend is expected to continue. Often, one or more children are involved. Of course, there are always widows and widowers who have children as well, and there are some men and women who choose to raise children outside wedlock.

Traditionally, child care needs were viewed as being outside the realm of the business world—a responsibility workers had to bear and manage alone. This situation was particularly difficult for single parents, but even working parent couples generally cannot afford a full-time live-in housekeeper. For many workers, child care has been managed with the help of family or friends. As evidence of the need for alternative arrangements, in 1950, only 12 percent of women with children under age six were in the labor force; that figure has now risen to almost 60 percent.[16]

Today, business has begun to see that providing child care services and workplace flexibility may influence workers' choice of employers. Many companies have begun providing day care services for employees. Some companies located in the same building or facility provide joint day care service. Other companies, such as IBM, provide day care referral services. More and more companies provide paid maternity leave, and some offer paternity leave. Still other firms give time off for children's visits to doctors, which can be charged against the parents' sick leave or personal time. Managers need to be sensitive to the needs of working parents. At times, management also needs to be creative in accommodating this most valuable segment of the workforce.

WOMEN IN BUSINESS

Today half the entry-level management positions are filled by women; this figure is up from 15 percent 15 years ago.[17] Because of the critical mass of talent, many believe that the 1990s will be remembered as the decade that saw women in mass break through to upper-level management. In one study, it appears that women no longer see careers and family as mutually exclusive. Sixty-nine percent of the women polled were married, and 63 percent had children.

Because of the number of women who are entering the workforce, there is an increasing number of nontraditional households in the United States. These households include those headed by single parents and those in which both partners work full time. Women who formerly remained at home to care for children and the household today need and want to work outside the home. If this valuable segment of the workforce is to be effectively utilized, organizations must fully recognize the importance of addressing work/family issues.[18]

DUAL-CAREER COUPLES

The increasing number of dual-career couples presents both challenges and opportunities for organizations. In a recent study by the Conference Board, a New York business research group, more than 50 percent of employers said employees in their organizations have turned down relocations because of spouses' jobs and concerns they had about their children.[19] As a result of this trend, some firms have revised their policies against nepotism to allow both partners to work for the same company. Other firms have developed polices to assist the spouse of an employee who is transferred. When a firm wishes to transfer an employee to another location, the employee's spouse may be unwilling to give up a good position or may be unable to find an equivalent position in the new location. Some companies are offering assistance in finding a position for the spouse of a transferred employee.

As the number of dual-career couples increases, organizations have to become even more flexible. For example, cafeteria benefit plans may need to offer more options for today's worker. With dual-career couples, only one of the spouses might pick up a health-care plan and additional vacation might be selected by the second spouse.[20] Some companies are actually designing their buildings to help dual-career couples. At Procter and Gamble, the company specifically incorporated into the plant a dry cleaner, a shoe-repair shop, and a cafeteria that prepares food employees can take home at night, relieving them of the need to prepare an evening meal.[21]

The dual-career challenge is especially difficult in the international environment. According to a survey of 176 companies conducted by Price Waterhouse/Bennett Associates, nearly 57 percent of couples that move internationally are dual-career families. Less than 3 percent of the accompanying spouses are offered employment by the company sponsoring the move.[22]

WORKERS OF COLOR

Workers of color often experience stereotypes about their group (including Hispanics, African Americans, and Asians). At times, they encounter misunderstandings and expectations based on ethnic or cultural differences. Members of ethnic or racial groups are socialized within their particular culture.

Many are socialized as members of two cultural groups—the dominant culture and their racial or ethnic culture. Ella Bell, professor of organizational behavior at MIT, refers to this dual membership as *biculturalism*. In her study of African-American women, she identifies the stress of coping with membership in two cultures simultaneously as bicultural stress. She indicates that *role conflict*—competing roles from two cultures—and *role overload*—too many expectations to fulfill comfortably—are common characteristics of bicultural stress. Although these issues can be applied to many minority groups, they are particularly intense for women of color. This is because this group experiences dynamics affecting *both* minorities and women.[23]

Socialization in one's culture of origin can lead to misunderstandings in the workplace. This is particularly true when the manager relies solely on the cultural norms of the majority group. According to these norms, within the American culture it is acceptable—even positive—to praise an individual publicly for a job well done. However, in cultures that place primary value on group harmony and collective achievement, this method of rewarding an employee causes emotional discomfort. Employees feel that if they are praised publicly, they will *lose face* within their group.

OLDER WORKERS

The U.S. population is growing older, a trend that is expected to continue beyond the year 2000. Life expectancies continue to increase, and the baby boom generation (people born from the end of World War II through 1964) had only half as many children as their parents did. Demographers estimate that by the year 2000, more than 60 million Americans will be over the age of 55.[24]

In addition, the trend toward earlier retirement appears to be reversing itself. This shift may have resulted from the 1986 amendment to the Age Discrimination in Employment Act. With certain exceptions, firms cannot force employees to retire because of age, no matter how old they are. Many older persons do not want to retire or even slow down. As many as one-third of retirees want to return to full- or part-time work.[25]

As the workforce grows older, the needs and interests of its members may change.[26] Many become bored with their present careers and desire different challenges. The *graying* of the workforce has required some adjustments. Some older workers favor less demanding full-time jobs, others choose semi-retirement, and still others prefer part-time work. Many of these individuals require retraining as they move through the various stages of their careers.

PEOPLE WITH DISABILITIES

A disability limits the amount or kind of work a person can do or makes its achievement unusually difficult. More common disabilities include limited hearing or sight, limited mobility, mental or emotional deficiencies, and various nerve disorders. Most disabled workers do as well as the unimpaired in terms of productivity, attendance, and average tenure. In fact, in certain high turnover occupations, handicapped workers have had lower turnover rates. The Americans with Disabilities Act (ADA), passed in 1990, prohibits discrimination against *qualified individuals with disabilities* and is discussed in detail in chapter 3.

A serious barrier to effective employment of disabled persons is bias or prejudice. Managers should examine their own biases and preconceived attitudes toward such individuals. Many individuals experience anxiety around workers with disabilities, especially if the disabilities are severe. Fellow workers may show pity or feel that a disabled worker is fragile. Some even show disgust. The manager can set the tone for proper treatment of workers with disabilities. If someone is unsure about how to act or how much help to offer, the disabled person should be asked for guidance. Managers must always strive to treat employees with disabilities as they treat other employees and must hold them accountable for achievement.

HRM IN ACTION
WHAT TO DO?

Duane Roberts, a paraplegic, has just been assigned to your division as a radio dispatcher for your delivery trucks. The human resource department has given you only limited information about Duane, but you know that he is 32 years old and has held similar jobs. You are in the dispatching office when you see a person you assume to be Duane coming up the sidewalk in his wheelchair. You think he might have a problem getting through the double glass doors in his path, which open against his direction of travel.

How would you handle the situation?

IMMIGRANTS

Today the permitted level of legal immigration in the United States is one million per year.[27] Large numbers of immigrants from Asia and Latin America have settled in many parts of the United States. Some are highly skilled and well educated and others are only minimally qualified, with little education. They have one thing in common—an eagerness to work.[28] They have brought with them attitudes, values, and mores particular to their home country cultures.

In the 1970s and 1980s, after the end of hostilities in Vietnam, Vietnamese immigrants settled along the Gulf Coast in Mississippi and Texas. At about the same time, thousands of Thais fleeing the upheaval in Thailand came to the Boston area to work and live. New York's Puerto Rican community has long been an economic and political force there. Cubans who fled Castro's regime congregated in southern Florida, especially Miami. A flood of Mexicans and other Hispanics continues across the southern border of the United States. The Irish, the Poles, the Italians, and others who came here in past decades have long since assimilated into—and indeed have become—the culture. Newer immigrants require time to adapt. Meanwhile, they generally take low-paying and menial jobs, live in substandard housing, and form enclaves where they cling to some semblance of the cultures they left.

Wherever they settle, members of these ethnic groups soon begin to become part of the regular workforce and break out of their isolation in certain occupations. They begin to adopt the English language and American customs. They begin to learn new skills and to adapt old skills to their new country. Human resource managers can place these individuals in jobs appropriate to their skills with excellent results for the organization. As corporations employ more foreign nationals in this country, managers must work to understand the different cultures and languages of their employees.

Young Persons with Limited Education or Skills

Each year, thousands of young, unskilled workers are hired, especially during peak periods, such as holiday buying seasons. These workers generally have limited education, sometimes even less than a high school diploma. Those who have completed high school often find that their education hardly fits the work they are expected to do. Most, for example, lack familiarity with computers. Many of these young adults and teenagers have poor work habits; they tend to be tardy or absent more often than experienced or better-educated workers.

Although the negative attributes of these workers at times seem to outweigh the positive ones, they are a permanent part of the workforce. There are many jobs they can do well. Also, more jobs can be *de-skilled*, making it possible for lower-skilled workers to do them. A well-known example of de-skilling is McDonald's substitution of pictures for numbers on its cash register keys. Managers should also look for ways to train unskilled workers and to further their formal education.

Educational Level of Employees

Another form of diversity now found in the workplace occurs in the educational level of employees. The United States is becoming a bipolar country with regard to education, with a growing number of very educated people on one side and an alarming increase in the illiteracy rate on the other. These functionally illiterate people want to join the workforce.[29] To complicate this situation, more than half the new jobs created through 2005 will probably require some education beyond high school.[30] Adding even more complexity is the trend in the workplace to empower workers. Empowerment is possible because of the advanced educational level of the new workforce. However, those with limited education will be left out of this empowerment effort.[31]

The Small Business

As mentioned in chapter 1, in the United States today, 90 percent of all businesses have fewer than 20 employees. Further, small businesses create two out of three new net jobs and provide 60 percent of all private sector jobs.[32] Every year, approximately 400,000 small businesses are established.[33] Every year, thousands of individuals, motivated by a desire to be their own boss, to earn a better income, and to realize the American dream, launch new business ventures. These individuals, often referred to as entrepreneurs, have been essential to the growth and vitality of the American free enterprise system. Entrepreneurs develop or recognize new products or business opportunities, secure the necessary start-up capital, and organize and operate the business. Most people who start their own businesses get a great deal of satisfaction from owning and managing them. Historically, approximately four out of five small businesses are thought to fail within five years. However, a recent study reported that over half survived in one form or another.[34] Almost every large corporation began as a small business. Many small businesses are so successful they become big businesses.

The environment of managers in large and small businesses is often quite different. Managers in large firms may be separated from top management by numerous managerial layers. They may have difficulty seeing how they fit into the overall organization. They often know managers one or two layers above them but seldom those higher up. In some large companies, supervisors are restricted by many written guidelines, and they may feel more loyalty to their workers than to upper management.

Managers in small businesses often identify more closely with the goals of the firm. They can readily see how their efforts affect the firm's profits. In many instances, lower-level managers know the company executives personally. These supervisors know the organization's success is closely tied to their own effectiveness.

Corporate Culture

Corporate culture: The system of shared values, beliefs, and habits within an organization that interacts with the formal structure to produce behavioral norms.

When beginning a new job, an employee may soon hear, "This is the way we do things around here." This bit of informal communication refers to something more formally known as corporate culture. **Corporate culture** is the system of shared values, beliefs, and habits within an organization that interacts with the formal structure to produce behavioral norms. It is the pattern of basic assumptions, values, norms, and artifacts shared by organizational members.[35] Corporate culture embodies the values and standards that guide people's behavior. It determines the organization's overall direction. Corporate culture governs what the company stands for and how it allocates resources; it determines the company's organizational structure, the systems it uses, the people it hires, the fit between jobs and people, and the results it recognizes and rewards; the culture decides what the company defines as problems and opportunities and how it deals with them.[36] As human resource executives become more like strategic partners, they will be major players in shaping the cultures of organizations.

Each individual forms perceptions of the job and organization over a period of time as he or she works under the general guidance of a superior and a set of organizational policies. For example, employees rapidly discover whether the firm's mission includes having a diverse workplace. A firm's culture has an impact on employee job satisfaction as well as on the level and quality of employee performance. However, each employee may assess the nature of an organization's culture differently. One person may perceive the culture negatively and another may view it positively. Employees who are quite dissatisfied may even leave an organization in the hope of finding a more compatible culture.

Businesses are being forced to make many changes to stay competitive. A means of shaping corporate culture is through organizational development, a topic of chapter 8. Companies must find ways to improve quality, increase speed of operations, and adopt a customer orientation. These changes are so fundamental that they must take root in a company's very essence, which means in its culture.[37] An organization's corporate culture is integral to the company's accomplishing its mission and objectives; therefore, the factors that determine corporate culture are also crucial to the company's success.

Factors That Influence Corporate Culture

The culture of a corporation evolves from the examples set by top management. It stems largely from what these executives do, not what they say. In addition, other factors can interact to shape the culture of a firm. Among those are work groups, managers' and supervisors' leadership styles, organizational characteristics, and administrative processes (see Figure 2-3). As in most management situations, the external environment also influences corporate culture.

WORK GROUP

The character of the immediate work group will affect a worker's perception of the nature of corporate culture. For example, commitment to the mission of the work group directly influences cultural perceptions. Commitment refers to whether the group is really working. If people in the work group are just going through the motions of work, individual members will have difficulty obtaining high levels of output and satisfaction. Hindrance may also occur when individuals work together as a group. Hindrance is concerned with the degree of busywork (work of doubtful value) given to the group. Morale and friendliness within the group are other factors that affect the environment of the work group and the perceived nature of the corporate culture.

MANAGER/SUPERVISOR LEADERSHIP STYLE

The leadership style of the immediate supervisor will have a considerable effect on the culture of the group, and vice versa. If the manager is aloof and distant in dealing with subordinates, this attitude could have a negative influence on the organization. If the supervisor is always pushing for output, this too alters the environment. Consideration is a desirable leadership characteristic that can influence group effectiveness positively. Thrust—managerial behavior characterized by hard work and example setting—is also a positive influence on the group.

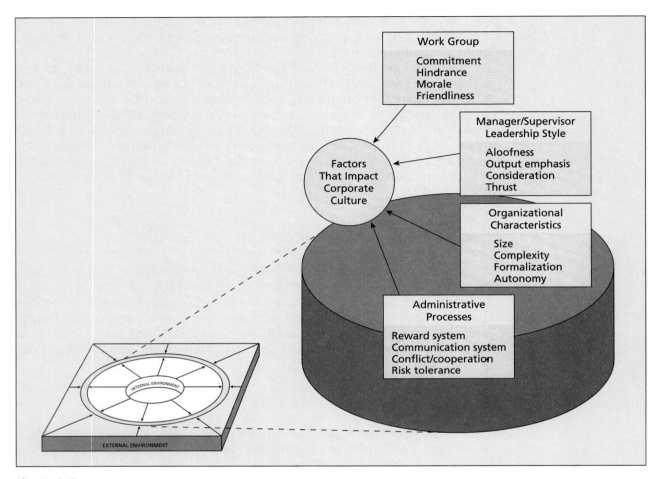

Figure 2-3
Factors That Influence Corporate Culture

ORGANIZATIONAL CHARACTERISTICS

The type of culture that develops is affected by organizational characteristics. For example, organizations vary by size and complexity. Large organizations tend toward higher degrees of specialization and impersonalization. Labor unions often find that large firms are easier to organize than smaller ones because smaller firms tend to be closer and have more informal relationships among employees and management. Complex organizations tend to employ a greater number of professionals and specialists, a condition that alters the general approach to solving problems. Organizations also vary in the degree to which they write things down and attempt to program behavior through rules, procedures, and regulations. They can be distinguished, too, by how much they decentralize decision-making authority, as this affects the level of autonomy and employee freedom.

ADMINISTRATIVE PROCESSES

Corporate culture may be affected by administrative processes. Firms that can develop direct links between performance and rewards tend to create cultures conducive to achievement. Communication systems that are open and free flowing tend to promote participation and creative atmospheres. The general attitudes toward the tolerance of conflict and the handling of risk have considerable influence on teamwork. They also affect the amount of workers' innovation and creativity.

From these and other factors, organization members develop a subjective impression of the organization as a place to work. This impression will affect the workers' performance, satisfaction, creativity, and commitment to the organization.

HR Web Wisdom

http://www.prenhall.com/mondy

CULTURE CHANGE STRATEGY

Questions and answers about culture change and human resources are addressed.

Changing the Corporate Culture

Environmental factors, such as governmental action, workforce diversity, and global competition, often require a firm to change its culture and even make a clean break with the past. For example, the present culture of AT&T is distinctly different from the company's culture of just a few years ago when it virtually monopolized its industry. After being dismantled by the government, the firm has had to deal with aggressive competitors and in doing so develop a new modus operandi.

A diverse American workforce reflects the increasing diversity of the country's population. To maximize the advantages of diversity—particularly the talents of women and minorities—companies are trying to create a culture in which each employee has the opportunity to contribute and to advance in the organization based on excellent performance. Human resource professionals know that critical factors, such as retention, motivation, and advancement, are highly dependent on the way employees react to their firm's culture.

A recent survey of a group of managers with high representations of women and minority employees identified several problem areas inherent in counterproductive cultures.[38]

- *Fighting stereotypes.* The number one problem reported by women and minority managers related to frustrations in coping with gender and race stereotypes.

- *Discrimination and harassment.* Whether experiencing discrimination personally or witnessing it, managers reported that such incidents caused them to question whether they fit in with the firm.

- *Exclusion and isolation.* Women and minority managers are often excluded from social activities and left out of informal communication networks.
- *Work-family balance.* Women managers expressed the view that playing the game often requires compromising personal values and conforming to the expectations of others.
- *Career development.* Observing how few women and minority managers there are in the organization can result in concerns about opportunities for career advancement.

These problem areas illustrate legitimate concerns that organizations must consider in revamping their corporate cultures. Taken together, women and minorities represent a majority of employees entering the workforce. If the talents of these key groups are to be utilized to the fullest, corporate cultures of the future must reflect their needs.

Global competition is another key factor impacting corporate cultures. Few firms have escaped the competitive pressure from foreign firms. This pressure has greatly increased the need for improved quality, competitive pricing, and better customer service. Because these critical factors are so dependent on a firm's culture, the culture itself must change if the firm is to survive, much less prosper.

In changing a firm's culture, as much of the organization should be involved as possible. The chief executive officer should have a proactive role. The necessity of the change, along with the goals sought, should be clearly communicated to all organizational members. They, too, should be involved either directly or indirectly. Change of this magnitude is often called organization development (discussed in chapter 8).

Human Resource Management in the Global Environment

Global corporation:
An organization that has corporate units in a number of countries; the units are integrated to operate as one organization worldwide.

Earlier in this chapter our discussion focused primarily on environmental factors affecting organizations located and doing business in only the United States. The external environment confronting global enterprises is even more diverse and complex than that facing domestic firms. A **global corporation** (GC) has corporate units in a number of countries that are integrated to operate as one organization worldwide. Thus, as illustrated in Figure 2-4, global operations add another environmental layer to human resource management. Although the basic human resources management tasks remain essentially the same, the manner in which they are accomplished may be altered substantially by the global firm's external environment. "A Global Perspective" is presented at the end of each chapter to emphasize the importance of the global environment on human resource management. Also, chapter 17, entitled "Global Human Resource Management," covers various global aspects of this topic.

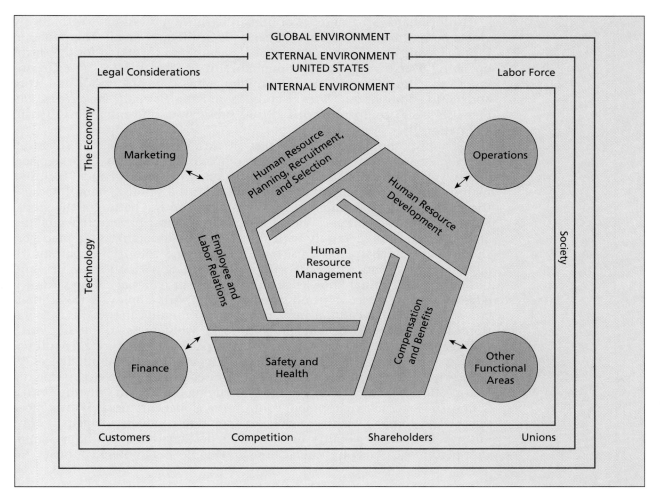

Figure 2-4
Human Resource Management in the Global Environment

A GLOBAL PERSPECTIVE
GLOBAL HR EXPERIENCE: THE TICKET TO SUCCESS

Adapting to the global environment is essential as the worldwide market-place expands and becomes more profitable. If exports and imports were combined, they would total almost 25 percent of the U.S. economy. This fig-ure is up from only 16 percent just 10 years ago.[39] Global competition, air travel, satellite communication technology, the Internet, and wage differen-tials have made doing business abroad both necessary and feasible. Compa-nies have responded by establishing more and more operations overseas.

Unfortunately, the number of human resource professionals with a truly global perspective and effective global skills is still quite small. This situation is problematic because the number of U.S. employees working for U.S. firms operating overseas is expanding dramatically. In fact, the U.S. State Department estimates that more than 2.2 million Americans now reside and work abroad. In addition, the *Directory of American Firms Operating in Foreign Countries* lists 2,500 companies with 18,500 subsidiaries and offices overseas in 132 nations.[40]

Obviously, human assets will play at least as large a role as advanced technology and economies of scale in competing in the global marketplace. Globally, HR professionals must manage human resources in an all-inclusive manner, thinking systematically and looking at the whole system.[41] Because the number of global employees is expanding and the nature of the global environment is so complex, global HR managers must have unique abilities and skills. To deal effectively with the global environment, these managers should have "global experience outside the home country; global knowledge, attitudes, and perspectives toward international issues, events, and business; multicultural knowledge and expertise of national cultures; knowledge of working effectively and simultaneously with employees from different countries; cross-cultural interaction and communication skills, adaptation skills for living in foreign cultures, a willingness to modify one's management style; and have a catalyst-type personality for creating cultural synergy through practicing key skills and integrating national differences."[42]

Earlier in this chapter our discussion focused primarily on environmental factors affecting organizations located and doing business in only the United States. The external environment confronting global enterprises is even more diverse and complex because a global corporation conducts a large part of its business outside the country in which it is headquartered and has a significant percentage of its physical facilities and employees in other countries. ■

SUMMARY

1. *Identify the environmental factors that affect human resource management.*

   External environmental factors include labor force, legal considerations, society, unions, shareholders, competition, customers, technology, and the economy.

2. *Distinguish between a proactive and a reactive response to the external environment.*

   A proactive response involves taking action in anticipation of environmental changes. A reactive response involves simply reacting to environmental changes after they occur.

3. *Define diversity and identify the diverse workforce that management now confronts.*

   Diversity refers to any perceived difference among people: age, functional specialty, profession, sexual orientation, geographic origin, lifestyle, tenure with the organization, or position. The diverse workforce consists of single parents and working mothers, women in business, dual-career couples, workers of color, older workers, people with disabilities, immigrants, young people with limited education or skills, and employees with an extremely wide range of educational levels.

4. ***Explain the importance of small business in today's work environment.***
   In the United States today, 90 percent of all U.S. businesses have fewer than 20 employees. Further, small businesses create two out of three new net jobs and provide 60 percent of all private sector jobs. Every year, approximately 400,000 such businesses are established.

5. ***Define* corporate culture.**
   Corporate culture is the system of shared values, beliefs, and habits within an organization that interacts with the formal structure to produce behavioral norms. It is the pattern of basic assumptions, values, norms, and artifacts shared by organizational members.

6. ***Identify factors that influence corporate culture.***
   The culture of a corporation evolves from the examples set by top management. It stems largely from what these executives do, not what they say. Other factors can also interact to shape the culture of a firm; among these are work groups, managers' and supervisors' leadership styles, organizational characteristics, and administrative processes.

QUESTIONS FOR REVIEW

1. What factors make up the external environment of human resource management? Briefly describe each of these factors.
2. Distinguish between a proactive and reactive response. Give an example of each.
3. Define *diversity*.
4. How is the composition of the U.S. labor force expected to change?
5. How important is small business to our economy?
6. Define *corporate culture*. What effect could it have on human resource management?

DEVELOPING HRM SKILLS

AN EXPERIENTIAL EXERCISE

Judy Flack has just been promoted from assistant to the human resource director to assistant general manager. Although the general manager, Jerry Connors, has mixed feelings about Judy, he did not directly oppose the promotion, but he did express his concerns to his immediate boss, Mr. Samuelson. Jerry's boss told him that he could *handle her* and that the company needed more female managers. Now, Jerry and Judy are about to have their first meeting since the promotion, which should prove very interesting.

If you like a little excitement, you will enjoy this exercise. It is obvious that Jerry and Judy will disagree on many aspects of supervision, and that diversity of opinions could lead to some interesting interactions. If you want to be in Jerry's shoes, or if you'd like to be Judy, volunteer quickly. Everyone else, observe carefully. Your instructor will provide the participants with additional information.

Take It to the Net

We invite you to visit the Mondy home page on the Prentice Hall Web site at:

http://www.prenhall.com/mondy

for updated information, Web-based exercises, and links to other HR-related sites.

HRM SIMULATION

In any organization, decisions should be based on the best available information. The same is true with this simulation. Each decision period, your team will have the opportunity to purchase industry research that will aid you in the decision-making process. The surveys available are industry average quality, morale, grievances, and absenteeism; industry average and local comparable wage rates; average industry training, safety, and quality budgets; and the number of firms with employee participation programs.

HRM INCIDENT

1

The Environment

As the largest employer in Ouachita County, Arkansas, International Forest Products Company (IFP) is an important part of the local economy. Ouachita County includes a mostly rural area of south central Arkansas. It employs almost 10 percent of the local workforce; few alternative job opportunities are available in the area.

Scott Wheeler, the human resource director at IFP, tells of a difficult decision he once had to make.

Everything was going along pretty well despite the economic recession, but I knew that sooner or later we would be affected. I got the word at a private meeting with the president, Mr. Deason, that we would have to cut the workforce by 30 percent on a crash basis. I was to get back to him within a week with a suggested plan. I knew that my plan would not be the final one, because the move was so major, but I knew that Mr. Deason was depending on me to provide at least a workable approach.

First, I thought about how the union would react. Certainly, workers would have to be let go in order of seniority. The union would try to protect as many jobs as possible. I also knew that all management actions during this period would be intensely scrutinized. We had to make sure we had our act together.

Then there was the impact on the surrounding community to consider. The economy of Ouachita County had not been in good shape recently. Aside from the effect on individual workers who were laid off, I knew our cutbacks would further depress the area's economy. I knew that a number of government officials and civic leaders would want to know how we were trying to minimize the harm done to the public in the area.

We really had to make the cuts, I believed. I had no choice because Mr. Deason had said we were going to do it. Also, I had recently read a news account that one of our competitors, Johns Manville Corporation in West Monroe, Louisiana, had laid off several hundred workers in a cost-cutting move. To keep our sales from being further depressed, we had to keep our costs as low as those of our competitors. The wood products market is very competitive and a cost advantage of even 2 or 3 percent would allow competitors to take many of our customers.

Finally, a major reason for the cutbacks was to protect the interests of our shareholders. A few years ago a shareholder group disrupted our annual meeting to insist that IFP make certain antipollution changes. In general, though, the shareholders seem to be more concerned with the return on their investment than with social responsibility. At our meeting, the president reminded me that, just like every other manager in the company, I should place the shareholders' interest foremost. I really was quite overwhelmed as I began to work up a personnel plan that would balance all the conflicting interests that I knew about.

Questions

1. List the elements in the company's environment that will affect Scott's suggested plan. How legitimate is the interest of each of these?
2. Is it true that Scott should be concerned first and foremost with protecting the interests of the shareholders? Discuss.

HRM INCIDENT

2

Implementing a New Culture

*W*hen Bruce Young retired because of ill health in 1995, he appointed his 26-year-old son, Jim, president of the family firm. The company, McDaniel Corporation of Marietta, Georgia, marketed a line of hospital beds. The company manufactured the metal frames for the beds and purchased hydraulic items, springs, and certain other parts. The company also sold hospital furniture items and maintained a crew to repair the McDaniel beds. Employment at the firm totaled about 500 people.

With an MBA degree from Georgia State University and two years' experience with the company, Jim was eager to take over. He believed that his college training and work experience had prepared him well. One of the first things Jim wanted to do was to give decision-making authority to the managers. He remarked, "I felt this would let me pay attention to the big picture while the day-to-day problems were solved lower in the organization." He felt that one effective tool for helping him shift more authority downward in the organization would be the use of work teams.

Bruce Young had been president and owner of Young Corporation for 30 years. During that time, the firm had grown from a small hospital supply company with three employees to its present size. Bruce had been a hard worker, often putting in 15 hours a day. Jim said that his dad was a *pleasant autocrat* because the elder Young insisted on making every important decision, but Bruce had such an affable personality that no one objected.

For a while, Jim tried to behave pretty much like his father had, making all decisions on matters that were brought to him. About a month after his father's retirement, however, Jim called a meeting to tell the managers that he was going to change things and give the managers more decision-making authority. This action would free him to look at the company's overall concerns. He made a brief presentation to the managers, explaining that they did not need his approval for day-to-day decisions. He especially emphasized that they would now have more responsibility and that he expected all supervisors to follow his instructions.

Questions
1. How would these changes affect the culture at Young Corporation?
2. Discuss any likely pitfalls to this rapid change in culture.

Notes

1. Kenneth E. Goodpaster and John B. Matthews, Jr., "Can a Corporation Have a Conscience?" *Harvard Business Review* 60 (January–February 1982): 132–141.
2. Robert J. Samuelson, "R.I.P.: The Good Corporation," *Newsweek* 122 (July 5, 1993): 41.
3. Aaron Bernstein, "Workplace: Unions: Sweeney's Blitz," *Business Week* (February 2, 1997): 56.
4. John E. Lyncheski and Joseph M. McDermott, "Unions Employ New Growth Strategies," *HR Focus* 73 (September 1996): 22.
5. Michael Schroeder and Joseph Weber, "Is Merck Ready for Marty Wygod?" *Business Week* (October 4, 1993): 80–84.
6. Marianne Kolbasuk McGee, "IT Management: Sign-On Bonuses Lure Top IT Talent," *Information Week* (April 12, 1997): 84.
7. Patricia Buhler, "Managing in the 90s," *Supervision* 58 (March 1997): 24.
8. Joseph Spiers, "Behind the Job Worries, Business Keeps Plodding Along," *Fortune* 128 (August 9, 1993): 19.
9. Patricia Sellers, "The Best Cities for Business," *Fortune* 122 (October 22, 1990): 49.
10. Sinclair E. Hugh, "Observations from the Witness Stand," *HRMagazine* 39 (August 1994): 176.
11. Matti F. Dobbs, "Managing Diversity: Lessons from the Private Sector," *Public Personnel Management* 25 (September 1996): 351.
12. Barbara Ettorre, Donald J. McNerny, and Bob Smith, "HR's Shift to a 'Center of Influence,'" (American Management Association's 67th Annual Human Resources Conference and Exposition) *HR Focus* 73 (June 1996): 12.
13. Amy Saltzman, Mary Lord, Scott McMurray, Jill Jordan Siede, Ilan Greenberg, and Barbara Burgower Hordern, "Making It in a Sizzling Economy," *U.S. News & World Report* 122 (June 23, 1997): 50.
14. Alice Cuneo, "Diverse by Design," *Business Week* (Reinventing America 1992): 72.
15. Lee Gardenswartz and Anita Rowe, *Managing Diversity* (San Diego: Business One Irwin/Pfeiffer & Company, 1993): 57–97; Mahalingam Subbiah, "Adding a New Dimension to the Teaching of Audience Analysis: Cultural Awareness," *IEEE Transactions on Professional Communication* 35 (March 1992); and Marcus Mabry, "Pin a Label on a Manager—and Watch What Happened," *Newsweek* 14 (May 1990): 43.

16. Dan Cordtz, "Hire Me, Hire My Family," *Finance World* 159 (September 18, 1990): 77.

17. Amanda Troy Segal and Wendy Zeller, "Corporate Women," *Business Week* (June 8, 1992): 74.

18. Charlene Marmer Solomon, "Work/Family's Failing Grade: Why Today's Initiatives Aren't Enough," *Personnel Journal* 73 (May 1994): 72.

19. Amy Saltzman, "A Family Transfer," *U.S. News & World Report* 122 (February 10, 1997): 60–62.

20. Buhler, "Managing in the 90s."

21. Joan Hamilton, Stephen Baker, and Bill Vlasic, "The New Workplace," *Business Week* (April 29, 1996): 106.

22. Karen Fawcett, "Trailing Spouse Often Must Fend for Self—Herself," *USA Today* (August 9, 1994): 2.

23. Ella Bell, "The Bicultural Life Experience of Career Oriented Black Women," *Journal of Organizational Behavior* 11 (November 1990): 459–478.

24. Suzanne Crampton, John Hodge, and Jetendra Mishra, "Transition-Ready or Not: The Aging of America's Work Force," *Public Personnel Management* 25 (June 1996): 243.

25. Joan L. Kelly, "Employers Must Recognize That Older People Want to Work," *Personnel Journal* 69 (January 1990): 44.

26. Anthony J. Buonocore, "Older and Wiser: Mature Employees and Career Guidance," *Management Review* 81 (September 1992): 54.

27. Yeh Ling-Ling, "Immigration Injures U.S. Environment," *Newsday* (March 1995): A42.

28. Michael J. Mandel, "The Immigrants," *Business Week* (July 13, 1992): 114.

29. Buhler, "Managing in the 90s."

30. Laurie J. Bassi, George Benson, and Scott Cheney, "The Top Ten Trends," *Training & Development* 50 (November 1996): 28.

31. Ibid.

32. Jack Faris, "Small Business Works for America," *Enterprise/Salt Lake City* 26 (June 1997): 18.

33. Gene Koretz, "A Surprising Finding on New-Business Mortality Rates," *Business Week* (June 14, 1993): 22.

34. Ibid.

35. Thomas G. Cummings and Christopher G. Worley, *Organization Development and Change*, 5th ed. (Minneapolis/St. Paul: West Publishing Company, 1993): 526.

36. Frank Petrock, "Corporate Culture Enhances Profits," *HRMagazine* 35 (November 1990): 64–66.

37. Brian Dumaine, "Creating a New Company Culture," *Fortune* 121 (January 15, 1990): 127.

38. Benson Rosen and Kay Lovelace, "Fitting Square Pegs into Round Holes," *HRMagazine* 39 (January 1994): 86–93.

39. Michael J. Mandel, Wendy Zeller, and Robert Hof, "Jobs, Jobs," *Business Week* (February 22, 1993): 70.

40. Marni Halasa, "Discrimination Overseas: New Law Offers Recourse for American Expats," *USA Today* (August 9, 1996): 7A.

41. Perry Pascarella, "Thinking Globally Is 'Sacred' Management Duty," *Management Review* 86 (April 1997): 58–59.

42. Clifford C. Hebard, "Managing Effectively in Asia," *Training & Development* 50 (April 1996): 34.

3
Equal Employment Opportunity and Affirmative Action

CHAPTER OBJECTIVES

1. Identify the major laws affecting equal employment opportunity.
2. Explain Presidential Executive Orders 11246 and 11375.
3. Describe the purpose of the Office of Federal Contract Compliance Programs.
4. Identify some of the major Supreme Court decisions that have had an impact on equal employment opportunity.
5. Explain the purpose of the Uniform Guidelines on Employee Selection Procedures.
6. Explain adverse impact and affirmative action programs.
7. Describe the Uniform Guidelines related to sexual harassment, national origin, and religion.

"*I agree with you Phyllis,*" *said Art Kurth, supervisor of the maintenance division of Allied Chemical. "Mary Martin is by far the best qualified to fill that vacant position in my department. She has done similar work at Olin for seven years and comes highly recommended. I really want to hire her, but do you think a woman could survive with that crew? They might not work with her, and you know how important cooperation is in that job. Remember what happened when we hired that woman a couple of years ago. She lasted a week before she walked out crying and didn't return. Also, I heard Mary is pregnant."*

Phyllis Jordon, production manager of Allied, was visibly upset when she heard Art's comments. Ten years ago when she joined Allied, she might have expected something like that, but not now. Allied has an aggressive nondiscrimination policy. "Listen, Art," she said, "I still recommend that you hire her. I know that you can find a way to see that she fits in. From all I can gather, she is a top-notch worker, and Allied is lucky to have an applicant of that quality. Regardless of whether Mary is pregnant, I'll help you make this work."

*I*n this chapter, we provide an overview of the major equal employment opportunity legislation that has had an impact on human resource management. We first discuss the significant equal employment opportunity laws affecting human resource management. Then we describe the importance of Presidential Executive Orders 11246 and 11375. Next, we review significant Supreme Court decisions and describe the Equal Employment Opportunity Commission. We discuss the Uniform Guidelines on Employee Selection Procedures, address the issue of adverse impact, and discuss additional guidelines. We devote the remainder of the chapter to affirmative action programs and employment standards that should be avoided.

Equal Employment Opportunity: An Overview

The concept of equal employment opportunity has undergone much modification and fine-tuning since the passage of the Civil Rights Act of 1964. Congress has passed numerous amendments to that act as well as other acts in response to oversights in the initial legislation. Major Supreme Court decisions interpreting the provisions of the act have also been handed down. Executive orders were signed into law that further strengthened equal employment opportunity. Over three decades have passed since introduction of the first legislation, and equal employment opportunity has become a part of the workplace.

Although equal employment opportunity has come a long way since the early 1960s, continuing efforts are required. For example, almost six of ten HR professionals responding to a recent SHRM survey reported that their firms had been sued over employment issues within the past five years.[1] While perfection is elusive, the majority of businesses today do attempt to make employment decisions based on which applicant is best qualified as opposed to whether he or she is of a certain gender, race, religion, color, national origin, or age. By and large, legislation, Supreme Court decisions, and executive orders have provided organizations—both public and private— the opportunity to tap the abilities of a workforce that was largely underutilized before the mid-1960s.

Laws Affecting Equal Employment Opportunity

Numerous national laws have been passed that have had an impact on equal employment opportunity. Enactment of these laws reflects society's attitude toward the changes that should be made to give everyone an equal opportunity for employment. We briefly describe the most significant of these laws in the following sections.

TITLE VII OF THE CIVIL RIGHTS ACT OF 1964—AMENDED 1972

One law that has greatly influenced human resource management is Title VII of the 1964 Civil Rights Act, as amended. This legislation prohibits discrimination based on race, color, sex, religion, or national origin. Title VII covers employers engaged in an industry affecting interstate commerce if the company employs 15 or more workers for at least 20 calendar weeks in the year in which a charge is filed or the year preceding the filing of a charge. Included in the definition of employers are state and local governments, schools, colleges, unions, and employment agencies. The act created the Equal Employment Opportunity Commission (EEOC), which is responsible for its enforcement.

VIETNAM ERA VETERANS READJUSTMENT ACT OF 1974

The Vietnam Era Veterans Readjustment Act relates only to government contractors or subcontractors who have contracts with the federal government in the amount of $10,000 or more. It covers honorably discharged persons who served more than 180 days on active duty between August 5, 1964, and May 7, 1975. To be covered by the act, the veteran must have been separated from the service within 48 months prior to the alleged discrimination action. The Department of Labor is responsible for administering the act.

A major provision of the act is that virtually all employment openings must be listed with the state employment office. Employers with 50 or more employees who have received contracts for over $50,000 must maintain an affirmative action program.

AGE DISCRIMINATION IN EMPLOYMENT ACT OF 1967—AMENDED IN 1978 AND 1986

As originally enacted, the Age Discrimination in Employment Act (ADEA) prohibited employers from discriminating against individuals who were 40 to 65 years old. The 1978 amendment provided protection for individuals who were at least 40 but less than 70 years old. In a 1986 amendment, employer discrimination against anyone over 40 years old became illegal. The latest amendment not only gives older employees the option of continuing to work after they are 70 years old, but the health care provision of the amendment also provides them with an additional incentive to continue doing so.[2] The act pertains to employers who have 20 or more employees for 20 or more calendar weeks (either in the current or preceding calendar year); unions of 25 or more members; employment agencies; and federal, state, and local government subunits. Administration of the act was transferred from the U.S. Department of Labor to the EEOC in 1979.

Enforcement begins when a charge is filed, but the EEOC can review compliance even if no charge is filed. The Age Discrimination in Employment Act differs from Title VII of the Civil Rights Act in providing for a trial by jury and carrying a possible criminal penalty for violation of the act. The trial-by-jury provision is important because juries may have great sympathy for older people who may have been discriminated against. The criminal penalty provision means that a person may receive more than lost wages if discrimination is proved. The 1978 amendment also makes class action suits possible.

The Older Workers Benefit Protection Act (OWBPA), an amendment to the Age Discrimination in Employment Act, was signed into law in 1990.[3] This act prohibits discrimination in the administration of benefits on the basis of age but also permits early retirement incentive plans as long as they are voluntary.[4] The act establishes wrongful termination waiver requirements as a means of protecting older employees by ensuring that waiver acceptance is made by fully informed and willful personnel.[5]

TRENDS & INNOVATIONS

AGE CAN BE A BONA FIDE OCCUPATIONAL QUALIFICATION

Contrary to the ADA, courts continue to support age limitations when elimination of the age policy would increase the likelihood of risk or harm to others. In July 1997, the U.S. Federal Court of Appeals ruled that the Federal Aviation Administration adequately explained its long-standing rule that pilots can be forced to retire at age 60. The age 60 rule was first imposed in 1959 and had long been controversial.[6]

This ruling supported the 1974 Seventh Circuit Court decision that Greyhound did not violate the ADA when it refused to hire persons 35 years of age or older as intercity bus drivers. Again, the likelihood of risk or harm to its passengers was involved. Greyhound presented evidence concerning degenerative physical and sensory changes that humans undergo at about age 35 that have a detrimental effect on driving skills and that are not detectable by physical tests.[7]

Thus, age can be a bona fide occupational qualification when it may reasonably affect business functions, and the employer has a rational or factual basis for believing that all or substantially all people within the age class would not be able to perform satisfactorily.

REHABILITATION ACT OF 1973

The Rehabilitation Act covers certain government contractors and subcontractors and organizations that receive federal grants in excess of $2,500. Individuals are considered disabled if they have a physical or mental impairment that substantially limits one or more major life activities or if they have a record of such impairment. If a contract or subcontract exceeds $50,000, or if the contractor has 50 or more employees, he or she must prepare an affirmative action program. In it, the contractor must specify the reasonable steps he or she is taking to hire and promote disabled persons. The Office of Federal Contract Compliance Programs (OFCCP) administers the act.

PREGNANCY DISCRIMINATION ACT OF 1978

Passed as an amendment to Title VII of the Civil Rights Act, the Pregnancy Discrimination Act prohibits discrimination in employment based on pregnancy, childbirth, or related medical conditions. The basic principle of the act is that women affected by pregnancy and related conditions must be treated the same as other applicants and employees on the basis of their ability or inability to work. A woman is therefore protected against such practices as being fired or refused a job or promotion merely because she is pregnant or has had an abortion. In the case of Allied Chemical, Mary is the best qualified and therefore should be given the job regardless of whether she is pregnant. She usually cannot be forced to take a leave of absence as long as she can work. If other employees on disability leave are entitled to return to their jobs when they are able to work again, so too are women who have been unable to work because of pregnancy.

The same principle applies in the benefits area, including disability benefits, sick leave, and health insurance. A woman unable to work for pregnancy-related reasons is entitled to disability benefits or sick leave on the same basis as employees unable to work for medical reasons. Also, any health insurance provided must cover expenses for pregnancy-related conditions on the same basis as expenses for other medical conditions. However, health insurance for expenses arising from an abortion is not required unless the life of the mother would be endangered if the fetus were carried to term or where medical complications have arisen from an abortion.

In a class action suit originally filed in 1978 but settled in July 1991, American Telephone & Telegraph Company (AT&T) agreed to settle a pregnancy discrimination suit with the EEOC for $66 million. This suit was the largest cash recovery in the agency's history and involved more than 13,000 present and former female AT&T workers. The 1978 suit charged that Western Electric required pregnant workers to leave their jobs at the end of their sixth month of pregnancy, denied them seniority credit, and refused to guarantee them a job when they returned.[8]

IMMIGRATION CONTROL ACTS

Three immigration control acts deserve mention as related to human resource management. These are the Immigration Reform and Control Act of 1986, the Immigration Act of 1990, and the Illegal Immigration Reform and Immigrant Responsibility Act of 1996.

The Immigration Reform and Control Act (IRCA).

The Immigration Reform and Control Act (IRCA) established criminal and civil sanctions against employers who knowingly hire an unauthorized alien. The act also makes unlawful the hiring of anyone unless the person's employment authorization and identity are verified. When dealing with the national origin provision of the Civil Rights Act, IRCA reduces the threshold coverage from 15 to four employees. The effect of this extension of the 1964 law will be to curtail hiring actions of some businesses. They may choose to hire only U.S. citizens and thereby avoid any potential violation of IRCA. However, many foreign nationals are in this country legally (many who are legal immigrants awaiting citizenship); refusing to hire them would violate their civil rights.[9]

Immigration Act. The Immigration Act of 1990 significantly revised U.S. policy on legal immigration. The law increased levels of immigration, particularly employment-based immigration of highly skilled professionals and executives. Apparently a problem resulted from this act. It opened the front door on immigration, but as some say, it did not close the back door and illegal immigration continued.[10]

Illegal Immigration Reform and Immigrant Responsibility Act. The Illegal Immigration Reform and Immigrant Responsibility Act was signed into law on September 30, 1996. The new law places severe limitations on people who have come to the United States and remain in the country longer than permitted by their visas as well as on those who have violated their nonimmigrant status. Anyone unlawfully present in the United States for 180 days but less than one year will be subject to a three-year ban on admission to this country. Anyone unlawfully present for one year or more is subject to a 10-year ban on legal entry to the United States. There are certain exceptions, however, such as extreme hardship.[11] The impact of this act is yet to be determined as the law took effect in April 1997.

THE AMERICANS WITH DISABILITIES ACT (ADA)

The Americans with Disabilities Act (ADA), passed in 1990, prohibits discrimination against *qualified individuals with disabilities*. Persons discriminated against because they have a known association or relationship with a disabled individual also are protected. The ADA defines an *individual with a disability* as a person who has or is regarded as having a physical or mental impairment that substantially limits one or more major life activities and has a record of such an impairment or is regarded as having such an impairment. Alcoholism is defined as a disability and so is drug addiction. However, the ADA does not protect people currently using illegal drugs. It does protect those in rehabilitation programs who are not currently using illegal drugs, those who have been rehabilitated, and those erroneously labeled drug users.[12] Further, a recent EEOC guidance stated that employers are required to provide reasonable accommodations for workers with psychiatric disabilities unless such measures would impose an undue hardship on the employer.[13]

The ADA prohibits discrimination in all employment practices, including job application procedures, hiring, firing, advancement, compensation, training, and other terms, conditions, and privileges of employment. It applies to recruitment, advertising, tenure, layoff, leave, fringe benefits, and all other employment-related activities. The employment provisions apply to private employers, state and local governments, employment agencies, and labor unions. Employers with 15 or more employees are covered.

The Equal Employment Opportunity Commission (EEOC) issued new guidelines in 1994 on preemployment inquiries and tests regarding disabilities. These guidelines clarify provisions in the Americans with Disabilities Act of 1990 (ADA) that prohibit inquiries and medical examinations intended to gain information about applicants' disabilities before a conditional job offer is made. The guiding principle is to ask only about potential employees' ability to do the job and not about their disabilities. Lawful inquiries include those regarding performance of specific functions or possession of training, whereas illegal inquiries include those that ascertain previous medical conditions or extent of prior drug use.[14]

CIVIL RIGHTS ACT OF 1991

The Civil Rights Act of 1991 amended the Civil Rights Act of 1964 and had the following purposes:

1. To provide appropriate remedies for intentional discrimination and unlawful harassment in the workplace
2. To codify the concepts of *business necessity* and *job-related* pronounced by the Supreme Court in *Griggs v Duke Power Co.*, and in the other Supreme Court decisions prior to *Wards Cove Packing Co., Inc. v Antonio*
3. To conform statutory authority and provide statutory guidelines for the adjudication of disparate impacts under Title VII of the Civil Rights Act of 1964
4. To respond to recent decisions of the Supreme Court by expanding the scope of relevant civil rights statutes to provide adequate protection to victims of discrimination

Under this act, a complaining party may recover punitive damages if the complaining party demonstrates that the company engaged in a discriminatory practice with malice or with reckless indifference to the law. However, the following limits, based on the number of people employed by the company, were placed on the amount of the award:

- Between 15 and 100 employees—$50,000
- Between 101 and 200 employees—$100,000
- Between 201 and 500 employees—$200,000
- More than 500 employees—$300,000

In each case, aggrieved employees must have been with the firm for 20 or more calendar weeks in the current or preceding calendar year.

With regard to burden of proof, a complaining party must show that a particular employment practice causes a disparate impact on the basis of race, color, religion, sex, or national origin. The case must also show that the company is unable to demonstrate that the challenged practice is job related for the position in question and consistent with business necessity.

The act also extends the coverage of the Civil Rights Act of 1964 to extraterritorial employment. However, the act does not apply to U.S. companies operating in another country if it would violate the law of the foreign country. Furthermore, the act reverses the following Supreme Court decisions: *Patterson v McLean Credit Union*, *Martin v Wilks*, and *Wards Cove Packing Co., Inc. v Antonio*. However, a Supreme Court decision ruled that the act does not apply to the cases that were pending when the act took effect.[15]

The act mandates the establishment of the Equal Employment Opportunity Commission's Technical Assistance Training Institute (TATI) and enhances the provisions of Title VII regarding education and outreach. The TATI provides technical assistance and training regarding the laws and regulations enforced by the commission. The commission is charged with carrying out educational and outreach activities (including dissemination of information in languages other than English) targeted to individuals who have historically been victims of employment discrimination and have not been equitably served by the commission. The act also extends the nondiscrimination principles to Congress and other government agencies, such as the General Accounting Office and the Government Printing Office.

HR Web Wisdom

http://www.prenhall.com/mondy

THE GLASS CEILING
The glass ceiling is explored including current court cases.

Glass ceiling: The invisible barrier in organizations that prevents many women and minorities from achieving top-level management positions.

Also included in the Civil Rights Act of 1991 is the Glass Ceiling Act of 1991. The **glass ceiling** is the invisible barrier in organizations that prevents many women and minorities from achieving top-level management positions. This act established a Glass Ceiling commission to study the manner in which businesses fill management and decision-making positions, the developmental and skill-enhancing practices used to foster the necessary qualifications for advancement to such positions, and the compensation programs and reward structures currently utilized in the workplace. The commission was to study the limited progress made by minorities and women. The act also established an annual award for excellence in promoting a more diverse skilled workforce at the management and decision-making levels in business.

In 1995, the Glass Ceiling Commission released its first report and found that only 5 percent of the senior-level managers in Fortune 1000 companies are women. The report identified three levels of artificial barriers to the advancement of women and minorities. First, societal barriers exist that are likely outside the control of business. Second, internal structural barriers are present that are under the direct control of business, including recruitment policies and corporate cultures. Finally, there are governmental barriers such as insufficient monitoring and enforcement.[16]

Companies have discovered that the courts are being forceful in eliminating such barriers. In one instance, a highly rated female supervisor was denied a promotion because her boss said it would be easier for employees to work with a man who was their *chum*. The employer reasoned that when it came to working long hours, the staff would work better with the male worker who was promoted. The courts disagreed and called this action unlawful discrimination.[17]

STATE AND LOCAL LAWS

Numerous state and local laws also affect equal employment opportunity. A number of states and some cities have passed fair employment practice laws prohibiting discrimination on the basis of race, color, religion, gender, or national origin. Even prior to federal legislation, several states had antidiscrimination legislation relating to age and gender. For instance, New York protected individuals between the ages of 18 and 65 prior to the 1978 and 1986 ADEA amendments, and California had no upper limit on protected age. However, when EEOC regulations conflict with state or local civil rights regulations, the legislation more favorable to women and minorities applies.

EQUAL EMPLOYMENT OVERSEAS

An interesting observation is that even as U.S. laws, such as ADA and the Civil Rights Act of 1991, are generating a growing number of employment-related claims here, overseas claims are also increasing rapidly. In the United Kingdom, Europe, and Japan, the court systems are becoming more accessible, and the number of employment related claims is increasing rapidly. According to Theodore Boundas of Peterson and Ross, the new laws written to govern the European Economic Community trading pact will greatly increase the number of employment-related claims filed annually.[18]

Executive Order 11246, as Amended by Executive Order 11375

Executive orders (EO): Directives issued by the president that have the force and effect of laws enacted by the Congress.

An **executive order (EO)** is a directive issued by the president and has the force and effect of laws enacted by Congress as they apply to federal agencies and federal contractors. In 1965, President Lyndon B. Johnson signed Executive Order 11246, which establishes the policy of the U.S. government as providing equal opportunity in federal employment for all qualified people. It prohibits discrimination in employment because of race, creed, color, or national origin. The order also requires promoting the full realization of equal employment opportunity through a positive, continuing program in each executive department and agency. The policy of equal opportunity applies to every aspect of federal employment policy and practice.

A major provision of EO 11246 requires adherence to a policy of nondiscrimination in employment as a condition for the approval of a federal grant, contract, loan, insurance, or guarantee. Every executive department and agency that administers a program involving federal financial assistance must include such language in its contracts. Contractors must agree not to discriminate in employment because of race, creed, color, or national origin during performance of a contract.

Affirmative action:
Stipulated by Executive Order 11246, it requires employers to take positive steps to ensure employment of applicants and treatment of employees during employment without regard to race, creed, color, or national origin.

Affirmative action, stipulated by EO 11246, requires covered employers to take positive steps to ensure employment of applicants and treatment of employees during employment without regard to race, creed, color, or national origin. Covered human resource practices relate to employment, upgrading, demotion, transfer, recruitment or recruitment advertising, lay-offs or termination, rates of pay or other forms of compensation, and selection for training, including apprenticeships. Employers are required to post notices explaining these requirements in conspicuous places in the workplace. In the event of contractor noncompliance, contracts can be canceled, terminated, or suspended in whole or in part, and the contractor may be declared ineligible for future government contracts. In 1968, EO 11246 was amended by EO 11375, which changed the word *creed* to *religion* and added sex discrimination to the other prohibited items. These EOs are enforced by the Department of Labor through the Office of Federal Contract Compliance Programs (OFCCP).

Significant U.S. Supreme Court Decisions

Knowledge of the law is obviously important for human resource managers. However, they must be aware of and understand much more than the words in the law itself. The manner in which the courts interpret the law is also vitally important. Also, interpretation continuously changes, even though the law may not have been amended. Discussions of some of the more significant U.S. Supreme Court decisions affecting equal employment opportunity follow.

GRIGGS V DUKE POWER COMPANY

A major decision affecting the field of human resource management was rendered in 1971. A group of black employees at Duke Power Company had charged job discrimination under Title VII of the Civil Rights Act of 1964. Prior to Title VII, the Duke Power Company had two workforces, separated by race. After passage of the act, the company required applicants to have a high school diploma and pass a paper-and-pencil test to qualify for certain jobs. The plaintiff was able to demonstrate that, in the relevant labor market, 34 percent of the white males but only 12 percent of the black males had a high school education. The plaintiff was also able to show that people already in those jobs were performing successfully even though they did not have high school diplomas. No business necessity could be shown for this educational requirement.

In an 8–0 vote, the Supreme Court ruled against Duke Power Company and stated, "If an employment practice which operates to exclude Negroes cannot be shown to be related to job performance, the practice is prohibited." A major implication of the decision is that when human resource management practices eliminate substantial numbers of minority or women applicants, the burden of proof is on the employer to show that the practice is job related. This court decision significantly affected the human resource practices of many firms.

ALBERMARLE PAPER COMPANY V MOODY

In 1966, a class action suit was brought against Albermarle Paper Company and the plant employees' labor union. A permanent injunction was requested against any policy, practice, custom, or usage at the plant that violated Title VII. In 1975, the Supreme Court, in *Albermarle Paper Co. v Moody* reaffirmed the idea that any test used in the selection process, or in promotion decisions, must be validated if its use has had an adverse impact on women and minorities. The employer has the burden of proof for showing that the test is valid by showing that any selection or promotion device actually measures what it is supposed to measure.

PHILLIPS V MARTIN MARIETTA CORPORATION

In 1971, the Court ruled that the Martin Marietta Corporation had discriminated against a woman because she had young children. The company had a rule prohibiting the hiring of women with school-age children. The company argued that it did not preclude all women from job consideration— only those with school-age children. Martin Marietta contended that this was a business requirement. The argument was obviously based on stereotypes and was rejected. A major implication of this decision is that a firm cannot impose standards for employment only on women. For example, a firm cannot reject divorced women if it does not also reject divorced men. Neither application forms nor interviews should contain questions for women that do not also apply to men.

ESPINOZA V FARAH MANUFACTURING COMPANY

In 1973, the Court ruled that Title VII does not prohibit discrimination on the basis of lack of citizenship. The EEOC had previously said that refusing to hire anyone who was a noncitizen was discriminatory as this selection

---

H R M   I N   A C T I O N
AN EQUAL EMPLOYMENT DILEMMA

You are the general manager of a great group of people, but you would rather be doing anything else. Today you must antagonize your friend Fred, who is the most productive dock foreman you have. You realize that Fred will not understand when you tell him he needs to consider hiring qualified minorities and women. You know Fred believes he understands best whom he needs to hire to get the job done. Fred has stated many times, "On the docks, we don't shuffle paper, we do real work, and it takes real men to do the work." According to Fred, "My men are the best dock workers on the pier. They have always exceeded the tonnage moved by any other group, and that is because they work so well together. Change the makeup of the work group, and the productivity of the group will be severely damaged."

What would you do?

standard was likely to have adverse impact on individuals of foreign national origin. As 92 percent of the employees at the Farah facility in question were Mexican Americans or native Mexicans who had become American citizens, the Court held that the company had not discriminated on the basis of national origin when it refused to hire a Hispanic who was not a U.S. citizen.

WEBER V KAISER ALUMINUM AND CHEMICAL CORPORATION

In 1974, the United Steelworkers of America and Kaiser Aluminum and Chemical Corporation entered into a master collective bargaining agreement covering terms and conditions of employment at 15 Kaiser plants. The agreement contained an affirmative action plan designed to eliminate conspicuous racial imbalances in Kaiser's then almost exclusively white craft workforce. Black craft hiring goals equal to the percentage of blacks in the respective local labor forces were set for each Kaiser plant. To enable the plants to meet these goals, on-the-job training programs were established to teach unskilled production workers—black and white—the skills necessary to become craft workers. The plan reserved 50 percent of the openings in the newly created in-plant training programs for black employees.

In 1974, only 1.83 percent (5 out of 273) of the skilled craft workers at the Gramercy, Louisiana, plant were black, even though the labor force in the Gramercy area was approximately 39 percent black. Thirteen craft trainees, of whom seven were black and six were white, were selected from Gramercy's production workforce. The most junior black selected for the program had less seniority than several white production workers whose bids for admission were rejected. Brian Weber subsequently instituted a class action suit alleging that the action by Kaiser and USWA discriminated against him and other similarly situated white employees in violation of Title VII. Although the lower courts ruled that Kaiser's actions were illegal because they fostered reverse discrimination, the Supreme Court reversed that decision, stating that Title VII does not prohibit race-conscious affirmative action plans. Because the affirmative action plan was voluntarily agreed to by the company and the union, it did not violate Title VII.

DOTHARD V RAWLINGSON

At the time Rawlingson applied for a position as a correctional counselor trainee, she was a 22-year-old college graduate whose major course of study had been correctional psychology. She was refused employment because she failed to meet the minimum height and weight requirements. In this 1977 case, the Supreme Court upheld the U.S. District Court's decision that Alabama's statutory minimum height requirement of five feet two inches and minimum weight requirement of 120 pounds for the position of correctional counselor had a discriminatory impact on women applicants. The contention was that minimum height and weight requirements for the position of correctional counselor were job related. However, the Court stated that this argument does not rebut prima facie evidence showing that these requirements have a discriminatory impact on women, whereas no evidence was produced correlating these requirements with a requisite amount of strength thought essential to good performance. The impact of the decision was that height and weight requirements must be job related.

UNIVERSITY OF CALIFORNIA REGENTS V BAKKE

In *University of California v Bakke*, the Supreme Court heard the first major test involving reverse discrimination. The University of California had reserved 16 places in each beginning medical school class for minority persons. Allen Bakke, a white man, was denied admission even though he scored higher on the admission criteria than some minority applicants who were admitted. The Supreme Court ruled 5–4 in Bakke's favor. As a result, Bakke was admitted to the university and later received his degree. At the same time, the Court reaffirmed that race may be taken into account in admission decisions.

AMERICAN TOBACCO COMPANY V PATTERSON

The 1982 Supreme Court decision concerning the American Tobacco Company versus Patterson allows the continuation of seniority and promotion systems established since Title VII, even though they unintentionally hurt minority workers. Under *Griggs v Duke Power Co.*, a prima facie violation of Title VII may be established by policies or practices that are neutral on their face and in intent but that nonetheless discriminate against a particular group. A seniority system would fall under the *Griggs* rationale if it were not for Section 703(h) of the Civil Rights Act, which provides the following:

> Notwithstanding any other provision of this subchapter, it shall not be an unlawful employment practice for an employer to apply standards of compensation, or different terms, conditions, or privileges of employment pursuant to a bona fide seniority or merit system . . . provided that such differences are not the result of an intention to discriminate because of race, color, religion, sex, or national origin, nor shall it be an unlawful employment practice for an employer to give and to act upon the results of any professionally developed ability test provided that such test, its administration or action upon the results is not designed, intended or used to discriminate because of race, color, religion, sex, or national origin.

Thus, the court ruled that a seniority system adopted after Title VII may stand even though it has an *unintended* discriminatory impact.

MERITOR SAVINGS BANK V VINSON

The first sexual harassment case to reach the U.S. Supreme Court was the 1986 case, *Meritor Savings Bank v Vinson*. In ruling for the plaintiff, the Court held that Title VII was not limited to discrimination having only economic or tangible effects. In this case, the plaintiff had obtained two promotions based on merit, even though sexual harassment was involved. The Court also ruled on whether an employee's voluntary participation in sexual acts with a manager constitutes a valid defense for an employer to a Title VII complaint. Here, the justices said that the appropriate test is whether the sexual activity was *unwelcome*, not whether the employee voluntarily engaged in sexual activity with her manager.[19]

CITY OF RICHMOND V J. A. CROSON CO.

The City of Richmond adopted a minority business utilization plan requiring prime contractors awarded city construction contracts to subcontract at least 30 percent of the dollar amount of each contract to one or more minority business enterprises (MBEs). The plan defined these enterprises as businesses anywhere in the country that were at least 51 percent owned and controlled by black, Spanish-speaking, Oriental, Native American, Eskimo, or Aleut citizens. After J. A. Croson Co. was denied a waiver and lost its contract, it brought suit alleging that the plan was unconstitutional under the Fourteenth Amendment's Equal Protection Clause. In 1989, the Supreme Court affirmed a Court of Appeals ruling that the city's plan was not justified by a compelling governmental interest because the record revealed no prior discrimination by the city itself in awarding contracts, and the 30 percent set-aside was not narrowly tailored to accomplish a remedial purpose. The decision forced 36 states and many cities and counties to review their programs.

HOPKINS V PRICE WATERHOUSE

In 1990, according to instructions from the Supreme Court, the trial court issued an order that required Price Waterhouse to make Ms. Hopkins a partner as of 1983 and award her back pay and full seniority. Back pay in the amount of $250,000 was to be collected in addition to all attorney fees and court costs. In this case, Price Waterhouse was found to have discriminated against Hopkins by sexually stereotyping her employment activities when the international accounting firm denied her partnership status. The court also issued an order against retaliating against Ms. Hopkins as a result of her being made a partner.

ADARAND CONSTRUCTORS V PENA

In a 5–4 opinion, the U.S. Supreme Court in 1995 criticized the moral justification for affirmative action, saying that race-conscious programs can amount to unconstitutional reverse discrimination and even harm those they seek to advance. The Adarand case concerned a Department of Transportation policy that gave contractors a bonus if they hired minority subcontractors. A white contractor challenged the policy in court after losing a contract to build guardrails, despite offering the lowest bid. A federal appeals court upheld the program as within the proper bounds of affirmative action. The Supreme Court decision did not uphold or reject that ruling, but instead sent the case back for further review under new, tougher rules. As a result, the ruling seems to invite legal challenges to other federal affirmative action programs. On August 14, 1997, the Clinton administration modified affirmative action policies for the Small Business Administration based on the Adarand ruling. A company can now be eligible for federal contracts if it meets the following criteria: it must be small; its owner must have a personal net worth of less than $250,000; and he or she must be "socially disadvantaged," a designation the law automatically bestows on blacks and Hispanic people, Indians, Asians, Eskimos and Native Hawaiians. Whites can now fall under the program if they prove they are socially disadvantaged by showing, for example, a history of discrimination or unfair denial of credit. By some estimates, an additional 3,000 firms will be eligible to apply for government contracts. Most of these firms will be headed by white women and they will likely claim to have been socially disadvantaged.[20]

O'CONNOR V CONSOLIDATED COIN CATERERS CORP.

A unanimous 1996 U.S. Supreme Court decided that an employee does not have to show that he or she was replaced by someone younger than 40 to bring suit under the ADEA. The High Court declared that discrimination is illegal even when all the employees are members of the protected age group. The case began in 1990 when James O'Connor's job as a regional sales manager was eliminated. The company did not select O'Connors, age 56, to manage either of its two remaining sales territories. He later was fired. His replacement was 40 years old. O'Connor was evidently doing so well that he earned a bonus of $37,000 the previous year. Apparently O'Connor's new boss told him he was *too damn old* for the kind of work he was doing and that what the company needed was *new blood*. Writing for the Court, Justice Scalia stated, "The ADEA does not ban discrimination against employees because they are aged 40; it bans discrimination against employees because of their age, but limits the protected class to those who are 40 or older." Thus, it is not relevant that one member in the protected class has lost out to another member in that class, so long as the person lost out because of his or her age. The Court found that being replaced by someone substantially younger was a more reliable indicator of age discrimination than being replaced by someone outside the protected class.[21]

HR
Web
Wisdom

http://www.prenhall.com/mondy

SHRM–HR LINKS
The diversity hot link covers various issues including affirmative action and equal employment opportunity.

Equal Employment Opportunity Commission

Title VII of the Civil Rights Act, as amended, created the Equal Employment Opportunity Commission. Under Title VII, filing a discrimination charge initiates EEOC action. Charges may be filed by one of the presidentially appointed EEOC commissioners, by any aggrieved person, or by anyone acting on behalf of an aggrieved person. Charges must be filed within 180 days of the alleged act. However, the time is extended to 300 days if a state or local agency is involved in the case.

Figure 3-1 shows that when a charge is filed, the EEOC typically proceeds in the following manner. First, an attempt at no-fault settlement is made. Essentially, the organization charged with the violation is invited to settle the case with no admission of guilt. Most charges are settled at this stage.

Failing settlement, the EEOC investigates the charges. Once the employer is notified that an investigation will take place, no records relating to the charge may be destroyed. During the investigative process, the employer is permitted to present a position statement. After the investigation has been completed, the district director of the EEOC will issue a *probable cause* or a *no probable cause* statement.

In the event of a probable cause statement, the next step involves attempted conciliation. In the event this effort fails, the case will be reviewed for litigation potential. Some of the factors that determine whether the EEOC will pursue litigation are (1) the number of people affected by the alleged practice, (2) the amount of money involved in the charge, (3) other charges against the employer, and (4) the type of charge. Recommendations for litigation are then passed on to the general counsel of the EEOC. If the

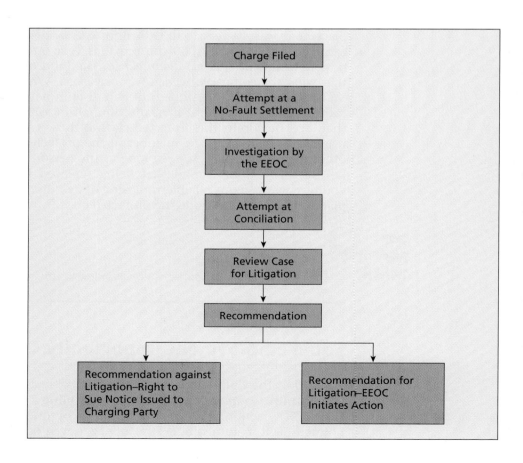

Figure 3-1
EEOC Procedure Once a
Charge Is Filed

recommendation is against litigation, a right to sue notice will be issued to the charging party.

Note that the Civil Rights Act of 1964 prohibits retaliation against employees who have opposed an illegal employment practice. The act also protects those who have testified, assisted, or participated in the investigation of discrimination.

There are certain exceptions to the coverage of Title VII. These exceptions include (1) religious institutions, with respect to the employment of persons of a specific religion in any of the institution's activities; (2) aliens; and (3) members of the Communist Party. Noncitizens are not protected from discrimination because of their lack of citizenship. However, they are protected from discrimination because of their national origin. Even with these exceptions, the impact of the law has been felt by virtually every organization.

Beginning in 1996, the EEOC began a new strategy of litigation. Priority is now given to class action suits, cases involving companywide discrimination, and cases likely to develop key legal principles. Recently the EEOC has been involved in discrimination suits against such companies as Mitsubishi, Texaco Inc., Home Depot Inc., and Publix Super Markets Inc.

Uniform Guidelines on Employee Selection Procedures

Prior to 1978, employers had to comply with several different selection guidelines. In 1978, the *Uniform Guidelines on Employee Selection Procedures* were adopted by the Equal Employment Opportunity Commission, the Civil Service Commission, the Department of Justice, and the Department of Labor. These *Guidelines* cover several federal equal employment opportunity statutes and executive orders including Title VII of the Civil Rights Act, EO 11246, and the Equal Pay Act. They do not apply to the Age Discrimination in Employment Act or the Rehabilitation Act.

The *Uniform Guidelines* provide a single set of principles that were designed to assist employers, labor organizations, employment agencies, and licensing and certification boards in complying with federal prohibitions against employment practices that discriminate on the basis of race, color, religion, gender, and national origin. The *Guidelines* provide a framework for making legal employment decisions about hiring, promotion, demotion, referral, retention, licensing and certification, the proper use of tests, and other selection procedures. Under the guidelines, recruiting procedures are not considered selection procedures and therefore are not covered.

Regarding selection procedures, the *Guidelines* state that a test is

> any measure, combination of measures, or procedures used as a basis for any employment decision. Selection procedures include the full range of assessment techniques from traditional paper and pencil tests, performance tests, testing programs or probationary periods and physical, education, and work experience requirement through informal or casual interviews and unscored application forms.

Using this definition, virtually any instrument or procedure used in the selection decision is considered a test.

The Concept of Adverse Impact

Prior to issuance of the *Uniform Guidelines on Employee Selection Procedures* in 1978, the only way to prove job relatedness was to validate each test. The *Guidelines* do not require validation in all cases. Essentially, it is required only in instances where the test or other selection device produces an adverse impact on a minority group. Under the *Guidelines*, adverse impact has been defined in terms of selection rates, the selection rate being the number of applicants hired or promoted, divided by the total number of applicants. **Adverse impact**, a concept established by the *Uniform Guidelines*, occurs if women and minorities are not hired at the rate of at least 80 percent of the best-achieving group. This standard has also been called the four-fifths rule, which is actually a guideline subject to interpretation by the EEOC. The groups identified for analysis under the guidelines are (1) blacks, (2) Native Americans (including Alaskan natives), (3) Asians, (4) Hispanics, (5) women, and (6) men.

Adverse impact: A concept established by the *Uniform Guidelines;* it occurs if women and minorities are not hired at the rate of at least 80 percent of the best-achieving group.

The following formula is used to compute adverse impact for hiring:

$$\frac{\text{Success rate for women and minorities applicants}}{\text{Success rate for best-achieving group applicants}} = \text{Determination of adverse impact}$$

The success rate for women and minority applicants is determined by dividing the number of members of a specific group *employed* in a period by the number of women and minority *applicants* in a period. The success rate of best-achieving group applicants is determined by dividing the number of people in the best-achieving group *employed* by the number of the best-achieving group *applicants* in a period.

Using the formula, let us determine whether there has been an adverse impact in the following case. During 1998, 400 people were hired for a particular job. Of the total, 300 were white and 100 were black. There were 1,500 applicants for these jobs, of whom 1,000 were white and 500 were black. Using the adverse formula, we have

$$\frac{100/500}{300/1,000} = \frac{0.2}{0.3} = 66.67\%$$

We conclude that adverse impact exists.

Evidence of adverse impact involves more than the total number of minority workers *employed*. Also considered are the total number of qualified *applicants*. For instance, assume that 300 blacks and 300 whites were hired.

But there were 1,500 black applicants and 1,000 white applicants. Putting these figures into the adverse impact formula, we conclude that adverse impact still exists.

$$\frac{300/1,500 \ = \ 0.2}{300/1,000 \ = \ 0.3} = 66.67\%$$

Thus, it is clear that firms must monitor their recruitment efforts very carefully. Obviously, they should attempt to recruit qualified individuals because once in the applicant pool, they will be used in computing adverse impact.

Assuming that adverse impact is shown, employers have two avenues available to them if they still desire to use a particular selection standard. First, they may validate a selection device by showing that it is indeed a predictor of success. If the device has proved to be a predictor of job performance, business necessity has been established. If the firm's selection device has not been validated, business necessity may be demonstrated in another manner: The employer can show a strong relationship between the selection device and job performance, and that if the firm did not use this procedure, its training costs would become prohibitive.

The second avenue available to employers should adverse impact be shown is the *bona fide occupational qualification* (BFOQ) defense. The BFOQ defense means that only one group is capable of performing the job successfully. As you might expect, this defense has been narrowly interpreted by courts because it almost always relates to sex discrimination. For instance, courts have rejected the concept that because most women cannot lift 50 pounds, all women would be eliminated from consideration for a job requiring heavy lifting.

Creators of the *Guidelines* adopted the bottom-line approach in assessing whether a firm's employment practices are discriminatory. For example, if a number of separate procedures is used in making a selection decision, the enforcement agencies will focus on the end result of these procedures to determine whether adverse impact has occurred. Essentially, the EEOC is concerned more with what is occurring rather than how it occurred. They admit the possibility that discriminatory employment practices that cannot be validated may exist. However, the net effect, or the bottom line, of the selection procedures is the focus of their attention.

Additional Guidelines

Since the *Uniform Guidelines* were published in 1978, they have been modified several times. Some of these changes reflect Supreme Court decisions; others clarify implementation procedures. Three major changes—*Interpretative Guidelines on Sexual Harassment, Guidelines on Discrimination because of National Origin,* and *Guidelines on Discrimination because of Religion*—merit additional discussion.

INTERPRETATIVE GUIDELINES ON SEXUAL HARASSMENT

In one survey, 42 percent of the women and 15 percent of the men reported that they had been sexually harassed on the job.[22] Perhaps because of the publicity caused by the Navy's Tailhook incident and the testimony of Anita Hill and Clarence Thomas, one of the most fervently pursued civil rights issues today relates to sexual harassment.[23] In fact, from 1990 to 1996 the number of sexual harassment complaints filed with the Equal Employment Opportunity Commission more than doubled—from 6,100 to 15,342.[24] As we previously mentioned, Title VII of the Civil Rights Act generally prohibits discrimination in employment on the basis of gender. The EEOC has also issued interpretive guidelines stating that employers have an affirmative duty to maintain a workplace free of sexual harassment. The OFCCP has issued similar guidelines. Managers in both for-profit and not-for-profit organizations should be particularly alert to the issue of sexual harassment. The EEOC issued the guidelines because of the belief that sexual harassment continued to be a widespread problem. Table 3-1 contains the commission's definition of sexual harassment.

According to these guidelines, employers are totally liable for the acts of their supervisors, regardless of whether the employer is aware of the sexual harassment act. Where co-workers are concerned, the employer is responsible for such acts if the employer knew, or should have known, about them. The employer is not responsible when it can show that it took immediate and appropriate corrective action on learning of the problem.

Another important aspect of these guidelines is that employers may be liable for acts committed by nonemployees in the workplace if the employer knew, or should have known, of the conduct and failed to take appropriate action. Firms are responsible for developing programs to prevent sexual harassment in the workplace. They must also investigate all formal and informal complaints alleging sexual harassment. After investigating, a firm must take immediate and appropriate action to correct the situation.[25] Failure to do so constitutes a violation of Title VII, as

---

TABLE 3-1

EEOC Definition of Sexual Harassment

Unwelcome sexual advances, requests for sexual favors, and verbal or physical conduct of a sexual nature that occur under any of the following situations:

1. When submission to such contact is made either explicitly or implicitly a term or condition of an individual's employment
2. When submission to or rejection of such contact by an individual is used as the basis for employment decisions affecting such individual
3. When such conduct has the purpose or effect of unreasonably interfering with an individual's work performance or creating an intimidating, hostile, or offensive working environment

One of the most fervently pursued civil rights issues today relates to sexual harassment.

interpreted by the EEOC. To prevail in court, companies must have clear procedures for handling sexual harassment complaints. Typically, employers choose an impartial ombudsperson to hear and investigate charges before lawyers get involved. If the sexual harassment complaint appears legitimate, the company must take *immediate* and *appropriate action* as established in the pivotal 1986 case, *Hunter v Allis-Chalmers*.[26]

The improper exercise of power is inappropriate and often costly. Sexual harassment is an improper exercise of power. Sexual harassment is also a costly abuse of power. Research by Freada Klein Associates, a workplace-diversity consulting firm, shows that 90 percent of Fortune 500 companies have dealt with power abuses that resulted in sexual harassment complaints. Klein estimates that this abuse of power costs the average large corporation $6.7 million a year.[27]

There have been numerous sexual harassment court cases. In *Miller v Bank of America*, a U.S. Circuit Court of Appeals held an employer liable for the sexually harassing acts of its supervisors, even though the company had a policy prohibiting such conduct, and even though the victim did not formally notify the employer of the problem. Another U.S. Circuit Court of Appeals ruled that sexual harassment, in and of itself, is a violation of Title VII. The court ruled that the law does not require the victim to prove that she or he resisted harassment and was penalized for that resistance. The first sexual harassment case to reach the U.S. Supreme Court was the 1986 case of *Meritor Savings Bank v Vinson*. In the Vinson decision, the Supreme Court recognized for the first time that Title VII could be used for offensive environment claims.[28] The 1993 Supreme Court decision of *Harris v Forklift Systems, Inc.* expanded the hostile workplace concept, and made it easier to win sexual harassment claims.[29] No longer does severe psychological injury have to be shown. Under this ruling, plaintiffs need only show that their employer allowed a hostile-to-abusive work environment to exist. According to the EEOC, specific actions that could create a hostile workplace include a pattern of threatening, intimidating or hostile acts and remarks, negative sexual stereotyping, or the display of written or graphic materials considered degrading. A hostile environment has been defined further as a workplace atmosphere or behavior that a *reasonable woman* would find offensive.[30]

GUIDELINES ON DISCRIMINATION BECAUSE OF NATIONAL ORIGIN

The EEOC broadly defined discrimination on the basis of national origin as the denial of equal employment opportunity because of an individual's ancestors or place of birth or because an individual has the physical, cultural, or linguistic characteristics of a national origin group. Because height or weight requirements tend to exclude individuals on the basis of national origin, firms are expected to evaluate their selection procedures for adverse impact regardless of whether the total selection process has an adverse impact based on national origin. Height and weight requirements are, therefore, exceptions to the bottom-line concept. As Table 3-2 shows, the EEOC has identified certain selection procedures that may be discriminatory.

Harassment on the basis of national origin is a violation of Title VII. Employers have an affirmative duty to maintain a working environment free from such harassment. Ethnic slurs and other verbal or physical conduct relating to an individual's national origin constitute harassment when this conduct (1) has the purpose or effect of creating an intimidating, hostile, or offensive working environment; (2) has the purpose or effect of unreasonably interfering with an individual's work performance; or (3) otherwise adversely affects an individual's employment opportunity.

Of current interest with regard to national origin is English-only rules. Courts have generally ruled in the employer's favor if the rule would

---

TABLE 3-2

Selection Procedures That May Be Discriminatory with Regard to National Origin

1. Fluency in English requirements: One questionable practice involves denying employment opportunities because of an individual's foreign accent or inability to communicate well in English. When this practice is continually followed, the Commission will presume that such a rule violates Title VII and will study it closely. However, a firm may require that employees speak only in English at certain times if business necessity can be shown.

2. Training or education requirements: Denying employment opportunities to an individual because of his or her foreign training or education, or practices that require an individual to be foreign trained or educated may be discriminatory.

promote safety, product quality and stop harassment. For example, suppose a company has a rule that only English must be spoken except during breaks. That rule must be justified by a compelling business necessity. A retail store will most likely be permitted to have an English-only rule in the sales area where the public is served, so that customers do not feel uncomfortable by sales representatives speaking to each other in another language.[31]

Perhaps the most important ruling to date on English-only rules is the 1993 *Garcia v Spun Steak*. The Ninth Circuit Court of Appeals (the Supreme Court refused to review) concluded that the rule did not necessarily violate Title VII. Spun Steak's management implemented the policy after some workers complained they were being harassed and insulted in a language they could not understand. The rule allowed workers to speak Spanish during breaks and lunch periods.[32]

GUIDELINES ON DISCRIMINATION BECAUSE OF RELIGION

Employers have an obligation to accommodate religious practices unless they can demonstrate a resulting hardship. The most common claims filed under the religious accommodation provisions involve either employees objecting to Sabbath employment or to membership in or financial support of labor unions.[33] Consideration is given to identifiable costs in relation to the size and operating costs of the employer and the number of individuals who actually need the accommodation. These guidelines recognize that regular payment of premium wages constitutes undue hardship, whereas these payments on an infrequent or temporary basis do not. Undue hardship would also exist if an accommodation required a firm to vary from its bona fide seniority system.

These guidelines identify several means of accommodating religious practices that prohibit working on certain days. Some of the methods suggested included voluntary substitutes, flexible scheduling, lateral transfer, and change of job assignments. Some collective bargaining agreements include a provision that each employee must join the union or pay the union a sum equivalent to dues. When an employee's religious beliefs prevent compliance, the union should accommodate the employee by permitting that person to make an equivalent donation to a charitable organization.

In recent years religious discrimination has been thrust to the forefront as employees demand more accommodation regarding their religious practices. In fact, since 1990, the number of claims filed against employers has risen by more than 30 percent according to the EEOC. A significant religious discrimination lawsuit was brought against Wal-Mart. In this case, an employee claimed that he was forced to quit his job after refusing to work on Sunday, his Sabbath. Although Wal-Mart denied any wrongdoing, it agreed to alter its human resource policies and conduct extensive training to prevent religious discrimination in its stores.[34]

HR Web Wisdom

http://www.prenhall.com/mondy

AFFIRMATIVE ACTION
The then and nows of affirmative action.

Affirmative Action Programs

Affirmative action program (AAP): A program that an organization develops to employ women and minorities in proportion to their representation in the firm's relevant labor market.

An **affirmative action program** (AAP) is an approach developed by certain organizations with government contracts to demonstrate that workers are employed in proportion to their representation in the firm's relevant labor market. The need for affirmative action programs was created by EO 11246, as amended by EO 11375, which places enforcement with the Office of Federal Contract Compliance Programs (OFCCP). An affirmative action program may also be voluntarily implemented by an organization. In such an event, goals are established and action is taken to hire and move minorities and women upward in the organization. In other situations, an AAP may be mandated by the OFCCP. The degree of control the office will impose depends on the size of the contract. Contracts of $10,000 or less are not covered. The first level of control involves contracts that exceed $10,000 but are less than $50,000. These contractors are governed by the equal opportunity clause, as shown in Table 3-3.

The second level of control occurs if the contractor (1) has 50 or more employees; (2) has a contract of $50,000 or more; (3) has contracts that in any 12-month period total $50,000 or more or reasonably may be expected to total $50,000 or more; or (4) is a financial institution that serves as a depository for government funds in any amount, acts as an issuing or redeeming agent for U.S. savings bonds and savings notes in any amount, or subscribes to federal deposit or share insurance. Contractors meeting these criteria must develop a written affirmative action program for each of its establishments and file an annual EEO-1 report (see Figure 3-2). The affirmative action program is the major focus of EO 11246, which requires specific steps to guarantee equal employment opportunity. Prerequisite to development of a satisfactory AAP is identification and analysis of problem areas inherent in employment of minorities and women and an evaluation of opportunities for utilizing minority and women employees.

The third level of control on contractors is in effect when contracts exceed $1 million. All previously stated requirements must be met; in addition, the OFCCP is authorized to conduct pre-award compliance reviews. The purpose of a compliance review is to determine whether the contractor is maintaining nondiscriminatory hiring and employment practices. The review also ensures that the contractor is utilizing affirmative action to guarantee that applicants are employed, placed, trained, upgraded, promoted, terminated, and otherwise treated fairly without regard to race, color, religion, gender, national origin, veteran status, or disability during employment. In determining whether to conduct a pre-award review, the OFCCP may consider, for example, the items presented in Table 3-4.

If an investigation indicates a violation, the OFCCP tries first to secure compliance through persuasion. If persuasion fails to resolve the issue, the office serves a notice to show cause or a notice of violation. A show cause notice contains a list of the violations, a statement of how the OFCCP proposes that corrections be made, a request for a written response to the findings, and a suggested date for a conciliation conference. The firm usually has 30 days to

TABLE 3-3

Equal Opportunity Clause—Government Contracts

1. The contractor will not discriminate against any employee or applicant for employment because of race, color, religion, sex, or national origin. The contractors will take affirmative action to ensure that applicants are employed, and that employees are treated during employment, without regard to their race, color, religion, sex, or national origin. Such action shall include, but not be limited to the following: employment, upgrading, demotions, or transfer; recruitment or recruitment advertising, layoff or termination; rates of pay or other forms of compensation; and selection for training, including apprenticeship. The contractor agrees to post in conspicuous places, available to employees and applicants for employment, notices to be provided by the contracting officer setting forth the provisions for this nondiscrimination clause.

2. The contractor will in all solicitations or advertisements for employees placed by or on behalf of the contractor, state that all qualified applicants will receive consideration for employment without regard to race, color, religion, sex, or national origin.

3. The contractor will send to each labor union or representative of workers with which he or she has a collective bargaining agreement or other contract or understanding, a notice to be provided by the agency contracting officer, advising the labor union or workers' representative of the contractor's commitments under section 202 of Executive Order 11246 of September 24, 1965, and shall post copies of the notice in conspicuous places available to employees and applicants for employment.

4. The contractor will comply with all provisions of Executive Order 11246 of September 24, 1965, and the rules, regulations, and relevant orders of the Secretary of Labor.

5. The contractor will furnish all information and reports required by Executive Order 11246 of September 24, 1965, and by the rules, regulations, and orders of the Secretary of Labor, or pursuant thereto, and will permit access to his or her books, records, and accounts by the contracting agency and the Secretary of Labor for purposes of investigation to ascertain compliance with such rules, regulations, and orders.

6. In the event of the contractor's noncompliance with the nondiscrimination clauses of this contract or with any of such rules, regulations, or orders, this contract may be canceled, terminated, or suspended in whole or in part and the contractor may be declared ineligible for further Government contracts in accordance with procedures authorized in Executive Order 11246 of September 24, 1965, or by rule, regulation, or order of the Secretary of State, or as otherwise provided by law.

7. The contractor will include the provisions of paragraphs (1) through (7) in every subcontract or purchase order unless exempted by rules, regulations, or orders of the Secretary of Labor issued pursuant to section 204 of Executive Order 12146 of September 24, 1965, so that such provisions will be binding upon each subcontractor or vendor. The contractor will take such action with respect to any subcontract or purchase order as may be directed by the Secretary of Labor as a means of enforcing such provisions including sanctions for noncompliance: Provided, however, that in the event the contractor becomes involved in, or is threatened with litigation with a subcontractor or vendor as a result of such direction, the contractor may request the United States to enter into such litigation to protect the interests of the United States.

Source: Federal Register, 45, no. 251 (Tuesday, December 30, 1980): 86230.

Joint Reporting Committee

- Equal Employment Opportunity Commission
- Office of Federal Contract Compliance Programs (Labor)

EQUAL EMPLOYMENT OPPORTUNITY

EMPLOYER INFORMATION REPORT EEO—1

1997

Standard Form 100 (Rev. 4-92)
O.M.B. No. 3048-0007
EXPIRES 12/31/93
100-213

Section A—TYPE OF REPORT
Refer to instructions for number and types of reports to be filled.

1. Indicate by marking in the appropriate box the type of reporting unit for which this copy of the form is submitted (MARK ONLY ONE BOX).

(1) ☐ Single-establishment Employer Report

Multi-establishment Employer:
(2) ☐ Consolidated Report (Required)
(3) ☐ Headquarters Unit Report (Required)
(4) ☐ Individual Establishment Report (submit one for each establishment with 50 or more employees)
(5) ☐ Special Report

2. Total number of reports being filed by this Company (Answer on Consolidated Report only) ______

Section B—COMPANY IDENTIFICATION *(To be answered by all employers)* — OFFICE USE ONLY

1. Parent Company
   a. Name of parent company (owns or controls establishment in item 2) omit if same as label — a.
   Address (Number and street) — b.
   City or town | State | ZIP code — c.
2. Establishment for which this report is filed. (Omit if same as label)
   a. Name of establishment — d.
   Address (Number and street) | City or town | County | State | ZIP code — e.
   b. Employer identification No. (IRS 9-DIGIT TAX NUMBER) ☐☐☐☐☐☐☐☐☐ — f.

Was an EEO–1 report filed for this establishment last year? ☐ Yes ☐ No

Section C—EMPLOYERS WHO ARE REQUIRED TO FILE *(To be answered by all employers)*

☐ Yes ☐ No 1. Does the entire company have at least 100 employees in the payroll period for which you are reporting?

☐ Yes ☐ No 2. Is your company affiliated through common ownership and/or centralized management with other entitles in an enterprise with a total employment of 100 or more?

☐ Yes ☐ No 3. Does the company or any of its establishments (1) have 50 or more employees AND (b) is not exempt as provided by 41 CFR 60–1.5, AND either (1) is a prime government contractor or first-tier subcontractor, and has a contract, subcontract, or purchase order amounting to $50,000 or more, or (2) serves as a depository or Government funds in any amount or is a financial institution which is an issuing and paying agent for U.S. Savings Bonds and Savings Notes?

If the response to question C–3 is yes, please enter your Dun and Bradstreet Identification number (if you have one): ☐☐☐☐☐☐☐☐☐

NOTE: If the answer is yes to questions 1, 2, or 3, complete the entire form, otherwise skip to Section G.

NSN 7540-00-180-6384

Figure 3-2
Equal Opportunity Employer Information Report

respond. Successful conciliation results in a written contract between the OFCCP and the contractor. In a conciliation agreement, the contractor agrees to take specific steps to remedy noncompliance with an EO. Firms that do not correct violations can be passed over in the awarding of future contracts.

Section D—EMPLOYMENT DATA

Employment at this establishment—Report all permanent full-time and part-time employees including apprentices and on-the-job trainees unless specifically excluded as set forth in the instructions. Enter the appropriate figures on all lines and in all columns. Blank spaces will be considered as zeros.

JOB CATEGORIES		OVERALL TOTALS (SUM OF COL. B THRU K) A	MALE WHITE (NOT OF HISPANIC ORIGIN) B	BLACK (NOT OF HISPANIC ORIGIN) C	HISPANIC D	ASIAN OR PACIFIC ISLANDER E	AMERICAN INDIAN OR ALASKAN NATIVE F	FEMALE WHITE (NOT OF HISPANIC ORIGIN) G	BLACK (NOT OF HISPANIC ORIGIN) H	HISPANIC I	ASIAN OR PACIFIC ISLANDER J	AMERICAN INDIAN OR ALASKAN NATIVE K
Officials and Managers	1											
Officials and Managers	2											
Officials and Managers	3											
Officials and Managers	4											
Officials and Managers	5											
Officials and Managers	6											
Officials and Managers	7											
Officials and Managers	8											
Service Workers	9											
TOTAL	10											
Total employment reported in previous EEO–1 report	11											

NOTE: Omit questions 1 and 2 on the Consolidated Report.
1. Date(s) of payroll period used:
2. Does this establishment employ apprentices? 1 ☐ Yes   2 ☐ No

Section E—ESTABLISHMENT INFORMATION (*Omit on the Consolidated Report*)

1. What is the major activity of this establishment? (Be specific, i.e., manufacturing steel castings, retail grocer, wholesale plumbing supplies, title insurance, etc. Include the specific type of product or type of service provided, as well as the principal business or industrial activity.)

OFFICE USE ONLY

g.

Section F—REMARKS

Use this item to give any identification data appearing on last report which differs from that given above, explain major changes in composition or reporting units and other pertinent information.

Section G—CERTIFICATION (*See Instructions G*)

Check one   1 ☐ All reports are accurate and were prepared in accordance with the instruction (Check on consolidated only)
2 ☐ This report is accurate and was prepared in accordance with the instructions.

Name of Certifying Official	Title	Signature	Date

Name of person to contact regarding this report (Type or print)	Address (Number and Street)		

Title	City and State	ZIP code	Telephone Number (including Area Code)	Extension

All reports and information obtained from individual reports will be kept confidential as required by Section 709(e) of Title VII.
WILLFULLY FALSE STATEMENTS ON THIS REPORT ARE PUNISHABLE BY LAW, U.S. CODE, TITLE 18, SECTION 1001.

Figure 3-2
Equal Opportunity Employer Information Report   *(continued from page 90)*

The procedures for developing affirmative action plans were published in the *Federal Register* of December 4, 1974. These regulations are referred to as Revised Order No. 4. The OFCCP guide for compliance officers, outlining what to cover in a compliance review, is known as Order No. 14.

TABLE 3-4

Factors That the OFCCP May Consider in Conducting a Pre-award Review

1. The past EEO performance of the contractor, including its current EEO profile and indications of underutilization
2. The volume and nature of complaints filed by employees or applicants against the contractor
3. Whether the contractor is in a growth industry
4. The level of employment or promotional opportunities resulting from the expansion of, or turnover in, the contractor's workforce
5. The employment opportunities likely to result from the contract in issue
6. Whether resources are available to conduct the review

The OFCCP is very specific about what should be included in an affirmative action program. A policy statement has to be developed that reflects the CEO's attitude regarding equal employment opportunity, assigns overall responsibility for preparing and implementing the affirmative action program, and provides for reporting and monitoring procedures. The policy should state that the firm intends to recruit, hire, train, and promote persons in all job titles without regard to race, color, religion, gender, or national origin, except where gender is a *bona fide organizational qualification* (BFOQ). The policy should guarantee that all human resource actions involving such areas as compensation, benefits, transfers, layoffs, return from layoffs, company-sponsored training, education, tuition assistance, and social and recreational programs will be administered without regard to race, color, religion, gender, or national origin. Revised Order No. 4 is quite specific with regard to dissemination of a firm's EEO policy, both internally and externally. An executive should be appointed to manage the firm's equal employment opportunity program. This person should be given the necessary support by top management to accomplish the assignment. Revised Order No. 4 specifies the minimum level of responsibility associated with the role of EEO manager.

An acceptable AAP must include an analysis of deficiencies in the utilization of minority groups and women. The first step in conducting a utilization analysis is to make a workforce analysis.

The second step involves an analysis of all major job groups. An explanation of the situation is required if minorities or women are currently being underutilized. A job group is defined as one or more jobs having similar content, wage rates, and opportunities. Underutilization is defined as having fewer minorities or women in a particular job group than would reasonably be expected by their availability. The utilization analysis is important because the calculations determine whether underutilization exists. For example, if the utilization analysis shows that the availability of blacks for a certain job group is 30 percent, the organization should have at least 30 percent black employment in that group. If actual employment is less than 30 percent, underutilization exists, and the firm should set a goal of 30 percent black employment for that job group.

The primary focus of any affirmative action program is on goals and timetables; the issue is how many, by when. Goals and timetables developed by the firm should cover its entire affirmative action program, including correction of deficiencies. These goals and timetables should be attainable; that is, they should be based on results that the firm, making good faith efforts, could reasonably expect to achieve.

Goals should be significant and measurable, as well as attainable. Two types of goals must be established regarding underutilization: annual and ultimate. The annual goal is to move toward elimination of underutilization, whereas the ultimate goal is to correct all underutilization. Goals should be specific in terms of planned results, with timetables for completion. However, goals should not establish inflexible quotas that must be met. Rather, they should be targets that are reasonably attainable.

Employers should also conduct a detailed analysis of job descriptions to ensure that they accurately reflect job content. Job specifications should be validated, with special attention given to academic, experience, and skills requirements. If a job specification screens out a disproportionate number of minorities or women, the requirements must be professionally validated in relation to job performance. Thus, a comprehensive job analysis program is required.

When an opening occurs, everyone involved in human resource recruiting, screening, selection, and promotion should be aware of the opening. In addition, the firm should evaluate the entire selection process to ensure freedom from bias. Individuals involved in the process should be carefully selected and trained in order to minimize bias in all human resource actions.

Firms should observe the requirements of the *Uniform Guidelines*. Selection techniques other than paper-and-pencil tests can also be used improperly and thus discriminate against minorities and women. Such techniques include unscored interviews; unscored or casual application forms; use of arrest records and credit checks; and consideration of marital status, dependency, and minor children. Where data suggest that discrimination or unfair exclusion of minorities and women exists, the firm should analyze its unscored procedures and eliminate them if they are not objective and valid. Some techniques that can be used to improve recruitment and increase the flow of minority and women applicants are shown in Table 3-5.

As previously discussed in the *Adarand Constructors v Pena* Supreme Court decision, affirmative action programs are presently receiving court challenges. As a result of this case, the future of affirmative action is yet to be determined. From now on, federal affirmative action programs will be subject to the most rigorous level of court review.[35]

Employment Standards to Avoid

Throughout this chapter, we have focused on laws, court cases, executive orders, and interpretive guidelines that affect human resources. As a result of all these decisions and actions, certain employment standards that should be avoided have evolved (see Table 3-6). Some of these standards relate to laws, others to court decisions, and still others to established guidelines. They relate to a multitude of human resource decisions such as selection, promo-

TABLE 3-5

Techniques to Improve Recruitment of Minorities and Women

- Identify referral organizations for minorities and women.
- Hold formal briefing sessions with representatives of referral organizations.
- Encourage minority and women employees to refer applicants to the firm.
- Include minorities and women on the Personnel Relations staff.
- Permit minorities and women to participate in Career Days, Youth Motivation Programs, and related activities in their community.
- Actively participate in job fairs and give company representatives the authority to make on-the-spot-commitments.
- Actively recruit at schools having predominant minority or female enrollments.
- Use special efforts to reach minorities and women during school recruitment drives.
- Undertake special employment programs whenever possible for women and minorities. These might include technical and nontechnical co-op programs, after school and/or work-study jobs, summer jobs for underprivileged, summer work-study programs, and motivation, training, and employment programs for the hardcore unemployed.
- Pictorially present minorities and women in recruiting brochures.
- Include the minority news media and women's interest media when expending help wanted advertising.

Source: Federal Register, 45, no. 251 (Tuesday, December 30, 1980): 86243.

tion, demotion, termination, and the like. In the case of Allied Chemical, Mary Martin should be hired even though she is a woman in a male-dominated work area. She is the best qualified, which is the ultimate determining factor. Everything else aside, hiring Mary is the right thing to do.

A GLOBAL PERSPECTIVE
GLOBAL EQUAL OPPORTUNITY PROTECTION: FACT OR FICTION?

U.S.-based global firms often find their human resource policies in conflict with the laws and accepted norms of the host country. For instance, the influence of Title VII of the Civil Rights Act of 1964, as amended, has been felt by virtually all firms operating in the United States, but most countries in the world do not have laws prohibiting discrimination. In fact, some countries practice overt discrimination against certain groups whose members would be protected if employed in the United States. In 1991, the Supreme Court ruled that when Congress passed the Civil Rights Act of 1964, it did not want the statute to apply outside the United States. Specifically, in

TABLE 3-6

Employment Standards to Avoid

Gender

Hiring people based on whether they are men or women is unlawful. The only exception is a case in which gender is a bona fide occupational qualification (BFOQ). However, the use of BFOQs has been narrowly interpreted by the Equal Employment Opportunity Commission (EEOC) and the courts. The specification of a man versus a woman must be made in view of whether gender is absolutely job related. For example, if the job in question is for an attendant for a women's restroom, gender can legitimately be specified.

Presuming that a particular job is physically too demanding for a woman to perform is also ill-advised. Instead, women applicants should be given the opportunity to prove that they can perform the job. For example, if a job requires frequent lifting of a 50-pound object, an employer may require applicants to demonstrate that they—both men and women—can regularly lift the required weight.

National Origin

Information regarding an applicant's national origin should not be sought. In addition, other data that might be used to determine national origin should not be requested. Questions regarding an applicant's place of birth and the place of birth of parents, grandparents, or spouse fall into this category.

Marital Status

Marital status is a difficult selection standard to defend and should be avoided. Although asking a person's marital status is not by itself illegal under federal law, the standard has often been applied differently to women and men.

Disabilities

The passage of the Americans with Disabilities Act (ADA) has caused large and small firms to reevaluate their hiring practices as well as their physical workplaces. Virtually all employers must provide equal employment opportunities to disabled persons who are qualified. This may include making reasonable accommodations for them.

Religion

Discrimination based on religious beliefs is generally unlawful. The only exception is when the employer is a religious corporation, association, educational institution, or society. Questions regarding the applicant's religious denomination, religious affiliation, church, parish, or observation of religious holidays are generally ill-advised. Another form of discrimination can occur when individuals' religious beliefs cause them to be away from work before sundown, on Saturdays, or at other times. In these situations, the practices should be reasonably accommodated unless undue hardships are imposed on the employer.

Race

Race is very rarely a legal employment requirement. Therefore selection decisions should be made without regard to this factor.

Age

Questions asked about an applicant's age or date of birth may be ill-advised. However, a firm may ask for age information to comply with the child labor law. For example, the question could be asked, "Are you under the age of 18?" With this exception, an applicant should not be asked his or her age or date of

(continued on page 96)

TABLE 3-6

Employment Standards to Avoid *(continued from page 95)*

birth. Also, questions about the ages of children, if any, could be potentially discriminatory because a close approximation of the applicant's age often is obtained through knowledge of the ages of the children.

Pregnancy

Discrimination in employment based on pregnancy, childbirth, or complications arising from either is illegal. Questions regarding a women's family and childbearing plans should not be asked. Similarly, questions relating to family plans, birth control techniques, and the like may be viewed as discriminatory because they are not also asked of men.

Physical Requirements

Specifications that set a minimum height or weight should be used only when these characteristic are necessary for performing a particular job. Hispanics, Asians, and Pacific Islanders are generally shorter and smaller than others, and women are generally smaller than men. Therefore, non-job-related physical requirements would tend to reject a disproportionate number of individuals in certain groups.

Standards relating to the ability to lift a certain amount of weight also should not be used unless they are clearly job related. At times, it may be feasible for the employer to redesign the job to overcome a weight-lifting requirement.

Credit Record

An individual's poor credit rating has been found to be an improper standard for rejecting applicants for cases in which this has a disproportionate negative effect on women and minorities. Members of certain groups are more likely to have credit problems than others. Therefore, the standard should not be used unless the employer has a business necessity for obtaining the information. Inquiries about charge accounts, credit references, and home or car ownership should not be made unless they are job related.

Background of Spouse

Basing employment decisions on the background of a spouse is very difficult, if not impossible, to support. Some employers believe that they need to know what the spouse does for a living in making selection decisions. Merely asking this type of question may be interpreted as sex discrimination. In certain instances, women have been turned down for employment because the employer believed that a woman with a working husband would be denying an unemployed man the opportunity for a job.

Care of Children

Employers have, at times, denied employment to women who have non-school-age children. If this standard is imposed on women and not on men, it amounts to sex discrimination. Although some woman find it difficult to work and take care of children at the same time, the same can be said for men. A person should be evaluated on his or her ability to perform a particular job.

Arrest Record

In our system of justice, an arrest is not an indication of guilt. Standards related to arrest records have been found to constitute race or national origin discrimination because the arrest rate for minority group members tends to be higher than that for nonminorities. Therefore, this selection criterion can rarely be used as a justification for rejecting applicants from certain minority groups.

(continued on page 97)

TABLE 3-6

Employment Standards to Avoid *(continued from page 96)*

Conviction Record

Unlike an arrest record, a conviction record is an indication of guilt. Even though some minorities have a greater conviction rate than nonminorities, this standard may be used if it is job related. It would be quite acceptable to reject a job applicant who had been convicted of robbery if the job required handling of large sums of money. On the other hand, it would be difficult to justify rejecting an applicant for a laborer job if that individual had been convicted only for failure to pay alimony.

Work Experience Requirements

Experience requirements should be reviewed to ensure that they are actually job related. Many women and minorities have not been in the labor force long enough to gain extensive work experience. Requiring that a person have, for example, 10 years' work experience may eliminate a large portion of women and minorities and would be discriminatory if this experience is not actually needed to perform the job.

Garnishment Record

As with arrest and conviction records, members of certain minority groups have had their wages garnished more than nonminorities. Therefore, if knowledge of this information cannot be shown to be job related, it should not be used as an employment standard.

Dress and Appearance

Employers have the right to establish standards relating to dress and appearance. This is especially true in situations in which the applicant is dealing directly with the public. Requiring hair to be a certain length has been found by the courts to be nondiscriminatory except when standards have varied by gender. Care should be taken when rejecting applicants strictly on their appearance. A person's appearance may be related to a special dress and style typical of a certain group.

Education Requirements

Non-job-related educational standards should not be used because of their potential for discrimination. For example, the ability to speak English should be required only if it is job related. A disproportionate number of certain minorities have not graduated from high school or college. Stating that a job requires a college degree when it could be accomplished effectively by a high school graduate can potentially be discriminatory. Any educational standard may be difficult to defend. Therefore, focusing on the knowledge, skills, and abilities needed to perform the job is advisable.

Relatives Working for the Company (Antinepotism Rule)

Standards established about an applicant's relatives working for the company may be discriminatory if they result in reducing employment opportunities for women and members of minorities. Some firms have rules that prohibit hiring the spouse of a current employee. On the surface, this rule appears to affect men and women similarly. In reality, because men have normally been in the labor force longer, the rule reduces employment opportunities much more for women. Therefore, antinepotism rules should be avoided unless they can be shown to be a business necessity.

Boureslan v Aramco (1991), the U.S. Supreme Court held that Title VII of the Civil Rights Act of 1964 did not apply beyond the geographical limits of the enacting state or nation but are still amenable to its laws.[36]

However, after years of no recourse for American expatriates who had been victims of employment discrimination, Congress in 1991 extended coverage of U.S. antidiscrimination law to American citizens employed by U.S.-owned or U.S.-controlled firms overseas. In 1991, Congress specifically amended Title VII and the Americans with Disabilities Act. The Age Discrimination in Employment Act had been previously amended in 1984 to apply to Americans abroad. According to Lairold M. Street, a former international lawyer with the Equal Employment Opportunity Commission, "More and more American companies were doing business overseas and we had been litigating more and more international discrimination cases [but] the courts in general didn't really know how to handle them." Since 1991, the number of expatriate discrimination cases has been increasing, but the EEOC does not track the cases because there are still so few complaints from abroad relative to the 75,000 to 90,000 annual U.S. cases.[37]

Even if a violation is identified, enforcing antidiscrimination laws abroad can be difficult. One problem is that neither expatriates nor U.S. companies are familiar with the law's new reach. According to Street, "Many expatriates generally think their rights stop at the border, and many companies don't realize how far American law applies." Another problem may be the informal procedures of the EEOC, the U.S. agency that primarily handles the enforcement of antidiscrimination law. Although the EEOC takes expatriate complaints seriously, pursuing these matters is not always easy because of the potential conflict with other nations' laws. In addition, district office investigators are scattered all over the country with differing experiences that often limit their understanding of the international implications of a violation. Legal experts believe that to counter discrimination, expatriates must become aware of what discrimination is and understand foreign social norms. For example, the United States in many cases will respect the laws of countries like Saudi Arabia, where women are not permitted to drive. When assigned abroad, expatriates should be prepared to have their personal rights curtailed because of cultural differences. The bottom line, however, is that unless expatriates file complaints, the problem is not going away.[38]   ▪

SUMMARY

1. Identify the major laws affecting equal employment opportunity.

Title VII of the Civil Rights Act of 1964, as Amended in 1972; Vietnam Era Veterans Readjustment Act of 1974; Age Discrimination in Employment Act of 1967, as Amended in 1978 and 1986; Rehabilitation Act of 1973; Pregnancy Discrimination Act of 1978; Immigration Reform and Control Act (IRCA) of 1986; Immigration Act of 1990; Illegal Immigration Reform and Immigrant Responsibility Act of 1996; Americans with Disabilities Act of 1990; and the Civil Rights Act of 1991.

2. Explain Presidential Executive Orders 11246 and 11375.

By EO 11246, the policy of the government of the United States expanded to provide equal opportunity in federal employment for all qualified persons. The order prohibited discrimination in employment because of race, creed, color, or national origin. EO 11246 was amended by EO 11375, which changed the word *creed* to *religion* and added sex discrimination to the other prohibited items.

3. ***Describe the purpose of the Office of Federal Contract Compliance Programs.***

   The Secretary of Labor established the Office of Federal Contract Compliance Programs (OFCCP) and gave it the power and responsibility for implementing EO 11246. The degree of control the OFCCP will impose depends on the size of the contract involved.

4. ***Identify some of the major Supreme Court decisions that have had an impact on equal employment opportunity.***

   Griggs v Duke Power Company, Albermarle Paper Company v Moody, Phillips v Martin Marietta Corp, Espinoza v Farah Manufacturing, Weber v Kaiser Aluminum Corporation, Dothard v Rawlingson, University of California Regents v Bakke, American Tobacco Co. v Patterson, Meritor Savings Bank v Vinson, City of Richmond v J. A. Croson Co., Hopkins v Price Waterhouse, Adarand Constructors v Pena, and *O'Connors v Consolidated Coin Caterers, Corp.*

5. ***Explain the purpose of the Uniform Guidelines on Employee Selection Procedures.***

   The guidelines adopted a single set of principles that were designed to assist employers, labor organizations, employment agencies, and licensing and certification boards in complying with requirements of federal law prohibiting employment practices that discriminated on the basis of race, color, religion, sex, and national origin. They were designed to provide a framework for determining the proper use of tests and other selection procedures.

6. ***Explain adverse impact and affirmative action programs.***

   Adverse impact is a concept established by the *Uniform Guidelines* and occurs if women and minorities are not hired at the rate of at least 80 percent of the best-achieving group. An affirmative action program (AAP) is an approach developed by an organization with government contracts to demonstrate that women or minorities are employed in proportion to their representation in the firm's relevant labor market. The need for affirmative action programs was addressed by the signing of EO 11246 as amended by EO 11375 and placed enforcement of these orders with the OFCCP.

7. ***Describe the* Uniform Guidelines *related to sexual harassment, national origin, and religion.***

   The EEOC has also issued interpretive guidelines stating that employers have an affirmative duty to maintain a workplace free from sexual harassment. The EEOC broadly defined discrimination on the basis of national origin as the denial of equal employment opportunity because of an individual's ancestors or place of birth or because an individual has the physical, cultural, or linguistic characteristics of a national origin group. Employers have an obligation to accommodate religious practices unless they can demonstrate a resulting hardship.

QUESTIONS FOR REVIEW

1. Briefly describe the following laws:
   a. Title VII of the Civil Rights Act of 1964, as amended in 1972
   b. Vietnam Era Veterans Readjustment Act of 1974
   c. Age Discrimination in Employment Act of 1967, as amended in 1978 and 1986
   d. Rehabilitation Act of 1973
   e. Pregnancy Discrimination Act of 1978
   f. Immigration Control Acts
   g. Americans with Disabilities Act of 1990
   h. the Civil Rights Act of 1991
2. What is a presidential executive order? Describe the major provisions of EO 11246, as amended by EO 11375.
3. What is the purpose of the Office of Federal Contract Compliance Programs?
4. Discuss the significant U.S. Supreme Court decisions that have had an impact on equal employment opportunity.
5. What is the purpose of the *Uniform Guidelines on Employee Selection Procedures*?
6. Distinguish between adverse impact and affirmative action programs.
7. How does the Equal Employment Opportunity Commission (EEOC) define sexual harassment?

DEVELOPING HRM SKILLS

AN EXPERIENTIAL EXERCISE

Many laws have been passed and court decisions rendered that affect the everyday actions of human resource management. Past decisions may no longer apply. Managers have a responsibility to ensure that actions affecting human resource management adhere to both the letter and intent of the law. Unfortunately, not everyone may share this view; this is when problems occur. In this situation, the human resource manager and a dock foreman for New York-based Hoffa Loading and Storage Company are having an employment disagreement.

A potential for conflict exists in this situation. Two individuals will participate in this exercise: one to serve as the human resource manager and the other to play the role of dock foreman. All students not playing a role should carefully observe the behavior of both participants. Your instructor will provide the participants with the additional information they will need.

 Take It to the Net

We invite you to visit the Mondy home page on the Prentice Hall Web site at:

http://www.prenhall.com/mondy

for updated information, Web-based exercises, and links to other HR-related sites.

HRM SIMULATION

*O*ne of the key elements of this simulation relates to affirmative action. The firm currently has fewer female and minority workers than the local working population. Hiring has been generally done on a walk-in basis, and there is no formal plan to increase the number of women and minorities in the firm. Although there is no litigation concerning this unbalanced workforce at the present time, your team has been directed by the CEO to begin integrating the workforce.

HRM INCIDENT

1

What to Do?

*E*ligha Guillory, human resource manager for Baxter Manufacturing, had a problem he did not know how to handle. His firm was unionized and the relationship between management and the union had generally been good. The firm also had a strong affirmative action program. Baxter had made major strides in implementing this program throughout the firm, with the notable exception of the machine department. In that department there were no minority or women employees.

Eligha had recommended many blacks and women to the production manager. Some of them had been hired but they never stayed long. In their exit interviews, they often made comments such as "I just wasn't part of the team. No one would even talk to me," or "They helped one another. But no one would help me," or "I was blamed if I was nearby when something went wrong."

The problem was further complicated by the uncooperativeness of the union employees. When Eligha attempted to talk to the workers, he was told in no uncertain terms that if he wanted problems, he could keep sending minority and women employees to the department. He knew that if this department were shut down by a strike, the entire company would have to close. Eligha wanted to maintain the affirmative action program but he also knew the impact a wildcat strike could have on the company.

Questions
1. How would you suggest that Eligha deal with this situation? Discuss.
2. What should be the union's responsibility in this situation?

HRM INCIDENT

2

Whom Should I Recommend?

*L*eroy Hasty was faced with a dilemma. He supervised 12 process technicians at the Indestro Chemical plant in El Dorado, Arkansas, but he was being transferred to a new job. The production manager, Jack Richards, had just asked Leroy to nominate one of his subordinates as a replacement. Two possible choices immediately came to mind; Carlos Chavez and James Mitchell.

Carlos was a very capable worker. He was 24 years old and married, and he had earned his bachelor's degree in management by attending night school. His heritage was Mexican American. He had done an excellent job on every assignment Leroy had given him. He had all the qualifications Leroy believed a good supervisor should have, including solid technical expertise. Leroy considered Carlos punctual, diligent, mature, and intelligent. A serious sort, Carlos often came to work early and stayed late and seemed to spend most of his spare time with his family.

James was a 25-year-old high school graduate. He was single, and Hasty knew he often went hunting or partying with several of the other technicians. Like most of his fellow workers, James was a WASP (white Anglo-Saxon protestant). He was a hard worker and was liked and respected by the others, including Carlos. On the basis of objective factors, Leroy believed James ran second to Carlos, although the call was a close one.

However, there was the race issue. Several times Leroy had heard fellow workers refer to Carlos as a *wetback*. Leroy believed some of the workers would prefer to have James as a supervisor, purely because of his national origin. In fact, he thought one or two of them might resist Carlos's authority to try to make him look bad. If productivity in the section fell because of administrative problems, Leroy knew that his own record with the company might be tarnished.

At that moment, the phone rang. It was Jack Richards. "Leroy," he said, "I need to see you. Could you come to my office in a few minutes?" As Leroy hung up the phone, he thought, "I know Jack is going to want to talk about my replacement."

Question
1. What decision would you recommend that Leroy make? Discuss.

Notes

1. "SHRM Survey Finds Many Employers Being Sued," *HR News* 16 (July 1997): 7.
2. Michael R. Carrell and Frank E. Kuzmits, "Amended ADEA's Effects on HR Strategies Remain Dubious," *Personnel Journal* 66 (May 1987): 112.
3. Rory Judd Albert and Neal S. Schelberg, "Highlighting the OWBPA," *Pension World* 27 (January 1991): 40.
4. Robert J. Noble, Esq., "To Waiver or Not to Waiver Is the Question of OWPWA," *Personnel* 68 (June 1991): 11.
5. Kate Colborn, "You Want Me to Sign What?" *EDN* 38 (March 11, 1993): 69.
6. Carol J. Castaneda, "Panel Backs FAA on Retire-at-60 Rule," *USA Today* (July 16, 1997): 6A.
7. Donald L. Caruth, Robert M. Noe, III, and R. Wayne Mondy, *Staffing the Contemporary Organization* (New York: Quorum Books, 1988): 49.
8. John J. Keller, "AT&T Will Settle EEOC Lawsuit for $66 Million," *The Wall Street Journal* 88, no. 13 (July 18, 1991): B8.
9. Art L. Bethke, "The IRCA: What's an Employer to Do?" *Wisconsin Small Business Forum* 6 (Fall 1987): 26.
10. Susan Martin, "U.S. Immigration Policy," *National Forum* 74 (June 1994): 12.
11. Dan P. Danilow, "New Immigration Law Signed," *Northwest Asian Weekly* (November 15, 1996): PG.

12. Eric Minton, "The ADA and Records Management," *Records Management Quarterly* 28 (January 1994): 12.

13. Stuart Silverstein, "Guidelines for Disabilities Cases," *Newsday* (May 11, 1997): F12.

14. Betty Southard Murphy, Wayne E. Barlow and D. Diane Hatch, "Manager's Newsfront," *Personnel Journal* 73 (August 1994): 26.

15. Robert L. Brady, "A Win for Employers: Civil Rights Act Is Not Retroactive," *Legal Insights* 71 (August 1994): 19.

16. Francy Blackwood, "Bipartisan Panel Finds Glass Ceiling Thicker Than It Looks," *Business Journal Serving Greater Sacramento* (January 1995): 30.

17. Jack Raisner, "When Workplace Relationships Cause Discrimination," *HRMagazine* 36 (January 1991): 75.

18. Brian Cox, "D&O Liability Risks Growing with Economy's Globalization," *National Underwriters* 97 (November 22, 1993): 2, 20.

19. Frederick L. Sullivan, "Sexual Harassment: The Supreme Court's Ruling," *Personnel* 63 (December 1986): 37–38.

20. Steven A. Holmes, "Minority Program May Be Opened Up for Bids by Whites," *Houston Chronicle* 96 (August 15, 1997): 2A.

21. Constance B. DiCesare, "Age Discrimination (*O'Connor v Consolidated Coin Caters Corp*)," *Monthly Labor Review* 119 (July 1996): 51.

22. Kelly Flynn, "Preventive Medicine for Sexual Harassment," *Personnel* 68 (March 1991): 17.

23. Michele Galen, "Ending Sexual Harassment: Business Is Getting the Message," *Business Week* (March 18, 1991): 98.

24. Larry Reynolds, "Sex Harassment Claims Surge," *HR Focus* 74 (March 1997): 8.

25. Theresa Brady, "Added Liability: Third-Party Sexual Harassment," *Management Review* 86 (April 1997): 45–47.

26. Anne B. Fisher, "Sexual Harassment: What to Do," *Fortune* 128 (August 23, 1993): 84–88.

27. Ibid.

28. Stacey J. Garvin, "Employer Liability for Sexual Harassment," *HRMagazine* 36 (June 1991): 107.

29. Reynolds, "Sex Harassment Claims Surge."

30. Amanda Troy Segal, "Sexual Harassment: The Age of Anxiety," *Business Week* (July 6, 1992): 16.

31. Theresa Brady, "The Downside of Diversity," *Management Review* 85 (June 1996): 29.

32. Ibid.

33. Stephanie Overman, "Good Faith Is the Answer," *HRMagazine* 39 (January 1994): 76.

34. Janell Kurtz, Elaine Davis, and Jo Ann Asquith, "Religious Beliefs Get New Attention," *HR Focus* 73 (July 1996): 12.

35. Melinda-Hawkeye Carlton, Philip Hawkey, Douglas Watson, William Donahue, Bobby Garcia, and Dan Johnson, "Affirmative Action," *Public Management* 79 (January 1997): 19.

36. Janice R. Franke and Maria Whittaker, "The Extraterritoriality Issue," *American Business Law Journal* (May 1992): 143–168.

37. Marni Halasa, "Discrimination Overseas New Law Offers Recourse for American Expats," *USA Today* (August 9, 1996): 7A.

38. Ibid.

4
Job Analysis

CHAPTER OBJECTIVES

1. Define *job analysis.*
2. Discuss the reasons that job analysis is a basic human resource tool.
3. Explain the reasons for conducting job analysis.
4. Describe the types of information required for job analysis.
5. Describe the various job analysis methods.
6. Identify who conducts job analysis.
7. Describe the components of a well-designed job description.
8. Define *job specification* and identify the components of the job specification.
9. Discuss why the timeliness of job analysis is important.
10. Identify the newer methods available for conducting job analysis.
11. Describe how job analysis helps satisfy various legal requirements.
12. Define *job design.*
13. Describe management by objectives, total quality management, and reengineering.

"*Mary, I'm having trouble figuring out what kind of machine operators you need,*" said John Anderson, the human resource director at Gulf Machineries. "*I've sent four people for you to interview who seemed to meet the requirements outlined in the job description. You rejected all of them.*"

"*To heck with the job description,*" replied Mary. "*What I'm concerned with is finding someone who can do the job. The people you sent me couldn't do the job. Besides, I've never even seen the job description.*"

John took a copy of the job description to Mary and went over it point by point. They discovered that either the job description never fit the job, or the job had changed a great deal since it was written. For example, the job description specified experience on an older model drill press, whereas the one in use was a new digital machine. Workers had to be more mathematically oriented to use the new machine effectively.

After hearing Mary describe the qualifications needed for the machine operator's job and explain the duties the operators perform, John said, "*I think that now we can write an accurate description of the job, and using it as a guide, find the right kind of people. Let's work more closely so this kind of situation won't happen again.*"

*T*he situation just described reflects a very common problem in human resource management: The job description did not adequately define the duties and skills needed to perform the job. Therefore, it became virtually impossible for John Anderson, the human resource director, to locate people with the required skills. Job analysis was critically needed to resolve the problem. As we stress throughout the remainder of this book, job analysis is a basic function of human resource management.

We begin the chapter by defining job analysis and explaining the reasons for conducting job analysis. Next, we review the types of information required for job analysis, discuss job analysis methods, and describe who conducts job analysis. Then we explain the use of job analysis data in preparing job descriptions and job specifications, the expanded job description, and discuss why the timeliness of job analysis is important. We describe other methods for conducting job analysis and the ways job analysis helps to satisfy various legal requirements. We end the chapter by explaining job design and describing various design approaches with regard to whether they are fad or fashion.

HR
Web
Wisdom

http://www.prenhall.com/mondy

JOB ANALYSIS
Job analysis research and classifications are briefly reviewed.

Job Analysis: A Basic Human Resource Tool

In this rapidly changing work environment, the need for a sound job analysis system is extremely critical.[1] New jobs are being created, and old jobs are being redesigned or eliminated. A job analysis that was conducted only a few years ago quite probably includes inaccurate data. Essentially, job analysis helps organizations address the fact that change is taking place.[2]

A **job** consists of a group of tasks that must be performed for an organization to achieve its goals. A job may require the services of one person, such as that of president, or the services of 75, as might be the case with data entry operators in a large firm. For Gulf Machineries, the job of machine operator would best be described as digital machine operator, not merely machine operator.

In a work group consisting of a supervisor, two senior clerks, and four word processing operators, there are three jobs and seven positions. A **position** is the collection of tasks and responsibilities performed by one person; there is a position for every individual in an organization. For instance, a small company might have 25 jobs for its 75 employees, whereas in a large company 2,000 jobs may exist for 50,000 employees. In some firms, as few as 10 jobs constitute 90 percent of a workforce.

Job analysis is the systematic process of determining the skills, duties, and knowledge required for performing jobs in an organization.[3] It is an

Job: A group of tasks that must be performed if an organization is to achieve its goals.

Position: The tasks and responsibilities performed by one person; there is a position for every individual in an organization.

Job analysis: The systematic process of determining the skills, duties, and knowledge required for performing specific jobs in an organization.

essential and pervasive human resource technique. The purpose of job analysis is to obtain answers to six important questions:

1. What physical and mental tasks does the worker accomplish?
2. When is the job to be completed?
3. Where is the job to be accomplished?
4. How does the worker do the job?
5. Why is the job done?
6. What qualifications are needed to perform the job?

Job analysis provides a summary of a job's duties and responsibilities, its relationship to other jobs, the knowledge and skills required, and working conditions under which it is performed. The job analysis conducted by Mary and John resulted in a different set of qualifications and duties for new machine operators. Job facts are gathered, analyzed, and recorded as the job exists, not as the job should exist. The latter function is most often assigned to industrial engineers, methods analysts, or others. Job analysis is conducted after the job has been designed, the worker has been trained, and the job is being performed.

Job analysis is performed on three occasions. First, it is done when the organization is founded, and a job analysis program is initiated for the first time. Second, it is performed when new jobs are created. Third, it is used when jobs are changed significantly as a result of new technologies, methods, procedures, or systems. Job analysis is most often performed because of changes in the nature of jobs. Job analysis information is used to prepare both job descriptions and job specifications.

Job description: A document that provides information regarding the tasks, duties, and responsibilities of a job.

The **job description** is a document that provides information regarding the tasks, duties, and responsibilities of the job. After John consulted with Mary regarding the new nature of the machine operator's job, he wrote a new job description that is accurate at that point in time. The minimum acceptable qualifications a person should possess to perform a particular job are contained in the **job specification**. We discuss both types of documents in greater detail later in the chapter.

Job specification: A document that outlines the minimum acceptable qualifications a person should possess to perform a particular job.

Reasons for Conducting Job Analysis

As Figure 4-1 shows, data derived from job analysis have an impact on virtually every aspect of human resource management. A major use of job analysis data is in the area of human resource planning. Merely knowing that the firm will need 1,000 new employees to produce goods or services to satisfy sales demand is insufficient. Each job requires different knowledge, skills, and ability levels. Obviously, effective human resource planning must take these job requirements into consideration.

Employee recruitment and selection would be haphazard if the recruiter did not know the qualifications needed to perform the job. Lacking up-to-

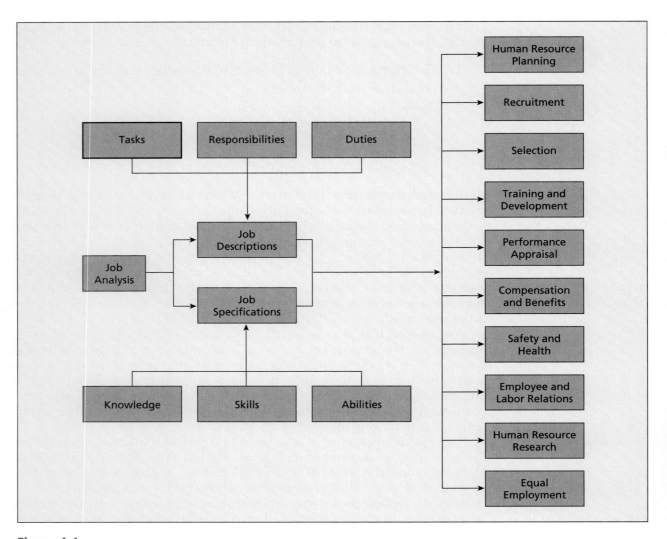

Figure 4-1
Job Analysis: The Most Basic Human Resource Management Tool

date job descriptions and specifications, a firm would have to recruit and select employees for jobs without having clear guidelines, and this practice could have disastrous consequences. Such a practice is virtually unheard of when firms procure raw materials, supplies, or equipment. For example, even when ordering personal computers, the purchasing department normally develops precise specifications. Surely, the same logic should apply when searching for a firm's most valuable asset!

Also, job specification information often proves beneficial in identifying training and development needs. If the specification suggests that the job requires a particular knowledge, skill, or ability—and the person filling the position does not possess all the qualifications required, training and/or development is probably in order. It should be directed at assisting workers in performing duties specified in their present job descriptions or preparing them for promotion to higher level jobs. With regard to performance appraisal, employees should be evaluated by how well they accomplish the duties specified in their job descriptions. A manager who evaluates an employee on factors not included in the job description is wide open to allegations of discrimination.

In the area of compensation, the relative value of a particular job to the company must be known before a dollar value can be placed on it. Relatively speaking, the more significant its duties and responsibilities, the more the job is worth. Jobs that require greater knowledge, skills, and abilities should be worth more to the firm. For example, the relative value of a job calling for a master's degree normally would be higher than that of a job that requires only a high school diploma.

Information derived from job analysis is also valuable in identifying safety and health considerations. For example, employers are required to state whether a job is hazardous. The job description/specification should reflect this condition. In addition, in certain hazardous jobs, workers may need specific information about the hazards to perform the jobs safely.

Job analysis information is also important to employee and labor relations. When employees are considered for promotion, transfer, or demotion, the job description provides a standard for comparison of talent. Regardless of whether the firm is unionized, information obtained through job analysis can often lead to more objective human resource decisions.

Finally, having properly accomplished job analysis is particularly important for supporting the legality of employment practices.[4] In fact, the importance of job analysis is well documented in the *Uniform Guidelines on Employee Selection Procedures*.[5] Job analysis data are needed to defend, for example, decisions involving promotion, transfers, and demotions.

Thus far, we have described job analysis as it pertains to specific HRM functions. In practice, however, these functions are interrelated. Job analysis provides the basis for tying the functional areas together and the foundation for developing a sound human resource program.

Types of Job Analysis Information

Considerable information is needed for successful accomplishment of job analysis. The job analyst identifies the actual duties and responsibilities of the job and gathers the other types of data shown in Table 4-1. Essential functions of the job are determined in this process. Note that work activities; worker-oriented activities; and the types of machines, tools, equipment, and work aids used in the job are important. This information is used later to help determine the job skills needed. In addition, the job analyst looks at job-related tangibles and intangibles, such as the knowledge needed, the materials processed, and the goods made or services performed.

TABLE 4-1

Types of Data Collected in Job Analysis

Summary of Types of Data Collected through Job Analysis*
1. **Work activities**
   a. Work activities and processes
   b. Activity records (in film form, for example)
   c. Procedures used
   d. Personal responsibility
2. **Worker-oriented activities**
   a. Human behaviors, such as physical actions and communicating on the job
   b. Elemental motions for methods analysis
   c. Personal job demands, such as energy expenditure
3. **Machines, tools, equipment, and work aids used**
4. **Job-related tangibles and intangibles**
   a. Knowledge dealt with or applied (as in accounting)
   b. Materials processed
   c. Products made or services performed
5. **Work performance†**
   a. Error analysis
   b. Work standards
   c. Work measurements, such as time taken for a task
6. **Job context**
   a. Work schedule
   b. Financial and nonfinancial incentives
   c. Physical working conditions
   d. Organizational and social contexts
7. **Personal requirements for the job**
   a. Personal attributes such as personality and interests
   b. Education and training required
   c. Work experience

* This information can be in the form of qualitative, verbal, narrative descriptions or quantitative measurements of each item, such as error rates per unit of time or noise level.
† All job analysis systems do not develop the work performance aspects.
Source: Reprinted by permission of Marvin D. Dunnette.

Some job analysis systems identify job standards. Work measurement studies may be needed to determine how long it takes to perform a task. With regard to job content, the analyst studies the work schedule, financial and nonfinancial incentives, and physical working conditions. Because many jobs are often performed in conjunction with others, organizational and social contexts are also noted. Finally, specific education, training, and work experience pertinent to the job are identified.

T R E N D S & *I N N O V A T I O N S*

JOB ANALYSIS FOR TEAMS

Historically, companies established permanent jobs and filled these with people who best fit the job description. The jobs were then maintained for years to come.[6] In some firms today, people are being hired and paid on a project basis. Better performance produces better income. Today, whenever someone asks "What your job description?" the reply might well be "Whatever." This means that if a project has to be completed, individuals do what has to be done to complete the task.[7]

In a traditional organization, work was compartmentalized into jobs or positions, defined by functional and occupational domains. The result was disjointed execution, high unit cost, and uncompetitively long cycle times. With team design, there are no narrow jobs. Today, departments and functional domains have disappeared in some organizations and work is bundled into teams. The members of these teams have a far greater depth and breadth of skills than would have been required in traditional jobs. In addition, the teams often include employees from more than one company. This versatility allows an employee to take an entire business process from start to finish in one rapid, seamless flow. Formerly, there might have been 100 separate job classifications in a facility. With team design, there may be just 10 or fewer broadly defined roles on teams.[8]

Another dimension is added to job analysis when groups or teams are considered. The ability to work in teams is an important consideration. Job analysis may determine how important it is for employees to be team players and work well in group situations. Other traits that might be discovered through job analysis include coordination skills and the ability to work in more than one system.[9]

Job Analysis Methods

Job analysis has traditionally been conducted in a number of different ways because organizational needs and resources for conducting job analysis differ. Selection of a specific method should be based on the ways the information is to be used (job evaluation, pay increases, development, and so on) and the approach that is most feasible for a particular organization. We describe the most common methods of job analysis in the following sections.

QUESTIONNAIRES

Questionnaires are typically quick and economical to use. The job analyst may administer a structured questionnaire to employees, who identify the tasks they perform. In some cases, employees may lack verbal skills, a condition that makes this method less useful. Also, some employees may tend to exaggerate the significance of their tasks, suggesting more responsibility than actually exists.

A portion of a job analysis questionnaire used by First Interstate Bancorp is presented in Figure 4-2. Although the entire questionnaire consists of six sections, only Section III, "Position Skills and Knowledge," is shown.

OBSERVATION

When using the observation method, the job analyst usually watches the worker perform job tasks and records his or her observations. This method is used primarily to gather information on jobs emphasizing manual skills, such as those of a machine operator. It can also help the analyst identify interrelationships between physical and mental tasks. However, observation alone is usually an insufficient means of conducting job analysis, particularly when mental skills are dominant in a job. Observing a financial analyst at work would not reveal much about the requirements of the job.

INTERVIEWS

An understanding of the job may also be gained through interviewing both the employee and the supervisor. Usually the analyst interviews the employee first, helping the worker describe the duties performed. Then the analyst normally contacts the supervisor for additional information, to check the accuracy of the information obtained from the worker, and to clarify certain points.

EMPLOYEE RECORDING

In some instances, job analysis information is gathered by having the employees describe their daily work activities in a diary or log. With this method, the problem of employees exaggerating job importance may have to be overcome. Even so, valuable understanding of highly specialized jobs, such as a recreation therapist, may be obtained in this way.

COMBINATION OF METHODS

Usually an analyst does not use one job analysis method exclusively. A combination of methods is often more appropriate. In analyzing clerical and administrative jobs, the analyst might use questionnaires supported by interviews and limited observation. In studying production jobs, interviews supplemented by extensive work observation may provide the necessary data. Basically, the analyst should employ the combination of techniques needed for accurate job descriptions/specifications.

First Interstate *Bancorp*

Job Analysis Questionnaire

Name _____

Position Title _____

Affiliate _____

Division/Group/Unit _____

City and State _____

Immediate Manager _____

General Instructions

This questionnaire is designed to provide information about your current position. It is *not* intended to measure your performance or productivity. It is a tool for analyzing and describing your job.

The questionnaire consists of six sections.

- **Section I** deals with the tasks and activities that comprise your job.
- **Section II** asks you to compare various job dimensions, which are groupings of similar tasks.
- **Section III** covers the skills and knowledge required to perform the tasks and activities of your position.
- **Section IV** identifies specific scope measures of your position.
- **Section V** focuses on individual factors that you may bring to your job.
- **Section VI** includes additional factors which may have an impact on your position.

Because this questionnaire covers a broad range of affiliates and jobs, a number of the questions may not apply to your position. However, *if you perform tasks that are not covered by the questionnaire, space has been provided for you to write them in*. Whether you perform a large number of tasks or only a few is not important. What is essential is that you respond to all of the questions (for example, you may perform certain financial management tasks, although you are in a marketing function), and in a manner which best describes your position as it typically performed by you.

In responding to the questions, please use the following definitions:

- *affiliate* refers to an individual bank (e.g., First Interstate Bank of Arizona) or a nonbank subsidiary (e.g., First Interstate Services Company).
- *customer* means any individual or group, inside or outside the company, with which you deal on a client or customer basis. For example, an affiliate bank can be a customer for the data processing unit, a small business can be a customer for the venture capital group, and an individual or a corporation can be a customer for a bank.
- *unit* is the organizational group in which you report or for which you have responsibility. This could be a functional group, a department, or a division of a company. For example, for a Cashier position, the unit might be the Cashier's Department; for a VP Operations, the unit might be the Operations Department; for a VP Administration, the unit would be the Administration Division; or for a Chief Executive Officer, the unit would be the entire bank.

The questionnaires will be returned directly to Towers, Perrin, Forster & Crosby (TPF&C), so all responses on this form will remain confidential. However, to ensure that the information about your position is accurate and consistent, you and your immediate manager will review the results of TPF°C's analysis of the questionnaire.

Please follow the specific instructions at the beginning of each section. Read each section in full before attempting to complete it so that you can respond as accurately as possible.

Thank you for your efforts in participating in this study.

(continued)

Figure 4-2
A Job Analysis Questionnaire
Source: Used with the permission of First Interstate Bancorp.

Section III. Position Skills and Knowledge

This section focuses on the type and depth of skills and knowledge that are 1) required to perform your job, and 2) that you may possess.

For each of the skills listed, you are asked to rate two items: the *level required* and the *level you possess*. In the appropriate boxes, write the number that best describes the skill or knowledge level, according to the following scale:

0 = Job neither requires nor do I possess skill/knowledge.
1 = Familiarity with skill/knowledge.
2 = General working skill/knowledge.
3 = Advanced skill/knowledge.
4 = Unique expertise in skill/knowledge.

In the first column, identify the *level of skill/knowledge* required to successfully perform your present job.

In the second column of boxes, identify the *level of skill/knowledge* that *you possess*, regardless of whether the job requires it.

The third column identifies sources of skills and knowledge. To indicate where you acquired each skill or knowledge that is required for the performance of your current position, identify up to, but no more than, two sources. Mark 1 in the column that represents the primary source. Mark 2 in the column that represents the secondary source.

Column headers (right side grids):
- Level required for position
- Level you possess
- On-the-job training
- College/university
- Formal banking program
- Internal training program
- External training program

A.   Planning, Policies, Procedures

1 Organization design
2 Short-term planning (setting budgets, goals, etc.)
3 Strategic planning
4 Pricing fee structuring

B.   Business Development/Marketing

5 Market research (identifying markets, competitive analyses and evaluation)
6 Market analysis (client needs, trends, strategies, etc.)
7 Marketing tools (advertising, promotional campaigns, etc.)
8 Products/services (bank unit services, systems, etc.)
9 Marketing/sales

C.   Customer Relations

10 Customer industry (objectives, economics, trends, etc.)
11 Customer counsel/problem solving
12 Account management
13 Profit analysis

For every statement
• If a task is not part of your job, mark X in the first box
• If a task is a part of your job, rate

Relative Time Spent
1 = Very small amount
2 = Small amount
3 = Moderate amount
4 = Large amount
5 = Very large amount

Relative Importance
A Unimportant
B Minor importance
C Important
D Very important
E Crucial

Column headers: Not part of the job | Relative time spent | Relative importance

A.   Planning

1 Develops business planning activities
2 Directs business planning activities
3 Develops annual unit goals and objectives
4 Approves annual unit goals and objectives
5 Develops longer-range strategic goals
6 Approves longer-range strategic goals
7 Develops specific strategy and action plans for unit
8 Approves specific strategy and action plans for unit
9 Reviews, approves, and monitors business plans
10 Prepares profit plans and updates
11 Approves profit plans and updates
12 Prepares operating budget
13 Approves operating budget
14 Approves requests for nonbudgeted items
15 Develops plans to improve administrative efficiency
16 Approves plans to improve administrative efficiency
17 Integrates the plans of other organizational units
18 Coordinates with other units to meet predetermined schedules
19 Proposes new or customized programs, services, products and research
20 Approves new or customized programs, services, products and research
21 Identifies impact of external conditions on unit
22 Coordinates units in the development of plans and programs
23 Monitors progress of specific projects
24 Recommends revisions to the unit organizational structure
25 Approves revisions to the unit organizational structure
26 Evaluates and recommends approval of affiliate facility projects
27 Recommends potential mergers, aquisitions or relocations
28 Approves potential mergers, aquisitions or relocations
29 *Other* please list task(s) and check boxes

a _____
b _____
c _____

From the above list of Planning tasks, please mark the numbers of the three most important tasks in rank order

1 ___
2 ___
3 ___

B.   Policies and Procedures

30 Formulates and recommends policies or procedures for others to follow
31 Approves policies or procedures for others to follow
32 Reviews agreements or documentation for compliance with appropriate policies and standards
33 Directs the establishment of review or control procedures
34 Evaluates operating policies or procedures against desired objectives
35 Develops or maintains standards for service
36 Develops quality control programs and procedures
37 Approves quality control programs and procedures
38 Formulates or recommends pricing policies
39 Approves pricing policies
40 Develops methods and procedures to evaluate business strategies
41 Establishes planning guidelines and procedures
42 Directs creation, handling and disposition of official records
43 Directs safeguarding or records and documents
44 Approves procedures for automating existing manual systems
45 Other please list task(s) and check boxes

a _____
b _____
c _____

From the above list of Policies and Procedures tasks, please mark the numbers of the three most important tasks in rank order

1 ___
2 ___
3 ___

Figure 4-2
A Job Analysis Questionnaire   *(continued from page 113)*
Source: Used with the permission of First Interstate Bancorp.

Conducting Job Analysis

The person who conducts job analysis is interested in gathering data on what is involved in performing a particular job. The people who participate in job analysis should include, at a minimum, the employee and the employee's immediate supervisor. Large organizations may have one or more job analysts, but in small organizations line supervisors may be responsible for job analysis. Organizations that lack the technical expertise often use outside consultants to perform job analysis. Regardless of the approach taken, before conducting job analysis, the analyst should learn as much as possible about the job by reviewing organizational charts and talking with individuals acquainted with the jobs to be studied. Before beginning, the supervisor should introduce the analyst to the employees and explain the purpose of the job analysis. Although employee attitudes about the job are beyond the job analyst's control, the analyst must attempt to develop mutual trust and confidence with those whose jobs are being analyzed. Failure in this area will detract from an otherwise technically sound job analysis. On completion of job analysis, two basic human resource documents—job descriptions and job specifications—can be prepared.

Job Description

Information obtained through job analysis is crucial to the development of job descriptions. Earlier, job description was defined as a document that states the tasks, duties, and responsibilities of the job. Job descriptions must be both relevant and accurate. They should provide concise statements of what employees are expected to do on the job and indicate exactly what employees do, how they do it, and the conditions under which the duties are performed. Job description takes on an even greater importance under the Americans with Disabilities Act (ADA) because the description of essential job functions may be critical to a defense regarding reasonable accommodation.[10] Although there is no legal mandate to do so, some firms present essential job functions in a separate section of the job description.

Among the items frequently included in a job description are these:

- Major duties performed
- Percentage of time devoted to each duty
- Performance standards to be achieved
- Working conditions and possible hazards
- Number of employees performing the job and to whom they report
- The machines and equipment used on the job

The contents of the job description vary somewhat with the purpose for which it will be used. The next section looks at the parts of a job description.

JOB IDENTIFICATION

The job identification section includes the job title, the department, the reporting relationship, and a job number or code. A good title will closely approximate the nature of the work content and will distinguish that job from others. Unfortunately, job titles are often misleading. An executive secretary in one organization may be little more than a highly paid clerk, whereas a person with the same title in another firm may practically run the company. For instance, one former student's first job after graduation was with a major tire and rubber company as an *assistant district service manager*. Because the primary duties of the job were to unload tires from trucks, check the tread wear, and stack the tires in boxcars, a more appropriate title would probably have been *tire checker and stacker*.

One information source that assists in standardizing job titles is the *Dictionary of Occupational Titles (DOT)*.[11] The *DOT* includes standardized and comprehensive descriptions of job duties and related information for over 200,000 occupations. Such standardization permits employers in different industries and parts of the country to match more accurately job requirements with worker skills.

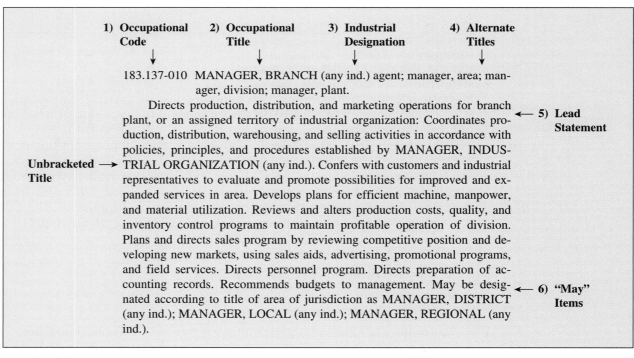

Figure 4-3
The Parts of the Dictionary of Occupational Titles Definition
Source: U.S. Department of Labor, *Dictionary of Occupational Titles.*

An example of a *DOT* definition—for a *branch manager*, occupational code 183.137-010—is provided in Figure 4-3. The first digit of the code identifies one of the following major occupations:

0/1   Professional, technical, and managerial

2   Clerical and sales

3   Service

4   Farming, fishing, forestry, and related

5   Processing

6   Machine trade

7   Bench work

8   Structural work

9   Miscellaneous

For the branch manager, the major classification would be *managerial* occupations. Thus, this example has a code *1*.

The next two digits represent breakdowns of the general occupation category. Digits four through six describe the job's relationship to data, people, and things. For the branch manager, a code *1* for data would be *coordinating*, a code *3* for people would be *supervising*, and a code *7* for things would be *handling*.

The final three digits indicate the alphabetical order of titles within the six-digit code group. These codes assist in distinguishing a specific occupation from other similar ones. The alphabetical order for *branch manager* is indicated by the digits 010.

DATE OF THE JOB ANALYSIS

The job analysis date is placed on the job description to aid in identifying job changes that would make the description obsolete. Some firms have found it useful to place an expiration date on the document. This practice ensures periodic review of job content and minimizes the number of obsolete job descriptions.

JOB SUMMARY

The job summary provides a concise overview of the job. It is generally a short paragraph that states job content.

DUTIES PERFORMED

The body of the job description delineates the major duties to be performed. Usually one sentence beginning with an action verb such as *receives, performs, establishes,* or *assembles,* adequately explains each duty. Essential functions are shown in a separate section to aid in complying with the Americans with Disabilities Act.

Job Specification

Recall that we defined job specification as a document containing the minimum acceptable qualifications that a person should possess to perform a particular job. Items typically included in the job specification are educational requirements, experience, personality traits, and physical abilities. In practice, job specifications are often included as a major section of job descriptions.

Figure 4-4 is a job description provided by Conoco for an administrative support position. Some of the critical skills needed for the job include interpersonal skills/team player, ability to influence others, and knowledge of

Position Title: **Administrative Support**		Code:	Salary Grade:
Work Location:		Report To:	Function:

Basic Purpose/Accountabilities:
Responsible for providing and coordinating administrative support to assigned functional groups. Focus is on aligning contributions to department needs and company goals.

Primary Functions/Responsibilities:	Critical Skills/Leadership Criteria:
-Preparation of time sheets -Track employee attendance -Manage fixtures, furniture and equipment necessary to support the function -Process invoices, monitor expenditures -Coordinate and support meetings -Participate in planning process on projects -Type documentation to individuals external to Conoco -Assist with presentation preparation and planning -Coordinate large scale documentation reproduction -External mailing/facsimile transmission -Coordinate central office supplies -Resource computer software applications -Coordinate work activities with other functions -Generate alternatives and make recommendations on improving area work process -Record retention/filing	**CRITICAL SKILLS** -Interpersonal skills/team player -Ability to influence others -Knowledge of business software applications -Confidentiality -Planning, organizing and time management -Written and oral communication -Customer orientation -Knowledge of operations and organization **LEADERSHIP CRITERIA** -Able to lead others -Engenders trust -Understands and uses functional expertise to contribute -Accepts ownership, is accountable and delivers on commitments -Oriented towards continuous learning

Quantitative Factors/Business Model Activities:	
Quantitative	Business Model

Figure 4-4
A Conoco Job Description
Source: Conoco Inc.

It cannot be denied that jobs are changing. They are getting bigger and more complex.

software applications. This type of information is extremely valuable in the recruiting and selection process.

After jobs have been analyzed and the descriptions written, the results should be reviewed with the supervisor and the worker to ensure that they are accurate, clear, and understandable. The courtesy of reviewing results with employees also helps to gain their acceptance. Because the job description and job specification are often combined into one form, we use the term *job description* in this book to include both documents.

The Expanded Job Description

When first hearing the news that he had died, Mark Twain responded "Reports of my death have been greatly exaggerated." As we hear report after report about the demise of the *job*, we have a similar response.[12] After talking with managers representing literally scores of business firms, we have yet to locate an organization void of jobs.

Nevertheless, it cannot be denied that jobs are changing. They are getting bigger and they are getting more complex. The last duty shown on the proverbial job description, "And any other duty that may be assigned," is increasingly becoming *THE* job description. This enlarged, flexible, complex job changes the way virtually every HR function is performed. Take recruitment and selection, for example. You cannot simply look for an individual who possesses narrow skills required to perform a job. You must go deeper and seek competencies, intelligence, ability to adjust, and ability and willingness to work in teams.

Training an individual for this *job* also, understandably, becomes more difficult. There is a lot more to learn. Appraising performance is also more complicated, especially if you want to evaluate more than output and also focus on means. Organizations have never really determined how to compensate anyone fairly. Persons performing the new *job* will present an even greater challenge.

HRM IN ACTION
WHAT KIND OF PERSON DO YOU NEED?

"I can't determine what kind of computer programmer you need, Alex," said Bob Sanders, the human resource director. "Every applicant I sent down was proficient in FORTRAN, just like the job description stated."

"Get real, Bob," replied Alex. "We haven't required FORTRAN in 10 years. The person I need has to be up-to-date on the latest software. None of the people you sent me were qualified."

How would you respond?

Timeliness of Job Analysis

The rapid pace of technological change makes the need for accurate job analysis even more important now and in the future. Historically, job analysis could be conducted and then set aside for a reasonable time. Today, however, job requirements are changing so rapidly that they must be constantly reviewed to keep them relevant. By one estimate, technological change is occurring so rapidly that people may have to change their entire skills three or four times during their careers.[13] If this projection is accurate, the need for accurate and timely job analysis is becoming ever more important.

On a downside, because of rapid technological changes, companies that do not constantly monitor their job analysis program will be in a difficult position. Recruiting for a position with an inaccurate job description may result in a poor match of skills the employee possesses and skills needed. Training may be irrelevant and the compensation system may be flawed. Thus, job analysis in today's environment is likely to be even more important than it was earlier.

Other Job Analysis Methods

Over the years, attempts have been made to provide more systematic methods of conducting job analysis. We describe several of these approaches next.

DEPARTMENT OF LABOR JOB ANALYSIS SCHEDULE

Job Analysis Schedule (JAS): A systematic method of studying jobs and occupations; developed by the U.S. Department of Labor.

The U.S. Department of Labor established a method of systematically studying jobs and occupations called the **Job Analysis Schedule (JAS)**. When the JAS method is used, information is gathered by a trained analyst.

A major component of the JAS is the work performed ratings section. Here, what workers do in performing a job with regard to data (D), people (P), and things (T) is evaluated. Each of these is viewed as a hierarchy of functions, with the higher in the category being more difficult. The codes in the worker functions section represent the highest level of involvement in each of the three categories.

The JAS component called Worker Traits Ratings relates primarily to job requirement data. The topics general education designation (GED), specific vocational preparation (SVP), aptitudes, temperaments, interests, physical demands, and environmental conditions are included. The description of tasks section provides a specific description of the work performed. Both routine tasks and occasionally performed tasks are included.

FUNCTIONAL JOB ANALYSIS

Functional job analysis (FJA): A comprehensive approach to formulating job descriptions that concentrates on the interactions among the work, the worker, and the work organization.

Functional Job Analysis (FJA) is a comprehensive job analysis approach that concentrates on the interactions among the work, the worker, and the organization. This approach is a modification of the job analysis schedule. It is a worker-oriented method of describing jobs that identifies what a person actually does rather than his or her responsibilities.[14] The fundamental elements of FJA are these:

1. A major distinction is made between what gets done and what workers do to get things done. It is more important in job analysis to know the latter. For instance, a word processing operator does not just keep the system running; he or she must perform a number of tasks to accomplish the job.
2. Each job is concerned with data, people, and things.
3. Workers function in unique ways as they relate to data, people, and things.
4. Each job requires the worker to relate to data, people, and things in some way.
5. Only a few definite and identifiable functions are involved with data, people, and things (Table 4-2).

TABLE 4-2

Worker Function Scale for Job Analysis Schedule

Data (4th digit)	*People (5th digit)*	*Things (6th digit)*
0 Synthesizing	0 Monitoring	0 Setting up
1 Coordinating	1 Negotiating	1 Precision working
2 Analyzing	2 Instructing	2 Operating—controlling
3 Compiling	3 Supervising	3 Driving—operating
4 Computing	4 Diverting	4 Manipulating
5 Copying	5 Persuading	5 Tending
6 Comparing	6 Speaking—signaling	6 Feeding—offbearing
7 No significant relationship	7 Serving	7 Handling
	8 No significant relationship	8 No significant relationship

Source: U.S. Department of Labor, *Dictionary of Occupational Titles.*

6. These functions proceed from the simple to the complex. The least complex form of data would be comparing and the most complex would be synthesizing. In addition, the assumption is that if an upper-level function is required, all the lower-level functions are also required.

7. The three hierarchies for data, people, and things provide two measures for a job. First, there is a measure of relative complexity in relation to data, people, and things—in essence, the amount of interrelationship among the three functions. Second, there is a measure of proportional involvement for each function. For instance, 50 percent of a person's time may be spent in analyzing, 30 percent in supervising, and 20 percent in operating.

POSITION ANALYSIS QUESTIONNAIRE

Position Analysis Questionnaire (PAQ): A structured job analysis questionnaire that uses a checklist approach to identify job elements.

The **Position Analysis Questionnaire (PAQ)** is a structured job analysis questionnaire that uses a checklist approach to identify job elements. Some 194 job descriptors relate to job-oriented elements. Advocates of the PAQ believe that its ability to identify job elements, behaviors required of job incumbents, and other job characteristics make its use applicable to analysis of virtually any type of job. Each job descriptor is evaluated on a specified scale such as extent of use, amount of time, importance of job, possibility of occurrence, and applicability.

Each job being studied is scored relative to the 32 job dimensions. The score derived represents a profile of the job; this can be compared with standard profiles to group the job into known job families—that is, jobs of a similar nature. In essence, the PAQ identifies significant job behaviors and classified jobs. With the PAQ, job descriptions can be based on their relative importance and emphasis placed on various job elements.

MANAGEMENT POSITION DESCRIPTION QUESTIONNAIRE

Management Position Description Questionnaire (MPDQ): A form of job analysis designed for management positions that uses a checklist method to analyze jobs.

The **Management Position Description Questionnaire (MPDQ)** is a method of job analysis designed for management positions; it uses a checklist to analyze jobs. The MPDQ has been used to determine the training needs of individuals who are slated to move into managerial positions. It has also been used to evaluate and set compensation rates for managerial jobs and to assign the jobs to job families.

GUIDELINES-ORIENTED JOB ANALYSIS

Guidelines-Oriented Job Analysis (GOJA): A method that responds to the growing amount of legislation affecting employment decisions by utilizing a step-by-step procedure to describe the work of a particular job classification.

The **Guidelines-Oriented Job Analysis (GOJA)** responds to the legislation affecting staffing and involves a step-by-step procedure for describing the work of a particular job classification.[15] It is also used for developing selection tools, such as application forms and for documenting compliance with various legal requirements. The GOJA obtains the following types of information: (1) machines, tools, and equipment; (2) supervision; (3) contacts; (4) duties; (5) knowledge, skills, and abilities; (6) physical and other requirements; and (7) differentiating requirements.

HR Web Wisdom

http://www.prenhall.com/mondy

SHRM–HR LINKS
This site covers various legal issues related to work.

Job Analysis and the Law

Effective job analysis is essential to sound human resource management as an organization recruits, selects, and promotes employees. In particular, human resource management has focused on job analysis because selection methods need to be clearly job related.[16] Legislation requiring thorough job analysis includes the following acts.

Fair Labor Standards Act: Employees are categorized as exempt or nonexempt, and job analysis is basic to this determination. Nonexempt workers must be paid time and a half when they work more than 40 hours per week. Overtime pay is not required for exempt employees.

Equal Pay Act: In the past (and to some extent today), men were often paid higher salaries than women, even though they performed essentially the same job. If jobs are not substantially different, the employees performing them must receive similar pay. When pay differences exist, job descriptions can be used to show whether jobs are substantially equal in terms of skill, effort, responsibility, or working conditions.

Civil Rights Act: As with the Equal Pay Act, job descriptions may provide the basis for adequate defenses against unfair discrimination charges in initial selection, promotion, and all other areas of human resource administration. When job analysis is not performed, defending certain qualifications established for the job is usually difficult. For instance, stating that a high school diploma is required without having determined its necessity through job analysis leaves the firm open to possible discrimination charges.

Occupational Safety and Health Act: Job descriptions are required to specify elements of the job that endanger health or are considered unsatisfactory or distasteful by the majority of the population. Showing the job description to the employee in advance is a good defense.

The Americans with Disabilities Act (ADA): Employers are required to make reasonable accommodations for workers with disabilities who are able to perform the essential functions of a job. It is important that organizations distinguish these essential functions from those that are marginal. The EEOC defines a reasonable accommodation as any modification or adjustment to a job, an employment practice, or the work environment that allows an individual with a disability to enjoy an equal employment opportunity. What constitutes reasonable accommodations depends on the disability and the skills of the person in question.[17]

Job design: A process of determining the specific tasks to be performed, the methods used in performing these tasks, and how the job relates to other work in an organization.

Job Design

Job design is the process of determining the specific tasks to be performed, the methods used in performing these tasks, and the way the job relates to other work in the organization. Several concepts related to job design including job enrichment and job enlargement will be discussed next.

HR Web Wisdom

http://www.prenhall.com/mondy

JOB ENRICHMENT
Included are the history, nature, and results of job enrichment.

JOB ENRICHMENT

Job enrichment: The restructuring of the content and level of responsibility of a job to make it more challenging, meaningful, and interesting to a worker.

In the past two decades, there has been considerable interest in and application of job enrichment in a wide variety of organizations. Strongly advocated by Frederick Herzberg, **job enrichment** consist of basic changes in the content and level of responsibility of a job so as to provide greater challenge to the worker. Job enrichment provides a vertical expansion of responsibilities. The worker has the opportunity to derive a feeling of achievement, recognition, responsibility, and personal growth in performing the job. Although job enrichment programs do not always achieve positive results, they have often brought about improvements in job performance and in the level of worker satisfaction in many organizations. One group that appears to be particularly receptive to job enrichment are Generation X employees. Generation X employees are the more than 40 million American workers in their 20s or early 30s. Generation Xers recognize the value of formal training and development programs that support individualized career goals, and they welcome both regular and ad hoc opportunities to learn on the job as well as from mentoring relationships. Also, because Generation Xers are independently motivated to learn and grow professionally, they are especially accepting of the expanded job responsibilities that are common in job enrichment.[18]

According to Herzberg, five principles should be followed when implementing job enrichment.

1. *Increasing job demands*: The job should be changed in such a way as to increase the level of difficulty and responsibility.

2. *Increasing the worker's accountability*: More individual control and authority over the work should be allowed, with the manager retaining ultimate accountability.

3. *Providing work scheduling freedom*: Within limits, individual workers should be allowed to schedule their own work.

4. *Providing feedback*: Timely periodic reports on performance should be made directly to workers rather than through their supervisors.

5. *Providing new learning experiences*: Work situations should encourage opportunities for new experiences and personal growth.[19]

JOB ENLARGEMENT

Job enlargement: A change in the scope of a job so as to provide greater variety to a worker.

There is a clear distinction between job enrichment and job enlargement. **Job enlargement** involves changes in the scope of a job so as to provide greater variety to the worker. It provides a horizontal expansion of duties. For example, instead of knowing how to operate only one machine, a person learns to operate two or even three but is given no higher level of responsibility. On the other hand, job enrichment gives a person additional responsibilities; it involves a vertical expansion of duties. For instance, the worker may be given the additional responsibility of scheduling the three machines. Increased responsibility means providing the worker with greater freedom to do the job; this includes making decisions and exercising more self-control over work.

Design Approaches: Fad or Fashion

Three management design approaches are described and analyzed next: management by objectives, total quality management, and reengineering. Management designs can have a major impact on jobs and subsequent job analysis.

MANAGEMENT BY OBJECTIVES

Management by objectives (MBO): A philosophy of management that emphasizes the setting of agreed-on objectives by superior and subordinate managers and the use of these objectives as the primary basis of motivation, evaluation, and self-control.

Management by objectives (MBO) is a philosophy of management that emphasizes the setting of agreed-on objectives by superior and subordinate managers and using these objectives as the primary basis for motivation, evaluation, and self-control. As a management approach that encourages managers to anticipate and plan for the future, MBO directs efforts toward attainable goals. It deemphasizes guessing or making decisions based on hunches.

Management by objectives is a dynamic process that must be continuously reviewed, modified, and updated. Top management must both initiate the MBO process by establishing long-range goals and support the process. The subordinate proceeds to work toward his or her goals. At the end of the appraisal period, both parties review the subordinate's performance and determine what can be done to overcome any problems encountered. Goals are then established for the next period and the process is repeated.

Some organizations continue to use various forms of management by objectives, whereas others view it as a passing fad.[20] General Motor's (GM) Saturn division utilized a version of MBO that was a model of cooperation between management and labor. The division currently has the authority to develop, make, and sell cars independent of the rest of General Motors. Saturn workers, unlike those at GM, take part in decision making even to the point of solving problems on the floor as soon as they occur. General Motors wants common parts and common methods as their model, not the model of Saturn. Saturn's form of MBO works, but it is expensive, and when General Motors CEO Jack Smith laid out the plan to streamline GM, it appears that MBO may be a victim of that effort.[21]

There are potential benefits to be realized from using management by objectives, but numerous problems are also associated with this practice. Without the full support of top management, for example, it is bound to fail. This commitment may be difficult to obtain because implementing such a system often takes from three to five years. In addition, goals may be difficult to establish. Another potential weakness is a tendency to concentrate on short-term plans: Short-term objectives may be achieved at the expense of long-term goals. The system also has the potential to create a seemingly insurmountable paper mill if it is not closely monitored. Finally, some managers believe that MBO is excessively time-consuming and excessively detailed. The Department of Defense remembers how MBO "fell under its own weight due to a shift from concentrating on the most critical aspects of an agency's mission to second, third, fourth tier objectives that were too detailed for a strategic view." [22]

TOTAL QUALITY MANAGEMENT

Total quality management (TQM): A top management philosophy that emphasizes the continuous improvement of the processes that result in goods or services.

Total quality management (TQM) is a commitment to excellence by everyone in an organization that emphasizes excellence achieved by teamwork and a process of continuous improvement. Today many companies have *total quality* programs that integrate every department from manufacturing to marketing and research in the effort to improve. Implied in the concept is a commitment to be the best and provide the highest quality products and services possible and which meet or exceed the hopes of the customer. Businesses are making many changes to stay competitive. They are constantly seeking ways to improve quality, increase speed of operations, and adopt a customer orientation. These changes are so fundamental that they must take root in a company's very essence, which means in its *culture*.

Total quality management often involves major cultural changes. It requires a new way of thinking and strong leadership at all levels. Individuals throughout the organization must be inspired to do things differently. They must understand what needs to be done and why, and this takes strong leadership. The ultimate goal of TQM is to alter the process by improving customer satisfaction. Instead of being content with the status quo, employees at all levels continually seek alternative methods or technologies that will improve existing processes. TQM provides a strategy for reducing the causes of poor quality and thereby increasing productivity.

Total quality management is a process of continuously improving quality over the long run. In the short run, once each of the linked processes within a firm is operating at or above a desired level of quality, reliance on costly inspection practices can be reduced or eliminated altogether. Attention can then be turned to monitoring the overall process to determine the sources of variation still present. If these sources are also eliminated, the process can be even more precise and produce fewer defects or errors. In the customer's view, quality will have exceeded the expected level. The customer, more than satisfied, will probably remain a customer. The increased employee participation required by TQM creates a new role for all organizational members. Top management, middle managers, first-level supervisors, and all workers must embrace the philosophy and work to ensure its acceptance throughout the organization. Operative employees are consulted for assistance in determining and analyzing sources of process variation, and they are relied on to develop proposals for reducing or eliminating these variances.

Cultural change must precede or accompany the introduction of total quality management. And the organizational culture required to support the concepts of this management method is not likely to be changed quickly. Five to ten years is generally needed for such changes in the top management value system to permeate the organization. TQM is not a body of regulations and cannot be forced on employees. As a company's culture is largely a product of positively reinforced behavior, the route to change is almost always through education and training.[23] In addition to training and development activities, employee selection practices will be a central component in implementing this management philosophy.

The perspective, "It sounds good in theory, but does it work in practice?" may also apply to total quality management. According to research by the consulting firms of Arthur D. Little, Ernst & Young, Rath & Strong, McKinsey & Co., and A. T. Kearney, "only about one-fifth—at best one-third—of TQM programs in the United States and Europe have achieved significant or even tangible improvements in quality, productivity, competitiveness or financial returns."[24] Many practitioners admit that the image of TQM is tarnished and is not the quick fix that U.S. management often seeks.[25] According to one researcher, "TQM is not synonymous with quality. Quality is essential for organizational success and competitive advantage. TQM is only one of many possible means to attain quality. In other words, quality is sacred; TQM is not."[26] At times it works and at other times it is unsuccessful. As with MBO, the theory may be valid but proper implementation is the key to success. Both approaches are management tools that must be carefully chosen and patiently implemented.

REENGINEERING

When business problems occur, workers are often blamed, even though the real obstacle lies in process design. Unfortunately, rather than looking for process problems, managers often focus on worker deficiencies, at least initially. This is true even though the design of the process may be causing problems. If process is the problem, it might be reengineered for a substantial improvement in productivity.

Reengineering: The fundamental rethinking and radical redesign of business processes to achieve dramatic improvements in critical, contemporary measures of performance, such as cost, quality, service, and speed.

Reengineering essentially requires the firm to rethink and redesign their business system to become more competitive. **Reengineering** is "the fundamental rethinking and radical redesign of business processes to achieve dramatic improvements in critical, contemporary measures of performance, such as cost, quality, service, and speed."[27] Reengineering emphasizes the radical redesign of work in which companies organize around process instead of by functional departments. Incremental change is not what is desired, as with TQM, instead, radical changes are wanted that will alter entire operations with the stroke of pens. Essentially, the firm must rethink and redesign its business system from the ground up. Reengineering focuses on the overall aspects of job designs, organizational structures, and management systems. It stresses that work should be organized around outcomes as opposed to tasks or functions. Reengineering should never be confused with downsizing (discussed in chapter 5), even though a workforce reduction often results from this strategy.[28]

In the language of reengineering, a term that is often used is *process manager.* As opposed to being a functional manager such as a production manager, a marketing manager, a finance manager, and so forth, a process manager is responsible for accomplishing all operations associated with a specific process. The structure is similar in nature to the matrix organization.

Reengineering evolved from a management fad to a $51 billion industry very rapidly. Today the star is slowly fading.[29] One study indicates that 85 percent of reengineering attempts failed.[30] Like TQM, reengineering can be effective in certain instances. There are numerous examples of very successful implementations. The use of reengineering at IBM to significantly change its benefit center is a high profile example of success.[31] There are other instances of failure, with Levi Strauss having had a very disappointing and costly experience.[32]

A GLOBAL PERSPECTIVE

Global Job Descriptions: The Domestic Blueprint Is Just Not Good Enough

Realistic global job descriptions are essential before a company makes global assignments. A systematic process of determining the necessary skills, duties, and knowledge required for a global assignment is essential and usually more complex. HR managers cannot simply take the domestic job description blueprint, require some language training, and then assume the job will be accomplished. Effective global job analysis and the development of accurate job descriptions may actually mean the difference between success and failure overseas.

According to Richard A. Guzzo of the University of Maryland/College Park, an estimated 20 percent of U.S. expatriates sent abroad return prematurely; many others endure global assignments but are ineffective in their jobs and social lives and often experience broken marriages.[33] Failures can be traced directly to a selection process that is based on inaccurate job descriptions. Determining the skills, duties, and knowledge required for performing global jobs is much more complex than making such determinations domestically. Whereas basic skills may be essentially the same for most domestic assignments, basic skills for an overseas assignment must often include foreign language skills, cultural adaptability, and the ability to cope with different work methods and procedures. For instance, research indicates that success in overseas work assignments depends on the possession of personal skills, people skills, and perceptual skills far beyond those needed to accomplish job-related tasks domestically. Personal skills are those techniques and attributes that facilitate the expatriate's mental and emotional well-being. They include means of finding solitude, such as meditation, prayer, and physical exercise routines, which tend to decrease the employee's stress level. An ability to manage time, to delegate, and to manage responsibilities are also essential personal skills.[34] Whereas domestic duties often are well defined, expatriates are actually representatives of the company and are also there to protect the company's best interest, often transmitting the domestic corporate culture overseas. Doing the job may require these individuals to accomplish duties not assigned to managers domestically. A job description for a global position must take into account the need for knowledge that extends far beyond the job being accomplished in the United States.

Issues that are addressed domestically are much more complicated when analyzed in global terms. The physical and mental tasks carry much higher demands globally. The job to be completed often involves intangible issues such as transferring the domestic corporate culture overseas. One of the main areas in which job descriptions become complex is location considerations. When the job is to be completed overseas, job performance is often more difficult. Also, how the worker does the job becomes more complex. Cultural and diversity considerations are important domestically, but such issues are compounded globally. Even the reasons the job is done may require more in-depth analysis because often locals could perform the job just as well; other considerations make expatriates necessary. The bottom line is that the qualifications needed to perform the job globally often go far beyond those needed to do the same job domestically. Because the job is more complex, global job descriptions must be much more involved. ■

SUMMARY

1. **Define job analysis.**

   Job analysis is the systematic process of determining the skills, duties, and knowledge required for performing jobs in an organization.

2. **Discuss the reasons that job analysis is a basic human resource tool.**

   Without a properly conducted job analysis, a human resource manager would find it difficult, if not impossible, to perform satisfactorily the other human resource-related functions. Job analysis information is used to prepare both job descriptions and job specifications. Job analysis data impacts virtually every aspect of human resource management—human resource planning, recruitment, selection, job specifications, job descriptions, performance appraisal, compensation, safety and health, human resource research, employee and labor relations, and legal employment practices.

3. **Explain the reasons for conducting job analysis.**

   The need for a sound job analysis system is extremely critical. New jobs are being created and old jobs are being redesigned. Referring to a job analysis that was conducted only a few years ago may provide inaccurate data. Essentially, job analysis helps organizations address the reality that change is taking place.

4. **Describe the types of information required for job analysis.**

   The job analyst identifies the actual duties and responsibilities associated with the job. Work activities and worker-oriented activities are quite important. In addition, knowledge of the types of machines, tools, equipment, and work aids that are used in performing the job are also important. The job analyst also looks for job-related tangibles and intangibles. Some job analysis systems identify the standards that are established for the job. With regard to job content, the analyst studies the work schedule, financial and nonfinancial incentives, and physical working conditions. Since jobs are often performed in conjunction with others, organizational and social contexts should also be noted. Also, specific education, training, and work experience pertinent to performing the job are identified.

5. *Describe the various job analysis methods.*

The job analyst administers a structured questionnaire to employees who then identify the tasks they perform in accomplishing the job. The job analyst witnesses the work being performed and records his or her observations when the observation method is used. An understanding of the job may also be gained through interviewing both the employee and the supervisor. Job analysis information may be gathered through the employees describing their daily work activities in a diary or log. A combination of the above job analysis methods are often used.

6. *Identify who conducts job analysis.*

The person who conducts job analysis is interested in gathering data regarding what is involved in performing a particular job. The people who participate in job analysis should include, at a minimum, the employee and the employee's immediate supervisor.

7. *Describe the components of a well-designed job description.*

The job identification section includes the job title, department, reporting relationship, and a job number or code. The job analysis date is placed on the job description to aid in identifying job changes that would make the description obsolete. The job summary provides a concise overview of the job. The body of the job description delineates the major duties to be performed and highlights essential job functions.

8. *Define* job specification *and identify the components of the job specification.*

A job specification is a document containing the minimum acceptable qualifications that a person should possess in order to perform a particular job. Items typically included in the job specification are educational requirements, experience, personality traits, and physical abilities.

9. *Discuss why the timeliness of job analysis is important.*

The rapid pace of technological change makes the need for accurate job analysis even more important now and in the future. Job requirements are changing so rapidly that they must be constantly reviewed to keep them relevant.

10. *Identify the newer methods available for conducting job analysis.*

The U.S. Department of Labor Job Analysis Schedule (JAS); Functional Job Analysis (FJA); Position Analysis Questionnaire (PAQ); Management Position Description Questionnaire (MPDQ); and Guidelines-Oriented Job Analysis (GOJA).

11. *Describe how job analysis helps satisfy various legal requirements.*

With the Fair Labor Standards Act, employees are categorized as exempt or nonexempt, and job analysis is basic to this determination. Nonexempt workers must be paid time and a half when they work more than 40 hours per week. Overtime pay is not required for exempt employees. According to the Equal Pay Act, if jobs are not substantially different, similar pay must be provided to employees in those similar jobs. Based on the Civil Rights Act, job descriptions may provide the basis for adequate defenses against unfair discrimination charges in initial selection, promotion, and all other areas of human resource administration. Based on the Occupational Safety and Health Act, job descriptions are required to specify elements of the job that endanger workers' health or are considered unsatisfactory or distasteful by the majority of the population. Based on the Americans with Disabilities Act, employers are required to make reasonable accommodations for workers with disabilities who are able to perform the essential functions of a job.

12. *Define* **job design.**

    Job design is the process of determining the specific tasks to be performed, the methods used in performing the task, and how the job relates to other work in the organization.

13. *Describe management by objectives, total quality management, and reengineering.*

    Management by objectives (MBO) is a philosophy of management that emphasizes the setting of agreed-on objectives by superior and subordinate managers and the use of these objectives as the primary basis for motivation, evaluation, and self-control. Total quality management (TQM) is a commitment to excellence by everyone in an organization that emphasizes excellence achieved by teamwork and a process of continuous improvement. Reengineering is the fundamental rethinking and radical redesign of business processes to achieve dramatic improvements in critical, contemporary measures of performance, such as cost, quality, service, and speed.

QUESTIONS FOR REVIEW

1. What is the distinction between a job and a position? Define job analysis.
2. Discuss what is meant by the statement, "Job analysis is a most basic human resource management tool."
3. Describe the traditional methods used to conduct job analysis.
4. List and briefly describe the types of data that are typically gathered when one is conducting job analysis.
5. What are the basic components of a job description? Briefly describe each.
6. What are the items typically included in a job specification?
7. Briefly define each of the following: (a) U.S. Department of Labor Job Analysis Schedule (JAS), (b) Functional Job Analysis (FJA), (c) Position Analysis Questionnaire (PAQ), (d) Management Position Description Questionnaire (MPDQ), and (e) Guidelines-Oriented Job Analysis (GOJA).

8. Describe how effective job analysis can be used to satisfy each of the following statutes: (a) Fair Labor Standards Act, (b) Equal Pay Act, (c) Civil Rights Act, (d) Occupational Safety and Health Act, and (e) Americans with Disabilities Act.
9. Distinguish among job design, job enrichment, and job enlargement.
10. Define each of the following:
    a. management by objectives (MBO)
    b. total quality management (TQM)
    c. reengineering

DEVELOPING HRM SKILLS

AN EXPERIENTIAL EXERCISE

Developing and updating job descriptions is an integral part of the job of any human resource professional. Without properly designed job descriptions, a human resource manager will find that performing necessary human resource management activities is extremely difficult. This exercise will permit you to gain a better appreciation of what is involved in preparing job descriptions. Job descriptions may vary even when the job analysis information is similar.

Each participant will use the *Pedal Cycle Company's Job Description Form* obtained from your instructor and develop an appropriate job description. Several class members can participate in this exercise. Your instructor will give the participants the additional information necessary to complete the exercise.

 *Take It to the Net*

We invite you to visit the Mondy home page on the Prentice Hall Web site at:

http://www.prenhall.com/mondy

for updated information, Web-based exercises, and links to other HR-related sites.

HRM SIMULATION

Incident A in the *Simulation Players Manual* involves an opportunity to conduct job analysis. Your team has been investigating the various methods and costs of doing a job analysis for your organization. Any job analysis program would include writing a job description for each job in the organization. You have discovered that job descriptions have many uses, such as recruitment, interviewing, orientation, training, job evaluation, wage compensation survey, performance appraisal, and out-placement. Because your organization does not have the personnel or in-house expertise to do the work, your team has received bids from various firms to write these. Your team is charged with the responsibility of choosing the best qualified and reasonably priced firm from a list of proposals.

HRM INCIDENT

1

Who Needs Job Descriptions?

*J*ohn Case, accounting supervisor, was clearly annoyed as he approached his boss, Gerald Jones. He began, "Gerald, this note you sent me says I have to update descriptions for all 10 of the jobs in my department within the next two weeks."

"Well, what's the problem with that?" asked Gerald.

John explained, "This is a waste of time, especially as I have other deadlines. It will take at least 30 hours. We still have two weeks of work left on the internal audit reviews. You want me to push that back and work on job descriptions? No way.

"We haven't looked at these job descriptions in years. They will need a great deal of revision. And as soon as they get into the hands of the employees, I'll get all kinds of flack."

"Why would you get flack for getting the job descriptions in order?" asked Gerald.

John answered, "This whole thing is a can of worms. Just calling attention to the existence of job descriptions will give some people the idea that they don't have to do things that aren't in the description. And if we write what the people in my division really do, some jobs will have to be upgraded and others downgraded, I'll bet. I just can't afford the morale problem and the confusion right now."

Gerald replied, "What do you suggest, John? I have been told just to get it done, and within two weeks."

"I don't want to do it at all," said John, "but certainly not during the audit period. Can't you just go back up the line and get it put off until next month?"

Questions
1. What have John and Gerald forgotten to do prior to the creation of job descriptions? Why is that step important?
2. Evaluate John's statement, "Just calling attention to the existence of job descriptions will give some people the idea that they don't have to do things that aren't in the description."

HRM INCIDENT

2

Job Analysis: Should We Do It?

*R*ichard Boudreaux was excited as he told his dad about his plan for developing job descriptions at their family-owned company, Boudreaux Gasket Company. Richard had been working with his father for some years after completing a stint in the Air Force. He was taking over more and more of the responsibilities for management because they both knew that it would not be long before Mr. Boudreaux retired. Richard had a degree in management and had just completed a symposium on job analysis.

"Dad," said Richard, "in two years the workforce here has gone from 30 to over 50. I don't believe we can keep our finger on everything without a little more formality than we have had in the past."

"I don't know son," said Mr. Boudreaux. "The way you describe it, creating job descriptions is pretty complicated. I don't know how to conduct job analysis. For my part, I wouldn't do it unless you can figure out how it can help us make rubber gaskets better, faster, or with fewer work hours than we use now."

Boudreaux Gasket Company is a small gasket maker near Gueydan, Louisiana. Most of the jobs involve operating punch presses. The operators place pieces of fiber-reinforced rubber sheeting into their machines, press the footpedals, and remove the gaskets that have been cut. Some of the workers make nonstandard gaskets. They cut these using various kinds of punches and cutters, which are hand operated. All workers are responsible for inspecting the items they make and packaging them for shipment. Even for standard items, a batch seldom exceeds 2,000 pieces in size. The gaskets are used throughout the country, primarily in the petrochemical industry.

Questions

1. Is Boudreaux Gasket Company big enough to justify formal job analysis? Explain your answer.
2. If you were Richard, what kinds of arguments would you use to convince your father that formal job analysis is justified?
3. Which method of obtaining job analysis data would you use?
4. What steps would you follow to accomplish formal job analysis at Boudreaux Gasket Company?

Notes

1. James Clifford, "Manage Work Better to Better Manage Human Resources: A Comparative Study of Two Approaches to Job Analysis," *Public Personnel Management* 25 (April 1996): 89.
2. James P. Clifford, "Job Analysis: Why Do It, and How Should It Be Done?" *Public Personnel Management* 23 (Summer 1994): 324.
3. R. Wayne Mondy, Robert M. Noe, and Robert E. Edwards, "What the Staffing Function Entails," *Personnel* 63 (April 1986): 55–58.

4. Clifford, "Job Analysis: Why Do It, and How Should It Be Done?"
5. *Uniform Guidelines on Employee Selection Procedures, Federal Register,* Friday, August 25, 1978, Part IV.
6. IBM Human Resources Conference, "IT Should Support HR Changes," October 23, 1996.
7. Mary Molina Fitzer, "Managing from Afar: Performance and Rewards in a Telecommmuting Environment," *Compensation & Benefits Review* 29 (January/February 1997): 65–73.
8. N. Fredric Crandall and Marc J. Wallace, Jr., "Inside the Virtual Workplace: Forging a New Deal for Work and Rewards," *Compensation & Benefits Review* 29 (January/February 1997): 27–36.
9. Gilbert B. Siegel, "Job Analysis in the TQM Environment," *Public Personnel Management* 25 (December 1996): 493.
10. Stuart Silverstein, "Guidelines for Disability Cases," *Newsday* (May 11, 1997): F12.
11. U.S. Department of Labor, *Dictionary of Occupational Titles,* 4th ed. (Washington, DC: U.S. Government Printing Office, 1977).
12. Howard Risher, "The End of Jobs: Planning and Managing Rewards in the New Work Paradigm," *Compensation & Benefits Review* 29 (January/February 1997): 13–17.
13. David Snyder, "The Revolution in the Workplace: What's Happening to Our Jobs?" *Futurist* 30 (March 1996): 8.
14. Felix M. Lopez, Gerald A. Kesselman, and Felix E. Lopez, "An Empirical Test of a Trait-Oriented Job Analysis Technique," *Personnel Psychology* 35 (August 1981): 480.
15. Stephen E. Bemis, Ann Holt Belenky, and Dee Ann Soder, *Job Analysis: An Effective Management Tool* (Washington, DC: Bureau of National Affairs, 1983), 42.
16. Clifford, "Job Analysis: Why Do It, and How Should It Be Done?"
17. Eric Minton, "The ADA and Records Management," *Records Management Quarterly* 28 (January 1994): 12.
18. Bruce Tulgan, "Managing Generation X," *HR Focus* 72 (November 1995): 22–24.
19. Frederick Herzberg, "One More Time: How Do You Motivate Employees?" *Harvard Business Review* 65 (September/October 1987): 109–120.
20. R. Henry-Gunn Migliore, "Strategic Planning/Management by Objectives," *Hospital Topics* 73 (July 1995): 26; and James Kennedy, "The Leisure Suits of Consulting Fads," *Boston Business Journal* 16 (September 1996): 21.
21. "GM Consolidation Plan Worries Saturn Workers," *USA Today* (July 28, 1997): 6B.
22. Alice C. Maroni, "DOD Implementation of the Government Performance and Result Act (GPRA)," *Armed Forces Controller* 41 (September 1996): 23.
23. Ellis Pines, "TQM Training: A New Culture Sparks Change at Every Level," *Aviation Week and Space Technology* 132 (May 21, 1990): S38.
24. Oren Harari, "Ten Reasons TQM Doesn't Work," *Management Review* 86 (January 1997): 38–41.
25. Ceel Pasterak, "TQM Worth It," *HRMagazine* 38 (August 1993): 30.
26. Harari, "Ten Reasons TQM Doesn't Work."
27. Michael Hammer and James Champy, *Reengineering the Corporation: A Manifesto for Business Revolution* (New York: HarperCollins, 1993), 32.
28. Michael Hammer and James Champy, "The Malapropian 'R' Word," *Industry Forum,* prepared by the American Management Association (September 1993), 1.

29. Oren Harari, "Why Did Reengineering Die?" *Management Review* 85 (July 1996): 49.

30. Ibid.

31. Edward Shugrue, Joan Berland, and Bob Gonzales, "Case Study: How IBM Reengineered Its Benefits Center into a National HR Service Center," *Compensation & Benefits Review* 29 (March/April 1997): 41–48.

32. Stratford Sherman and Eanne C. Lee, "Levi's as Ye Sew, So Shall Ye Reap Vastly Successful, Immensely Rich, a Little Smug: The World's Premier Blue Jeans Maker Has Created a Unique Bond with Employees. Will Layoffs Wreck It?" *Fortune* 135 (May 1997): 104.

33. Daniel B. Moskowitz, "How to Cut It Overseas," *International Business* 5 (October 1992): 76–78.

34. Ibid.

ABCNEWS VIDEO CASE

Sexual Harassment in the Workplace

Sexual harassment has long been illegal in the United States. Yet, organizations continue to pay millions of dollars each year to victims because of this illicit behavior. Some forms of sexual harassment are easily identified whereas others are not. The most easily recognizable form of sexual harassment is called quid pro quo, or something for something. It might occur, for example, when a supervisor promises a subordinate a pay raise or promotion in exchange for sexual favors. A form of sexual harassment that is more difficult to define is sexual harassment that results from the creation of a hostile work environment. This type of harassment stems from sexual behavior that involves, for example, the telling of off-color jokes or other behavior that creates an intimidating or offensive work environment or interferes with job performance.

A hostile work environment is not easy to determine because its presence is based on the perception of the harassed individual. Knowing how each person interprets a situation is difficult, at best. Consider whether the following events may lead to a hostile work environment:

- A male manager and a female employee have worked together for almost 20 years. When the woman is presented a pen for her long service, her boss bends over and kisses her on the cheek.
- Several men are gathered near a work station occupied by a female employee and are enjoying the exchange of off-color jokes. The female employee is indignant and immediately exits her workplace.
- A female employee is being urged by her boss to have another date with him. He implies that their last meeting focused too much on business and that a return engagement would let them get to know each other better. The woman is obviously turned off and makes a hasty retreat. The manager continues his pursuit.

QUESTIONS:

1. Most examples of sexual harassment involve a man harassing a woman. Explain this phenomenon.
2. You have a picture of a person clad in a very revealing outfit on the wall near your desk. Could this possibly create a hostile work environment?
3. Some people have asserted that gender-based instincts make it very difficult for men and women to work together in a physically close environment. Do you agree? Why or why not?
4. As a manager, what would you do to ensure that your unit remained free of sexual harassment?

Source: Based on "Men, Women, and Work," *Primetime Live,* ABC News; aired on July 21, 1994.

HUMAN RESOURCE PLANNING, RECRUITMENT, AND SELECTION

5
Strategic Human Resource Planning

CHAPTER OBJECTIVES

1. Define *strategic planning*.
2. Describe the levels of strategic planning.
3. Explain the strategic planning process.
4. Identify the factors to be considered in strategy implementation.
5. Explain the human resource planning process.
6. Describe some human resource forecasting techniques.
7. Define requirement and availability forecasts.
8. Differentiate management inventory from skills inventory.
9. Distinguish between succession planning and succession development.
10. Identify what a firm can do when a surplus of workers exists.
11. Describe the concept of downsizing.
12. Define *human resource information system (HRIS)* and identify the type of information an HRIS should provide.

*M*ark Swann, the marketing director for Sharpco Manufacturing, commented at the weekly executive directors' meeting, "I have good news. We can get the large contract with Medord Corporation. All we have to do is complete the project in one year instead of two. I told them we could do it."

Linda Crane, vice president of strategic human resources, brought everyone back to reality by asserting, "As I understand it, our present workers do not have the expertise required to produce the quality that Medord's particular specifications require. Under the two-year project timetable, we planned to retrain our present workers gradually. With this new time schedule, we will have to go into the job market and recruit workers who are already experienced in this process. We may need to analyze this proposal further to see whether that is really what we want to do. Human resource costs will rise considerably if we attempt to complete the project in one year instead of two. Sure, Mark, we can do it, but with these constraints, will the project be cost effective?"

*I*n this instance, Mark failed to consider the strategic nature of human resource planning in his projections. In today's fast-paced, competitive environment, failure to recognize the strategic nature of human resource planning will often destroy an otherwise well-thought-out plan.

Our overall purpose in this chapter is to explain the role and nature of strategic human resource planning in organizations today. First, we describe HR and strategic planning and the levels of strategic planning. Next, strategy implementation and the human resource planning process is described. Then, we examine some human resource forecasting techniques. Next, we discuss forecasting human resource requirements and availability and examine action to be taken when a firm has a surplus of workers. Downsizing is then discussed, followed by an example of effective human resource planning. We devote the final sections of the chapter to a discussion of the human resource information system.

HR and Strategic Planning

Strategic planning: The determination of overall organizational purposes and goals and how they are to be achieved.

In chapter 1, we stressed that HR executives are focusing their attention on how human resources can assist the organization achieve its strategic objectives.[1] They now function as strategic partners with line executives in assuring that the organization achieves its mission. Thus, HR must be highly involved in the strategic planning process. Essentially, it is moving from a *micro* to a *macro* view of its mission.[2] **Strategic planning** is the process by which top management determines overall organizational purposes and objectives and how they are to be achieved.

When a firm's mission is clearly defined and its guiding principles understood, employees and managers are likely to put forth maximum effort in pursuing company objectives. Top management expects HR activities to be closely aligned to this mission and strategic goals and to add value toward achieving these goals.[3] Mark Swann of Sharpco Manufacturing excluded HR from the strategic planning process and wants to accept a contract that will not be cost effective because of HR constraints. The advantage of strategic planning is most evident as firms respond to rapidly changing environments. This realization should make strategic planning even more important now as the Economic Community in Europe removes its barriers to trade and with Asian markets, especially those of China, opening up. As the globalization of business becomes more pervasive, strategic planning may well provide companies with a competitive edge. It allows managers in changing environments to chart their courses carefully, and it helps their organizations expand and survive.

The Levels of Strategic Planning

Strategic planning should be considered according to the organizational levels at which it occurs, particularly with the growth in recent decades of such complex organizations as General Electric, United Technologies, Allied Cor-

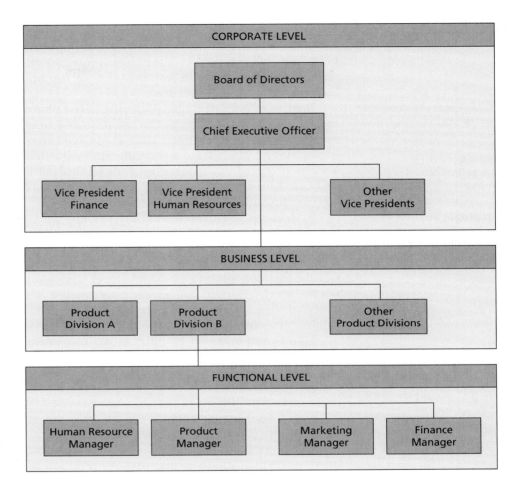

Figure 5-1
The Levels of Strategic Planning

Source: R. Wayne Mondy and Shane R. Premeaux, *Management: Concepts, Practices, and Skills*, 7th ed. (Prentice Hall: Upper Saddle River, NJ, 1995): 171.

poration, and Textron. Figure 5-1 illustrates the organizational levels of a typical complex corporation and the corresponding levels of strategic planning. Because each level has its own distinctive characteristics, there are differences in the tools and processes that are useful in formulating strategy at the three levels.

If an organization produced a single product or service, then a single strategic plan would encompass everything the corporation did. However, many organizations are in diverse businesses, some of which are only vaguely related. Because so many organizations are engaged in multiple activities, it is important to understand the differences among corporate-level strategic planning, business-level strategic planning, and functional-level strategic planning.

Corporate-level strategic planning is the process of defining the overall character and purpose of the organization, the businesses it will enter and leave, and the way its resources will be distributed among those businesses. This type of planning will determine what line of businesses the corporation should be in. Corporate-level strategy typically concerns the mix and utilization of business divisions called *strategic business units* (discussed later in the

Corporate-level strategic planning: The process of defining the overall character and purpose of the organization, the businesses it will enter and leave, and the way resources will be distributed among those businesses.

Business-level strategic planning: The planning process concerned primarily with how to manage the interests and operations of a particular business.

Strategic business unit (SBU): Any part of a business organization that is treated separately for strategic planning purposes.

Functional-level strategic planning: The process of determining policies and procedures for relatively narrow areas of activity that are critical to the success of the organization.

chapter). Corporate-level strategic planning addresses the actions the organization will take and determines the roles of each business in the organization's grand strategy. Note again in Figure 5-1 that corporate-level strategic planning is primarily the responsibility of the organization's top executives, including the top HR executive.

Business-level strategic planning is the planning process concerned primarily with how to manage the interests and operations of a particular business. As many organizations have extensive interests in different businesses, top managers often have a difficult time organizing the complex companies and their varied activities. One way to deal with this problem is to create strategic business units, which are meant to facilitate the management of large organizations.

A **strategic business unit (SBU)** is any part of a business organization that is treated separately for strategic planning purposes. It can be a single business or a collection of related businesses. The corporate-level strategy provides the general direction, and a business-level strategy provides the direction for each SBU. The business-level strategic plan is reviewed at the corporate level, changes are made if necessary, and the final business-level strategic plan for the unit is approved. Each SBU has a unique mission and product line and its own competitors and markets.[4]

Many companies set up SBUs as separate profit centers, sometimes giving them virtual autonomy. Other companies have tight control over their SBUs, enforcing corporate policies and standards down to very low levels in the organization. In general, SBU business-level strategic planning is the responsibility of vice presidents or division heads.

Functional-level strategic planning is the process of determining policies and procedures for relatively narrow areas of activity that are critical to the success of the organization. Practically every large organization is divided into functional subdivisions, usually production, marketing, finance, and human resources. Each of these functional subdivisions is vital to the success of the organization. Functional-level strategic plans conform to both corporate-level and business-level strategic plans. As Figure 5-1 shows, a human resource manager may be assigned to each strategic business unit.

The Strategic Planning and Implementation Process

Strategic planning at all levels of the organization can be divided into four steps: (1) determination of the organizational mission, (2) assessment of the organization and its environment, (3) setting of specific objectives or direction, and (4) determination of strategies to accomplish those objectives (see Figure 5-2).[5] The strategic planning process described here is basically a derivative of the SWOT (strengths, weaknesses, opportunities, and threats) framework that affects organizational performance, but it is less structured. We believe the step-by-step approach just described guides the understanding of the strategic planning process.

Despite its complexity, strategic planning can be thought of usefully as a sequential process. By individually examining the four steps of the strategic

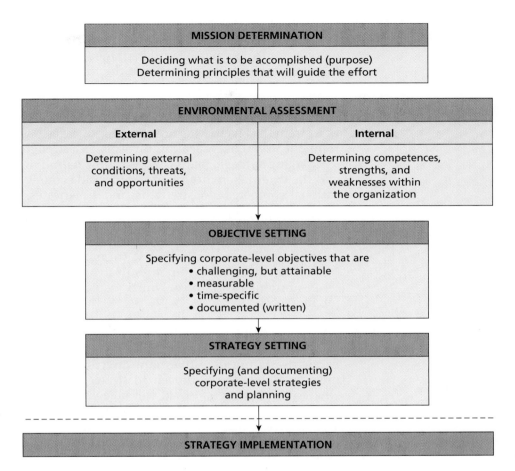

Figure 5-2
Formulating Strategy
and Implementation

Source: R. Wayne Mondy
and Shane R. Premeaux,
*Management: Concepts,
Practices, and Skills*, 7th ed.
(Prentice Hall, Inc.: Upper
Saddle River, NJ: 1995):
175.

planning process and the final step of strategy implementation, we can bring into focus the desirability of a systematic approach to strategic planning and implementation.

MISSION DETERMINATION

The first step of the strategic planning process is to determine the corporate mission. The corporate mission is the sum total of the organization's ongoing purpose. Arriving at a mission statement should involve answering these questions: What are we in management attempting to do for whom? Should we maximize profit so that shareholders will receive higher dividends or so share price will increase? Alternatively, should we emphasize stability of earnings so that employees will remain secure?

There are many other mission possibilities. Mission determination also requires deciding on the principles on which management decisions will be based. To what extent will the corporation stress diversity, promotion from within, or a competitive compensation system? The answers to such questions tend to become embedded in a corporate culture and help determine the organizational mission.

ENVIRONMENTAL ASSESSMENT

Once the mission has been determined, the organization must be assessed for strengths and weaknesses, and the threats and opportunities in the external environment must be evaluated. Specific objectives can be established, and strategies can be developed for accomplishing those objectives. A firm that has a highly skilled and motivated workforce would list that workforce as a strength. Likewise, a firm that has a diverse workforce in a global environment would likely see this diversity as a strength.

Making strategic plans involves information flows from both the internal and the external environment. From inside comes information about organizational competencies, strengths, and weaknesses. Scanning the external environment allows organizational strategists to identify threats and opportunities as well as constraints. In brief, the job in the planning phase is to develop strategies that take advantage of the company's strengths and minimize its weaknesses, allowing it to grasp opportunities and avoid threats. Linda Crane was quick to point out to Mark Swann the company's weakness of an untrained workforce, which would necessitate going external into the job market.

OBJECTIVE SETTING

Explicitly stating objectives and directing all activities toward their attainment is a common approach to strategic management. If you don't know where you're going, no road will take you there. Setting objectives has been generally accepted as a means for improving the process of management. This is no less true at the corporate level of strategic management than it is for the runner who wishes to better the existing world record for running a mile.

STRATEGY SETTING

Once objectives are established or direction is determined, strategies can be formulated. Many organizations limit their written strategic plans to financial budgets—and some do not even have budgets. Most authorities, however, consider putting strategies in writing a worthwhile activity. Whether or not strategies are written, the task of organizational strategists is to communicate clearly how the organization intends to accomplish its goals.

Strategy Implementation

Once the strategic planning process is complete, the strategy must be implemented. Some people argue that strategy implementation is the most difficult and important part of strategic management. No matter how creative and well formulated the strategic plan, the organization will not benefit if the plan is incorrectly implemented. Strategy implementation involves several dimensions of the organization. It requires changes in the organization's behavior; this can be brought about by changing one or more organizational

Once the strategic planning process is complete, the strategy must be implemented.

dimensions, including management's leadership ability, organizational structure, information and control systems, technology, and human resources.

LEADERSHIP

A leader is able to get others to do what he or she wants them to do. Managers must influence organization members to adopt the behaviors needed for strategy implementation. Top-level managers seeking to implement a new strategy may find it useful to build coalitions and persuade middle-level managers to go along with the strategic plan and its implementation. If leaders involve other managers during strategy formulation, implementation will be easier because managers and employees will better understand and be more fully committed to the new strategy. Basically, leadership is used to encourage employees to adopt supportive behaviors and, when necessary, to accept the required new values and attitudes.

ORGANIZATIONAL STRUCTURE

A company's organizational structure is typically illustrated by its organizational chart. This structure indicates individual managers' responsibilities and degrees of authority, and it incorporates jobs into departments. The structure also reflects the company's level of centralization and the types of departments that will be utilized.

INFORMATION AND CONTROL SYSTEMS

Among the information and control systems are reward systems; incentives; budgets for allocating resources; information systems; and the organization's rules, policies, and procedures. Certainly, human resource executives would be proactive in securing this information. A proper mix of information and control systems must be developed to support implementation of the strategic plan. Managers and employees must be rewarded for adhering to the new strategy and making it a success, or the intensity of implementation will be reduced substantially.

TECHNOLOGY

The knowledge, tools, and equipment used to accomplish an organization's assignments make up its technology. If an organization adopts a strategy of producing a new product, managers must often redesign jobs and construct new buildings and facilities. New technology may also be required for implementing a low-cost strategy if the technology can improve efficiency. As with other aspects of strategy implementation, the appropriate level of technology must be found for proper implementation of the strategic plan.

HUMAN RESOURCES

The organization's human resources are its employees. The human resource function involves such tasks as recruitment, selection, training, transfers, promotions, and layoffs of employees as these actions help to implement the strategic plan properly. In certain situations, employees simply may be incompatible with a new strategy and they may have to be retrained or even replaced. The new strategy may foster resentment and resistance among both managers and employees, a matter that must be resolved quickly before it hinders strategy implementation. In essence, a proper balance of human resources must be developed to support strategy implementation.

The Human Resource Planning Process

The HR executive works with upper management to formulate corporate-level strategy. Once the corporate-level strategy has been agreed on, human resource planning can occur.

Human resource plan-ning (HRP): The process of systematically reviewing human resource requirements to ensure that the required number of employees, with the required skills, are available when they are needed.

Human resource planning (HRP) is the process of systematically reviewing human resource requirements to ensure that the required number of employees, with the required skills, are available when they are needed.[6] Linda Crane was aware of her workforce's capabilities. She realized that the planned gradual training schedule would not work under the proposed contractual timetable. The new plan would definitely involve the costly step of recruiting employees externally on the job market.

Human resource planning involves matching the internal and external supply of people with job openings anticipated in the organization over a specified period of time. However, there is a growing mismatch between emerging jobs and qualified people available to fill them. The labor pool is changing as U.S. companies try to cope with rapid technological shifts and increasing globalization of the economy. The adequacy of the labor pool is vital to the success of the global organization. If global employees are to be developed properly, they must be technologically and cross-culturally trained to help broaden their perspectives and relationships, preparing them to deal effectively with organizational changes.[7] The human resource planning process is illustrated in Figure 5-3. Note that strategic planning precedes human resource planning.

After an organization's strategic plans have been formulated, human resource planning can be undertaken. Strategic plans are reduced to specific quantitative and qualitative human resource plans. For example, note in Figure 5-3 that human resource planning has two components: requirements and availability. Forecasting human resource requirements involves determining the number and type of employees needed, by skill level and location. These projections will reflect various factors, such as production plans and changes in productivity. In order to forecast availability, the human re-

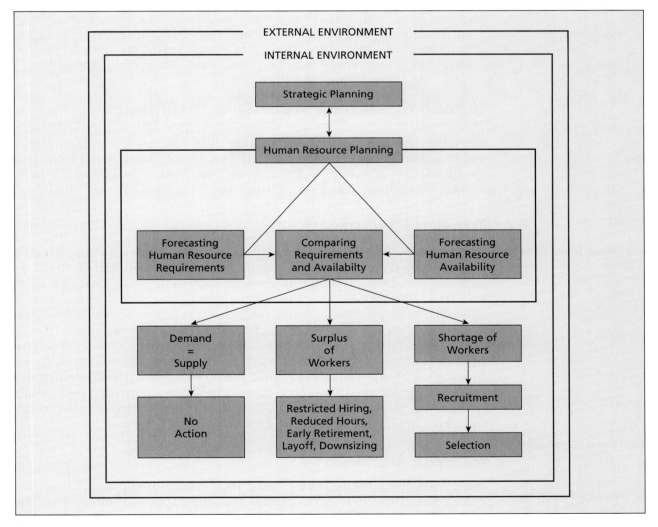

Figure 5-3
The Human Resource Planning Process

source manager looks to both internal sources (presently employed employees) and external sources (the labor market). When employee requirements and availability have been analyzed, the firm can determine whether it will have a surplus or a shortage of employees. Ways must be found to reduce the number of employees if a surplus is projected. Some of these methods include restricted hiring, reduced hours, early retirements, and layoffs. If a shortage is forecast, the firm must obtain the proper quantity and quality of workers from outside the organization. External recruitment and selection is required in this situation.

Because conditions in the external and internal environments can change quickly, the human resource planning process must be continuous. Changing conditions could affect the entire organization, thereby requiring extensive modification of forecasts. Planning in general enables managers to anticipate and prepare for changing conditions, and human resource planning in particular allows flexibility in the area of human resource management. During the past 10 years, various factors have caused some organizations to downsize (reduce the size of their workforces). Human resource planning allows workforce reductions with a minimum of disruption.

Human Resource Forecasting Techniques

Several techniques for forecasting human resource requirements and availability are currently used by those in the profession. Some of the techniques are qualitative in nature, and others are quantitative. Several of the better known methods are described in this section.

ZERO-BASE FORECASTING

Zero-base forecasting:
A method for estimating future employment needs using the organization's current level of employment as the starting point.

The **zero-base forecasting** approach uses the organization's current level of employment as the starting point for determining future staffing needs. Essentially the same procedure is used for human resource planning as for zero-base budgeting, in which each budget must be justified each year. If an employee retires, is fired, or leaves the firm for any other reason, the position is not automatically filled. Instead, an analysis is made to determine whether the firm can justify filling it. Equal concern is shown for creating new positions when they appear to be needed. The key to zero-base forecasting is a thorough analysis of human resource needs. In today's globally competitive environment, an open position is thoroughly analyzed before a replacement is approved. More often than not, the position is not filled and the work is spread out among the remaining employees.

BOTTOM-UP APPROACH

Bottom-up approach: A forecasting method beginning with the lowest organizational units and progressing upward through an organization ultimately to provide an aggregate forecast of employment needs.

Some firms use what might be called the bottom-up approach to employment forecasting. It is based on the reasoning that the manager in each unit is most knowledgeable about employment requirements. In the **bottom-up approach**, each successive level in the organization—starting with the lowest—forecasts its requirements, ultimately providing an aggregate

HRM IN ACTION
WHAT, ME JUSTIFY?

"Cynthia, what do you mean by saying that I'm going to have to justify my need for the typesetter's position? One of my 10 employees in this job just quit, and I want a replacement now! We've had 10 typesetters in my department for the 13 years that I've been here, and probably a long time before that. If we've needed them in the past, certainly we will need them in the future."

This is the beginning of a conversation between Richard Wiley, a first-line supervisor with Allen Industries, and Cynthia Larger, its human resource manager.

How should Cynthia respond?

forecast of employees needed. Human resource forecasting is often most effective when managers periodically project their human resource needs, comparing their current and anticipated levels, and give the human resource department adequate lead time to explore internal and external sources.

USE OF PREDICTOR VARIABLES

Predictor variables: Factors known to have an impact on a company's employment levels.

Another means of forecasting human resource requirements is to use past employment levels to predict future requirements. **Predictor variables** are factors known to have had an impact on employment levels. One of the most useful predictors of employment levels is sales volume. The relationship between demand and the number of employees needed is a positive one. In Figure 5-4, a firm's sales volume is depicted on the horizontal axis,

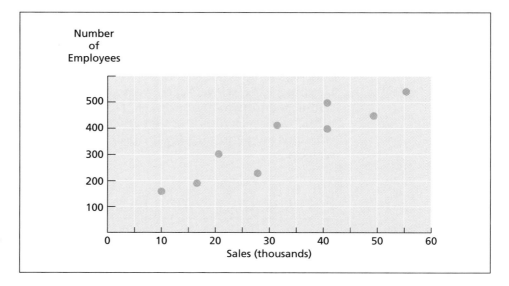

Figure 5-4
The Relationship of Sales Volume to Number of Employees

and the number of employees actually required is shown on the vertical axis. In this illustration, as sales decrease, so does the number of employees needed. Using such a method, managers can approximate the number of employees required at different demand levels.

SIMULATION

Simulation: A technique for experimenting with a real-world situation by means of a mathematical model that represents the actual situation.

Simulation is a technique for experimenting with a real-world situation through a mathematical model representing that situation. A model is an abstraction of the real world. Thus, a simulation model is an attempt to represent a real-world situation through mathematical logic to predict what will occur. Simulation assists human resource managers by permitting them to ask many *what if* questions without having to make a decision having real-world consequences.

In human resource management, a simulation model might be developed to represent the interrelationships among employment levels and many other variables. The manager could then ask *what if* questions such as these:

- What would happen if we put 10 percent of the present workforce on overtime?
- What would happen if the plant utilized two shifts? Three shifts?

The model permits managers to gain considerable insight into a particular problem before making an actual decision.

Forecasting Human Resource Requirements

Requirements forecast: An estimate of the numbers and kinds of employees an organization will need at future dates to realize its stated objectives.

A **requirements forecast** is an estimate of the numbers and kinds of employees the organization will need at future dates to realize its stated goals. Before human resource requirements can be projected, demand for the firm's goods or services must first be forecast. This forecast is then converted into people requirements for the activities necessary to meet this demand. For a firm that manufactures personal computers, activities might be stated in terms of the number of units to be produced, number of sales calls to be made, number of vouchers to be processed, or a variety of other activities. For example, manufacturing 1,000 widgets each week might require 10,000 hours of work by assemblers during a 40-hour week. Dividing the 10,000 hours by the 40 hours in the workweek indicates that 250 assembly workers are needed. Similar calculations are performed for the other jobs needed to produce and market the widgets.

Forecasting Human Resource Availability

Forecasting requirements provides managers with the means of estimating how many and what types of employees will be required. But there is another side to the coin, as this example illustrates:

A large manufacturing firm on the West Coast was preparing to begin operations in a new plant. Analysts had already determined that there was a large, long-term demand for the new product. Financing was available and equipment was in place. But production did not begin for two years! Management had made a critical mistake: It had studied the demand side of human resources but not the supply side. There were not enough qualified workers in the local labor market to operate the new plant. New workers had to receive extensive training before they could move into the newly created jobs.

Availability forecast: A process of determining whether a firm will be able to secure employees with the necessary skills from within the company, from outside the organization, or from a combination of the two sources.

Determining whether the firm will be able to secure employees with the necessary skills and from what sources is called an **availability forecast.** It helps to show whether the needed employees may be obtained from within the company, from outside the organization, or from a combination of the two sources.

INTERNAL SOURCES OF SUPPLY

Many of the workers that will be needed for future positions may already work for the firm. If the firm is small, management probably knows all the workers sufficiently well to match their skills and aspirations with the company's needs. Suppose the firm is creating a new sales position; common knowledge in the company may be that Mary Garcia, a five-year employee, has both the skills and the desire to take over the new job. This unplanned process of matching people and positions may be sufficient for smaller firms. As organizations grow, however, the matching process becomes increasingly difficult. Both skills and management inventories are being used by organizations that take human resources seriously. Also, succession planning helps ensure an internal supply of highly qualified management personnel.

Skills inventory: Information maintained on nonmanagerial employees in a company regarding their availability and preparedness to move either laterally or into higher level positions.

Skills Inventories. A **skills inventory** is information maintained on the availability and preparedness of nonmanagerial employees to move either into higher level positions or laterally in the organization. Although the process and the intent of the skills inventory are essentially the same as for a management inventory, the information differs somewhat. Generally included in a skills inventory is this information about a worker:

- Background and biographical data
- Work experience
- Specific skills and knowledge
- Licenses or certifications held
- In-house training programs completed
- Previous performance appraisal evaluations
- Career goals

A properly designed and updated skills inventory system permits management to readily identify employees with particular skills and match them as well as possible to the changing needs of the company.

Management inventory: Detailed data regarding each manager in an organization; used in identifying individuals possessing the potential to move into higher level positions.

Management Inventories. Managerial positions require a broad range of skills. Thus, firms may maintain additional data for their managers. A **management inventory** contains detailed information about each manager and is used to identify individuals who have the potential to move into higher level positions. Essentially, this type of inventory provides information for replacement and promotion decisions. It would likely include data such as the following:

- Work history and experience
- Educational background
- Assessment of strengths and weaknesses
- Developmental needs
- Promotion potential at present and with further development
- Current job performance
- Field of specialization
- Job preferences
- Geographic preferences
- Career goals and aspirations
- Anticipated retirement date
- Personal history, including psychological assessments

Management and Skills Inventories in the High-Tech Environment. Companies are beginning to use their intranets to help manage their people. Through their own computers, employees maintain their own electronic resumes through a well-structured database. This database can then be searched when a certain department needs people with specific skills.[8] Information vital to identifying those qualified for positions can be easily found.

HR Web Wisdom

http://www.prenhall.com/mondy

SUCCESSION PLANNING
The essence of business succession planning is briefly reviewed.

The Need for Succession Planning. The fatal crash of Commerce Secretary Ron Brown's plane on April 3, 1996, with a dozen CEOs on board suddenly caught the attention of many company executives across the nation. Was a replacement ready to take over the position of leadership? Also, it does not take a plane crash to cause sudden loss of leadership for a company. A month after the April crash, Texas Instruments' CEO Jerry Junkins, with no history of heart disease, died suddenly of a heart attack at age 58. Fortunately, Junkins had personally groomed his successor and continuity in the company was assured.[9] **Succession planning** is the process of ensuring that a qualified person is available to assume a managerial position once the position is vacant. This definition includes untimely deaths, resignations, terminations, or the orderly retirement of a company official.

Succession planning: The process of ensuring that a qualified person is available to assume a managerial position once the position is vacant.

Because of the tremendous changes that will confront management in the next century, succession planning is taking on more importance than

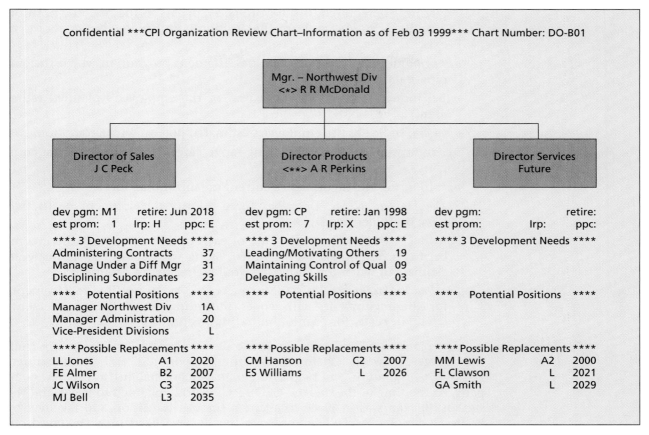

Figure 5-5
Career Planning Inventory Organization Review Chart

perhaps ever before. In view of these expected changes, organizations need to develop a profile of the types of individuals who can effectively lead the organization both now and in the future.[10] At Corning there is a list of candidates for each of the 35 top jobs and this list is reviewed two or three times a year.[11] Many companies are performing similar tasks. In a recent survey of over 400 boards of large U.S. companies, nearly three-quarters of the firms questioned had a succession plan.[12]

One of the outcomes of a management inventory is a succession plan. Detroit Edison calls its plan a Career Planning Inventory Organization Review Chart. In Figure 5-5, the chart shows a manager in the top box with immediate subordinates in the lower boxes. Information shown on the chart includes the following:

Position Box: Shows the position title and the incumbent's name in each box. The symbol * preceding the name identifies incumbents who will retire between 1997 and 2003, indicating that short-range planning is required. The symbol ** preceding the name identifies incumbents who will retire between 2001 and 2007, indicating that long-range planning is required. If the word *open* appears in the box, the position is unfilled. If *future* appears, the position is anticipated but does not yet exist.

dev pgm: Identifies the particular development program in which the employee participates.

retire: Indicates the month and year of the employee's planned retirement.

est prom: Indicates the employee's estimated potential for promotion.

lrp: Indicates the employee's long-range career potential with the company.

ppc: Indicates the incumbent's current organizational level.

3 Development Needs: Describes three priority development needs that have been identified.

Potential Positions: Shows the title of each position to which the incumbent can potentially be promoted, along with codes that indicate an estimate of when the employee would be ready for promotion.

Possible Replacements: Lists the names of up to 10 possible replacements for the incumbent, with codes indicating when the replacements would be ready for promotion to this position.

The planned CEO succession at the new Chemical Bank, resulting from the merger between Chemical Banking Corporation and Manufacturers Hanover Corporation, will help assure management stability at the new company. At the time of the merger, CEO McGillicuddy planned to leave, and the succession plan was in place to assure a smooth transition and takeover by Walter V. Shipley. McGillicuddy would really have liked to have stayed on, because he loved the people and what he was doing. However, he also believed that the succession was necessary. According to McGillicuddy, he felt even more strongly that he had had his time. With proper succession planning, McGillicuddy believes that often the best thing a leader can do is "put your hat on, say, 'Good luck, gang,' and go out and do something else."[13]

A recent concept related to succession planning is succession development. **Succession development** is the process of determining a comprehensive job profile of the key positions and then ensuring that key prospects are properly developed to match these qualifications. In succession planning, replacement candidates often do not know that they are being considered for a future position whereas in succession development, candidates are kept informed and encouraged to participate in their development process.[14]

Succession development: The process of determining a comprehensive job profile of the key positions and then ensuring that key prospects are properly developed to match these qualifications.

EXTERNAL SUPPLY

Unless a firm is experiencing declining demand, it will have to recruit some employees from outside the organization. However, finding and hiring new employees capable of performing immediately is usually quite difficult. The best source of supply varies by industry, firm, and geographic location. Some organizations find that their best sources of potential employees are colleges and universities. Others get excellent results from vocational schools, competitors, or even unsolicited applications.

If the company has information revealing where its present employees were recruited, it can develop statistics and project the best sources. A firm may discover that graduates from a particular college or university adapt well to the firm's environment and culture. One large farm equipment manufacturer has achieved excellent success in recruiting from regional schools located in rural areas. Managers in this firm believe that because many students come from a farming environment, they can adapt more quickly to the firm's method of operation. Pepsi often recruits from second-tier schools because graduates of top business schools are seldom willing to start out in menial jobs.

Other firms may discover from past records that the majority of their more successful employees grew up no more than 20 miles from their place of work. This information may suggest concentrated recruiting efforts in that particular geographic area.

Forecasting can assist not only in identifying where potential employees may be found but also in predicting the types of individuals that will likely succeed in the organization. For example, a regional medical center—located far from any large metropolitan area—reviewed its employment files of registered nurses. It discovered that nurses born and raised in smaller towns adapted better to the medical center's small town environment than those who grew up in large metropolitan areas. After studying these statistics, management modified its recruiting efforts.[15]

Forecasting at times has pitfalls, and examples of improper forecasting often occur. Managers of one large convenience store chain, for instance, were disturbed by their unusually high employee turnover rate. When they analyzed their recruiting efforts, they discovered that the large majority of short-term employees had merely seen a sign in the store window announcing that a position was available. These individuals, often unemployed at the time, were highly transient. The recruitment method used tapped a source of supply that virtually guaranteed a high turnover rate. After the managers discovered this fact, they utilized new approaches, which significantly reduced turnover.

Surplus of Employees

A comparison of requirements and availability may indicate a worker surplus in the making; with this knowledge, restricted hiring, reduced hours, early retirements, and layoffs may be required to correct the situation. Downsizing, one result of worker surpluses, is discussed later in the chapter as a separate topic.

RESTRICTED HIRING

When a firm implements a restricted hiring policy, it reduces the workforce by not replacing employees who leave. New workers are hired only when the overall performance of the organization may be affected if strategic jobs are not filled. For instance, if a quality control department that consisted of four inspectors lost one to a competitor, this individual probably would not be replaced. However, if the firm lost all its inspectors, it would probably replace at least some of them to ensure continued operation.

REDUCED HOURS

A company can also react to a reduced workload requirement by reducing the total number of hours employees work. Instead of continuing a 40-hour week, management may decide to cut each employee's time to 30 hours. This cutback normally applies only to hourly employees because management and other professionals typically are salaried (not paid on an hourly basis).

EARLY RETIREMENT

Early retirement of some present employees is another way to reduce the number of workers. Some employees will be delighted to retire, but others will be somewhat reluctant. The latter may be willing to accept early retirement if the total retirement package is made sufficiently attractive. A key point to remember is that because of the Age Discrimination in Employment Act, as amended, retirement can no longer be mandated by age.

LAYOFFS

At times, a firm has no choice but to lay off part of its workforce. A layoff is not the same as a firing, but it has the same basic effect—the worker is no longer employed. When the firm is unionized, layoff procedures are usually stated clearly in the labor-management agreement. Typically, workers with the least seniority are laid off first. If the organization is union free, it may base layoff on a combination of factors, such as seniority and productivity level. When managers and other professionals are laid off, the decision is likely to be based on ability, although internal politics may be a factor.

HR Web Wisdom

http://www.prenhall.com/mondy

DOWNSIZING
A factual look at corporate downsizing.

Downsizing

Downsizing: A reduction in the number of people employed by a firm (also known as *restructuring* and *rightsizing*).

Tied very closely to layoffs is **downsizing**, also known as restructuring and rightsizing. This situation is essentially the reverse of company growth and suggests a one-time change in the organization and the number of people employed. Typically, both the organization and the number of people in the organization shrink. The trend among many companies in the 1980s and early 1990s was to cut staff and downsize. Job losses, which traditionally impacted blue-collar workers, this time centered on white-collar workers. One study estimates that between 1985 and 1995, almost 14 million white-collar jobs disappeared.[16]

Many companies that have had a long-term policy of no layoffs have changed their position. For example, IBM's 40-year policy of not laying off anyone employed on a regular basis was shattered in the mid-1980s. At the peak of the no-layoff policy, employees in the company numbered 405,000. Today, IBM has around 225,000 workers, and they are not shielded by a no-layoff policy. Other examples abound. Sears eliminated 50,000 positions in the 1990s whereas AT&T shed 40,000 white-collar workers in 1995.[17]

In some cases, downsizing was successful. IBM might not have survived with a workforce of 405,000. However, downsizing does not always turn a company around. The reason is that downsizing often does not solve the fundamental causes of the problems. Organizations have not developed appropriate strategies for growth; instead, they focus on reducing costs, which is merely attacking a symptom of the problem. Downsizing at such firms as American Express, Westinghouse, and Sears Roebuck did not achieve the expected results.[18]

One result of downsizing is that many layers are often pulled out of an organization, making advancement in the organization more difficult. In addition, when one firm downsizes, often others must follow if they are to be competitive. Thus, more and more individuals are finding themselves plateaued in the same job until they retire. To reinvigorate demoralized workers, some firms are providing additional training, lateral moves, short sabbaticals, and compensation based on a person's contribution, not his or her title.[19] Some firms are restoring their employees' enthusiasm by providing raises based on additional skills the workers acquire and use.

Historically, firms have downsized in difficult times and rehired when times got better. Today, with firms competing globally, managers are rethinking their automatic rehiring strategies. For instance, Arvin Industries, a manufacturer of automotive components, cut its workforce by 10 percent to just under 16,000, but the company rebounded with profits estimated to grow at an annual rate of 20 percent through the 1990s. Even with enhanced business success, Arvin is not rehiring; instead, it is trying to trim its staff further. According to Arvin's human resources director Ray Mack, "To remain globally competitive, we must continue to streamline operations and keep a tight rein on labor costs."[20]

The philosophy of downsizing is not merely a U.S. undertaking. An Australian study of 302 downsized companies with over 100 employees found that after four years, 28 percent of the firms continued to shrink, 24 percent had started to grow again, and the remainder had stabilized. On a very negative side, approximately 48 percent of the downsizers had ceased to exist; they had either closed, been taken over, or had merged.[21]

One result of downsizing is that employee trust is often significantly reduced. For workers who remain after downsizing, the trust level is low. These workers believe that they might be let go the next time. A common pattern of thought is that "I must take care of myself, the company won't." Employees who would never have considered changing jobs prior to downsizing are now thinking about this option, especially if their present company does not provide them with the necessary development to keep up with industry trends. One of the main goals of HR in today's environment is to reestablish this lost worker trust.[22]

The rush to downsize appears to be slowing down. A recent survey by the American Management Association determined that for every job eliminated these days, another was being created. Also, 68 percent of responding firms were creating jobs.[23] Downsizing no longer appears to be the major impetus for change in the United States.

Human Resource Planning: An Example

The human resource planning model presented in Figure 5-3 is a generalized one. Each firm must tailor human resource planning to fit its specific needs. Figure 5-6 shows the human resource planning process for Honeywell, Inc., which we discuss in the following sections.

Organizational Goals

To be relevant, a human resource planning process should be clearly tied to the organization's strategic goals. It must rest on a solid foundation of information about sales forecasts, market trends, technological advances, and major changes in processes and productivity. Considerable effort should be devoted to securing reliable data on business trends and needs—in terms of quantity and quality of labor—as the basic input for human resource planning.

Human Resource Needs Forecast

A second element of the planning process is forecasting human resource needs based on business strategies, production plans, and the various indicators of change in technology and operating methods. Forecasting is usually accomplished by utilizing historical data and reliable ratios (such as indirect/direct labor) and adjusting them for productivity trends. The result of this forecast is a spreadsheet showing employees in terms of numbers, mix, cost, new skills, job categories, and numbers and levels of managers needed to accomplish the organization's goals. Experience has shown that producing this forecast is the most challenging part of the planning process because dealing with business and technical uncertainties several years in the future requires creativity and a high level of participation.

Employee Information

A third element of the planning process is maintaining accurate information concerning the composition, assignments, and capabilities of the current workforce. This information includes job classifications, age, gender, minority status, organization level, rate of pay, and functions. Employee information may also include data, such as skills, education, training received, and career interests.

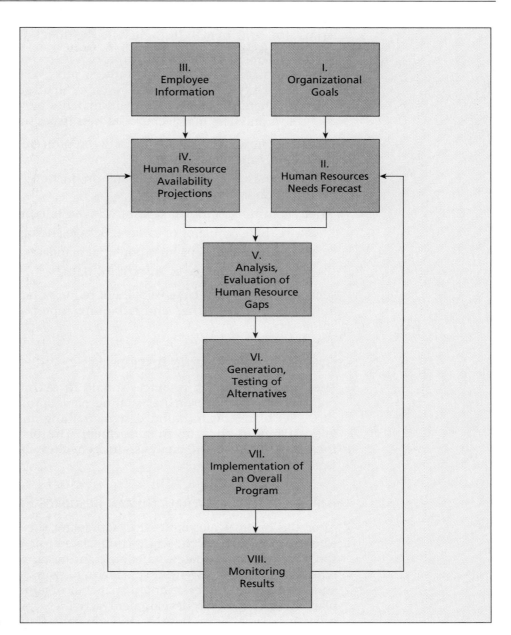

Figure 5-6
Elements of a Human
Resource Plan

Source: Used with the permission of Honeywell, Inc.

HUMAN RESOURCE AVAILABILITY PROJECTIONS

The fourth element of the planning process is estimating which current employees will be available in the future. By projecting past data about the size,
organization, and composition of the workforce and about turnover, aging,
and hiring, availability at a specific future date can be estimated. The result is
a picture of the organization's current human resources and how they can be
expected to evolve over time in terms of turnover, retirement, obsolescence,
promotability, and other relevant characteristics.

ANALYZING AND EVALUATING HUMAN RESOURCE GAPS

The fifth element of the planning process is to compare what is needed with what is available in terms of numbers, mix, skills, and technologies. This comparison permits the human resource manager to determine gaps and evaluate where the most serious mismatches are likely to be. This type of analysis should help management address issues such as the following:

- Are imbalances developing between projected human resource requirements and availability?
- What is the effect of current productivity trends and pay rates on workforce levels and costs?
- Do turnover problems exist in certain jobs or age levels?
- Are there problems of career blockage and obsolescence?
- Are there sufficient high-potential managers to fulfill future needs?
- Is there a shortage of any critical skills?

Such an analysis permits development of long-range plans for recruiting, hiring, training, transferring, and retraining appropriate numbers and types of employees.

GENERATING AND TESTING ALTERNATIVES

The analysis of human resources should reveal much about a wide range of policies and practices, such as staffing plans, promotion practices and policies, EEO plans, organization design, training and development programs, salary planning, and career management. This phase of the process explores the implications of the analysis and generates alternatives to current practices and policies.

IMPLEMENTING AN OVERALL HUMAN RESOURCE PROGRAM

After the optimal alternative for addressing the organization's human resource issues has been chosen, it is translated into operational programs with specific plans, target dates, schedules, and resource commitments. The analytical steps described—from considering organizational goals to generating and testing alternatives—should shape an organization's staffing plan, EEO plan, human resource development activities, mobility plans, productivity programs, bargaining strategies, and compensation programs.

MONITORING RESULTS

The final element in any human resource planning process is to provide a means for management to monitor results of the overall program. This step should address questions such as the following:

- How well is the plan working?
- Is the plan cost effective?
- What is the actual versus planned impact on the workforce?

- Where are the plan's weaknesses?
- What changes will be needed during the next planning cycle?

http://www.prenhall.com/mondy

SHRM—HR LINKS
This site covers various human resource information system issues.

Human Resource Information Systems

Human resource information system (HRIS):
Any organized approach to obtaining relevant and timely information on which to base human resource decisions.

A **human resource information system (HRIS)** is any organized approach for obtaining relevant and timely information on which to base human resource decisions. An effective system is crucial to sound human resource decision making; it typically employs computers and other sophisticated technologies to process data that reflect day-to-day operations of a company, organized in the form of information to facilitate the decision-making process.

An HRIS should be designed to provide information that is

- *Timely*—A manager must have access to up-to-date information.
- *Accurate*—A manager must be able to rely on the accuracy of the information provided.
- *Concise*—A manager can absorb only so much information at any one time.
- *Relevant*—A manager should receive only the information needed in a particular situation.
- *Complete*—A manager should receive complete, not partial, information.

The absence of even one of these characteristics reduces the effectiveness of an HRIS and complicates the decision-making process. Conversely, a system possessing all these characteristics enhances the ease and accuracy of the decision-making process. An effective system also produces several important reports and forecasts related to business operations:

- *Routine Reports.* Business data summarized on a scheduled basis are referred to as routine reports. Weekly and monthly employment status reports may be sent to the general manager, whereas quarterly reports may be forwarded to top management.
- *Exception Reports.* Exception reports highlight variations in operations that are serious enough to require management's attention. One type of exception report is the quality-exception report, completed when the number of product defects exceeds a predetermined maximum. The human resource manager may be interested in this type of information in order to identify additional training needs.
- *On-Demand Reports.* An on-demand report provides information in response to a specific request. The number of engineers with five years'

work experience who speak fluent Spanish is an example of an on-demand report that the human resource manager could request from the database.[24]

■ *Forecasts*. A forecast applies predictive models to specific situations. Managers need forecasts of the numbers and types of employees required to satisfy projected demand for the firm's product.

Firms realize that a properly developed HRIS can provide tremendous benefits to the organization. Figure 5-7 presents an overview of the human resource information system designed for one organization. Utilizing numerous types of input data, the system makes available many types of output data that have far-reaching human resource planning and operational value. The HRIS ties together all human resource information into a system. Data from various input sources are integrated to provide the needed outputs. Information needed in the firm's human resource decision-making process is readily available when the system is properly designed. For instance, many firms are now studying historical trends to determine the best means of securing qualified applicants. In addition, complying with statutes and government regulations would be extremely difficult were it not for the modern HRIS.

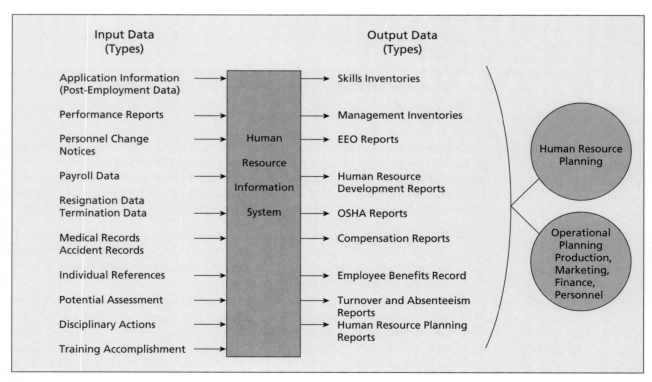

Figure 5-7
A Human Resource Information System

T R E N D S & I N N O V A T I O N S

VIRTUAL HR

Today's HR professionals use a word processing program to update the employee manual, a spreadsheet program to conduct a payroll analysis, and a database for storing employee evaluations and skills. Company employees approach virtual HR by updating or changing their own data without interfacing with the human resource department. Employees are able to change 401(k) plans with a voice response system. HR professionals perform preemployment credit checks on job applicants.[25] As one human resource professional stated, "All human resources services will be available instantaneously on demand, at the place most convenient to the employee—anywhere in the world."[26] The ease of access and availability of human resource services to employees is analogous to banking with an automated teller machine. Additional virtual HR systems are being developed to further benefit the human resource manager in the areas of strategic planning, compensation, executive development, and succession studies.[27]

A GLOBAL PERSPECTIVE

HRIS: Helping to Take Complexity Out of Global HR Management

Human resource managers must follow trends toward globalization, and this requires them to use technological advancements in information technology.[28] An effective global human resource information system (GHRIS) is essential because of the complexity involved in managing a global labor force. A global HRIS is an organized approach for obtaining relevant and timely information on which to base human resource decisions. An ideal information system exists when users are supplied with all the information they need when they need it. Such a utopian situation has not yet arrived for most companies, but new technology allows companies to cope more effectively with HR issues.[29]

Global HR may require activities such as cutting paychecks in various currencies; often, the regulations of multiple taxing agencies must be adhered to. Some HR practices must be consistent across the company whereas others must change to accommodate local customs that require an advanced global human resource information system.[30] Regardless of the nature of the information system, information concerning the many relevant factors affecting human resources must be available in a timely fashion to ensure that the best human resource decisions are made. Companies must often redesign their operations to keep up with global demands. Departmental lines will continue to fade, and HR will be pulled in many directions. Successfully managing HR on a global level can be facilitated with a global human resource information system, taking advantage of new technology such as client/server computing, supernetworks, and groupware.[31]

According to Ralph W. Stevens, vice president of personnel and employee relations for the Denver-based Hamilton Oil Corporation, human resource professionals in each location must be experts on local laws, customs, salary structures, and so on. It is, therefore, essential that these professionals have high-quality information. Through an effective GHRIS, Hamilton Oil's human resource management approach is becoming much more integrated. All of Hamilton Oil's human resource managers are linked electronically with a PC-based network. This system allows them to have and access a database of human resource statistics and other relevant material.[32]

Technology, in and of itself, cannot run a global human resources system. However, a state-of-the-art global human resource information system, properly implemented, can improve the effectiveness of an HR department by automating administrative tasks, reducing paperwork, simplifying work processes, and distributing better information to HR professionals and others who manage people in the global organization and each of its foreign operations.[33]

SUMMARY

1. *Define* **strategic planning**.

Strategic planning is the process by which top management determines overall organizational purposes and objectives and how they are to be achieved.

2. ***Describe the levels of strategic planning.***

The process of defining the overall character and purpose of the organization, the businesses it will enter and leave, and how resources will be distributed among those businesses is corporate-level strategic planning. The planning process concerned primarily with how to manage the interests and operations of a particular business is business-level strategic planning. The process of determining policies and procedures for relatively narrow areas of activity that are critical to the success of the organization is functional-level strategic planning.

3. ***Explain the strategic planning process.***

Strategic planning at all levels of the organization can be divided into four steps: (1) determination of the organizational mission, (2) assessment of the organization and its environment, (3) setting of specific objectives or direction, and (4) determination of strategies to accomplish those objectives.

4. ***Identify the factors to be considered in strategy implementation.***

Factors to be considered include leadership, organizational structure, information and control systems, technology, and human resources.

5. ***Explain the human resource planning process.***

After strategic plans have been formulated, human resource planning can be undertaken. Organizational plans identified in the strategic planning process are reduced to specific quantitative and qualitative human resource plans. Human resource planning has two components: requirements and availability. When the requirements and availability of employees have been analyzed, the firm is in a position to determine whether there will be a surplus or shortage of employees. Ways must be found to reduce the number of employees if a surplus of workers is projected.

6. *Describe some human resource forecasting techniques.*
   Zero-base forecasting uses the organization's current level of employment as the starting point for determining future staffing needs. The bottom-up approach is a forecasting method that projects progress upward in the organization from small units to ultimately provide an aggregate forecast of employment needs. Using predictor variables, managers can forecast human resource requirements, with past employment needs serving as a predictor of future requirements.

7. *Define a* requirements *and an* availability forecast.
   A requirements forecast is an estimate of the numbers and kinds of employees the organization will need at future dates to realize its goals. Determining whether the firm will be able to secure employees with the necessary skills and from what sources these individuals may be obtained is called availability forecasting.

8. *Differentiate management inventory from skills inventory.*
   A management inventory contains detailed information about each manager and is used to identify individuals who have the potential to move into higher level positions. A skills inventory is information maintained on the availability and preparedness of nonmanagerial employees to move either into higher level positions or laterally in the organization.

9. *Distinguish between succession planning and succession development.*
   Succession planning is the process of ensuring that a qualified person is available to assume a managerial position once the position is vacant. Succession development is the process of producing a comprehensive job profile of the key positions and then ensuring that key prospects are properly developed to match these qualifications.

10. *Identify what a firm can do when a surplus of workers exists.*
   When a surplus of workers exists, a firm may implement one or more of the following: restricted hiring, reduced hours, early retirement, and layoffs.

11. *Describe the concept of downsizing.*
   Downsizing, also known as restructuring and rightsizing, is essentially the reverse of company growth; it suggests a one-time change in the organization and the number of people who are employed by a firm. The purpose is to make the organization more efficient.

12. *Define* human resource information system (HRIS) *and identify the type of information an HRIS should provide.*
   A human resource information system (HRIS) is any organized approach for obtaining relevant and timely data on which to base human resource decisions. The information provided in an HRIS should be timely, accurate, concise, relevant, and complete.

QUESTIONS FOR REVIEW

1. Define *strategic planning*. What role does HR play in strategic planning?
2. List the levels of strategic planning. Give an example of each.
3. What are the steps in the strategic planning process? Briefly describe each.
4. Describe the major factors for consideration in strategy implementation.
5. Describe the human resource planning process.
6. Identify and briefly describe the methods used to forecast human resource needs.
7. Distinguish between forecasting human resource requirements and availability. Use definitions and examples.
8. What actions could a firm take if it had a worker surplus?
9. Distinguish between a management inventory and a skills inventory. What are the essential components of each?
10. Why is it important to have succession planning?
11. Define and describe the purpose of downsizing.
12. What is the purpose of a human resource information system?

DEVELOPING HRM SKILLS

AN EXPERIENTIAL EXERCISE

This exercise is designed to give participants experience in dealing with some aspects of planning that a typical human resource manager faces. Students will also be exposed to some of the activities that human resource managers confront on a daily basis. The old axiom, "plan your work and work your plan" will probably have new meaning after this exercise.

You are the human resource manager at a large canning plant. Your plant produces several lines of canned food products that are shipped to wholesale distributors nationwide. You are responsible for the human resource activities at the plant.

It is Monday morning, August 30. You have just returned from a week-long corporate executives' meeting at the home office. The meeting was attended by all human resource managers from each of the company's plants. You returned with notes from the meeting and other materials concerning the company's goals and plans for the next six months. When you arrive at your office (an hour early), you find your in-basket full of notes, messages, and other correspondence.

Your instructor will provide you with additional information necessary to participate.

 Take It to the Net

We invite you to visit the Mondy home page on the Prentice Hall Web site at:

http://www.prenhall.com/mondy

for updated information, Web-based exercises, and links to other HR-related sites.

HRM SIMULATION

*H*uman resource planning and forecasting are key elements of this simulation. Your team will be furnished with the total number of operations/production employees needed each quarter and an estimate of how many employees may quit during the quarter. Your team will then need to hire and/or promote employees to fill jobs at all levels. If your team does not hire sufficient people, the firm will need to schedule overtime work to fill production quotas, and your team will be charged for this extra expense. Because of the nature of the work and wage rates that are lower than local rates, your organization has fairly high turnover when the simulation begins. First, you will need to develop a strategy to decrease this costly turnover rate.

HRM INCIDENT

1

A Degree for Meter Readers?

*J*udy Anderson was assigned as a recruiter for South Illinois Electric Company (SIE), a small supplier of natural gas and electricity for Cairo, Illinois, and the surrounding area. The company had expanded rapidly during the last half of the 1980s, and this growth was expected to continue. In January 1998, SIE purchased the utilities system serving neighboring Mitchell County. This expansion concerned Judy. The company workforce had increased by 30 percent the previous year, and Judy had found it a struggle to recruit enough qualified job applicants. She knew that new expansion would intensify the problem.

Judy is particularly concerned about meter readers. The tasks required in meter reading are relatively simple. A person drives to homes served by the company, finds the gas or electric meter, and records its current reading. If the meter has been tampered with, it is reported. Otherwise no decision making of any consequence is associated with the job. The reader performs no calculations. The pay is $8.00 per hour, high for unskilled work in the area. Even so, Judy has been having considerable difficulty keeping the 37 meter reader positions filled.

Judy was thinking about how to attract more job applicants when she received a call from the human resource director, Sam McCord. "Judy," Sam said, "I'm unhappy with the job specification calling for only a high school education for meter readers. In planning for the future, we need better educated people in the company. I've decided to change the education requirement for the meter reader job from a high school diploma to a college degree."

"But, Mr. McCord," protested Judy, "the company is growing rapidly. If we are to have enough people to fill those jobs, we just can't insist on finding college applicants to perform such basic tasks. I don't see how we can meet our future needs for this job with such an unrealistic job qualification."

Sam terminated the conversation abruptly by saying, "No, I don't agree. We need to upgrade all the people in our organization. This is just part of a general effort to do that. Anyway, I cleared this with the president before I decided to do it."

Questions

1. Should there be a minimum education requirement for the meter reader job? Discuss.
2. What is your opinion of Sam's effort to upgrade the people in the organization?
3. What legal ramifications, if any, should Sam have considered?

HRM INCIDENT 2

A Busy Day

Dave Johnson, human resource manager for Eagle Aircraft, had just returned from a brief vacation in Cozumel, Mexico. Eagle is a Wichita, Kansas, maker of small commercial aircraft. Eagle's workforce in 1998 totaled 236. Dave's friend Carl Edwards, vice president for marketing, stopped by to ask Dave to lunch, as he often did. In the course of their conversation Carl asked Dave's opinion on the president's announcement concerning expansion. "What announcement?" was Dave's response.

Carl explained that there had been a special meeting of the executive council to announce a major expansion, involving a new plant to be built near St. Louis, Missouri. He continued, "Everyone at the meeting seemed to be completely behind the president. Joe Davis, the controller, stressed our independent financial position. The production manager had written a complete report on the equipment we are going to need, including availability and cost information. And I have been pushing for this expansion for some time. So I was ready. I think it will be good for you too, Dave. The president said he expects employment to double in the next year."

As Carl left, Rex Schearer, a production supervisor, arrived. "Dave," said Rex, "the production manager jumped on me Friday because maintenance doesn't have anybody qualified to work on the new digital lathe that's being installed."

"He's right," Dave replied, "Maintenance sent me a requisition last week. We'd better get moving and see if we can find someone." Dave knew that it was going to be another busy Monday.

Questions

1. What should Dave do, if anything, about being kept in the dark regarding the expansion? Explain.
2. Discuss any additional problems highlighted by the case and suggest what should be done to solve them.

Notes

1. Connie Freeman, "Strategy: Training HR Pros to Fit Your Culture," *HR Focus* 74 (May 1997): 9.
2. James Down, "From Paper Pushing to Strategic Planning," *Boston Business Journal* 16 (January 24, 1997): 6.
3. Melody Jones, "Four Trends to Reckon With," *HR Focus* 73 (July 1996): 22.

4. Frederick Gluck, Stephen Kaufman, and A. Steven Walleck, "The Four Phases of Strategic Management," *Journal of Business Strategy* 2 (Winter 1982): 11–12.

5. Ian Wilson, "The Strategic Management Technology: Corporate Fad or Strategic Necessity," *Long-Range Planning* 19 (1986): 21–22.

6. R. Wayne Mondy, Robert M. Noe, and Robert E. Edwards, "What the Staffing Function Entails," *Personnel* 63 (April 1986): 55–56.

7. Paul A. Evans, "Management Development as Glue Technology," *Human Resource Planning* 15 (December 1992): 85–106.

8. James Martin, "HR in the Cybercorp," *HR Focus* 74 (April 1997): 3.

9. Gale Dutton, "Future Shock: Who Will Run the Company?" *Management Review* 85 (August 1996): 19.

10. James E. McElwain, "Succession Plans Designed to Manage Change," *HRMagazine* 36 (February 1991): 67.

11. Ibid.

12. "Heirs and Races," *The Economist* 318 (March 9, 1991): 69.

13. Kelley Holland, "Why the Chemistry is Right at Chemical," *Business Week* (June 7, 1993): 90–93.

14. Kenneth Nowack, "The Secrets of Succession," *Training & Development* 48 (November 1994): 49.

15. R. Wayne Mondy and Harry N. Mills, "Choice Not Chance in Nurse Selection," *Supervisor Nurse* 9 (November 1978): 35–39.

16. N. Fredric Crandall and Marc J. Wallace, Jr., "Inside the Virtual Workplace: Forging a New Deal for Work and Rewards," *Compensation & Benefits Review* 29 (January/February 1997): 27–36.

17. Joseph Nocer and Ed Brown, "Living with Layoffs," *Fortune* 131 (May 1996): 69.

18. Elizabeth Lesly and Larry Light, "When Layoffs Alone Don't Turn the Tide," *Business Week* (December 7, 1992): 100–101.

19. Jaclyn Fierman, "Beating the Midlife Career Crisis," *Fortune* 128 (September 6, 1993): 53.

20. Louis S. Richman, "When Will the Layoffs End?" *Fortune* 128 (September 20, 1993): 54.

21. "Downsizing Doesn't Work, Says Aussie Academic," *Newsbytes News Network* (July 15, 1997): 1.

22. Shari Caudron, "Rebuilding Employee Trust," *Training & Development* 50 (August 1996): 18.

23. Jenny C. McCune, "Downsizing the Downswing," *HR Focus* 74 (January 1997): 6.

24. Janet Bensu, "Use Your Data Base in New Ways," *HRMagazine* 35 (March 1990): 33–34.

25. Beth Slick, "Technology and the Human Factor (reprinted from PC Today)," *Softbase* (April 29, 1996): 10.

26. James L. Wilkerson, "The Future Is Virtual HR," *HR Focus* 74 (March 1997): 15.

27. Wilkerson, "The Future Is Virtual HR."

28. Row Henson, "Globalization: A Human Resources Mandate," *SoftBase* (March 3, 1996): 62–64.

29. Gale Eisenstodt, "Information Power," *Forbes* 151 (June 21, 1993): 44–45.

30. Ibid.

31. Henson, "Globalization: A Human Resources Mandate."

32. Ellen Brandt, "Global HR," *Personnel Journal* 70 (March 1991): 38–39.

33. Row Henson, "HRIMS for Dummies: A Practical Guide to Technology Implementation," *HR Focus* 73 (November 1996): 3–6.

6
Recruitment

CHAPTER OBJECTIVES

1. Define *recruitment*.
2. Identify alternatives that a firm might consider before resorting to outside recruitment.
3. Describe the recruitment process.
4. Define *promotion from within*.
5. Explain and describe internal recruitment methods.
6. Identify external sources of recruitment.
7. Identify the external methods of recruitment.
8. Explain what needs to be accomplished to recruit for diversity.

*D*orothy Bryant, recruiting supervisor for International Manufacturing Company, had been promoted to her position after several years as a group leader in the production department. One of Dorothy's first assignments was to recruit two software design engineers for International. After considering various recruitment alternatives, Dorothy placed the following ad in a local newspaper with a circulation in excess of 1,000,000:

EMPLOYMENT OPPORTUNITY
FOR SOFTWARE DESIGN ENGINEERS
*2 positions available for software design engineers
desiring career in growth industry.
Prefer recent college graduates with good appearance.
Apply Today! Send your resumé,
in confidence, to D. A. Bryant
International Manufacturing Co., P.O. Box 1515
Alexandria, VA 22314*

More than 300 applications were received in the first week, and Dorothy was elated. When she reviewed the applicants, however, it appeared that few people possessed the desired qualifications for the job.

*D*orothy learned, the hard way, the importance of proper recruiting practices. She obviously failed to include specific job requirements in her newspaper ad. As a result, an excessive number of unqualified persons applied. Also, the road is paved for a potential legal problem because Dorothy uses a subjective criterion, *good appearance*, which may not be job related. In addition, stating a preference for a *recent college graduate* may also prove to be ill-advised because of the age implication. Adding further to Dorothy's dilemma is the potential liability her ad creates for the firm by implying a *career* for employees. Her corporate attorney will probably advise her to avoid any semblance of creating an implied contract for a candidate who is hired. The individual may later be discharged and then sue the company for breach of contract. Dorothy has found that preparing an effective, legally sound recruitment ad is not as simple as it once was.

Recruitment: The process of attracting individuals on a timely basis, in sufficient numbers and with appropriate qualifications, and encouraging them to apply for jobs with an organization.

Recruitment is the process of attracting individuals on a timely basis, in sufficient numbers, and with appropriate qualifications, and encouraging them to apply for jobs with an organization. Finding the appropriate way of encouraging qualified candidates to apply for employment is extremely important when a firm needs to hire employees. Tapping productive sources of applicants and using suitable recruitment methods are essential for the greatest recruiting efficiency and effectiveness. Some firms, however, may prefer options other than recruitment. We begin the chapter by describing these alternatives. Next, we discuss the recruitment process and external and internal environments of recruitment. We present methods used in external and internal recruitment and explore ways to tailor methods to sources. Finally, we cover recruiting efforts specifically aimed at assuring a diverse workforce and at the same time satisfying legal requirements.

HR Web Wisdom

http://www.prenhall.com/mondy

RECRUITMENT
Creative recruitment solutions are offered which can empower the hiring manager or employment team.

Alternatives to Recruitment

Even when human resource planning indicates a need for additional or replacement employees, a firm may decide against increasing the size of its workforce. Recruitment and selection costs are not insignificant when all the related expenses are considered: the search process, interviewing, agency fee payment, and relocation and processing of the new employee. Although selection decisions are not irreversible, once employees are placed on the payroll, they may be difficult to remove, even if their performance is marginal. Therefore, a firm should consider its alternatives carefully before engaging in recruitment. Alternatives to recruitment commonly include outsourcing, use of contingent workers, employee leasing, and overtime.

OUTSOURCING

As defined in chapter 1, outsourcing is the process of transferring responsibility for an area of service and its objectives to an external provider. Subcontracting of various functions to other firms has been a common practice in industry for many decades. This decision is usually made when the subcontractor is viewed as an organization that can perform a given function such as sales or production with perhaps even greater efficiency and effectiveness. Within the past few years, this practice has become widespread and increasingly a popular alternative involving virtually every functional area of business. The decision to outsource functions may be made to avoid hiring additional employees or to implement reengineering programs and the subsequent downsizing of the firm. As with other alternatives, there is a downside to outsourcing. The primary obstacles seem to be twofold; cost issues and concern about loss of control.[1] To accommodate the current popularity of outsourcing, a number of organizations have been created. IBM's own human resource function spawned one such firm.

IBM's Workforce Solutions WFS is a full-service human resource company that was spun off from its human resource operation. It was originally designed to serve IBM's other independent units but now markets its services to external customers. These services are grouped into several areas: human resource research and consulting services, leadership development, workforce diversity programs, equal opportunity programs/compliance, resources planning services, compensation and benefits programs, recruiting and employment services, occupational health services, relocation programs, international assignment services, employment involvement/suggestion programs, and testing and assessment. As an independent company, WFS Workforce Solutions is expected to compete for business within and outside IBM and to make a profit.[2]

CONTINGENT WORKERS

Described by the secretary of labor as the *disposable American workforce*, contingent workers—also known as part-timers, temporaries, and independent contractors—make up the fastest growing segment of the U.S. economy. In 1993, part-time workers alone numbered 21 million, or 17 percent of the total labor force. Currently, there are over 3,500 independent temporary help agencies operating more than 10,000 offices nationwide.[3]

What accounts for the rapid growth of jobs for these workers? According to a recent Conference Board survey, over 80 percent of the respondents indicated their number one reason was to achieve flexibility. Global competition and changing technology prevent employers from accurately forecasting their employment needs months in advance. To avoid hiring people one day and resorting to layoffs the next, firms look to a temporary workforce as a buffer.[4] In addition to needing flexibility, companies want to control cost. The total cost of a permanent employee is generally estimated at 30 percent to 40 percent above the person's gross pay; this figure does not include, among other things, the costs of recruitment. To avoid some of these costs and to maintain flexibility as workloads vary, many organizations use part-time or temporary employees. Companies that provide temporary workers assist their clients in handling excess or special workloads. These companies assign their own employees to their customers and fulfill all the obligations normally associated with an employer. The expenses of recruitment, absenteeism and turnover, and employee benefits are avoided.

During periods of downsizing, contingent workers are the human equivalents of just-in-time inventory. These *disposable workers* permit maximum flexibility for the employer and lower labor costs. The huge unanswered question is whether this approach to staffing is healthy for our society in the long run. For the shorter term, however, the advantages gained by using contingent workers may be essential for the success or even survival of many companies.

EMPLOYEE LEASING

Another alternative to recruitment that is growing in popularity is employee leasing. Using this approach, a firm terminates some or most of its employees. A leasing company then hires them, usually at the same salary, and leases them back to the former employer, who becomes the client. The employees continue to work as before, with the client supervising their activities. The leasing company, however, assumes all responsibilities associated with being the employer.

A primary advantage of employee leasing to the client is being free from human resource administration, including payroll withholdings, employee benefits, pensions, medical, dental and disability insurance, educational allowances, and vacations.[5] The firm writes only one check per payroll period to cover wages, taxes, benefits, and an administrative fee to the leasing company that may range from 2 percent to 8 percent of payroll.

Leasing has advantages for employees, also. Because leasing companies provide workers for many companies, they often enjoy economies of scale that permit them to offer excellent, low-cost benefit programs. In addition, workers frequently have greater opportunities for job mobility. Some leasing firms operate throughout the nation, so if one employed spouse is relocated in a dual-career family, the leasing company may offer the other a job in the new location, too. Also, if a client organization suffers a downturn in business, the leasing company can transfer employees to another client, avoiding both layoff and loss of seniority.

A potential disadvantage to the client is erosion of employee loyalty—because workers receive pay and benefits from the leasing company. Regardless of any shortcomings, use of employee leasing is growing. By 2005, the industry could involve $185 billion in revenues and more than 9 million employees.[6]

Smaller firms, with fewer than 35 employees, have typically been most attracted to employee leasing. However, as leasing firms grow and become more mature, larger companies have begun using their services to a greater extent. Leasing provides companies with a body of well-trained, long-term employees that can expand or contract as business conditions dictate.

OVERTIME

Perhaps the most commonly used method of meeting short-term fluctuations in work volume is having permanent employees work overtime. Overtime may help both employer and employees. The employer benefits by avoiding recruitment, selection, and training costs. The employees gain from increased income during the overtime period.

There are potential problems with overtime, however. Many managers believe that when they work employees for unusually long periods of time, the company pays more and receives less in return. Employees may become fatigued and lack the energy to perform at a normal rate, especially when excessive overtime is required.

Two other possible problems are related to the use of prolonged overtime. Employees may, consciously or not, pace themselves so that overtime will be assured. They may also become accustomed to the added income resulting from overtime pay. Some may even elevate their standard of living to the level permitted by this additional income. Then, when overtime is no longer required and the paycheck shrinks, employees may become disgruntled.

When alternatives to hiring additional employees are considered but determined to be inappropriate, organizations turn to ways of attracting potential employees and encouraging them to apply for the open positions.

HR
Web
Wisdom

http://www.prenhall.com/mondy

SHRM–HR LINKS
This site covers various recruitment issues including interviewing and on-line recruiting directories.

The Recruitment Process

Recruitment is the process of attracting individuals on a timely basis, in sufficient numbers, and with appropriate qualifications, and encouraging them to apply for jobs with an organization. Applicants with qualifications most closely related to job specifications may then be selected. Dorothy Bryant was quite disappointed when she reviewed over 300 applications and found that only a few applicants had the desired qualifications. The main reason could be Dorothy's ad, which did not focus on specific qualifications.

How many times do we hear CEOs state, "Our most important assets are human"? This axiom has probably always been true, but an increasing number of executives are beginning to believe it. Hiring the best people available has never been more critical than today because of global competition, but hiring decisions can be no better than the alternatives presented through recruitment efforts. Marketing know-how is an especially important skill in recruitment. The task is to *sell* your product to target customer groups. In recruitment, these groups include potential candidates both inside and outside the firm.[7] In small firms lacking specialized expertise, recruitment is normally handled by individual managers. Regardless of who is responsible,

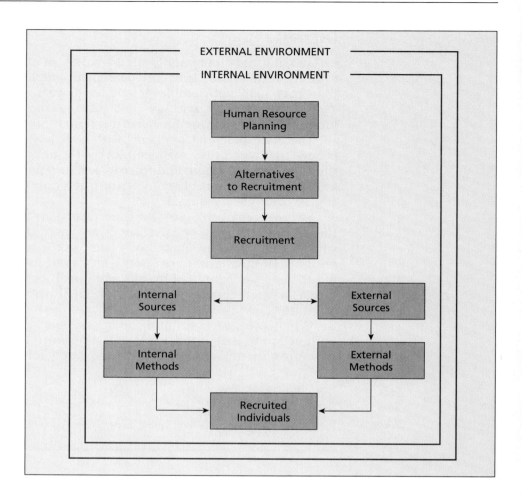

Figure 6-1
The Recruitment Process

recruitment in some form is essential for every firm desiring additional employees.

Figure 6-1 shows that when human resource planning indicates a need for employees, the firm may evaluate alternatives to recruitment. If these alternatives are found to be inappropriate, the recruitment process starts. Frequently, recruitment begins when a manager initiates an employee requisition. The **employee requisition** is a document that specifies job title, department, the date the employee is needed for work, and other details. An employee requisition for Raytheon E-Systems appears in Figure 6-2. With this information, managers can refer to the appropriate job description to determine the qualifications the recruited person needs. These qualifications, however, are becoming less clear-cut. According to Joanne Jorz, vice president of program development for Conceptual Systems Inc., an HRM consulting firm, "Job descriptions aren't cleanly defined any longer . . . When you recruit and hire for task X, it won't be long before the employee will be asked to do A, B, C and D as well."[8] With such broad expectations from the company, the employee will obviously need a broader range of skills and abilities. Some firms deal with this situation by striving to employ individuals

Employee requisition:
A document that specifies a particular job title, the appropriate department, and the date by which an open job should be filled.

EMPLOYMENT REQUISITION - Greenville   Requisition Number: __NO   30560__
(This Document Must Be Typed)

Title Of Position		Job Code	Date Needed	☐ Supervisory
				☐ Non-Supervisory

Job Status (Please Check One)

☐ Regular (Standard Hours)_____ am/pm to_____ am/pm

☐ Part-Time (Less Than 40 Hours/Week)

☐ Temporary For _____ days

☐ Co-Op Alternating

☐ Co-Op Parallel (part time)

☐ Temporary For _____ days

☐ Job Shop / Consultant

☐ New Grad

☐ ICT or VOE Trainee

Department Name: Account Number

Department Number	CBN Number	Extension of Time (Temp)
		☐ Yes ☐ No

Please Check One:

☐ Indirect   ☐ Direct Contract Number _____

Department Interviewer

1._____ Ext. _____

2._____ Ext. _____

Justification

☐ Addition ☐ Replacement For (Name) _____

Security Clearance

Level _____ Access _____

Recommended Billed Hourly Rate

(Temps only) _____ / Hr.

Not to Exceed $ _____ / Total Effort

Per Diem Authorized   ☐ Yes   ☐ No

Knowledge and Skills

Indicate Type(s) of Computer   Indicate Type(s) of Software

☐ Mainframe   ☐ MS Word

☐ IBM PC   ☐ Excel

☐ Macintosh   ☐ Power Point

☐ Other _____   ☐ Other _____

Other Skills Required _____

_____

_____

APPROVALS

Section/Department Head _____ Date _____

VP Organization _____ Date _____

VP Finance _____ Date _____

Vice President and General Manager _____ Date _____

FOR HUMAN RESOURCES USE ONLY

☐ Received In Labor Relations   Date _____   Date Approval for Staffing _____

☐ Released In Labor Relations   Date _____

Temporary Agency _____   ☐ Reviewed For ETOP   Posted ☐ Yes ☐ No

8-98999-1 (June 1996)

Figure 6-2
An Employee Requisition for Raytheon-E-Systems

who are bright and adaptable and can work effectively in teams. Hiring for organizational *fit* is discussed in Chapter 7.

The next step in the recruitment process is to determine whether qualified employees are available within the firm (the internal source) or must be recruited from external sources, such as colleges, universities, and other organizations. Because of the high cost of recruitment, organizations need to use the most productive recruitment sources and methods available.

Recruitment sources:
Various locales in which qualified individuals are sought as potential employees.

Recruitment methods:
The specific means by which potential employees are attracted to an organization.

Recruitment sources are the locations where qualified individuals can be found. **Recruitment methods** are the specific means by which potential employees can be attracted to the firm. When the sources of potential employees have been identified, appropriate methods for either internal or external recruitment are used to accomplish recruitment objectives.

Companies may discover that some recruitment sources and methods are superior to others for locating and attracting potential executive talent. For instance, one large equipment manufacturer determined that medium-size, state-supported colleges and universities located in rural areas were good sources of potential managers. Other firms may arrive at different conclusions. To maximize recruiting effectiveness, a company should use recruitment sources and methods tailored to its specific needs.

External Environment of Recruitment

Like other human resource functions, the recruitment process does not take place in a vacuum. Factors external to the organization can significantly affect the firm's recruitment efforts. Of particular importance is the demand for and supply of specific skills in the labor market. If demand for a particular skill is high relative to supply, a company may have to make an extraordinary recruiting effort.

As the unemployment rate nears record lows nationwide, some small business firms have implemented creative approaches to recruitment. For example, certain business owners in Milwaukee are paying bonuses to churches whose pastors will work the pews to recruit entry-level workers. Another small firm in Los Angeles, Benji Electronics Inc., has expanded its labor market by hiring people with few if any qualifications. The firm is then willing to spend much time and money training them—often in remedial subjects.[9]

When the unemployment rate in an organization's labor market is high, the firm's recruitment process may be simplified. For any announced job vacancy, the number of unsolicited applicants is usually greater, and the increased size of the labor pool improves the company's likelihood of attracting qualified applicants. Conversely, as the unemployment rate drops, recruitment efforts must be increased and new sources explored.

Local labor market conditions are of primary importance in recruitment for most nonmanagerial, many supervisory, and even some middle-management positions. However, recruitment for executive and professional positions often extends to national or even global markets. Although the recruiter's day-to-day activities provide a *feel* for the labor market, accurate employment data—found in professional journals and U.S. Department of Labor reports—can be extremely helpful.

Legal considerations also play a significant role in recruitment practices in the United States. The individual and the employer first make contact during the recruitment process. One survey found that about one-fourth of all discrimination claims resulted from the employers' recruitment and selection actions.[10] Therefore, nondiscriminatory practices at this stage are absolutely essential. We discuss this topic later in the chapter.

The firm's corporate image is another important factor that affects recruitment. If employees believe their employer deals with them fairly, the positive word-of-mouth support they provide is of great value to the firm. It assists in establishing credibility with prospective employees. When good reputations are earned in this manner, more and better qualified applicants will seek employment with the firm. Prospective employees are more inclined to respond positively to the organization's recruitment efforts if the firm is praised by employees. The firm with a positive public image is one believed to be a *good place to work*, and its recruitment efforts are greatly enhanced.

Internal Environment of Recruitment

Although the labor market and the government exert powerful external influences, the organization's own practices and policies also affect recruitment. One major internal factor that can greatly aid recruitment is human resource planning. In most cases, a firm cannot attract prospective employees in sufficient numbers and with the required skills overnight. Examining alternative sources of recruits and determining the most productive methods for obtaining them often takes time. After identifying the best alternatives, managers can make appropriate recruitment plans.

An organization's promotion policy can also have a significant impact on recruitment. An organization can stress promotion from within its own ranks or fill positions from outside the organization. Depending on the circumstances, either approach may have merit.

Promotion from within (PFW): The policy of filling vacancies above entry-level positions with employees presently employed by a company.

Promotion from within (PFW) is the policy of filling vacancies above entry-level positions with current employees. When an organization emphasizes promotion from within, its workers have an incentive to strive for advancement. When employees see co-workers being promoted, they become more aware of their own opportunities. Motivation provided by this practice often improves employee morale. Today's flatter organizational structures, with fewer levels of management, restrict upward mobility to a degree. However, the opportunity to move up in an organization will continue to serve as a motivating factor for some employees.

Another advantage of internal recruitment is that the organization is usually well aware of its employees' capabilities. An employee's job performance may not, by itself, be a reliable criterion for promotion. Nevertheless, many of the employee's personal and job-related qualities will be known. The employee has a track record, as opposed to being an unknown quantity. Also, the company's investment in the individual may yield a higher return. Still another positive factor is the employee's knowledge of the firm, its policies, and its people.

It is unlikely, however, that a firm can—or would even desire to—adhere rigidly to a practice of promotion from within. The vice president of human resources for a major automobile manufacturer offers this advice: "A strictly applied 'PFW' policy eventually leads to inbreeding, a lack of cross-fertilization, and a lack of creativity. A good goal, in my opinion, is to fill 80 percent of openings above entry-level positions from within." Frequently, new blood is needed to provide new ideas and innovation that must take place for firms to remain competitive. In such cases, even organizations with promotion from within policies may opt to look outside the organization for new talent. In any event, a promotion policy that first considers insiders is great for employee morale and motivation and is often beneficial to the organization.

Policies related to the employment of relatives may also affect a firm's recruitment efforts. The content of such policies varies greatly, but it is not uncommon for companies to have anti-nepotism policies that discourage the employment of close relatives, especially when related employees would be placed in the same department, under the same supervisor, or in supervisor-subordinate roles.

Methods Used in Internal Recruitment

Management should be able to identify current employees who are capable of filling positions as they become available. Helpful tools used for internal recruitment include skills inventories, job posting, and bidding procedures. As mentioned in chapter 5, skills and management inventories permit organizations to determine whether current employees possess the qualifications for filling open positions. As a recruitment device, these inventories have proved to be extremely valuable to organizations when they are kept current. Inventories can be of tremendous value in locating talent internally and supporting the concept of promotion from within.

Job posting: A procedure for communicating to company employees the fact that a job opening exists.

Job bidding: A technique that permits individuals in an organization who believe that they possess the required qualifications to apply for a posted job.

Job posting is a procedure for informing employees that job openings exist. **Job bidding** is a technique that permits employees who believe they possess the required qualifications to apply for a posted job. Table 6-1 shows the procedure a medium-sized firm might use. Some firms provide employees with an up-to-date computer list of job openings, or they may post openings on the company's intranet.

The job posting and bidding procedure minimizes the complaint commonly voiced in many companies that insiders never hear of a job opening until it has been filled. It reflects an openness that most employees generally value highly. In addition, this system can assist in college recruitment efforts. A firm that offers freedom of choice and encourages career growth has a distinct advantage over firms that do not. However, a job posting and bidding system does have some negative features. An effective system requires the expenditure of considerable time and money. When bidders are unsuccessful, someone must explain to them why they were not chosen. If care has not been taken to ensure that the most qualified applicant is chosen, the system will lack credibility. Even successful implementation of such a system cannot completely eliminate complaints.

TABLE 6-1

Job Posting and Bidding Procedure

Responsibility	*Action Required*
Human Resource Assistant	1. Upon receiving a Human Resource Requisition, send an e-mail or memo to each appropriate supervisor stating that a job opening exists. The message should include a job title, job number, pay grade, salary range, summary of the basic duties performed, and the essential qualifications required for the job (data to be taken from the job description/specification).
Supervisors	2. Ensure that the message is communicated to all within his or her section.
Interested Employees	3. Contact Human Resources

External Sources of Recruitment

At times, a firm must look beyond itself to find employees, particularly when expanding its workforce. The following needs require external recruitment: (1) filling entry-level jobs, (2) acquiring skills not possessed by current employees, and (3) obtaining employees with different backgrounds to provide new ideas. As Figure 6-3 shows, even when promotions are made internally, entry-level jobs must be filled from the outside. Thus, after the president of a firm retires, a series of internal promotions is made. Ultimately, however, the firm has to recruit externally to fill the entry-level position of salary analyst. If the president's position had been filled from the outside, the chain-reaction of promotions from within would not have occurred. Depending on the qualifications desired, employees may be attracted from a number of outside sources.

HIGH SCHOOLS AND VOCATIONAL SCHOOLS

Organizations concerned with recruiting clerical and other entry-level operative employees often depend heavily on high schools and vocational schools. Many of these schools have outstanding training programs for specific occupational skills, such as home appliance repair and small engine mechanics. Some companies work with schools to ensure a constant supply of trained individuals with specific job skills. In some areas, companies even lend employees to schools to assist in the training programs.

COMMUNITY COLLEGES

Many community colleges are sensitive to the specific employment needs in their local labor markets and graduate highly sought after students with marketable skills. Typically, community colleges have two-year programs

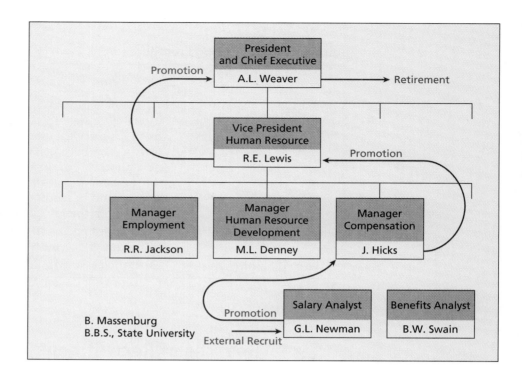

Figure 6-3
Internal Promotion and
External Recruitment

designed for both a terminal education and preparation for a four-year university degree program. Many community colleges also have excellent mid-management programs combined with training for specific trades. In addition, career centers often provide a place for employers to contact students, thereby facilitating the recruitment process.

COLLEGES AND UNIVERSITIES

Colleges and universities represent a major recruitment source for many organizations. Potential professional, technical, and management employees are typically found in these institutions. Many firms routinely utilize this source for prospective employees.

Placement directors, faculty, and administrators can be helpful to organizations in their search for recruits. Because on-campus recruitment is mutually beneficial, both employers and universities should take steps to develop and maintain close relationships. When a company establishes recruitment programs with educational institutions, it should continue those programs year after year to maintain an effective relationship with each school. It is important that the firm know the school and that the school know the firm.

COMPETITORS AND OTHER FIRMS

Competitors and other firms in the same industry or geographic area may be the most important source of recruits for positions in which recent experience is required. The fact that approximately 5 percent of the working population, at any one time, is either actively seeking or receptive to change of position emphasizes the importance of these sources.

Even organizations that have policies of promotion from within occasionally look elsewhere to fill important positions. Volkswagen drew the ire of General Motors when it hired José Ignacio Lopez de Arriortua, head of GM's huge purchasing operation. Not only was GM fearful that Lopez would divulge company trade secrets, but it also alleged that Volkswagen stepped up its efforts to lure away other key GM executives. The chairman of Opel claimed that VW had targeted more than 40 managers at Opel and General Motors.[11] Although the ethics of corporate raiding may be debatable, it is apparent that competitors and other firms do serve as external sources of recruitment for high-quality talent.

Smaller firms, in particular, look for employees who have been trained by larger organizations that have greater developmental resources. For instance, one optical firm believes that its own operation is not large enough to provide extensive training and development programs. Therefore, a person recruited by this firm for a significant management role is likely to have held at least two previous positions with a larger competitor.

THE UNEMPLOYED

The unemployed often provide a valuable source of recruits. Qualified applicants join the unemployment rolls every day for various reasons. Companies may go out of business, cut back operations, or be merged with other firms, leaving qualified workers without jobs. Employees are also fired sometimes merely because of personality differences with their bosses. Not infrequently, employees become frustrated with their jobs and simply quit.

OLDER INDIVIDUALS

Older workers, including those who are retired, may represent a valuable source of employees. Although these workers are often victims of negative stereotyping, the facts support the notion that older people can perform some jobs extremely well. When Kentucky Fried Chicken Corporation had difficulty recruiting younger workers, it turned to older individuals and those with disabilities. The results were dramatically reduced vacancies and turnover rates within six months. Management surveys indicate that most employers have high opinions of their older workers; they value them for many reasons, including their knowledge, skills, work ethic, loyalty, and good basic literacy skills.[12]

MILITARY PERSONNEL

Operation Transition is a program begun to ease downsizing of the armed services. The Defense Outplacement Referral System (DORS) provides recently discharged service members' resumés to employers via e-mail, fax, or mail through 350 offices worldwide. Employers may place job ads on electronic bulletin boards kept by transition offices. The bulletin boards contain business opportunities, a calendar of transition seminars and events, and other helpful information.

Hiring of former service members may make sense to many employers because these individuals typically have a proven work history and are flexible, motivated, and drug free. Another valuable characteristic of veterans is their goal and team orientation.[13] As skills possessed by veterans are wide ranging, this source of employees should not be overlooked.

SELF-EMPLOYED WORKERS

Finally, the self-employed worker may also be a good potential recruit. Such individuals may constitute a source of applicants for any number of jobs requiring technical, professional, administrative, or entrepreneurial expertise within a firm.

Conventional External Methods of Recruitment

By examining recruitment sources, a firm determines the location of potential job applicants. It then seeks to attract these applicants by specific recruitment methods. Some conventional external methods of recruitment are discussed next.

ADVERTISING

Advertising: A way of communicating the firm's employment needs to the public through media such as radio, newspaper, or industry publications.

Advertising communicates the firm's employment needs to the public through media such as radio, newspapers, television, and industry publications. Dorothy Bryant's method is a newspaper with a circulation in excess of 1,000,000. In determining the content of an advertising message, a firm must decide on the corporate image it wants to project. Obviously, the firm should give prospective employees an accurate picture of the job and the organization. Dorothy's ad did not provide an accurate picture of the job and was limited in other ways, including legal aspects and the use of subjective criteria. At the same time, the firm should attempt to appeal to the self-interest of prospective employees, emphasizing the job's unique qualities. The ad must tell potential employees why they should be interested in that particular job and organization. The message should also indicate how an applicant is to respond: apply in person, by telephone, or submit a resumé by fax or e-mail.

The firm's previous experience with various media should suggest the approach to be taken for specific types of jobs. A common form of advertising that provides broad coverage is the newspaper ad. The greatest problem with this method of external recruitment is the large number of unqualified individuals who respond to such ads. This situation increases the likelihood of poor selection decisions.

Although few base their decision to change jobs on advertising, an ad creates awareness, generates interest, and encourages a prospect to seek more information about the firm and the job opportunities it provides. Examination of the Sunday edition of any major newspaper reveals the extensive use of advertising in recruiting.

Certain media attract audiences that are more homogeneous in terms of employment skills, education, and orientation. Advertisements placed in such publications as the *Wall Street Journal* relate primarily to managerial, professional, and technical positions. The readers of these publications are generally individuals qualified for many of the positions advertised. Focusing on a specific labor market minimizes the likelihood of receiving marginally qualified or even totally unqualified applicants.

Virtually every professional group publishes a journal that is widely read by its members. Advertising for a marketing executive position in *Marketing Forum*, for example, would hit the target market because it is read almost exclusively by marketing professionals. Trade journals are also widely utilized. The use of journals does, however, present some problems. For example, they lack scheduling flexibility; their publishing deadlines may be weeks prior to the issue date and may be even further in advance for four-color material. Staffing needs cannot always be anticipated far in advance, so the use of journals for recruitment obviously has limitations.

Qualified prospects who read job ads in newspapers and professional and trade journals may not be so dissatisfied with their present jobs that they will pursue opportunities advertised. Therefore, in high demand situations, a firm needs to consider all available media resources.

Other conventional media that can also be used include radio, billboards, and television. These methods are likely to be more expensive than newspapers or journals, but they have been used with success in specific situations. For instance, a regional medical center used billboards successfully to attract registered nurses. One large manufacturing firm achieved considerable success in advertising for production trainees by means of spot advertisements on the radio. A large electronics firm used television to attract experienced engineers when it opened a new facility and needed more engineers immediately. Thus, in situations where hiring needs are urgent, television and radio may provide good results even though these media may not be sufficient by themselves. Broadcast messages can let people know that an organization is seeking recruits. They are, however, limited in the amount of information they can transmit. Advertising jobs on the Internet does not have such a limitation. Although it is a relatively new approach, this medium offers great potential as an advertising channel and is discussed later in the chapter.

EMPLOYMENT AGENCIES — PRIVATE AND PUBLIC

Employment agency: An organization that assists firms in recruiting employees and also aids individuals in their attempts to locate jobs.

An **employment agency** is an organization that helps firms recruit employees and, at the same time, aids individuals in their attempts to locate jobs. These agencies perform many recruitment and selection functions that have proven quite beneficial to many organizations.

Private employment agencies: Agencies utilized by firms for virtually every type of position; best known for recruiting white-collar employees.

Private employment agencies are utilized by firms to help fill virtually every type of position. However, they are best known for recruiting white-collar employees and offer an important service in bringing qualified applicants and open positions together. They should not be overlooked by either the organization or the job applicant. Candidates are often turned off by the one-time fees that some agencies charge. However, other private employment agencies deal primarily with firms that pay the fees.

Public employment agencies: Employment agencies that are operated by each state but receive overall policy direction from the U.S. Employment Service; best known for recruiting and placing individuals in operative jobs.

The **public employment agencies** operated by each state receive overall policy direction from the U.S. Employment Service. Public employment agencies are best known for recruiting and placing individuals in operative jobs, but they have become increasingly involved in matching people with technical, professional, and managerial positions. Some public agencies use computerized job matching systems to aid in the recruitment process. Public employment agencies provide their services without charge to either the employer or the prospective employee.

RECRUITERS

The most common use of recruiters is with technical and vocational schools, community colleges, colleges, and universities. After a decline of nearly two decades, campus recruitment is on the rise nationwide. A recent survey found that each responding firm recruited from an average of 30 schools in 1995; this is double the number of schools visited in 1993.[14] The key contact for recruiters on college and university campuses is often the director of student placement. This administrator is in an excellent position to arrange interviews with students possessing the qualifications desired by the firm. Placement services help organizations use their recruiters efficiently. Qualified candidates are identified, interviews are scheduled, and suitable rooms are provided for interviews.

The company recruiter plays a vital role in attracting applicants. The interviewee often perceives the recruiter's actions as a reflection of the character of the firm. If the recruiter is dull, the interviewee may think the company dull; if the recruiter is apathetic, discourteous, or vulgar, the interviewee may well attribute all these negative characteristics to the firm. Recruiters must always be aware of the image they present at the screening interview because it makes a lasting impression.

Some American firms have discovered an innovative use of recruiters. All it takes is a $5,000 computer system with a terminal at both corporate headquarters and on a college campus. Recruiters can communicate with college career counselors and interview students through a video conferencing system without leaving the office. Connie Thanasoulis-Cerrachio of Citibank states that "$1,000 versus the cost of $12 or $13 an interview is an amazing savings." According to Citibank, these systems have grown fivefold to more than 150 on campuses in the past year.[15]

SPECIAL EVENTS

Special events: A recruitment method that involves an effort on the part of a single employer or group of employers to attract a larger number of applicants for interviews.

Holding **special events** is a recruiting method that involves an effort by a single employer or group of employers to attract a large number of applicants for interviews. Job fairs, for example, are designed to bring together applicants and representatives of various companies. From an employer's viewpoint, a primary advantage of job fairs is the opportunity to meet a large

A primary advantage of job fairs is that they provide the employer with the opportunity to meet a large number of candidates in a short time.

number of candidates in a short time. More than a dozen commercial firms operate job fairs, but government agencies, charitable organizations, and business alliances also frequently sponsor them. As a recruitment method, job fairs offer the potential for a much lower cost per hire than traditional approaches.

INTERNSHIPS

Internship: A special form of recruitment that involves placing students in temporary jobs with no obligation either by the company to hire the student permanently or by the student to accept a permanent position with the firm following graduation.

An **internship** is a special form of recruiting in which a student is placed in a temporary job. In this arrangement, there is no obligation by the company to hire the student permanently or by the student to accept a permanent position with the firm following graduation. An internship typically involves a temporary job for the summer months or a part-time job during the school year. In many instances, students alternate their schedules by working full-time one semester and becoming full-time students the next. During the internship, the student gets to view business practices firsthand. At the same time, the intern contributes to the firm by performing needed tasks. Through this relationship, a student can determine whether a company would be a desirable employer. Similarly, having a relatively lengthy period of time to observe the student's job performance, the firm can make a better judgment regarding the person's qualifications. In addition to other benefits, internships provide opportunities for students to bridge the gap from business theory to practice.

Firms, including Andersen Consulting based in Chicago, have learned that student interns can also serve as effective recruiters. If the intern has a good experience, he or she will tell other students about it. Each year, Andersen employs more than 250 college interns—a number that represents 10 percent of the graduates Andersen hires annually for full-time employment.[16]

Internships are also an effective public relations tool, providing visibility for the company name and assisting in recruitment. Allstate Insurance

Company has carried the concept of internships one step further. Ken Marques, employment director for the firm, believes that internships can also be a strategic retention tool. He set a goal of hiring 60 percent of his company's entry-level staff from its internship program. He calls the program *the 10-week interview* and states that his firm prefers to have its turnover up front, eliminating the mismatches before the individuals are hired rather than two years later.[17]

EXECUTIVE SEARCH FIRMS

Executive search firms:
Organizations retained by a company to search for the most qualified executive available for a specific position.

Executive search firms may be used by organizations in their recruitment efforts to locate experienced professionals and executives when other sources prove inadequate. **Executive search firms** are organizations that seek the most qualified executive available for a specific position. They are generally retained by the companies needing specific types of individuals.

Executive search is a rapidly growing industry with estimated global revenue reaching $3.5 billion annually. The American market, which generates nearly $2 billion, is expected to grow by 10 percent to 12 percent each year. European revenues are expected to grow by around 30 percent and in Asia, the fastest growing market, revenues are set to rise by up to 40 percent.[18] The executive search industry has evolved from a basic recruitment service to a highly sophisticated profession serving a greatly expanded role. Search firms now assist organizations in determining their human resource needs, establishing compensation packages, and revising organizational structures.

An executive search firm's representatives often visit the client's offices and interview the company's management. This enables them to gain a clear understanding of the company's goals and the job qualifications required. After obtaining this information, they contact and interview potential candidates, check references, and refer the best-qualified person to the client for the selection decision. Search firms maintain databases of resumés that are used during this process. Other sources used include networking contacts, files from previous searches, specialized directories, personal calls, previous clients, colleagues, and unsolicited resumés. The search firm's fee is generally a percentage of the individual's compensation for the first year. Expenses, as well as the fee, are paid by the client.

The relationship between a client company and a search firm should be based on mutual trust and understanding. Both parties gain most from their relationship when they interact often and maintain good communication.[19] To be successful, the search firm must understand in detail the nature of the client's operations, the responsibilities of the position being filled, and the client's corporate culture. Similarly, the client must understand the search process, work with the consultant, and provide continuous, honest feedback.

PROFESSIONAL ASSOCIATIONS

Many functional business areas including finance, marketing, accounting, and human resource professional associations provide recruitment and placement services for their members. The Society for Human Resource Management, for example, operates a job referral service for members seeking new positions and employers with positions to fill.

EMPLOYEE REFERRALS

Many organizations have found that their employees can serve an important role in the recruitment process by actively soliciting applications from their friends and associates. One recent study involving over 200 human resource executives indicated that employee referrals, along with college recruiting and executive search firms, produced the best employees for their organizations.[20] For example, at NEC Technologies, hires from employee referrals rose from 15 percent to 52 percent within only a few years. This firm found that as referrals became their primary recruitment and retention approach, the costs previously incurred from advertising and using placement agencies were significantly reduced. With a goal not only to attract employees but also retain them, NEC discovered that this recruitment method results in effective employee/employer bonding.[21]

UNSOLICITED WALK-IN APPLICANTS

If an organization has the reputation of being a good place to work, it may be able to attract qualified prospects even without extensive recruitment efforts. Acting on their own initiative, well-qualified workers may seek out a specific company to apply for a job. Unsolicited applicants who apply because they are favorably impressed with the firm's reputation often prove to be valuable employees.

Innovative External Methods of Recruitment

Technology has also had an impact on how recruitment is conducted. Some of these ways include Internet recruiting, recruitment databases/automated applicant tracking systems, and virtual job fairs. In addition, sign-on bonuses are also being used.

INTERNET RECRUITING

Print advertising will probably not be abandoned soon. However, advertising job openings on the Internet is becoming increasingly popular. Recruiters may search a number of electronic mail bulletin boards and use their own firm's web page. A web page can be put up inexpensively compared to print, which must be paid for by the word and the length of time the ad appears in a publication. Job postings on the web page are easy to update and can be paid for with a flat fee for the site. Also, the firm may be able to attract individuals otherwise inaccessible. This includes, according to one executive, the passive job seekers—those who may be the best qualified but who are not presently looking for a job. Also, firms may be able to attract the attention of candidates worldwide. One small software firm, Geometrics Corporation, posted a listing for a software engineer on a worldwide electronic-mail bulletin board and received 200 resumés, some from as far away as Israel, Germany, and Hong Kong.[22] IBM, which hires between 1,500 and 1,600 college graduates a year, has created a web site it calls *Club Cyberblue*. This page is accessible 24 hours a day, seven days a week. The college page has generic company information rather than specific job postings. Interested candidates can find out when IBM recruitment activities will be held on their campus and get information concerning cooperative programs. The page also helps candidates prepare resumés by providing a standardized form that includes information important to the company.[23] According to one survey of 150 executives, a full 40 percent reported that they are using the Internet to snare new recruits.[24] This response is somewhat surprising considering the newness of the approach.

Another study found that 67 percent of HR professionals use the Internet as a recruitment tool. A majority of their firms began employing this alternative within the past year. However, although most respondents to this survey plan to continue using the Internet, the HR professionals included are generally only moderately satisfied with it as a recruitment method. The same study concluded that a relatively small number of positions are currently being filled through the Internet and that both newspaper advertisements and executive recruiters are usually more effective for recruiting potential employees.[25] Nevertheless, expanded use of the Internet by employers and job seekers alike is a certainty. Candidates for employment, especially those with technical skills, will continue to explore the web for job possibilities. The most commonly used web sites are shown in Figure 6-4.

Impressive results using the Internet for recruiting are not achieved by simply posting jobs and waiting for applicants to e-mail resumés. Silicon Graphics, a California-based manufacturer of computer workstations, created a site that's both enticing and fruitful. Their site has many jazzy graphics and games and a benefits page that describes what the company has to offer. In addition, a College Connection page includes a resumé builder, a list of job fairs, and an explanation of the company's philosophy and culture.[26]

The caveat to Internet recruiting is to be sure not to let the web page become outdated. An incomplete page or obsolete web address is sure to present a negative view of the firm.[27]

HOST WEB SITES

CareerWeb	**Monster Board**
careerweb.com	monsterboard.com
E-Span	**Online Career Center**
espan.com	occ.com
Intellimatch	**Diversity Virtual Job Fair**
intellimatch.com	jwtworks.com/dvjf

Figure 6-4
Most Commonly Used Web Sites for Employers and Job Seekers

Source: "Networking '97: A Research Study on Employment and the Internet," *JWT Specialized Communications* (1997): 3.

TRENDS & INNOVATIONS

REAL-TIME RECRUITMENT

Relaxing on the deck of his beach hotel in Cancun, Mexico, Jack Hicks is job hunting using his personal digital assistant (PDA) linked by a satellite to various electronic professional job posting services. Hicks, a petroleum engineer, is enjoying a three-week vacation after a fairly long period of employment with a Saudi-based oil company. He is a professional contract employee working on a just-in-time basis rather than being a permanent employee of one firm. Just before completing each free-lance assignment Hicks posts his resumé, compensation requirements, and availability date on the electronic bulletin board of his professional engineering organization. Very much like the various electronic professional job posting services, this bulletin board also serves as a global link for employers and job seekers.

Guy Newman, vice president of Explore All Recovery, needs to assemble a joint U.S.-Canadian-Russian team of engineers to recover oil reserves from Siberian oil fields. Newman is seeking the remaining specialist needed for the team with specialized software capable of searching on-line databases for key words related to job experience and training. Once individuals with the needed specialties are isolated from databases of various bulletin boards and electronic job posting services, they are downloaded into Newman's desktop computer. Newman then reviews the various matches and identifies individuals who have the skills and experiences needed, have reasonable compensation requirements, and are available immediately. Hicks's resumé is directly in line with Newman's needs and he was familiar with Hicks's excellent reputation. In addition, Hicks had experience working in the inhospitable conditions of Siberia.

Newman e-mails Hicks indicating a strong interest in working with him on the upcoming Siberian project. The e-mail reaches Hicks, who is still relaxing in his lounge chair. Hicks is interested in the Siberian project, also having heard good things about Newman. Hicks uses his PDA to call Newman and leaves a voice-mail message indicating his strong interest. Newman e-mails Hicks an employment contract via his PDA. Newman and Hicks discuss the possibilities, utilizing their visual/voice/data link capabilities. Several contractual changes are made and Hicks initials them on screen. Both Hicks and Newman sign the revised contract with their styluses, completing the deal. Newman goes back to work assembling the remaining team members while Hicks heads back to the beach.[28]

RECRUITMENT DATABASES/AUTOMATED APPLICANT TRACKING SYSTEMS

Computers have greatly facilitated many HRM functions, a trend that is sure to accelerate. Resumé databases have already begun to shape the way college recruitment is approached. By using a database system, recruiters can receive copies of students' resumés before they visit the campus. This makes college recruitment much more effective. Schools offering the most promising prospects can be determined as well as the specific students the recruiter wishes to interview.[29] Firms continue to seek ways to cut costs and universities strive to secure more jobs for their students.

The size of databases operated by several independent networks continues to grow as some firms downsize and others become more aware of what computers can do. Others offer resumé banks of individuals at all career levels in a wide variety of fields. Central databases can be accessed by corporate clients using their own personal computers. When a candidate's background matches an open position, the client may obtain a copy of the resumé to review. The process of matching candidates with positions dramatically reduces paperwork costs. For example, a job search through a national database firm may cost less than $1,000. An executive search firm, on the other hand, normally charges about one-third of the candidate's first-year salary and bonus.[30] The cost and time efficiency of databases may make some recruiting methods obsolete, but they will not completely replace currently used systems. For example, searches for CEOs will always be politically sensitive and require special handling.

Internal databases make automated applicant tracking systems possible. In an automated system, information can be drawn from a firm's database to produce fast and accurate requisitions. Next, applicant information can be accessed from the database. In seconds, the few individuals who meet specific selection criteria can be identified from a group of many applicants. The selection procedure, discussed in the next chapter, can also be facilitated. With a few simple keystrokes, managers can get a detailed picture of each candidate's background.

An automated tracking system streamlines the recruitment process and permits managers to spend more time finding high-quality candidates. A firm gains a sophisticated means of handling all steps of the process, from generating routine correspondence to tracking requisitions and scheduling interviews. Such a system provides detailed documentation of hiring practices and is a tremendous help in meeting EEO guidelines.

HR Web Wisdom

http://www.prenhall.com/mondy

CYBER FAIR REVIEW
An example of an on-line virtual job fair is reviewed.

VIRTUAL JOB FAIRS

Virtual job fair: A recruitment method in which students meet recruiters face-to-face in interviews conducted over special computers that have lenses that transmit head-and-shoulder images of both parties.

In a **virtual job fair** students meet recruiters face-to-face in interviews conducted over special computers; which have lenses that transmit head-and-shoulder images of both parties. This recruitment method is a project of VIEWnet Inc., producer of the technology, and career centers in 21 universities from the Atlantic Coast and Southeastern Conferences. In what was advertised as the nation's first Virtual Job Fair, recruiters at 20 major corporations, after reviewing 12,000 resumés, chose 1,000 students to interview for 300 jobs. The recruiters can visit all schools without having to leave their offices.[31]

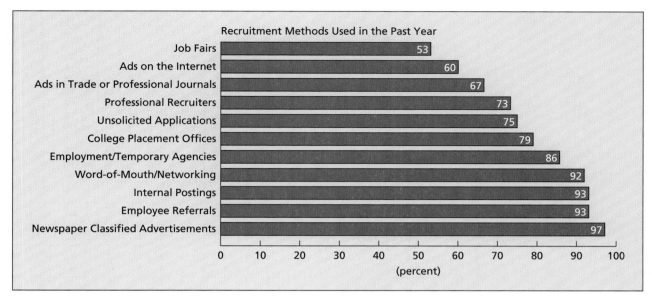

Figure 6-5
Currently Used Recruitment Methods

Source: "Networking '97: A Research Study on Employment and the Internet," *JWT Specialized Communications* (1997): 14.

SIGN-ON BONUSES

As mentioned in chapter 2, some firms are following the practice of the sports industry by offering sign-on bonuses to high-demand prospects. This strategy is especially prevalent in industries with severe shortages of highly skilled workers, such as information systems workers. As discussed in chapter 12, lump-sum payments have broad appeal because they provide a way for companies to compensate employees (in this case recruit them) while controlling fixed pay rates.[32]

As the preceding sections indicate, a number of recruitment methods are used by organizations to attract applicants. One national survey of HR professionals revealed the extent to which these methods are currently used. Figure 6-5 shows that newspaper classified advertisements are used by virtually every firm included in the survey. Although ads on the Internet are used less frequently than all others except for job fairs, the rapid increase in use of the Internet will surely change these data—and rather quickly.

Tailoring Recruitment Methods to Sources

Each organization is unique in many ways, so the types and qualifications of workers needed to fill positions vary greatly. Thus, to be successful, recruitment must be tailored to the needs of each firm. In addition, recruitment sources and methods often vary according to the type of position being filled.

	Advertising	Private employment agencies	Public employment agencies	Recruiters	Special events	Internships	Executive search firms	Unsolicited applications	Professional associations	Employee referrals	Unsolicited applicants	Automated applicant tracking system	Resume databases
High schools													
Vocational schools													
Community colleges													
Colleges and universities													
Competitors and other firms	X	X					X		X				
Unemployed													
Self-employed													

Figure 6-6
Methods and Sources of Recruitment for an Information Systems Manager

Figure 6-6 shows a matrix of the methods and sources of recruitment for an information systems manager. Managers must first identify the *source* (where prospective employees are) before choosing the *methods* (how to get them). Suppose, for example, that a large firm has an immediate need for an accounting manager with a minimum of five years' experience, and no one within the firm has these qualifications. It is most likely that such an individual is employed by another firm, very possibly a competitor, or is self-employed. After considering the recruitment source, the recruiter must then choose the method (or methods) of recruitment that offers the best prospects for attracting qualified candidates. Perhaps the job can be advertised in the classified section of the *Wall Street Journal*, *National Employment Weekly*, or *The CPA Journal*. Alternatively, an executive search firm may be used to locate qualified candidates. In addition, the recruiter may attend meetings of professional accounting associations. One or more of these methods will likely yield a pool of qualified applicants.

In another scenario, consider a firm's need for 20 entry-level machine operators whom the firm is willing to train. High schools and vocational schools would probably be good recruitment sources. Methods of recruitment might include running newspaper ads, working through public employment agencies, sending recruiters to vocational schools, and encouraging employee referrals.

The specific recruitment methods used will be affected by external environmental factors, including market supply and job requirements. Each organization should maintain employment records and conduct its own research to determine which recruitment sources and methods are most appropriate under various circumstances. Studies show that firms that conduct internal studies of recruitment effectiveness are significantly more profitable than those that do not.[33]

Recruitment for Diversity

Equal opportunity legislation outlaws discrimination in employment based on race, gender, disability, and other factors. Some firms abide by the law solely to avoid the legal consequences of violating these laws. Others, however, also recognize the inherent advantages of heterogeneous groups, the creativity they possess, and the ability they bring to a firm in expanding its customer base. Global competition mandates that firms be innovative. Therefore, forward-thinking organizations actively engage in acquiring a workforce that reflects society and helps the company expand into untapped markets.[34] To accomplish this objective, firms may need to use nontraditional recruitment approaches.

Because of past unequal opportunity, women, minorities, and individuals with disabilities may not respond to traditional recruitment methods. These groups may be omitted altogether from the typical recruitment process unless specific action is taken to attract them. Therefore, any organization that seeks diversity must implement recruitment and other employment programs that assure women, minorities, and those with disabilities of inclusion in decision-making processes. Otherwise, organizations will overlook a great deal of much needed talent.

ANALYSIS OF RECRUITMENT PROCEDURES

To ensure that its recruitment program is oriented toward diversity, a firm must analyze its recruitment procedures. For example, a wise move might be to reconsider the use of employee referrals or unsolicited applicants as primary recruitment methods. Most referrals from an organization consisting

HRM IN ACTION
ONLY ABLE-BODIED MEN?

Mark Smith and Debra Coffee, two executives from competing firms, met at their annual professional conference. They were discussing the effect of the Americans with Disabilities Act on their firms. Mark said, "I don't think we will have any difficulty at our company. We don't employ any handicapped people. All our production jobs require able-bodied men."

"Have you considered making reasonable accommodations for applicants with disabilities?" Debra asked.

After thinking a moment, Mark replied, "I don't believe so, Debra. You see, our executive group is very pleased with the productivity in our plant. I really don't think they want to fix something that isn't broke."

How would you respond?

primarily of white males would likely be more white males. If so, this behavior would perpetuate the composition of the organization's workforce. To support this assumption, in cases where minorities and women are not well represented at all levels, the courts have ruled that reliance on these particular practices is discriminatory.

In identifying sources of continuing discrimination, a helpful approach is to develop a *record of applicant flow*. This record may be mandatory if the firm has been found guilty of discrimination or operates under an affirmative action program. An applicant flow record includes personal and job-related data about each applicant. It indicates whether a job offer was extended and, if no such offer was made, an explanation of the decision. Such records enable the organization to analyze its recruitment and selection practices and take corrective action when necessary.

UTILIZATION OF MINORITIES, WOMEN, AND INDIVIDUALS WITH DISABILITIES

Recruiters should be trained in the use of objective, job-related standards because these individuals occupy a unique position in terms of encouraging or discouraging minorities, women, and the disabled to apply for jobs. Qualified members of these groups may be used effectively in key recruitment activities, such as visiting schools and colleges and participating in career days. They are also in an excellent position to provide valuable input for recruitment planning and can effectively serve as referral sources. Pictures of minority, women, and disabled employees in help-wanted advertisements and company brochures give credibility to the message, "We are an equal opportunity employer."

ADVERTISING

With few exceptions, jobs must be open to all individuals. Therefore, gender-segregated ads, for example, must not be used unless gender is a bona fide occupational qualification (BFOQ). The BFOQ exception provided in Title VII of the Civil Rights Act requires that qualifications be job related. This definition is narrowly interpreted by EEOC and the courts. The burden of proof is on the employer to show that the requirements are essential for successful performance of the job. Dorothy may have a problem with her ad specifying someone with a *good appearance*, as this criterion is subjective and may not be job related. Other advertising practices designed to provide equal opportunity include these:

- Ensuring that the content of advertisements does not indicate preference for any race, gender, or age, or that these factors are a qualification for the job.
- Utilizing media that are directed toward minorities, such as appropriate radio stations.
- Emphasizing the intent to recruit without regard to race, gender, or disabled status by including the phrase EEO/AA/ADA (Equal Employment Opportunity, Affirmative Action, and American with Disabilities) in job ads (see Figure 6-7).

Corporate Controller

Sureway Development Company offers an outstanding opportunity in its Financial Analysis Division for a Certified Public Accountant (CPA). A minimum of 4 years' experience in financial analysis and budgeting is required. Real estate development experience preferred.

For confidential consideration, mail, fax, or e-mail your resumé to Sureway Development Co., Box 1951, Dayton, OH 45401

Toll Free Fax: 1-888-760-9151 or e-mail: Sureway@realest.com

An Equal Employment Opportunity Employer EEO/AA/ADA

Figure 6-7
A Newspaper Ad
Stressing Equal
Employment Opportunity

EMPLOYMENT AGENCIES

An organization should emphasize its nondiscriminatory recruitment practices when utilizing employment agencies. Even when a business works with private agencies, which are also covered under Title VII, jobs at all levels should be listed with the state employment service. These agencies can provide valuable assistance to organizations seeking to fulfill diversity goals. In addition, agencies and consultant firms that specialize in minority and women applicants should be contacted.

OTHER SUGGESTED RECRUITMENT APPROACHES

Personal contact should be made with counselors and administrators at high schools, vocational schools, and colleges with large minority and/or female enrollments. Counselors and administrators should be made aware that the organization is actively seeking minorities, women, and disabled individuals for jobs they have not traditionally held. Also, counselors and administrators should be familiar with the types of jobs available and the training and education needed to perform these jobs. The possibilities for developing internships and summer employment should be carefully investigated. Firms should develop and maintain contacts with minority, women's, and other community organizations. These organizations include the National Association for the Advancement of Colored People (NAACP), the League of United Latin American Citizens, the National Urban League, the American Association of University Women, the Federation of Business and Professional Women's Talent Bank, the National Council of Negro Women, and the Veterans Administration. The EEOC's regional offices will assist employers in locating appropriate local agencies.

A GLOBAL PERSPECTIVE

Understand the Global Workforce for Effective Worldwide Recruitment

Global recruitment is vital if U.S. firms are to be successful internationally. Unfortunately, competition for qualified workers in the international labor market is just as intense as it is in the product market. To be effective, global

HR professionals must understand the demographics and variances in the international labor force as well as the needs of each separate operation. These include skill deficiencies and skills training, labor shortages and surpluses, unemployment rates, layoffs, wage rates, and education.

Recruiting the most productive employees requires an acute understanding of all segments of the global workforce. For example, workers throughout the world, particularly those in industrialized countries, expect more flexibility in their work schedules. In many countries, part-time and temporary work, flexible schedules, and working at home are growing in popularity as the workforce prefers more flexible forms of employment. When recruiting in this type of environment, organizations must be as accommodating as possible.[35]

The most formidable task facing many global firms is the recruitment and development of a cadre of employees who can operate effectively in the global market environment. Unfortunately, there is an unwillingness to recruit and develop women internationally. This is of particular concern because recent research suggests that women are more sensitive to cultural differences and are, therefore, often better able to work effectively in other countries. Human resource professionals must be sure they do not ignore any portion of the labor pool or they will not be able to recruit effectively worldwide.[36] However, even when women are assigned overseas, their path to success is often more difficult than the way for their male counterparts. Women managers expatriated to Asia may find themselves doing business in cultures in which women are secondary to men and do not have equal status in the workplace. In Japan, for example, sexual harassment, withholding paychecks, and breaking contracts are common treatment of women, even at the managerial level.

Even with these impediments, possibly the biggest drawback for businesswomen in Japan is that they cannot participate on an equal footing in after-hours activities. The *social grease* of Japanese business is harder for women to access. Still, acceptance of women in Asian business is growing, and as economies develop, there will be an even greater need for the best and brightest regardless of gender.[37]

SUMMARY

1. *Define* **recruitment.**
   Recruitment is the process of attracting individuals on a timely basis, in sufficient numbers, and with appropriate qualifications, and encouraging them to apply for jobs with an organization.

2. *Identify alternatives that a firm might consider before resorting to outside recruitment.*
   Alternatives include outsourcing, contingent workers, employee leasing, and overtime.

3. *Describe the recruitment process.*
   Frequently recruitment begins when a manager initiates an employee requisition. Next, determine whether qualified employees are available

within the firm (the internal source) or must be recruited externally from sources such as colleges, universities, and other firms. Sources are where qualified individuals are located, and methods are the specific means to attract potential employees to the firm. Once the sources of potential employees are isolated, appropriate methods for either internal or external recruiting are used to accomplish recruitment goals.

4. *Define* **promotion from within.**

A policy that stresses promotion from within its own ranks.

5. *Explain and describe internal recruitment methods.*

A management inventory is a file that contains detailed data regarding each manager and is used to identify individuals with the potential to move into higher level positions. A skills inventories is a file that contains data regarding nonmanagerial employees' abilities. Job posting is a method of internal recruitment that is used to communicate that job openings exist. Job bidding is a system that permits individuals in an organization to apply for a specific job within the firm.

6. *Identify external sources of recruitment.*

External sources of recruitment include high schools and vocational schools, community colleges, colleges and universities, competitors and other firms, unemployed, older individuals, military personnel, and self-employed workers.

7. *Identify the external methods of recruitment.*

External methods of recruitment include advertising, employment agencies, recruiters, special events, internships, executive search firms, professional associations, employee referrals, unsolicited applicants, resumé databases/automated applicant tracking systems, the Internet, virtual job fairs, and sign-on bonuses.

8. *Explain what needs to be accomplished to recruit for diversity.*

To ensure that an organization's recruitment program is nondiscriminatory, the firm must analyze its recruitment procedures. Each individual who engages in recruitment should be trained in the use of objective, job-related standards. With few exceptions, jobs must be open to all individuals. When placing job orders with employment agencies, an organization should emphasize its nondiscriminatory recruitment practices. Organizations engaged in affirmative recruitment should develop contacts with minority, women's, and other community organizations.

QUESTIONS FOR REVIEW

1. What are some actions that can be taken prior to engaging in recruitment?
2. Describe the basic components of the recruitment process.
3. List and discuss the various external and internal factors that may affect recruitment.
4. What is meant by the term *internal recruitment*? Describe the advantages and disadvantages of internal recruitment.

5. Describe the methods commonly used in internal recruitment. Briefly define each.
6. Discuss the reasons for an external recruitment program.
7. Distinguish between sources and methods of external recruitment.
8. Describe the various conventional methods of external recruitment.
9. Describe the various innovative methods of external recruitment.
10. How can a firm improve its recruiting efforts to achieve diversity?

DEVELOPING HRM SKILLS

AN EXPERIENTIAL EXERCISE

Human resource managers often have the responsibility for preparing job descriptions. From these job descriptions, profiles of the types of individuals needed to fill various positions in the firm can be developed and recruitment efforts can be designed. The human resource manager must determine where the best applicants are located (recruitment sources) and how to entice them to join the organization (recruitment methods). This exercise is designed to provide an understanding of the relationship between recruitment sources and methods.

Participants will attempt to determine the most appropriate recruitment sources and methods for the job description that will be given to them. Your instructor will provide the participants with additional information necessary to complete the exercise.

 Take It to the Net

We invite you to visit the Mondy home page on the Prentice Hall Web site at:

http://www.prenhall.com/mondy

for updated information, Web-based exercises, and links to other HR-related sites.

HRM SIMULATION

*I*ncident C in the *Simulation Players Manual* involves recruiting for temporary positions. Your organization has been instructed by a customer (or client) to augment your product (or service) for the next quarter's production. No additional units are to be produced, but you need to do the work according to the customer/client's specific instructions. This will require the addition of 50 employees for only one quarter. Your team must recommend which recruitment method should be used to handle this temporary situation.

HRM INCIDENT 1
Right Idea, Wrong Song

*R*obert Key is a human resource manager at Epler Manufacturing Company in Greenfield, Wisconsin. He was considering the need to recruit qualified blacks for Epler when Betty Alexander walked into his office. "Got a minute?" asked Betty. "I need to talk to you about the recruiting trip to Michigan State next week."

"Sure," Robert replied, "but first, I need your advice about something. How can we get more blacks to apply for work here? We're running ads on WBEZ radio along with the classified ads in the *Tribune*. I think you and John have made recruiting trips to every community college within 200 miles. We've encouraged employee referral, too, and I still think that's our most reliable source of new workers. But we just aren't getting any black applicants."

From the president on down, the management at Epler claimed commitment to equal employment opportunity. According to Robert, the commitment went much deeper than posting the usual posters and filing an affirmative action program with the federal government. However, the percentage of black employees at Epler remained at only 5 percent although the surrounding community was 11 percent black. Epler paid competitive wages and had a good training program.

Epler had a particular need for machine operator trainees. The machines were not difficult to operate, and no special educational requirement was needed for the job. There were also several clerical and management trainee positions open.

Question
1. Evaluate the current recruitment effort. How could Robert better the firm's goal of equal employment?

HRM INCIDENT 2
A Dilemma

*A*s the human resource director for KBH Stores in St. Louis, Missouri, Virginia Knickerbocker knew that she had her work cut out for her. Company management had just announced a goal of opening 10 new stores during the next 12 months. KBH employed 480 people in the 35 stores they had in operation. Virginia knew that staffing the new stores would require hiring and training about 150 people. She felt that her own small office was inadequately funded and staffed to handle this task.

Virginia found out about the expansion plans from a friend who knew the president's secretary. Although she did not like being kept in the dark, she was not surprised that she had not been told. Glenn Sullivan, the president of KBH, was noted for his autocratic leadership style. He tended to tell subordinates only what he wanted them to know. He expected everyone who worked for him to follow orders without question. He was not an unkind person, though, and Virginia had always gotten along with him pretty well. She had never confronted Mr. Sullivan about anything, so it was with some concern that she approached his office that day.

"Mr. Sullivan," she began, "I hear that we are going to be opening 10 new stores next year."

"That's right, Virginia," said Mr. Sullivan. "We've already arranged the credit lines and have picked out several of the sites."

"What about staffing?" asked Virginia.

"Well, I presume that you will take care of that, Virginia, when we get to that point."

"What about my own staff?" asked Virginia. "I think I am going to need at least three or four more people. We are already crowded for space, so I hope you plan to expand the office."

"Not really," said Mr. Sullivan. "You will have to get by with what you have for at least a year or so. It's going to be hard enough to afford the new stores and the people we need to staff them without spending money for more office space."

Questions
1. What recruiting sources and methods should Virginia use? Explain.
2. Describe the elements of the internal environment that the case highlights. How does each affect Virginia?

Notes

1. "HR-Executive Review: Outsourcing HR Services," *The Conference Board* 1 (1994): 3.
2. Ibid.
3. Allison Thomson, "The Contingent Workforce," *Occupational Outlook Quarterly* (Spring 1995): 46.
4. Cassandra Hayes and Charlene Solomon, "The Lure of Temping," *Black Enterprise* 26 (February 1996): 120–122.
5. Allan Harcrow, "The Changing Workforce," *Workforce Tools* (Supplement to the January 1997 Issue, *Workforce*): 5–6.
6. Jay Finegan, "Look Before You Lease," *Inc* 19 (February 1997): 106.
7. Steve Mamarchev, "Think Like a Marketing Pro," *HR Focus* 73 (October 1996): 9.
8. Martha I. Finney, "Playing a Different Tune: Using the Hidden Assets of Employees," *HRMagazine* 41 (December 1996): 73.
9. Dale D. Buss, "Help Wanted Desperately," *Nation's Business* 84 (April 1996): 17–19.
10. Ken Dubrowski, "What Employers Can and Cannot Ask," *HR Focus* 72 (June 1995): 3.
11. John Templeton and David Woodruff, "The Aftershock from the Lopez Affair," *Business Week* (April 19, 1993): 31.
12. Stephanie Overman, "Myths Hinder Hiring of Older Workers," *HRMagazine* 38 (June 1993): 51.
13. Stephanie Overman, "Heroes for Hire," *HRMagazine* 38 (December 1993): 61–62.
14. Shannon Peters Talbott, "Boost Your Campus Image to Attract Top Grads," *Personnel Journal* 75 (March 1996): 6.

15. Fred Katayama, (1997) "Recruiting in the 90s," *CNNfn, Digital Jam,* httP://cnnfn.com/digitaljam/9701/29/job_pkg/index.htm (24 May 1997).
16. Talbott, "Boost Your Campus Image to Attract Top Grads."
17. Mary E. Scott, "Internships Add Value to College Recruitment," *Personnel Journal* 71 (April 1992): 25.
18. Bob Curley, "Don't Call Us . . . ," *Economist* 337 (January 1995): 71–72.
19. Paul DiMarchi, "The Two Faces of Search Firms," *Financial Executive* 10 (January–February 1994): 53.
20. David E. Terpstra, "The Search for Effective Methods," *HR Focus* 73 (May 1996): 16.
21. Albert H. McCarthy, "The Human Touch Helps Recruit Quality Workers," *Personnel Journal* 70 (November 1991): 68.
22. Molly Klimas, "How to Recruit a Smart Team," *Nation's Business* 83 (May 1995): 26.
23. Samantha Drake, "HR Departments Are Exploring the Internet," *HRMagazine* 41 (December 1996): 53.
24. "Recruiting On-Line," Hr News Capsules *HR Focus* 73 (December 1996): 6.
25. "Networking '97: A Research Study on Employment and the Internet, *JWT Specialized Communications* (1997): 4.
26. Samuel Greengard, "Leverage the Power of the Internet," *Workforce* 76 (March 1997): 78.
27. Samantha Drake, "HR Departments Are Exploring the Internet," *HRMagazine* 41 (December 1996): 53–56.
28. Adapted from Lyle M. Spencer, Jr., *Reengineering Human Resources* (New York: Wiley, 1995): 6–7.
29. Bill Leonard, "Resumé Databases to Dominate Field," *HRMagazine* 38 (April 1993): 59–60.
30. Barbara Hetzer, "Personal Business: Careers: When the Headhunter Comes Calling," *Business Week* (May 5, 1997): 40.
31. Beth Ashley, "Job Interview Come to Cyberspace," *USA Today,* http://wsf2.usa today.com/life/cyber/tech/ct351.htm (30 May 1997).
32. Carrie Mason-Draffen, "Companies Find New Ways to Pay/Workers' Performance Tied to Stock Options, Bonuses, Raises," *Newsday* (January 5, 1997): F08.
33. Terpstra, "The Search for Effective Methods."
34. Jim Roberts, "Workforce Diversity Helping Companies Boost Bottom Line," *Fairfield County Business Journal* 34 (December 11, 1995): 8.
35. David Cherrington and Laura Middleton, "An Introduction to Global Business Issues," *HRMagazine* 40 (June 1995): 124.
36. Hugh Scullion, "Attracting Management Globetrodders," *Personnel Management* 24 (January 1992): 28–32.
37. Clifford C. Hebard, "Managing Effectively in Asia," *Training & Development* 50 (April 1996): 34.

7
Selection

CHAPTER OBJECTIVES

1. Define *selection*.
2. Identify the environmental factors that affect the selection process.
3. Describe the general selection process.
4. Explain the importance of the preliminary interview.
5. Identify the types of questions that should be asked on an application form.
6. Describe the basic conditions that should be met if selection tests are to be used in the screening process.
7. Explain the types of validation studies.
8. Describe types of employment tests.
9. Identify the types of information that should be gained from the interview.
10. Describe the basic types of interviewing.
11. Describe the various methods of interviewing.
12. Define a *realistic job preview*.
13. Explain the legal implications of interviewing.
14. Explain why reference checks and background investigations are conducted.
15. Explain negligent hiring and retention.
16. Explain the reasons for preemployment physical examinations.

*B*ill Jenkins is the printing shop owner/ manager of Quality Printing Company. Because of an increase in business, shop employees have been working overtime for almost a month. Last week, Bill put an ad in the newspaper to hire a printer. Three people applied for the job. Bill considered only one of them, Mark Ketchell, to be qualified. Bill called Mark's previous employer in Detroit, who responded, "Mark is a diligent, hardworking person. He is as honest as the day is long. He knows his trade, too." Bill also found that Mark had left Detroit after he was divorced a few months ago and that his work had deteriorated slightly prior to the divorce. The next day, Bill asked Mark to operate one of the printing presses. Mark did so competently, and Bill immediately decided to hire him.

Mary Howard is the shipping supervisor for McCarty-Holman Warehouse, a major food distributor. One of Mary's truck drivers just quit. She spoke to the human resource manager, Tom Sullivan, who said that he would begin the search right away. The next day an ad appeared in the local paper for the position. Tom considered three of the 15 applicants to be qualified and called them in for an initial interview. The next morning Tom called Mary and said, "I have three drivers who look like they can do the job. When do you want me to set up an interview for you with them? I guess you'll want to give them a driving test at that time."

Mary interviewed the three drivers and gave them each a driving test; then she called Tom to tell him her choice. The next day the new driver reported to Mary for work.

*T*hese incidents provide only a brief look at the all-important selection process. In the first case, Bill, as owner/manager of a small printing shop, handled the entire selection process himself. In the second case, Tom, the human resource manager, was heavily involved in the selection process, but Mary, the shipping supervisor, made the actual decision. However, knowledge of the selection process was important in both situations.

We begin the chapter by discussing the significance of employee selection and the environmental factors that affect it. Then we describe the selection process, the preliminary interview, and review of the application and resume for employment. Next, we cover administration of selection tests and types of validity studies and employment tests. In the ensuing sections, we present the employment interview, the types of interviews, and methods of interviewing. We follow those topics with a discussion of the legal implications of interviewing, reference checks, background investigations, negligent hiring and retention, and polygraph tests. We then describe factors related to the selection decision, physical examination, and notification of acceptance or rejection of job applicants.

HR Web Wisdom

http://www.prenhall.com/mondy

PRESCREENING

Prescreening for a productive, dependable, customer- and sales-oriented workforce is briefly reviewed.

The Significance of Employee Selection

Selection: The process of choosing from a group of applicants those individuals best suited for a particular position and an organization.

Whereas recruitment encourages individuals to seek employment with a firm, the purpose of the selection process is to identify and employ the best qualified individuals for specific positions. **Selection** is the process of choosing from a group of applicants the individual best suited for a particular position and an organization. As you might expect, a firm's recruitment success has a significant impact on the quality of the selection decision. The organization may be forced to employ marginally qualified workers if recruitment efforts do not produce some highly qualified applicants. There are many ways to improve productivity, but none is more powerful than making the right hiring decision. Superior performers are often two or three times more productive than those who are barely acceptable.[1] A firm that selects qualified employees can reap substantial benefits, and these may be repeated every year the employee is on the payroll.

Most managers recognize employee selection as one of their most difficult and most important business decisions. Peter Drucker has stated, "No other decisions are so long lasting in their consequences or so difficult to unmake. And yet, by and large, executives make poor promotion and staffing decisions."[2] However, if a firm hires too many mediocre or poor performers, it cannot be successful long, even if it has perfect plans, a sound organizational structure, and finely tuned control systems. These organizational factors are not self-actuating. Competent people must be available to ensure that organizational goals are attained. Today, with many firms having access to the same technology, it is the people who make the real difference. An organization's distinctive advantage has become increasingly grounded in its human resources.[3]

As mentioned in chapter 2, small businesses, more than any other type, cannot afford to make hiring mistakes. An incompetent person's foul-up in a large firm may have insignificant consequences. However, a similar error in the small company may have devastating effects. In the smaller, less specialized firm, each person typically accounts for a larger part of the business's activity.[4] Bill Jenkins's small print shop business could suffer greatly if Bill selects an incompetent printing press operator. The impact of Mary's hiring one less competent driver would probably have a lesser effect on McCarty-Holman Warehouse's entire operation.

The selection process affects, and is also affected by, the other HR functions. For instance, if the selection process only provides the firm with marginally qualified workers, the organization may have to intensify its training efforts. If the compensation package is inferior to those provided by the firm's competition, attracting the best-qualified applicants may be difficult or impossible.

The goal of the selection process is to make a proper match of people with jobs and the organization. If individuals are overqualified, underqualified, or for any reason do not *fit* either the job or organization, they will probably leave the firm. In fact, a large percent of all U.S. workers have been in their jobs for less than two years.

Although some turnover may be positive for an organization, a high turnover rate makes achieving superior performance almost impossible. For example, product research and development is delayed, manufacturing loses efficiency, and marketing penetration is slowed. These hidden consequences of turnover, not the visible costs of recruitment, relocation, and training, constitute the major costs. Two studies conducted almost a decade apart indicate that such expenses, although they are rarely measured, account for 80 percent or more of turnover costs.[5] Turnover in Bill Jenkins's small printing shop could be particularly costly because any turnover may well have a major impact on Bill's profitability, as small business profits are often quite sensitive to cost increases.

HR
Web
Wisdom

http://www.prenhall.com/mondy

SHRM–HR LINKS
This site covers various selection issues.

Environmental Factors Affecting the Selection Process

A standardized screening process that can be followed consistently would greatly simplify the selection process. However, circumstances may require exceptions to be made. The following section describes environmental factors that impact the selection process.

LEGAL CONSIDERATIONS

Human resource management is influenced by legislation, executive orders, and court decisions. Managers who hire employees must have extensive knowledge of the legal aspects of selection. They must see the relationship between useful and legally defensible selection tools. This necessity was highlighted in the chapter 3 section, "Employment Standards to Avoid." What makes good business sense is not at odds with the intent of federal legislation.

SPEED OF DECISION MAKING

The time available to make the selection decision can also have a major effect on the selection process. Suppose, for instance, that the production manager for a manufacturing firm comes to the human resource manager's office and says, "My only quality control inspectors just had a fight and both resigned. I can't operate until those positions are filled." Speed is crucial in this instance, and two interviews, a few phone calls, and a prayer may constitute the entire selection process. Mary Howard needs a truck driver now; one just quit and someone must be found to drive the truck. Possibly, Bill Jenkins does not feel as much time pressure because other employees have been covering the vacant position for nearly a month by working overtime. On the other hand, selecting a chief executive officer in a national search may take an entire year. In this case, considerable attention may be devoted to a careful study of resumes, intensive reference checking, and hours of interviews.

Following selection policies and procedures closely always helps to provide protection against legal problems. However, at times, the pressure of business dictates that exceptions must be made.

ORGANIZATIONAL HIERARCHY

Different approaches to selection are generally taken for filling positions at varying levels in the organization. For instance, consider the differences in hiring a top-level executive and a person to fill a clerical position. Extensive background checks and interviewing would be conducted to verify the experience and capabilities of the applicant for the executive position. On the other hand, an applicant for a clerical position would most likely take only a word processing test and perhaps have a short employment interview.

APPLICANT POOL

The number of qualified applicants for a particular job can also affect the selection process. The process can be truly selective only if there are several qualified applicants for a particular position. However, only a few applicants with the required skills may be available. The selection process then becomes a matter of choosing whoever is at hand. Expansion and contraction of the labor market also exerts considerable influence on availability and, thus, the selection process. This was the problem confronting many businesses in the summer of 1997 when the unemployment rate was under 5 percent.

Selection ratio: The number of people hired for a particular job compared to the total number of individuals in the applicant pool.

The number of people hired for a particular job compared to the individuals in the applicant pool is often expressed as a **selection ratio**, or

$$\frac{\text{Selection}}{\text{Ratio}} = \frac{\text{Number of persons hired to fill a particular job}}{\text{Number of available applicants}}$$

A selection ratio of 1.00 indicates that there is only one qualified applicant for each position. An effective selection process is impossible if this situation exists. People who might otherwise be rejected are often hired. The lower the ratio falls below 1.00, the more alternatives the manager has in making a selection decision. For example, a selection ratio of 0.10 indicates that there are 10 qualified applicants for each position.

Type of Organization

The sector of the economy in which individuals are to be employed—private, governmental, or not-for-profit—can also affect the selection process. A business in the private sector is heavily profit oriented. Prospective employees are screened with regard to how they can help achieve profit goals. Consideration of the total individual, including personality factors that are job related, is involved in the selection of future employees for this sector.

Government civil service systems typically identify qualified applicants through competitive examinations. Often a manager is allowed to select from only the top three applicants for a position. A manager in this sector frequently does not have the prerogative of interviewing other applicants.

Individuals being considered for positions in not-for-profit organizations (such as the Boy and Girl Scouts, YMCA, or YWCA) confront still a different situation. The salary level may not be competitive with private and governmental organizations. Therefore, a person who fills one of these positions must not only be qualified but also dedicated to this type of work.

Probationary Period

Many firms use a probationary period that permits them to evaluate an employee's ability based on established performance. This practice may be either a substitute for certain phases of the selection process or a check on the validity of the process. The rationale is that if an individual can successfully perform the job during the probationary period, other selection tools may not be needed. In any event, newly hired employees should be monitored to determine whether the hiring decision was a good one.

Even though a firm may be unionized, a new employee typically is not protected by the union-management agreement until after a certain probationary period. This period is typically from 60 to 90 days. During that time, an employee may be terminated with little or no justification. When the probationary period is over, terminating a marginal employee may prove to be quite difficult. When a firm is unionized, identification of the most productive workers through the selection process becomes especially important. Once workers come under the union-management agreement, its terms must be followed in changing an employee's status, and these terms may not include productivity.

The Selection Process

Figure 7-1 illustrates a generalized selection process. It typically begins with the preliminary interview, after which obviously unqualified candidates are quickly rejected. Next, applicants complete the firm's application for em-

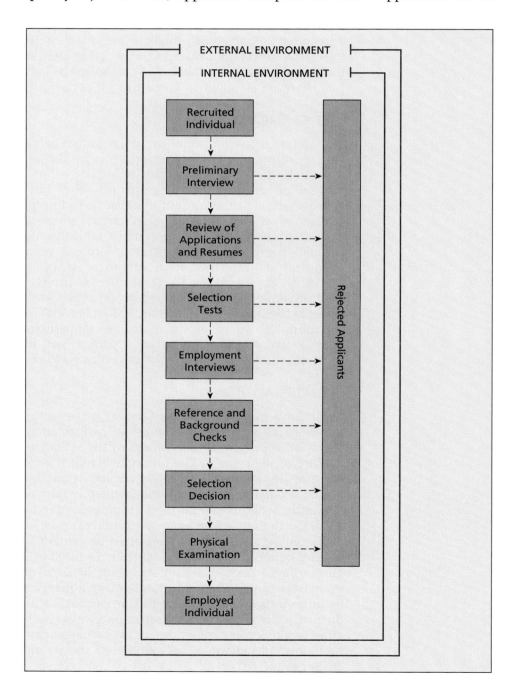

Figure 7-1
The Selection Process

ployment. Then, they progress through a series of selection tests, the employment interview, and reference and background checks. The successful applicant receives a company physical examination. The individual is employed if results of the physical examination are satisfactory. Several external and internal factors impact the selection process, and the manager must take them into account in making selection decisions.

Preliminary Interview

The selection process often begins with a preliminary interview. The purpose of this initial screening of applicants is to eliminate those who obviously do not meet the position's requirements. At this stage, the interviewer asks a few straightforward questions. For instance, a position may require considerable work experience. If the interview fails to reveal relevant experience, any further discussion wastes time for both the firm and the applicant regarding this particular position.

In addition to eliminating obviously unqualified job applicants quickly, a preliminary interview may produce other positive benefits for the firm. Possibly, the position for which the applicant applied is not the only one available. A skilled interviewer will know about other vacancies in the firm and may be able to steer the prospective employee to another position. For instance, an applicant may obviously be unqualified to fill the advertised position of senior programming analyst but be well qualified to work as a computer operator. This type of interviewing not only builds goodwill for the firm but also can maximize recruitment and selection effectiveness.

Review of Applications

Another early step in the selection process may involve having the prospective employee complete an application for employment. The employer then evaluates it to see whether there is an apparent match between the individual and the position. A well-designed and properly used application form can be a real time-saver because it collects essential information and presents it in a standardized format. (See figure 7-2.) For these reasons, an application form can be used more effectively than resumes to reduce dozens of applicants to a few bona fide candidates.

The specific type of information requested on an application for employment may vary from firm to firm, and even by job type within an organization. An application form typically contains sections for name, address, telephone number, military service, education, and work history. Preprinted statements that are very important when the applicant signs the form include certification that everything on the form is true, and if not, the candidate can be released. When not prohibited by state law, the form should also state that the position is employment at will, and that the employer or the employee can terminate employment at any time for any reason or no reason. Finally, the form should contain a statement whereby the candidate gives permission for his or her references to be checked.

Application for Employment

Application No. 125413

Equal Employment Opportunity—It is our policy to provide equal employment opportunity throughout the Company for all qualified persons without regard to race, color, religion, age, sex, national origin, disability, or veteran status.

Instructions
• **Please print in black ink or type information.**

Name (Last, First, Middle)	Are you over 18 years of age? ☐ Yes ☐ No	Social Security Number

Present Address (Street, City, State, ZIP Code)	Phone Number (Area Code First) ( )

Permanent Address (Street, City, State, ZIP Code)	Phone Number (Area Code First) ( )

Date Available for Employment	Employment Desired ☐ Temporary ☐ Regular, Full-Time	Would you accept temporary employment? ☐ Yes ☐ No	Will you perform shift work? ☐ Yes ☐ No

Position Desired—First Preference	Second Preference

Geographical Location Preferred	Geographical Location Where You Will Not Consider Employment

Will you work overtime? ☐ Yes ☐ No	Are you legally authorized to work in the United States on a regular, full-time basis? ☐ Yes ☐ No

Have you been previously employed by Conoco?
☐ No ☐ Yes   If yes, where _____ when _____

Do you have relatives currently employed by Conoco?
☐ No ☐ Yes   If yes, Name _____

Relationship _____ Department _____ Location _____

If you are presently employed, may we contact your employer for a reference?
☐ Yes ☐ No

Indicate Source Which Referred You

☐ Campus Placement Office   ☐ Walk-in   ☐ Private Employment Agency   ☐ Published Advertisement
☐ Employee Referral   ☐ Write-In   ☐ Governmental Employment Agency   ☐ Other (Specify)
☐ Rehire

Employment Record (List below your employment in reverse chronological order. Include part-time and summner experience)

From Mo./Yr	To Mo./Yr	/	/	/	/	/	/	/	/
Employer									
Address									
Supervisor's Name and Telephone No. (Area Cose First)		( )		( )		( )		( )	
Position(s) Held									
Reason for Leaving									

Identify and explain any time lapses in your above employment record.

Figure 7-2
An Application for Employment: Conoco, Inc.

Education—Circle Highest Grade Completed 1 2 3 4 5 6 7 8 9 10 11 12	Course of Study Major—Minor	Degree Received	Grade Average		Degree Date
			Overall	Major	
High School Attended and Location		Diploma ☐ Yes ☐ No			
Vocational or Technical School Attended		Completed ☐ Yes ☐ No			
College or University					
College or University					
College or University					

Other—1) Include information you believe is important, such as: special training, apprenticeships completed, military experience, other education, or foriegn language fluency.

—2) List those machines and/or equipment you are qualified to operate and any other skills you possess.

—3) Titles of these and special research projects.

Completion of this section is optional.

Conoco Inc. is a government contractor subject to Section 503 of the Rehabilitation Act and Section 402 of the Veterans Readjustment Act. As such, we must take affirmative action to employ and advance in employment individuals with disabilities, special disabled veterans, and veterans of the Vietnam era. If you are such an individual and would like to be considered under the affirmative action program, please indicate below.

☐ I am a **special disabled veteran** because **either:** (1) I am entitled to compensation under VA law for disability rated at 30% or more, or for disability rated at 10% or 20% for a serious employment handicap; **or** (2) I was discharged or released from active duty because of a service-connected disability.

☐ I am a **veteran of the Vietnam era** because part or all of my active military service occured between 8/5/64 and 5/7/75 **and either:** (1) I was on active duty for more than 180 days and my discharge or release was not dishonorable; **or** (2) I was discharged or released from active duty because of a service-connected disability.

Submission of this information is voluntary, and disclosure or refusal to provide it will not subject you to adverse treatment. This information shall be used only as allowed by law and shall be kept confidential except that (i) supervisors and managers may be informed about restrictions on work or job duties and necessary accommodations, (ii) first aid or safety personnel may be informed where appropriate in case of an emergency, and (iii) government officials investigating compliance with the law shall be informed.

You may omit references in this section which you feel might reveal age, race, color, sex, national origin, or handicap.

Name and description of scholastic honors received including scholarships.

Name honorary, technical and professional organizations of which you have been a member, or other extracurricular activities in which you have participated, including offices held. (List professional licences held.)

This form will usually provide the necessary information. It may be supplemented, however, by a letter or personal resume.

PLEASE READ THE FOLLOWING CAREFULLY BEFORE SIGNING.

I authorize any third parties, including former employers, schools, law enforcement authorities, and any persons named above, to give to Conoco Inc. any information they may have regarding me and my background, whether or not such information is contained in written records. I hereby release these third parties from all liability for any damage whatsoever for providing information to Conoco Inc. in connection with this application. I also release Conoco Inc., its agents, employees, and representatives from any liability in connection with their collection and use of information obtained from third parties during the application process. I certify that all information furnished in this application, signed and dated by me this date, is true and complete to the best of my knowledge and belief and that falsification or omission of information requested in this application or in the application process shall be grounds for disqualification from further consideration or for termination.

I understand that if an employment offer is extended, I may be required to undergo a physical examination and/or drug screen test at the expense of Conoco Inc. I further understand that if I do not successfully complete the physical examination or drug screen test, Conoco Inc. may refuse to hire me, and I agree to hold Conoco Inc. harmless for such refusal. I also understand that employment is conditional on my ability to verify my identity and eligibility for employment as required by the Immigration Reform and Control Act of 1986.

I agree and understand that any employment which may be offered to me will not be for any definite period of time and that such employment is subject to termination by me or by Conoco Inc. at any time, with or without cause. I also agree and understand that nothing contained in this application nor any verbal statements made during the application process or during my employment shall be deemed to constitute an employment contract between me and Conoco Inc.

Signature	Date

12-21 (R), 3-92

Figure 7-2
An Application for Employment: Conoco, Inc. *(continued)*

An employment application form must reflect not only the firm's informational needs but also EEO requirements. (You may want to refer again to the section in chapter 3 entitled "Employment Standards to Avoid.") Even so, one study of 151 Fortune 500 firms found that more than 98 percent of their forms contained items that were either not necessary for personnel decisions or questionable with respect to Title VII. Another study of 50 national U.S. companies determined that 48 out of 50 forms contained inappropriate items. The most common problems related to questions about arrest records, physical disabilities, military background, and education.[6]

Conoco provides an example of a properly designed application form in Figure 7-2. Notice in the employee release and privacy section, the following statement: "I understand that any employment which may be offered to me will not be for any definite period of time and that such employment is subject to termination by me or by Conoco Inc. at any time, with or without cause." Potentially discriminatory questions inquiring about such factors as gender, race, age, and number of children living at home do not appear on the form.

The information contained in a completed application for employment is compared to the job description to determine whether a potential match exists between the firm's requirements and the applicant's qualifications. As you might expect, this comparison is often difficult. Applicants frequently attempt to present themselves in an exaggerated, somewhat unrealistic light. Comparing past duties and responsibilities with those needed for the job the applicant is seeking is not always easy.

Some companies now have computer terminals in their lobbies on which applicants can complete a job application form. Also, optical scanning programs that can handle the first-level screening of applications may be used. These programs may scan applications for other jobs that the applicants do not know they are qualified to fill. This comprehensive approach is not only more objective but also less expensive.

HR Web Wisdom

http://www.prenhall.com/mondy

RESUME TIPS
Resumé tips are offered to improve resumé preparation.

Review of Resumés

Resumé: A common method used by job seekers to present their qualifications.

A **resumé** is a common method applicants use to present their qualifications. Even when resumés are not required by prospective employers, they are frequently submitted by job seekers. Although there are no hard and fast rules for designing resumés, some general guidelines can be followed, depending on the type and level of position sought. An example of a resumé submitted by a recent college graduate for a position in a public accounting firm is shown in Figure 7-3. As you see in this example, there is much *white space*, which makes the resumé easier to read. The current and permanent addresses and telephone numbers of the applicant are prominently located. An *objective* statement is written to describe the type of opportunity desired. As

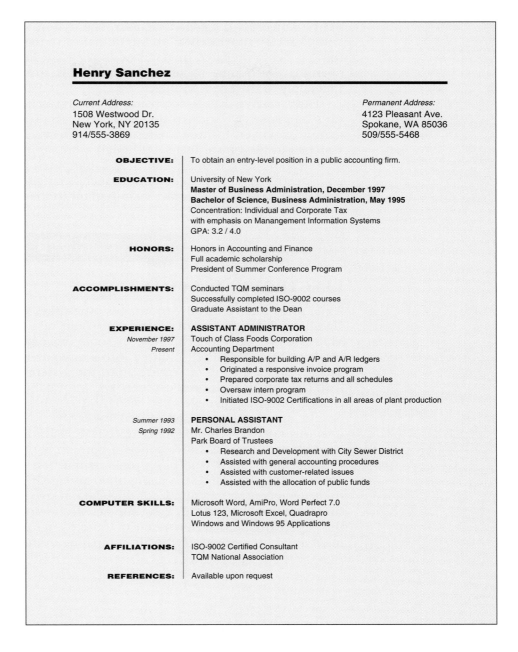

Henry Sanchez

Current Address:
1508 Westwood Dr.
New York, NY 20135
914/555-3869

Permanent Address:
4123 Pleasant Ave.
Spokane, WA 85036
509/555-5468

OBJECTIVE:	To obtain an entry-level position in a public accounting firm.
EDUCATION:	University of New York **Master of Business Administration, December 1997** **Bachelor of Science, Business Administration, May 1995** Concentration: Individual and Corporate Tax with emphasis on Manangement Information Systems GPA: 3.2 / 4.0
HONORS:	Honors in Accounting and Finance Full academic scholarship President of Summer Conference Program
ACCOMPLISHMENTS:	Conducted TQM seminars Successfully completed ISO-9002 courses Graduate Assistant to the Dean
EXPERIENCE: *November 1997* *Present*	**ASSISTANT ADMINISTRATOR** Touch of Class Foods Corporation Accounting Department • Responsible for building A/P and A/R ledgers • Originated a responsive invoice program • Prepared corporate tax returns and all schedules • Oversaw intern program • Initiated ISO-9002 Certifications in all areas of plant production
Summer 1993 *Spring 1992*	**PERSONAL ASSISTANT** Mr. Charles Brandon Park Board of Trustees • Research and Development with City Sewer District • Assisted with general accounting procedures • Assisted with customer-related issues • Assisted with the allocation of public funds
COMPUTER SKILLS:	Microsoft Word, AmiPro, Word Perfect 7.0 Lotus 123, Microsoft Excel, Quadrapro Windows and Windows 95 Applications
AFFILIATIONS:	ISO-9002 Certified Consultant TQM National Association
REFERENCES:	Available upon request

Figure 7-3
Example of Resumé for
an Entry-Level Position

most recent graduates are being hired for their potential value to a firm, education is a vital factor at this stage of their careers, and the applicant's education level is shown next. Work experience follows, especially internships in which students have worked in their degree field; this should be shown in reverse chronological order, with the most recent experience shown first. Prospective employers spend little time reading resumés. Therefore, especially in firms that have not automated their resumé handling procedures, the document must be concise. A typical college graduate's resumé should not be longer than a page in length. The resumé's appearance must be neat and correct. Typographical and grammatical errors can be killers. If the resumé is being prepared in response to an ad or knowledge of a specific job opening, the resumé should reflect the skills and abilities of the applicant that apply to the open position.

Firms such as Hewlett-Packard, AT&T, Texas Instruments, and Ford Motor Company have turned to virtual recruiters. The software programs used permit employers to store the resumés they receive in a database that can be searched to fill job vacancies. Although a human recruiter cannot search for qualifications as fast or efficiently as a computer, the computer is unable to go beneath the surface to determine such intangibles as whether the person is a team player and other factors important to the employer.[7]

TRENDS & INNOVATIONS

ELECTRONIC RESUMÉS

Some firms receive literally thousands of resumés weekly for open positions. Handling these documents manually would take an army of clerical staff. This task is effectively dealt with by some organizations. When resumés are received, they are either inputted into a computer directly from the source, such as fax or e-mail, or scanned into the system using an optical scanner. Artificial intelligence then captures key information from each resumé. Recruiters or hiring managers can search the database for applicants who have certain qualifications. A prioritized list is then available for each position opening, ranked according to the specified qualifications in the search.[8]

Although there is a divergence of opinion at OFCCP headquarters, some feel that individuals who place their resumés on electronic bulletin boards are expressing an interest in being hired and are, therefore, to be included in the federal contractor's applicant flow data. If specific guidelines—which are sure to follow—reflect this view, the new technologies meant to help reduce the paperwork burden may result in a more onerous record-keeping requirement and hurt employers who are competing in the global marketplace.[9]

Administration of Selection Tests

Evidence suggests that the use of tests is becoming more prevalent for assessing an applicant's qualifications and potential for success. A recent study indicates that more than half the organizations surveyed require skills tests for hourly jobs. Twenty-three percent of firms use skills tests for management job seekers.[10] Tests are used more in the public sector than in the private sector and in medium-size and large companies more than in small companies. Large organizations are likely to have trained specialists to run their testing programs.

ADVANTAGES OF SELECTION TESTS

Selection testing can be a reliable and accurate way to select qualified candidates from a pool of applicants. An extreme example of the contribution of effective selection tests to productivity was provided years ago by the Philadelphia Police Department. Labor savings in this 5,000 member organization from the use of cognitive ability tests to select officers was estimated to be $18 million for each year's hires.[11]

As with all selection procedures, an important element is identifying the essential functions of each job and determining the skills needed to perform them. Selection tests must be job related and must meet standards as outlined in the EEOC's *Uniform Guidelines on Employee Selection Procedures*.

POTENTIAL PROBLEMS IN USING SELECTION TESTS

Job performance is related primarily to an individual's ability and motivation to do the job. Selection tests may accurately predict an applicant's *ability* to perform the job, but they are less successful in indicating whether the individual will *want* to perform it. The most successful employees share two things in common: They identify with their firm's goals and they are highly motivated.[12] For one reason or another, many employees with high potential never seem to reach it. The factors related to success on the job are so numerous and complex that selection may always be more of an art than a science.

Another potential problem, related primarily to personality tests and interest inventories, has to do with applicants' honesty. An applicant may be strongly motivated to respond to questions untruthfully or provide answers that he or she believes the firm expects. To prevent this occurrence, some tests have built-in lie detection scales.

A common problem is test anxiety. Applicants often become quite anxious when confronting yet another hurdle that might eliminate them from consideration. The test administrator's reassuring manner and a well-organized testing operation should help to reduce this threat. Actually, although a great deal of anxiety is detrimental to test performance, a slight amount is helpful.

The dual problems of hiring unqualified or less qualified candidates and rejecting qualified candidates will continue regardless of the procedures followed. Organizations can minimize such errors through the use of well-developed tests administered by competent professionals. Nevertheless, selection tests rarely, if ever, are perfect predictors. With even the best test, errors will be made in predicting success. For this reason, tests should not be used alone in the selection process but in conjunction with other tools.

CHARACTERISTICS OF PROPERLY DESIGNED SELECTION TESTS

Properly designed selection tests are standardized, objective, based on sound norms, reliable, and—of utmost importance—valid. Application of these concepts is discussed next.

Standardization: The degree of uniformity of the procedures and conditions related to administering tests.

Standardization. **Standardization** refers to the uniformity of the procedures and conditions related to administering tests. If the performances of several applicants on the same test are to be compared fairly, all must take the test under conditions that are as close to identical as possible. For example, the content of instructions provided and the time allowed must be the same, and the physical environment must be similar. If one person takes a test in a noisy room and another takes it in a quiet environment, differences in test results are likely. Dissimilar conditions may affect an applicant's performance. Even though test administration procedures may be specified by a test's developers, test administrators are responsible for ensuring standardized conditions.

Objectivity: The condition that is achieved when all individuals scoring a given test obtain the same results.

Objectivity. **Objectivity** in testing is achieved when everyone scoring a test obtains the same results. Multiple-choice and true-false tests are said to be objective. The person taking the test either chooses the correct answer or does not. Scoring these tests is a highly mechanical process, which lends itself to machine grading.

Norm: A distribution that provides a frame of reference for comparing an applicant's performance with that of others.

Norms. A **norm** provides a frame of reference for comparing an applicant's performance with that of others. Specifically, a norm reflects the distribution of many scores obtained by people similar to the applicant being tested. The scores will tend to be distributed according to the normal probability curve shown in Figure 7-4. Standard deviations measure the amount of dispersion

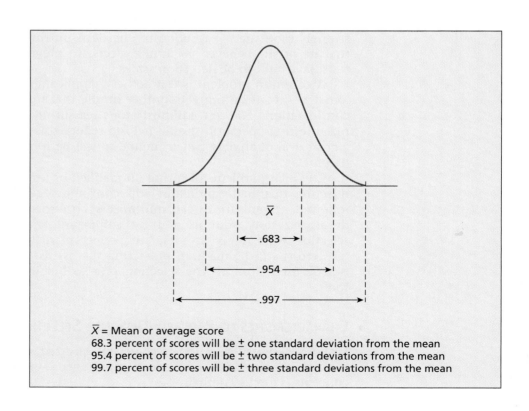

$\bar{X}$ = Mean or average score
68.3 percent of scores will be ± one standard deviation from the mean
95.4 percent of scores will be ± two standard deviations from the mean
99.7 percent of scores will be ± three standard deviations from the mean

Figure 7-4
A Normal Probability
Curve

of the data. In a normalized test, approximately 68.3 percent of the scores will fall within ±1 standard deviation from the mean. Individuals scoring in this range would be considered average. Individuals achieving scores outside the range of ±2 standard deviations would probably be highly unsuccessful or highly successful, based on the particular criteria used.

When a sufficient number of employees are performing the same or similar work, employers can standardize their own tests. Typically, this is not the case, and a national norm for a particular test must be used. A prospective employee takes the test, the score obtained is compared to the norm, and the significance of the test score is determined.

Reliability: The extent to which a selection test provides consistent results.

Reliability. **Reliability** is the extent to which a selection test provides consistent results. Reliability data reveal the degree of confidence that can be placed in a test. If a test has low reliability, its validity as a predictor will also be low. The existence of reliability does not in itself guarantee validity, however.

Validity: The extent to which a test measures what it purports to measure.

Validity. The basic requirement for a selection test is that it be valid. **Validity** is the extent to which a test measures what it purports to measure. If a selection test cannot indicate ability to perform the job, it has no value as a predictor.

Validity is commonly reported as a correlation coefficient, which summarizes the relationship between two variables. For example, these variables may be the score on a selection test and some measure of employee performance. A coefficient of 0 shows no relationship, while coefficients of either +1.0 or −1.0 indicate a perfect relationship, one positive and the other negative. Naturally, no test will be 100 percent accurate, yet organizations strive for the highest feasible coefficient. The cumulative body of previous research indicates that tests yield correlation coefficients of .30 to .60, depending on the test and the position.[13] If a test is designed to predict job performance and validity studies of the test indicate a high correlation coefficient, most prospective employees who score high on the test will probably later prove to be high performers.

Employers are not required to validate their selection tests automatically. Generally, validation is required only when the selection process as a whole results in an adverse impact on women or minorities. Validation of selection tests is expensive. However, an organization cannot know whether the test is actually measuring the qualities and abilities being sought without validation.

Types of Validation Studies

The *Uniform Guidelines* established three approaches that may be followed to validate selection tests: criterion-related validity, content validity, and construct validity.

CRITERION-RELATED VALIDITY

Criterion-related validity: A test validation method that compares the scores on selection tests to some aspect of job performance as determined—for example, by performance appraisal.

Criterion-related validity is determined by comparing the scores on selection tests to some aspect of job performance as determined, for example, by performance appraisal. Performance measures might include quantity and quality of work, turnover, and absenteeism. A close relationship between the score on the test and job performance suggests that the test is valid.

There are two basic forms of criterion-related validity: concurrent and predictive validity. With **concurrent validity**, the test scores and the criterion data are obtained at essentially the same time. For instance, all currently employed telemarketers may be given a test. Company records contain current information about each employee's job performance. If the test is able to identify productive and less-productive workers, one could say that it is valid. A potential problem in using this validation procedure results from changes that may have occurred within the work group. For example, the less-productive workers may have been fired, and the more productive employees may have been promoted out of the group.

Predictive validity involves administering a test and later obtaining the criterion information. For instance, a test might be administered to all applicants but test results not used in the selection decision; employees would be hired on the basis of other selection criteria. After employee performance has been observed over a period of time, the test results are analyzed to determine whether they differentiate the successful and less successful employees. Predictive validity is considered to be a technically sound procedure. However, because of the time and cost involved, its use is often not feasible.

CONTENT VALIDITY

Although statistical concepts are not involved, many practitioners believe that content validity provides a sensible approach to validating a selection test. **Content validity** is a test validation method whereby a person performs certain tasks that are actually required by the job or completes a paper-and-pencil test that measures relevant job knowledge. Thorough job analysis and carefully prepared job descriptions are needed when this form of validation is used. An example of the use of content validity is giving a data entering test to an applicant whose primary job would be to enter data. In *Washington v Davis*, the Supreme Court supported assessment based on content validity.

CONSTRUCT VALIDITY

Construct validity is a test validation method that determines whether a test measures certain traits or qualities that are important in performing the job. For instance, if the job requires a high degree of teamwork, a test would be used to measure the applicant's ability to work effectively in teams. Traits or qualities such as teamwork, leadership, and planning or organizational ability must first be carefully identified through job analysis. Remember from chapter 4 that job analysis determines what traits are needed for the job.

After a test has been shown to be valid, an appropriate cutoff score may be established. A **cutoff score** is the score below which an applicant will not be selected. Cutoff scores will vary over time because they are directly related to the selection ratio. The more individuals applying for a job, the more selective the firm can be and, therefore, the higher the cutoff scores can be. Cutoff scores should normally be set to reflect a reasonable expectation of acceptable proficiency.

Concurrent validity: A validation method in which test scores and criterion data are obtained at essentially the same time.

Predictive validity: A validation method that involves administering a selection test and later obtaining the criterion information.

Content validity: A test validation method in which a person performs certain tasks that are actual samples of the kind of work a job requires or completes a paper-and-pencil test that measures relevant job knowledge.

Construct validity: A test validation method to determine whether a selection test measures certain traits or qualities that have been identified as important in performing a particular job.

Cutoff score: The score below which an applicant will not be considered further for employment.

Types of Employment Tests

Individuals differ in characteristics related to job performance. These differences, which are measurable, relate to cognitive abilities, psychomotor abilities, job knowledge, work samples, vocational interests, and personality. Other tests that may be administered include drug testing, genetic testing, and testing for AIDS. Assessment centers are also used by some firms in selecting employees. This technique is also used for assessing the potential capabilities of employees. It is discussed in chapter 10.

COGNITIVE APTITUDE TESTS

Cognitive aptitude tests: Tests that measure an individual's ability to learn as well as to perform a job.

Cognitive aptitude tests are used to determine general reasoning ability, memory, vocabulary, verbal fluency, and numerical ability. They may be helpful in identifying job candidates who have extensive knowledge bases. As the content of jobs become broader and more fluid, employees must be able to adapt quickly to job changes and rapid technological advances. It is likely that more general selection methods will be needed to determine the broader range of characteristics required for success.[14]

PSYCHOMOTOR ABILITIES TESTS

Psychomotor abilities tests: Aptitude tests that measure strength, coordination, and dexterity.

Psychomotor abilities tests measure strength, coordination, and dexterity. The development of tests to determine these abilities has been accelerated by miniaturization in assembly operations. Much of the work of miniaturization is so delicate that workers must use magnifying lenses, and the psychomotor abilities required to perform the tasks are critical. Standardized tests are not available to cover all these abilities, but those that are involved in many routine production jobs and some office jobs can be measured.

JOB KNOWLEDGE TESTS

Job knowledge tests: Tests designed to measure a candidate's knowledge of the duties of a job for which he or she is applying.

Job knowledge tests are designed to measure a candidate's knowledge of the duties of the position for which he or she is applying. Such tests are commercially available but may also be designed specifically for any job, based on the data derived from job analysis.

WORK-SAMPLE TESTS (SIMULATIONS)

Work-sample tests: Tests requiring the identification of a task or set of tasks that are representative of a particular job.

Work-sample tests, or **simulations**, require an applicant to perform a task or set of tasks representative of the job. Therefore, such tests by their nature are job related. Not surprising, the evidence to date concerning this type of test is that it produces a high predictive validity, reduces adverse impact, and is more acceptable than other tests to applicants. If a position requires writing quickly on short deadlines, for example, a simulation would require the applicant to take a timed writing test. The applicant can then demonstrate his or her ability to write satisfactorily under the pressure imposed by time and the interview environment itself.[15] A real test with any kind of validity, in the opinion of some experts, should be a performance assessment: Take individuals to a job and give them the opportunity to perform it.[16]

VOCATIONAL INTEREST TESTS

Vocational interest tests indicate the occupation in which a person is most interested and is most likely to receive satisfaction from. These tests compare the individual's interests with those of successful employees in a specific job. Although interest tests may possibly have application in employee selection, their primary use has been in counseling and vocational guidance.

PERSONALITY TESTS

Personality tests have been used to identify individuals who are highly motivated, flexible, and able to work well in teams. Some firms use these tests to classify personality types. With this information, firms can create diverse teams for creativity or homogeneous teams for compatibility.[17] As selection tools, personality tests have been controversial because they lack face validity. Nevertheless, a recent study indicated that the use of personality tests was on the rise. Eighteen percent of the firms surveyed ask hourly workers to take a personality test and 22 percent of the firms ask managers to take one.[18]

DRUG TESTING

Few issues generate more controversy today than drug testing. Proponents of drug testing programs contend that it is necessary to ensure workplace safety, security, and productivity. It is also viewed as an accurate measure of drug use and a means to deter it. Critics of drug testing argue just as vigorously that drug testing is an unjustifiable intrusion into private lives.[19]

Although the controversy remains, along with legal questions, drug testing in the United States seems to be becoming more commonplace. For example, an American Management Association survey indicated that by 1995, 48 percent of Fortune 1000 firms engaged in some type of drug testing.[20] Nationally, drug testing reveals only about a 2 to 6 percent positive rate among tested applicants. The explanation for this low rate is that many applicants who use *hard* drugs avoid their use for several days prior to the test. Only marijuana is retained in the body for over a week.[21]

In addition to concerns about privacy, some employers may worry that applicants denied employment may seek protection as persons with a disability under the Americans with Disabilities Act. The act, however, is actually supportive of testing when it is carefully performed. Persons engaging in the illegal use of drugs are excluded from the act's definition of the term *qualified individual with a disability*. Note, however, that persons who have successfully completed or who are participating in a supervised drug-rehabilitation program and who no longer engage in illegal drug use are not automatically excluded from this definition.[22]

Preemployment alcohol testing may also be done by assessing breath, urine, blood, saliva, or hair samples. The method of choice among law enforcement agencies and the transportation industry is breath alcohol analysis. However, most experts regard blood tests as the forensic benchmark against which others should be compared. The problem with this approach is that it is an invasive method and requires trained personnel for administration and analysis. The use of hair samples is unique in that drug traces will remain in the hair and will not likely diminish over time. Unlike detection in urine or blood, detection of drug or alcohol use in hair analysis cannot be avoided by abstention for a period of time before the test.[23]

GENETIC TESTING

Genetic testing: An approach that can show whether a person carries the gene mutation for certain diseases.

As genetic research progresses, confirmed links between specific gene mutations and diseases are emerging. **Genetic testing** can now determine whether a person carries the gene mutation for certain diseases, including heart disease, colon cancer, breast cancer, and Huntington's disease.[24] Gene tests tell of a person's predisposition to a disease. Usually they cannot tell whether a person is certain to get the disease or whether the individual would become ill at age 30 or 90. In addition, everyone has some disposition to genetic disease and a genetic predisposition is not the same as a preexisting condition. However, anecdotal evidence suggests that some employers are using this information for employment decisions.[25]

A major concern about genetic testing is employee privacy. Once the results of a genetic test are in a medical record, the results may be available to employers and insurers without an individual's knowledge or consent.

Guidelines issued by the EEOC in 1995 interpreted the Americans with Disabilities Act as covering discrimination on the basis of genetic information. In addition, states have begun to act. Since 1990, 12 states have passed laws against genetic discrimination in employment and similar bills are pending in 13 more.[26] Several top geneticists and health advocates have recommended uniform regulations across the country. At least two bills on genetic privacy issues have been introduced in Congress but no action has yet been taken.[27]

TESTING FOR ACQUIRED IMMUNE DEFICIENCY SYNDROME (AIDS)

Individuals with AIDS and those who test positive for the human immunodeficiency virus (HIV) are protected by both the Rehabilitation Act and the Americans with Disabilities Act. It is not common practice to test for these conditions unless the nature of the work creates a high potential for employee exposure to infected co-workers. Health care institutions, for example, may be able to show the business necessity for using this selection tool. We discuss AIDS further in chapter 13.

The Employment Interview

Employment interview: A goal-oriented conversation in which an interviewer and an applicant exchange information.

The **employment interview** is a goal-oriented conversation in which the interviewer and applicant exchange information. Historically, interviews have not been shown to be valid predictors of success on the job. Most interviews

The employment interview is especially significant because the applicants who reach this stage are considered to be the most promising candidates.

have correlation coefficients in the 0.00 to .30 range.[28] Nevertheless, they continue to be the primary method used to evaluate applicants, and they are utilized by virtually every company. As we discuss later in the chapter, progress has been made by some firms in improving the validity of interviews.

The employment interview is especially significant because the applicants who reach this stage are considered to be the most promising candidates. They have survived the preliminary interview and scored satisfactorily on selection tests. At this point, the candidates appear to be qualified, at least on paper. Every seasoned manager knows, however, that appearances can be quite misleading. Additional information is needed to indicate whether the individual is willing to work and can adapt to that particular organization.

INTERVIEW PLANNING

Interview planning is essential to effective employment interviews. The physical location of the interview should be both pleasant and private, providing for a minimum of interruptions. The interviewer should have a pleasant personality, empathy, and the ability to listen and communicate effectively. He or she should become familiar with the applicant's qualifications by reviewing the data collected from other selection tools. As preparation for the interview, a job profile should be developed based on the job description. After job requirements have been listed, it is helpful to have an interview checklist that includes these hints:

- Compare an applicant's application and resume with job requirements.
- Develop questions related to the qualities sought.
- Prepare a step-by-step plan to present the position, company, division, and department.
- Determine how to ask for examples of past applicant behavior, not what future behavior might be.

CONTENT OF THE INTERVIEW

Both the interviewer and the candidate have agendas for the interview. After establishing rapport with the applicant, the interviewer seeks additional job-related information to complement data provided by other selection tools. The interview permits clarification of certain points, the uncovering of additional information, and the elaboration of data needed to make a sound selection decision. In addition, providing information about the company, the job, and expectations of the candidate is important. Other areas typically included in the interview are discussed next.

Occupational Experience. The interviewer will explore the candidate's knowledge, skills, abilities, and willingness to handle responsibility. Although successful performance in one job does not guarantee success in another, it does provide an indication of the person's ability and willingness to work.

Academic Achievement. In the absence of significant work experience, a person's academic record takes on greater importance. A grade point average, however, should be considered in light of other factors. For example, involvement in work or extracurricular activities may have affected an applicant's grades.

Interpersonal Skills. An individual may possess important technical skills significant to accomplishing a job. However, if the person cannot work well with others, chances for success are slim. This is especially true in today's world with increasing use of teams.

Personal Qualities. Personal qualities normally observed during the interview include physical appearance, speaking ability, vocabulary, poise, adaptability, and assertiveness. These attributes, as with all selection criteria, should be considered only if they are relevant to job performance.

Organizational Fit. A hiring criterion that is not prominently mentioned in the literature is *organizational fit*. Organizational fit is ill defined but refers to management's perception of the degree to which the prospective employee will fit in, for example, with the firm's culture or value system.[29] A candidate's proficiency credentials are obviously important, but personal credentials may be even more indicative of potential success on the job. When you consider the reasons many individuals fail on the job, most failed, in all likelihood because of inadequate personal skills, an inability to communicate, or because they simply did not fit in with the culture—in other words, bad chemistry.[30]

Remember the discussion of corporate culture in chapter 2. Although using *fit* as a criterion raises legal and diversity questions, there is evidence that it is nevertheless used in making selection decisions. For example, one professional stated: "Finding a 'fit,' while meeting the legal guidelines of questions we can ask, is our greatest challenge . . . a skilled interviewer must be able to legally steer the interviewee to answer any questions that have an impact in determining a mutual fit."[31]

Remembering that interviewees also have objectives for the interview is important. These may be summarized as follows:[32]

- To be listened to and understood
- To have ample opportunity to present their qualifications
- To be treated fairly and with respect
- To gather information about the job and the company
- To make an informed decision concerning the desirability of the job

The specific content of employment interviews varies greatly according to an organization's strategic mission and the nature of the job. For example, David Pritchard, director of recruiting for Microsoft, has stated, "The best thing we can do for our competitors is hire poorly." One of the things Microsoft managers look for in a candidate is intelligence and experience, but they also want to know what a prospective employee will bring to the firm in the long term. Because of the dynamic nature of the industry, where things change virtually daily, they must have people who are flexible and capable of learning new things. Mr. Pritchard notes, "We might even teach them an algorithm in a morning interview and then ask them about [it] in the afternoon to see how much they have learned."[33]

After the interview is concluded, the interviewer must determine whether the candidate is suitable for the open position. If the conclusion is positive, the process continues; if there appears to be no match, the candidate is eliminated from consideration.

Types of Interviews

Interviews may be broadly classified as structured or unstructured. These are discussed next.

THE UNSTRUCTURED (NONDIRECTIVE) INTERVIEW

Unstructured interview: A meeting with a job applicant during which the interviewer asks probing, open-ended questions.

In the **unstructured interview**, the interviewer asks probing, open-ended questions. This type of interview is comprehensive, and the interviewer encourages the applicant to do much of the talking. The nondirective interview is often more time-consuming than structured interviews and obtains different information from different candidates. This diversity adds to the potential legal woes of organizations using this approach. Compounding the problem is the likelihood that ill-advised, potentially discriminatory information will be discussed. The applicant who is being encouraged to pour his or her heart out may volunteer information the interviewer does not need or want to know. Unsuccessful applicants subjected to this interviewing approach may later claim in court that the reason for his or her failure to get the job was the employer's use of this information.

THE STRUCTURED (DIRECTIVE OR PATTERNED) INTERVIEW

Structured interview:
A process in which an interviewer consistently presents the same series of job-related questions to each applicant for a particular job.

Situational questions:
Questions that pose a hypothetical job situation to determine what the applicant would do in such a situation.

Job knowledge questions: Questions that probe the knowledge a person possesses for performing a particular job.

Job-sample simulation questions: Situations in which an applicant may be required to actually perform a sample task from a particular job.

Worker requirements questions: Questions that seek to determine the applicant's willingness to conform to the requirements of a job.

Behavior description interview: A structured interview that uses questions designed to probe an applicant's past behavior in specific situations.

The **structured interview** consists of a series of job-related questions that are asked of each applicant for a particular job. Although interviews have historically been very poor predictors for making good selection decisions, use of structured interviews increases reliability and accuracy by reducing the subjectivity and inconsistency of unstructured interviews.

A structured job interview typically contains four types of questions.

- **Situational questions** pose a typical job situation to determine what the applicant did in a similar situation.
- **Job knowledge questions** probe the applicant's job-related knowledge; these questions may relate to basic educational skills or complex scientific or managerial skills.
- **Job-sample simulation questions** involve situations in which an applicant may be required to perform a sample task from the job.
- **Worker requirements questions** seek to determine the applicant's willingness to conform to the requirements of the job. For example, the interviewer may ask whether the applicant is willing to perform repetitive work or move to another city.

BEHAVIOR DESCRIPTION INTERVIEWING

The **behavior description interview** is a structured interview that uses questions designed to probe the candidate's past behavior in specific situations. It avoids making judgments about applicants' personalities and avoids hypothetical and self-evaluative questions. The situational behaviors are carefully selected for their relevance to job success. Questions are formed from the behaviors by asking applicants how they performed in the described situation. For example, a candidate for an engineering position might be asked, "Tell me about a time when you had to make an important decision without having all the information you needed." Benchmark answers derived from behaviors of successful employees are prepared for use in rating applicant responses. The best responses to a given situation provide the means for developing a good insight into the job candidate's potential.[34]

Behavior-based interviewing has been described as a thorough, systematic way to gather and evaluate information about what applicants have done in the past to show how they would handle future situations. The method would likely include these steps:[35]

- Analyze the job to determine the knowledge, skills, abilities, and behaviors important for job success.
- Determine which behavioral questions to ask about the particular job to elicit the desired behaviors.
- Develop a structured format tailored for each job.
- Set benchmark responses—examples of *good*, *average*, and *bad* answers to questions.
- Train the interviewers.

Questions asked in behavior description interviewing are legally safe because they are job related. Equally important, as both questions and answers are related to successful job performance, they are more accurate in predicting whether applicants will be successful for the job they are hired to perform. Validity coefficients for behavior description interviewing have been shown to be several times higher than those for traditional interviewing.[36] One caveat, however, is that the correct answer for evaluating responses may reflect behavior of the traditional white male employee. Women and minorities may not have the experiences in life that provide similar responses. Individuals from other cultures may experience similar problems.

Methods of Interviewing

Interviews may be conducted in several ways. The level of the position to be filled and the labor market to be tapped determine the most appropriate approach.

ONE-ON-ONE INTERVIEW

In a typical employment interview, the applicant meets one-on-one with an interviewer. As the interview may be a highly emotional occasion for the applicant, meeting alone with the interviewer is often less threatening. The environment this method provides may allow an effective exchange of information to take place.

GROUP INTERVIEW

Group interview: A meeting in which several job applicants interact in the presence of one or more company representatives.

Unlike a one-on-one interview, in a **group interview** several applicants interact in the presence of one or more company representatives. This approach, while not mutually exclusive of other interview types, may provide useful insights into the candidates' interpersonal competence as they engage in group discussion. Another advantage of this technique is that it saves time for busy professionals and executives.

BOARD INTERVIEW

Board interview: A meeting in which one candidate is interviewed by several representatives of a company.

In a **board interview**, one candidate is interviewed by several representatives of the firm. Although a thorough examination of the applicant is likely, the interviewee's anxiety level is often quite high. A vice president of industrial relations for an aircraft firm stated, "We use a three-person board to screen each applicant, asking a series of questions designed to ferret out the individual's attitudes toward former employers, jobs, etc. Then, a week later, we bring successful applicants and their spouses in for a family-night meeting with top management and their spouses, where we further screen them while discussing the company and employee benefits." Naturally, the amount of time devoted to a board interview will differ depending on the type and level of job.

STRESS INTERVIEW

Most interview sessions are designed to minimize stress on the part of the candidate. However, the **stress interview** intentionally creates anxiety to determine how an applicant will react to stress on the job. The interviewer deliberately makes the candidate uncomfortable by asking blunt and often discourteous questions. The purpose is to determine the applicant's tolerance for stress. Knowledge of this factor may be important if the job requires the ability to deal with a high level of stress. On the other hand, some human resource professionals believe that the stress interview is not only inconsiderate but is also ineffective. Proponents of this view feel that information exchange in a stressful environment is often distorted and misinterpreted. These critics maintain that the data obtained are not the type of information on which to base a selection decision. In any event, the stress interview does not seem to be appropriate for the majority of situations.

VIDEOTAPED INTERVIEW

When a company is conducting a national search to fill a high-level position, interviewing a number of candidates may be desirable. However, with increasing pressure to reduce costs, videotaped interviews may be the solution. There are consulting firms that have many interviewers available throughout the nation. Using a structured interview format provided by the hiring firm, the interviewer can videotape the candidate's responses. To assure standardized treatment of other similarly conducted interviews, the interviewer may not interact with the candidate but only repeat the question, if necessary.

The videotaped interview is not intended to replace personal interviews. However, its use may permit a firm to take a better look at more candidates and it may assist in the screening process. The less personal approach has definite shortcomings. However, it does allow a firm to conduct a broader search and to get more people in the selection pool.[37]

COMPUTER INTERVIEW

At times, the computer is used in the interviewing process. Brooks Mitchell, a former human resource director, was hired by a West Virginia garment manufacturer to reduce its high turnover among sewing machine operators. From the job applications of 100 successful operators and 100 who had quit or been fired, he identified 10 variables that appeared to predict job success. He then designed a weighted job application and a scoring key that gave points for the best answers to the predictive questions. He then hired a computer hacker to write a program that would permit applicants to take the job interview on a computer. The results showed that applicants were more honest with the computer than they had been with human interviewers. For example, a number admitted to the computer that they intended to quit their job within six months. By eliminating applicants who were likely to quit or be fired, the apparel firm halved its turnover rate in three years.[38]

Figure 7-5
Typical Consequences of Job Procedures

Traditional Procedures	Realistic Procedures
Set initial job expectations too high	Set job expectations realistically
↓	↓
Job is typically viewed as attractive	Job may or may not be attractive, depending on individual's needs
↓	↓
High rate of job offer acceptance	Some accept, some reject job offer
↓	↓
Work experience disconfirms expectations	Work experience confirms expectations
↓	↓
Dissatisfaction and realization that job not matched to needs	Satisfaction; needs matched to job
↓	↓
Low job survival, dissatisfaction, frequent thoughts of quitting	High job survival, satisfaction, infrequent thoughts of quitting

REALISTIC JOB PREVIEWS[39]

Many applicants have unrealistic expectations about the prospective job and employer. This inaccurate perception, which may have negative consequences, is often encouraged by firms that present themselves in overly attractive terms. Too many interviewers paint false, rosy pictures of the job and company. This practice leads to mismatches of people and positions. The problem is further compounded when candidates also engage in exaggerating their own qualifications.[40] To correct this situation from the employer's side, a realistic job preview should be given to applicants early in the selection process and definitely before a job offer is made.

Realistic job preview (RJP): A method of conveying job information to an applicant in an unbiased manner, including both positive and negative factors.

A **realistic job preview (RJP)** conveys job information to the applicant in an unbiased manner, including both positive and negative factors. An RJP conveys information about tasks the person would perform, behavior expected if the applicant is to fit into the organization, and company policies and procedures. This approach helps applicants develop a more accurate perception of the job and the firm. Considerable research confirms the effectiveness of realistic job previews. Although applicants subjected to an RJP tend to accept job offers less often than those who are not, their productivity is virtually the same as candidates selected without one. The important results are that employees who had a realistic job preview exhibit lower turnover and greater job satisfaction. A comparison of the results of traditional preview procedures and realistic preview procedures is shown in Figure 7-5. Note that traditional procedures result in low job survival and dissatisfaction, whereas realistic previews help to overcome these difficulties.

Legal Implications of Interviewing

The definition of a test in the *Uniform Guidelines* included "physical, education and work experience requirements from informal or casual interviews." Because the interview is considered to be a test, it is subject to the same validity requirements as any other step in the selection process, should adverse impact be shown. For the interview, this constraint presents special difficulties. To begin with, few firms are willing to pay the cost of validating interviews. They can be validated only by a long-term follow-up—a method that requires collecting much data over a long period of time. However, significant evidence indicates that if two managers in a firm interview the same applicant at different times, the outcomes will differ. In fact, the interview is perhaps more vulnerable to charges of discrimination than any other tool used in the selection process. Some interviewers are inclined to ask questions that are not job related and that reflect their personal biases. Interviewing in this manner is risky and can lead to charges of discrimination. Interviewing is governed by one simple rule: All questions must be job related. In addition to being a waste of time, irrelevant or personal questions are dangerous and often improper.[41]

To elicit needed information, the interviewer must create a climate that encourages the applicant to speak freely. However, the conversation should not become too casual. Whereas engaging in friendly chitchat with candidates might be pleasant, in our litigious society, it may be the most dangerous thing an interviewer can do.

> When the office manager at a Midwestern newspaper made friendly inquiries about a job applicant's children, he thought he was merely breaking the ice and setting the tone for an effective dialogue. A year later, however, he was the target of a lawsuit filed by the applicant who had not been selected. The applicant claimed to have been the victim of sexual discrimination because she had told the manager she had need of a day care facility when she went to work. She claimed that a man would not have been asked questions about his children.

To avoid the appearance of discrimination, employers should ask all applicants for a position the same questions.[42] It is also critical to record the applicant's responses. If a candidate begins volunteering personal information that is not job related, the interviewer should steer the conversation back on course. It might do well to begin the interview by tactfully stating, "This selection decision will be based strictly on qualifications. Let's not discuss topics such as religion, social activities, national origin, gender, or family situations. We are definitely interested in you, personally. However, these factors are not job related and will not be considered in our decision."[43] Table 7-1 shows potential problems that can threaten the success of employment interviews.

The Americans with Disabilities Act also provides warning for interviewers. There are three situations in which interviewers can ask about reasonable accommodations:

- The applicant has an obvious disability that will require an accommodation. For example, if the applicant uses a wheelchair; this condition will require an employer to provide a ramp.
- The applicant voluntarily discloses a hidden disability, such as a heart attack or diabetes.
- The disabled applicant asks for some reasonable accommodation.[44]

Employers should refrain from asking applicants about their disabilities, if any. Instead, interviewers should frame questions in terms of whether

TABLE 7-1

Potential Interviewing Problems

Inappropriate Questions

Although no questions are illegal, many are clearly inappropriate. When they are asked, the responses generated create a legal liability for the employer. The most basic interviewing rule is this: "Ask only job-related questions!"

Premature Judgments

Research suggests that interviewers often make judgments about candidates in the first few minutes of the interview. When this occurs, a great deal of potentially valuable information is not considered.

Interviewer Domination

In successful interviews, relevant information must flow both ways. Therefore, interviewers must learn to be good listeners as well as suppliers of information.

Inconsistent Questions

If interviewers ask all applicants essentially the same questions and in the same sequence, all the applicants are judged on the same basis. This enables better decisions to be made while decreasing the likelihood of discrimination charges.

Central Tendency

When interviewers rate virtually all candidates as average, they fail to differentiate between strong and weak candidates.

Halo Error

When interviewers permit only one or a few personal characteristics to influence their overall impression of candidates, the best applicant may not be selected.

Contrast Effects

An error in judgment may occur when, for example, an interviewer meets with several poorly qualified applicants and then confronts a mediocre candidate. By comparison, the last applicant may appear to be better qualified than he or she actually is.

Interviewer Bias

Interviewers must understand and acknowledge their own prejudices and learn to deal with them. The only valid bias for an interviewer is to favor the best-qualified candidate for the open position.

Lack of Training

When the cost of making poor selection decisions is considered, the expense of training employees in interviewing skills can be easily justified.

Behavior Sample

Even if an interviewer spent a week with an applicant, the sample of behavior might be too small to judge the candidate's qualifications properly. In addition, the candidate's behavior during an interview is seldom typical or natural.

Nonverbal Communication

Interviewers should make a conscious effort to view themselves as applicants do to avoid sending inappropriate or unintended nonverbal signals.

the applicants can perform the essential functions of the jobs they are applying for.[45]

When the interviewer has obtained the necessary information and answered the applicant's questions, the interview should be concluded. At this point, the interviewer should tell the applicant that he or she will receive notification of the selection decision shortly. When this promise is broken, a positive relationship between the applicant and the organization may be destroyed.

Personal Reference Checks

Reference checks: A way to gain additional insight into the information provided by an applicant and a way to verify the accuracy of the information provided.

Personal **reference checks** may provide additional insight into the information furnished by the applicant and allow verification of its accuracy. In fact, applicants are often required to submit the names of several references who can provide additional information about them. The basic flaw with this step in the selection process is that virtually every living person can name three or four individuals willing to make favorable statements about him or her. Furthermore, personal references are likely to focus on personal characteristics of the candidate. Objective, job-related data are seldom gathered from these sources. For this reason, most organizations place more emphasis on investigations of previous employment.

Background Investigations

Background investigations primarily seek data from references supplied by the applicant including his or her previous employers. The intensity of background investigations depends on the level of responsibility inherent in the position to be filled. The employer faces several potential problems at this stage of the selection process. If a *reasonable* background investigation is not conducted, the employer may be legally liable for negligent hiring, or if the investigation reveals negative information about the applicant, invasion of privacy or defamation charges may be filed. A true *catch 22* situation is created for employers. Carefully checking references reduces the risks of a lawsuit stemming from the failure to exercise reasonable care when selecting new employees. Reasonable care varies according to the job. The risk of harm to third parties, for example, requires a higher standard of care when hiring a taxi driver than a bank teller.[46]

A related problem in obtaining information from previous employers is their general reluctance to reveal such data. The Privacy Act of 1974, although limited to the public sector, provides a major reason for this hesitancy. Employers and employees in the private sector have become very sensitive to the privacy issue. About a dozen states have passed laws to protect employers who provide good-faith job references of former and current employees. The intent of this legislation is to make it easier for employers to give and receive meaningful information. However, there has been some hesitancy on the part of firms to take advantage of it. Apparently, there is a wait-and-see attitude; although a protective law does exist, litigation and a court ruling are required before the statute is fully understood.[47]

There are two schools of thought with regard to supplying information about former employees. One is, "Don't tell them anything." The other is "Honesty is the best policy." In the more conservative approach, the employer typically provides only basic data, such as starting and termination dates and last job title. The *honesty* approach is based on the reality that facts honestly given or opinions honestly held constitute a solid legal defense. When former employers are unwilling to give any information about a job applicant, both the potential employer and the applicant are disadvantaged. A red flag is quickly raised when a former employer refuses to talk about a one-time employee.

Regardless of the difficulties encountered in background investigations, employing organizations have no choice but to engage in them. One compelling reason is that credential fraud has increased in recent years. Some 7 percent to 10 percent of job applicants are not what they present themselves to be. Some applicants are not even who they say they are. They may also exaggerate their skills, education, and experience when given the chance. One firm gave applicants a list of equipment and asked them to identify the items they were qualified to operate. A high percentage of the candidates indicated they could operate equipment that did not exist.[48]

Prospects for employment should be asked to sign a liability waiver for employers who desire to obtain background checks.[49] A comprehensive waiver releases former employers, business references, and others from liability. The waiver can also authorize checks of court records and the verification of the applicant's educational history and other credentials.[50] The results of all reference and background checks should be fully documented.

Small firms may not possess the staff to screen backgrounds of prospective employees thoroughly. Even large organizations may prefer to use the specialized services of professional screening firms. An alternative is presented by consultants who may electronically tap into public records, buy computerized records of credit reporting firms, and serve their clients effectively and efficiently. Some background checks may be performed within 24 hours for a few dollars per search. Pinkerton Security and Investigation Services screens more than one million job applicants each year for its own operations and for its clients.[51]

Regardless of how they are accomplished, background investigations have become increasingly important for companies in making sound selection decisions and avoiding charges of negligent hiring. The investigations may provide information critical to selection decisions as virtually every qualification an applicant lists can be verified.

Negligent Hiring and Retention

Negligent hiring has become a critical concern in the selection process. An employer can be held responsible for an employee's unlawful acts if the hiring firm does not reasonably investigate applicants' backgrounds and then assigns potentially dangerous persons to positions where they can inflict harm. This liability exists for an employer even if the employee's actions are not job related. A firm should not go overboard with the investigation, however, because invasion of privacy is a possibility. Negligent retention, a related potential liability, involves keeping persons on the payroll whose records indicate strong potential for wrongdoing.

Employers are beginning to be held responsible for actions outside the scope of the employees' duties. For example, if an employer hired a manager of an apartment complex without investigating the person's background and the individual later assaulted a tenant, the employer could be held responsible for the action. Employers are required by law to provide employees a safe place to work. This duty has been extended to providing safe employees because the courts have reasoned that a dangerous worker is comparable to a defective machine.

Negligent hiring cases often involve awards in the hundreds of thousands of dollars. In addition, they are likely to be upheld on appeal. The primary consideration in negligent hiring is whether the risk of harm from a dangerous employee was reasonably foreseeable. The nature of the job also has a critical bearing on the employer's obligation. If the job gives employees access to homes or property (as in the case of meter readers, security guards, and exterminators), the hiring firm may be found to have an obligation to make a reasonable investigation into the person's background. Occupations that are especially sensitive to the negligent hiring dilemma include landlords, common carriers, workers in hospitals and other patient care facilities, and taxi drivers.

A case in point is a Fort Worth, Texas, cab company. One of its drivers picked up a young mother and her daughters at a bus station and took them to a deserted area, where he raped and robbed the mother. The young woman sued the cab company and won a judgment of $4,500,000 for *negligent hiring*.[52] The Texas Supreme Court determined that a reasonable background investigation would have made it quite clear that the cab driver should not have been hired. He had been previously convicted of robbery and forgery, and before that, he had been arrested and charged for using a hammer to assault a woman. To avoid cases of this sort, employers should consider the type of interaction employees have with customers. Employers should also make reasonable background investigations and keep written records of the investigations.[53] A hiring organization cannot avoid the possibility of legal action. However, interviewing a minimum of three references is one of the surest ways to avoid a charge of negligent hiring.[54]

Polygraph Tests

For many years, another way used to verify background information has been the polygraph, or lie detector test. One purpose of the polygraph was to confirm or refute the information an applicant provided on the job application. However, the Employee Polygraph Protection Act of 1988 severely limited the use of polygraph tests in the private sector. It made unlawful the use of a polygraph test by any employer engaged in interstate commerce. Even so, the act does not apply to government employers, and there are limited exceptions for ongoing investigations and for drug security, drug theft, or drug diversion investigations.

The Selection Decision

After obtaining and evaluating information about the finalists in a job selection process, the manager must take the most critical step of all: making the actual hiring decision. The final choice will be made from among those still in the running after reference checks, selection tests, background investigations, and interview information have been evaluated. The individual with the best overall qualifications may not be hired. Rather, the person whose qualifications most closely conform to the requirements of the open position and the organization should be selected. If a firm is going to invest thousands of dollars to recruit, select, and train an employee, the manager must hire the most qualified available candidate for the position.

Human resource professionals may be involved in all phases leading up to the final employment decision. However, especially for higher level positions, the person who normally makes the final selection is the manager who will be responsible for the new employee's performance. In making this decision, the operating manager will review results of the selection methods used. All will not likely be weighted the same. The question then becomes, "Which data are most predictive of job success?"

In a survey of over 200 HR executives, five selection methods were rated as above average in their ability to predict employees' job performance.[55] These included work samples, references/recommendations, unstructured interviews, structured interviews, and assessment centers. Academic research confirms that work samples, assessment centers, and structured interviews are good methods. For each firm, the best optimum selection method may be different.

Physical Examination

After the decision has been made to extend a conditional job offer, the next phase of the selection process may involve a physical examination of the applicant. Typically, a job offer is contingent on the applicant's passing this examination. The basic purpose of the physical examination is to determine whether an applicant is physically capable of performing the work. For instance, if the work is physically demanding and the examination clearly reveals a condition prohibiting the performance of required tasks, the individual will likely be rejected. In addition, the physical examination information may be used to determine whether certain physical capabilities differentiate successful from less-successful employees.

Managers must be aware of the legal liabilities related to physical examinations. The *Uniform Guidelines* state that these examinations should be used to reject applicants only when the results show that job performance would be adversely affected.

The Rehabilitation Act of 1973 and the Americans with Disabilities Act of 1990 do not prohibit employers from requiring physical examinations. However, they have encouraged employers who are considering hiring covered employees to examine carefully each job's physical requirements. The acts require employers to take affirmative action to hire qualified disabled persons who, with reasonable accommodation, can perform the essential components of a job.

Notification of Candidates

The selection process results should be made known to candidates—successful and unsuccessful—as soon as possible. Any delay may result in the firm's losing a prime candidate, as top prospects often have other employment options. As a matter of courtesy and good public relations, the unsuccessful candidates should also be promptly notified.

If currently employed by another firm, the successful candidate customarily gives between two and four weeks' notice. Even after this notice, the individual may need some personal time to prepare for the new job. This transition time is particularly important if the new job requires a move to another city. Thus, the amount of time before the individual can join the firm is often considerable—but necessary.

The firm may also want the individual to delay the date of employment. If, for example, the new employee's first assignment upon joining the firm is to attend a training school, the organization may request that the individual delay joining the firm until the school begins. This practice, which would only benefit the company, should not be abused, especially if it places an undue hardship on the individual.

Applicants may be rejected during any phase of the selection process. Research has indicated that most people can accept losing if they lose fairly.[56] Problems occur when the selection process appears to be less than objective. It is therefore important for firms to develop and utilize rational selection tools.

HRM IN ACTION
NEEDING A FAVOR

Julie Thompson, the production manager for Ampex Manufacturing, called her friend, Bill Alexander, in human resources, to ask a favor. "Bill, I have a friend I'd like you to consider for the new sales manager's position. I really like the fellow and would appreciate anything you could do."

"Tell me about the person," said Bill.

"He just graduated from State University with a degree in history, I believe. He has no real work experience, but I'm sure he could learn quickly. His parents are real good friends of mine, and I sure would like to help him out."

How would you respond?

When considerable time has been spent on the individual in the selection process, a company representative may sit down with the applicant and explain why another person was offered the job. Increasingly, however, time constraints may force the firm to write a rejection letter. However, such a letter can still be personalized. A personal touch will often reduce the stigma of rejection and the chance that the applicant will have negative feelings about the company. An impersonal letter is likely to have the opposite effect. The best an organization can do is to make selection decisions objectively and to hope that most individuals can, with time, accept the fact that they were not chosen.

A GLOBAL PERSPECTIVE

Global Selection: Not Adaptive, Not Successful

Globally, organizations are facing a growing mismatch between new jobs requiring higher level skills and the people available to fill them. Global human resource management is becoming an even greater challenge because, according to the Commission on Workforce Quality and Labor Market Efficiency, unless government and business undertake a vast increase in their investment in human capital, U.S. companies will not be able to hire the types of workers needed to compete in global markets.[57]

According to the Council on Competitiveness, Washington, D.C., human resources are the key to global competitiveness. Therefore, employee selection for overseas assignments must be carefully addressed. Selecting employees for expatriate assignments is often difficult and complex. Selecting the correct individual involves more than just selecting an individual who is qualified to do the job domestically. The selection process must ensure that the individual chosen is adaptive to the foreign culture and will be receptive to training.

Further complicating the issue of expatriate selection, most employees will have families, so the selection process involves profiling the appropriateness of the candidate and his or her family. Therefore, expatriate selection is actually a dual-selection process, involving the individual and his or her family. When selecting a potentially successful candidate for a global assignment, a company needs to remember that, in most cases, it is sending the entire family, not just the employee, overseas. Crucial to the success of an international assignment is selecting the right employee with a family compatible with the assignment. Basically, the professional skills and job qualifications are important, but the ability of the employee and family to adapt to living in a different culture can be even more of a factor in determining the overall success of a global assignment.[58]

SUMMARY

1. *Define* selection.

Selection is the process of choosing from a group of applicants those individuals best suited for a particular position.

2. *Identify the environmental factors that affect the selection process.*
The environmental factors that affect the selection process include legal considerations, organizational hierarchy, applicant pool, type of organization, and probationary period.

3. *Describe the general selection process.*
The selection process typically begins with the preliminary interview in which obviously unqualified candidates are rejected. Next, applicants complete the firm's application form, and this is followed by the administration of selection tests and a series of employment interviews, with reference and background checks. Once the selection decision has been made, the prospective employee may be given a company physical examination.

4. *Explain the importance of the preliminary interview.*
The selection process begins with an initial screening of applicants to remove individuals who obviously do not fulfill the position requirements. In addition to quickly eliminating the obviously unqualified job applicants, a preliminary interview may produce other positive benefits for the firm.

5. *Identify the type of questions that should be asked on an application form.*
The specific type of information requested in an application blank may vary from firm to firm and even by job types within a given organization, but the information sought should be job related. Sections of an application typically include name, address, telephone number, military service, education, and work history.

6. *Describe the basic conditions that should be met if selection tests are to be used in the screening process.*
Standardization refers to uniformity of procedures and conditions related to administering tests. Objectivity means ensuring that all individuals scoring a given test will obtain the same results. A norm is a distribution of scores obtained by people similar in nature to applicants being tested. Reliability is the extent to which a selection test provides consistent results. Validity is the extent to which a test measures what it purports to measure.

7. *Explain the types of validation studies.*
Criterion-related validity is determined by comparing the scores on selection tests to some aspect of job performance. Content validity is a test validation method whereby a person performs certain tasks that are actually required in the job, or he or she completes a paper-and-pencil test that measures relevant job knowledge. Construct validity is a test validation method to determine whether a test measures certain traits or qualities that are important in performing the job.

8. *Describe types of employment tests.*
Cognitive aptitude tests measure an individual's ability to learn as well as to perform a job. Job-related abilities may be classified as verbal, numerical, perceptual speed, spatial, and reasoning. Psychomotor abilities tests measure strength, coordination, and dexterity. Job knowledge tests

are designed to measure a candidate's knowledge of the duties of the position for which he or she is applying. Work-sample tests (simulations) identify a task or set of tasks that are representative of the job. Vocational interest tests indicate the occupation in which a person is most interested and is most likely to experience satisfaction. As selection tools, personality tests have been controversial.

9. *Identify the types of information that should be gained from the interview.*

The interview should provide information about occupational experience, academic experience, interpersonal skills, personal qualities, and organizational fit.

10. *Describe the basic types of interviewing.*

An unstructured interview is one in which probing, open-ended questions are asked. A structured interview consists of a series of job-related questions that are asked of each applicant for a particular job. The behavior description interview is a structured interview that uses questions designed to probe the candidate's past behavior in specific situations.

11. *Describe the various methods of interviewing.*

In a typical employment interview, the applicant meets one-on-one with an interviewer. An interview consisting of several applicants interacting in the presence of one or more company representatives is a group interview. In the board interview, one candidate is quizzed by several interviewers. A form of interview that intentionally creates anxiety to determine how an applicant will react in certain types of environments is a stress interview. In a national search for a high-level position, it may be desirable to interview a number of candidates. However, with increasing pressure to reduce costs, a videotaped interview may be the solution. At times, the computer is used in the interviewing process.

12. *Define a* **realistic job preview.**

A realistic job preview (RJP) conveys job information to the applicant in an unbiased manner, including both positive and negative factors.

13. *Explain the legal implications of interviewing.*

The definition of a test in the *Uniform Guidelines* included "physical, education and work experience requirements from informal or casual interviews." Because the interview is considered to be a test, it is subject to the same validity requirements as any other step in the selection process, should adverse impact be shown. For the interview, this constraint presents special difficulties.

14. *Explain why reference checks and background investigations are conducted.*

Reference checks are ways to provide additional insight into the information provided by the applicant and to verify the accuracy of the information provided. The background investigation may be helpful in determining whether the person's past work experience is related to the qualifications needed for the new position and in avoiding charges of negligent hiring.

15. *Explain negligent hiring and retention.*

An employer can be held responsible for an employee's unlawful acts if the company does not reasonably investigate applicants' backgrounds and then assigns potentially dangerous persons to positions where they can inflict harm. This liability exists for an employer even if the employee's actions are not job related. Negligent retention involves keeping persons on the payroll when their records indicate strong potential for wrongdoing.

16. *Explain the reasons for preemployment physical examinations.*

One of the reasons for requiring a physical exam is to screen out individuals who have a contagious disease. Also, the physical exam assists in determining whether an applicant is physically capable of performing the work. Finally, the physical examination information may be used to determine whether there are certain physical capabilities that differentiate between successful and less-successful employees.

QUESTIONS FOR REVIEW

1. What basic steps normally are followed in the selection process?
2. Identify and describe the various factors outside the control of the human resource manager that could affect the selection process.
3. What would be the selection ratio if there were 15 applicants to choose from and only one position to fill? Interpret the meaning of this selection ratio.
4. If a firm wants to use selection tests, how should they be used to avoid discriminatory practices?
5. What is the general purpose of the preliminary interview?
6. What types of questions should be asked on an application form?
7. What basic conditions should be met if selection tests are to be used in the screening process? Briefly describe each.
8. What are the types of approaches that the *Uniform Guidelines* say should be followed to validate selection tests?
9. What is a cutoff score?
10. Identify and describe the various types of employment tests.
11. What information should be gained from the interview?
12. What are the basic types of interviews?
13. Describe the various methods of interviewing?
14. What is a realistic job preview?
15. What are the legal implications of interviewing?
16. What is the purpose of reference checks and background investigations?
17. Why should an employer be concerned with negligent hiring and retention?
18. What are the reasons for administering a physical examination?

DEVELOPING HRM SKILLS

AN EXPERIENTIAL EXERCISE

Selecting the best person to fill a vacant position is one of the most important tasks of human resource management. As all managers recognize, many factors must be considered to ensure proper selection. The selection decision you will be dealing with in this exercise is necessary because George Winston has just been promoted; before he starts his new job, he must determine his replacement. George's firm is an affirmative action employer, and presently there are few women in management. George has some excellent employees to choose from, but he must consider many factors before he makes a decision. The people upstairs made it perfectly clear that they expect George to select an individual who can perform as well as he did over the last six years.

Four individuals will have roles in this exercise: one to serve as George Winston, the current supervisor, and three to be the candidates for the promotion. Your instructor will provide the participants with additional information necessary to complete the exercise.

Take It to the Net

We invite you to visit the Mondy home page on the Prentice Hall Web site at:

http://www.prenhall.com/mondy

for updated information, Web-based exercises, and links to other HR-related sites.

HRM SIMULATION

*Y*our team will have to make a critical selection decision with Incident D in the *Simulation Players Manual*. Four applicants have applied for a Level 3 supervisor's job, and your team has been provided a job description. Your team will have a tough decision because all applicants have different strengths and weaknesses.

HRM INCIDENT

1

Business First!

*A*s production manager for Thompson Manufacturing, Jack Stephens has the final authority to approve the hiring of any new supervisors who work for him. The human resource manager performs the initial screening of all prospective supervisors and then sends the most likely candidates to Jack for interviews.

One day recently, Jack received a call from Pete Peterson, the human resource manager: "Jack, I've just spoken to a young man who may be just who you're looking for to fill that final line supervisor position. He has some good work experience and it appears as if his head is screwed on straight. He's here right now and available if you could possibly see him."

Jack hesitated a moment before answering, "Gee, Pete," he said, "I'm certainly busy today but I'll try to squeeze him in. Send him on down."

A moment later Allen Guthrie, the new applicant, arrived at Jack's office and introduced himself. "Come on in, Allen," said Jack. "I'll be right with you after I make a few phone calls." Fifteen minutes later Jack finished the calls and began talking with Allen. Jack was quite impressed. After a few minutes, Jack's door opened and a supervisor yelled, "We have a small problem on line number 1 and need your help." Jack stood up and said, "Excuse me a minute, Allen." Ten minutes later Jack returned, and the conversation continued for 10 more minutes before a series of phone calls again interrupted them.

The same pattern of interruptions continued for the next hour. Finally, Allen looked at his watch and said, "I'm sorry, Mr. Stephens, but I have to pick up my wife." "Sure thing, Allen," Jack said as the phone rang again. "Call me later today."

Questions
1. What specific policies should a company follow to avoid interviews like this one?
2. Explain why Jack, not Pete, should make the selection decision.

HRM INCIDENT

2

Should We Investigate?

*P*atsy Swain, district sales manager for Avco Electronics, was preparing to interview her first applicant, Ray Wyscup, for a sales representative position. She had advertised for an individual with detailed knowledge of computers and spreadsheet software in addition to a minimum of five years' sales experience.

"Hello Ray, I'm Pat Swain. I've looked at your resumé and am anxious to talk to you about this job. You have a very impressive sales record."

"It's nice to meet you, Pat. Your ad in the *Journal* certainly caught my attention. I would like to work with a firm offering such a promising career."

"Glad you saw it Ray. We like to believe that our firm is unique and truly has something to offer top caliber people such as you. Why don't you begin this session by telling me all about yourself? We are a very close knit group here, and I would like to learn about you and your family."

Ray appeared to be very relaxed and comfortable in Pat's presence. He began, "Well, I'm a single parent with two preschool children. Since I'm only 41 years old, I'm pretty well able to keep up with their various activities. Of course, you understand that one gets sick occasionally, and this causes me to take a few personal days off, but I've always been able to handle it. This circumstance wouldn't affect my job performance."

"Well, I'm sure it wouldn't. I also have some youngsters at home," Pat replied. "Would you now tell me about your last job with IBX?"

Ray, feeling more confident than ever, began, "Well, Pat, I had a brief, but very successful stint with them. But I would prefer that you not contact them about me. You see, my regional manager and I had a personality conflict, and I'm afraid he might not tell a straight story."

"I see," Pat said. "What about your position before that, your job with Uniserv?"

"I did well there too," Ray stated. "But that outfit went belly up. I have no idea where any of those people are now."

After the interview had continued for about an hour, Pat said, "Well, I guess that about wraps it up, Ray, unless you have questions for me?"

"No," Ray responded, "I believe I understand the nature of the position, and I can assure you that I will do a great job for you."

Pat smiled and nodded and the two shook hands as Ray departed.

Questions
1. Do you agree with the interview format provided by Patsy Swain? Explain.
2. How will Patsy handle a background investigation of Ray Wyscup?

Notes

1. Clyde E. Witt, "Get Smart about Productivity," *Material Handling Engineering* (January 1996): 22.
2. Peter F. Drucker, "Getting Things Done: How to Make People Decisions," *Harvard Business Review* 63 (July/August 1985): 22.
3. Patricia Buhler, "Managing in the 90s," *Supervision* 57 (May 1996): 26.
4. Michael Barrier, "Hiring the Right People," *Nation's Business* 84 (June 1996): 20.
5. J. Douglas Phillips, "The Price Tag on Turnover," *Personnel Journal* 69 (December 1990): 58–61.
6. Stephen J. Vodanovich and Rosemary H. Lowe, "They Ought to Know Better: The Incidence and Correlates of Inappropriate Application Blank Inquiries," *Public Personnel Management* 21 (Fall 1992): 363–364.
7. Glenn Rifkin, "Virtual Recruiter: Software That Reads Resumés," *The New York Times* (March 24, 1996): F12.
8. Shannon Peter Talbott, "Get the Most from Automated Resumé-tracking Software," *Personnel Journal* 75 (Supplement to March 1996 Issue): 18.
9. Elizabeth Sheley, "High Tech Recruiting Methods," *HRMagazine* 40 (September 1995): 63.
10. Ellen Neuborne, "Putting Job Seekers to the Test: Employers Score New Hires," *USA Today* (July 9, 1997): 1B.
11. John E. Hunter and Frank L. Schmidt, "Ability Tests: Economic Benefits versus the Issue of Fairness," *Industrial Relations* 21 (Fall 1982): 293.
12. Valerie Frazee, "Do Your Job-Applicant Tests Make the Grade?" *Personnel Journal* 75 (August 1996 Supplement): 17.
13. T. L. Brink, "A Discouraging Word Improves Your Interviews," *HRMagazine* 37 (December 1992): 49.

14. David E. Terpstra, "The Search for Effective Methods," *HR Focus* 73 (May 1996): 16–17.
15. Jonathan A. Segal, "Take Applicants for a Test Drive," *HRMagazine* 41 (December 1996): 120.
16. Carla Joinson, "Is After-Hire Testing the Best Solution," *HRMagazine* 42 (July 1997): 122.
17. Terpstra, "The Search for Effective Methods."
18. Ellen Neuborne, "Putting Job Seekers to the Test: Employers Score New Hires," *USA Today* (July 9, 1997): 01B.
19. Robert M. Solomon and Sydney J. Usprich, "Employment Drug Testing," *Business Quarterly* 58 (Winter 1993): 73.
20. Tyler D. Hartwell, Paul D. Steele, and Nathaniel F. Rodman, "Prevalence of Drug Testing in the Workplace," *Monthly Labor Review* 119 (November 1996): 35.
21. Gerald L. White, "Employee Turnover: The Hidden Drain on Profits," *HR Focus* 72 (January 1995): 15–17.
22. Samuel J. Bresier and Roger D. Sommer, "Take Care in Administering Tests under ADA," *HRMagazine* 37 (April 1992): 49–50.
23. Kevin R. Murphy, "Why Pre-Employment Alcohol Testing is Such a Bad Idea," *Business Horizons* 38 (September–October 1995): 69–70.
24. Maureen Minehan, "The Right to Medical Privacy," *HRMagazine* 42 (March 1997): 160.
25. Joanne Kenen, "Experts Urge Limits to Genetic Tests in Workplace," *Reuters Business Report* (March 20, 1997): 1.
26. Andy Seiler, "Genetic Test Threat Grows," *USA Today* (April 19, 1996): 13A.
27. Kenen, "Experts Urge Limits to Genetic Tests in Workplace."
28. Brink, "A Discouraging Word Improves Your Interviews."
29. Timothy A. Judge and Gerald R. Ferris, "The Elusive Criterion of Fit in Human Resources Staffing Decisions," *Human Resources Management: Perspectives, Context, Functions and Outcomes* (Englewood Cliffs, NJ: Prentice Hall, 1995): 217.
30. Clifford E. Montgomery, "Organizational Fit Is Key to Job Success," *HRMagazine* 41 (January 1996): 95.
31. Ann Sanders-Means, "Recruiting: It's Not a Perfect Science," *Nashville Business Journal* (August 1995): 30.
32. *Selection Interviewing for the 1990s* (New York: DBM Publishing, a Division of Drake Beam Morin, Inc, 1993): 28.
33. Erin M. Davies, "Wired for Hiring: Microsoft's Slick Recruiting Machine," *Fortune* 133 (February 5, 1996): 123–124.
34. Mary H. Yarborough, "New Variations on Recruitment Prescreening," *HR Focus* 71 (October 1994): 1.
35. Alice M. Starcke, "Tailor Interviews to Predict Performance," *HRMagazine* 41 (July 1996): 49.
36. Tom Janz, Lowell Hellervik, and David C. Gilmore, *Behavior Description Interviewing* (Boston, MA: Allyn & Bacon, 1986): 15.
37. Robin Rimmer Hurst, "Video Interviewing," *HRMagazine* 41 (November 1996): 101–104.
38. Suzanne Oliver, "Slouches Make Better Operators," *Forbes* 152 (August 16, 1993): 104.
39. John P. Wanous, "Tell It Like It Is at Realistic Job Previews," in Kendrith M.

Rowland, Manual London, Gerald R. Ferris, and Jay L. Sherman (eds.), *Current Issues in Personnel Management* (Boston: Allyn & Bacon, 1980): 41–50.

40. Brink, "A Discouraging Word Improves Your Interviews."

41. Ellen C. Auwarter and Darlene Orlov, "How to Screen without Getting Sued," *Industry Forum* (January 1997), 12.

42. Jonathan A. Segal, "Looking for Trouble?" *HRMagazine* 42 (July 1997): 78.

43. Phillip M. Perry, "Your Most Dangerous Legal Traps When Interviewing Job Applicants," *Editor & Publisher* 126 (February 27, 1993): 21–23.

44. Robert L. Brady, "The ADA and Job Interviews," *HR Focus* 73 (April 1996): 20.

45. Segal, "Looking for Trouble?"

46. Paul W. Barada, "Reference Checking Is More Important Than Ever," *HRMagazine* 41 (November 1996): 49.

47. Bill Leonard, "Reference-Checking Laws: Now What?" *HRMagazine* 40 (December 1996): 57–58.

48. Stevan P. Payne, "A Closer Look at Hiring and Firing," *Security Management* 33 (June 1989): 50.

49. Robert LoPresto, "Reference Checking: Getting Information—Safely," *Inc* 17 (December 1995): 120.

50. Barada, "Check References with Care."

51. Bob Smith, "The Evolution of Pinkerton," *Management Review* 82 (September 1993): 56.

52. Caleb S. Atwood and James M. Neel, "New Lawsuits Expand Employer Liability," *HRMagazine* 35 (October 1990): 74.

53. Joseph W. Ambash, "Knowing Your Limits: How Far Can You Go When Checking an Applicant's Background?" *Management World* 19 (March/April 1990): 8–10.

54. Barada, "Check References with Care," 56.

55. Terpstra, "The Search for Effective Methods."

56. Ken Jordan, "Play Fair and Square When Hiring from Within," *HRMagazine* 42 (January 1997): 49.

57. Elizabeth Coinor, "Will Our Human Resources Measure Up?" *HR Focus* 72 (October 1995): 22–23.

58. David E. Molnar and G. Michael Loewe, "Global Assignments: Seven Keys to International HR Management," *HR Focus* 74 (May 1997): 11–12.

| ABCNEWS | VIDEO CASE |

Genetic Testing: Is It Ethical?

Medical scientists continue to learn more about our genetic maps. One research organization even hopes to map out human DNA by the year 2005. Genetic testing can now determine such things as whether a person carries a mother's gene for breast cancer or a father's marker for heart disease. The problem is that the tests cannot determine when a person will become ill or even whether the person will definitely get the disease. Although the Americans with Disabilities Act has been interpreted to cover discrimination on the basis of genetic information, there is evidence that some employers use the test for employment decisions.

There are positive and negative aspects to genetic testing. On the positive side, if people know what their future risk of illness is going to be, preventive medicine can be practiced; they can focus on the things that they are specifically at risk for. For example, if a person is at risk for colon cancer, that individual can have a colonoscopy once a year in order for a physician to detect and surgically remove polyps when they are still small and treatable. On the negative side, if genetic testing indicates that someone falls into a high-risk category for colon cancer, once the tests results are available, other people are going to have access to that information. If a business organization provides this test and uses it as a selection device, that employer will obviously know the results as will all future employers. Most likely insurance companies will know the results as well.

Because genetic research holds the promise of alleviating suffering for the human race, it will no doubt continue. There are, however, many ethical questions that remain to be answered about the use of genetic testing including the way these tests are used to make employment selection decisions.

QUESTIONS:

1. Should organizations be permitted to use genetic testing as a selection tool? Explain your answer.
2. What ethical problems do you see related to genetic testing?
3. Would you like to know the diseases that you are likely to contract during your lifetime? Why would (or wouldn't) you?
4. What should Congress do (if anything) about the question of genetic testing?

Source: "Genetic Testing: Do You Really Want to Know?" *Nightline*, ABC News; aired April 26, 1996.

PART FOUR

HUMAN RESOURCE DEVELOPMENT

8
Training and Development

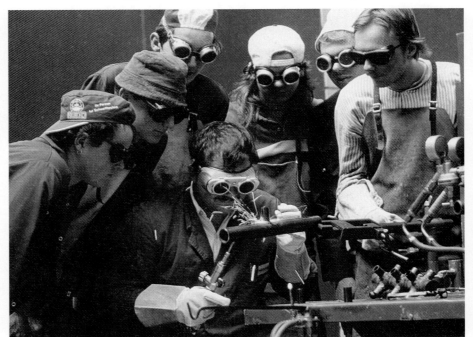

CHAPTER OBJECTIVES

1. Define *training and development* (T&D).
2. Describe the T&D process.
3. Explain factors influencing T&D.
4. Identify the various training and development methods.
5. Describe management development.
6. Identify the means by which T&D programs are evaluated.
7. Describe the Job Training Partnership Act.
8. Define *orientation* and identify the purposes of orientation.
9. Define *organizational development* (OD).
10. Describe various OD techniques.

*L*ou McGowen was worried as she approached the training director's office. She is the supervisor of six punch press operators at Keller-Globe, a maker of sheet metal parts for the industrial refrigeration industry. She had just learned that her punch presses would soon be replaced with a continuous-feed system that would double the speed of operations. She was thinking about how the workers might feel about the new system when the training director, Bill Taylor, opened the door and said, "Come on in, Lou. I've been looking forward to seeing you."

After a few pleasantries, Lou told Bill of her concerns. "The operators really know their jobs now, but this continuous-feed system is a whole new ball game. I'm concerned, too, about how the workers will feel about it. The new presses are going to run faster. They may think that their job is going to be harder."

Bill replied, "After talking with the plant engineer and the production manager, I have made up a tentative training schedule that might make you feel a little better. I think we first have to let the workers know why this change is necessary. You know that both our competitors changed to this new system last year. After that, we will teach your people to operate the new presses."

"Who's going to do the teaching?" Lou asked. "I haven't even seen the new system."

"Well, Lou," said Bill, "the manufacturer has arranged for you to visit a plant with a similar system. They'll also ship one of the punch presses in early so you and your workers can learn to operate it."

"Will the factory give us any other training help?" Lou asked.

"Yes, I have asked them to send a trainer down as soon as the first press is set up. The trainer will conduct some classroom sessions and then work with your people on the new machine."

After further discussion about details, Lou thanked Bill and headed back to the production department. She was confident that the new presses would be a real benefit to her section and that her workers could easily learn the skills required.

*L*ou was lucky to have a training professional to help her prepare the operators for the change in their jobs. Many times managers have to perform the training personally. As we see in this chapter, training and development (T&D) is a most important managerial function.

We devote the first portion of this chapter to defining and explaining the scope of training and development and current trends in the field. Next, the T&D process is described. Then we discuss organization change and factors that influence T&D. Next, we consider determining T&D needs and establishing T&D objectives. Then we look at the numerous T&D methods. Sections on management development, supervisory management training programs, and training programs for entry-level professionals and operative employees are presented. Special training topics precede sections dealing with implementing training and development programs and evaluating T&D programs. The Job Training Partnership Act is discussed along with a section describing employee orientation. The final section of the chapter deals with organization development.

Training and Development: Definition and Scope

Training and develop-ment: A planned, continuous effort by management to improve employee competency levels and organizational performance.

Training: Activities designed to provide learners with the knowledge and skill needed for their present jobs.

Development: Learning that looks beyond the knowledge and skill needed for a present job.

Learning organiza-tions: Firms that recognize the critical importance of continuous performance-related training and development and take appropriate action.

Training and development (T&D) is a planned, continuous effort by management to improve employee competency levels and organizational performance. Although the terms may be used interchangeably, a distinction is sometimes made between the two. **Training** is designed to provide learners with the knowledge and skills needed for their present jobs.[1] Showing a worker how to operate a lathe or a supervisor how to schedule daily production are examples of training. Lou McGowen and her punch press operators will receive training in preparation for the new press. On the other hand, **development** involves learning that looks beyond today's job; it has a more long-term focus.[2] It prepares employees to keep pace with the organization as the company changes and grows. Training and development activities have the potential to align employees of a firm with its corporate strategies.[3]

In virtually every market, customers are demanding higher quality, lower costs, and faster cycle times. To meet these requirements, firms must continually improve their overall performance. Rapid advances in technology and improved processes have been important factors in helping businesses meet this challenge. However, the most important competitive advantage for any firm is its workforce, and these workers must remain competent through continuous training and development efforts. Improved performance—the bottom-line purpose of T&D—is a strategic goal for many organizations. A number of forward-thinking firms have become or are striving to become learning organizations. **Learning organizations** are firms that recognize the critical importance of continuous performance-related training and development and take appropriate action to provide them. They view training as a strategic investment rather than a budgeted cost.

In a recent year, budgeted formal training expenditures were estimated to be over $52 billion.[4] It is important to note that *formal* training refers to training activity that is planned, structured, and occurs when people are called away from their workstation to participate in it. It does not include the informal training that occurs on the job in the form of on-the-job-training.[5] Continued growth in both forms of training appears to be a given. Most organizations invest in T&D because they believe that higher profits will result—and this often happens. Training frequently improves workers' skills and boosts their motivation. This, in turn, leads to higher productivity and increased profitability.

Although training budgets are increasing in many firms, most organizations do not offer any formal training. Fortunately, this was not the case for Lou McGowen. However, just 15,000 companies (0.5 percent of the total) account for 90 percent of the billions spent on formal training annually. In addition, most of these training efforts are directed toward executives and managers, overlooking the majority of American operative employees. Notable exceptions are Motorola, Federal Express, and Corning. These firms have been cited for allocating more than 3 percent of their payroll for training. The president of Motorola once stated, "When you buy a piece of equipment, you set aside a percentage for maintenance. Shouldn't you do the same for people?"[6]

Training and development costs should be accepted for what they are— an investment in human resources. It is clear that training and development is not merely a nice thing to provide; it is a strategic resource that firms must tap to move their organizations into the next century.[7]

HR Web Wisdom

http://www.prenhall.com/mondy

SHRM—HR LINKS
Various training and development issues are addressed.

Training and Development Trends

Managers involved with training and development should be aware of the developing trends that may impact the way they perform. These trends include the following:

- Skill requirements will continue to increase in response to rapid technological change. More complex equipment and processes will boost the need for more highly skilled workers.

- The U.S. workforce will become significantly better educated and more diverse.

- Corporate restructuring will continue to reshape businesses. Although large firms have historically provided most of the training, small firms that typically provided little training offer the most promising future prospects for training.

- As outsourcing of training increases, training departments have shrunk. Much of the training provided will be by independent consultants outside conventional training and development departments.

- Although traditional classroom delivery of training still predominates, advances in technology will revolutionize the way certain training is delivered.

- The role of training departments will change significantly. Increasingly, these departments will act as brokers of learning services, no longer functioning as the sole providers of training.

- Training professionals will shift their focus from traditional training classes to flexible courses aimed more specifically at performance improvement.

- Integrated high-performance work systems will proliferate. Training will be integrated with actual work. Just-in-time and just-what's-needed training will be commonplace.

- More firms will strive to become learning organizations.

- Emphasis on human performance management will accelerate. The idea that people are a firm's most important asset will be put into action.[8]

Predictions about the future aren't always accurate. However, it behooves managers to keep an eye to the future in order to anticipate it and to act proactively. This seems to be particularly true regarding the T&D process where some of the prophecies are already coming true.

The Training and Development Process

Major adjustments in the external and internal environments necessitate corporate change. The general training and development process that anticipates or responds to change is shown in Figure 8-1. Once the need for change is recognized and the factors that influence intervention are considered, the process of determining training and development needs begins. Essentially, two questions must be asked: "What are our training needs?" and "What do we want to accomplish through our T&D efforts?" The objectives might be quite narrow if they are limited to the supervisory ability of one or two managers. Alternatively, they might be broad enough to include improving the management skills of all first-line supervisors.

After stating the T&D objectives, management can determine the appropriate methods for accomplishing them. Various methods and media are available; the selection depends on the nature of the T&D goals. Naturally, T&D must be continuously evaluated to facilitate change and accomplish organizational objectives.

As with other HRM functions, training and development is undergoing rapid change. As T&D units are being downsized, line managers are becoming more involved and much of the training is being outsourced. There is an increased need for *just-in-time training*, available when and where it is needed; also, the training must be more closely related to organizational goals. Recognizing that T&D must be a continuous process, there is a trend for firms to become learning organizations. In a dynamic environment, it is especially important for firms to provide training initiatives that address several critical needs:

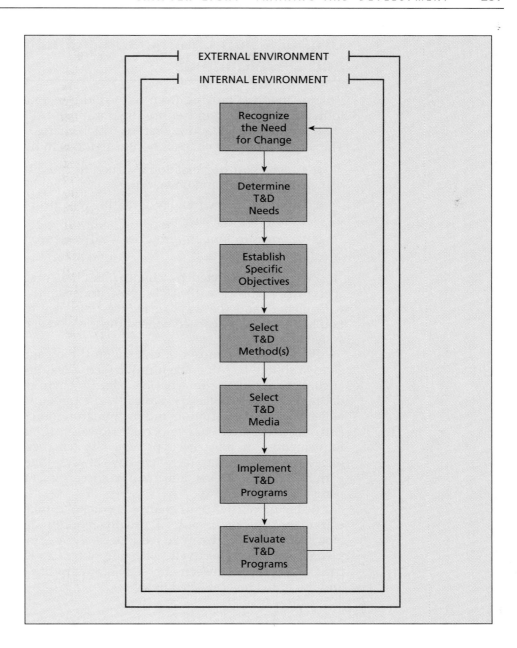

Figure 8-1
The Training and
Development (T&D)
Process

- To guide individual employees in planning and managing their careers
- To help managers coach and mentor employees
- To help managers and employees deal with change

The only constant in our lives is said to be change, and change is the force that brings about the critical need for T&D. This phenomenon is discussed next.

Organization Change and Training and Development

Change involves moving from one condition to another, and it will affect individuals, groups, and entire organizations. All organizations experience change of some sort, and the rate at which change takes place is accelerating. The most prominent changes occurring today in business include these:

- Changes in organizational structure caused by mergers, acquisitions, rapid growth, and downsizing
- Changes in technology and the way people work, resulting largely from computerization
- Changes in human resources—a diverse workforce consisting of many groups

Everyone is affected by change. As change agents, managers and staff specialists involved with T&D must understand the difficulties associated with change and the ways to reduce resistance to change. Remember that Lou McGowen was worried about how the workers would feel about the new system.

Because of the impact of change on the organization and its employees, change should be undertaken only when a real need for it exists. Of course, circumstances in the internal or external environments may make change desirable or even necessary. Basically, the impetus for change comes from a belief that the organization and its human resources can be more productive and successful after change occurs. However, if change is to be successfully implemented, it must be approached systematically. There may be a tendency for employees to feel, "We have always done it this way, so why argue with success?" However, a firm's past success guarantees neither future prosperity nor even survival.

Reducing resistance to change is crucial to success. At times, this may be extremely difficult because it usually requires shifts in people's attitudes. However, if resistance can be reduced, or even eliminated, change can be implemented more effectively. Bringing about a change in attitude requires trust and respect between the people attempting to implement the change and the individuals affected by it.

Factors Influencing Training and Development

Obviously, change is one factor that impacts T&D. Several of the other important factors that influence training and development are shown in Figure 8-2. How these factors are addressed often determines whether a firm achieves its T&D objectives.

First, training and development programs must have the full support of top management. This support must be real—not merely lip service—and it should be communicated to the entire organization. True support becomes evident when executives provide the resources needed for the T&D function.

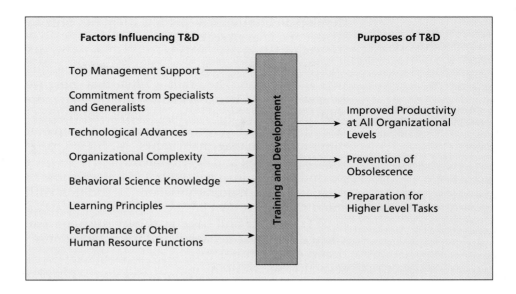

Figure 8-2
Factors Influencing
Training and
Development

In addition, all managers should be committed to and involved in the T&D process. According to one prominent director of corporate management development, "The primary responsibility for training and development lies with line managers, from the president and chairman of the board on down. T&D management merely provides the technical expertise."

To ensure effective programs, managers must be convinced that there will be a tangible payoff if resources are committed to this effort. Although training is not the only reason for Motorola's success, it is obviously an important factor. This industry leader's training program is considered a model in corporate circles because it is strongly tied to the firm's business strategy. In a recent year, Motorola was scheduled to spend about $150 million to provide at least 40 hours of training to each of its 132,000 employees. The firm dedicates more than 4 percent of its payroll for training; much above the 1 percent average invested by most American industry. During a recent five-year period, Motorola experienced annual sales increases averaging 18 percent, and earnings growth has soared at a 26 percent clip. Productivity as measured by sales per employee has grown 139 percent even though the firm's work force increased substantially. Anthony Carnevale, a labor economist with the Committee for Economic Development, stated, "Training is the strongest variable we see contributing to higher returns, and its importance grows over time."[9] One study was conducted recently to determine the relationship between education and productivity at more than 3,000 U.S. workplaces. The findings showed that on average, a 10 percent increase in workforce education level led to an 8.6 percent gain in total productivity. A 10 percent increase in the value of capital equipment increased productivity only 3.4 percent.[10]

In recent years, the increasingly rapid changes in technology, products, systems, and methods have had a significant impact on job requirements. Thus, employees face the need to upgrade their skills constantly and to develop an attitude that permits them not only to adapt to change but also to accept and even seek it.

Many organizations have changed dramatically as a result of downsizing, technological innovations, and customer demands for new and better products and services. The result is often that more work must be accomplished by fewer people. Employees must not only do more work, but they must perform work at a more complex level. Supervisors and operative employees performing in self-directed teams are taking up much of the slack from dwindling middle-management ranks. All these changes translate into a greater need for training and development.

Individuals involved with T&D must know more than the topic to be presented in a training program. In addition to having a thorough understanding of their own business, they must be aware of current behavioral science knowledge and basic learning principles. The purpose of training is to change employee behavior, and information must be learned if change is to occur. Although much remains to be discovered about the learning process, several generalizations may be helpful in understanding this phenomenon. Some general concepts—fundamentals related to learning—include:

- Behavior that is rewarded (reinforced) is more likely to recur.
- Reinforcement, to be most effective, must immediately follow the desired behavior and be clearly connected with that behavior.
- Learners progress in an area of learning only as far as they need to in order to achieve their purposes.
- Individuals are more likely to be enthusiastic about a learning situation if they themselves have participated in the planning and implementation of the project.
- What is learned is more likely to be available for use if it is learned in a situation much like that in which it is to be used and immediately preceding the time it is needed.
- The best time to learn is when the learning can be useful. Motivation is then at its strongest peak.
- Providing continuous feedback on the learner's progress enhances learning. By tracking an individual's progress, a *learning curve* can be prepared to reflect the trainee's progress over a period of time. Knowledge of results permits managers to establish realistic goals for future training.
- Practice may not make perfect but it does make "better." Repeating the performance of a task is an almost certain approach for performance improvement.
- Depending on the type of training, a wise move may be to space the training sessions. For example, the period of time between training sessions for highly complex tasks may need to be increased to permit the learning to be assimilated.

Most of these concepts clearly relate to the management and development of human resources. For example, behavior that is rewarded (reinforced) is more likely to recur. As the security and success of most employees today lies in their level of knowledge and skills, the motivation to participate in and perform well in T&D programs should be easily obtained.

Successful accomplishment of other human resource functions can also have a crucial impact on T&D. For instance, if recruitment and selection efforts attract marginally qualified workers, a more extensive T&D program will be needed to train entry-level workers. Training and development efforts may also be influenced by the firm's compensation package. Firms with competitive pay systems or progressive health and safety programs will find it easier to attract qualified workers. Reputations in these, and other HRM areas may substantially influence the type of training required.

Determining Training and Development Needs

To compete effectively, firms must keep their employees well trained. The question often asked is this: "What type of training is needed?" A study conducted by the Olsten Corporation found that for three levels of employees—management, support staff, and professional/technical employees—the skills most needed were basic computer, written communications, listening, and interpersonal communications.[11] A summary of the results of this study appears in Table 8-1.

The next step in the T&D process is to determine specific training and development needs. In today's highly competitive business environment, undertaking programs simply because other firms are doing it is asking for

TABLE 8-1

Skill Needs by Employee Level

Type of Skill	Support Staff	Professional/ Technical	Management
Basic computer	63%	50%	65%
Written communications	65%	58%	52%
Listening	60%	58%	69%
Interpersonal communications	62%	63%	67%
Organizational	50%	53%	50%
Customer service	61%	50%	39%
Quality awareness	55%	50%	48%
Analytical	42%	38%	33%
Cross-cultural communications	47%	47%	54%
Sales/marketing	27%	34%	32%
Basic math	43%	14%	9%
Reading comprehension	42%	19%	12%

Source: "Skills for Success," *The Olsten Forum*™ *on Human Resource Issues and Trends,* the Olsten Corporation, Fall 1994, p. 7.

trouble. A systematic approach to addressing bona fide needs must be undertaken.

Three types of analysis are often performed to determine an organization's training and development needs: organization analysis, task analysis, and person analysis.[12] In this context, *organization analysis* examines the entire firm to determine where training and development should be conducted. The firm's strategic goals and plans should be studied along with the results of human resource planning.

In conducting *task analysis*, two primary factors should be determined: importance and proficiency. Importance relates to the relevance of specific tasks and behaviors in a particular job and the frequency with which they are performed. Proficiency is the employees' competence in performing these tasks. Job descriptions, performance appraisals, and interviews or surveys of supervisors and job incumbents should provide the data needed.[13]

Person analysis, which focuses on the individual employee, deals with two questions: "Who needs to be trained?" and "What kind of training is needed?" The first step in a person analysis is to compare employee performance with established standards. If the person's work is acceptable, training may not be needed. Because of the need to reduce costs, some firms feel that "sheep-dip training"—in which all employees are trained whether they need it or not—should be avoided.[14] However, another school of thought is that no employee is exempt from the need for self-improvement and professional development.[15] Tests and role playing and use of assessment centers may also be helpful in conducting person analysis. The results of career planning programs may prove to be quite revealing as well.

Although employee training needs are obviously an important first step in providing T&D programs, a recent Conference Board survey indicated that the chief executive officer's vision and values were credited by 80 percent of the respondents as the most important factor influencing management development programs. The CEO's role was viewed as more critical than the firm's strategic plan, its operating needs, or its corporate culture.[16]

Establishing Training and Development Objectives

Clear and concise objectives must be formulated for training and development. Without them, designing meaningful T&D programs would not be possible. Worthwhile evaluation of a program's effectiveness would also be difficult at best. Consider these purposes and objectives for a training program involving employment compliance:

Training Area: Employment Compliance

Purpose. To provide the supervisor with

1. Knowledge and value of consistent human resource practices
2. The intent of EEO legal requirements
3. The skills to apply them

Objectives. To be able to

1. Cite the supervisory areas affected by employment laws on discrimination.
2. Identify acceptable and unacceptable actions.
3. State how to get help on equal employment opportunity matters.
4. Describe why we have discipline and grievance procedures.
5. Describe our discipline and grievance procedures, including who is covered.

As you see, the purpose is clearly established first. The specific learning objectives that follow leave little doubt of what participants should learn from the training. With these types of objectives, managers may determine whether a person has obtained the necessary knowledge from the training. For instance, a trainee either can or cannot state how to get help on equal employment opportunity matters.

Training and Development Methods

When a person is working on a car, some tools are more helpful than others for certain tasks. The same logic applies to various training and development methods. Note the diverse methods shown in Table 8-2. Some methods are more applicable to managers and professionals and others to operative employees. The majority of T&D methods generally apply to all employees.

Again referring to Table 8-2, note that T&D methods are used both on and off the job. Often, learning at the same time they are performing jobs is not feasible for employees. Thus, although a large portion of training and development takes place on the job, many T&D programs occur away from the work setting.

Regardless of whether programs are presented in-house or by an outside source, a number of methods are used to impart information and skills to managers and operative employees. These methods are discussed next.

COACHING

Coaching: An on-the-job approach in which a manager has the opportunity to teach an employee on a one-to-one basis.

Coaching is an on-the-job approach in which a manager provides instruction on a one-to-one basis. The trainee, in addition to having the opportunity to observe, is assigned significant tasks requiring decision-making skills. The experiences provided must teach the individual to be flexible and adaptive and to have a broad perspective. These characteristics, along with the ability to value and use diversity, are essential in today's environment.

To be effective, coach-counselor managers must have a thorough knowledge of the job and how it relates to the firm's goals. They should also have a strong desire to share information with the trainee and be willing to take the time—which can be considerable—for this endeavor. The relationship between the supervisor and subordinate must be based on mutual trust and confidence for this approach to be effective.

TABLE 8-2

Training and Development Methods

Method	Utilized Generally for			Conducted Primarily	
	Managers and Professionals	Operative Employees	All Employees	On-the-Job	Off-the-Job
Coaching			X	X	
Mentoring	X				X
Business Games			X		X
Case Study			X		X
Videotapes			X		X
In-basket Training			X		X
Internships	X			X	
Role Playing			X		X
Job Rotation			X	X	
Programmed Instruction			X		X
Computer-based Training			X		X
Cyberlearning:					
Internet/Intranet			X		X
Virtual Reality			X		X
Distance Learning					
and Videoconferencing			X		X
Classroom Programs			X		X
Corporate Universities			X		X
Community Colleges			X		X
On-the-job Training			X	X	
Apprenticeship Training		X		X	
Simulators			X		X
Vestibule Training		X			X

Every manager will not be a good candidate to serve as a coach. The basic problem is that many people who have become successful managers became so using skills that are different from the ones needed today. For this reason, some organizations are institutionalizing coaching as a T&D method.

MENTORING

Mentoring: An on-the-job approach to training and development in which the trainee is given an opportunity to learn on a one-to-one basis from more experienced organizational members.

Mentoring is an approach to T&D in which the trainee is given the opportunity to learn on a one-to-one basis from more experienced organizational members. The mentor is usually an older, experienced executive who serves as a host, friend, confidant, and advisor to a new firm member. The mentor can be located anywhere in the organization. The relationship may be formally planned or it may develop informally. The concept of mentoring has some prestigious advocates, such as Ortho Pharmaceutical Corporation, Bell Labs, and AT&T. Mentoring has received considerable attention, most of which has emphasized its advantages. There have even been suggestions that mentoring is necessary for an individual to make it to the top and that lack of it is the reason women and minorities have encountered the glass ceiling.

For mentoring to work, the parties' interests must be compatible, and they must understand each other's personalities. Getting teachers and students together can obviously have advantages. In a mentoring relationship, this combination has the potential for positive results.[17]

BUSINESS GAMES

Business games: Simulations that represent actual business situations.

Simulations that represent actual business situations are referred to as **business games**. These simulations attempt to duplicate selected factors in a particular situation, which are then manipulated by the participants. Business games involve two or more hypothetical organizations competing in a given product market. The participants are assigned roles, such as president, controller, and marketing vice president. They make decisions affecting price levels, production volumes, and inventory levels. Their decisions are manipulated by a computer program, with the results simulating those of an actual business situation. Participants are able to see how their decisions affect other groups and vice versa. The best part about this type of learning is that if a decision is made that costs the company $1 million, no one gets fired, and still the business lesson is learned.

> One game, originally designed for elementary grade students, involves putting together a brightly colored, plastic, six-foot high, 20-foot-long toy locomotive. The one-third scale model with moving parts is assembled by four teams of four to eight participants. Team members wear colored aprons to designate their team and get a stack of color-coded parts, a five-gallon bucket of fasteners, and some blueprints. Initially, the required organization structure is hierarchical and orders come from above. Supervisors only are permitted to talk to subordinates. Progress, if any, comes slowly. Then, halfway through the two-and-a-half hour exercise, the rules are changed. Participants get an accelerated course in total quality principles and are invited to suggest new approaches to doing the work. The pace picks up and the locomotive gets assembled. Despite the apparent simplicity of the exercise, it has been successful in giving trainees an unprecedented insight into team dynamics. As the chemical plant engineer at BP Oil Company noted, it has "taken the teamwork concept and put it at the third-grade level. But you know what? I finally get it."[18]

CASE STUDY

Case study: A training method that presents simulated business problems for trainees to solve.

The **case study** is a training method in which trainees solve simulated business problems. The individual is expected to study the information given in the case and make decisions based on the situation. If the student is provided a case involving an actual company, he or she is expected to research the firm to gain a better appreciation of its financial condition and environment. Typically, the case study method is used in the classroom with an instructor who serves as a facilitator.

VIDEOTAPES

The use of videotapes continues to be a popular training method. This method may be especially appealing to small businesses that cannot afford more expensive approaches.[19] In addition, videotapes provide the flexibility that is desired by any firm.

Behavior modeling: A training method that utilizes videotapes to illustrate effective interpersonal skills and the ways managers function in various situations.

An illustration of the use of videotapes is provided by behavior modeling. **Behavior modeling** has long been a successful training approach that uses videotapes to illustrate effective interpersonal skills and to show how managers function in various situations. The trainees observe the model's actions. Behavior modeling has been used successfully to train supervisors in such tasks as conducting performance appraisal reviews, correcting unacceptable performance, delegating work, improving safety habits, handling discrimination complaints, overcoming resistance to change, orienting new employees, and mediating between individuals or groups in conflict.[20]

IN-BASKET TRAINING

In-basket training: A simulation in which the participant is asked to establish priorities for and then handle a number of business papers, such as memoranda, reports, and telephone messages, that would typically cross a manager's desk.

In-basket training is a simulation in which the participant is given a number of business papers such as memoranda, reports, and telephone messages that would typically cross a manager's or team leader's desk. The papers, presented in no particular order, call for actions ranging from urgent to routine handling. The participant is required to act on the information contained in these papers. In this method, the trainee assigns a priority to each particular situation before making the decisions called for by each one.

HR Web Wisdom

http://www.prenhall.com/mondy

NATIONAL INTERNSHIPS
National internships, which many believe are the bridge between academia and business, are listed in the available guide, with comments.

INTERNSHIPS

As we mentioned in Chapter 6, an internship program is a recruitment method typically involving university students who divide their time between attending classes and working for an organization. Internships also serve as an effective training method.

From the employer's viewpoint, an internship provides an excellent way to view a potential permanent employee at work. Internships also provide advantages for students. The experience they obtain through working enables them to integrate theory learned in the classroom with the practice of management. At the same time, the interns' experience will help them determine whether a particular type of firm and job appeals to them.

ROLE PLAYING

Role playing: A training method in which participants are required to respond to specific problems they may actually encounter in their jobs.

In **role playing**, participants are required to respond to specific problems they may actually encounter in their jobs. Rather than hearing about how a problem might be handled or even discussing it, they learn by doing. Role playing is often used to teach such skills as interviewing, grievance handling, performance appraisal, conference leadership, team problem solving, effective communication, and leadership style analysis. The Developing HRM Skills section at the end of each chapter is a role-playing exercise that demonstrates the benefits of this training approach.

JOB ROTATION

Job rotation: A training method that involves moving employees from one job to another to broaden their experience.

In **job rotation**, employees move from one job to another to broaden their experience. This breadth of knowledge is often needed for performing higher level tasks. Rotational training programs help new employees understand a variety of jobs and their interrelationships. Job rotation has much potential as a T&D method, but it also has some potential problems. The new hires may have such short assignments that they feel more like visitors in the department than a part of the workforce. Because they often do not develop a high level of proficiency, the new hires can lower the overall productivity of the work group. In addition, employees who observe or have to work with an individual rotating through their department may resent having to help a fast-track employee who may in time become their boss.

PROGRAMMED INSTRUCTION

Programmed instruction (PI): A teaching method that provides instruction without the intervention of an instructor.

A teaching method that provides instruction without the intervention of an instructor is called **programmed instruction**. With this teaching method, information is broken down into small portions (frames). The learner reads each frame in sequence and responds to questions, receiving immediate feedback on response accuracy. If correct, the learner proceeds to the next frame. If not, the learner repeats the frame. Primary features of this approach are immediate reinforcement and the ability of learners to proceed at their own pace. Programmed instruction material may be presented in a book or by more sophisticated means, such as computers.

HR Web Wisdom

http://www.prenhall.com/mondy

COMPUTER-BASED TRAINING
The benefits of computer-based training are listed.

COMPUTER-BASED TRAINING

Computer-based training: A teaching method that takes advantage of the speed, memory, and data manipulation capabilities of the computer for greater flexibility of instruction.

Computer-based training takes advantage of the speed, memory, and data manipulation capabilities of the computer for greater flexibility of instruction. The increased speed of presentation and decreased dependence on an instructor are advantages of this training approach. Computer-based training

Multimedia: A computer application that enhances learning through presentations combining automation, stereo sound, full-motion video, and graphics.

may also utilize multimedia. **Multimedia** enhances learning with audio, animation, graphics, and interactive video using the computer. Instruction can be provided either in a central location or a satellite office.

W. R. Grace employees are required to pass periodic safety examinations. Their computer-based testing system presents safety materials followed by tests. If a participant misses a question, material regarding the question is displayed again and the answers are scrambled when the question is again presented a second time. This method enables employees to take tests at their workstation terminals throughout the plant when it fits into their work schedule.

On the downside, some students object to the absence of a human facilitator in certain computer-based programs. Another disadvantage is the cost of hardware and software. However, with enough trainees, the cost may quickly reach an acceptable level. One way to achieve this is for firms to join together as some have done to form LearnShare, a consortium of large, noncompeting manufacturing companies. This group, which includes Owens Corning, General Motors, Motorola, and 3M, plus three research universities, has combined resources to develop a Web site and buy the materials required for multimedia training. Although the firms are in different types of business, a survey indicated that 74 percent of their training needs were the same. For example, diversity training for General Motors employees should vary little from that needed by Reynolds Metals, Deere & Company, or others in the consortium. As these participants consolidate their power to take advantage of technology, their consortium can distribute educational materials anywhere on earth almost instantly and with less cost than would be incurred if each company acted alone.[21]

Technology is revolutionizing the way training and development programs can be delivered. One executive has stated, "It allows a human resources department to provide on-demand information that can be updated constantly and distributed nationally or globally."[22] Computer-based training is clearly more than a fad. In fact, a vast majority of large organizations use computers in training.

CYBERLEARNING[23]

As we move rapidly toward just-in-time delivery of information, training and development professionals must have the expertise to develop strategies that optimize a firm's technological capabilities. *Cyberlearning* is a term used to identify these high-tech training methods, some of which are discussed next.

The Internet, Intranets, and Just-in-Time Training.

Intranets: Proprietary electronic networks that permit delivery of programs that have been developed specifically for an organization's particular learning needs.

E-mail on the Internet may be used for distributing course material and sharing information. Interactive tutorials on the Internet and intranets also permit trainees to take courses on-line.

Intranets, proprietary electronic networks, permit delivery of programs that have been developed specifically for an organization's particular learning needs. To implement an intranet, an organization needs little more than a set of networked PCs loaded with inexpensive browser software.

Organizations may share a little of their intranet with outsiders but probably not all.[24]

Just-in-time training becomes feasible with computers and the Internet or intranets. This application is illustrated in the following example.

> Roy Jackson, a recent business school graduate, is in his first job as a district sales manager. He hasn't been in this position nearly long enough to feel confident in confronting one of his top sales reps, Glen Dikes. Glen has led the district in sales for the past eight years and is currently on track for a record year. Glen has a serious problem with alcohol abuse, however, and came to the office drunk for the third time this month.
>
> Uncertain as to his next action, Roy turns to his personal computer and clicks on an icon that takes him to his firm's intranet program "Management Advisor/Drug and Alcohol Abuse/Confronting an Employee." This program, developed by the training department and several line managers, plays a video that describes the firm's policy on providing help to an employee with a substance abuse problem. It also details the steps of a confrontation interview.
>
> The program then asks if the viewer would like to see an example of a confrontation interview. When Roy clicks on "yes," he sees a 10-minute tape of a confrontation interview showing the steps and points the manager should make, typical employee responses, and how a manager can deal with each.
>
> Dikes, suspecting that he may be fired, uses a company kiosk and clicks on the human resource icon. He reaches a program on "Employee Assistance/Drug Abuse & Alcohol/Telling Your Boss You Have a Problem." He then views a tape advising him how to inform his boss that he needs assistance for a personal problem and how to get help without being terminated.[25]

Virtual Reality. Using virtual reality, trainees can view objects from a perspective otherwise impractical or impossible. For example, it is not feasible to turn a drill press on its side so it can be inspected from the bottom. A computer easily permits this type of manipulation.

Distance Learning and Videoconferencing. For the past decade, a number of firms in the United States have used videoconferencing and satellite classrooms for training. This approach to training is now going interactive and appears to offer the flexibility and spontaneity of a traditional classroom. A great deal of training is beginning to take place using this technology, offering the prospect of increasing the number of trainees and at the same time saving a lot of money for the company.[26]

Global companies in particular can benefit from this new technology. With far-flung operations, travel is getting more frequent and expensive. Distance learning, videoconferencing, and similar technology can be used to increase employees' access to training, ensure consistency of instruction, and reduce the cost of delivering training and development programs. Although the heaviest users to date have been universities, one study indicated that about 10 percent of U.S. organizations with more than 100 employees had used videoconferencing for some type of training.[27]

At an IBM subsidiary, for example, programs are offered over a satellite-based network. At each of the 44 sites in the system, a 25-inch monitor is used on a desk equipped with a student response unit. These units allow interconnection with other classrooms and the instructor. The student response unit has a voice-activated microphone, question and question-cancel buttons, and keypads that allow students to answer questions from the instructor. Other firms such as AT&T, DuPont, Ford, General Electric, Mobil Oil, Sears, and Wal-Mart also use this type of service. Stentor, an alliance of Canadian telephone companies, has announced an $8-billion, 10-year initiative that will bring broadband, multimedia services to 90 percent of all homes and business in Canada by 2004.

TRENDS & INNOVATIONS

TRAINING IN THE INFORMATION AGE

What do General Motors and the Army National Guard have in common? They are trying to solve one of the growing challenges of the Information Age: helping workers keep pace with the exponential growth of on-the-job knowledge.

As Kevin Rogers, president of Interactive Solutions, said, "People can't remember all the information they learn in a classroom. They have to put it on their hip and take it with them wherever they go." GM and the military came together to solve their common training problem and brought Rogers into the group. The company has designed a wearable, multimedia, voice-controlled computer that provides on-the-spot training for technicians under the hood of a car or a tank. Users speak into the computer, the heart of which is a 7 1/2-inch by 5 1/2-inch black box packed with a Pentium microprocessor and multimedia cards that process applications such as speech recognition and video. It is equipped with software designed for on-the-job training or instant tutorials.

Training people for a high-tech world is a growing necessity. By 2005, three-quarters of all new jobs will require technical skills, according to a spokesperson for Interactive Solutions. It's impossible to put a price on the cost of addressing that training crisis nationwide, but it will be expensive if the auto industry is any indication. Interactive Solutions claims that 30 percent of the automotive industry's warranty repair costs are the result of faulty diagnoses by technicians. That creates billions of dollars a year in waste associated with unnecessary labor and parts.

"We have literally hundreds of thousands of pages we have to reference. It's becoming more of an issue in the technical world," says Jim Roach, head of service technology research at GM. Some new GM car models have as many as 19 microprocessors, testing traditional training methods.

At a model GM car dealership in Warren, Michigan, mechanics are testing five of Interactive Solutions' Mentis computers to see how well they work in the field. If the trial goes well, GM will distribute computers to car dealers around the country within 12 months, Roach says. Wearable computers could also find a broad application in medicine, education, and other knowledge-rich fields.[28]

CLASSROOM PROGRAMS

Classroom programs continue to be effective for certain types of employee training. In fact, as shown in Figure 8-3 on page 272, classroom teaching heads the list of training delivery methods used by American firms. Ninety-one percent of respondents to a recent survey stated an intention to use classroom programs for at least some of their training courses.[29]

One advantage of classroom programs is that the instructor may convey a great deal of information in a relatively short period of time. The effectiveness of classroom programs can be improved when groups are small enough to permit discussion, when the instructor is able to capture the imagination of the class, and when multimedia can be used in an appropriate manner. Louise McGowen, the supervisor mentioned at the beginning of the chapter, planned to have her workers attend classroom sessions.

CORPORATE UNIVERSITIES

A decade ago, there were about 400 corporate training institutions in the United States. Today, that number likely exceeds 1,000. The rapid growth of these institutions is tied to the need for gaining a competitive advantage and to relate learning to more specific organizational goals. Also, firms are now better able to control the quality of training and to ensure that their employees all receive the same message.

Firms often partner with universities or other organizations with training expertise such as the American Management Association. The best-known corporate universities are those at McDonalds, Disney, Motorola, and Sears. The number of such institutions is expected to grow over the next few years.[30]

TRAINING IN COMMUNITY COLLEGES

Some employers, including giant General Motors, have discovered that community colleges can provide certain types of training better and more cost effectively than alternatives. Rapid technological changes and corporate restructuring have created a new demand by industry for community college training resources. Among the examples are these:[31]

■ Sematech, the semiconductor industry association, is working with Maricopa Community College in Phoenix to develop a national curriculum for training manufacturing technicians.

■ Pennsylvania Power & Light has created a technology demonstration center with Northampton Community College in Bethlehem, Pennsylvania, to test-run new developments.

■ Aegon US, the Cedar Rapids insurer, built a $10 million corporate data center at Kirkwood Community College in Cedar Rapids, Iowa, to be shared by college students and company employees.

■ General Motors and Toyota donated $2 million of equipment and 75 demonstration cars to Gateway Community-Technical College in

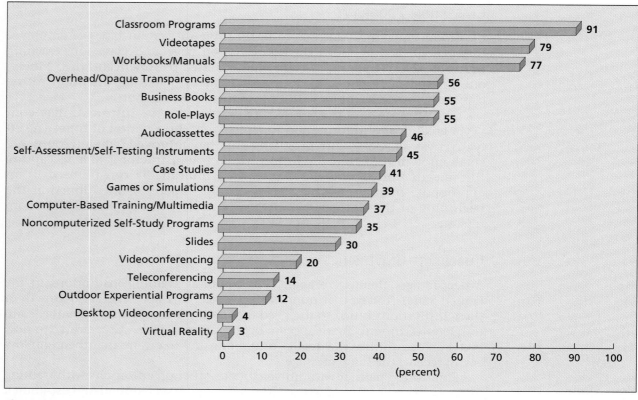

Figure 8-3
Training and Development Methods and Media

Source: "The Industry Report 1996," *Training* 34 (October 1996): 61.

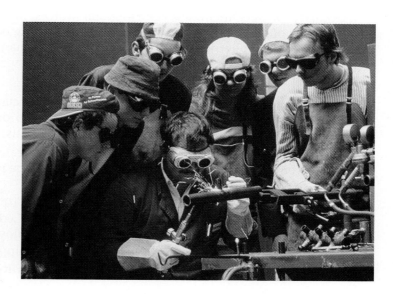

Rapid technological changes and corporate restructuring have created a new demand by industry for community college training resources.

North Haven, Connecticut, to prepare service technicians to work at area dealerships. GM has similar programs at more than 50 other schools.

ON-THE-JOB TRAINING

On-the-job training (OJT): An informal approach to training in which an employee learns job tasks by actually performing them.

On-the-job-training (OJT) is an informal approach to training that permits an employee to learn job tasks by actually performing them. It is the most commonly used approach to training and development. With OJT, there is no problem for participants in later transferring what they have learned to the task. Individuals may also be more highly motivated to learn because they see clearly that they are acquiring the knowledge they need to perform their jobs. At times, however, the emphasis on production may detract from the training process. The trainee may feel so much pressure to perform that learning is negatively affected.

Firms should be selective about who provides on-the-job training. The trainers can be either supervisors or peers. However, the main requirement is that they have a good work ethic and can correctly model desired behavior.[32]

APPRENTICESHIP TRAINING

Apprenticeship training: A combination of classroom instruction and on-the-job training.

Another approach, **apprenticeship training**, combines classroom instruction with on-the-job training. Such training is traditionally used in craft jobs, such as those of plumber, barber, carpenter, machinist, and printer. While in training, the employee earns less than the master craftsperson who is the instructor. The training period varies according to the craft. For instance, the apprenticeship training period for barbers is two years; for machinists, four years; and for pattern makers, five years.

German-owned Siemens Stromberg-Carlson has a background in apprenticeship training that spans 100 years. A program at its Lake Mary, Florida, plant involves both high school students and students from Seminole Community College. The high school students work at Siemens three hours a day, twice a week. Community college students complete a two-and-a-half-year curriculum while working 20 hours a week.[33] Employees recruited from the apprenticeship program are expected to hit the ground running. Siemens's experience had shown that this was not possible with other recruits.[34]

SIMULATORS

Simulators: Training devices of varying degrees of complexity that duplicate the real world.

Simulators are training devices of varying degrees of complexity that model the real world. They range from simple paper mock-ups of mechanical devices to computerized simulations of total environments. Training and development specialists may use simulated sales counters, automobiles, and airplanes. Although simulator training may be less valuable than on-the-job training for some purposes, it has certain advantages. A prime example is the training of airline pilots: Simulated training crashes do not cost lives or deplete the firm's fleet of jets.

VESTIBULE TRAINING

Vestibule training:
Training that takes place away from the production area on equipment that closely resembles the actual equipment used on the job.

Vestibule training takes place away from the production area on equipment that closely resembles equipment actually used on the job. For example, a group of lathes may be located in a training center where the trainees will be instructed in their use. A primary advantage of vestibule training is that it removes the employee from the pressure of having to produce while learning. The emphasis is on learning the skills required by the job.

Management Development

A firm's future lies largely in the hands of its managers. This group performs certain functions that are essential to the organization's survival and prosperity. Managers must make the right choice in most of the numerous decisions they make. Otherwise, the firm will not grow and may even fail. Therefore, it is imperative that managers keep up with the latest developments in their respective fields and—at the same time—manage an ever-changing workforce operating in a dynamic environment. **Management development** consists of all learning experiences provided by an organization resulting in an upgrading of participants' skills and knowledge required in current and future managerial positions. Whereas critical knowledge and skills are provided by organizations in development programs, the process also requires personal commitment of the individual manager. In fact, taking responsibility for one's own development may be the most important aspect.[35]

Management development: Learning experiences provided by an organization for the purpose of upgrading skills and knowledge required in current and future managerial positions.

First-line supervisors, middle managers, and executives may all be expected to participate in management development programs. These programs are offered in-house, by professional organizations, and colleges and universities. In-house programs are often planned and presented by a firm's T&D specialists in conjunction with line managers. Organizations, such as the Society for Human Resource Management and the American Management Association, conduct conferences and seminars in a number of specialties. Numerous colleges and universities also provide management training and development programs. At times, colleges and universities possess expertise not available within business organizations. In some cases, academicians and management practitioners can advantageously present T&D programs jointly. One survey revealed the most frequently mentioned reasons for conducting management training outside the company:

- An outside perspective
- New viewpoints
- Possibility of taking executives out of the work environment
- Exposure to faculty experts and research
- Broader vision

The most frequently mentioned reasons for keeping management training inside the company are listed below:

- Training that is more specific to needs
- Lower costs

TABLE 8-3

General Types of Training

Types of Training	% Providing
Basic computer skills	88
Technical skills/knowledge	85
Management skills/development	84
Communication skills	83
Supervisory skills	81
New methods/procedures	78
Customer relations/services	74
Executive development	72
Personal growth	68
Clerical/secretarial skills	62
Customer education	58
Employee/labor relations	58
Wellness	55
Sales	55
Remedial/basic education	42

Source: Paul Froiland, "Who's Getting Trained?" *Training* (October 1996): 58.

- Less time
- Consistent, relevant material
- More control of content and faculty
- Development of organizational culture and teamwork

Basically, companies have various training and development options. A survey of organizations with 100 or more employees revealed numerous types of training currently being used. These data are shown in Table 8-3. Basic computer skills was the most popular type of training, followed by technical skills/knowledge, and management skills/development. Basic computer skills training of all employees was provided by 88 percent of the responding firms but 94 percent of large firms provided this type of training.[36]

Executive and Management Development at IBM

At IBM, formal management development programs are conducted for various organizational levels. These programs vary from three-day sessions for recently appointed managers to two-week programs for newly named executives having worldwide responsibilities. Specifically, the following programs are provided: New Manager Training–U.S. Policy and Practices; New Manager School–IBM Leadership Program; IBM Business Management Institute; and IBM Global Executive Program.

New Manager Training–U.S. Policy and Practices is provided for newly appointed managers at various locations. The purpose of this three-day program is for participants to develop an understanding of IBM's basic management policies, practices, and skills. It focuses on performance management, compensation, diversity, career development, and management of individuals.

New Manager School–IBM Leadership Program is designed for all individuals appointed to the initial level of management responsibility. The three-and-a-half-day school normally begins within 60 to 90 days after the appointment and is held at the Central Headquarters Management Development Center in Armonk, New York.

IBM Business Management Institute is an eight-day program held worldwide. It is for individuals newly appointed to responsibility for an organization having significant impact on IBM's success in the marketplace. The program focuses on profitability and customer satisfaction. Case studies and business models are utilized to work on actual IBM business problems.

IBM Global Executive Program is for newly named executives with worldwide responsibilities. This two-week program is conducted in New York and La Hulpe, Belgium. The program focuses on building global perspectives, fostering performance and change, and leveraging IBM's capabilities. A significant part of the program is addressing a strategic business issue, including the presentation of results to the sponsoring senior executive.

Supervisory Management Training Programs

Many firms also conduct supervisory training programs. Often these are provided some time after the individual has served as supervisor. Until they receive training, supervisors *practice* on their subordinates. This approach is questioned by those who strongly believe that the training should precede the promotion. Today, more firms have adopted this philosophy and see the wisdom of training potential supervisors before they are put in a position to manage others. Supervisory training may include these areas:[37]

- Time management
- Planning, organizing, decision making, and problem solving
- How to motivate, discipline, and appraise the performance of employees
- Supervision, including delegation and giving constructive feedback
- Interviewing skills
- Conflict resolution
- Diversity training
- Oral presentations

If traditional T&D methods are used, training supervisors one at a time may not be feasible. When this is the case, individuals with supervisory potential are trained in groups. One oil firm believes so much in its supervisory training that it trains not only those viewed as having managerial potential but other hourly employees as well. The rationale is to have these individuals develop a better understanding of the supervisor's role, company goals, and the firm's commitment to help employees improve themselves.[38] This perspective may gain support as firms increasingly turn to self-managed teams in which operative employees perform many tasks previously reserved for managers.

Training Methods for Entry-Level Professional Employees

Firms have a special interest in college-trained employees hired for entry-level professional positions, including management trainees. Of all the technologies affecting management in today's business world, information management is experiencing the most rapid change. This fast-paced development is expected to continue well into the future. To prepare enterprising minds for this challenge, General Electric (GE) conducts the Information Management Leadership Program (ISMP). This is a two-year program combining rotational work assignments with graduate-level seminars. It prepares employees to design, program, and implement integrated computerized and manual information systems.

General Electric's ISMP emphasizes challenging work assignments in such areas as programming, systems analysis and design, computer center operation, project management, and functional work. The length of these assignments varies, and individual progress is determined by employee performance and demonstrated potential.

A candidate for ISMP will most likely have a degree in computer science, information systems, or engineering. However, a strong interest in technical applications must be balanced with business acumen. Therefore, individuals possessing degrees in business or liberal arts with a minor in computer science will be considered if other criteria are met. Given GE's diverse businesses and unique needs, a wide range of candidates is considered for this program. Candidates' overall qualifications are considered, including their course curriculum, academic records, leadership in extracurricular activities, and work experience.

Other training programs for college graduates may have more or less structure than General Electric's ISMP. However, most of them also emphasize training provided on the job. *Hands-on* experience, alone or in combination with other methods, appears to be an essential component of these programs.

Training Methods for Operative Employees

In many firms today, especially those using self-directed work teams, operative employees make numerous decisions previously made exclusively by managers. Perhaps for this reason, most of the training methods previously described are applicable to all employees. The jobs of operative employees still differ from those of managers, however, in that their *primary* role does not involve achieving goals through the efforts of others. Basically, they are the *other people*. Therefore, although the methods utilized in training are often similar to those used for other employees, the training is more likely to be narrowly focused on skills rather than on the more general development provided to managers and professional employees. Nevertheless, the contributions of operative employees are essential and collectively vital to the production of goods and services. Organizations rely heavily on their senior clerks, systems analysts, and other operative employees. Every position in an organization is necessary or it would not (or should not) exist. Therefore, training and development for operative employees should also be given high priority.

Special Training Areas

Some firms have changed their focus from conventional training programs to special training approaches that provide immediate assistance for employees. At Westinghouse, for example, executives no longer attend traditional training courses. Instead, a team of top executives is brought together to discuss the best way to meet their developmental needs. These focus groups discuss a topic and then feed back solutions. This approach is thought to meet the firm's needs more directly and provide the flexibility to react quickly to a given concern.[39]

Topics of special training sessions and the methods of delivery will vary according to the specific needs of an organization, but several areas are currently popular. Included in this category are diversity training, conflict resolution, values training, teamwork and empowerment, and customer service.

Implementing Training and Development Programs

A perfectly conceived training program can fail if management cannot convince the participants of its merits. Participants must believe that the program has value and will help them achieve their personal and professional goals. The credibility of T&D programs may depend on a series of successful programs.

Implementing T&D programs is often difficult. One reason is that managers are typically action oriented and feel that they are too busy for T&D. According to one management development executive, "Most busy executives are too involved chopping down the proverbial tree to stop for the purpose of sharpening their axes." Another difficulty in program implementation is that qualified trainers must be available. In addition to possessing communication skills, the trainers must know the company's philosophy, its objectives, its formal and informal organization, and the goals of the training program. Training and development requires more creativity than perhaps any other human resource function.

A new program must be monitored carefully, especially during its initial phases. Training implies change, which employees may resist vigorously.

Others may sit back waiting, perhaps even hoping, that the program will fail. Participant feedback is vital at this stage because there will be bugs in any new program. The sooner these problems are resolved, the better will be the chances for success.

Implementing training programs presents unique problems. For example, it may be difficult to schedule the training around present work requirements. Unless the employee is new to the firm, he or she undoubtedly has specific full-time duties to perform.

Another difficulty in implementing T&D programs is record keeping. Records should be maintained on all training the employee receives and how well he or she performs during training and on the job. This information is important in terms of measuring program effectiveness and charting the employee's progress in the company.

Training conducted outside the organization also requires considerable coordination. As previously discussed, many business functions have been outsourced. This trend has included training and development for various types of employees. As you see in Figure 8-4, some training is provided by in-house staff only and some by outside suppliers only. A majority of training for all groups is provided by both inside and outside suppliers.

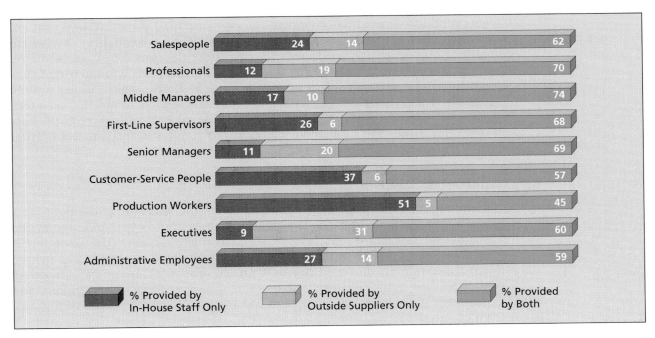

Figure 8-4
Sources of Training
Despite much recent talk of outsourced training, the percentage of training handled by in-house staff only versus outsiders only has changed remarkably little in the past five years. That's not to say more outsourcing isn't taking place at those companies that use a mix of insiders and outsiders. Still, the unchanged numbers under the in-house heading suggest that trainers have not rushed to outsouce entire chunks of their work.

Source: Paul Froland, "Who's Getting Trained?" *Training* 34 (October 1996): 57.

Evaluating Training and Development

Although corporate America spends billions of dollars a year on employee training, there is no clear consensus within the training community on how to determine its value. Obviously, the credibility of T&D can be greatly enhanced if the tangible benefits to the organization from such programs can be shown. Thus, the training and development department must document its efforts and clearly show that it provides a valuable service.

Organizations have taken several approaches to determining the worth of specific programs. These include measuring (1) the participants' opinions of the program, (2) the extent to which participants have learned the material, (3) the participants' behavioral change, (4) whether the stated training goals have been achieved, (5) return on investment, and, the last approach, (6) benchmarking.

PARTICIPANTS' OPINIONS

Evaluating training and development program by asking the participants' opinions of it is an inexpensive approach that provides a response and suggestions for improvements. However, obtaining feedback from participants after they've returned to their jobs is sometimes difficult. To help overcome this problem, Texas Instruments developed an e-mail survey system that enables course managers to register courses online for evaluation. An e-mail message is sent to all participants 90 days after they complete a course asking them to respond to a short questionnaire. The emphasis is on getting information about skills transfer to the job. These responses are recorded on-line and the results are stored in a database that is accessible to course managers. This automated system has increased the use of evaluations, reduced data collection time, and provided a standard measure for evaluating the transfer of skills and behavior to the job.[40]

EXTENT OF LEARNING

Some organizations administer tests to determine what the participants in a T&D program have learned. The pretest-posttest control group design is one evaluation procedure that may be used. In this procedure, the same test is used before and after training. It also calls for both a control group (which does not receive the training) and an experimental group (which does). Trainees are randomly assigned to each group. Differences in pretest and posttest results between the groups are then attributed to the training provided.

BEHAVIORAL CHANGE

Tests may indicate fairly accurately what participants have learned, but they give little insight into whether the training leads participants to change their behavior. For example, it is one thing for a manager to learn about motivational techniques but quite another matter for this person to apply the new knowledge. Consider the situation involving Pat Sittel:

Pat Sittel sat in the front row at the supervisory training seminar her company sponsored. The primary topic of the program was empowering employees. As the lecturer made each point, Pat would nod her head in agreement. She thoroughly understood what was being said during the two-day period of the seminar. At the end of the program, Pat returned to her department and continued the management style she had followed for 10 years, one that involved little empowerment of anyone except herself. Although she had understood the material presented in the seminar, Pat's failure to apply what she had learned didn't benefit the organization.

ACCOMPLISHMENT OF T&D OBJECTIVES

Still another approach to evaluating T&D programs involves determining the extent to which stated objectives have been achieved. For instance, if the objective of an accident prevention program is to reduce the number and severity of accidents by 15 percent, comparing accident rates before and after training provides a useful measurement of success. The problem is that many programs dealing with broader topics are more difficult to evaluate. A group of executives may, for example, be sent to a state university for a one-week course in management and leadership development. Before and after performance appraisals of the participants may be available. Following the course, the managers may actually perform at a higher level, but other variables may distort the picture. For instance, a mild recession may force the layoff of several key employees, a competing firm may be successful in luring away one of the department's top engineers, or the company president could pressure the employment director to hire an incompetent relative for a key position. These and many other factors could cause the performance level of the group to decline, even though the managers had benefited from the developmental program. If Lou McGowen's press operators are able to operate the new presses successfully after the training, her training objectives will have been accomplished.

RETURN ON INVESTMENT (ROI)[41]

In return on investment evaluation, the training's monetary benefits is compared with its costs. The return on investment (ROI) may be calculated by subtracting the costs from the total benefits of the training to produce the net benefits. Next, the net benefits are divided by the costs. An alternative method is to find the benefit/cost ratio (BCR). Here, you simply divide the total benefits by the cost. A literacy-skills training program at Magnavox provides an illustration:

> The training program produced benefits of $321,600 with a cost of $38,233. The BCR is 8.4. For every dollar invested, $8.40 was returned in the form of benefits. The net benefits are $283,367 ($321,600 − $38,233). ROI is 741 percent ($283,367/$38,233 × 100). Using ROI, for every dollar invested in this training, there was a return of $7.41 in net benefits.

Usually, the benefits are the amount saved or gained in the year after training is completed. These benefits may continue but the effects may diminish over time. There are obviously difficulties in calculating either the ROI or the BCR—for example, it is difficult to determine how much of the benefits are due strictly to the training. However, estimates for other purposes are also imprecise. A key factor is developing an approach that is acceptable to top management.

BENCHMARKING[42]

Benchmarking uses exemplary practices of other organizations to evaluate and improve training and development programs. By some estimates, up to 70 percent of American firms engage in a type of benchmarking. Most of this effort involves monitoring and measuring a firm's internal processes, such as operations, and then comparing the data with data from companies that excel in those areas. The use of benchmarking is expanding beyond core business operations and is being used by training functions. Because training programs for individual firms are unique, the training measures should be broad. For example, benchmarking questions often ask about the cost of training, the ratio of training staff to employees, and whether new or more traditional delivery systems are used. Information derived from these questions probably lacks the detail to permit specific improvements to the training curricula. However, a firm may recognize, for example, that another organization is able to deliver a lot of training for relatively little cost. This information could then trigger the firm to follow up with interviews or site visits to determine whether that phenomenon represents a *best practice*. As training and development becomes more crucial to organizational success, determining model training practices and learning from them will become increasingly important.

In evaluating T&D programs, managers should strive for proof that the program is effective. Although such proof may be difficult to establish, the effect of training on performance should at least be estimated to show whether the training achieved its desired purpose. In spite of problems associated with evaluation, managers responsible for T&D must continue to strive for solid evidence of its contributions in achieving organizational goals.

In recent years, government funds to support training have been dwindling. However one federal program is still important—the Job Training Partnership Act. It is discussed next.

Job Training Partnership Act

The **Job Training Partnership Act (JTPA)** provides training through local-level partnerships between business and government. The federal government has some 154 training programs, administered by 14 agencies, that cost nearly $25 billion per year.[43] The JTPA is the largest of these programs.[44] It provides funds each year to the states, which, in turn, give grants to local governments and private entities. Job training and employment services are then provided for economically disadvantaged adults and youth, dislocated workers, and other persons who face exceptional employment hurdles. No

HRM IN ACTION
IS THAT TRAINING IMPORTANT?

Your boss has just returned from a conference. He has called all the supervisors into his office. "I want every employee in this place trained in CPR (cardiopulmonary resuscitation)," he says. Just this morning you got word of a *big push* to increase production for the upcoming seasonal surge in sales. You sure hope they get the CPR training done soon—you may need the treatment. The boss has just asked you, "When do you want to schedule your people for the four hours of CPR training?"

▶ *How would you respond?*

more than 20 percent of the funds may be spent on administrative costs and no less than 50 percent may be spent on direct training services.[45] The act first became operational in 1983 with the goal of moving the unemployed into permanent, unsubsidized, self-sustaining jobs. Initially criticized for inadequate cost controls and failure to target the most disadvantaged individuals, the act was amended in 1992 to address these problems.

Job Training Partnership Act programs are overseen by the Private Industry Council (PIC). PIC members represent business, education, labor, rehabilitation, and economic development agencies, community-based organizations, and public employment services. More than half the council's members come from the business community. These business-led organizations assist in allocating funds to local training and employment services. The JTPA gives local councils considerable power to choose their trainee population and determine the job placement methods. On-the-job training programs are also offered. In these programs, the sponsoring business firms are reimbursed for a portion of their cost for training eligible new hires. On-the-job training places participants in jobs that are determined by the Private Industry Council to be in high demand in their area. The purpose of all JTPA training is to provide better employment, higher earnings, increased skills, and decreased welfare dependency for participants. The ultimate goal is to improve the quality of the workforce and to enhance the nation's productivity.[46]

The overall success of the JTPA appears to be controversial. Very little research has been conducted to determine its impact, and the federal government has given states little encouragement to do such evaluations.

A study conducted by James Heckman of the University of Chicago found that for trainees under 21, the training had no effect in improving earnings and may have even caused some to lose earnings. Adult participants, however, did improve their earnings.[47]

Orientation

Orientation: The guided adjustment of new employees to the company, the job, and the work group.

The initial T&D effort designed for employees is orientation. **Orientation** is the guided adjustment of new employees to the company, the job, and the work group. It is a common type of formal training in U.S. organizations, and some firms have developed sophisticated approaches. For example, Federal Express uses computer-based training for orienting new employees in a two-hour program that offers detailed information on the corporate culture, benefits, policies, and procedures. It also outlines the company's organizational structure and features a video message from the chief executive officer.[48]

In a typical orientation program, company policies and rules are spelled out along with the mechanics of promotion, demotion, transfer, resignation, discharge, layoff, and retirement. These data are also likely to be included in handbooks given to each new employee. A summary of employee benefits is often provided.

To perform effectively, new employees need information that not only permits them to do their jobs but also provides information that will help them understand their co-workers' behavioral patterns. Although orientation is often the joint responsibility of the training staff and the line supervisor, peers have been found to serve as excellent information agents. There are several reasons for peers' success in performing this function. For one thing, they are accessible to newcomers—often more so than the boss. Peers also tend to have a high degree of empathy for new people. In addition, they have the organizational experience and technical expertise to which new employees need access.

A new employee's first few days on the job may be spent in orientation. However, some firms feel that learning is more effective if spread out over a period of time. For example, Web Industries' program is delivered in a system of 20 one-hour sessions over a period of four weeks.[49]

Purposes of Orientation

Orientation formats are unique to each firm. However, almost all emphasize these areas: the employment situation (job, department, and company), company policies and rules, compensation and benefits, corporate culture, team membership, employee development, and dealing with change and socialization.

THE EMPLOYMENT SITUATION

A basic purpose, from the firm's viewpoint, is to have the new employee become productive as quickly as possible. Therefore, specific information about performing the job may be provided at an early point in time. Knowledge of how the job fits into the departmental goals and goals of the company tend to illustrate its importance and provide meaning to the work.

COMPANY POLICIES AND RULES

Every job within an organization must be performed within the guidelines and constraints provided by policies and rules. Employees must understand these to have a smooth transition to the workplace. This information may be quite detailed, so common practice is to include it in the form of an employee handbook.

COMPENSATION AND BENEFITS

Employees will have a special interest in obtaining information about the reward system. This information is usually provided during the recruitment and selection process, but a review of the data is appropriate during orientation.

CORPORATE CULTURE

The firm's culture reflects, in effect, "how we do things around here." This relates to everything from the way employees dress to the way they talk. Companies have a number of ways to communicate their culture, and knowledge of it is critical to a new employee's orientation. The topic of corporate culture was discussed in Chapter 2.

TEAM MEMBERSHIP

A new employee's ability and willingness to work in teams is most likely determined before he or she is hired. In orientation, the importance of becoming a valued member of the company team may be emphasized. Even though the individual is now and will always be important to organizations, many processes can be more effectively accomplished through teams. It is imperative that team spirit be instilled in each employee—and the sooner the better.

EMPLOYEE DEVELOPMENT

Employee development has become essentially a do-it-yourself process. However, some firms provide assistance in this area. Employees should know exactly what is expected of them and what is required by the firm for advancement in the job or for promotion. An individual's employment security is increasingly becoming dependent upon his or her ability to acquire needed knowledge and skills that are constantly changing. Thus, employees should be kept aware of company-sponsored developmental programs and those available externally, and they should receive encouragement to take advantage of any appropriate opportunities.

DEALING WITH CHANGE

The significance of change was discussed at the beginning of this chapter. Simply put, employees at all levels must learn to deal effectively with change to survive in their jobs. The best way individuals can be prepared for change is to develop and expand their skills continually. It is mutually advantageous for both employee and employer for this to occur as it provides security for the employee and a more valuable performer for the firm.

SOCIALIZATION

To reduce the anxiety that new employees may experience, attempts should be made to integrate the person into the informal organization. Many years ago, Texas Instruments conducted research that clearly revealed the importance of this purpose. The experimental design included randomly assigning new employees to one of two training groups—either the traditional orientation program or the experimental group's socialization program. The latter group covered such subjects as career management, the importance of politics, picking the right boss, and the importance of being in the right place at the right time. At the end of two years, the learning rates of the two groups were compared. Employees in the socialization program proved to be significantly superior on all measures to those in the traditional group. The most dramatic finding was the impact on turnover among professionals, such as engineers and computer specialists. The turnover rate for those who had completed the socialization program was 40 percent lower than for those in the traditional group.[50]

Although orientation programs are typically conducted for new employees, programs designed for those who have been on the payroll for a longer period of time may also be needed. As organizations change, different management styles may develop, communication methods may be altered, and the structure of the organization itself may, and typically does, take on a new form. Even the corporate culture may evolve into something different over time. Any of these changes may warrant reorientation. Without it, employees may find themselves in organizations they do not even recognize.

Organization Development

Organization development (OD): An organizationwide application of behavioral science knowledge to the planned development and reinforcement of a firm's strategies, structures, and processes for improving its effectiveness.

Remember from the discussion of corporate culture in chapter 2 that various factors affect employees' behavior on the job. To bring about desired changes in these factors and behavior, organizations must be transformed into market-driven, innovative, and adaptive systems if they are to survive and prosper in the highly competitive global environment of the next decade. Many firms are beginning to face this urgent need by practicing organization development, a training and development approach that involves the entire system. **Organization development (OD)** is an organizationwide application of behavioral science knowledge to the planned development and reinforcement of a firm's strategies, structures, and processes for improving its effectiveness.[51] Organization development is a major means of achieving change in the corporate culture, a topic of chapter 2. This type of development is increasingly important as the workforce diversifies and as the way work is accomplished changes. Because 75 percent of new entrants in the workforce are expected to be women and minorities, developing effective work behaviors that can cope with greater diversity is vital.[52]

Organization development applies to an entire system, such as a company or a plant. Early applications of the approach focused on employee satisfaction. It appears that employee and organizational performance are now being emphasized as well. Although organization development does not produce a blueprint for how things should be done, it does provide an adaptive strategy for planning and implementing change. In addition, it ensures a long-term reinforcement of change. Organization development may involve changes in the firm's strategy, structure, and processes. A firm's strategy affects how it relates to its wider environment and how to improve those relationships. In dealing with structure, the focus is on how people are grouped in the organization. The firm's processes include methods of communication and solving problems.[53] Organization development efforts include survey feedback, quality circles, sensitivity training, and team building.

SURVEY FEEDBACK

Survey feedback: A survey method and research technique that systematically collects information about organizations and employee attitudes and makes the data available in aggregate form to employees and management so that problems can be diagnosed and plans developed to solve them.

Survey feedback is a process of collecting data from an organizational unit with a questionnaire or survey. A developing trend has been to combine survey feedback, a powerful intervention in its own right, with other organization development interventions.[54]

Survey feedback generally involves the following steps:

- Members of the organization, including top management, are involved in planning the survey.
- The survey instrument is administered to all members of the organizational unit.
- The organization development consultant analyzes the data, tabulates results, suggests approaches to diagnosis, and trains participants in the feedback process.
- Data feedback begins at the top level of the organization and flows downward to groups reporting at successively lower levels.
- Feedback meetings provide an opportunity to discuss and interpret data, diagnose problem areas, and develop action plans.[55]

An example of a management survey feedback instrument is provided in Figure 8-5. This instrument is used to analyze management performance in leadership, motivation, communication, decision making, goals, control, and other critical areas. Employees are asked to check—along a continuum—the point that best describes their organization. They are also asked to indicate their views of a desired state. Averaging the responses and charting them produces an organizational profile. Referring again to Figure 8-5, note that the present state of leadership is perceived as being quite negative. The employees surveyed apparently felt that their company's leadership was *condescending*. The consensus was that the leader should show *substantial* confidence in subordinates (the desired state).

QUALITY CIRCLES

Quality circles: Groups of employees who meet regularly with their supervisors to identify production problems and recommend solutions.

Another organization development approach is the use of quality circles. **Quality circles** are groups of employees who voluntarily meet regularly with their supervisors to identify production problems and recommend solutions. These recommendations are then presented to higher level management for review, and the approved actions are implemented with employee participation.

In spite of numerous successful applications, the quality circle concept has not worked well for some organizations. To implement a successful quality circle program, the firm must set clear goals for the program, gain the

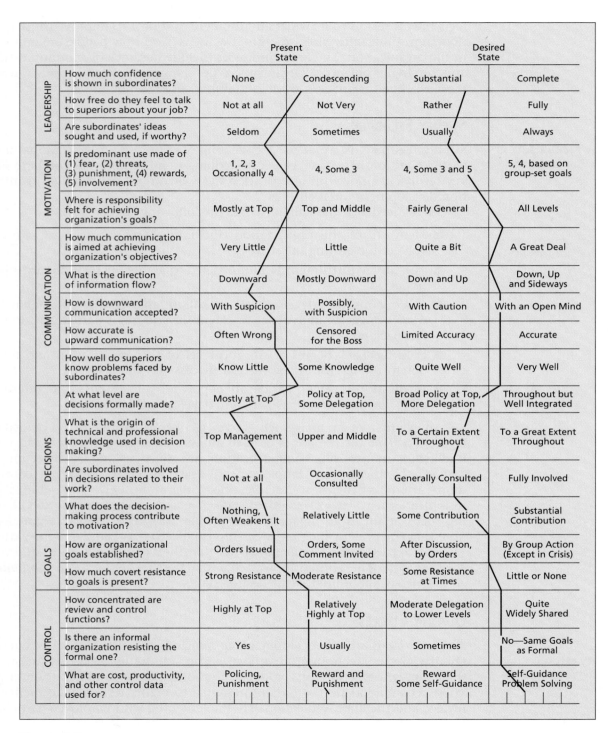

		Present State		Desired State	
LEADERSHIP	How much confidence is shown in subordinates?	None	Condescending	Substantial	Complete
	How free do they feel to talk to superiors about your job?	Not at all	Not Very	Rather	Fully
	Are subordinates' ideas sought and used, if worthy?	Seldom	Sometimes	Usually	Always
MOTIVATION	Is predominant use made of (1) fear, (2) threats, (3) punishment, (4) rewards, (5) involvement?	1, 2, 3 Occasionally 4	4, Some 3	4, Some 3 and 5	5, 4, based on group-set goals
	Where is responsibility felt for achieving organization's goals?	Mostly at Top	Top and Middle	Fairly General	All Levels
COMMUNICATION	How much communication is aimed at achieving organization's objectives?	Very Little	Little	Quite a Bit	A Great Deal
	What is the direction of information flow?	Downward	Mostly Downward	Down and Up	Down, Up and Sideways
	How is downward communication accepted?	With Suspicion	Possibly, with Suspicion	With Caution	With an Open Mind
	How accurate is upward communication?	Often Wrong	Censored for the Boss	Limited Accuracy	Accurate
	How well do superiors know problems faced by subordinates?	Know Little	Some Knowledge	Quite Well	Very Well
DECISIONS	At what level are decisions formally made?	Mostly at Top	Policy at Top, Some Delegation	Broad Policy at Top, More Delegation	Throughout but Well Integrated
	What is the origin of technical and professional knowledge used in decision making?	Top Management	Upper and Middle	To a Certain Extent Throughout	To a Great Extent Throughout
	Are subordinates involved in decisions related to their work?	Not at all	Occasionally Consulted	Generally Consulted	Fully Involved
	What does the decision-making process contribute to motivation?	Nothing, Often Weakens It	Relatively Little	Some Contribution	Substantial Contribution
GOALS	How are organizational goals established?	Orders Issued	Orders, Some Comment Invited	After Discussion, by Orders	By Group Action (Except in Crisis)
	How much covert resistance to goals is present?	Strong Resistance	Moderate Resistance	Some Resistance at Times	Little or None
CONTROL	How concentrated are review and control functions?	Highly at Top	Relatively Highly at Top	Moderate Delegation to Lower Levels	Quite Widely Shared
	Is there an informal organization resisting the formal one?	Yes	Usually	Sometimes	No—Same Goals as Formal
	What are cost, productivity, and other control data used for?	Policing, Punishment	Reward and Punishment	Reward Some Self-Guidance	Self-Guidance Problem Solving

Figure 8-5
An Example of a Survey Feedback Questionnaire
Source: Adapted by permission of Michael McGill, School of Business Administration, Southern Methodist University. All Rights Reserved.

support of top management, and create a climate conducive to participative management. In addition, a qualified manager must be selected for the program, and the program's goals must be communicated to all concerned. Individuals participating in the program must receive quality circle training.

SENSITIVITY TRAINING

Sensitivity training: An organizational development technique that is designed to make people aware of themselves and their impact on others.

An organization development technique designed to make us more aware of ourselves and our impact on others is referred to as **sensitivity training**. It is quite different from traditional forms of training, which stress the learning of a predetermined set of concepts.[56]

Sensitivity training features a group—often called a training group or T-group—in which there is no preestablished agenda or focus. The trainer's purpose is merely to serve as a facilitator in this unstructured environment. Participants are encouraged to learn about themselves and others in the group. Some objectives of sensitivity training are to increase the following:

1. Self-awareness and insight into the participant's behavior and its meaning in a social context
2. Sensitivity to the behavior of others
3. Awareness and understanding of the types of processes that facilitate or inhibit group functioning and the interactions between different groups
4. Diagnostic skills in social, interpersonal, and intergroup situations
5. The participant's ability to intervene successfully in intergroup or intragroup situations so as to increase member satisfaction, effectiveness, and output
6. The participant's ability to analyze continually his or her own interpersonal behavior in order to achieve more effective and satisfying interpersonal relationships.[57]

When sensitivity training begins, there is no agenda—and no leaders, no authority, and no power positions. Essentially, a vacuum exists until participants begin to talk. Through dialogue, people begin to learn about themselves and others. Participants are encouraged to look at themselves as others see them. Then, if they want to change, they can attempt to do so.

Although the purpose of sensitivity training (to assist individuals to learn more about how they relate to other people) cannot be questioned, the technique has been roundly criticized. Sensitivity training often involves anxiety-provoking situations as stimulants for learning. In addition, some critics believe that it is one matter for participants to express true feelings in the psychological safety of the laboratory but quite another to face their co-workers back on the job.[58] Information learned in a sensitivity group may prove to be irrelevant or even damaging unless the participant returns to an organizational environment that supports the use of that knowledge. Individuals may be encouraged to be more open and supportive in the T-group, but when they return to their jobs, they often have not really changed. In addition, participants often undergo severe emotional stress during training.

Sensitivity training flourished in the 1970s. Use of poorly trained, uncertified trainers may be the primary reason for the decline in popularity of this method.

TEAM BUILDING AND SELF-DIRECTED TEAMS

Individualism has deep roots in American culture. This trait has been a virtue and will continue to be an asset in our society. Now, however, there are work situations that make it imperative to subordinate individual autonomy to cooperation with a group. Lives in an industrial setting are not normally in jeopardy, but jobs certainly are. Performance by teams has been shown to be clearly superior in accomplishing many of the tasks required by organizations. The building of effective teams, therefore, has become a business necessity.

Team building: A conscious effort to develop effective work groups throughout an organization.

Much training effort must be expended prior to efficient and effective functioning of work teams. Fortunately, most managers know this. A conscious effort to develop effective work groups throughout the organization is referred to as **team building**. Team building uses self-directed teams, each composed of a small group of employees responsible for an entire work process or segment. Team members work together to improve their operation or product, to plan and control their work, and to handle day-to-day problems. They may even become involved in broader, companywide issues, such as vendor quality, safety, and business planning.[59] Team building is one of the more popular approaches to organization development. For instance, Team Saturn—the revolutionary approach to car manufacturing that resulted in the Saturn automobile being named by J. D. Powers & Associates the best built car in the United States—is based on the concept of teamwork. Unlike other General Motors plants, Saturn is really built on a team effort, not just an exercise in lip service. Line worker, Deborah Wikaryasz, could not believe the difference between teamwork at Saturn and at the Cadillac plant where she worked previously. Wikaryasz is very impressed with the environment at Saturn, stating, "We don't have the backstabbing and the yelling." Her team not only assembles fixtures on the left side of each Saturn, but they also hire workers, approve parts from suppliers, and handle administrative matters such as its budget. Wikaryasz is proud that her team "keeps down costs and passes the savings along to customers." This plant was started from scratch with a team approach calling for all team members to be selected from the best General Motors had to offer. At Saturn, teams were kept small and were composed of people with complementary skills, who were committed to the common purpose of not compromising quality.[60]

A nation-wide survey conducted by a human resources consulting firm found that 27 percent of the respondents use self-directed teams. Half the respondents predicted that the majority of their workforce will be organized in teams within the next five years. The reason? Teams produce extra performance results![61]

Advocating the use of teams years before they became commonplace, Douglas McGregor identified characteristics of effective management teams (see Table 8-4). His version of an effective team emphasizes an infor-

TABLE 8-4

Characteristics of Effective Teams

1. The atmosphere, which can be sensed in a few minutes of observation, tends to be informal, comfortable, and relaxed. There are no obvious tensions.

2. There is a lot of discussion in which virtually everyone participates, but it remains pertinent to the task of the group.

3. The task or the objective of the group is well understood and accepted by the members.

4. The members listen to each other! The discussion does not have the quality of jumping from one idea to another unrelated one. Every idea is given a hearing. People are not afraid of seeming foolish by expressing a creative thought, even if it seems fairly extreme.

5. There is disagreement. The group is comfortable with this and shows no signs of having to avoid conflict or to keep everything light and on a plane of sweetness. Disagreements are not suppressed or overridden by premature group action. Individuals who disagree do not appear to be trying to dominate the group or to express hostility. Their disagreement is an expression of a genuine difference of opinion, and they expect a hearing in order for a solution to be found.

6. Most decisions are reached by a kind of consensus in which it is clear that everybody is in general agreement and willing to go along.

7. Criticism is frequent, frank, and relatively comfortable. There is little evidence of personal attack, either open or hidden. The criticism has a constructive flavor in that it is oriented toward removing an obstacle that prevents the group from getting the job done.

8. People freely express their feelings as well as their ideas on both the problem and the group's operation. There is little pussyfooting; there are few hidden agendas. Everybody appears to know quite well how everybody else feels about any matter under discussion.

9. When action is taken, clear assignments are made and accepted.

10. The chairperson of the group does not dominate it, nor to the contrary, does the group defer unduly to him or her. In fact, the leadership shifts from time to time, depending on the circumstances. At various times, different members, because of their knowledge or experience, are in a position to act as "resources" for the group. The members utilize them in this fashion and they occupy leadership roles while they are thus being used. There is little evidence of a struggle for power as the group operates. The issue is not who controls but how to get the job done.

11. The group is conscious of its own operations. Frequently, it will stop to examine how well it is doing or what may be interfering with its operation. The problem may be a matter of procedure, or it may be that an individual's behavior is interfering with the accomplishment of the group's objectives. Whatever the problem, it is openly discussed until a solution is found.

Source: Adapted from Douglas McGregor, *The Human Side of Management* (New York: McGraw-Hill, 1960), 232–235. Reprinted by permission of the McGraw-Hill Book Company. All rights reserved.

mal organizational culture that is relatively free from tension. The team's decision-making process involves much discussion and broad participation. Communications are open, with an emphasis placed on listening to the views of others. Members feel free to disagree but do so in an atmosphere of acceptance. The team pursues goals that its members understand and accept.

Effective work teams focus on solving actual problems while building efficient management teams. The team-building process begins when the team leader defines a problem that requires organizational change. The team diagnoses the problem to determine the underlying causes. These causes may be related to breakdowns in communication, inappropriate leadership styles, deficiencies in the organizational structure, or other factors. The team then considers alternative solutions and selects the most appropriate one. The result of open and frank discussions is likely to be commitment to the proposed course of action. The interpersonal relations developed by team members improve the chances for implementing the change. Team building is a process in which participants and facilitators experience increasing levels of trust, openness, and willingness to explore core issues that affect excellent team functioning.

The American Society for Training and Development (ASTD) conducted a survey that asked for the areas most improved through the use of trained, self-directed teams. The factors that had noticeably or significantly improved are in the following list. The figure in parentheses indicates the percentage of respondents who felt the factor had improved.[62]

- Productivity (77%)
- Quality (72%)
- Job satisfaction (65%)
- Customer service (57%)
- Waste reduction (55%)

A GLOBAL PERSPECTIVE

Global Orientation: For the Employee and the Family

Effective employee orientation is essential for employee success overseas. Global orientation is the guided adjustment of employees to the company's overseas operation, the global job, the global work groups, and the country that will be the expatriates' home for the term of the assignment. Orientation for global employees varies in its complexity, but global orientation will almost certainly be more complex than any domestic orientation program. Because of the extreme cost of global staffing and the staggering cost of failed expatriate assignments, global orientation takes on increased importance. However, regardless of how effective the global orientation program is, it cannot overcome poor selection; therefore, the selection process should be carefully considered and executed. Companies must interview candidates for global assignments carefully, even to the point of interviewing the employee's spouse to determine his or her adaptability to the overseas assignment.[63]

The candidate must be adequately profiled with his or her family. When determining who might be a good candidate for an international assignment, a company needs to keep in mind that, in most cases, it is sending the entire family overseas, not just the employee. Therefore, the entire family must be adaptable and be subjected to a well-developed orientation program. Although professional skills and job qualifications are important, the ability of the employee and the family to adapt to living in a different culture can be even more of a factor in determining the overall success of an assignment.[64]

Once the correct employee is selected and all adaptability issues are resolved, orientation begins. An effective global orientation program prepares the employee and the family for relocation. Inadequate attention to the *soft* issues is often a problem. Many companies focus on the *hard* issues surrounding expatriate assignments, such as taxes, cost-of-living allowances, and premiums, and they overlook the so-called soft issues. Companies should give overseas employees and their families language training, cultural training, and a general orientation to everyday living in the host country, such as information about schools, banks, and shopping. Such an introduction should also include an overview of the history, traditions, and corporate values of partners, if any. Then it should include a description of the new venture, its organization, and its management structure, followed by an introduction of the employee to the manager, department, and co-workers.[65] In addition, an employee sent on an international assignment needs a tremendous amount of overseas logistical support that includes locating housing in the host country, transporting the employee and family to the foreign location, securing immigration and visa clearance for the employee and family to work and live in the host country, and ensuring that the family receives adequate insurance and medical care during the assignment. Global orientations must consider international differences and prepare everyone involved for a stressful situation.

Global orientations provide much more support and assistance than domestic orientations. Compared to domestic orientations, where there is little involvement in the personal affairs of an employee and family, international moves place the company in much more intimate contact with its employees and their families. Global orientation cannot be a sketchy overview of the basics. It should be an in-depth process that has been thoroughly planned in advance, taking a long-term approach that includes provisions for follow-up and evaluation. Basically, international success requires preparing employees to deal with the social context of their jobs and cope with the insecurities and frustrations of a new global work situation.

SUMMARY

1. *Define* training and development (T&D).
Although the terms are often used interchangeably, a distinction is sometimes made. Training is designed to help learners acquire knowledge and skills needed for their present jobs. Development involves learning that looks beyond today's job; it has a more long-term focus.

2. *Describe the T&D process.*
Once the need for change is recognized and the factors that influence intervention are considered, the process of determining training and development needs begins. Essentially, two questions must be asked: "What are our training needs?" and "What do we want to accomplish through our T&D efforts?" After stating the T&D objectives, management can determine the appropriate methods for accomplishing them.

Various methods and media are available; the selection depends on the nature of the training and development goals. Naturally, T&D must be continuously evaluated to facilitate change and accomplish organizational objectives.

3. *Explain factors influencing T&D.*

First, training and development programs must have the full support of top management. In addition, all managers should be committed to and involved in the T&D process. To ensure effective programs, managers must be convinced that there will be a tangible payoff if resources are committed to this effort. In recent years, the increasingly rapid changes in technology, products, systems, and methods have had a significant impact on job requirements.

4. *Identify the various training and development methods.*

Training and development methods include coaching, mentoring, business games, videotapes, in-basket training, internships, role playing, job rotation, programmed instruction, computer-based training, cyberlearning, classroom programs, corporate universities, community colleges, on-the-job training, apprenticeship training, simulators, and vestibule training.

5. *Describe management development.*

Management development consists of all learning experiences provided to management employees by an organization to help them acquire or upgrade the skills and knowledge required in current and future positions. A firm's future lies primarily with its management. This group performs the essential functions necessary for the organization to survive and prosper.

6. *Identify the means by which T&D programs are evaluated.*

Training and development programs are evaluated by several measures: participants' opinions, extent of learning, behavioral change, accomplishment of T&D objectives, return on investment (ROI), and benchmarking.

7. *Describe the Job Training Partnership Act.*

The Job Training Partnership Act (JTPA) provides training through local-level partnerships between business and government. It results in the largest single training effort sponsored by the federal government.

8. *Define* orientation *and identify the purposes of orientation.*

Orientation is the guided adjustment of new employees to the company, the job, and the work group. Orientation acquaints employees with the employment situation, company policies and rules, compensation and benefits and corporate culture. Orientation may also cover employee development, dealing with change, and socialization.

9. *Define* organization development (OD).

Organization development is an organizationwide application of behavioral science knowledge to the planned development and reinforcement of a firm's strategies, structures, and processes for improving its effectiveness.

10. *Describe various OD techniques.*

Survey feedback is a process of collecting data from an organizational unit through the use of a questionnaire or survey. Quality circles are groups of employees who voluntarily meet regularly with their supervisors to identify production problems and recommend solutions. Sensitivity training is an OD technique designed to make participants more aware of themselves and their impact on others. Team building is a conscious effort to develop effective work groups throughout the organization.

<table>
<tr><td>

QUESTIONS
FOR
REVIEW

</td><td>

1. Distinguish between training and development.
2. What are some current training and development trends?
3. Describe the training and development process.
4. Describe the factors that influence training and development.
5. List and describe the primary training and development methods.
6. Define management development. Why is it important?
7. What are some of the means of evaluating human resource development programs? Discuss.
8. What is the purpose of the Job Training Partnership Act?
9. Define orientation and explain the purposes of orientation to a firm.
10. Define each of the following:
   a. Organization development
   b. Survey feedback
   c. Quality circles
   d. Sensitivity training
   e. Team building

</td></tr>
</table>

DEVELOPING
HRM
SKILLS

AN EXPERIENTIAL EXERCISE
Training and development is very important to any organization as it faces change and deals with the continual development of its employees. Training can often be used to improve employee productivity. However, effective training cannot occur in a vacuum; therefore, training requires the support and understanding of the entire organization.

Two individuals will play roles in this exercise: one to serve as the training specialist and the other to play the supervisor. Each participant should carefully follow his or her role. All students not playing roles should carefully observe the behavior of both participants. Your instructor will provide the participants with additional information necessary to complete the exercise.

 *Take It to the Net*

We invite you to visit the Mondy home page on the Prentice Hall Web site at:

http://www.prenhall.com/mondy

for updated information, Web-based exercises, and links to other HR-related sites.

HRM SIMULATION

*T*raining is another major element of the simulation. Training programs prepare an employee for new job responsibilities, provide general managerial and career development training, and update an employee's technical skills. Currently, your organization does not have any training programs. Failure to train a person who has been promoted will result in a higher than normal turnover rate in that level, reduced productivity, and decreased morale when the employee fails at his or her new job and must be placed back in the old position.

HRM INCIDENT 1

What to Do?

"I'm a little discouraged," said Susan Matthews to the training officer. "I keep making mistakes running the new printing press. It's a lot more complicated than the one I operated before, and I just can't seem to get the hang of it."

"Well, Susan," responded George, "maybe you're just not cut out for the job. You know we sent you to the two-week refresher course in Atlanta to get you more familiar with the new equipment."

"Yes," said Susan, "they had modern equipment at the school, but it wasn't anything like this machine."

"What about the factory rep?" asked George. "Didn't he spend some time with you?"

"No; I was on vacation at that time," said Susan.

George responded, "Have you asked your boss to get him back for a day or two?"

"I asked him," said Susan, "but he said training was your responsibility. That's why I'm here." After she was gone, George began writing a letter to the printing press manufacturer.

Questions
1. What steps in the training and development process has the company neglected?
2. Is George taking the proper action? What would you do?

HRM INCIDENT 2

Management Support of Training and Development?

*A*s the initial training session began, John Robertson, the hospital administrator, spoke of the tremendous benefits he expected from the management development program the hospital was starting. He also complimented Brenda Short, the human resource director, for her efforts in arranging the program. As he finished his five-minute talk, he said, "I'm not sure what Brenda has in store for you, but I know that management development is important, and I'll expect each of you to put forth your best efforts to make it work." Mr. Robertson then excused himself from the meeting and turned the program over to Brenda.

For several years, Brenda had been trying to convince Mr. Robertson that the supervisors could benefit from a management development program. She believed that many problems within the hospital were management related. Reluctantly, Mr. Robertson had agreed to authorize funds to employ a consultant. Through employee interviews and self-administered questionnaires completed by the supervisors, the consultant attempted to identify development needs. The consultant recommended 12 four-hour sessions emphasizing communication, leadership, and motivation. Each session was to be repeated once so that supervisors who missed it the first time could attend the second offering.

Mr. Robertson had signed the memo that Brenda had prepared, directing all supervisors to support the management development program. There was considerable grumbling, but all the supervisors agreed to attend. As Brenda replaced Mr. Robertson at the podium, she could sense the lack of interest in the room.

Questions
1. Have any serious errors been made so far in the management development program? What would you have done differently?
2. What advice do you have for Brenda at this point to help make the program effective?

Notes

1. William Fitzgerald, "Training versus Development," *Training & Development* 46 (May 1992): 81.
2. Ibid.
3. Richard Koonce, "How to Find the Right Organizational Fit," *Training & Development* 51 (April 1997): 15.
4. Bob Filipczak, "Training Cheap," *Training* 33 (May 1996): 29.
5. "Industry Report Symposium," *Training* 30 (October 1993): 29–30.
6. Ronald Henkoff, "Companies That Train Best," *Fortune* 127 (March 22, 1993): 62–63.
7. Martha H. Peak, "Go Corporate U," *Management Review* 86 (February 1997): 37.
8. Laurie J. Bassi, George Benson, et al., "The Top Ten Trends," *Training & Development* 50 (November 1996): 28.
9. Linda Grant, "A School for Success," *U.S. News & World Report* 120 (May 22, 1995): 53–54.
10. Thomas A. Steward, "How a Little Company Won Big by Betting on Brainpower," *Fortune* 132 (September 4, 1995): 122.
11. "Skills for Success," *The Olsten Forum ™ on Human Resource Issues and Trends*, the Olsten Corporation (Fall 1994): 7.
12. Kenneth N. Wexley and Gary P. Latham, *Developing and Training Human Resources in Organizations*, 2nd ed. (New York: HarperCollins, 1991): 36.
13. Kenneth M. Nowack, "A True Training Needs Analysis," *Training & Development* 45 (April 1991): 69.

14. Filipczak, "Training Cheap."

15. Joseph T. Straub (1997). "Dan Davis: Manager of Continuing Education, Chaparral Steel," *Training and Development Forum* http://www.3.elibrary.com/getdoc.cgi?id=73'e=Training_Development_Forum&puburl=0 (June 25, 1997).

16. Peak, "Go Corporate U."

17. Don Barnes, "What Is This Thing Called Mentoring?" *National Underwriter* 94 (May 28, 1990): 9.

18. Marc Hequet, "Games That Teach," *Training* 32 (July 1995): 53–54.

19. Tim McCollum, "Handy Tools for Training," *Nation's Business* 85 (April 1997): 49.

20. William M. Fox, "Getting the Most from Behavior Modeling Training," *National Productivity Review* 7 (Summer 1988): 238.

21. Michael Blumfield, "Learning to Share," *Training* 34 (April 1997): 38.

22. Samuel Greengard, "How Technology Is Advancing HR," *Personnel Journal* 72 (September 1993): 81.

23. Michael J. Marquardt, "Cyberlearning: New Possibilities for HRD," *Training & Development* 50 (November 1996): 56–57.

24. Martha I. Finney, "Harness the Power Within," *HRMagazine* 42 (January 1997): 66–74.

25. Lyle M. Spencer, Jr., *Reengineering Human Resources* (New York: John Wiley, 1995): 8–9.

26. Samuel Greengard, "Interactive Satellite Learning Improves Training Programs," *Personnel Journal* 72 (September 1993): 86.

27. Michael Emery and Margaret Schubert, "A Trainer's Guide to Videoconferencing," *Training* 30 (June 1993): 59–61.

28. Steve Rosenbush, "Mechanics Road Test Mentis," *USA Today* (August 12, 1997): 6B.

29. "The Industry Report 1996 Symposium," *Training* 33 (October 1996): 61.

30. Peak, "Go Corporate U."

31. Susan Jackson, "Your Local Campus: Training Ground Zero," *Business Week* (September 1996): 68.

32. Filipczak, "Training Cheap."

33. After 11 months' training in Siemens's Florida program, American apprentices scored higher on their intermediary tests than did their German counterparts. This finding suggests that American youths may be more talented than they are often given credit for.

34. Beth Rogers, "The Making of a Highly Skilled Worker," *HRMagazine* 39 (July 1994): 62–63.

35. William K. Fitzgerald and Scott Allen, "Personal Empowerment Key to Manager's Development," *HRMagazine* 38 (November 1993): 84–85.

36. Paul Froiland, "Who's Getting Trained?" *Training* 34 (October 1996): 58.

37. Martin M. Broadwell, "The Case for Pre-Supervisory Training," *Training* 33 (October 1996): 103–104.

38. Ibid.

39. Margaret Olesen, "Coaching Today's Executives," *Training & Development* 50 (March 1996): 24.

40. Leslie Overmyer-Day and George Benson, "Training Success Stories," *Training & Development* 50 (June 1996): 28.

41. Jack J. Phillips, "ROI: The Search for Best Practices," *Training & Development* 50 (February 1996): 42–47. This is the first of a three-article series dealing with return on investment as a training and development evaluation approach.

42. Leslie E. Overmyer Day, "Benchmarking Training," *Training & Development* 49 (November 1995): 27–30.

43. Chris Lee, "Out of the Maze: Can the Federal Job-Training Mess Be Fixed?" *Training* 32 (February 1995): 30.

44. "What Works? (Government-Funded Job Training is Ineffective)," *The Economist* 339 (April 1996): 19.

45. Job Training Partnership Act (JTPA), Title II-A, Adult Training Program. (1997). Http://www.ezec.gov/toolbox/guide/emp/rg_emp2.html.

46. Kathleen Barnes, "Government Program Supports On-the-Job Training," *HR Focus* 71 (June 1994): 12.

47. "What Works? (Government-Funded Job Training is Ineffective)."

48. Samuel Greengard, "How Technology Is Advancing HR," *Personnel Journal* 72 (September 1993): 85.

49. Leslie Brokaw, "The Enlightened Employee Handbook," *Inc* 13 (October 1991): 49.

50. Ron Zemke, "Employee Orientation: A Process, Not a Program," 34.

51. Thomas G. Cummings and Christopher G. Worley, *Organization Development and Change*, 5th ed. (Minneapolis/St. Paul: West, 1993): 2.

52. Don McNerney, "The Bottom-Line Value of Diversity," *HR Focus* 71 (May 1994): 22–23.

53. Ibid.

54. Cummings and Worley, *Organization Development and Change*, 136–137.

55. Ibid, p. 137.

56. James L. Gibson and John M. Ivancevich, *Organizations: Behavior, Structure, Processes*, 4th ed. (Plano, Texas: Business Publications, 1982): 580–581.

57. John P. Campbell and Marvin D. Dunnette, "Effectiveness of T-Group Experiences in Managerial Training and Development," *Psychological Bulletin* 70 (August 1968): 23–104.

58. Irwin L. Goldstein, *Training in Organizations: Needs Assessment, Development, and Evaluation*, 2nd ed. (Monterey, CA: Brooks/Cole, 1986): 243.

59. Richard Wellins and Jill George, "The Key to Self-Directed Teams," *Training & Development* 45 (April 1991): 27.

60. David Woodruff, James B. Treece, Sunita Wadekar Bhargava, and Karen Lowry Miller, "Saturn," *Business Week* (August 17, 1992): 88.

61. Shari Caudron, "Are Self-Directed Teams Right for Your Company?" *Personnel Journal* 72 (December 1993): 78.

62. Wellins and George, "The Key to Self-Directed Teams."

63. Donald J. McNerney, "Global Staffing: Some Common Problems—and Solutions," *HR Focus* 73 (June 1996): 1–4.

64. David E. Molnar, "Global Assignments: Seven Keys to International HR Management," *HR Focus* 74 (May 1997): 11–12.

65. Wayne F. Cascio and Manuel G. Serapio, Jr., "Human Resource Systems in an International Alliance: The Undoing of a Deal?" *Organizational Dynamics* 19 (Winter 1991): 68.

9
Career Planning and Development

CHAPTER OBJECTIVES

1. Define *career planning* and *career development*.
2. Explain the evolution of work as it impacts career planning and development.
3. Describe career-impacted life stages.
4. Identify the career anchors that account for the way people select and prepare for a career.
5. Explain the importance of individual career planning and how a thorough self-assessment is crucial to career planning.
6. Describe the strength/weakness balance sheet.
7. Define *organizational career planning (OCP)* and identify the objectives of OCP.
8. Describe the various types of career paths.
9. Explain plateauing.
10. Explain the concept of adding value to retain a present job.
11. Describe the concept of job revitalization and career enhancement.
12. Identify some of the methods of organizational career planning and development.
13. Describe Generation X employees and the *new* factory workers.

ven little shops like Northeast Tool & Manufacturing Company, outside Charlotte, are making the commitment to innovate. Rote assembly-line work is being replaced with an industrial vision that requires skilled and nimble workers to think while they work. This move toward innovation has made career planning and development essential. The past nature of work has little bearing on the future of work. Factory workers at Northeast Tool now must deal with industrial robots and computers that control massive steel casters and stamp presses. Factory workers are constantly funneling information through computers so they can work on the floor and even perform some duties previously performed by management.

Fred Price is being affected as others are on the line. Fred leaves for work at 4 A.M., and while on the job, this 29-year-old North Carolina factory worker

schedules orders as usual for the tiny tool-and-die shop, where he doubles as a supervisor when he's not bending metal. At midday today, test results are coming in from the state Labor Department in Raleigh. These aptitude exams for all 43 workers at Northeast Tool measured everything from math and mechanical skills to leadership and adaptability. Fred's life is about to change—less leisure and less family time—because Fred, like tens of thousands of employees across America, is going back to school. Because even factory work is increasingly defined by blips on a computer screen, a structured developmental program designed to retrain, reeducate, and continually prepare Fred and his co-workers for future careers is essential. Fred Price realizes that to develop to his full potential he must go beyond Northeast's requirements because his career plan is to develop to the point of someday actually managing the plant.[1]

*T*he impact of innovations on Northeast Tool's workforce will be dramatic. Obviously, Northeast Tool has a well-thought-out career planning and development program. The company is using employee tests to develop customized training and development programs for each worker. Based on their developmental plans, some employees will enroll at a nearby community college, others will take computer courses at the plant, and still others will attend afternoon classes right in the plant. However, this is only the beginning of their developmental journey. Career planning and development are important to companies like Northeast, because these businesses must ensure that people with the necessary skills and experience will be available to adapt with the changing nature of work. This planning and developmental process is continual for the workforce of this real company, which is innovating for future survival.

In this chapter, we first discuss the concept of career planning and development. Next, we discuss the environment impacting career planning and development. Then we identify several factors that affect career planning and discuss the nature of this type of planning. We next address career planning and career paths. Adding value, plateauing, job revitalization, and career enhancement are reviewed. Following this, we describe career development, career development responsibility, and the methods used in organizational career planning and development. We devote the last part of the chapter to a discussion of developing unique segments of the workforce.

HR
Web
Wisdom

http://www

http://www.prenhall.com/mondy

SHRM–HR LINKS
This site covers various issues dealing with careers, including career planning.

Career Planning and Development Defined

Career: A general course of action a person chooses to pursue throughout his or her working life.

A **career** is a general course that a person chooses to pursue throughout his or her working life. Fred Price's career is in extreme flux as Northeast Tool innovates their work processes. Usually, a career is a sequence of work-related positions an individual occupies during a lifetime, although probably not with the same company. In today's world, however, the days are numbered for relatively static jobs that required infrequent training and virtually no development for maintaining acceptable productivity levels. Such jobs are going overseas in great numbers. Because jobs are no longer static, neither can be the workers performing these jobs. One of the primary responsibilities of HR is to develop employees so they can accomplish organizational goals more effectively.[2]

Career planning: An ongoing process through which an individual sets career goals and identifies the means to achieve them.

Career planning is an ongoing process whereby an individual sets career goals and identifies the means to achieve them. Career planning by Fred Price includes a career path that he expects to take him from the factory floor to the plant manager's office. Fred fully realizes the need for development to achieve his career plans, even beyond that outlined in his organizational career plan. The major focus of career planning should be on matching personal goals and opportunities that are realistically available. Career planning should not concentrate only on advancement opportunities, as the present work environment has reduced many of these opportunities. Also, from a practical standpoint, there have never been enough high-level positions to make upward mobility a reality for everyone. At some point, career planning needs to focus on achieving successes that do not necessarily entail promotions.

Organizational career planning: The process of establishing career paths within a firm.

In **organizational career planning**, the organization identifies paths and activities for individual employees as they develop. Northeast Tool is committed to innovation that necessitates organizational career planning for all their employees, including Fred Price. Organizational career planning is necessary to help ensure that an organization improve its ability to perform by identifying needed capabilities and the type of people required to perform in an ever-evolving business environment.[3]

Individual and organizational career planning are not separate and distinct. A person whose individual career plan cannot be followed within the organization will probably leave the firm sooner or later. If opportunities are not available elsewhere, employees may leave the firm virtually by permitting their productivity to decline. Thus, organizations should assist employees in career planning so that both can satisfy their needs. A **career path** is a flexible line of movement through which an employee may progress during employment with a company. Following an established career path, the employee can undertake career development with the firm's assistance.

Career path: A flexible line of progression through which an employee may move during his or her employment with a company.

Career development: A formal approach taken by an organization to ensure that people with the proper qualifications and experience are available when needed.

Career development is a formal approach used by the organization to ensure that people with the proper qualifications and experiences are available when needed. Northeast Tool did extensive employee testing to identify the developmental needs of their current workforce. According to Pat McLagan, author of *The Models*, effective career development should result in a competitive advantage for a company.[4] The career development tools, which are specified during career planning and utilized in the career development program, most notably include various types of training and the application of organizational development techniques. Career planning and development benefit both the individual and the organization and must therefore be carefully considered by both.

HR Web Wisdom

http://www.prenhall.com/mondy
CAREER PLANNING
The steps in the career planning process are reviewed.

The Evolution of Work Impacting Career Planning and Development

The work environment in which career planning takes place has changed rapidly in recent years. Across the country and around the world, downsizing has occurred in many firms, with workers and managers alike being displaced. Therefore, a very important factor affecting career planning and development is the work environment individuals confront. As noted by Charles W. Sweet, president of A. T. Kearney's executive recruiting firm in Chicago, Illinois, "The way people approached their careers in the past is history. It will never, never, never return."[5] For many workers, career planning involves devising ways to retain their present jobs in this drastically changing work environment.

Regardless of whether such predictions are true, corporate restructuring probably has become a permanent feature of American life. Companies cut jobs and change work processes continuously, in spite of soaring profits and a growing economy. Even in this environment, HR professionals must ensure that a qualified and motivated workforce exists, regardless of whether their company calls for regular cuts in the workforce or new ways to get work done without a net reduction in employees. Companies that accept layoffs as a way of life tend to develop HR practices that suit a mobile workforce. Companies that avoid layoffs tend to develop HR practices that are more consistent with maintaining a permanent workforce. Regardless of the corporate strategy used to cope with the ever-changing business environment, career planning and development are essential for success. The need for career planning and development is even more critical now, in a fluid job market with current labor shortages, particularly of better skilled employees.

According to an American Management Association (AMA) survey, member firms continue to cut jobs. However, job cuts are no longer tied to the business cycle but to structural changes in the economy, some of which can be overcome by career development. Eric Rolfe Greenberg, AMA research director, believes that "job eliminations are no longer driven by market demand, [with] only 3 percent of surveyed firms cutting jobs solely because of current market conditions." An interesting finding is that 60 percent of the companies in the AMA survey that cut jobs created jobs at the same time. This action appears to indicate that if these companies had developed workers already employed, providing such training could have been a cost-effective business decision.[6]

According to Greenberg, "What we see are jobs being taken off the organizational chart because their functions are no longer necessary to the organization, while new jobs are being added to the chart—jobs with very different skill sets, different demands, and at somewhat different pay levels." As the cost of hiring new employees continues to increase, most firms would rather prepare current employees through career planning and development than hire new ones. Basically, "as new technologies, new business opportunities and new competitive situations arise—and they do all the time—this reexamination of the business becomes perpetual" and so must the reexamination of careers and career development. The evolution of business means that "from time to time it may lead to a decision to eliminate jobs [and] from time to time it may lead to a decision to create jobs."[7] Fortunately, companies are discovering that productivity gains can result from continual developmental activities that can save jobs and create careers.[8]

TRENDS & INNOVATIONS

THE CHANGING NATURE OF EMPLOYMENT IMPACTING HR DEVELOPMENTAL PRACTICES

Fewer and fewer companies focus on offering real employment security. Instead of employment security, these companies offer career security through career planning and development. With such development, workers are offered opportunities to improve their skills—and thus their employability in an ever-changing work environment. Under this so-called employability doctrine, employees owe the company their commitment while they are on board, and the company owes its workers the opportunity to learn new skills—but that's as far as the commitment goes in the firms following this doctrine. Loyalty is not expected in either direction. United Technologies Corporation (UT), Hartford, Connecticut, a supplier of products and services to the aircraft, aerospace, and automobile industries, has adopted a unique approach to development in line with the employability doctrine. UT unveiled an ambitious plan to help employees reeducate themselves. Under the plan, workers can study whatever they wish—creative writing, nursing, science, and so on—and UT pays. The responsibility rests on the employee to define what skills are most important to his or her career development and follow through.[9]

According to Tom Pierson, manager of HR planning, staffing, and relocations at Hewlett-Packard (HP) in Palo Alto, California, not every firm buys into the employability issue, with its emphasis on job cuts and mobile employees. HP rejects the employability doctrine outright, as just a rationalization for not being able to provide employment security. Hewlett-Packard continues to offer employment security to its workers, avoiding layoffs and making every effort to keep employees on board, even during business downturns. HP "feels very strongly about employment security, [and] still cherishes careers [with the company]." Employment security is possible because of a commitment to career planning and development that prepares employees to contribute as the nature of work changes. Because the way work is accomplished changes, sometimes quickly and dramatically, the workforce must be continually developed to add value to themselves and the company.[10]

Regardless of whether the doctrine of employability with no job security is adhered to, or whether employment security is a top corporate priority, career planning and development are essential to ensure a qualified internal workforce, to decrease turnover and attrition rates, and to reduce the cost of retraining and educating new hires. A study by the Center for Creative Leadership in San Diego, California, indicates that companies with a greater emphasis on employee development enjoy better retention rates and higher productivity levels. By contrast, even well-intentioned bosses may kill off their business by focusing on profit at the expense of people.[11] As employees change jobs, even within a firm, developmental planning is necessary to help ensure a qualified workforce.

Factors Affecting Career Planning

Several factors affect a person's view of a career. According to William Bridges, author of *JobShift* and president of William Bridges & Associates, the individual's place in the new economy is a product of the work environment, which was previously discussed, and the person's desires, abilities, temperament, and assets.[12] From the standpoint of the newer entrants into the job market, the real prize is career security, which results from effective career development. **Career security** is the goal of developing a person's marketable skills and expertise, actions that help to ensure employment for the individual within a range of careers. Career security is different from job security, or even employment security; job security implies long-term tenure in one job, often with one company, whereas career security results from a person's ability to perform within a career designation, often in more than one organization. The individual should recognize and consider the most important factors when planning a career. Beyond the environmental and business conditions that shape the future of work—such as technology versus physically demanding labor—there are two major factors that impact career planning: career-impacted life stages and career anchors.

Career security: The development of marketable skills and expertise that helps ensure employment within a range of careers.

CAREER-IMPACTED LIFE STAGES

Each person's career goes through stages that influence the individual's knowledge of and preference for various occupations. People change constantly and thus view their careers differently at various stages of their lives. Some of these changes result from the aging process and others from opportunities for growth and status. The basic life stages are shown in Figure 9-1. The main stages of the career cycle include the growth, exploration, establishment, maintenance, and decline.[13]

Growth Stage.
The growth stage is roughly from birth to age 14 and is a period during which an individual develops a self-concept by identifying and interacting with other people. Toward the beginning of this period, children experiment with different ways of acting. What they observe from these experiences helps them learn how other people react to different behaviors and contributes to their developing unique personalities. Toward the end of this stage, adolescents begin to think realistically about alternative occupations. During this stage, teenagers establish their own identities.

Exploration Stage.
The exploration stage is the period from roughly 15 to 24 years of age; during this time, an individual seriously explores various occupational alternatives. The person attempts to match these occupational alternatives with his or her own interests and abilities formed or discovered through education, leisure activities, and work. Young people generally make tentative and broad occupational choices during the beginning of this period. Near its end, they make what seems to them to be an appropriate choice and try to secure a beginning job. Probably the individual's most important accomplishment at this point is developing a realistic understanding

of his or her abilities and talents. Also, he or she makes educational decisions based on credible sources of information about occupational alternatives. During this stage, young people explore career alternatives and begin to move into the adult world.

Establishment Stage. A person goes through the establishment stage when he or she is roughly 25 to 44 years of age; this period is the major part of most people's work lives. The fortunate individuals find a suitable occupation during this period and engage in those activities that help establish a permanent career. In these years, people are continually testing their personal capabilities and ambitions against the requirements of their initial occupational choice. The establishment stage itself has three substages: the trial substage, the stabilization substage, and the midcareer crisis.

The *trial substage* lasts from about age 25 to age 30. In these years, the person determines whether the chosen field is suitable; if it is not, he or she will probably try to change directions. Between 30 and 40, the individual goes through a *stabilization substage*. At this time, he or she will set more rigid occupational goals and engage in explicit career planning to determine the sequence of promotions, job changes, and/or any educational activities necessary for accomplishing these goals. Then, somewhere in the thirties and forties, the individual may enter the *midcareer crisis substage*. During this period, many people make a major reassessment of their career progress, relative to their original ambitions and goals. Also at this point, individuals decide the importance of family and leisure versus career. Frequently, this is the time when people must deal with the difficult choices among what is really important to them, what they can realistically accomplish, and how much they must sacrifice to achieve the reevaluated goals.

Maintenance Stage. Between the ages of 45 and 65, many people move from the stabilization substage into the maintenance stage. By now, the individual has usually created a place in the work world and most efforts are directed at maintaining the career gains.

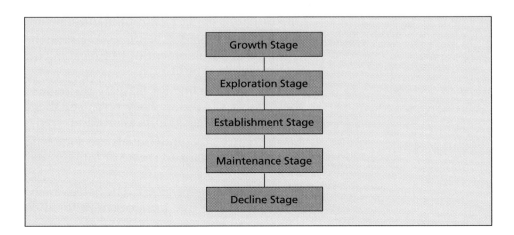

Figure 9-1
Career-Impacted Life Stages

Decline Stage. As retirement becomes an inevitable reality, in the decline stage, there is frequently a period of adjustment; at this time, many begin to accept reduced levels of power and responsibility. During this period, individuals either withdraw from the work environment or accept new roles such as mentoring younger employees. Diminishing physical and mental capabilities may accelerate this stage. A person may have lower aspirations and less motivation during the decline stage, resulting in additional career adjustments.

Even though most individuals have career development needs throughout their working lives, the majority of developmental activities have been directed at new, younger workers. Since the last amendment of the Age Discrimination in Employment Act, there has been no mandatory retirement age; therefore, the self-maintenance and self-adjustment stage is likely to be extended. Future employees will probably need career development as much in their later years as they do in the initial years of their working lives. Also, as a result of downsizing and eliminating layers of management in organizations, development has become much more important as workers are expected to accomplish a wider variety of tasks. This was the case with the workforce at Northeast Tool. "There's much more emphasis on enhancing skills that are broad-based and not necessarily related to one's present organization [or job]," says Vikesh Mahendroo, president of William M. Mercer Inc., a consulting firm based in New York.[14]

CAREER ANCHORS

All of us have different aspirations, backgrounds, and experiences. Our personalities are molded, to a certain extent, by the results of our interactions with our environments as well as the career-impacted life stages we experience. Edgar Schein's research identified five different motives that account for the way people select and prepare for a career; one additional anchor is added to better reflect the evolving nature of the new workforce. He called these motives *career anchors*.[15]

1. *Managerial Competence.* The career goal of managers is to develop qualities of interpersonal, analytical, and emotional competence. People using this anchor want to manage people.

2. *Technical/Functional Competence.* The anchor for technicians is the continuous development of technical talent. These individuals do not seek managerial positions.

3. *Security.* The anchor for security-conscious individuals is to stabilize their career situations. They often see themselves tied to a particular organization or geographical location.

4. *Creativity.* Creative individuals are somewhat entrepreneurial in their attitude. They want to create or build something that is entirely their own.

5. *Autonomy and Independence.* The career anchor for independent people is a desire to be free from organizational constraints. They value au-

tonomy and want to be their own boss and work at their own pace. This also includes an entrepreneurial spirit exhibited by many Generation X workers currently in their twenties and early thirties.

6. *Technological Competence.* A natural affinity for technology and a desire to work with technology whenever possible indicate technical competence, which is also a characteristic of Generation X workers. These individuals often readily accept change and therefore are very adaptable.

A primary implication of career-impacted life stages and career anchors is that companies must be flexible enough to provide alternative career paths to satisfy people's varying needs at various times during their lives.

Career Planning

Through career planning—the process by which individuals plan their life's work—a person evaluates his or her own abilities and interests, considers alternative career opportunities, establishes career goals, and plans practical developmental activities. According to trend analyst Arnold Brown, more responsibility is shifting from employers to individuals. This trend is also true in career planning, "where people are being asked to take more control of their own careers and act like entrepreneurs."[16] As previously discussed, organizational career planning involves the identification of paths and activities for individual employees as they develop. Career planning, at the individual level, and organizational career planning are interrelated and interdependent; therefore, success requires parallel planning at both levels.

In addition to a self-assessment, an individual would be wise to follow the guidelines presented in Table 9-1 to prepare for a new career path. Career planning should begin with a person's placement in an entry-level job and initial orientation. Management will observe the employee's job performance and compare it with job standards. At this stage, strengths and weaknesses will be noted, enabling management to assist the employee in making a tentative career decision. Naturally, this decision can be altered later as the process continues. This tentative career decision is based on a number of factors, including the person's needs, abilities, and aspirations and the organization's needs. Management can then schedule human resource development programs that relate to the employee's specific needs. For instance, a person who wants a career in human resources may require some legal training.

Remember that career planning is an ongoing process. It takes into consideration the changes that occur in people, in organizations, and in the environment. This type of flexibility is absolutely necessary in today's dynamic organizational environment. Not only do the firm's requirements change, but individuals may choose to revise their career expectations. Some prefer the old-fashioned way—up; but in today's less vertical corporate world, workers may have to consider other directions that may eventually lead to a higher plane. For example, they can move sideways, with no change in

TABLE 9-1

Fourteen Steps on a New Career Path

1. **Accept the new values of the workplace by showing how you can help a company meet its bottom-line needs:** increasing profits, cutting costs, increasing productivity and efficiency, improving public relations, even getting new clients. . . .

2. **Continually look for newer and better ways to be of more value to your employer.** Too many who did a good job 15 or 20 years ago are today doing the same thing and thinking that they are still doing a good job. Your company has changed; you need to change with it.

3. **Don't keep yourself stuck in an "information vacuum."** Today you can no longer afford to be unaware of what is happening to your company, industry, your community, your country, or, for that matter, the world. . . .

4. **Don't be reactive.** Those who are successful today are those who prepare ahead of time, anticipate problems and opportunities, and get ready.

5. **Continually seek out a new education.** Expanded knowledge, increased information, and new skills are appearing at record pace. Those who are successful are those who find out what new skills and knowledge they need and who are taking the extra time and trouble to learn them. The others simply will not be competitive.

6. **Develop significant career and financial goals and detailed plans to reach them.** Otherwise, you are vulnerable.

7. **Avoid a state of denial.** When a person is in denial, he or she will ignore signs that something is wrong. Denial is one of the major reasons why people become immobilized and are not prepared for a problem or a change in the company.

8. **Prepare for survival in your present career and for taking the next job or career step.** Have you explored alternatives? Are your job search skills those of today, or are you using antiquated job search methods.

salary or title, to a more dynamic department; leave the company perhaps for a more rewarding career elsewhere; remain in the same position and try to enhance their skills and explore new horizons; or move down to a job that may carry less weight but promises more growth.[17]

INDIVIDUAL CAREER PLANNING

Careers have begun to look less like the steady upward progressions of yesterday and more like patchwork quilts. Dave Ulrich, professor of business at the University of Michigan, calls this emerging pattern the *new career mosaic*. The mosaic means that careers are built in pieces that make sense to the individual. Subsequently, career development for the individual is not a clean picture but more of a mosaic in terms of the path that will accomplish the ultimate career goals.[18] Because of this career mosaic, career planning must begin with self-understanding. Then, the person will be in a position to establish realistic goals and determine what to do to achieve these goals. This action also lets the person know whether his or her goals are realistic.

TABLE 9-1

Fourteen Steps on a New Career Path *(Continued)*

9. **Become motivated by your goals, not by anger, fear, or hopelessness.** In difficult and uncertain career situations, it is human nature to have strong feelings. The problem is that too many of us let those feelings guide our actions and our words.

10. **Market yourself aggressively.** Whether you have a job or are looking for a job, today's world demands that in order to survive and be successful, you must learn to market yourself; network with others, let others know the good work that you do, and don't burn your bridges by making unnecessary enemies. In particular, learn to market yourself within your present company.

11. **Improve your motivation and commitment.** Employers are no longer looking for those who are good enough, they are looking for those who are the most highly motivated. Demand and get the best out of yourself. Go to seminars and get counseling if there is a motivational block. Rejuvenate your enthusiasm and demonstrate it at work.

12. **Place your weaknesses and inadequacies in perspective;** do not allow them to loom so large in your mind that all you can see when you look in the mirror is failure. Remember that no one is without weaknesses, inadequacies, and mistakes.

13. **Realize that to survive and prosper in today's world, your primary job is to change yourself.** You are the one who has to keep up with your training and education. You are the one who has to learn new skills in networking. You are the one who has to develop a different perspective on your career and your employment.

14. **There's no reason HR professionals can't take advantage of the same professional counseling and guidance available to others.** Give yourself the edge and you can confidently move forward to define the career path you want.

Source: Sander I. Marcus and Jotham G. Friedland, "Fourteen Steps on a New Career Path," *HRMagazine* 38 (March 1993): 55–56.

HR Web Wisdom

http://www.prenhall.com/mondy

SELF-ASSESSMENT
Individual self-assessment tools are presented.

Self-assessment: The process of learning about oneself.

Learning about oneself is referred to as **self-assessment**. Anything that could affect one's performance in a future job should be considered. Realistic self-assessment may help a person avoid mistakes that could affect his or her entire career progression. Often an individual accepts a job without considering whether it matches his or her interests and abilities. This approach often results in failure. A thorough self-assessment will go a long way toward helping match an individual's specific qualities and goals with the right job or profession.

Some useful tools include a strength/weakness balance sheet and a likes and dislikes survey. However, any reasonable approach that assists self-understanding is helpful.

Strength/weakness balance sheet: A self-evaluation procedure, developed originally by Benjamin Franklin, that helps people to become aware of their strengths and weaknesses.

Strength/Weakness Balance Sheet.

A self-evaluation procedure, developed originally by Benjamin Franklin, that assists people in becoming aware of their strengths and weaknesses is called a **strength/weakness balance sheet.** Employees who understand their strengths can use them to maximum advantage. By recognizing their weaknesses, they avoid having to utilize those qualities or skills. Furthermore, by recognizing weaknesses, they are in a better position to overcome them. This attitude is summed up by the statement "If you have a weakness, understand it and make it work for you as a strength; if you have a strength, do not abuse it to the point that it becomes a weakness."

To use a strength/weakness balance sheet, the individual lists strengths and weaknesses as he or she perceives them. This is quite important because believing, for example, that a weakness exists can equate to a real weakness. Thus, a person who believes that he or she will make a poor first impression when meeting someone will probably make a poor impression. The perception of a weakness often becomes a self-fulfilling prophecy.

The mechanics for preparing the balance sheet are quite simple. To begin, draw a line down the middle of a sheet of paper. Label the left side *strengths* and the right side *weaknesses*. Record all perceived strengths and weaknesses. You may find it difficult to write about yourself. Remember, however, that no one else need see the results. The primary consideration is complete honesty.

Figure 9-2 shows an example of a strength/weakness balance sheet. Obviously, Wayne (the person who wrote the sheet) did a lot of soul searching in making these evaluations. Typically, a person's weaknesses will outnumber strengths in the first few iterations. However, as the individual repeats the process, some items that first appeared to be weaknesses may eventually be recognized as strengths and should then be moved from one column to the other. A person should devote sufficient time to the project to obtain a fairly clear understanding of his or her strengths and weaknesses. Typically, the process should take a minimum of one week. The balance sheet will not provide all the answers regarding a person's strengths and weaknesses, but many people have gained a better understanding of themselves by completing it.

Likes and Dislikes Survey.

Likes and dislikes survey: A procedure that helps individuals recognize restrictions they place on themselves.

An individual should also consider likes and dislikes as part of a self-assessment. A **likes and dislikes survey** assists individuals in recognizing restrictions they place on themselves. For instance, some people are not willing to live in certain parts of the country, and such feelings should be noted as a constraint. Some positions require a person to spend a considerable amount of time traveling. Thus, an estimate of the amount of time a person is willing to travel would also be helpful. Recognition of such self-imposed restrictions may reduce future career problems. Another limitation is the type of firm an individual will consider working for.

The size of the firm might also be important. Some people like a major organization whose products are well known; others prefer a smaller organization, believing that the opportunities for advancement may be greater or that the environment is better suited to their tastes. All factors that could affect an individual's work performance should be listed in the likes and dislikes survey. An example of this type of survey is shown in Figure 9-3.

Strengths	Weaknesses
Work well with people.	Get very close to few people.
Like to be given a task and get it done in my own way.	Do not like constant supervision.
Good manager of people.	Don't make friends very easily with individuals classified as my superiors.
Hard worker.	Am extremely high-strung.
Lead by example.	Often say things without realizing consequences.
People respect me as being fair and impartial.	Cannot stand to look busy when there is no work to be done.
Tremendous amount of energy.	Cannot stand to be inactive. Must be on the go constantly.
Function well in an active environment.	Cannot stand to sit at a desk all the time.
Relatively open-minded.	Basically a rebel at heart but have portrayed myself as just the opposite. My conservatism has gotten me jobs that I emotionally did not want.
Feel comfortable in dealing with high-level businesspersons.	Am sometimes nervous in an unfamiliar environment.
Like to play politics. (This may be a weakness.)	Make very few true friends.
Get the job done when it is defined.	Not a conformist but appear to be.
Excellent at organizing other people's time. Can get the most out of people who are working for me.	Interest level hits peaks and valleys.
Have an outgoing personality—not shy.	Many people look on me as being unstable. Perhaps I am. Believe not.
Take care of those who take care of me. (This could be a weakness.)	Divorced.
Have a great amount of empathy.	Not a tremendous planner for short range. Long-range planning is better.
Work extremely well through other people.	Impatient—want to have things happen fast.
	Do not like details.
	Do not work well in an environment where I am the only party involved.

Figure 9-2
Strength/Weakness Balance Sheet
Source: Wayne Sanders.

Likes	Dislikes
Like to travel.	Do not want to work for a large firm.
Would like to live in the East.	Will not work in a large city.
Enjoy being my own boss.	Do not like to work behind a desk all day.
Would like to live in a medium-size city.	Do not like to wear suits all the time.
Enjoy watching football and baseball.	
Enjoy playing racquetball.	

Figure 9-3
Likes and Dislikes Survey
Source: Wayne Sanders.

A self-assessment, such as this one, helps a person understand his or her basic motives, setting the stage for pursuing a management career or seeking further technical competence. A person with little desire for management responsibilities should probably not accept a promotion to supervisor or enter management training. People who know themselves can more easily make the decisions necessary for successful career planning. Many people get sidetracked because they choose careers based on haphazard plans or the wishes of others rather than on what they believe to be best for themselves.

Getting to know oneself is not a singular event. As individuals progress through life, priorities change. Individuals may think they know themselves quite well at one stage of life and later begin to see themselves quite differently. Therefore, self-assessment should be viewed as a continuous process. Career-minded individuals must heed the Red Queen's admonition to Alice: "It takes all the running you can do, to keep in the same place."[19] This admonition is so very true in today's work environment.

ORGANIZATIONAL CAREER PLANNING

Although the primary responsibility for career planning rests with the individual, organizational career planning identifies the paths and activities for individual employees.[20] Therefore, organizations must actively assist in the process. Organizational career planning must begin with a virtual redefinition of the way work is done. The once stable, well-defined jobs of years past are now continually evolving, with the overall purpose of making the organization more adaptable in changing markets. Creativity, resourcefulness, flexibility, innovation, and adaptability are becoming much more important than the ability to perform a precisely specified job. Through effective organizational career planning, human resources will do better in developing a pool of men and women who can thrive in any number of organizational structures in the future. The HR function should help redefine the concept of work by developing employees with multiple skills to fill broadly defined roles. Competence in a given job is less important than core competencies or the special skills that enable employees to be more productive. For example, the core competency at Walt Disney Co., Burbank, California, is the distinctive integration of creative, engineering, and marketing skills, which the company calls imagineering.[21] From the organization's viewpoint, career planning involves a conscious attempt to maximize a person's potential contributions. Consider your workers' aspirations and they will stay happier—a simple formula, but often hard to execute.[22] Firms that promote organizational career planning programs for their employees reap many benefits.

The process of establishing career paths and activities for individuals within a firm is referred to as organizational career planning. Firms should undertake organizational career planning programs only when the programs contribute to achieving current and future organizational goals. Therefore, the rationale and approach to career planning programs varies among firms. This rationale is very important in today's environment in which traditional vertical mobility has been stifled in many organizations. In most organizations, career planning programs are expected to achieve one or more of the following objectives:

- More effective development of available talent. Individuals are more likely to be committed to development that is part of a specific career plan. This way, they can better understand the purpose of development.

- Self-appraisal opportunities for employees considering new or nontraditional career paths. Some excellent workers do not view the traditional upward mobility as a career option as firms today have fewer and fewer promotion options available. Other workers see themselves in dead-end jobs and seek relief. Rather than lose these workers, a firm can offer career planning to help them identify new and different career paths.

- More efficient development of human resources within and among divisions and/or geographic locations. Career paths should be developed that cut across divisions and geographic locations.

- A demonstration of a tangible commitment to equal employment opportunity and affirmative action. Adverse impact can occur at virtually any level in an organization. Firms that are totally committed to reducing adverse impact often cannot find qualified women and minorities to fill vacant positions. One way to overcome this problem is to have an effective career planning and development program. Frequently, affirmative action programs require companies to set up career development programs for women and minorities.

- Satisfaction of employees' personal development needs. Individuals who see their personal development needs being met tend to be more satisfied with their jobs and the organization.

- Improvement of performance through on-the-job training experiences provided by horizontal and vertical career moves. The job itself is the most important influence on career development. Each job can provide different challenges and experiences.

- Increased employee loyalty and motivation, leading to decreased turnover. Individuals who believe that the firm is interested in their career planning will be more likely to remain with the organization.

- A method of determining training and development needs. If a person desires a certain career path and does not presently have the proper qualifications, this identifies a training and development need.[23]

All these objectives may be desirable, but successful career planning depends on a firm's ability to satisfy those it considers most crucial to employee development and the achievement of organizational goals.

Career Paths

Recall that a career path is a flexible line of progression through which an employee typically moves during employment. Information regarding career options and opportunities must be available before individuals can begin to set realistic career objectives. One way to provide this information is to develop career path data for each job. This information can be developed from

HRM IN ACTION
LEGITIMATE COMPLAINT?

Five years ago, when Bobby Bret joined Crystal Productions as a junior accountant, he felt that he was on his way up. He had just graduated with a B+ average from college, where he was well liked by his peers and the faculty. As an officer in several student organizations, Bobby had shown a natural ability to get along with people as well as to get things done. He remembered what Roger Friedman, the controller at Crystal, had told him when he was hired, "I think you will do well here, Bobby. You've come highly recommended. You are the kind of guy who can expect to move right on up the ladder."

Bobby felt that he had done a good job at Crystal, and everybody seemed to like him. In addition, his performance appraisals had been excellent. However, after five years he was still a junior accountant. He had applied for two senior accountant positions that had come open, but they were both filled by people hired from outside the firm. When the accounting supervisor's job came open two years ago, Bobby had not applied. He was surprised when his new boss turned out to be a hotshot graduate of State University whose only experience was three years with a major accounting firm. Bobby had hoped that Ron Green, a senior accountant he particularly respected, would get the job.

On the fifth anniversary of his employment at Crystal, Bobby decided it was time to do something. He made an appointment with Mr. Friedman. At that meeting Bobby explained that he had worked hard to obtain a promotion and shared his frustration about having been in the same job for so long.

"Well," said Mr. Friedman, "you don't think you were all that much better qualified than the people we hired, do you?"

"No," said Bobby, "but I think I could have handled the senior accountant job. Of course, the people you have hired are doing a great job, too."

The controller responded, "We just look at the qualifications of all the applicants for each job and, considering everything, try to make a reasonable decision."

➤ Do you believe that Bobby has a legitimate complaint? Explain.

job descriptions, based on historical trends within the organization, or based on similarities to other jobs in the same job family. All this information must be reevaluated in light of the changing nature of work. Career path information is particularly useful because it shows each employee how his or her job relates to other jobs, presents career alternatives, describes educational and experience requirements for a career change, and points out the orientations of other jobs.[24] Career paths have historically focused on upward mobility within a particular occupation. However, there are four types of career paths an individual may chose including traditional, network, lateral skill, and dual-career paths.

TRADITIONAL CAREER PATH

Traditional career path: A vertical line of career progression from one specific job to the next.

The **traditional career path** is one in which an employee progresses vertically upward in the organization from one specific job to the next. The assumption is that each preceding job is essential preparation for the next higher level job. Therefore, an employee must move, step-by-step, from one job to the next to gain needed experience and preparation.

One of the biggest advantages of the traditional career path is that it is straightforward. The path is clearly laid out, and the employee knows the specific sequence of jobs through which he or she must progress.

Today, however, the traditional approach has become flawed because of business trends and changes in the workforce. Some of these factors include the following:

- A massive reduction in management ranks due to mergers, downsizing, stagnation, and growth cycles
- Extinction of paternalism and job security
- Erosion of employee loyalty
- A work environment where new skills must constantly be learned

The certainties of yesterday's business methods and growth have vanished in many industries, and neither organizations nor individuals can be assured of ever regaining them.

NETWORK CAREER PATH

Network career path: A method of job progression that contains both vertical and horizontal opportunities.

The **network career path** contains both a vertical sequence of jobs and a series of horizontal opportunities. The network career path recognizes the interchangeability of experience at certain levels and the individual's need to broaden his or her experience at one level before being promoted to a higher level. This approach more realistically represents opportunities for employee development in an organization than does the traditional career path. The vertical and horizontal options lessen the probability of blockage. One disadvantage of this type of career path is the difficulty of explaining to employees the specific route their careers may take for a given line of work.

LATERAL SKILL PATH

Lateral skill path: A career path that allows for lateral moves within the firm; these permit an employee to become revitalized and find new challenges.

Traditionally, a career path was viewed as moving upward to higher levels of management in the organization. The previous two career path methods focused on such an approach. The availability of these two options has diminished considerably in recent years, but this does not mean that an individual has to remain in the same job for life. The **lateral skill path** allows for lateral moves within the firm that permit an employee to become revitalized and find new challenges. No pay or promotion is involved, but by learning a different job, an employee can increase his or her value to the organization and also become revitalized.

DUAL CAREER PATH

Dual career path: A method of rewarding technical specialists and professionals who can, and should be allowed to, continue to contribute significantly to a company without having to become managers.

The dual career path was originally developed to deal with the problem of technically trained employees who had no desire to move into management through the normal procedure for upward mobility in an organization. The **dual career path** recognizes that technical specialists can—and should be allowed to—contribute their expertise to a company without having to become managers. In organizations such as National Semiconductor, a high-tech worldwide firm headquartered in Santa Clara, California, a dual career approach was set up to encourage and motivate individual contributors in engineering, sales, marketing, finance, human resources, and other areas.[25] Individuals in these fields can increase their specialized knowledge, make contributions to their firms, and be rewarded without entering management. Whether on the management or technical side of the path, compensation would be comparable at each level.

The dual career path is becoming increasingly popular. In our high-tech world, specialized knowledge is often as important as managerial skill. Rather than creating poor managers out of competent technical specialists, the dual career path permits an organization to retain both highly skilled managers and highly skilled technical people.[26] Dow Corning has created what they describe as multiple ladders. As shown in Figure 9-4, individuals can progress upward in research, technical service and development, and process engineering without being forced into management roles.

Level	Managerial	Research	Technical Service and Development (TS&D)	Process Engineering
	Vice President, R&D Director			
VIII	Manager	Senior Research Scientist	Senior Development Scientist	Senior Process Engineering Scientist
VII	Manager	Research Scientist	Development Scientist	Process Engineering Scientist
VI	Section Manager	Associate Research Scientist	Associate Development Scientist	Associate Process Engineering Scientist
V	Group Leader	Senior Research Specialist	Senior TS&D Specialist	Senior Engineering Specialist
IV		Research Specialist	TS&D Specialist	Senior Project Engineer
III		Project Chemist	TS&D Representative	Project Engineer
II		Associate Project Chemist	TS&D Engineer	Development Engineer
I		Chemist	Engineer	Engineer

Figure 9-4
Multiple Ladders at Dow Corning

Source: Charles W. Lentz, "Dual Ladders Become Multiple Ladders at Dow Corning," *Research Technology Management* 33 (May–June 1990): 28.

Today's workers need to develop a plan in which they are viewed as continually adding value to the organization.

Adding Value to Retain Present Job

Adding value to retain a person's present job may seem to be a strange topic to include under career planning, but regardless of the career path pursued, today's workers need to develop a plan whereby they are viewed as continually *adding value* to the organization. William J. Morin, chairman of the outplacement firm Drake Beam Morin, said, "Employees will have to anticipate where they can add value to their companies and take charge of their own destiny."[27] If employees cannot add value, the company does not need them, and much of the evolving work environments cannot use them either. Workers must anticipate what tools will be needed for success in the future and obtain these skills. These workers must look across company lines to other organizations to determine what skills are transferable, and then go and get them. Essentially, today's workers must manage their own careers as never before. According to Pat Milligan, a partner in Towers Perrin, a human resources consulting firm, the new attitude among companies is this: "There will never be job security. You will be employed by us as long as you add value to the organization, and you are continuously responsible for finding ways to add value. In return, you have the right to demand interesting and important work, the freedom and resources to perform it well, pay that reflects your contribution, and the experience and training needed to be employable here or elsewhere."[28] Although this representation may be a bit dramatic, the new business environment will require everyone to add value.

As a worker increases his or her value to an organization, that value also increases in the overall job market. In today's work environment, *job security* is often replaced with career security, which is the ability to go out and find another job. It might be called enlightened self-interest. A person must discover what companies need and then develop the necessary skills to meet these needs as defined by the marketplace. As one Avon executive stated, "Always be doing something that contributes significant, positive change to the organization. That's the ultimate job security."[29] Basically, the only tie that binds a worker to the company, and vice versa, is a common commitment to mutual success and growth.

Plateauing

Plateauing: A career condition that occurs when an employee's job functions and work content remain the same because of a lack of promotional opportunities within a company.

A problem for many individuals who aspire to move upward in an organization is plateauing. **Plateauing** occurs when an employee's job functions and work content remain the same because of a lack of promotional opportunities within the firm. By some estimates, virtually all of the workforce has experienced plateauing at least once in their career.[30] Plateauing has become more common recently because many organizations are downsizing, hierarchies are flattening, middle-management layers are being eliminated, and the baby boom generation is just reaching its prime. In addition, women and minorities are now competing for positions that once were not available to them.

In the 1950s, 1960s, and 1970s, many companies offered extraordinary opportunities for advancement. However, the picture today is quite different, as a large number of people with similar educational backgrounds compete for fewer promotions. In our society, promotion has always been an important measure of success. Thus, plateauing presents new challenges for those involved with career planning and development.

Several approaches may be used to deal with this problem. As previously mentioned, one possibility is to move individuals laterally within the organization. Although status or pay may remain unchanged, the employee is given the opportunity to develop new skills. Firms that want to encourage lateral movement may choose to utilize a skill-based pay system that rewards individuals for the type and number of skills they possess. Another approach, already discussed, is job enrichment. This approach rewards (without promoting) an employee by increasing the challenge of the job, giving the job more meaning, and giving the employee a greater sense of accomplishment. Today, roughly one in 10 midsize to large companies offers such enrichment opportunities.

Exploratory career development is yet another way of dealing with plateauing. It gives an employee the opportunity to test ideas in another field without committing to an actual move. Demotions have long been associated with failure, but limited promotional opportunities in the future may make them more legitimate career options. If the stigma of demotion can be removed, more employees—especially older workers—might choose to make such a move. In certain instances, this approach might open up a clogged promotional path and, at the same time, permit a senior employee to escape unwanted stress without being thought of as a failure.

Job Revitalization and Career Enhancement

Many organizations are not able to reward workers with raises and promotions and remain competitive in the new global workplace. This climate has often caused productivity to suffer and absenteeism to soar. Says Chevron's head of personnel development, Sarah Clemens, "We're working to help people revitalize their jobs in a way that will benefit them and the company."[31] Companies need to reinvigorate diminished and demoralized ranks. They are trying to spur productivity by offering employees a host of ways to spice up their jobs with additional training, lateral moves, short sabbaticals, and compensation based on a person's contribution, not title.[32]

Compensation is another way flattened organizations are spurring enthusiasm. Broadbanding, discussed in greater detail in chapter 11, provides the opportunity for people to obtain pay increases without the necessity of being promoted. Pay for skills furnishes another means: the more skills you acquire and use, the more you can earn—even if you do not jump to the next rung in the corporate ladder.[33] In addition, broadening individual development also enhances career security should an individual decide to join another company.

As companies reduce the levels of management, lower the number of workers employed, and increase the pressure on those who remain, lateral moves have become the commonest way to reenergize the troops. Chevron, which has slimmed down by 6,500 employees in the past two years, has redeployed over 1,000 people to different areas of the company. As CEO Kenneth Derr puts it, "That's not as easy as it sounds. Relocation and retraining expenses can run around $75,000 a person." General Motors, which by 1995 had cut its vast white-collar workforce nearly in half to about 70,000, is paying some $10 million a year for 6,100 employees to be retrained and to enhance their skills in everything from carpentry to the nuts and bolts of automotive design.[34]

Career Development

Career developmental tools: Consist of skills, education, experiences as well as behavioral modification and refinement techniques that allow individuals to work better and add value.

As previously mentioned, a career path is a flexible line of movement through which an employee may travel during employment. Career development is a formal approach taken by the organization to ensure that people with the proper qualifications and experiences are available when needed. Career development benefits both the organization and the employee because properly developed employees are better prepared to add value. Thus, career development includes exposure to any and all activities that prepare a person for satisfying the needs of the firm both now and in the future. **Career developmental tools** consist of skills, education, and experiences as well as behavioral modification and refinement techniques that allow individuals to work better and add value. Specific methods were discussed in chapter 8 under the heading of Training and Development Methods. The methods can apply to employee training at all levels, even nonmanagerial. Once, only managers were allowed to participate in many of these developmental methods, but with the current move toward a team-based environment, where the line between manager and employee is blurring, such developmental methods are important for nonmanagerial employees as well as managerial. Nonmanagerial employees can no longer be considered hands, without brains. Developmental efforts, therefore, are often quite important for nonmanagerial workers.

Although skills, education, and experiences are very important, the behaviors that accomplish work are becoming more important as the workforce diversifies. Therefore, the need for organizational development of employees is often essential. Organizational development is important because it helps develop appropriate employee behaviors. Organizational development efforts include survey feedback, quality circles, sensitivity training, and team building; these were discussed in Chapter 8 under the heading Organization Development. As was previously mentioned, one company that has adopted this broad-based approach to development is United Technologies Corporation (UT), which help employees reeducate themselves by studying whatever they wish—creative writing, nursing, science, and so on—and UT picks up the tab. The responsibility rests on the employee to define what skills are most important to his or her career development. Today's workers realize that if they do not continuously add value to the organization, their future with the firm and in the workplace is greatly diminished. Essentially everyone in the company should be involved in continual career development.[35]

Certain principles should be observed with regard to career development. First, the job itself has the greatest influence on career development, and because jobs are no longer static, this fluidity further complicates career development. When each day presents a different challenge, what is learned on the job is very important; but because of the ever-changing nature of work, formally planned development is also quite important. Second, the type of developmental skills that will be needed is determined by specific job demands, and these change frequently. Third, development is continual because the skills demanded by a particular job are often in a state of flux.

Responsibility for Career Development

Many key individuals must work together if an organization is to have an effective career development program. Management must first make a commitment to support the program by making policy decisions and allocating resources to the program. Human resource professionals are then responsible for implementing the career development program by providing the necessary information, tools, guidance, and program liaison with top management.

The worker's immediate supervisor is responsible for providing support, advice, and feedback. Through the supervisor, a worker can find out how supportive of career development the organization actually is. Finally, individual employees are ultimately responsible for developing their own careers.[36] "You can lead a horse to water but you can't make it drink" is an appropriate analogy for career development. However, without career development, good-paying jobs will not be forthcoming in the future, something more and more employees now realize.

Organization Career Planning and Development Methods

Organizations can assist individuals in career planning and development in numerous ways. Some currently utilized methods, most of which are used in various combinations, are listed here:

- *Superior/Subordinate Discussions*. The superior and subordinate jointly agree on career planning and development activities. The resources made available to achieve these objectives may well include development programs. Human resource professionals are often called on for assistance, as are psychologists and guidance counselors. Colleges and universities often provide such services.

- *Company Material*. Some firms provide material specifically developed to assist their workers in career planning and development. Such material is tailored to the firm's special needs.

- *Performance Appraisal System*. The firm's performance appraisal system can also be a valuable tool in career planning. Noting and discussing an employee's weaknesses can uncover development needs. If overcoming a particular weakness seems difficult or even impossible, an alternate career path may be the solution.

- *Workshops*. Some organizations conduct workshops lasting two or three days for the purpose of helping workers develop careers within the company. Employees define and match their specific career objectives with the needs of the company.

Developing Unique Segments of the Workforce

Career planning and development are essential for the continual evolution of the labor force and the success of organizations, as well as individuals. Certain groups of employees are unique because of the specific characteristics of the work they do or who they are. The newer groups include Generation X employees and *new* factory workers. Because of certain differences between these groups and more traditional workers, and because of differences in the methods of accomplishing work, each group must be developed in rather unique ways. Although generalizations about a group are risky, these generalizations are offered simply to provide additional insight into what some members of each group may require developmentally.

DEVELOPING GENERATION X EMPLOYEES

The more than 40 million American workers in their twenties or early thirties are sometimes referred to as Generation Xers. Generation X is one of the most widely misunderstood phenomena facing the HR professional today. Generation Xers do indeed differ from previous generations in some significant ways including their natural affinity for technology and their entrepreneurial spirit. Job instability and the breakdown of traditional employer-employee relationships in today's era of restructuring brought a realization to Generation Xers that the world of work is different for them than it was for past generations.

Managers who understand how these circumstances have shaped Generation Xers' outlook on career issues can begin to develop a positive relationship with young workers and harness their unique abilities. In fact, a company's success in the coming decades will depend on its ability to turn the extraordinary promise of Generation Xers into reality.

Developing Generation X employees requires supporting their quest to acquire skills and expertise. Given the demise of the old *employment contract*, Generation Xers recognize that their careers cannot be founded securely on a relationship with any one employer. They think of themselves more as free agents in a mobile workforce and expect to build career security—not job security—by acquiring marketable skills and expertise. Fortunately, the surest way to gain Xers' loyalty is to help them develop self-building career security. When a company helps them expand their knowledge and skills—in essence, preparing them for the job market—Xers will often want to stay on board to learn those very skills. The result should be lower turnover rates and greater commitment from Generation Xers, a situation benefiting everyone.[37]

To support Xers' career development goals, the organization must provide them with opportunities to learn new skills, processes, and technologies. Generation Xers recognize the value of formal training and development programs that support individualized career goals, and they welcome both regular and ad hoc opportunities to learn on the job, as well as mentoring relationships. Also, because Generation Xers are independently motivated to learn and grow professionally, they are especially good at lateral moves that are becoming more common. Supporting Xers in building self-based career security is also the key to recruiting the best young talent today. Basically, the developmental program must have self-building security as one of its main goals. First, managers must understand that Xers expect to develop career security by acquiring marketable job skills and expertise. Second, an implicit contract should exist whereby the company fully supports Xers' pursuit of marketable skills and expertise; in exchange, the company receives their commitment to the company's vision and goals during their tenure with the firm.[38]

DEVELOPING THE *NEW* FACTORY WORKERS

Today, life on the factory line requires more brains than brawn, so laborers are taking evaluation examinations to identify skill and educational strengths and weaknesses and adaptability. After being evaluated, *new* factory workers are heading for development in the form of training, classroom lectures, computer-aided learning, organizational development techniques, and so on. Tens of thousands of factory workers across America are going back to school. These days, in an economy where even factory work increasingly is defined by blips on a computer screen, more schooling is the road to success. Northeast Tool & Manufacturing, introduced earlier, is using employee tests over the next several months to determine how to develop each worker. Some will enroll at a nearby community college; others will take remote courses through computers set up at the plant. A few will attend afternoon classes with professors brought right into the plant.

Over the past decade, the thinned-out ranks of managers have been equipping factory workers with industrial robots and teaching them to use computer controls to operate technologically advanced manufacturing processes. At the same time, managers are funneling information through the computers, thereby bringing employees into the data loop. Workers are trained to watch inventories and to know suppliers and customers in addition to being aware of costs and prices. Knowledge that long separated brain workers from brawn workers is now available from computers on the factory floor. Rusty Arant of Northeast Tool points to a powerful computer he rigged up to a milling machine and says: "I crammed it with memory because I want these guys to be managing the business from the shop floor."[39]

The trend toward high-skills manufacturing began in the mid-1980s with innovative companies such as Corning, Motorola, and Xerox. They replaced rote assembly-line work with an industrial vision that requires skilled and nimble workers to think while they work. In the 1990s, what was once the industrial avant-garde is now mainstream as its practices spread across the manufacturing sector. Large, old-line companies finally are learning that investments in people boost productivity, often at less cost than capital investments. Even little shops such as Northeast Tool see high skills as essential for competition.[40]

Subsequently, there has been an intensifying transformation of the American factory and the corresponding workforce. During this period of transformation, the share of the country's 19 million factory workers with a year or two of college has jumped to 25 percent versus 17 percent in 1985, according to the Bureau of Labor Statistics. An additional 19 percent have college diplomas today, up from 16 percent a decade ago. Pamela J. Tate, president of the Council for Adult & Experiential Learning, a Chicago consulting group, believes "there's a real rise in companies' willingness to invest in their workforces." This investment, though, carries a loud and clear message for America's manufacturing workers: "Hone your skills or risk being left behind." Workers in the United States are being pushed to raise their technical savvy to the level of the best foreign workers. At the same time, many are being asked to develop leadership skills and to take a role in managing.[41]

Indeed, the old formula of company loyalty, a strong back, and showing up on time no longer guarantees job security, or even a decent paycheck. Today, industrial workers will thrive only if they use their wits and keep adding to their skills base by continual development. It's a rich irony that "millions of Americans who headed for the factory because they didn't like school, among other reasons, are now faced with a career-long dose of it." Across the economy, in manufacturing and services alike, there has been a surge in demand for higher skills as employers reorganize work around new technologies and human capital-investments.[42]

Closing the skills gap requires carefully considered career development programs to ensure that workers can compete in the factory of the future. More companies are recognizing that they cannot afford not to develop employees, and are therefore willing to develop employees with the profile of a lifelong learner. In fact, according to David P. Jones, an official of Aon Consulting, a Chicago firm that assists manufacturers in testing and hiring, "We look for people who want change, who don't see it as troublesome, but as an opportunity." To earn higher paychecks or save their jobs from rivals abroad, U.S. blue-collar factory workers must add value to themselves through continual development, and thereby add value to the company. Basically, American blue-collar workers must help carry U.S. industry, but this time, "not on their shoulders, but instead with their heads."[43]

A GLOBAL PERSPECTIVE

Global Expatriate Development: The Costs Are Too High Not to Develop Managers Properly

Managers must be properly developed so they can work effectively across cultures. Effective international managers must think globally and have an understanding of international economic, social, and political developments in the region and the industry. According to George Renwick, president of Renwick and Associates, development is essential for success and recommends certain guidelines for managerial development. Developing global managers requires at least one month of intensive language training; one month of orientation in the country to learn about the people, the issues, and how the company operates; intensive cross-cultural training on cultural adaptation and professional performance in such skills as negotiations as they apply to the particular culture; and one month of working closely with one of the company's experienced managers in the region.[44]

Renwick also believes that "a job that's a little over a person's head is often the most effective way of developing him or her." According to Renwick, generally, there are three weaknesses in developmental programs: insufficient language training; cross-cultural training that favors adaptation over job performance; and a lack of follow-up or ongoing support. Bob Wilner, McDonald's director of international human resources, believes that people skills are especially important when managers are working in different cultures. At McDonald's, expatriate managers must be able to motivate and lead teams, counsel employees, and conduct performance reviews, and this is reflected in McDonald's U.S. developmental programs. Basically, enlisting expatriate managers with people, technical, and influencing skills and who are good at strategic thinking is the key to proper development and subsequent global success.[45]

SUMMARY

1. **Define career planning and career development.**
   Career planning is an ongoing process whereby an individual sets career goals and identifies the means to achieve them. Career development is a formal approach taken by the organization to ensure that people with the proper qualifications and experience are available when needed.

2. **Explain the evolution of work as it impacts career planning and development.**
   The work environment in which career planning takes place has changed rapidly in recent years. Across the country and around the world, downsizing has occurred, with workers and managers alike being

displaced. Therefore, a very important factor affecting career planning and development is the work environment individuals confront.

3. *Describe career-impacted life stages.*

Each person's career goes through stages that influence the person's knowledge of and preference for various occupations. People change constantly; thus, they view their careers differently at various stages of their lives. Some of these changes result from the aging process and others from opportunities for growth and status. The main stages of the career cycle include growth, exploration, establishment, maintenance, and decline.

4. *Identify the career anchors that account for the way people select and prepare for a career.*

The career anchors are managerial competence, technical/functional competence, security, creativity, autonomy and independence, and technological competence.

5. *Explain the importance of individual career planning and how a thorough self-assessment is crucial to career planning.*

Career planning begins with self-understanding. Then, the person is in a position to establish realistic goals and determine what to do to achieve these goals.

6. *Describe the strength/weakness balance sheet.*

A self-evaluation procedure, developed originally by Benjamin Franklin, that assists people in becoming aware of their strengths and weaknesses is called a strength/weakness balance sheet. The individual lists strengths and weaknesses as he or she perceives them. The perception of a weakness often becomes a self-fulfilling prophecy.

7. *Define* organizational career planning (OCP) *and identify the objectives of OCP.*

The process of establishing career paths within a firm is referred to as organizational career planning. In most organizations, career planning programs are expected to achieve one or more of the following objectives: (1) more effective development of available talent; (2) self-appraisal opportunities for employees considering new or nontraditional career paths; (3) more efficient development of human resources within and among divisions and/or geographic locations; (4) a demonstration of a tangible commitment to equal employment opportunity and affirmative action; (5) satisfaction of employees' personal development needs; (6) improvement of performance through on-the-job training experiences provided by horizontal and vertical career moves; (7) increased employee loyalty and motivation, leading to decreased turnover; and (8) a method of determining training and development needs.

8. *Describe the various types of career paths.*

The traditional career path is one in which an employee progresses vertically upward in the organization from one specific job to the next. The network career path contains both a vertical sequence of jobs and a series of horizontal opportunities. The horizontal path is often lateral moves within the firm that allow an employee to become revitalized and find new challenges. The dual career path is a career path method that recognizes that technical specialists can and should be allowed to continue to contribute their expertise to a company without having to become managers.

9. *Explain plateauing.*

Plateauing occurs when an employee's job functions and work content remain the same because of a lack of promotional opportunities within the firm. Several approaches may be used to deal with this problem: lateral employment moves, job enrichment, and exploratory career development.

10. *Explain the concept of adding value to retain a present job.*

Regardless of the career path pursued, today's workers need to develop a plan whereby they are viewed as continually *adding value* to the organization. If employees cannot add value, the company does not need them, and much of the evolving work environments cannot use them either. Workers must anticipate the tools that will be needed for success in the future and obtain these skills.

11. *Describe the concept of job revitalization and career enhancement.*

Many organizations are not able to reward workers with raises and promotions and remain competitive in the new global workplace. This climate has often caused productivity to suffer and absenteeism to soar. Companies need to reinvigorate diminished and demoralized ranks. They are trying to spur productivity by offering employees a host of ways to spice up their jobs with additional training, lateral moves, short sabbaticals, and compensation based on a person's contribution, not title.

12. *Identify some of the methods of organizational career planning and development.*

Methods of organizational career planning and development include superior/subordinate discussions, company material, performance appraisal system, and workshops.

13. *Describe Generation X employees and the* new *factory workers.*

Generation Xers differ from previous generations in some significant ways including their natural affinity for technology and their entrepreneurial spirit. Job instability and the breakdown of traditional employer-employee relationships in today's era of restructuring brought a realization to Generation Xers that the world of work is different for them from the way it was for past generations.

Today, life on the factory line requires more brains than brawn—so laborers are taking evaluation examinations to identify skill and educational strengths and weaknesses and adaptability. After being evaluated, *new* factory workers are heading for development in the form of training, classroom lectures, computer-aided learning, organizational development techniques, and so on.

QUESTIONS FOR REVIEW

1. Define the following terms:

  a. *Career*
  b. *Career planning*
  c. *Organizational career planning*

    d. *Career path*

    e. *Career development*

2. Explain the evolution of work as it impacts career planning and development.

3. Identify and discuss the basic career-impacted life stages that people pass through.

4. List and briefly define the types of career anchors.

5. How should a strength/weakness balance sheet and a likes and dislikes survey be prepared?

6. What objectives are career planning programs expected to achieve?

7. What are the types of career paths? Briefly describe each.

8. Why is it important for an individual to constantly add value to the company?

9. Define *plateauing.*

10. What is involved in job revitalization and career enhancement?

11. Who is responsible for career development?

12. Identify and describe some of the methods of organizational career planning and development.

13. Explain the nature of the following:

    a. Developing Generation X Employees

    b. Developing the *New* Factory Workers

DEVELOPING HRM SKILLS

AN EXPERIENTIAL EXERCISE

Career planning and development is extremely important to many individuals. Workers want to know how they fit into the future of the organization. Employees who believe they have a future with the company are often more productive than those who do not. This exercise is designed to help you understand what it takes for a certain human resource professional to climb the organizational ladder. This climb is partially dependent on the individual's self-perceptions and perceptions of past experiences with the company. This exercise provides one method of individual career planning.

    Everyone in the class can participate in this exercise. Your instructor will provide the participants with additional information necessary to complete the exercise.

 *Take It to the Net*

We invite you to visit the Mondy home page on the Prentice Hall Web site at:

http://www.prenhall.com/mondy

for updated information, Web-based exercises, and links to other HR-related sites.

HRM SIMULATION

*I*ncident F in the *Simulation Players Manual* involves training and development. Your team has several requests for training and/or management development on its desk. Your team must make a decision concerning which, if any, it will grant.

HRM INCIDENT

1

In the Dark

"*C*ould you come to my office for a minute, Bob?" asked Terry Greech, the plant manager.

"Sure, be right there," said Bob Glemson. Bob was the plant's quality control director. He had been with the company for four years. After completing his degree in mechanical engineering, he worked as a production supervisor and then as a maintenance supervisor prior to moving to his present job. Bob thought he knew what the call was about.

"Your letter of resignation catches me by surprise," began Terry. "I know that Wilson Products will be getting a good person, but we sure need you here, too."

"I thought about it a lot," said Bob, "but there just doesn't seem to be a future for me here."

"Why do you say that?" asked Terry.

"Well," replied Bob, "the next position above mine is yours. You're only 39, so I don't think it's likely that you'll be leaving soon."

"The fact is that I *am* leaving soon," said Terry. "That's why it's even more of a shock to learn that you're resigning. I think I'll be moving to the corporate office in June of next year. Besides, the company has several plants that are larger than this one, and we need good people in those plants from time to time, both in quality control and in general management."

"Well, I heard about an opening in the Cincinnati plant last year," said Bob, "but by the time I checked, the job had already been filled. We never know about opportunities in the other plants until we read about the incumbent in the company paper."

"All this is beside the point now. What would it take to get you to change your mind?" asked Terry.

"I don't think I will change my mind now," replied Bob, "because I've given Wilson Products my word that I'm going to join them."

Questions
1. Evaluate the career planning and development program at this company.
2. What actions might have prevented Bob's resignation?

HRM INCIDENT

2

Self-Development?

J. D. Wallace, a 30-year-old employee with Bechtel Engineering, head quartered in Houston, Texas, describes his assessment of career development.

My present job is to work with an engineering software design program, Plant Design System (PDS) that is used to create a three-dimensional model of petro-chem refineries. PDS is the fastest growing and most demanded skill in my industry. The system has grown into a major design system that clients prefer. It has become very difficult for designers to find new jobs, or keep their current job, if they do not have the ability to run this system. Unfortunately, a lot of the designers have been caught with their pants down. They didn't see the need to get new skills. They believed, "I've done it this way for 20 years and never needed computer skills. Computers will never replace board drafting. This company needs me and they will not be able to replace me because of my many years of experience.

On the other hand, some designers have seen the importance of learning new technology. These designers can, for the most part, write their own ticket. They have become the highest paid and most sought after employees. I believe it is very important to constantly increase your value to the company. For example, my college degree opened the door for me. Once the door opened, it was up to me to keep learning. I had to continue to train, retrain, and learn new systems. Some of the systems I invested time learning quickly became obsolete. However, I have not lost anything in the process. Improving your skills is never a waste of time. It is amazing how fast the industry can change. Skills that you obtain and thought you would never use can be the only reason you have a job tomorrow.

Workers today must do whatever it takes to get the training needed to keep their jobs. Some of the things you could do include going back to school or changing companies to get the necessary training. Very few companies spend the time and money needed to give workers all the training they need. Everybody must realize that he or she must stay current or be left behind.

In the last year alone, the market for designers with PDS training has grown so fast that companies can no longer be assured of having an adequate work pool to draw from. The pay scale has expanded rapidly and is still growing. A good friend of mine has recently quit his present job for a 35 percent pay increase. Another company has lost many 10 year plus employees due to huge salary offers. Workers with the needed skills now have a lot of options. They can (for the most part) pick the company they want—by location, benefits, permanent staff, or contract. They currently have a lot of leverage. Workers without those skills have very limited choices because they do not add value to their companies.

Questions
1. Do you agree with J. D.'s assessment of what it takes to be successful in today's workplace? Discuss.
2. Do you agree with J. D.'s statement, "Improving your skills is never a waste of time," considering that he has learned obsolete systems in the learning process? Discuss.

Notes

1. Adapted from a real case presented in an article by Stephen Baker and Larry Armstrong, "Special Report—The New Factory Worker," *Business Week* (September 30, 1996): 59.

2. Donald J. McNerney, "As HR Changes, So Do HR Career Paths," *HR Focus* 73 (February 1996): 1–4.

3. Jenny C. McCune, "HR's Top Concerns," *HR Focus* 74 (March 1997): 6.

4. Donald J. McNerney, "'Designer' Downsizing: Accent on Core Competencies: Business Strategy," *HR Focus* 72 (February 1995): 1–3.

5. Louis S. Richman, "How to Get Ahead in America," *Fortune* 129 (May 14, 1994): 46.

6. Donald J. McNerney, "HR Adapts to Continuous Restructuring," *HR Focus* 73 (May 1996): 1–4.

7. Janin Friend, "Enterprise: Management: Workforce: 'How Ya Gonna Keep Em?'" *Business Week* (June 3, 1996): 4.

8. Paul Krugman, "Lower Wages Weren't Enough to Keep U.S. Company Abroad," *USA Today* (June 16, 1997): 19A.

9. Friend, "Enterprise: Management: Workforce: 'How Ya Gonna Keep Em?'"

10. Keith H. Hammonds, "Social Issues: The Issue Is Employment, not Employability," *Business Week* (June 10, 1996): 64.

11. Friend, "Enterprise: Management: Workforce: 'How Ya Gonna Keep Em?'"

12. Donald J. McNerney, "Life in the Jobless Economy," *HR Focus* 73 (August 1996): 9–10.

13. Edgar Schein, *Career Dynamics: Matching Individual and Organizational Needs* (Reading, MA: Addison-Wesley, 1978); Thomas A. Kochan and Thomas A. Barocci, *Human Resource Management and Industrial Relations: Text, Readings, and Cases* (Glenview, Illinois: Scott, Foresman, 1985): 105.

14. McNerney, "HR Adapts to Continuous Restructuring."

15. Edgar Schein, "How 'Career Anchors' Hold Executives to Their Career Paths," *Personnel* 52 (May–June 1975): 11–24.

16. Donald J. McNerney, "Trend Analysis: Know What's Happening before It Happens," *HR Focus* 72 (March 1995): 1–3.

17. Jaclyn Fierman, "Beating the Midlife Career Crisis," *Fortune* 128 (September 6, 1993): 54.

18. McNerney, "Career Development: As HR Changes, So Do HR Career Paths."

19. Lewis Carroll, *Through the Looking Glass* (New York: Norton, 1971): 127.

20. Lewis Newman, "Career Management Starts with Goals," *Personnel Journal* 68 (April 1989): 91.

21. G. William Dauphnais, "Who's Minding the Middle Manager?" *HR Focus* 73 (October 1996): 12–13.

22. Friend, "Enterprise: Management: Workforce: 'How Ya Gonna Keep Em?'"

23. Milan Moravec, "A Cost-Effective Career Planning Program Requires a Strategy," *Personnel Administrator* 27 (January 1982): 29.

24. Donald L. Caruth, Robert M. Noe, III, and R. Wayne Mondy, *Staffing the Contemporary Organization* (Westport, CT: Quorum Books, 1988): 42.

25. Milan Moravec and Beverly McKee, "Designing Dual Career Paths and Compensation," *Personnel* 67 (August 1990): 5.

26. Caruth, Noe, and Mondy, *Staffing the Contemporary Organization*, 253–254.

27. Richman, "How to Get Ahead in America," 47.

28. Brian O'Reilly, "The New Deal: What Companies and Employees Owe One Another," *Fortune* 129 (June 13, 1994): 44.

29. Richman, "How to Get Ahead in America," 49.

30. Susan Sonnesyn Brooks, "Moving Up Is Not the Only Option," *HRMagazine* 39 (March 1994): 79.

31. Fierman, "Beating the Midlife Career Crisis."

32. Ibid, 53–54.

33. Ibid.

34. Ibid, 58.

35. Zandby B. Leibowitz and Sherry H. Mosley, "Career Development Works Overtime at Corning, Inc.," *Personnel* 67 (April 1990): 38.

36. Loretta D. Foxman and Walter L. Polsky, "Aid in Employee Career Development," *Personnel Journal* 69 (January 1990): 22.

37. Bruce Tulgan, "Managing Generation X," *HR Focus* 72 (November 1995): 22–24.

38. Ibid.

39. Baker and Armstrong, "Special Report—The New Factory Worker."

40. Ibid.

41. Ibid.

42. Ibid.

43. Ibid.

44. Clifford C. Hebard, "Managing Effectively in Asia," *Training & Development* 50 (April 1996): 34.

45. Ibid.

10
Performance Appraisal

1. Define *performance appraisal.*
2. Identify the uses of performance appraisal.
3. Describe the performance appraisal process.
4. Identify the aspects of a person's performance that an organization should evaluate.
5. Identify who may be responsible for performance appraisal.
6. Identify the various performance appraisal methods used.
7. List the problems that have been associated with performance appraisal.
8. Explain the characteristics of an effective appraisal system.
9. Describe the legal implications of performance appraisal.
10. Explain how the appraisal interview should be conducted.
11. Describe assessment centers.

"*Doug, we simply must increase our productivity,*" *exclaimed Marco Ghignoni, vice president of production for Block and Becker. "If we don't, the foreign competition is 'going to eat our lunch.' Worker productivity hasn't declined much, but our people seem to have little incentive to work together to improve it."*

"I agree with you Marco," said Doug Overbeck, vice president for human resources. "We really don't have a good system for evaluating team results while at the same time recognizing differences in individual performance. I'm convinced that our team approach in manufacturing is sound, but it does bring us new problems with performance appraisal and our reward system. We need to take some action in these areas—and fast!"

Marco and Doug had begun to realize a need for identifying both team and individual performance. When a performance appraisal system is geared totally toward individual results, it is not surprising that employees show little interest in working in teams.[1] On the other hand, individual contributions must also be taken into account.

We begin this chapter by defining *performance appraisal* and its primary role in performance management. We then explain the performance appraisal process, what to evaluate, and responsibility for appraisal. We follow this with a discussion of the performance appraisal period, methods, and problems. Next, we describe the characteristics of an effective appraisal system, legal implications, the appraisal interview, and assessment centers. The overall purpose of this chapter is to emphasize the importance of performance appraisal as it relates to organizational effectiveness and its special implications for developing the firm's human resources.

HR Web Wisdom

http://www.prenhall.com/mondy

PERFORMANCE ASSESSMENT TOOLS
Various performance assessment tools are presented and defined.

Performance Appraisal Defined

Performance appraisal (PA): A formal system of periodic review and evaluation of an individual's or team job performance.

As emphasized many times, virtually every American business firm is affected by global competition. For survival and success, it is imperative that these organizations remain competitive. Continued competence can only be maintained through ceaseless development of human resources. A potential mechanism for this growth is employee performance appraisal. Managers must realize that performance appraisal has to be comprehensive and that it is a continuous process rather than an event that occurs once a year. **Performance appraisal (PA)** is a system of review and evaluation of an individual's or team's job performance. While the performance of teams should also be evaluated, the focus of PA in most firms remains on the individual employee. Regardless of the emphasis, an effective system assesses accomplishments and evolves plans for development.[2]

Conducting performance appraisals is often a frustrating human resource management task. One management guru, Edward Lawler, noted the considerable documentation showing that performance appraisal systems do not motivate individuals nor effectively guide their development. Instead, they create conflict between supervisors and subordinates and lead to dysfunctional behaviors.[3] General disenchantment with appraisal systems was expressed by another executive who stated, "the ugly truth . . . most employees dread receiving them almost as much as managers hate giving them."[4]

Because performance appraisal is so often perceived as a negative, disliked activity—and one that seems to elude mastery—why don't organizations just stop doing it? Actually, some might if managers did not have to make decisions about developmental needs, promotions, pay raises, terminations, transfers, admission to training programs, and areas with legal ramifications. If managers could be guaranteed that they would never be required to defend themselves in court against wrongful termination suits or charges of discrimination, perhaps performance appraisal would not be such a critical management task. However, considering the multiple needs for appraisal data, most organizations are led to one conclusion: Although the appraisal process is difficult to devise and administer, there is a genuine organizational and employee need to conduct such evaluations.

For the reasons cited, developing an effective performance appraisal system has been and will continue to be a high priority of human resource management. In this effort, performance appraisal must not be seen as an end in itself but rather the means to influence performance management. **Performance management** is a process that significantly affects organizational success by having managers and employees work together to set expectations, review results, and reward performance. It has been described as a three-step process:[5]

Performance management: A process which significantly affects organizational success by having managers and employees work together to set expectations, review results and reward performance.

1. Performance planning by managers and employees for determining performance expectations
2. Performance coaching, which is an ongoing process throughout the appraisal period
3. Performance review, a formal step that results in the individual and/or team evaluation.

According to one study, firms that have effective performance management processes in place outperformed those without such systems on several critical measures including profits, cash flow, and stock market performance.[6]

Performance appraisal is only one technique designed to enhance performance management. Mentoring and coaching, along with other developmental activities, are also involved. However, performance appraisal is a critical component. It is also one of many human resource activities that must be essentially owned by line managers. Whereas human resource professionals play an important role in developing and coordinating appraisal systems, for the process to be successful, line personnel must be key players in the system. Approached in this manner, performance appraisal has the best chance for successful implementation.

Uses of Performance Appraisal

For many organizations, the primary goal of an appraisal system is to improve performance. However, other goals may be sought as well. A potential problem, and possibly a primary cause of much dissatisfaction with appraisal, may result from expecting too much from one appraisal plan. In developing a new appraisal system to fit a changed corporate culture, Eastman Chemical Company found that it needed three separate assessments: one to address development and coaching, another specifically for compensation, and a third for selection.[7]

A system that is properly designed and communicated can help achieve organizational objectives and enhance employee performance. In fact, performance appraisal data are potentially valuable for use in virtually every human resource functional area.

HUMAN RESOURCE PLANNING

In assessing a firm's human resources, data must be available that describe the promotability and potential of all employees, especially key executives. Management succession planning, discussed in chapter 5, is a key concern for all firms. A well-designed appraisal system provides a profile of the organization's human resource strengths and weaknesses to support this effort.

RECRUITMENT AND SELECTION

Performance evaluation ratings may be helpful in predicting the performance of job applicants. For example, appraisal data may show that successful managers in a firm (identified through performance evaluations) exhibit certain behaviors when performing key tasks. These data may then provide benchmarks for evaluating applicant responses obtained through behavior description interviews (discussed in chapter 7). Also, in validating selection tests, employee ratings may be used as the variable against which test scores are compared. In this instance, determination of the selection test's validity would depend on the accuracy of appraisal results.

TRAINING AND DEVELOPMENT

A performance appraisal should point out an employee's specific needs for training and development. For instance, if Mary Jones's job requires skill in technical writing and she receives a marginal evaluation on this factor, she may need additional training in written communication. If the human resource manager finds that a number of first-line supervisors are having difficulty administering discipline, training sessions addressing this problem may be suggested. By identifying deficiencies that adversely affect performance, human resource and line managers are able to create training and development programs that permit individuals to build on their strengths and minimize their deficiencies. An appraisal system does not guarantee that employees will be properly trained and developed. However, the task of determining training and development needs is aided when appraisal data are available.

CAREER PLANNING AND DEVELOPMENT

Career planning and development may be viewed from either an individual or organizational viewpoint. In either case, performance appraisal data are essential in assessing an employee's strengths and weaknesses and in determining the person's potential. Managers may use such information to counsel subordinates and assist them in developing and implementing their career plans.

COMPENSATION PROGRAMS

Performance appraisal results provide a basis for rational decisions regarding pay adjustments. Most managers believe that outstanding job performance should be rewarded tangibly with pay increases. They believe that *what you reward is what you get*. To encourage good performance, a firm should design and implement a fair performance appraisal system and then reward the most productive workers and teams accordingly.

INTERNAL EMPLOYEE RELATIONS

Performance appraisal data are also frequently used for decisions in several areas of internal employee relations, including motivation, promotion, demotion, termination, layoff, and transfer. For example, self-esteem is essential for motivation. Therefore, appraisal systems must be designed and implemented in a way to maintain employees' self-esteem. Appraisal systems that result in brutally frank descriptions of performance result in demotivating people.[8] On the other hand, ignoring deficiencies in a person's performance may hinder that individual's opportunity to improve and achieve his or her potential.

An employee's performance in one job may be useful in determining his or her ability to perform another job on the same level, as is required in the consideration of transfers. When the performance level is unacceptable, demotion or even termination may be appropriate. When employees working under a labor agreement are involved, employee layoff is typically based on seniority. However, when management has more flexibility, an employee's performance record may be a more significant criterion.

ASSESSMENT OF EMPLOYEE POTENTIAL

Some organizations attempt to assess employee potential as they appraise job performance. The best predictors of future behavior are said to be past behaviors. However, an employee's past performance in a job may not accurately indicate future performance in a higher level or different position. The best salesperson in the company may not have what it takes to become a successful district sales manager. The best computer programmer may, if promoted, be a disaster as a data processing manager. Over-emphasizing technical skills and ignoring other equally important skills is a common error in promoting employees into management jobs. Recognition of this problem has led some firms to separate the appraisal of performance, which focuses on past behavior, from the assessment of potential, which is future oriented. These firms have established *assessment centers*, which are discussed in a later section.

HR
Web
Wisdom

http://www.prenhall.com/mondy
SHRM—HR LINKS
Various HR management topics are addressed including assessment of employee potential.

The Performance Appraisal Process

Many of the external and internal environmental factors discussed in chapter 2 can influence the appraisal process. Legislation, for example, requires that appraisal systems be nondiscriminatory. In the case of *Mistretta v Sandia Corporation* (a subsidiary of Western Electric Company, Inc.), a federal district court judge ruled against the company, stating, "There is sufficient circumstantial evidence to indicate that age bias and age based policies appear throughout the performance rating process to the detriment of the protected age group." The *Albermarle Paper v Moody* case supported validation requirements for performance appraisals as well as for selection tests. Organizations should avoid using any appraisal method that results in a disproportionately negative impact on a protected class.

The labor union is another external factor that might affect a firm's appraisal process. Unions have traditionally stressed seniority as the basis for promotions and pay increases. They may vigorously oppose the use of a management-designed performance appraisal system that would be used for these purposes.

Factors within the internal environment can also affect the performance appraisal process. For instance, the type of corporate culture in a firm can assist or hinder the process. In today's dynamic organizations, which increasingly use teams to perform jobs, overall team results as well as individual contributions must be recognized. A closed, nontrusting culture does not provide the environment needed to encourage high performance by either individuals or teams. In such an atmosphere, performance will suffer even though employees may try to do a good job.

Identification of specific goals is the starting point for the performance appraisal process (see Figure 10-1). An appraisal system probably will not be able to serve every desired purpose effectively. Therefore, management should select the specific appraisal goals it believes are most important and can be realistically achieved. For example, some firms may want to stress employee development; other organizations may want to focus on administrative decisions, such as pay adjustments. Too many performance appraisal systems fail because management expects too much from one method and does not determine specifically what it wants the system to accomplish.

After specific appraisal goals have been established, workers and teams must understand what is expected from them in their tasks. This understanding is greatly facilitated when the employees have had an input into the established goals.

At the end of the appraisal period, the appraiser and the employee together review work performance and evaluate it against established performance standards. This review helps determine how well employees have accomplished the goals, determines reasons for deficient areas, and sets a plan to correct the problems. The discussion also results in establishing goals for the next evaluation period.

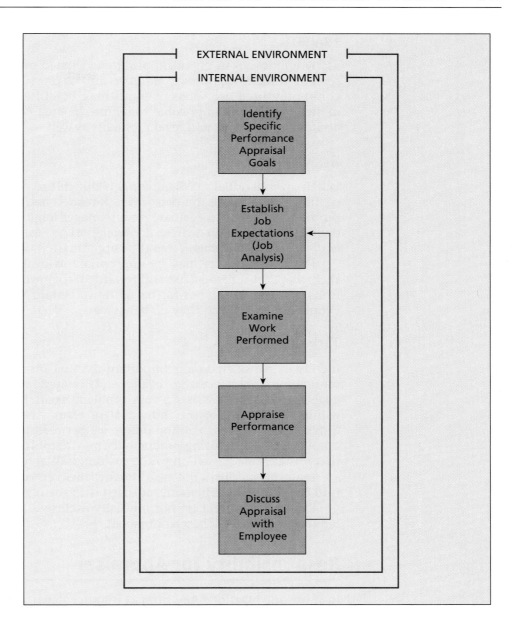

Figure 10-1
The Performance
Appraisal Process

What to Evaluate

What aspect of a person's performance should an organization evaluate? In practice, the most common sets of appraisal criteria are traits, behaviors, and task outcomes.

TRAITS

Many employees in organizations are evaluated on the basis of certain traits such as *attitude, appearance, initiative,* and so on. However, many of the traits commonly used are subjective and may be either unrelated to job performance or virtually impossible to define. In such cases, the result may be inaccurate evaluations and legal problems as well.

BEHAVIORS

When an individual's task outcome is difficult to determine, a common procedure is to evaluate the person's task-related behavior. For example, an appropriate behavior to evaluate for a manager might be *leadership style*. For individuals working in teams, *developing others, teamwork and cooperation*, or *customer service orientation* might be appropriate.

Desired behaviors may be appropriate as evaluation criteria because of the belief that if recognized and rewarded, they will be repeated. In addition, firms pay people salaries for behaving in certain ways that produce results. People don't do traits; they do behaviors.[9]

TASK OUTCOMES

If ends are considered more important than means, task outcomes become the most appropriate factor to evaluate. This approach is encouraged when a goals-oriented process is used. A problem exists here if the results are not within the control of the individual or team. Another problem might be a firm's failure to recognize the difference between productivity and quality of output. Overemphasizing productivity may result in such a frenzied work pace that mistakes are passed on to the customer. Total focus on quality may generate fantastic products but also botched delivery dates. The obvious answer is to balance the requirement for speed with the need to do the job right.[10]

Evaluation criteria are not mutually exclusive. In fact, most appraisal systems are a hybrid of these approaches.[11]

Responsibility for Appraisal

In most organizations, the human resource department is responsible for coordinating the design and implementation of performance appraisal programs. However, an essential element is that line managers play a key role from beginning to end. These individuals will likely have responsibility for actually conducting the appraisals, and they must directly participate in the program if it is to succeed. Several possibilities exist as to who will actually rate the employee, and these are presented next.

IMMEDIATE SUPERVISOR

An employee's immediate supervisor has traditionally been the most common choice for evaluating performance. This continues to be the case, and there are several reasons for this approach. In the first place, the supervisor is usually in an excellent position to observe the employee's job performance. Another reason is that the supervisor has the responsibility for managing a particular unit. When the task of evaluating subordinates is given to someone else, the supervisor's authority may be undermined. Finally, subordinate training and development is an important element in every manager's job, and appraisal programs and employee development are most often closely related.

On the negative side, the immediate supervisor may emphasize certain aspects of employee performance and neglect others. Also, managers have been known to manipulate evaluations to justify their decisions concerning pay increases and promotions. In project or matrix organizations, the functional supervisor may not have the opportunity to observe performance sufficiently to evaluate it. However, in most instances, the immediate supervisor will probably continue to be involved in evaluating performance. Organizations will seek alternatives, though, because of the organizational innovations that have occurred and a desire to broaden the perspective of the performance appraisal.

SUBORDINATES

Some firms have concluded that evaluation of managers by subordinates is feasible. They reason that subordinates are in an excellent position to view their superior's managerial effectiveness. Advocates of this approach believe that supervisors appraised in such a manner will become especially conscious of the work group's needs and will do a better job of managing. Critics are concerned that the manager will be caught up in a popularity contest or that employees will be fearful of reprisal. If this approach has a chance for success, one thing is clear: Anonymity of the evaluators must be guaranteed. Assuring this might be particularly difficult in a small department and especially if demographic data are included in the evaluation that could identify raters.

PEERS

Peer appraisal has long had proponents who believed that such an approach is reliable if the work group is stable over a reasonably long period of time and performs tasks that require considerable interaction. Organizations are increasingly using teams, including those that are self-directed. The rationale for evaluations conducted by team members includes the following:[12]

1. Team members know each other's performance better than anyone and can, therefore, evaluate performance more accurately.
2. Peer pressure is a powerful motivator for team members.
3. Members who recognize that peers within the team will be evaluating their work show increased commitment and productivity.
4. Peer review involves numerous opinions and is not dependent on one individual.

Problems with peer evaluations include the reluctance of people who work closely together, especially on teams, to criticize each other. Also, many team members will have little or no training in appraisal. Training in performance appraisal is obviously needed for team members as it is for anyone evaluating performance.

Peer evaluation works best in a participative culture. However, the approach is not always satisfactory, even in this type of environment. Quaker Oats had such a plan in one of its plants for 10 years before it crashed. An explanation for its demise was that "there was no incentive for people to be strict about it." One of the success stories comes from W. L. Gore, of Newark, Delaware. Gore associates (not called employees) are organized in work teams that handle performance problems. They also perform other traditional human resource functions, such as hiring and firing. With the growth in using self-directed work teams, peer appraisal is expected to grow in popularity.[13]

SELF-APPRAISAL

If employees understand the objectives they are expected to achieve and the standards by which they are to be evaluated, they are in a good position to appraise their own performance. Many people know what they do well on the job and what they need to improve. If they are given the opportunity, they will criticize their own performance objectively and take action needed to improve it.[14] Also, because employee development is self-development, employees who appraise their own performance may become more highly motivated. Self-appraisal, as a complement to other approaches, has great appeal to managers who are primarily concerned with employee participation and development. For compensation purposes, however, its value is considerably less.

CUSTOMER APPRAISAL

The behavior of customers determines the degree of success a firm achieves. Therefore, some organizations believe it is important to obtain performance input from this critical source. One study revealed that at least six winners of the Malcolm Baldrige National Quality Award use this approach because it demonstrates a commitment to the customer, holds employees accountable, and fosters change. Customer-related goals for executives generally are of a broad, strategic nature such as to achieve a specified rating for overall quality for a given evaluation period. Targets for lower level employees tend to be more specific—for example, to improve the rating for accurate delivery or reduce the number of dissatisfied customers by half. It is important to have employee participation in setting goals and to include only those factors within the employee's control.[15]

HR Web Wisdom

http://www.prenhall.com/mondy

360 SYSTEM
A state-of-the-art system for conducting 360-degree performance appraisals is presented.

T R E N D S & I N N O V A T I O N S

360-DEGREE FEEDBACK

360-degree feedback:
An increasingly popular appraisal method that involves input from multiple levels within the firm and external sources as well.

The approaches just described are not mutually exclusive. In fact, **360-degree feedback**, or multirater evaluation, is an increasingly popular appraisal method that involves input from multiple levels within the firm and external sources as well. This method is used by a growing number of companies including General Electric, AT&T, Digital Equipment Corporation, Nabisco, Warner Lambert, and Mobil Oil.[16] In fact, 90 percent of Fortune 1,000 companies use some form of multirater evaluation.[17]

360-Degree Feedback, unlike traditional approaches, focuses on skills needed across organizational boundaries. Also, by shifting the responsibility for evaluation from one person, many of the common appraisal errors can be reduced or eliminated. Having multiple raters also makes the process more legally defensible.

An appraisal system involving numerous evaluators will naturally take more time and, therefore, be more costly. A high degree of trust among participants and training in the appraisal system are needed regardless of how it is conducted. Nevertheless, the way firms are being organized and managed may require innovative alternatives to traditional top-down appraisals.

The Appraisal Period

Formal performance evaluations are usually prepared at specific intervals. Although there is nothing magic about the interval, in most organizations, they are made either annually or semiannually. In high-tech organizations, however, the speed of change mandates that a performance period be shorter—perhaps three or four months. The need is to link performance communication to the actual work cycle. Discussions of accomplishments can then keep pace with new goals and priorities.[18] In the current business climate, it may be well for all firms to consider monitoring performance often. Changes occur so fast that employees need to look at objectives and their own role throughout the year to see if they need to be altered. A study by Hewitt Associates found that companies conducting multiple performance reviews had better results in terms of total shareholder return, return on equity, sales growth, and cash flow.[19]

The appraisal period may begin with each employee's date of hire, or all employees may be evaluated at the same time. In the interest of consistency, it may be advisable to perform evaluations on a calendar basis, not on anniversaries. If the appraisals are not done at the same time, it may not be feasible to make needed comparisons between employees.[20]

Performance Appraisal Methods

Managers may choose from among several appraisal methods. The type of performance appraisal system used depends on its purpose. If the major emphasis is on selecting people for promotion, training, and merit pay increases, a traditional method such as rating scales may be appropriate. Collaborative methods may prove to be more appropriate for developing employees and helping them become more effective.

RATING SCALES

Rating scales method:
A widely used performance appraisal method that rates employees according to defined factors.

A widely used appraisal method, which rates employees according to defined factors, is called the **rating scales method.** Using this approach, judgments about performance are recorded on a scale. The scale is divided into categories—normally 5 to 7 in number—that are often defined by adjectives, such as *outstanding, average,* or *unsatisfactory.* Although an overall rating may be provided, the method generally allows for the use of more than one performance criterion. One reason for the popularity of the rating scales method is its simplicity, which permits many employees to be evaluated quickly.

The factors chosen for evaluation are typically of two types: job-related and personal characteristics. Note that in Figure 10-2, job-related factors include quantity and quality of work, whereas personal factors include such attributes as dependability, initiative, adaptability, and cooperation.[21] The rater (evaluator) completes the form by indicating the degree of each factor that is most descriptive of the employee and his or her performance.

Some firms provide space for the rater to comment on the evaluation given for each factor. This practice may be especially encouraged, or even required, when the rater gives either the highest or lowest rating. For instance, if an employee is rated *unsatisfactory* on initiative, the rater provides written justification for this low evaluation. The purpose of this type of requirement is to avoid arbitrary and hastily made judgments.

As shown in Figure 10-2, each factor and each degree have been defined. In order to receive an *exceptional* rating for the factor *quality of work*, a person must consistently exceed the prescribed work requirements. The more precisely the various factors and degrees are defined, the better the rater can evaluate worker performance. Evaluation agreement throughout the organization is achieved when each rater interprets the factors and degrees in the same way. This ability may be acquired through training in performance appraisal.

Many rating scale performance appraisal forms also provide for an assessment of the employee's growth potential. The form shown in Figure 10-2 contains four categories relating to a person's potential for future growth and development. They range from *now at or near maximum performance in present job* to *no apparent limitations.* Although there are drawbacks in attempting to evaluate both past performance and future potential at the same time, this practice is often followed.

Employee's Name _____

Job Title _____

Department _____

Supervisor _____

Evaluation Period:
  From _____ to _____

Instructions for Evaluation:
1. Consider only one factor at a time. Do not permit rating given for one factor to affect decision for others.
2. Consider performance for entire evaluation period. Avoid concentration on recent events or isolated incidents.
3. Remember that the average employee performs duties in a satisfactory manner. An above average or exceptional rating indicates that the employee has clearly distinguished himself or herself from the average employee.

EVALUATION FACTORS	Unsatisfactory. Does not meet requirements.	Below average. Needs improvement. Requirements occasionally not met.	Average. Consistently meets requirements.	Good. Frequently exceeds requirements.	Exceptional. Consistently exceeds requirements.
QUANTITY OF WORK: Consider the volume of work achieved. Is productivity at an acceptable level?					
QUALITY OF WORK: Consider accuracy, percision, neatness, and completeness in handling assigned duties.					
DEPENDABILITY: Consider degree to which employee can be relied on to meet work commitments.					
INITIATIVE: Consider self-reliance, resourcefulness, and willingness to accept responsibility.					
ADAPTABILITY: Consider ability to respond to changing requirements and conditions.					
COOPERATION: Consider ability to work for, and with, others. Are assignments, including overtime, willingly accepted?					

POTENTIAL FOR FUTURE GROWTH AND DEVELOPMENT:
☐ Now at or near maximum performance in present job.
☐ Now at or near maximum performance in this job, but has potential for improvement in another job, such as:

_____

☐ Capable of progressing after further training and experience.
☐ No apparent limitations.

EMPLOYEE STATEMENT: I agree ☐   disagree ☐   with this evaluation
  Comments:

_____

_____

Employee	Date
Supervisor	Date
Reviewing Manager	Date

Figure 10-2
Rating Scales Method of Performance Appraisal

COMPUTERIZED RATING SCALES

HR tasks such as performance appraisal may seem too personal to relegate to machines. However, software programs are available to assist raters in this chore, which may be time-consuming and often unpleasant. For instance, the *expert system* might begin by notifying the supervisor when reviews for employees are scheduled. They can assist in recording performance data relevant to employee performance throughout the rating period so they can easily be inserted in the final appraisal report. Based on information supplied by the rater, the program creates the text of the appraisal based on data entered by the manager. For example, David's supervisor gives him a "3" (average on a graphic rating scale) for being competent in the factor job knowledge and a "4" (above average) for supervision required. The firm's performance appraisal procedure requires the rating supervisor to comment on each rating. Based on these ratings, the computer spits out, "David needs a minimal amount of supervision to fulfill his responsibilities. He demonstrates competency in the skills and knowledge required."

The program can create a complete paragraph, structuring it from the most positive to the most negative according to how the employee is rated on each factor. It allows for generating and modifying text and even scans the document to seek out language that might pose legal difficulties. If the report appears excessively positive, for example, a keystroke will revise it to make it less so. Once the review is completed, the program can be consulted for advice as to how the review should be presented to the employee. Specific suggestions are available for how the manager might approach problem workers to assist them in improving their performance.[22]

CRITICAL INCIDENTS

Critical incident method: A performance appraisal technique that requires a written record of highly favorable and highly unfavorable employee work behavior.

The **critical incident method** requires that written records be kept of highly favorable and highly unfavorable work actions. When such an action affects the department's effectiveness significantly, either positively or negatively, the manager writes it down. It is called a critical incident. At the end of the appraisal period, the rater uses these records, along with other data, to evaluate employee performance. With this method, the appraisal is more likely to cover the entire evaluation period and not, for example, focus on the last few weeks or months.

ESSAY

Essay method: A performance appraisal method in which the rater writes a brief narrative describing an employee's performance.

In the **essay method**, the rater simply writes a brief narrative describing the employee's performance. This method tends to focus on extreme behavior in the employee's work rather than routine day-to-day performance. Ratings of this type depend heavily on the evaluator's writing ability. Some supervisors, because of their excellent writing skills, can make even a marginal worker sound like a top performer. Comparing essay evaluations might be difficult because no common criteria exist. However, some managers believe that the essay method is not only the most simple but also the best approach to employee evaluation.

WORK STANDARDS

Work standards method: A performance appraisal method that compares each employee's performance to a predetermined standard or expected level of output.

The **work standards method** compares each employee's performance to a predetermined standard or expected level of output. Standards reflect the normal output of an average worker operating at a normal pace. Work standards may be applied to virtually all types of jobs, but they are most frequently used for production jobs. Several methods may be used in determining work standards, including time study and work sampling.

An obvious advantage of using standards as appraisal criteria is objectivity. However, for employees to perceive that the standards are objective, they should understand clearly how the standards were set. The rationale for any changes to the standards must also be carefully explained.

RANKING

Ranking method: A job evaluation method in which the rater examines the description of each job being evaluated and arranges the jobs in order according to their value to the company; also a performance appraisal method in which the rater places all employees in a given group in rank order on the basis of their overall performance.

Paired comparison: A variation of the ranking method of performance appraisal in which the performance of each employee is compared with that of every other employee in the particular group.

In using the **ranking method**, the rater simply places all employees from a group in rank order of overall performance. For example, the best employee in the department is ranked highest, and the poorest is ranked lowest. A major difficulty occurs when individuals have performed at comparable levels.

Paired comparison is a variation of the ranking method in which the performance of each employee is compared with every other employee in the group. The comparison is often based on a single criterion, such as overall performance. The employee who receives the greatest number of favorable comparisons is ranked highest.

Some professionals in the field argue for using a comparative approach, such as ranking, whenever human resource decisions are made. For example, they feel that employees are not promoted because they achieve their objectives but rather because they achieve them better than others in their work group. Such decisions go beyond a single individual's performance and, therefore, should be considered on a broader basis.

FORCED DISTRIBUTION

Forced distribution method: An appraisal approach in which the rater is required to assign individuals in a work group to a limited number of categories similar to a normal frequency distribution.

In the **forced distribution method**, the rater is required to assign individuals in the work group to a limited number of categories similar to a normal frequency distribution. As an example, employees in the top 10 percent are placed in the highest group, the next 20 percent in the next group, the next 40 percent in the middle group, the next 20 percent in the second to lowest group, and the remaining 10 percent in the lowest category. This approach is based on the rather questionable assumption that all groups of employees will have the same distribution of excellent, average, and poor performers. If one department has done an outstanding job in selecting employees, the supervisor might be hard pressed to decide who should be placed in the lower categories.

Forced-Choice and Weighted Checklist Performance Reports

The **forced-choice performance report** requires that the appraiser choose from a series of statements about an individual those that are most or least descriptive of the employee. One difficulty with this method is that the descriptive statements may be virtually identical.

Using the **weighted checklist performance report**, the rater completes a form similar to the forced-choice performance report, but the various responses have been assigned different weights. The form includes questions related to the employee's behavior, and the evaluator answers each question either positively or negatively. The evaluator is not aware of each question's weight, however.

As with forced-choice performance reports, the weighted checklist is expensive to design. Both methods strive for objectivity, but the evaluator does not know which items contribute most to successful performance. Employee development, therefore, cannot result from this approach.

Behaviorally Anchored Rating Scales

The **behaviorally anchored rating scale (BARS) method** combines elements of the traditional rating scales and critical incidents methods. Using BARS, job behaviors derived from critical incidents—effective and ineffective behavior—are described more objectively. Individuals familiar with a particular job identify its major components. They then rank and validate specific behaviors for each of the components. Because BARS typically requires considerable employee participation, it may be accepted more readily by both supervisors and subordinates.

In BARS, various performance levels are shown along a scale and described in terms of an employee's specific job behavior. For example, suppose the factor chosen for evaluation is *Ability to Absorb and Interpret Policies*. On the *very positive* end of this factor might be "This interviewer could be expected to serve as an information source concerning new and changed policies for others in the organization." On the *very negative* end of this factor might be "Even after repeated explanations, this interviewer could be expected to be unable to learn new procedures." There might be several levels in between the very negative and very positive level. Instead of using adjectives at each scale point, BARS uses behavioral anchors related to the criterion being measured. This modification clarifies the meaning of each point on the scale. Instead of providing a box to be checked for a category such as *Very Positive* performance, the BARS method provides examples of such behavior. This approach facilitates discussion of the rating because specific behaviors can be addressed. This method was developed to overcome weaknesses in other evaluation methods. Reports on the effectiveness of BARS are mixed, and it does not seem to be superior to other methods in overcoming rater errors or in achieving psychometric soundness. A specific deficiency is that the behaviors used are activity oriented rather than results oriented. This characteristic poses a potential problem for supervisors because they must rate employees who are performing the activity but not necessarily accomplishing the desired goals.

OBJECTIVE-ORIENTED APPROACHES

In an objective-oriented system, the superior and the subordinate jointly agree on objectives for the next appraisal period. For instance, one objective might be to cut waste by 1 percent. At the end of the appraisal period, the worker's evaluation is based on how well these objectives were accomplished. One advantage of this approach is that the objectives, once jointly established, can be used in coaching subordinates. Objective-oriented appraisals are most often used to evaluate managers, not workers.

Problems in Performance Appraisal

Many performance appraisal methods have been severely criticized. The rating scales method seems to have received the greatest attention. In all fairness, many of the problems commonly mentioned are not inherent in the method; rather, they reflect improper usage. For example, raters may be inadequately trained or the appraisal criteria used may not be job related.

LACK OF OBJECTIVITY

A potential weakness of traditional performance appraisal methods is that they lack objectivity. In the rating scales method, for example, commonly used factors such as attitude, loyalty, and personality are difficult to measure. In addition, these factors may have little to do with an employee's job performance.

Some subjectivity will always exist in appraisal methods. However, the use of job-related factors does increase objectivity. Employee appraisal based primarily on personal characteristics may place the evaluator—and the company—in untenable positions with the employee and equal employment opportunity guidelines. The firm would be hard pressed to show that these factors are job related.

HALO ERROR

Halo error: The perception by an evaluator that one factor is of paramount importance and then gives a good or bad overall rating to an employee based on this particular factor.

Halo error occurs when the evaluator perceives one factor as having paramount importance and gives a good or bad overall rating to an employee based on this one factor. For example, Ted Ball, accounting supervisor, placed a high value on *neatness*, which was a factor used in the company's performance appraisal system. As Ted was evaluating the performance of his senior accounting clerk, Jack Hicks, he noted that Jack was not a very neat individual and gave him a low ranking on this factor. Also, consciously or unconsciously, Ted permitted the low ranking on neatness to carry over to other factors, giving Jack undeserved low ratings on all factors. Of course, if Jack were very neat, the opposite could have occurred. Either way, the halo error does a disservice to the employee involved and the organization.

LENIENCY/STRICTNESS

Leniency: Giving undeserved high performance appraisal rating to an employee.

Giving undeserved high ratings is referred to as **leniency.** This behavior is often motivated by a desire to avoid controversy over the appraisal. It is most prevalent when highly subjective (and difficult to defend) performance criteria are used, and the rater is required to discuss evaluation results with employees. A recently conducted research study found that when managers know they are evaluating employees for administrative purposes, such as pay increases, they are likely to be more lenient than when evaluating performance to achieve employee development.[23] Leniency may result in a number of organizational problems.[24]

1. When deficiencies are not recognized, organizations are denied accurate information regarding the effectiveness of their operations, potentially jeopardizing their success. Employees may not understand the need to improve their performance and the status quo will continue.

2. When appraisal data are used for determining merit pay, as is generally the case, leniency may lead to rapid depletion of the merit budget and reduce the reward available for superior employees. Thus, the potential motivational impact of the merit pay program is reduced.

3. Finally, an organization will find it difficult to terminate a poor performing employee if he or she has a record of satisfactory evaluations.

Strictness: Being unduly critical of an employee's work performance.

Being unduly critical of an employee's work performance is referred to as **strictness.** Although leniency is usually more prevalent than strictness, some managers apply an evaluation more rigorously than the company standard. This behavior may be due to a lack of understanding of various evaluation factors. When one manager is overly strict on an entire unit, workers in that group suffer with regard to pay raises and promotion. Strictness applied to a particular individual has the potential for charges of discrimination.

One study revealed that over 70 percent of responding managers believe that inflated and lowered ratings are intentionally given to subordinates. Table 10-1 shows these managers' explanations for their rationale. The results suggest that the validity of many performance appraisal systems is flawed. Evaluator training should be provided to emphasize the negative consequences of rater errors.

CENTRAL TENDENCY

Central tendency: A common error in performance appraisal that occurs when employees are incorrectly rated near the average or middle of a scale.

Central tendency is a common error that occurs when employees are incorrectly rated near the average or middle of the scale. Some rating scale systems require the evaluator to justify in writing extremely high or extremely low ratings. With such a system, the rater may avoid possible controversy or criticism by giving only average ratings.

RECENT BEHAVIOR BIAS

Virtually every employee knows precisely when he or she is scheduled for a performance review. Although his or her actions may not be conscious, an employee's behavior often improves and productivity tends to rise several

TABLE 10-1

Reasons for Intentionally Inflating or Lowering Ratings

Inflated Ratings

- The belief that accurate ratings would have a damaging effect on the subordinate's motivation and performance
- The desire to improve an employee's eligibility for merit raises
- The desire to avoid airing the department's dirty laundry
- The wish to avoid creating a negative permanent record of poor performance that might hound the employee in the future
- The need to protect good performers whose performance was suffering because of personal problems
- The wish to reward employees displaying great effort even when results are relatively low
- The need to avoid confrontation with certain hard-to-manage employees
- The desire to promote a poor or disliked employee up and out of the department

Lowered Ratings

- To scare better performance out of an employee
- To punish a difficult or rebellious employee
- To encourage a problem employee to quit
- To create a strong record to justify a planned firing
- To minimize the amount of the merit increase a subordinate receives
- To comply with an organization edict that discourages managers from giving high ratings

Source: Clinton Longenecker and Dean Ludwig, "Ethical Dilemmas in Performance Appraisal Revisited," *Journal of Business Ethics* 9 (December 1990): 963. Reprinted by permission of Kluwer Academic Publishers.

days or weeks before the scheduled evaluation. It is only natural for a rater to remember recent behavior more clearly than actions from the more distant past. However, performance appraisals generally cover a specified period of time, and an individual's performance should be considered for the entire period.

PERSONAL BIAS

Supervisors doing performance appraisals may have biases related to their employees' personal characteristics such as race, religion, gender, disability, or age. Although federal legislation protects such employees, discrimination continues to be an appraisal problem.

Discrimination in appraisal can be based on many factors in addition to those mentioned. For example, mild-mannered people may be appraised

HRM IN ACTION
WHAT SHOULD I DO?

Janice is just completing her first year of service. It is time to make out her annual performance appraisal. She has consistently done good work and has been a fine employee except for one morning last week. For some reason, Janice lost her temper and cursed a major client on the phone. Then she got up and went home without any explanation. You observed this episode but chose to say nothing about it. She has not mentioned the incident either, although she was back at work the next day. You have come to the attitude section on her performance appraisal.

➡ *How would you fill it in?*

more harshly simply because they do not raise serious objections to the results. This type of behavior is in sharp contrast to the *hell raisers* who often confirm the adage, "the squeaking wheel gets the grease."

JUDGMENTAL ROLE OF EVALUATOR

Supervisors conducting performance evaluations are at times accused of playing God with their employees. In some instances, supervisors control virtually every aspect of the process. Manipulating evaluations to justify their decisions about pay increases and promotions is one example of how supervisors may abuse the system. They make decisions about the ratings and often try to sell their version to the employees. The highly judgmental role of some evaluators often places employees on the defensive. Such relationships are hardly conducive to employee development, morale, and productivity.

Characteristics of an Effective Appraisal System

The basic purpose of a performance appraisal system is to improve performance of individuals, teams, and the entire organization. The system may also serve to assist in making administrative decisions such as pay increases. In addition, the appraisal system must be legally defensible. Although a perfect system does not exist, every system should possess certain characteristics. An accurate assessment of performance should be sought that permits developing a plan to improve individual and group performance. The system must honestly inform people how they stand with the organization.[25] The following factors assist in accomplishing this purpose.

JOB-RELATED CRITERIA

The criteria used for appraising employee performance must be job related. The *Uniform Guidelines* and court decisions are quite clear on this point. More specifically, job information should be determined through job analysis. Subjective factors, such as initiative, enthusiasm, loyalty, and cooperation, are obviously important. Unless they can be clearly shown to be job related, however, they should not be used.

PERFORMANCE EXPECTATIONS

Managers and subordinates must agree on performance expectations in advance of the appraisal period. Evaluating employees using criteria that they know nothing about is not reasonable.

The establishment of highly objective work standards is relatively simple in many areas, such as manufacturing, assembly, and sales. For numerous other types of jobs, however, this task is more difficult. Still, evaluation must take place, and performance expectations, however elusive, should be defined in understandable terms.

STANDARDIZATION

Employees in the same job category under the same supervisor should be appraised using the same evaluation instrument. Also important is that appraisals be conducted regularly for all employees and that they cover similar periods of time. Although annual evaluations are most common, employees are evaluated more frequently by many successful firms. Feedback sessions and appraisal interviews should be regularly scheduled for all employees.

A legal aspect of standardization is formal documentation. Employees should sign their evaluations. If the employee refuses to sign, the manager should document this behavior. Records should also include a description of employee responsibilities, expected performance results, and the way these data will be viewed in making appraisal decisions. However, smaller firms are not expected to maintain performance appraisal systems that are as formal as those used by large organizations. Courts have reasoned that objective criteria are less important in firms with fewer than 30 employees because a smaller firm's top managers are more familiar with their employees' work.[26]

TRAINED APPRAISERS

Responsibility for evaluating employee performance should be assigned to the individual or individuals who directly observe at least a representative sample of the worker's job performance. Usually, this person is the employee's immediate supervisor. However, as previously discussed, other approaches are gaining in popularity.

Situations that lessen the immediate supervisor's ability to appraise performance objectively include those found in matrix organizations. In these firms, certain employees may be formally assigned to a supervisor but actually work under various project managers. Also, a supervisor who is in a new position may have insufficient knowledge of employee performance initially. In such instances, multiple raters may be used as in 360-degree feedback. This method, along with self-directed work teams, requires employees as well as supervisors to be trained in performance appraisal.[27]

Training in performance appraisal should be an ongoing process to ensure consistency. The training should cover how to rate employees and conduct appraisal interviews. Instructions should be rather detailed and stress the importance of making objective and unbiased ratings.

OPEN COMMUNICATION

Most employees have a strong need to know how well they are performing. A good appraisal system provides highly desired feedback on a continuing basis. A worthwhile goal is to avoid surprises during the appraisal interview. Even though the interview presents an excellent opportunity for both parties to exchange ideas, it should never serve as a substitute for day-to-day communication and coaching required by performance management.

EMPLOYEE ACCESS TO RESULTS

For the many appraisal systems that are designed to improve performance, withholding appraisal results would be unthinkable. Employees would be severely handicapped in their developmental efforts if denied access to this information. Also, employees' review of appraisal results allows them to detect any errors that may have been made. An employee may simply disagree with the evaluation and may want to challenge it. Employees who receive a substandard appraisal should be offered needed training and guidance. Supervisors must make an effort to salvage marginal employees. Individuals in this category should, however, be told the specific consequences if their performance does not reach an acceptable level.

As a result of the Federal Privacy Act of 1974, employees of the federal government and federal contractors must be given access to their employment files. These records may include performance appraisal data. This requirement does not currently apply to all employees in the private sector, but there are good reasons—aside from the threat of broader legislation coverage—for allowing such access. Most important, employees will not trust a system they do not understand. Secrecy will invariably breed suspicion and thereby thwart efforts to obtain employee participation.

DUE PROCESS

Ensuring due process is vital. If a formal policy does not exist, one should be developed to permit employees to appeal appraisal results they consider inaccurate or unfair. They must have a procedure for pursuing their grievances and having them addressed objectively.

Legal Implications

A review of court cases shows clearly that legally defensible performance appraisal systems should be in place. Perfect systems are not expected and neither is it anticipated that supervisory discretion should be removed from the process. However, the courts normally require these conditions:

1. Either the absence of adverse impact on members of certain groups or validation of the process. As with the selection process, an invalid performance appraisal system has the potential for negative impact on members of certain groups.

2. A review process that prevents one manager from directing or controlling a subordinate's career. The performance appraisal should be reviewed and approved by someone or some group higher in the organization.

3. A rater who has personal knowledge and contact with the employee's job performance. This requirement may appear to be obvious, but there are instances in which raters do not have an adequate opportunity to observe performance. When this situation exists, the chances of a valid appraisal are nil.

4. Formal appraisal criteria that limit the manager's discretion. A system is needed that forces managers to base evaluations on certain predetermined criteria.

Mistakes in appraising performance and decisions based on these invalid results can have serious repercussions. For example, discriminatory allocation of money for merit pay increases can result in costly legal action. In settling cases, courts have held employers liable for back pay, court costs, and other costs related to training and promoting certain employees in protected classes. An employer may also be vulnerable to a negligent retention claim if an employee in a potentially hazardous environment who continually receives unsatisfactory appraisals is kept on the payroll, and he or she causes injury to a third party. In this instance, the firm's liability might be reduced if the substandard performer had received appropriate training.

It is unlikely that any appraisal system will be totally immune to legal challenge, but systems that possess the characteristics discussed here are apparently more legally defensible. At the same time, they can provide a more effective means for achieving performance management goals.

The Achilles' heel of the entire evaluation process is the appraisal interview itself.

The Appraisal Interview

The Achilles' heel of the entire evaluation process is the appraisal interview itself. In spite of the problems involved, supervisors usually conduct a formal appraisal interview at the end of an employee's appraisal period. This interview is essential for employee development. However, effective performance appraisal systems require more than this single interview. Instead, supervisors should maintain a continuous dialogue with employees, emphasizing their own responsibility for development and management's supportive role.

A successful appraisal interview should be structured in a way that allows both the supervisor and the subordinate to view it as a problem-solving rather than a fault-finding session. The supervisor should consider three basic purposes when planning an appraisal interview:

1. Discussing the employee's performance
2. Assisting the employee in setting objectives and personal development plans
3. Suggesting means for achieving established objectives, including support to be provided by the manager and firm

For instance, a worker may be rated as average on the factor *quality of production*. In the interview, both parties should agree as to the specific improvement needed during the next appraisal period. In suggesting ways to achieve a higher level objective, the supervisor might recommend specific actions, including his or her own assistance.

The interview should be scheduled soon after the end of the appraisal period. Employees usually know when their interview should take place, and their anxiety tends to increase when it is delayed. Interviews with top performers are often pleasant experiences for all concerned. However, supervisors may be reluctant to meet face-to-face with poor performers. They tend to postpone these anxiety-provoking interviews.

The amount of time devoted to an appraisal interview varies considerably with company policy and the position of the evaluated employee. Although costs must be considered, there is merit in conducting separate interviews for discussing (1) employee performance and development, and (2) pay increases. Many managers have learned that as soon as pay is mentioned in an interview it tends to dominate the conversation. For this reason, a rather common practice is to defer pay discussions for one to several weeks after the appraisal interview. At American Express's IDS Financial Services unit in Minneapolis, most employees receive formal evaluations at the end of each year. The salary review is conducted one day to three weeks later. Avon Products and Harley-Davidson have also separated their performance and salary evaluations at some locations.[28]

Conducting an appraisal interview is often one of management's more difficult tasks. It requires tact and patience on the part of the supervisor. Praise should be provided when warranted, but it can have only limited value if not clearly deserved. Criticism is especially difficult to give. So-called constructive criticism is often not perceived that way by the employee. Yet it is difficult for a manager at any level to avoid criticism when conducting appraisal interviews. The supervisor should realize that all individuals have some deficiencies that may not be changed easily, if at all. Continued criticism may lead to frustration and have a damaging effect on employee development. Again, this possibility should not allow unacceptable employee behavior to go unnoticed. However, discussions of sensitive issues should focus on the deficiency, not the person. Threats to the employee's self-esteem should be minimized whenever possible.

A serious error that a supervisor sometimes makes is to surprise the subordinate by bringing up some past mistake or problem. For example, if an incident had not been previously discussed, it would be most inappropriate for the supervisor to state, "Two months ago, you failed to properly coordinate your plans for implementing the new automated resumé review system." Good management practice and common sense dictate that such situations be dealt with when they occur and not be saved for the appraisal interview.

The entire performance appraisal process should be a positive experience for the employee. In practice, however, it often is not. Negative feelings can frequently be traced to the appraisal interview and the manner in which it was conducted by the supervisor. Ideally, employees will leave the interview with positive feelings about the supervisor, the company, the job, and themselves. The prospects for improved performance will be bleak if the employee's ego is deflated. Past behavior cannot be changed, but future performance can. Specific plans for the employee's development should be clearly outlined and mutually agreed on. Cessna Aircraft Company has developed several hints for supervisors that have been helpful in conducting appraisal interviews (see Figure 10-3 on page 360).

Assessment Centers

Many employee performance appraisal systems evaluate an individual's past performance and at the same time attempt to assess his or her potential for advancement. Other organizations have developed a separate approach for assessing potential. This process often takes place in what is appropriately referred to as an assessment center. As previously mentioned, this technique is also used by some firms to select new employees.

Assessment center: An employee selection or appraisal approach that requires individuals to perform activities similar to those they might encounter in an actual job.

In an **assessment center**, employees perform activities similar to those they might encounter in an actual job. These simulated exercises are based on a thorough job analysis. The assessors usually observe the employees somewhere other than their normal workplace over a certain period of time. The assessors selected are typically experienced managers who both participate in the exercises and evaluate performances. Assessment centers are used increasingly to (1) identify employees who have higher level management potential, (2) select first-line supervisors, and (3) determine employee developmental needs. Assessment centers are used by more than 1,000 organizations, including small firms and large corporations, such as General Electric Company, J. C. Penney Company, Ford Motor Company, and AT&T. An advantage of the assessment center approach is the increased reliability and validity of the information provided. Assessment centers have been shown to be more successful than aptitude tests in predicting performance.

1. Give the employee a few days' notice of the discussion and its purpose. Encourage the employee to give some preparatory thought to his or her job performance and development plans. In some cases, have employees read their written performance evaluation prior to the meeting.
2. Prepare notes and use the completed performance appraisal form as a discussion guide so that each important topic will be covered. Be ready to answer questions employees may ask about why you appraised them as you did. Encourage your employees to ask questions.
3. Be ready to suggest specific developmental activities suitable to each employee's needs. When there are specific performance problems, remember to "attack the problem, not the person."
4. Establish a friendly, helpful, and purposeful tone at the outset of the discussion. Recognize that it is not unusual for you and your employee to be nervous about the discussion, and use suitable techniques to put you both more at ease.
5. Assure your employee that everyone on Cessna's management team is being evaluated so that opportunities for improvement and development will not be overlooked and each person's performance will be fully recognized.
6. Make sure that the session is truly a discussion. Encourage employees to talk about how they feel they are doing on the job, how they might improve, and what developmental activities they might undertake. Often an employee's viewpoints on these matters will be quite close to your own.
7. When your appraisal differs from the employee's, discuss these differences. Sometimes employees have hidden reasons for performing in a certain manner or using certain methods. This is an opportunity to find out if such reasons exist.
8. These discussions should contain both constructive compliments and constructive criticism. Be sure to discuss the employee's strengths as well as weaknesses. Your employees should have clear pictures of how you view their performance when the discussions are concluded.
9. Occasionally the appraisal interview will uncover strong emotions. This is one of the values of regular appraisals; since they can bring out bothersome feelings, they can be dealt with honestly. The emotional dimension of managing is very important. Ignoring it can lead to poor performance. Deal with emotional issues when they arise because they block a person's ability to concentrate on other issues. Consult personnel for help when especially strong emotions are uncovered.
10. Make certain that your employees fully understand your appraisal of their performance. Sometimes it helps to have an employee orally summarize the appraisal as he or she understands it. If there are any misunderstandings, they can be cleared up on the spot. Ask questions to make sure you have been fully understood.
11. Discuss the future as well as the past. Plan with the employee specific changes in performance or specific developmental activities that will allow fuller use of potential. Ask what you can do to help.
12. End the discussion on a positive, future-improvement-oriented note. You and your employee are a team, working toward the development of everyone involved.

Figure 10-3
Suggestions
for Conducting
Appraisal Interviews

Source: Used with the permission of Cessna Aircraft Company.

A typical schedule for General Electric's Supervisory Assessment Center (SAC) is shown in Table 10-2. The SAC program is used for selecting new employees and assessing the management potential of current employees. Note the number of exercises that are utilized in evaluating a participant's behavior.

An evaluation of the General Electric SAC process revealed the following:

The SAC was based on a job analysis of a supervisor's job and is considered to have content validity.[29] The SAC provides all candidates an equal opportunity to demonstrate their skills and does not discriminate against any employee group. For example, a study of more than 1,000 candidates from 14 company locations showed that the success ratios were acceptable for Caucasians, minorities, and

TABLE 10-2

Typical Schedule for General Electric Company's Supervisory Assessment Center

---

Day 1

Approximately four hours per candidate are required for the background interview and an in-basket exercise. The interview covers such traditional areas as work experience, educational background, and leadership experience. The in-basket exercise provides an opportunity for the individual to demonstrate how he or she would handle administrative problems including day-to-day "fire-fighting." All Day 1 activities are scheduled on an individual basis and are typically administered by persons in Employee Relations.

Day 2

An additional four hours are devoted to group and individual exercises. Group exercises related to reallocation of resources allow an individual's performance to be observed as the candidate solves problems in peer group situations. In the individual exercises each candidate assumes the role of a supervisor to handle four typical work-related problems. Six operating managers serve as the SAC staff for Day 2 activities. They observe and evaluate the performance of six candidates. The staff completes structured rating forms on each candidate's performance immediately following each exercise. After all exercises have been completed and the candidates dismissed, the staff conducts an overall evaluation of each individual's potential for a supervisory position. Over fifty pieces of data from each candidate's performance are reviewed along with information obtained from the interview. The staff then arrives at a consensus decision and a recommended course of action for each candidate.

Source: Used with permission of the General Electric Company.

women. Those individuals who scored highest in the SAC are the same individuals who have subsequently received the greatest number of job promotions. Thus, one area of predictive validity of the SAC was demonstrated.

As many as half a dozen assessors may evaluate each participant, as at General Electric. The participant's position in the organization often determines the amount of time he or she spends in the center. First-line supervisory candidates may spend only a day or two, whereas more time may be needed for those being considered for middle-management and executive jobs. After the session is over, the participants return to their jobs and the assessors prepare their evaluations. Interestingly, because the assessors are often not full-time members of the human resource development staff, they frequently gain further insight into how managers in their organization should function. Even though a primary purpose of assessment centers is to identify management potential, the J. C. Penney experience indicates that the participants gain valuable insights into their own strengths, weaknesses, and interests. These insights permit management and the individual to make plans for the employee's development.

Accurately assessing potential and evaluating performance are critical to productivity, yet poorly conceived or improperly implemented systems can actually impair employee performance. Performance appraisal definitely presents management with a double-edged sword. However, as long as employee and organizational performance must be improved and certain administrative decisions made, firms must strive for the best system possible.

A GLOBAL PERSPECTIVE

Global Performance Appraisal: Factoring in Appropriate Employee Behaviors

A performance appraisal system mandates a formal periodic review and evaluation of an employee's job performance. A general management survey on perceptions of national management style was given to 707 managers representing diverse industries from the United States, Indonesia, Malaysia, and Thailand. Results from survey items relating to the design of performance appraisal systems revealed significant differences in the management styles of these countries. Such differences may translate into distinct differences in the optimal management of performance appraisal, thus suggesting important reservations about the transferability of traditional performance appraisal principles across cultural boundaries. The appropriate performance appraisal system of Pacific Rim managers may not be satisfied by traditional Western guiding principles.[30]

The development of an appropriate global performance appraisal system will undoubtedly be a complex process, but an effective global system is essential for credible employee evaluations.[31] Valid performance appraisal is difficult enough to achieve in the United States; evaluating overseas employees makes a normally complex problem nearly impossible. What usually works in one culture might not work in another. What is a strength in one culture might be considered a weakness in another. When performance appraisals are done overseas, the issue of what performance standards to use comes into question. Differences in performance appraisal practices are almost always necessary. An improper performance appraisal system can create a great deal of misunderstanding and personal offense.

A unique aspect of global performance appraisals is the need to factor in how to properly develop appropriate employee behaviors that best accomplish global objectives. Sprint's appraisal system faced this challenge when that company's managers were determining how to keep 48,000 worldwide employees focused on the bottom line in the rapidly changing, intensely competitive telecommunications industry.

In Sprint's performance appraisal system, raters look at the importance of employee behavior in achieving objectives. Appraisals measure and reward employees both on what they achieve and how they achieve it. Basically, to achieve a satisfactory performance appraisal, an employee must meet established objectives and demonstrate expected behaviors in accomplishing these objectives. If an employee meets his objectives but does not demonstrate the expected behaviors he may not receive a salary increase or incentive compensation. To date, 70 percent of Sprint's exempt employees have made the transition to this two-phase appraisal system. A study of employees who had participated in the system since 1994 attributed nearly $118 million in increased sales and/or reduced costs to the system, for a return on investment of more than 3,700 percent.[32] As with a domestic performance appraisal system, a global one should result in a realistic review and evaluation of employees' job performances.

SUMMARY

1. **Define performance appraisal.**
   Performance appraisal (PA) is a system of review and evaluation of an individual's or team's job performance. Performance management is a process that significantly affects organizational success by having managers and employees work together to set expectations, review results, and reward performance.

2. **Identify the uses of performance appraisal.**
   Performance appraisal data are potentially valuable for use in numerous functional areas of human resources including human resource planning, recruitment and selection, training and development, career planning and development, compensation programs, internal employee relations, and assessment of employee potential.

3. **Describe the performance appraisal process.**
   The steps in the performance appraisal process include these: identify the specific performance appraisal goals, establish job expectations (job analysis), examine work performed, appraise performance, and discuss appraisal with employee.

4. **Identify the aspects of a person's performance that an organization should evaluate.**
   The aspects of a person's performance that an organization should evaluate include traits, behaviors, and task outcomes.

5. **Identify who may be responsible for performance appraisal.**
   People usually responsible for performance appraisal include immediate supervisor, subordinates, peers, groups; other types of evaluation are self-appraisal, customer appraisal, and 360-degree feedback.

6. **Identify the various performance appraisal methods used.**
   Performance appraisal methods include rating scales, critical incidents, essay, work standards, ranking, forced distribution, forced choice, weighted checklist, behaviorally anchored rating scales, and an objective-oriented system.

7. **List the problems that have been associated with performance appraisal.**
   The problems associated with performance appraisals include lack of objectivity, halo error, leniency/strictness, central tendency, recent behavior bias, personal bias, and judgmental role of evaluator.

8. **Explain the characteristics of an effective appraisal system.**
   The criteria used for appraising employee performance must be job related. Managers must clearly explain their performance expectations

to their subordinates in advance of the appraisal period. Employees in the same job categories under a given supervisor should be appraised using the same evaluation instrument. Responsibility for evaluating employee performance should be assigned to the individual or individuals who directly observe at least a representative sample of the person's job performance. A good appraisal system provides highly desired feedback on a continuing basis. Employees should be provided adequate feedback on their performance. A formal procedure should be developed to permit employees the means for appealing appraisal results they do not consider accurate or fair.

9. *Describe the legal implications of performance appraisal.*
    With regard to performance appraisal, the courts normally require the following four conditions to exist: (1) either the absence of adverse impact on members of certain groups or validation of the process, (2) a review process that prevents one manager from directing or controlling a subordinate's career, (3) a rater who has personal knowledge and contact with the employee's job performance, and (4) the use of formal appraisal criteria that limit the manager's discretion.

10. *Explain how the appraisal interview should be conducted.*
    A successful appraisal interview should be structured in a way that allows both the supervisor and the subordinate to view it as a problem-solving rather than a fault-finding session. The interview should be scheduled soon after the end of the appraisal period. Discussions of sensitive issues should focus on the deficiency, not the person. The entire performance appraisal process should be a positive experience for the employee.

11. *Describe assessment centers.*
    The assessment center method is an appraisal approach that requires employees to participate in a series of activities similar to what they might be expected to do in an actual job. These situational activity exercises are developed as a result of thorough job analysis. The assessors observe the employees in a secluded environment, usually separate from the workplace, over a certain period of time.

QUESTIONS FOR REVIEW

1. Define *performance appraisal* and briefly discuss its basic purposes.
2. What are the basic steps in the performance appraisal process?
3. What aspect of a person's performance should an organization evaluate?
4. Many different people can conduct performance appraisals. Briefly describe the various alternatives.
5. Briefly describe each of the following methods of performance appraisal:
   a. Rating scales
   b. Critical incidents
   c. Essay
   d. Work standards
   e. Ranking

    f. Forced distribution

    g. Forced-choice and weighted checklist performance reports

    h. Behaviorally anchored rating scales

    i. Objectives-oriented approaches

6. What are the various problems associated with performance appraisal? Briefly describe each.

7. What are the characteristics of an effective appraisal system?

8. What are the legal implications of performance appraisal?

9. Why is the following statement often said: "The Achilles' heel of the entire evaluation process is the appraisal interview itself."

10. Describe how an assessment center could be used as a means of performance appraisal.

DEVELOPING HRM SKILLS

AN EXPERIENTIAL EXERCISE

Performance appraisal (PA) is an essential aspect of human resource management. It is a formal system that provides a periodic review and evaluation of an individual's or team's job performance. Developing an effective performance appraisal system is difficult. However, some managers do not take performance appraisal as seriously as they should. Such attitudes are counterproductive, and they frequently lower individual and group productivity.

Larry Beavers, supervisor of an electrical department, and Alex Martin, one of his employees meet today for Alex's performance appraisal interview. When these two get together, it will be a meeting of two quite different minds; in all likelihood, the meeting will be filled with disagreement, dissatisfaction, and maybe even hard feelings. This exercise will require active participation from two of you. One person will play the supervisor conducting the performance appraisal, and the other will be the evaluated employee. Only two can play; the rest of you should observe carefully. Your instructor will provide the participants with additional information necessary to complete the exercise.

 *Take It to the Net*

We invite you to visit the Mondy home page on the Prentice Hall Web site at:

http://www.prenhall.com/mondy

for updated information, Web-based exercises, and links to other HR-related sites.

HRM SIMULATION

*Y*our firm does not currently have a formal performance appraisal system. Some employees complain that the supervisors and managers give raises and perks to those they like and not necessarily to those who are most productive. A formal system could be established and maintained, but it costs money. However, decreased turnover, increased morale, and higher productivity might result.

In addition, in Incident E in the *Simulation Players Manual*, the CEO has instructed your team to recommend a system of performance appraisal for supervisors and managers. Choosing an appraisal system is not difficult but explaining your rationale may be more demanding.

HRM INCIDENT

1

Let's Get It Over With

"*T*here, at last it's finished," thought Tom Baker, as he laid aside the last of 12 performance appraisal forms. It had been a busy week for Tom, who supervises a road maintenance crew for the Georgia Department of Highways.

The governor, in passing through Tom's district a few days earlier, had complained to the area superintendent that repairs were needed on several of the highways. Because of this, the superintendent assigned Tom's crew an unusually heavy workload. In addition, Tom received a call from the personnel office that week telling him that the performance appraisals were late. Tom explained his predicament, but the personnel specialist insisted that the forms be completed right away.

Looking over the appraisals again, Tom thought about several of the workers. The performance appraisal form had places for marking *quantity of work, quality of work*, and *cooperativeness*. For each characteristic, the worker could be graded *outstanding, good, average, below average*, or *unsatisfactory*. As Tom's crew had completed all the extra work assigned for that week, he marked every worker *outstanding* in *quantity of work*. He marked Joe Blum *average* in *cooperativeness* because Joe had questioned one of his decisions that week. Tom had decided to patch a pothole in one of the roads, and Joe thought the small section of road surface ought to be broken out and replaced. Tom didn't include this in the remarks section of the form, though. As a matter of fact, he wrote no remarks on any of the forms.

Tom felt a twinge of guilt as he thought about Roger Short. He knew that Roger had been sloughing off, and the other workers had been carrying him for quite some time. He also knew that Roger would be upset if he found that he had been marked lower than the other workers. Consequently, he marked Roger the same to avoid a confrontation. "Anyway," Tom thought, "these things are a pain in the neck, and I really shouldn't have to bother with them."

As Tom folded up the performance appraisals and put them in the envelope for mailing, he smiled. He was glad he would not have to think about performance appraisals for another six months.

Question
1. What weaknesses do you see in Tom's performance appraisals?

HRM INCIDENT

2

Objectives?

*I*t was performance appraisal time again and Alex Funderburk knew that he would receive a low evaluation this time. Janet Stevens, Alex's boss, opened the appraisal interview with this comment, "The sales department had a good increase this quarter. Also, departmental expenses are down a good bit. But we nowhere near accomplished the ambitious goals you and I set last quarter."

"I know," said Alex. "I thought we were going to make it, though. We would have, too, if we had received that big Simpson order and if I could have gotten us on the computer a little earlier in the quarter."

"I agree with you, Alex," said Janet. "Do you think we were just too ambitious or do you think there was some way we could have made the Simpson sale and speeded up the computerization process?"

"Yes," replied Alex, "we could have gotten the Simpson order this quarter. I just made a couple of concessions to Simpson and their purchasing manager tells me he can issue the order next week. The delay with the computer was caused by a thoughtless mistake I made. I won't let that happen again."

The discussion continued for about 30 minutes longer. Alex discovered that Janet was going to mark him very high in all areas despite his failure to accomplish the goals that they had set.

Prior to the meeting, Janet had planned to suggest that the unattained goals for last period be set as the new goals for the coming quarter. After she and Alex had discussed matters, however, they both decided to establish new, somewhat higher goals. As he was about to leave the meeting, Alex said, "Janet, I feel good about these objectives, but I don't believe we have more than a 50 percent chance of accomplishing them."

"I believe you can do it," replied Janet. "If you knew for sure, though, the goals wouldn't be high enough."

"I see what you mean," said Alex, as he left the office.

Questions
1. What was wrong or right with Janet's appraisal of Alex's performance?
2. Should the new objectives be higher or lower than they are? Explain.

Notes

1. "The Team Building Tool Kit," *Compensation and Benefits Review* 26 (March/April 1994): 67.
2. Iris Randall, "Performance Appraisal Anxiety," *Black Enterprise* 25 (January 1995): 60.
3. Edward E. Lawler, III, "Performance Management: The Next Generation," *Compensation & Benefits Review* 26 (May/June 1994): 16.
4. Chris Lee, "Performance Appraisal," *Training* 33 (May 1996): 44.
5. Steven E. Gross, *Compensation for Teams* (New York: American Management Association, 1995): 87.
6. Robert B. Campbell and Lynne M. Garfinkel, "Performance Management: Strategies for Success," *HRMagazine* 41 (June 1996): 98.

7. Robert C. Joines, Steve Quisenberry, and Gary W. Sawyer, "Business Strategy Drives Three-Pronged Assessment System," *HRMagazine* 38 (December 1993): 68–70.

8. Ibid., 70.

9. Tom Payne, "Management by Behaviors," *Supervision* 57 (June 1996): 8–9.

10. Philip Ricciardi, "Simplify Your Approach to Performance Measurement," *HRMagazine* 41 (March 1996): 99.

11. Stephen E. Gross, *Compensation for Teams*, 90.

12. "The Team Building Tool Kit," 68.

13. Mathew Budman and Berkeley Rice, "The Rating Game," *Across the Board* 31 (February 1994): 34–38.

14. James G. Goodale, "Seven Ways to Improve Performance Appraisals," *HRMagazine* 38 (May 1993): 80.

15. Michelle A. Yakovac, "Paying for Satisfaction," *HR Focus* 73 (June 1996): 10–11.

16. Robert Hoffman, "Ten Reasons You Should Be Using 360-Degree Feedback," *HRMagazine* 40 (April 1995): 82.

17. Bob Filipczak, Marc Hequet, Chris Lee, Michele Picard, and David Stamps, "360-Degree Feedback: Will the Circle Be Broken?" *Training* 33 (October 1996): 24.

18. Robert B. Campbell and Lynne M. Garfinkel, "Performance Management: Strategies for Success," *HRMagazine* 41 (June 1996): 102.

19. Michelle Neely Martinez, "Rewards Given the Right Way," *HRMagazine* 42 (May 1997): 116.

20. Steps to Maximize Consistency. *HRMagazine* http://www.shrm.org/hrmagazine/articles/10steps.html (1 July 1997).

21. Because the system depicted makes liberal use of personal factors that may not be job related, it has been described by one reviewer as "a good example of a poor method."

22. Adapted from Richard O'Reilly, "The Cutting Edge: Computing/Technology/Innovation: Employee Review Software," *Los Angeles Times* (June 28, 1995): D–5.

23. "Research on Performance Appraisals Wins Award," *HR News* 16 (July 1997): 13.

24. Jeffrey S. Kane, H. John Bernardin, Peter Villanova, and Joseph Peyrefitte, "Stability of Rater Leniency: Three Studies," *Academy of Management Journal* 39 (August 1995): 1036–1037.

25. Larry L. Axline, "Ethical Considerations of Performance Appraisals," *Management Review* 83 (March 1994): 62.

26. Barry J. Baroni, "The Legal Ramifications of Appraisal Systems," *Supervisory Management* 27 (January 1982): 41–42.

27. William S. Hubbartt, "Bring Performance Appraisal Training to Life," *HRMagazine* 40 (May 1995): 168.

28. Julie Amparano Lopez, "Companies Split Reviews on Performance and Pay," *Wall Street Journal* (May 10, 1993): B1.

29. Content validity is inherent in the assessment center process when the exercises developed are based on job analysis. This type of validity is acceptable according to the *Uniform Guidelines*.

30. Charles M. Vance, Shirley R. McClaine, David M. Boje, and H. Daniel Stage, "An Examination of Transferability of Traditional Performance Appraisal Principles across Cultural Boundaries," *Management International Review* (Fourth Quarter, 1992): 313–326.

31. Wayne F. Cascio and Manuel G. Serapio, Jr., "HR Systems in an International Alliance: The Undoing of a Done Deal?" *Organizational Dynamics* 19 (Winter 1991): 65.

32. Karen Mailliard, "Case Study: Linking Performance to the Bottom Line," *HR Focus* 74 (June 1997): 17–18.

ABCNEWS VIDEO CASE

Job Security or Employment Security: Which Is More Important?

The length of time a person worked for a company used to be an important consideration in many employment decisions. For example, a person's seniority might play a major role in determining salary increases, vacation time, and work schedules. The longer an employee worked for a company, the more advantages that individual had. The implied message to these workers was that loyalty to the company would be rewarded. Today, this is no longer the case. In fact, job security has virtually vanished in many organizations. Changes due to global competition, technology, and organizational designs have resulted in the downsizing of many firms and caused many jobs to disappear along with job security. The message seems clear: If you have job skills that are needed in the workforce and keep these skills current, you have employment security; you can find another job. You do not necessarily, however, have job security with your current firm. The resulting problem is that a climate of employment uncertainty is generally not a one of efficiency and high morale.

One alternative approach to downsizing involves management communicating with workers, explaining to them the pressures that the organization is facing. Management then gives the employees the opportunity to demonstrate that they have the skills necessary for making a contribution to the organization and thus can remain with the firm. This relationship between management and employees de-emphasizes seniority. Loyalty is a consideration only insofar as employees maintain the skills required by the organization.

Pinnacle Brands is one company that has taken this approach. When the company fell on hard times, it did not engage in wholesale downsizing. Instead, Pinnacle workers demonstrated that they could achieve important outcomes, make positive contributions, and thus retain their jobs.

DISCUSSION QUESTIONS

1. What are the benefits of a firm providing job security in return for employee loyalty? What are the costs?
2. Do you think that Pinnacle Brands' approach is preferable to one that emphasizes security and loyalty? Why or why not?
3. Which is more important, job security or employment security? Although you may have little control over job security, what can you do to enhance your employment security?
4. Identify some of the key things a company must do to implement an approach that emphasizes employee contributions to organizational goals as a successful alternative to downsizing. Describe the circumstances under which downsizing might be preferable.

Source: "The End of Job Security and Loyalty," *Nightline*, ABC News; aired on April 9, 1996.

COMPENSATION AND BENEFITS

11
Compensation

CHAPTER OBJECTIVES

1. Describe the various forms of compensation.
2. Explain the concept of compensation equity.
3. Identify the determinants of financial compensation.
4. Identify the organizational factors that should be considered as determinants of financial compensation.
5. Describe factors that should be considered when the labor market is a determinant of financial compensation.
6. Describe how government legislation affects compensation.
7. Define *job evaluation.*
8. Explain the various forms of job evaluation.
9. Describe the Hay Guide Chart-Profile Method of job evaluation.
10. Explain pay for performance.
11. Identify factors related to the employee that are essential in determining pay and employee equity.
12. Define job pricing.
13. Describe factors to be considered in job pricing.
14. Explain the concepts of flextime, the compressed workweek, job sharing, flexible compensation, telecommuting, part-time work, and modified retirement.

ℰarl Lewis and his wife are full of excitement and anticipation as they leave their home for a shopping trip. Earl has just learned that his firm is implementing a new variable pay system and that his long record of high performance will finally pay off. He looks forward to the opportunity to increase his income so he can purchase some needed items for a new home.

Inez Scoggin's anxiety over scheduled minor surgery is somewhat relieved. Her supervisor has assured her that a major portion of her medical and hospitalization costs will be covered by the firm's health insurance plan.

Trig Ekeland, executive director of the local YMCA, returns home dead tired from his job each evening no earlier than six o'clock. His salary is small compared to the salaries of many other local managers who have similar responsibilities. Yet Trig is an exceptionally happy person who believes that his work with youth, civic leaders, and other members of the community is extremely important and worthwhile.

Joanne Abrahamson has been employed by a large manufacturing firm for eight years. Although her pay is not what she would like it to be, her job in the accounts payable department enables her to have contact with some of her best friends. She likes her supervisor and considers the overall working environment to be great. Joanne would not trade jobs with anyone she knows.

Compensation and benefits are obviously important to Earl Lewis and Inez Scoggin, as they are to most employees. However, for Trig and Joanne, other factors in a total compensation package also assume great importance. These components include a pleasant work environment and job satisfaction. Because it has many elements and a far-reaching impact on performance, compensation administration is one of management's most difficult and challenging human resource areas.

We begin this chapter with an overview of compensation and an explanation of compensation equity. Next, we discuss determinants of individual financial compensation, including the influence of the organization and the labor market. This is followed by a discussion of the job and the employee as determinants of financial compensation. Job pricing is presented next. We devote the final portion of the chapter to nonfinancial compensation and workplace flexibility.

HR Web Wisdom

http://www.prenhall.com/mondy

COMPENSATION LINK

Compensation link was designed by compensation professionals for those working in the compensation area.

Compensation: An Overview

Compensation: The total of all rewards provided employees in return for their labor.

Direct financial compensation: Pay that a person receives in the form of wages, salary, bonuses, and commissions.

Indirect financial compensation: All financial rewards that are not included in direct compensation.

Nonfinancial compensation: The satisfaction that a person receives from the job itself or from the psychological and/or physical environment in which the job is performed.

Compensation is the total of all rewards provided to employees in return for their services. The components of a total compensation program are shown in Figure 11-1. **Direct financial compensation** consists of the pay that a person receives in the form of wages, salaries, bonuses, and commissions. Earl Lewis just received word that by continuing his high level of performance he may now increase the size of his paycheck. **Indirect financial compensation** (benefits) includes all financial rewards that are not included in direct compensation. Inez Scoggin will receive indirect financial compensation because her company pays for a major portion of her medical and hospital costs. As you can see in Figure 11-1, this form of compensation includes a wide variety of rewards that are normally received indirectly by the employee.

Nonfinancial compensation consists of the satisfaction that a person receives from the job itself or from the psychological and/or physical environment in which the person works. Trig Ekeland and Joanne Abrahamson are receiving important forms of nonfinancial compensation. Trig is extremely satisfied with the job he performs. This type of nonfinancial compensation consists of the satisfaction received from performing meaningful job-related tasks. Joanne's job permits her to have contact with close friends. This form of nonfinancial compensation involves the psychological and/or physical environment in which the person works.

All such rewards make up a total compensation program. The rewards employees receive may be based on several factors including membership in

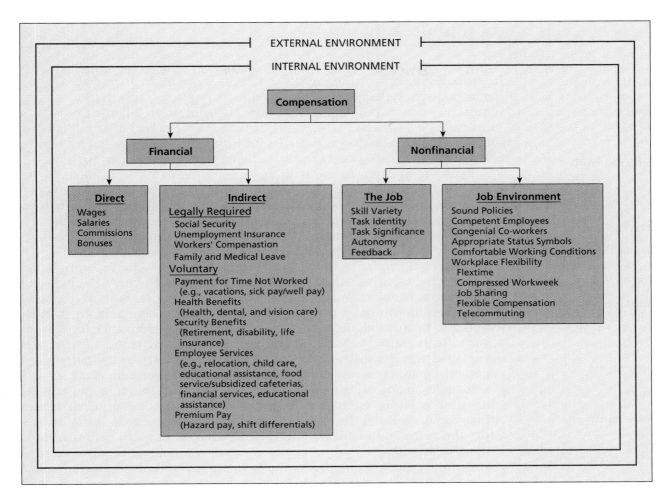

Figure 11-1
Components of a Total Compensation Program

the organization, seniority, or other elements. To remain competitive, organizations are increasingly rewarding performance outcomes that are required to achieve its key goals.[1] In determining effective rewards, the uniqueness of employees must be considered. People have different reasons for working, and the most appropriate compensation package depends in large measure on those reasons. When individuals are being stretched financially to provide food, shelter, and clothing for their families, money may well be the most important reward. However, some people work many hours each day, receive relatively little pay, and yet love their work because it is interesting or provides an environment that satisfies other needs. To a large degree, adequate compensation is in the mind of the receiver. It is often more than the financial compensation received in the form of a paycheck.

Compensation Equity

Equity: The perception by workers that they are being treated fairly.

External equity: Payment of employees at rates comparable to those paid for similar jobs elsewhere.

Internal equity: Payment of employees according to the relative values of their jobs within an organization.

Employee equity: A condition that exists when individuals performing similar jobs for the same firm are paid according to factors unique to the employee, such as performance level or seniority.

Team equity: Paying more productive teams in an organization at a higher rate than less productive teams.

Organizations must attract, motivate, and retain competent employees. Because achievement of these goals is largely accomplished through a firm's compensation system, organizations must strive for compensation equity. **Equity** is workers' perceptions that they are being treated fairly. Compensation must be fair to all parties concerned and be perceived as fair. It is fairly obvious that Earl Lewis was not happy with the previous pay system which, evidently did not adequately reward his long record of high performance.

External equity exists when a firm's employees are paid comparably to workers who perform similar jobs in other firms. Trig Ekeland did not receive a salary comparable to other local managers with similar responsibilities. Compensation surveys help organizations determine the extent to which external equity is present. **Internal equity** exists when employees are paid according to the relative value of their jobs within the same organization. Job evaluation is a primary means for determining internal equity. Joanne Abrahamson may not believe there is internal equity regarding salary, but her work environment is such that she forgoes other opportunities. **Employee equity** exists when individuals performing similar jobs for the same firm are paid according to factors unique to the employee, such as performance level or seniority. **Team equity** is achieved when more productive teams are rewarded more than less productive groups. Performance levels may be determined through appraisal systems, which were discussed in the previous chapter.

Inequity in any category can result in morale problems. If employees feel they are being compensated unfairly, they may leave the firm. Even greater damage may result for the firm if the employees do not leave but stay and restrict their efforts. In either event, the organization's overall performance is damaged. Regarding employee equity, for example, suppose that two accountants in the same firm are performing similar jobs, and one is acknowledged to be far superior to the other in performance. If both workers receive equal pay increases, employee equity does not exist and the more productive employee is likely to be unhappy. Most workers are concerned with pay equity, both internal and external. From an employee relations perspective, internal pay equity is probably more important. Employees simply have more information about pay matters within their own organization, and these data are used to form perceptions of equity. On the other hand, an organization must be competitive in the labor market to remain viable. External equity, therefore, must always be a prominent consideration. Maintaining equity on all fronts has long been an organizational dilemma and in some cases is simply not possible.

Determinants of Individual Financial Compensation

Compensation theory has never been able to provide a completely satisfactory answer to what an individual is worth for performing jobs. While no scientific approach is available, a number of relevant factors are typically

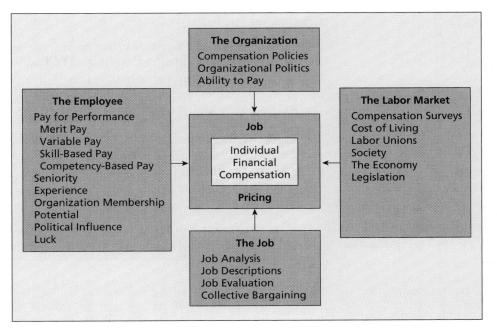

Figure 11-2
Primary Determinants of Individual Financial Compensation

used to determine individual pay. These determinants are shown in Figure 11-2. Historically, the organization, the labor market, the job, and the employee all have impacted job pricing and the ultimate determination of an individual's financial compensation. These factors continue to play an important role. However, for more and more business firms, the world has become the marketplace. As global economics increasingly establish the cost of labor, the global labor market grows in importance as a determinant of financial compensation for individuals.[2] Global compensation is discussed in chapter 17.

The Organization as a Determinant of Financial Compensation

Managers tend to view financial compensation as both an expense and an asset. It is an expense in the sense that it reflects the cost of labor. In service industries, for example, labor costs account for more than 50 percent of all expenses. However, financial compensation can be viewed as an asset when it induces employees to put forth their best efforts and to remain in their jobs. Compensation programs have top management's attention because they have the potential to influence employee work attitudes and behavior, and these, when positive, can lead to improved organizational performance.

COMPENSATION POLICIES

Corporate culture has a major effect on an individual's financial compensation. An organization often establishes—formally or informally—compensation policies that determine whether it will be a pay leader or a pay follower, or strive for an average position in the labor market. **Pay leaders** are organizations that pay higher wages and salaries than competing firms. Using this strategy, they feel that they will be able to attract high-quality, productive employees with the result of achieving lower per unit labor costs. Higher paying firms usually attract more and better qualified applicants than do lower paying companies in the same industry.

Pay leaders: Organizations that pay higher wages and salaries than competing firms.

HR Web Wisdom

http://www.prenhall.com/mondy

SHRM—HR LINKS
Various compensation and benefit issues including salary surveys are addressed.

Market (going) rate: The average pay that most employers provide for the same job in a particular area or industry.

The **market rate, or going rate**, is the average pay that most employers provide for the same job in a particular area or industry. Many organizations have a policy that calls for paying the market rate. In such firms, management believes that it can employ qualified people and still remain competitive by not having to raise the price of goods or services. Employers with this policy evidently believe they can acquire the skills needed for their particular operations.

Companies that choose to pay below the market rate because of poor financial condition or a belief that they simply do not require highly capable employees are **pay followers**. Difficulties often occur when this policy is followed. Consider the case of Melvin Denney.

Pay followers: Companies that choose to pay below the going rate because of a poor financial condition or a belief that they simply do not require highly capable employees.

Melvin Denney managed a large, but financially strapped farming operation in the Southwest. Although no formal policies had been established, Melvin had a practice of paying the lowest wage possible. One of his farmhands, George McMillan, was paid minimum wage. During a period of three weeks, George wrecked a tractor, severely damaged a combine, and stripped the gears in a new pickup truck. George's actions prompted Melvin to remark, "George is the most expensive darned employee I've ever had."

As Melvin discovered, paying the lowest wage possible did not save money; actually, the practice was quite expensive. In addition to hiring unproductive workers, organizations that are pay followers may have a high turnover rate as their most qualified employees leave to join organizations that pay more. Equally important, in situations where incompetent or disgruntled employees come in contact with customers, they may not provide the kind of customer service management desires. If management does not treat its employees well, their customers may also suffer, and this spells disaster for any firm in today's environment.

The organizational level in which compensation decisions are made can also have an impact on pay. These decisions are often made at a high management level to ensure consistency. However, there are advantages to making pay decisions at lower levels where better information may exist regarding employee performance. Top-level executives err when they make decisions in isolation from lower level managers.

ORGANIZATIONAL POLITICS

Take another look at Figure 11-2 and you will see that compensation surveys, job analysis, job evaluation, and performance appraisal are all involved in setting base pay. Political considerations may also enter into the equation in these ways:[3]

- Determination of firms included in the compensation survey. Managers could make their firm appear to be a wage leader by including in the survey those organizations that are *pay followers*.
- Choosing compensable factors for the job evaluation plan. Again, the job value determined by this process could be manipulated.
- Emphasis placed on either internal or external equity.
- Results of employee performance appraisal. Remember from Chapter 10 the various reasons rating supervisors may intentionally distort the ratings.

A sound, objective compensation system can be destroyed by organizational politics. Managers should become aware of this possibility and take appropriate action.

ABILITY TO PAY

An organization's assessment of its ability to pay is also an important factor in determining pay levels. Financially successful firms tend to provide higher-than-average compensation. However, an organization's financial strength establishes only the upper limit of what it will pay. To arrive at a specific pay level, management must consider other factors.

The Labor Market as a Determinant of Financial Compensation

Labor market: The geographical area from which employees are recruited for a particular job.

Potential employees located within the geographical area from which employees are recruited comprise the **labor market**. Labor markets for some jobs extend far beyond the locality of a firm's operations. An aerospace firm in Seattle, for example, may be concerned about the labor market for engineers in Wichita, Kansas, or Orlando, Florida. Managerial and professional employees are often recruited from a wide geographical area. In fact, some firms engage in global recruitment for certain skills and top executives.

Moreover, pay for jobs within these markets may vary considerably. Secretarial jobs, for example, may carry an average salary of $29,000 per year in a large, urban community but only $18,000 or less in a small, rural town. Compensation managers must be aware of these differences in order to compete successfully for employees. The market rate is an important guide in determining pay. Many employees view it as the standard for judging the fairness of their firm's compensation practices.

COMPENSATION SURVEYS

Compensation survey:
A means of obtaining data regarding what other firms are paying for specific jobs or job classes within a given labor market.

A **compensation survey** strives to obtain data regarding what other firms are paying for specific jobs or job classes within a given labor market. Organizations use surveys for two basic reasons; to identify their relative position with respect to the chosen competition in the labor market and to provide input in developing a budget and compensation structure.[4] Of all the wage criteria, market rates remain the most important standard for determining pay. Economic worth is determined by the marketplace,[5] and in a competitive environment, this is the critical factor.

Large organizations routinely conduct compensation surveys to determine market pay rates within labor markets. These surveys typically provide the low, high, and average salaries for a given position. The market rate, or going rate, may be defined as the 25th to 75th percentile range of pay for jobs rather than a single, specific pay point.[6] This range provides a sense of what other companies are paying employees in various jobs.

A primary difficulty in conducting a compensation survey involves determining comparable jobs. As the scope of jobs becomes broader, this difficulty grows. Employees are increasingly being paid for skills and competencies they bring to the job rather than performing traditional job descriptions. Therefore, the need is to match compensation levels to these broader roles. Although the specific information a company requires depends on its business needs, for many firms this trend changes the nature of the data needed and makes the task of conducting a compensation survey more complex.

Compensation surveys provide information for establishing both direct and indirect compensation. Before a compensation survey is conducted, the following determinations must be made:

- The geographic area of the survey
- The specific firms to contact
- The jobs to include

The geographic area to involve in the survey is often determined from employment records. Data from this source may indicate maximum distance or time that employees are willing to travel to work. Also, the firms to be contacted in the survey may be product line competitors or competitors for certain skilled employees. However, only 50 percent to 75 percent of the firms may be willing to share data.[7] Because obtaining data on all jobs in the organization may not be feasible, compensation surveys often include only benchmark jobs. A **benchmark job** is one that is well known in the company and industry, one that represents the entire job structure, and one in which a large percentage of the workforce is employed.

Benchmark job: A well-known job, in which a large percentage of a company's workforce is employed, that represents the entire job structure.

In addition to surveys, there are other ways to obtain compensation data. Some professional organizations, such as the American Compensation Association and the Society for Human Resource Management, periodically conduct surveys as do several industry associations. Consulting firms, including Hay Management Consultants, Towers & Perrin, and William M. Mercer, Inc., also conduct surveys. The U.S. Bureau of Labor Statistics conducts the following five surveys that may be considerably valuable:

- Area wage surveys
- White-collar pay survey
- Employee benefits in small private establishments
- Employee benefits in medium and large private establishments
- Employee benefits in state and local governments[8]

COST OF LIVING

Although not a problem in recent years, the logic for using cost of living as a pay determinant is simple: When prices rise over a period of time and pay does not, *real pay* is actually lowered. A pay increase must be roughly equivalent to the increased cost of living if a person is to maintain a previous level of real wages. For instance, if someone earns $24,000 during a year in which the average rate of inflation is 5 percent, a $100 per month pay increase will be necessary merely to maintain that person's standard of living.

People living on fixed incomes (primarily the elderly and the poor) are especially hard hit by inflation, but they are not alone; most employees also suffer financially. Recognizing this problem, some firms index pay increases to the inflation rate. In fact, some organizations sacrifice *merit pay* to provide across-the-board increases designed to offset the results of inflation.

LABOR UNIONS

An excerpt from the Wagner Act, which is discussed in chapter 14, prescribes the areas of mandatory collective bargaining between management and unions as "wages, hours, and other terms and conditions of employment." These broad bargaining areas obviously have great potential impact on compensation decisions.

When a union uses comparable pay as a standard in making compensation demands, the employer must obtain accurate labor market data. When a union emphasizes cost of living, management may be pressured to include a **cost-of-living allowance (COLA)**. This is an escalator clause in the labor agreement that automatically increases wages as the U.S. Bureau of Labor Statistics cost-of-living index rises.

Unions may also attempt to create, preserve, or even destroy pay differentials between wages for craft workers and unskilled workers. The politics of a given situation will determine the direction taken. For instance, if the unskilled workers have the largest union membership, an attempt may be made to eliminate pay differentials.

Management may want to use incentive plans to encourage greater productivity. However, decisions to implement such plans may be scrapped if the union strongly opposes this approach. Employee acceptance of such a plan is essential for successful implementation, and union opposition may make it unworkable.

Cost-of-living allowance (COLA): An escalator clause in a labor agreement that automatically increases wages as the U.S. Bureau of Labor Statistics' cost-of-living index rises.

SOCIETY

Compensation paid to employees often affects a firm's pricing of its goods or services. For this reason, consumers may also be interested in compensation decisions. At times in the past, the government has responded to public opinion and stepped in to encourage businesses to hold down wages and prices.

Businesses in a local labor market are also concerned with the pay practices of new firms locating in their area. For instance, when the management of a large electronics firm announced plans to locate a branch plant in a relatively small community, it was confronted by local civic leaders. Their questions largely concerned the wage and salary rates that would be paid. Subtle pressure was applied to keep the company's wages in line with other wages in the community.

THE ECONOMY

The economy definitely affects financial compensation decisions. For example, a depressed economy generally increases the labor supply. This, in turn, serves to lower the market rate. Historically, the cost of living has risen as the economy has expanded. Recently, however, the inflation rate has been both low and stable even as the economy has grown. This condition serves to minimize the prevalence of cost-of-living increases.

LEGISLATION

Federal and state laws can also affect the amount of compensation a person receives. Equal employment legislation—including the Civil Rights Act, the Age Discrimination in Employment Act, the Americans with Disabilities Act and the Family and Medical Leave Act—all prohibit discrimination against specified groups in employment matters, including compensation. The same is true for federal government contractors or subcontractors who are covered by Executive Order 11246 and the Rehabilitation Act. States and municipal governments also have laws that affect compensation practices. Our focus in the next section, however, is the federal legislation that provides broad coverage and specifically deals with compensation issues.

Davis-Bacon Act of 1931. The Davis-Bacon Act of 1931 was the first national law to deal with minimum wages. It requires federal construction contractors with projects valued in excess of $2,000 to pay at least the prevailing wages in the area. The secretary of labor has the authority to make this determination, and the prevailing wage is often the average local union rate.

Walsh-Healy Act of 1936. The Walsh-Healy Act of 1936 requires companies with federal supply contracts exceeding $10,000 to pay prevailing wages. The act also requires one-and-a-half times the regular pay rate for hours over eight per day or 40 per week.

Fair Labor Standards Act of 1938, as Amended (FLSA).

The most significant law affecting compensation is the Fair Labor Standards Act of 1938 (FLSA). It establishes a minimum wage, requires overtime pay and record keeping, and provides standards for child labor. This act is administered by the Wage and Hour Division of the U.S. Department of Labor (DOL).

The act provides for a minimum wage of not less than $5.15 an hour.[9] It also requires overtime payment at the rate of one-and-one-half times the employee's regular rate after 40 hours of work in a 168-hour period. Although most organizations and employees are covered by the act, certain classes of employees are specifically exempt from overtime provisions. However, nonexempt employees, many of whom are paid salaries, must receive overtime pay.

Exempt employees:
Those categorized as executive, administrative, or professional employees and outside salespersons.

Exempt employees are categorized as executive, administrative, and professional employees and outside salespersons. An *executive employee* is essentially a manager (such as a production manager) with broad authority over subordinates. An *administrative employee*, although not a manager, occupies an important staff position in an organization and might have a title such as systems analyst or assistant to the president. A *professional employee* performs work requiring advanced knowledge in a field of learning, normally acquired through a prolonged course of specialized instruction. This type of employee might have a title such as company physician, legal counsel, or senior statistician. *Outside salespeople* sell tangible or intangible items away from the employer's place of business. Employees in jobs not conforming to these definitions are considered nonexempt.

In 1995, federal wage and hour law investigators examined more than 20,000 workplaces. FLSA violations were uncovered in 80 percent of the visits and called for $120 million in back pay for more than 200,000 employees. An additional $21 million was owed employees to meet minimum wage standards. The vast majority of these cases were solved administratively with employers agreeing to correct the problem. Only about 1 percent of all FLSA compliance actions cannot be resolved administratively. These are referred to the solicitor's office for legal action. Investigations of FLSA violations are conducted by the U.S. Department of Labor's Employment Standards Administration (ESA). This agency oversees the FLSA and about 40 other federal statutes governing employment.[10]

For medium and large organizations with many white-collar employees, the most common violations involve jobs that have been incorrectly identified as exempt. Another common violation relates to the failure of employers to include payments such as bonuses and other forms of compensation in calculating the pay rate for overtime purposes. If firms offer employees a bonus for achieving a certain goal, therefore giving up discretion as to whether it will be received, the bonus payment must be included in figuring the regular rate of pay for overtime purposes. Special occasion bonuses given at the employer's discretion do not need to be included.

Most violations result from ignorance of the law and can be resolved at an early stage of the investigation. If an employer has doubts about any aspect of complying with the FLSA, he or she would be advised to check with the Wage-Hour Division. This practice may insulate the employer from violations without raising a red flag. The absolute worst thing an employer can do is to try to conceal a problem.

Business and professional groups, such as (SHRM), are urging Congress to update FLSA and revise rules written for a bygone era. For example, the law requires that workers in nonexempt jobs be paid time-and-a-half for any hours worked over 40 hours a week. The problems here are twofold: Employees may prefer compensatory time off instead. Also, this requirement conflicts with some applications of flextime (which is discussed later in this chapter) that might benefit both employees and employers. Still another problem relates to the FLSA's prohibiting private employers from docking an exempt worker's pay for less than a full day's absence. If an employer does this and the practice is discovered, the Labor Department can assume that all employees in this exempt category are being treated as nonexempt workers. The firm can then lose the exempt status for all its administrative and professional employees.[11]

Equal Pay Act of 1963. The Equal Pay Act of 1963 (an amendment to the FLSA) has also influenced the field of compensation. In 1972, amendments expanded the act to cover employees in executive, administrative, professional, and outside sales force categories as well as employees in most state and local governments, hospitals, and schools. The purpose of this legislation is to prohibit discrimination in pay on the basis of gender. The act has teeth, as evidenced by the millions of dollars paid to women employees to compensate them for past discriminatory pay policies.

The act applies to all organizations and employees covered by the FLSA, including the exempt categories. The act requires equal pay for equal work for both men and women. *Equal work* is defined as work requiring equal skill, effort, and responsibility that is performed under the same or similar working conditions. Even if two positions have the same title, the two may still not be equal within the EPA's definition. In one EPA case, a court found that two positions with the same job title were not equal when the male employee was less closely supervised than his female counterpart and when he had more employees under his supervision.[12]

The EPA does not prohibit the establishment of different wage rates based on seniority or a merit system. Also permitted are pay systems based on the quantity or quality of production and differentials based on any factor other than gender. The effect of the act has become less significant because a violation of the Equal Pay Act may also be a violation of Title VII of the Civil Rights Act.

The Job as a Determinant of Financial Compensation

The individual employee and market forces have become most prominent as wage criteria in some firms. However, the job itself continues to be a factor, especially in firms that have internal pay equity as a primary consideration. These organizations pay for the value they attach to certain duties, responsibilities, and other job-related factors such as working conditions. Management techniques utilized for determining a job's relative worth include job analysis, job descriptions, and job evaluation. Unions, when present in a firm, normally prefer to determine compensation through the process of collective bargaining. This topic is covered in chapter 15.

JOB ANALYSIS AND JOB DESCRIPTIONS

Before an organization can determine the relative difficulty or value of its jobs, it must first define their content. Normally, it does this by analyzing jobs. Recall from chapter 4 that job analysis is the systematic process of determining the skills and knowledge required for performing jobs. Remember also that the job description is the primary by-product of job analysis, consisting of a written document that describes essential job duties, or functions, and responsibilities. Job descriptions are used for many different purposes, including job evaluation. They are essential to all job evaluation methods, the success of which depends largely on their accuracy and clarity.

JOB EVALUATION

Job evaluation: That part of a compensation system in which a company determines the relative value of one job in relation to another.

Job evaluation is that part of a compensation system in which a firm determines the relative value of one job in relation to another. The basic purpose of job evaluation is to eliminate internal pay inequities that exist because of illogical pay structures. For example, a pay inequity exists if the mailroom supervisor earns more money than the accounting supervisor. Obviously, organizations prefer internal pay equity. However when a pay rate ultimately determined following job evaluation conflicts with the market rate, the latter is almost surely to take precedence. Job evaluation measures job worth in an administrative rather than an economic sense.[13] The latter can be determined only by the marketplace via compensation surveys. Nevertheless, many firms continue to use job evaluation for these purposes:

- To identify the organization's job structure
- To bring equity and order to the relationships among jobs
- To develop a hierarchy of job value that can be used to create a pay structure

The human resource department is typically responsible for administering job evaluation programs. However, actual evaluation is often done by committee. A typical committee might include the chief human resource executive and representatives from other functional areas such as finance, production, and marketing. If a labor union is present, representation from this group might also be involved if the union is not opposed to the concept of job evaluation. The composition of the committee usually depends on the type and level of the jobs that are being evaluated. In all instances, it is important for the committee to keep personalities out of the evaluation process and to remember it is the job that should be evaluated, not the person(s) performing the job.

Small- and medium-size organizations often lack job evaluation expertise and may elect to use an outside consultant. When employing a qualified consultant, management should require that the consultant develop an internal job evaluation program and train company employees to administer it properly.

The four historic job evaluation methods are ranking, classification, factor comparison, and point. There are innumerable variations of these and a firm may choose one method and modify it to fit the firm's particular purposes. The ranking and classification methods are nonquantitative; the factor comparison and point methods are quantitative approaches.

Ranking method: A job evaluation method in which the rater examines the description of each job being evaluated and arranges the jobs in order according to their value to the company; also a performance appraisal method in which the rater places all employees in a given group in rank order on the basis of their overall performance.

Classification method: A job evaluation method in which classes or grades are defined to describe a group of jobs.

Ranking Method. The simplest of the four job evaluation methods is the ranking method. In the **ranking method**, the raters examine the description of each job being evaluated and arrange the jobs in order according to their value to the company. The procedure is essentially the same as that discussed in chapter 10 regarding the ranking method for performance appraisal. The only difference is that jobs, not people, are being evaluated. The first step in this method—as with all the methods—is conducting job analysis and writing job descriptions.

Classification Method. The **classification method** involves defining a number of classes or grades to describe a group of jobs. In evaluating jobs by this method, the raters compare the job description with the class description. Class descriptions are prepared that reflect the differences of groups of jobs at various difficulty levels. The class description that most closely agrees with the job description determines the classification for that job. For example, in evaluating the job of word processing clerk, the description might include these duties:

1. Handle data entry of letters from prepared drafts
2. Address envelopes
3. Deliver completed correspondence to unit supervisor

Assuming that the remainder of the job description includes similar routine work, this job would most likely be placed in the lowest job class.

Probably the best-known illustration of classification method is the Office of Personnel Management's General Schedule (GS). This federal government system has 18 classes, or grades, which are distinguished by level of difficulty.[14]

Factor comparison method: A job evaluation method in which raters (1) need not keep an entire job in mind as they evaluate it and (2) make decisions based on the assumption that there are five universal job factors.

Factor Comparison Method. The factor comparison method is somewhat more involved than the two previously discussed qualitative methods. In the **factor comparison method**, raters need not keep the entire job in mind as they evaluate; instead, they make decisions on separate aspects, or factors, of the job. A basic underlying assumption is that there are five universal job factors:

■ Mental requirements, which reflect mental traits, such as intelligence, reasoning, and imagination.

■ Skills, which pertain to facility in muscular coordination and training in the interpretation of sensory impressions.

■ Physical requirements, which involve sitting, standing, walking, lifting, and so on.

■ Responsibilities, which cover areas such as raw materials, money, records, and supervision.

■ Working conditions, which reflect the environmental influences of noise, illumination, ventilation, hazards, and hours.

The committee first ranks each of the selected benchmark jobs on the relative degree of difficulty of each of the five factors. The committee then allocates the total pay rates for each job to each factor based on the importance of the respective factor to the job. This step is probably the most difficult to explain satisfactorily to employees because the decision is highly subjective.

A job comparison scale, reflecting rankings and money allocations, is developed next (see Figure 11-3). All jobs shown, except for programmer

	Mental	Skill	Physical	Responsibility	Working Conditions
$4.00	Systems Analyst (Programmer Analyst)			Systems Analyst	
3.80					
3.50	Programmer				
3.00				Programmer	
2.50		Data Entry Clerk Console Operator Programmer			
	Console Operator				
2.00		Systems Analyst		Console Operator	
1.50	Data Entry Clerk				Data Entry Clerk Console Operator Systems Analyst Programmer
				Data Entry Clerk	
1.00			Data Entry Clerk Systems Analyst Programmer Console Operator		
.50					
.00					

Figure 11-3
Job Comparison Scale

analyst, are original benchmark jobs. The scale is then used to rate other jobs in the group being evaluated. The raters compare each job, factor by factor, with those appearing on the job comparison scale. Then, they place the jobs on the chart in an appropriate position. For example, assume that the committee is evaluating the job of *programmer analyst*. The committee determines that this job has fewer mental requirements than that of *systems analyst* but more than those of *programmer*. The job would then be placed on the chart between these two jobs at a point agreed on by the committee. In this example, the committee evaluated the mental requirements factor at $3.80 (a point between the $4.00 and $3.40—values that had been allocated to the benchmark jobs of systems analyst and programmer, respectively). The committee repeats this procedure for the remaining four factors and then for all jobs to be evaluated. Adding the values of the five factors for each job yields the total value for the job.

The factor comparison method provides a systematic approach to job evaluation. However, at least two problems with it should be noted. The assumption that the five factors are universal has been questioned because certain factors may be more appropriate to some job groups than others. Also, while the steps are not overly complicated, they are somewhat detailed and may be difficult to explain to employees.

Point method: An approach to job evaluation in which numerical values are assigned to specific job components and the sum of these values provides a quantitative assessment of a job's relative worth.

Point Method.

In the **point method**, raters assign numerical values to specific job components, and the sum of these values provides a quantitative assessment of a job's relative worth. Historically, some variation of the point plan has been the most popular option.

The point method requires selection of job factors according to the nature of the specific group of jobs being evaluated. Because job factors vary from one group to another, a separate plan for each group of similar jobs (job clusters) is appropriate. Production jobs, clerical jobs, and sales jobs are examples of job clusters. The procedure for establishing a point method is illustrated in Figure 11-4. After determining the group of jobs to be studied, analysts conduct job analysis and write job descriptions. The job evaluation committee will later use these descriptions as the basis for making evaluation decisions.

Next, the analysts select and define the factors to be used in measuring job value. These factors become the standards used for the evaluation of jobs. They can best be identified by individuals who are thoroughly familiar with the content of the jobs under consideration. Education, experience, job knowledge, mental effort, physical effort, responsibility, and working conditions are examples of factors. Each should be significant in helping to differentiate jobs. Factors that exist in equal amounts in all jobs obviously would not serve this purpose. As an example, in evaluating a company's clerical jobs, the working conditions factor would be of little value in differentiating jobs if all jobs in the cluster had approximately the same working conditions. The number of factors used varies with the job cluster under consideration. It is strictly a subjective judgment. Different firms value jobs differently. For example, a relatively new organization in a fast-growing market will value job factors that relate to its growth in revenue and market share more than will a mature organization in a stable or declining market.[15]

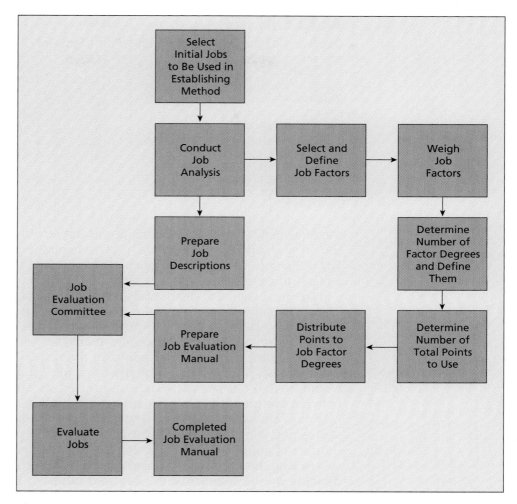

Figure 11-4
Procedure for Establishing the Point Method of Job Evaluation

The committee must establish factor weights according to their relative importance in the jobs to be evaluated. For example, if experience is considered quite important for a particular job cluster, this factor might be weighted as much as 35 percent. Physical effort (if used at all as a factor in an office cluster) would likely be low—perhaps less than 10 percent.

The next consideration is to determine the number of degrees for each job factor and define each degree. Degrees represent the number of distinct levels associated with a particular factor. The number of degrees needed for each factor depends on job requirements. If a particular cluster required virtually the same level of experience, for example, a smaller number of degrees would be appropriate compared to some clusters that required a broad range of experience.

The committee then determines the total number of points to be used in the plan. The number may vary, but 500 or 1,000 points may work well. The

TABLE 11-1

Overview of the Point System (500-Point System)

Job Factor	Weight	Degree of Factor				
		1	2	3	4	5
1. Education	50%	50	100	150	200	250
2. Responsibility	30%	30	70	110	150	
3. Physical effort	12%	12	24	36	48	60
4. Working conditions	8%	8	24	40		

use of a smaller number of points (for example, 50) would not likely provide the proper distinctions among jobs, whereas a larger number (such as 50,000) would be unnecessarily cumbersome. The total number of points in a plan indicates the maximum points that any job could receive.

The next step is to distribute point values to job factor degrees (see Table 11-1). The table shows that factor 1 (education) has five degrees, factor 2 (responsibility) has four, factor 3 (physical effort) has five, and factor 4 (working conditions) has three. Maximum points for each factor are easily calculated by multiplying the total points in the system by the assigned weights. For example, the maximum points any job could receive for education would be 250 (50 percent weight multiplied by 500 points). If the interval between factors is to be a constant number, points for the minimum degree may take the value of the percentage weight assigned to the factor. For instance, the percentage weight for education is 50 percent, so the minimum number of points would also be 50. The degree interval may be calculated by subtracting the minimum number of points from the maximum number and dividing by the number of degrees used minus 1. For example, the interval for factor 1 (education) is this:

$$\text{Interval} = \frac{250 - 50}{5 - 1} = 50$$

As you can see in Table 11-1, the interval between each degree for Education is 50.

This approach to determining the number of points for each degree is referred to as *arithmetic progression*. An arithmetic progression is simple to understand and explain to employees. In the example, the assumption is that the factors have been defined so that the intervals between the degrees are equal. However, if this is not the case, another method, such as a geometric progression, may be more appropriate.

The next step involves preparing a job evaluation manual. Although there is no standard format, the manual often contains an introductory section, factor and degree definitions, and job descriptions. As a final step, the job evaluation committee then evaluates jobs in each cluster by comparing each job description with the factors in the job evaluation manual. Point plans require time and effort to design. Historically, a redeeming feature of the method is that, once developed, the plan is useful over a long period of time. In today's environment, the shelf-life may be considerably less. In any event, as new jobs are created and the content of old jobs substantially changed, job analysis must be conducted and job descriptions rewritten. The job evaluation committee evaluates the jobs and updates the manual. Only when job factors change, or for some reason the weights assigned become inappropriate, does the plan become obsolete.

The Hay Guide Chart-Profile Method (Hay Plan).[16]

Hay Guide Chart-Profile Method (Hay Plan): A highly refined version of the point method of job evaluation that uses the factors of know-how, problem solving, accountability, and additional compensable elements.

A refined version of the point method is the **Hay guide chart-profile method**. The Hay Plan uses the compensable factors of know-how, problem solving, accountability, and additional compensable elements. Point values are assigned to these factors to determine the final point profile for any job.

Know-how is the total of all knowledge and skills needed for satisfactory job performance. It has three dimensions: the amount of practical, specialized, or scientific knowledge required; the ability to coordinate many functions; and the ability to deal with and motivate people effectively.

Problem solving is the degree of original thinking required by the job for analyzing, evaluating, creating, reasoning, and making conclusions. Problem solving has two dimensions: the thinking environment in which problems are solved (from strict routine to abstractly defined), and the thinking challenge presented by the problems (from repetitive to uncharted). Problem solving is expressed as a percentage of know-how, as people use what they know to think and make decisions.

Accountability is the responsibility for action and accompanying consequences. Accountability has three dimensions: the degree of freedom allowed the job incumbent to act, the impact of the job on end results, and the extent of the monetary impact of the job.

The fourth factor, *additional compensable elements*, addresses exceptional conditions in the environment in which the jobs are performed.

Because the Hay Plan is a job evaluation method used by employers worldwide,[17] it facilitates job comparison among firms. Thus, the method serves to determine both internal and external equity.

The Employee as a Determinant of Financial Compensation

In addition to the organization, the labor market, and the job, factors related to the employee are also essential in determining pay equity. These factors are covered in this section.

PAY FOR PERFORMANCE

As previously discussed, individual financial compensation may be influenced by many factors. The factor most controllable by employees is their performance on the job. This performance is typically reflected in the performance appraisal. Appraisal data provide the input for such approaches as merit pay, variable pay, skill-based pay, and competency-based pay. Each of these plans is discussed next.

Merit Pay.

Merit pay: Pay increase given to employees based on their level of performance as indicated in the appraisal.

Merit pay typically stems from the results of employee performance appraisal. In theory, **merit pay** is a pay increase given to employees based on their level of performance as indicated in the appraisal. In practice, however, it is often merely a cost-of-living increase in disguise. For example, the average annual merit increases over an 11-year period, adjusted for the Consumer Price Index, have not exceeded 2 percent.

A primary disadvantage in the typical merit pay increase is that it is added to an employee's base pay. It is therefore received each year the person is on the payroll regardless of later performance levels. Merit pay increases based on a previous employment period but added perpetually to base pay are difficult to justify.

Although many companies continue with their merit pay plans, others seek to control fixed costs by using variable pay. Actually, the two approaches are not mutually exclusive. In fact, they are often used together. Merit pay, which increases base salary, may be used to recognize lasting contributions of employees; variable pay, including lump-sum bonuses, may be used to recognize annual accomplishments.

Variable Pay.

Variable pay: Compensation based on performance.

Bonus (lump-sum payment): A one-time award that is not added to employees' base pay.

Variable pay is compensation based on performance. The most common type of variable pay for performance is the bonus. The **bonus**, or **lump-sum payment**, is a one-time award that is not added to employees' base pay. Firms are pushing these forms of pay—once reserved for high-ranking executives—down through the ranks. In a recent Towers Perrin, Inc., survey, 35 percent of responding firms stated that they plan to provide lump-sum payments. While 63 percent of these will limit the payments to employees at the top of their pay ranges, 14 percent plan to pay lump sums to all employees.[18] Another survey conducted by the American Compensation Association indicated that more than half the companies included in the study had established variable pay budgets.[19] At least 20 percent of American companies use variable pay plans of some type and growing numbers of middle managers and nonmanagers are included in these plans.[20]

With increasing domestic and international competition, maintaining high performance levels and controlling labor costs are essential. Variable pay addresses these requirements by rewarding, and therefore encouraging, high performance. It is cost effective in that the rewards provided for one period are not added to base pay. Therefore, they are not automatically carried over into subsequent periods unless performance is maintained. As previously stated, there are potential advantages to using a two-component approach: including merit pay but emphasizing variable pay. Among the powerful advantages of such a system are these:[21]

- Reducing fixed payroll expenses. This strategy will enable firms to relate total pay levels more equitably with their ability to pay.

- Reducing benefits costs. Many benefits are tied to base salary, including life insurance, disability insurance, and retirement.
- Supporting employee development initiatives. Merit increases can be used to reward employee development.
- Providing motivational rewards. By reducing merit increases, firms will be able to provide greater funds for variable pay.

The downside to variable pay relates to employee morale, which may affect performance. Whereas variable rewards allow for significant upside potential if performance exceeds the standard, they also allow for reduced rewards if performance is below par.[22] The financial insecurity inherent in variable pay may adversely affect employees' sense of financial security. In turn, the result may have negative consequences for workers' attitude toward their work and their employer. Perhaps this potential problem explains why most firms consider variable pay a supplement to rather than a replacement for merit pay.[23]

The disadvantage to employees in not having their base rate increased may be offset by the magnitude of the reward. For example, an employee earning $30,000 a year might get excited about receiving a pretax $1,500 lump-sum payment (5 percent increase) in lieu of having it doled out $125 each month. The potential problem would lie in the duration of the excitement.

Since 1988, the number of domestic firms offering variable pay to all salaried employees rose from 47 percent to 68 percent. Some of the advantages that have been cited for using performance-based pay include the following:[24]

- Increases job satisfaction
- Increases productivity
- Reduces avoidable absenteeism
- Decreases voluntary turnover
- Improves the quality of the employee mix

A prerequisite for any pay system tied to performance is a sound performance appraisal program. A valid means for determining varying performance levels is absolutely essential.

Skill-based pay: A system that compensates employees on the basis of job-related skills and the knowledge they possess.

Skill-Based Pay. **Skill-based pay** is a system that compensates employees on the basis of job-related skills and knowledge they possess, not for their job titles. It is premised on the belief that employees who know more are more valuable to the firm and therefore should be rewarded accordingly.[25] The purpose of this approach is to encourage employees to gain additional skills that will increase their value to the organization and improve its competitive position. Today's downsizing and elimination of many middle-management jobs have left fewer promotional opportunities. Room for growth needs to be possible within jobs, and employees should be motivated by factors other than promotions and titles.

TRENDS & INNOVATIONS

A PAY FOR SKILLS PROGRAM AT MCDONNELL DOUGLAS

McDonnell Douglas Helicopter Company, in Mesa, Arizona, determined that their automatic wage progression system was not working well. In developing an alternative—a pay for skills program—they found that the program should be done by teams rather than individuals. The implementation team was multidisciplinary and included a compensation specialist, an organizational development expert, a trainer, a systems analyst, and an employee relations professional. The purpose of this team was to provide leadership, create guidelines, facilitate the development process, and coordinate plan approvals. Its first task was to establish the structure for the development of teams; these were formed for each job family and involved both hourly employees and managers. The purpose of these teams included identifying relevant skills, determining how these skills would be verified, and deciding the type of training required. A majority of employees and managers at McDonnell Douglas have positive feelings about the new program, which has resulted in productivity improvements greater than anticipated.[26]

When employees obtain additional job-relevant skills, both individuals and the departments they serve may benefit. Employees may receive both tangible and intangible rewards: pay increases, job security, greater mobility, and the satisfaction of being more valuable. With additional skills, employees can often increase their earnings without having to move permanently to a higher level job. This factor gains additional importance in a highly competitive environment in which promotional opportunities are more limited than in the past. Organizational units are provided with a greater degree of versatility in dealing with absenteeism and turnover.

Skill-based pay is often used with autonomous work groups or other job enrichment programs. A high commitment to human resource development is necessary to implement such a program successfully. In addition, employees involved in skill-based pay programs must have the desire to grow and increase their knowledge and skills.

Skill-based pay appears to have advantages for both employer and employee, but it does present some challenges for management. Adequate training opportunities must be provided to workers or the system can become a demotivator. Research has revealed that workers reach their maximum level in a skill-based pay system in an average of only three years. What, then, will keep employees motivated? One answer has been to couple the plan with a pay-for-performance system. An additional challenge associated with skill-based pay is that payroll costs will escalate. It is conceivable that a firm could have, in addition to high training and development costs, a very expensive workforce possessing an excess of skills.[27] In spite of these negative possibilities, a number of firms have achieved lower operating costs and other benefits with their pay-for-skills programs.

Competency-based pay:
A compensation plan that rewards employees for their demonstrated expertise.

Competency-Based Pay. **Competency-based pay** is a compensation plan that rewards employees for their demonstrated expertise. Competencies include skills but also involve other factors such as motives, traits, values, attitudes, and self-concepts.[28] Core competencies may be unique to each company, but one service firm identified these:

- Team-centered: Builds productive working relationships at levels within and outside the organization
- Results-driven: Is focused on achieving key objectives
- Client-dedicated: Works as a partner with internal and external clients
- Innovative: Generates and implements new ideas, products, services, and solutions to problems
- Fast cycle: Displays a bias for action and decisiveness[29]

Pay for performance focuses on end results; competency-based pay examines how an employee accomplishes the objectives. The criteria used in competency-based pay would seem to be more difficult to evaluate.

SENIORITY

The length of time an employee has been associated with the company, division, department, or job is referred to as *seniority*. Management generally prefers performance as the primary basis for compensation changes; labor unions tend to favor seniority. They believe the use of seniority provides an objective and fair basis for pay increases. Many union leaders consider performance evaluation systems as too subjective, permitting management to reward favorite employees arbitrarily. Labor unions generally prefer collective bargaining for achieving their compensation goals, and seniority is usually the preferred criterion.

EXPERIENCE

Regardless of the nature of the task, experience has potential for enhancing a person's ability to perform. However, this possibility can be realized only if the experience acquired is positive. Knowledge of the basics is usually a prerequisite if a person's experience is to be put to effective use. This is true for someone beginning to play golf, learn a foreign language, or manage people in organizations. People who express pride in their long tenure as managers may be justified in their sentiments but only if their experience has been beneficial. Those who have been bull-of-the-woods autocrats for a dozen years or so would likely not find their experience highly valued by a Malcolm Baldrige Award-winning firm. Nevertheless, experience is often indispensable for gaining the insights necessary to perform many tasks.

Employees are often compensated on the basis of their experience. This practice is justified if the experience has been positive and is relevant to the job to be performed.

MEMBERSHIP IN THE ORGANIZATION

Some components of individual financial compensation are given to employees without regard for the particular job they perform or their level of productivity. These rewards are provided to all employees simply because they are members of the organization. For example, an average performer occupying a job in pay grade 1 may receive the same number of vacation days, the same amount of group life insurance, and the same reimbursement for educational expenses as a superior employee working in a job classified in pay grade 10. In fact, the worker in pay grade 1 may get more vacation time if he or she has been with the firm longer. Rewards based on organizational membership are intended to maintain a high degree of stability in the workforce and to recognize loyalty.

POTENTIAL

Potential is useless if it is never realized. However, organizations do pay some individuals based on their potential. To attract talented young people to the firm, for example, the overall compensation program must appeal to those with no experience or any immediate ability to perform difficult tasks. Many young employees are paid well, not because of their ability to add value to the firm immediately, but because they have the potential to become a first-line supervisor, manager of compensation, vice president of marketing, or possibly even chief executive officer.

POLITICAL INFLUENCE

Political influence is a factor that obviously should not be used to determine financial compensation. However, to deny its existence would be unrealistic. There is an unfortunate element of truth in the statement, "It's not *what* you know; it's *who* you know." To varying degrees in business, government, and not-for-profit organizations, a person's *pull* or political influence may sway pay and promotion decisions. It may be natural for a manager to favor a friend or relative in granting a pay increase or promotion. Nevertheless, if the person receiving the reward is not deserving, this fact will soon become known throughout the work group. The result may be devastating to employee morale.

LUCK

You've undoubtedly heard the expression, "It helps to be in the right place at the right time." There is more than a little truth in this statement as it relates to a person's compensation. Opportunities are continually presenting themselves in firms. Realistically, there is no way for managers to foresee many of the changes that occur. For instance, who could have known that the purchasing agent, Joe Flynch, an apparently healthy middle-age man, would suddenly die of a heart attack? Although the company may have been grooming several managers for Joe's position, none may be capable of immediately assuming the increased responsibility. The most experienced person,

Tommy Loy, has been with the company only six months. Tommy had been an assistant buyer for a competitor for four years. Because of his experience, Tommy receives the promotion and the increased financial compensation. Tommy Loy was lucky; he was in the right place at the right time.

When asked to explain their most important reasons for success and effectiveness as managers, two chief executives responded candidly. One said, "Success is being at the right place at the right time and being recognized as having the ability to make timely decisions. It also depends on having good rapport with people, a good operating background, and the knowledge of how to develop people." The other replied, "My present position was attained by being in the right place at the right time with a history of getting the job done." Both executives recognize the significance of luck combined with the ability to perform. Their experiences lend support to the idea that luck works primarily for the efficient.

Job Pricing

Job pricing: Placing a dollar value on the worth of a job.

The primary considerations in pricing jobs are the organization's policies, the labor market, and the job itself. If allowances are to be made for individual factors, they too must be considered. Recall that the process of job evaluation results in a job hierarchy. It might reveal, for example, that the job of senior accountant is more valuable than the job of computer operator, which, in turn, is more valuable than the job of senior invoice clerk. At this point, the relative value of these jobs to the company is known, but their absolute value is not. Placing a dollar value on the worth of a job is called **job pricing**. It takes place after the job has been evaluated and the relative value of each job in the organization has been determined. However, as shown in Figure 11-2, additional factors should be considered in determining the job's absolute value. Firms often use pay grades and pay ranges in the job-pricing process.

PAY GRADES

Pay grade: Similar jobs grouped to simplify the job-pricing process.

A **pay grade** is the grouping of similar jobs to simplify pricing jobs. It is much more convenient for organizations to price 15 pay grades rather than 200 separate jobs. The simplicity of this approach is similar to the practice of a college or university in grouping grades of 90 to 100 into an *A* category, grades of 80 to 89 into a *B* category, and so on. A false implication of preciseness is also avoided. Job evaluation plans may be systematic, but none is scientific.

Plotting jobs on a scatter diagram is often useful to managers in determining the appropriate number of pay grades for a company. In Figure 11-5, each dot on the scatter diagram represents one job as it relates to pay and evaluated points, which reflect its worth. When this procedure is used, a certain point spread will probably work satisfactorily (100 points was used in this illustration). Each dot represents one job but may involve dozens of individuals who fill that one job. The large dot at the lower left represents the job of data entry clerk, which was evaluated at 75 points. The data entry

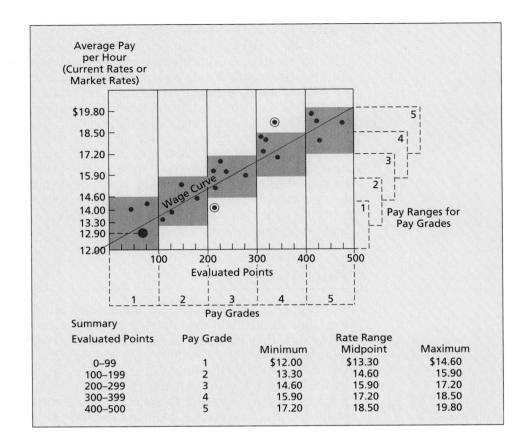

Figure 11-5
Scatter Diagram of
Evaluated Jobs
Illustrating the Wage
Curve, Pay Grades, and
Rating Ranges

Summary Evaluated Points	Pay Grade	Rate Range Minimum	Rate Range Midpoint	Rate Range Maximum
0–99	1	$12.00	$13.30	$14.60
100–199	2	13.30	14.60	15.90
200–299	3	14.60	15.90	17.20
300–399	4	15.90	17.20	18.50
400–500	5	17.20	18.50	19.80

Wage curve: The fitting of plotted points on a curve to create a smooth progression between pay grades (also known as the *pay curve*).

clerk's hourly rate of $12.90 represents either the average wage currently being paid for the job or its market rate. This decision depends on how management wants to price its jobs.

A **wage curve** (or pay curve) is the fitting of plotted points to create a smooth progression between pay grades. The line that is drawn to minimize the distance between all dots and the line—a line of best fit—may be straight or curved. However, when the point system is used (normally considering only one job cluster), a straight line is the usual result, as in Figure 11-5. This wage line can either be drawn freehand or be charted by using a statistical method.

PAY RANGES

Pay range: A minimum and maximum pay rate for a job, with enough variance between the two to allow for some significant pay difference.

After pay grades have been determined, the next decision is whether all individuals performing the same job will receive equal pay or whether pay ranges will be used. A **pay range** includes a minimum and maximum pay rate with enough variance between the two to allow for a significant pay difference. Pay ranges are generally preferred over single pay rates because they allow employees to be paid according to length of service and performance.

Pay then serves as a positive incentive. When pay ranges are used, a method must be developed to advance individuals through the range.

Referring again to Figure 11-5, note that anyone can readily determine the minimum, midpoint, and maximum pay rates per hour for each of the five pay grades. For example, for pay grade 5, the minimum rate is $17.20, the midpoint is $18.50, and the maximum is $19.80. The minimum rate is often the *hiring in* rate that a person receives when joining the firm. The maximum pay rate represents the maximum that an employee can receive for that job, regardless of how well the job is performed. A person at the top of a pay grade will have to be promoted to a job in a higher pay grade to receive a pay increase unless (1) an across-the-board-adjustment is made, raising the entire pay range, or (2) the job is reevaluated and placed in a higher pay grade. This situation has caused numerous managers some anguish as they attempt to explain the pay system to an employee who is doing a tremendous job but is at the top of a pay grade. Consider this situation:

> Everyone in the department realized that Beth Smithers was the best secretary in the company. At times, she appeared to do the job of three secretaries. Bob Marshall, Beth's supervisor, was especially impressed. Recently, he had a discussion with the human resource manager to see what could be done to get a raise for Beth. After Bob described the situation, the human resource manager's only reply was, "Sorry, Bob. Beth is already at the top of her pay grade. There is nothing you can do except have her job upgraded or promote her to another position."

Situations such as Beth's present managers with a perplexing problem. Many would be inclined to make an exception to the system and give Beth a salary increase. However, this action would violate a traditional principle, which holds that every job in the organization has a maximum value, regardless of how well it is performed. The rationale is that making exceptions to the compensation plan would result in widespread pay inequities. We should recognize that many traditional concepts are being challenged today as firms make decisions necessary to retain top performing employees. For example, if Beth Smithers was employed by Microsoft or Motorola, she would probably get a raise.

The rate ranges established should be large enough to provide an incentive to workers to do a better job. At times, pay differentials may need to be greater to be meaningful, especially at higher levels. There may be logic in having the rate range become increasingly wide at each consecutive level. Consider, for example, what a $200 per month salary increase would mean to a file clerk earning $2,000 per month (a 10 percent increase) and to a senior cost accountant earning $5,000 per month (a 4 percent increase). Assuming an inflation rate of 4 percent, the accountant's *real pay* would remain unchanged.

HR Web Wisdom

http://www.prenhall.com/mondy

BROADBANDING
A description of the broadband concept is provided.

BROADBANDING

The pressure on U.S. businesses to do things better, faster, and less expensively has brought all internal systems under close scrutiny. Compensation, in particular, has received attention because of its ability to affect job behavior. Responding to this need, an approach termed *broadbanding* was devised. **Broadbanding** is a technique that collapses many pay grades (salary grades) into a few wide bands to improve organizational effectiveness. Organizational downsizing and restructuring of jobs create broader job descriptions, with the result that employees perform more diverse tasks than they did previously. Broadbanding creates the basis for a simpler compensation system that deemphasizes structure and control and places greater importance on judgment and flexible decision making. Currently, only about 200 companies use broadbanding, and most of these programs are less than two years old.[30] However, a study conducted by ACA/Hewitt Associates found that 92 percent of human resource managers responding indicated that broadbanding should either be maintained or expanded within their organizations. Positive responses were also received from other executives and employees; 91 percent and 75 percent, respectively. The data from this survey indicate that numerous benefits may be derived from the use of broadbanding, including a company's improved ability to do these:[31]

- Provide flexibility in the way work is performed
- Promote lateral development of employees
- Support business goals
- Develop employee skills and encourage a team focus
- Direct employee attention away from vertical promotional opportunities

The decreased emphasis on job levels should encourage employees to make cross-functional moves to jobs that are on the same or even a lower level as their pay rate would remain unchanged. The problem of employees becoming stuck at the top of their pay grade would also be minimized.

Moving an employee's job to a new band would occur only when there was a significant increase in accountability.[32] However, considerable advancement in pay is possible within each band. This is particularly important in firms with flat organizational structures that offer fewer promotional opportunities. Figure 11-6 illustrates broadbanding as it relates to pay grades and rate ranges.

Broadbanding is not the only means for improving the effectiveness and efficiency of a compensation system and is not appropriate for every organization. However, it is an approach that should be considered in light of its potential benefits. For example, even massive General Electric has managed to place all its exempt jobs into five bands.[33]

Although broadbanding has been implemented successfully in some organizations, the practice is not without pitfalls. Because each band consists of a broad range of jobs, the market value of these jobs may vary considerably. Unless carefully monitored, employees in jobs at the lower end of the band could progress to the top of the range and become overpaid.

Figure 11-6
Broadbanding and Its Relationship to Traditional Pay Grades and Ranges

Source: Adapted from Joseph J. Martocchio, *Strategic Compensation* (Upper Saddle River, NJ: Prentice Hall, 1998): 36.

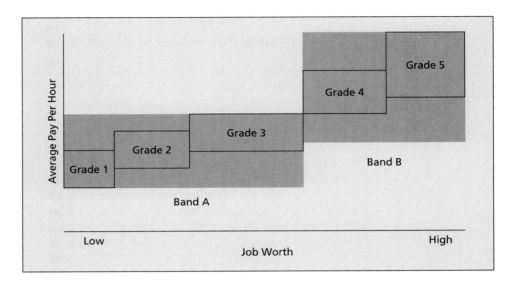

SINGLE-RATE SYSTEM

Pay ranges are not appropriate for some workplace conditions such as assembly line operations. For instance, when all jobs within a unit are routine, with little opportunity for employees to vary their productivity, a single- or fixed-rate system may be more applicable. When single rates are used, everyone in the same job receives the same base pay, regardless of seniority or productivity. This rate may correspond to the midpoint of a range determined by a compensation survey.

ADJUSTING PAY RATES

When pay ranges have been determined and jobs assigned to pay grades, it may become obvious that some jobs are overpaid and others underpaid. Underpaid jobs are normally brought to the minimum of the pay range as soon as possible. Referring again to Figure 11-5, you can see that a job evaluated at about 225 points and having a rate of $14.00 per hour is represented by a circled dot immediately below pay grade 3. The job was determined to be difficult enough to fall in pay grade 3 (200–299 points). However, employees working in the job are being paid 60 cents per hour less than the minimum for the pay grade ($14.60 per hour). Good management practice would be to correct this inequity as rapidly as possible by placing the job in the proper pay grade and increasing the pay of those who work that job.

Overpaid jobs present more of a problem. An overpaid job for pay grade 4 is illustrated in Figure 11-5 (note the circled dot above pay grade 4). Employees in this job earn $19.00 per hour, or 50 cents more than the maximum for the pay grade. This type of overpayment, as well as the kind of underpayment discussed above is referred to as *red circle rate*.

An ideal solution to the problem of an overpaid job is to promote the employee. This might be a reasonable approach if the employee is qualified

---

---

for a higher rated job and a job opening is available. Another possibility would be to bring the job rate and employee pay into line through a pay cut. This type of action may appear logical, but it is not consistent with good management practice. This action would punish employees for a situation they did not create. Somewhere between these two possible solutions is a third: to freeze the rate until across-the-board pay increases bring the job into line. In an era where this type of increase is declining in popularity, it might take a long time for this to occur.

Nonfinancial Compensation

Compensation departments in organizations do not normally deal with nonfinancial factors. However, nonfinancial compensation is often a very powerful factor in the compensation equation. Consider the situation described below.

> The workplace atmosphere is highly invigorating. Roy, Ann, Jack, Sandra, Walton, and Patsy are excited as they try to keep up with double-digit growth in sales orders. They do whatever it takes to get the job done, wearing multiple hats that would be difficult to cover in a job description. Their jobs have no salary grades and their performance is never formally reviewed. This doesn't worry them, however, because they enjoy the camaraderie and teamwork at their firm. They have complete trust in the firm's highly visible management and they have total confidence that their leaders will do what's right for them and the company. Believe it or not, this is a real-life scene from a real-life company, and thousands of firms like it exist across the country.[34]

Trig and Joanne, mentioned at the beginning of the chapter, also provided illustrations of the importance of nonfinancial compensation. This component of a total compensation system includes the job and the job environment.

Management's task is to create jobs that are meaningful and staff them with individuals whose interests and abilities match the positions.

THE JOB

Jobs that people are given to do may be boring or even so distasteful that employees dread going to work. This situation is very sad considering the time people devote to their jobs. Most of us spend a large part of our lives, not on the beach, but working. When work is a drag, life may not be very pleasant. As we discuss in chapter 13, the stressed person may eventually become emotionally or physically ill.

A more rewarding scenario involves an individual who has a job that is interesting and provides some challenge. When a job of this type is performed, employees often realize a sense of achievement. Of course, what is interesting and challenging to one person may not be to another. The task of management is to create work that is meaningful and staff these jobs with individuals whose interests and abilities match the work to be done.

As previously described, a job is a group of tasks that must be performed for an organization to achieve its goals. The demise of the job as a way of organizing work has been predicted in some quarters because of rapidly changing duties in a dynamic environment.[35] However, it seems that as long as tasks must be completed by humans, a job—by whatever name or however broad in scope—will be necessary whether performed by employees, temporary workers, part-timers, consultants, or contract workers. As long as employees are required by organizations, a major management objective will be to match job requirements satisfactorily with employee abilities and aspirations. There is no question that as the scope of many jobs expands and as they become more complex, this challenge will also increase in difficulty.

The job is a central issue in many theories of motivation, and it is also a vital component of a total compensation program. Employees may receive important rewards by performing meaningful jobs. This type of reward is intrinsic in nature, but management arranges required tasks into job content; therefore, the job's compensation possibilities are largely controlled by the organization. The selection and placement processes are extremely important in this context. The collection of tasks making up a job that is challenging to one person may be quite boring to another, and failure to recognize this difference often leads to major problems.

According to job characteristics theory, employees experience intrinsic compensation when their jobs rate high on five core job dimensions:

- Skill variety
- Task identity
- Task significance
- Autonomy
- Feedback

In this theory, jobs providing skill variety, task identity, and task significance lead employees to perceive their work as meaningful. Jobs that give autonomy allow employees to feel responsible for the outcomes of their work, and jobs that provide feedback let employees know how well they have performed. The ultimate benefits of these characteristics are increased performance, lower absenteeism and turnover, and higher employee satisfaction.[36]

JOB ENVIRONMENT

Performing a challenging, responsible job in a pig sty would not be rewarding to most people. The job environment must also be satisfactory. Employees can draw satisfaction from their work through nonfinancial factors such as a highly compatible work group and management that is both trusted and respected.

Sound Policies. Human resource policies and practices reflecting management's concern for its employees can serve as positive rewards. If a firm's policies show consideration rather than disrespect, fear, doubt, or lack of confidence, the result can be rewarding to both the employees and the organization.

Competent Employees. Successful organizations emphasize continuous development and assure that competent managers and nonmanagers are employed. Today's competitive environment and the requirement for teamwork will not permit any other behavior.

Congenial Co-workers. Although a few individuals in this world may be quite self-sufficient and prefer to be left alone, they will become lonely indeed in the team-oriented organizations that exist today. The American culture has historically embraced individualism; however, most people possess, in varying degrees, a desire to be accepted by their work group. It is very important that management develop and maintain compatible work groups.

Appropriate Status Symbols. **Status symbols** are organizational rewards that take many forms such as office size and location, desk size and quality, private secretaries, floor covering, and title. Some firms make liberal use of these types of rewards; others tend to minimize them. The latter approach reflects a concern about the adverse effect they may have in creating and

Status symbols: Organizational rewards that take many forms such as office size and location, desk size and quality, private secretaries, floor covering, and title.

maintaining a team spirit among members of various levels in the firm. If the team spirit is to permeate all levels of an organization, symbols should be dispensed with care.

Comfortable Working Conditions. Good working conditions are taken for granted in many organizations today. However, a brief return to non-air-conditioned offices would quickly remind us of their importance. The view that working conditions can be a form of compensation is reinforced by pay plans that increase the financial reward for jobs to be performed in relatively poor working conditions.

A flexible workplace featuring such practices as flextime and telecommuting can also enhance the nonfinancial compensation package. These topics are discussed in the following section.

TRENDS & INNOVATIONS

FLEXIBILITY AT AT&T GLOBAL BUSINESS COMMUNICATION SYSTEMS

In the early 1990s, AT&T Global Business Communications Systems (GBCS) was losing well over a half billion dollars a year. Fewer than 4 in 10 employees held a positive view of the business. At the same time, advances in technology allowed companies from other industries to move into their business. The highly competitive situation that resulted called for drastic action. By decentralizing operations and introducing flexibility programs, GBCS recovered. The firm is now well over a $4 billion business and returns extremely good profits as it continues to expand.

Dana Becker Dunn, vice president of the multimedia market office for GBCS, cites these tangible results of using flexibility programs: increased employee morale and satisfaction, higher employee retention rates, and lowered real-estate costs from widespread use of telecommuting. Becker Dunn adds, "The offering of flexibility options communicates to the associates that they are valued; that management has respect for their well-being and will accommodate them when feasible." The flexibility options offered by GCBS—all on a voluntary basis—include telecommuting, compressed work schedules, flexible hours, and job sharing.[37]

Workplace Flexibility

Flexible work arrangements do more than just assist new mothers return to full-time work. They comprise an aspect of nonfinancial compensation that allows many families to manage a stressful work/home juggling act. For employers, workplace flexibility can be a key strategic factor in attracting and retaining the most talented employees.[38] Discussed next are the concepts of flextime, compressed workweek, job sharing, flexible compensation, tele-commuting, part-time work, and modified retirement.

FLEXTIME

Flextime: The practice of permitting employees to choose, with certain limitations, their own working hours.

The practice of permitting employees to choose their own working hours, with certain limitations, is referred to as **flextime**. It was introduced in Germany in the late 1960s and has since spread throughout Europe and the United States. Currently, over 400,000 organizations use flextime.[39] A study conducted by Towers and Perrin indicated that 90 percent of companies that offered flextime reported it as their most popular work/life benefit.[40]

In a flextime system, employees work the same number of hours per day as they would on a standard schedule. However, they are permitted to work these hours within what is called a *band width*, which is the maximum length of the work day (see Figure 11-7). *Core time* is that part of the day when all employees must be present. *Flexible time* is the time period within which employees may vary their schedules. A typical schedule permits employees to begin work between 6:00 A.M. and 9:00 A.M. and to complete their work day between 3:00 P.M. and 6:00 P.M.

Perhaps the most important feature of flextime is allowing employees to schedule their time to minimize conflicts between personal needs and job requirements. With flextime, employees can accommodate their personal needs without being tempted to use sick leave illegitimately. Flextime also permits employees to work at hours when they feel they can function best. It caters to those who are early risers or those who prefer to work later in the day. The public also seems to reap benefits from flextime. Transportation services, recreational facilities, medical clinics, and other services can be better utilized as a result of reduced competition for service at conventional peak times. Benefits accruing to organizations are also impressive. Studies at such firms as AT&T Global Business Communications Systems indicate that assisting employees resolve work and family conflicts not only boosts morale but also increases productivity.

Flextime is not suitable for all types of organizations. For example, its use may be severely limited in assembly line operations and companies utilizing multiple shifts. However, flextime is feasible in many situations, benefiting both the employee and the employer. Clearly, the use of plans such as flextime are compatible with the desire of employees (especially younger ones) to have greater control over their work situations.

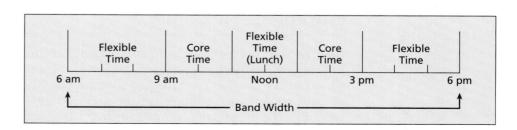

Figure 11-7
Illustration of Flextime

THE COMPRESSED WORKWEEK

Compressed work-week: Any arrangement of work hours that permits employees to fulfill their work obligation in fewer days than the typical five-day workweek.

Any arrangement of work hours that permits employees to fulfill their work obligation in fewer days than the typical five-day workweek is referred to as the **compressed workweek**. A common compressed workweek is four 10-hour days. Working under this arrangement, employees have reported greater job satisfaction. In addition, the compressed workweek offers the potential for better use of leisure time for family life, personal business, and recreation. Employers in some instances have cited advantages such as increased productivity and reduced turnover and absenteeism. In other firms, however, work scheduling and employee fatigue problems have been encountered. In some cases, these problems have resulted in lower product quality and reduced customer service. Nevertheless, a number of organizations feel the advantages of compressed workweeks outweigh the disadvantages. A recent study by William M. Mercer of 800 firms with 1,000 or more employees found that 34 percent use compressed workweeks for some part of their workforce and an additional 14 percent are considering this plan.[41]

JOB SHARING

Job sharing: The filling of a job by two part-time people who split the duties of one full-time job in some agreed-on manner and are paid according to their contributions.

Job sharing is an approach to work that is attractive to people who want to work fewer than 40 hours per week. In job sharing, two part-time people split the duties of one job in some agreed-on manner and are paid according to their contributions. A Conference Board survey of 131 firms offering flexible options found that 74 percent offer job sharing. The survey revealed that job sharing had significant benefits including the broader range of skills the partners bring to the job as opposed to a single employee. The survey also discovered the most important qualities inherent in a good job share situation: compatibility of partners, strong communication skills, trust between job sharers and managers, and dependability.[42]

FLEXIBLE COMPENSATION (CAFETERIA COMPENSATION)

Flexible compensation plans: A method that permits employees to choose from among many alternatives in deciding how their financial compensation will be allocated.

Flexible compensation plans permit employees to choose from among many alternatives in deciding how their financial compensation will be allocated. Employees are given considerable latitude in determining, for example, how much they will take in the form of salary, life insurance, pension contributions, and other benefits. Cafeteria plans permit flexibility in allowing each employee to determine the compensation package that best satisfies his or her particular needs.

Twenty years ago, firms offered a uniform package that generally reflected what a *typical* employee needed. Today, the workforce has become considerably more heterogeneous, and this prototype is no longer representative. To accommodate such diversity, flexible compensation plans appear to provide a satisfactory solution. Recent studies suggest that flexible compensation programs are becoming increasingly popular among employers.

The rationale behind cafeteria plans is that employees have individual needs and preferences. A 60-year-old man would probably not desire maternity benefits in an insurance plan. At the same time, a 25-year-old woman who regularly jogs three miles each day might not place a high value on a

TABLE 11-2

Compensation Vehicles Utilized in a Cafeteria Compensation Approach

Accidental death, dismemberment insurance	Health maintenance organization fees
Birthdays (vacation)	Home health care
Bonus eligibility	Hospital-surgical-medical insurance
Business and professional membership	Incentive growth fund
Cash profit sharing	Interest-free loans
Club memberships	Long-term disability benefit
Commissions	Matching educational donations
Company medical assistance	Nurseries
Company provided automobile	Nursing home care
Company provided housing	Outside medical services
Company provided or subsidized travel	Personal accident insurance
Day care centers	Price discount plan
Deferred bonus	Recreation facilities
Deferred compensation plan	Resort facilities
Dental and eye care insurance	Sabbatical leaves
Discount on company products	Salary continuation
Education costs	Savings plan
Educational activities (time off)	Scholarships for dependents
Free checking account	Severance pay
Free or subsidized lunches	Sickness and accident insurance
Group automobile insurance	Stock appreciation rights
Group homeowners' insurance	Stock bonus plan
Group life insurance	Stock purchase plan

parking space near the firm's entrance. Some of the possible compensation vehicles utilized in a cafeteria approach are shown in Table 11-2.

Obviously, organizations cannot permit employees to select all their financial compensation vehicles. For one thing, benefits required by law must be provided. In addition, it is probably wise to require that each employee have core benefits, especially in areas such as retirement and medical insurance. Some guidelines would likely be helpful for most employees in the long run. However, the freedom to select highly desired benefits would seem to maximize the value of an individual's compensation. Involvement in determining tailored compensation plans should also effectively communicate the cost of benefits to employees.

The existing information regarding employee satisfaction with flexible compensation plans is limited. However, the available evidence shows that workers' overall job satisfaction, pay satisfaction, and understanding of benefits increased after implementation of flexible plans. These outcomes are desirable as many of these elements are related to reduced absenteeism and turnover.[43]

Development and administrative costs for flexible compensation plans exceed those for more traditional plans. For example, a firm with 10,000 employees might incur developmental costs of about $500,000.[44] Even though flexible compensation programs add to the organization's administrative burden, the advantages seem to greatly outweigh the shortcomings. Therefore, systems of this type will likely become more common in the future.

TELECOMMUTING

Telecommuting: A procedure allowing workers to remain at home or otherwise away from the office and perform their work over data lines tied to a computer.

Telecommuting is a work arrangement that allows employees to remain at home or otherwise away from the office and perform their work over telephone lines tied to a computer. Modern communications and data processing technologies permit people to work just about anywhere they want. The number of telecommuters has skyrocketed from 4 million in 1990, to 8 million in 1995, to 11 million in 1997. More than 14 million home-based workers are expected by the year 2000.[45] A recent survey of senior executives revealed that nearly two-thirds of North American companies encourage telecommuting. More than 40 percent of the respondents to the survey have a formal telecommuting program in place.[46]

Telecommuters are generally information workers. They accomplish jobs that require, for example, analysis, research, writing, budgeting, data entry, or computer programming. Teleworkers also include illustrators, loan executives, architects, attorneys, and desktop publishers.[47] Using a personal computer in a location away from the office and connected to a computer network, both training and job duties are carried out without loss of efficiency and quality. Advantages of telecommuting accrue to the company, the employee, and the community. These advantages are shown in Figure 11-8.

Another advantage of telecommuting is that it eliminates the need for office space. As one manager put it, "The expense of an employee is not just the person; it's also the fact that I pay $90,000 a year for the office that person sits in."[48]

Commuting distances are not a factor for teleworkers. Therefore, firms may hire the best available employees located virtually anywhere. The size of the U.S. workforce should also increase with the ability of telecommuting to expand the utilization of disabled workers and workers with small children.

With its many advantages, telecommuting also has some potential pitfalls. For example, ties between employees and their firms may be weakened, and successful programs will require a higher degree of trust between employees and their supervisors. In addition to the way people are supervised, firms considering telecommuting will need to think about changes in other policy areas as well. Questions such as the following will need to be addressed:

- Will compensation and benefits be affected? If so, how?
- Who will be responsible for workers injured at home?
- What about responsibility for purchasing and providing insurance coverage for equipment?
- How will taxes be affected by telecommuting?
- Will overtime be allowed?

For the Company	For the Employee	For the Community
Helps attract new employees, especially those needing flexibility	Reduces transportation costs and commuting time	Decreases the environmental impact of commuting
Can increase retention rates	Allows personal control over working conditions	Conserves energy
Helps in ADA[1] compliance		Decreases traffic congestion
Complies with various EPA[2] regulations	Eliminates unplanned meetings or "drop ins"	Reduces the need for road repair
Reduces sick time and absenteeism	Provides more flexible child and elder care options	Takes pressure from public transportation
Increases productivity	Increases privacy	
Increases employee job satisfaction	Reduces the stress of commuting	
Maximizes office space	Allows work to be done when one is most productive	
Decreases relocation costs	Reduces clothing costs	
Reduces overtime	Creates more time to spend with family	
	Enhances communications with supervisor	
	Provides the ability to work without interruption	

Figure 11-8
Advantages of Telecommuting

[1]ADA = Americans with Disabilities Act

[2]EPA = Environmental Protection Act

Source: George M. Piskurich, "Making Telecommuting Work," *Training & Development* 50 (February 1996): 22.

- Will security be provided for the telecommuter's work? How?
- Will the firm have safety requirements for the home?

These kinds of questions seem to suggest that telecommuting poses insurmountable problems, yet there are few examples of unsuccessful telecommuting. One note of caution does exist, however: Telecommuting should not be used as a means to reduce other standard benefits provided to employees.[49]

PART-TIME WORK

Use of part-time workers on a regular basis has begun to gain momentum in the United States. This approach adds many highly qualified individuals to the labor market by permitting both employment and family needs to be addressed. Part-time employees have historically been regarded as second-class workers. This perception must be changed if a part-time program is to be successful.

MODIFIED RETIREMENT

Modified retirement:
An option that permits older employees to work fewer than regular hours for a certain period of time preceding retirement.

Modified retirement is an option that permits older employees to work fewer than regular hours for a certain period of time preceding retirement. This option allows an employee to avoid an abrupt change in lifestyle and move into retirement more gracefully.

To prosper with a diverse workforce, organizations will need to develop workplace flexibility. This shift is apparently resisted in some firms. For example, the view that "presence equals productivity" remains part of many corporate cultures. Flexible options seem to work best in environments characterized by freedom, trust, responsibility, and respect. An encouraging sign is that some organizations are altering traditional approaches to jobs and work not only to cut costs but also to ease conflicts between work and family responsibilities and to attract and retain qualified people.[50] If these goals are achieved, it seems reasonable that organizations will become more productive.

A GLOBAL PERSPECTIVE

Global Compensation: Don't Pay Too Much

Designing total compensation programs for expatriates and local nationals is often quite complex. In the United States, many firms have a single policy that covers all employees. However, firms overseas may have numerous standards depending on the employee's situation. Global compensation must establish and maintain a consistent relationship between equitable pay and acceptable productivity. The programs should also maintain compensation levels that are reasonable in relation to the practices of leading competitors. Failure to establish a uniform compensation policy can result in predictably adverse results, especially for employees doing the same jobs. Such compensation policies will inevitably lead to low morale, motivational problems, and less productive employees.[51] Apparently, the financial compensation provided to most expatriate managers is satisfactory. According to a recent survey, 80 percent of the respondents were satisfied with their financial perks.[52]

The level of pay offered to both expatriates and host country nationals will vary by country and by the skills required. Normally, expatriates are paid much higher wages when they accept global assignments. To avoid overcompensating expatriates, companies must have well-thought-out global compensation policies. Frequently, expatriates get whatever they ask for rather than what they need. Paying an expatriate enough to preserve the person's home-country standard of living in a foreign country is often impractical. According to Roberta Davis, expatriate services manager at Chubb & Son, Inc., "It is really not possible, nor does it make sense, for somebody going to Tokyo to expect to be able to rent a four-bedroom Colonial home; if it did exist, it would be prohibitively expensive."[53] Expatriate pay should start at modest levels and increase if necessary. To avoid extraordinary expenses for the company, expatriates must be paid wages equitable to others in the firm; but more important is selecting the right candidates, preparing them properly, and developing them to complete global assignments and return to the United States as effective and productive employees.

Although the costs and importance of expatriates cannot be denied, the most significant portion of the total overseas payroll will go to host-country nationals who are local employees in their own countries. The assumption is often made that host-country national payrolls will be relatively low. However, overseas local payrolls are rising. The assumption is made that local personnel in developing countries will work for little money, but this is not always the case. With qualified locals in such short supply, their cost is escalating. This trend is quite evident throughout Asia, where salaries have been rising by more than 10 percent a year in most labor markets since the early 1990s and by even larger amounts for skilled professionals and managers. The phenomenon is occurring in other developing markets as well. In Turkey, for example, the bidding war for talent is quite surprising. According to Bill Fontana, a veteran of many foreign assignments for Citibank and now vice president of NFTC, "When I was involved in Turkey, a new local venture offered one of my senior people double his base salary, or $100,000 U.S. currency deposited in a Swiss bank account." Although the bidding war for talented host-country nationals is increasing salaries, U.S. companies can take some steps to alleviate escalating local payrolls. These companies should not allow employees to bid one employer's salary offer against another; make sure that the total compensation package, beyond the salary is competitive; and don't make it a common practice to pirate employees from competitors. According to Fontana, "When Western companies pirate people away at double or triple their salary, we inflate salary scales."[54]

SUMMARY

1. **Describe the various forms of compensation.**

   Compensation is the total of all rewards provided employees in return for their services. Direct financial compensation consists of the pay a person receives in the form of wages, salaries, bonuses, and commissions. Indirect financial compensation (benefits) includes all financial rewards that are not included in direct compensation. Nonfinancial compensation consists of the satisfaction a person receives from the job itself or from the psychological and/or physical environment in which the person works.

2. **Explain the concept of compensation equity.**

   Equity involves workers' perceptions that they are being treated fairly. Compensation must be fair to all parties concerned and be perceived as fair. External equity exists when a firm's employees are paid comparably to workers who perform similar jobs in other firms. Internal equity exists when employees are paid according to the relative value of their jobs within an organization. Employee equity exists when individuals performing similar jobs for the same firm are paid according to factors unique to the employee, such as performance level or seniority. Team equity is achieved when more productive teams are rewarded more than less productive teams.

3. **Identify the determinants of financial compensation.**

   The organization, the labor market, the job, and the employee all have an impact on job pricing and the ultimate determination of an individual's financial compensation.

4. *Identify the organizational factors that should be considered determinants of financial compensation.*

Organizational factors that should be considered include compensation policies, organizational politics, and ability to pay.

5. *Describe factors that should be considered when the labor market is a determinant of financial compensation.*

Large organizations routinely conduct compensation surveys to determine prevailing pay rates within labor markets. Cost-of-living increases should be considered if a person is to maintain a previous level of real wages. When a union uses comparable pay as a standard for making compensation demands, the employer must obtain accurate labor market data. Consumers may also be interested in compensation decisions. The economy's health exerts a major impact on pay decisions. The amount of compensation a person receives can also be affected by certain federal and state legislation.

6. *Describe how government legislation affects compensation.*

The Davis-Bacon Act of 1931 requires federal construction contractors with projects valued in excess of $2,000 to pay at least the prevailing wages in the area. The Walsh-Healy Act of 1936 requires companies with federal supply contracts exceeding $10,000 to pay prevailing wages. The act also requires one-and-a-half times the regular pay rate for hours over eight per day or 40 per week. The Fair Labor Standards Act of 1938 establishes a minimum wage, requires overtime pay, mandates record keeping, and provides standards for child labor. The Equal Pay Act of 1963 prohibits discrimination in pay on the basis of gender.

7. *Define job evaluation.*

Job evaluation is the part of a compensation system in which a firm determines the relative value of one job compared with another.

8. *Explain the various forms of job evaluation.*

In the ranking method, raters examine the description of each job being evaluated and arrange the jobs in order according to their value to the company. A job evaluation method by which a number of classes or grades are defined to describe a group of jobs is the classification method. The factor comparison method of job evaluation method involves these steps: (1) raters need not keep the entire job in mind as they evaluate; (2) raters make decisions on separate aspects, or factors, of the job; and (3) the method assumes the existence of five universal job factors: mental requirements; skills; physical requirements; responsibilities; and working conditions. The point method is a job evaluation system in which numerical values are assigned to specific job components; summing these values provides a quantitative assessment of a job's relative worth.

9. *Describe the Hay Guide Chart-Profile Method of job evaluation.*

The Hay Guide Chart-Profile Method is a highly refined version of the point method that uses the factors of know-how, problem solving, accountability, and additional compensable elements.

10. *Explain pay for performance.*

Merit pay is a pay increase given to employees based on their level of performance as indicated in their performance appraisal. The bonus is a one-time award that is not added to employees' base pay. Skill-based pay compensates employees on the basis of job-related skills and knowledge they possess, not for their job titles. Competency-based pay rewards employees for their demonstrated expertise.

11. *Identify factors related to the employee that are essential in determining pay and employee equity.*

The factors include pay for performance, seniority, experience, membership in the organization, potential, political influence, and luck.

12. *Define job pricing.*

Placing a dollar value on the worth of a job is referred to as job pricing.

13. *Describe factors to be considered in job pricing.*

A pay grade is the grouping of similar jobs together to simplify the job-pricing process. A wage curve (or pay curve) is the fitting of plotted points to create a smooth progression between pay grades. A pay range includes a minimum and maximum pay rate with enough variance between the two to allow some significant pay difference. Broadbanding is a technique that collapses many pay grades (salary grades) into a few wide bands in order to improve organizational effectiveness. Pay ranges are not appropriate for some workplace conditions. When single rates are used, everyone in the same job receives the same base pay, regardless of seniority or productivity. When pay ranges have been determined and jobs assigned to pay grades, it may become obvious that some jobs are overpaid and others underpaid. Underpaid jobs normally are brought to the minimum of the pay range as soon as possible.

14. *Explain the concepts of flextime, the compressed workweek, job sharing, flexible compensation, telecommuting, part-time work, and modified retirement.*

Flextime is the practice of permitting employees to choose their own working hours, with certain limitations. The compressed workweek is any arrangement of work hours that permits employees to fulfill their work obligation in fewer days than the typical five-day workweek. Job sharing is an approach to work that is attractive to people who want to work fewer than 40 hours per week. Flexible compensation plans permit employees to choose from among many alternatives in deciding how their financial compensation will be allocated. Telecommuting is a work arrangement that allows employees to remain at home, or otherwise away from the office, and perform their work over telephone lines tied to a computer. Use of part-time workers permits both employment and family needs to be addressed. Modified retirement is an option allowing older employees to work fewer regular hours for a certain period of time preceding retirement.

QUESTIONS FOR REVIEW

1. Define each of the following terms:
   a. *Compensation*
   b. *Direct financial compensation*
   c. *Indirect financial compensation*
   d. *Nonfinancial compensation*

2. Distinguish among external equity, internal equity, employee equity, and team equity.

3. What are the primary determinants of individual financial compensation? Briefly describe each.

4. What organizational factors should be considered as determinants of financial compensation?

5. What factors should be considered when the labor market is a determinant of financial compensation?

6. How has government legislation affected compensation?

7. What factors should be considered when the job is a determinant of financial compensation?

8. Give the primary purpose of job evaluation.

9. Distinguish between the following job evaluation methods: ranking, classification, factor comparison, and point.

10. Describe the Hay Guide Chart-Profile Method of job evaluation.

11. Define each of the following:
    a. merit pay
    b. bonus
    c. skill-based pay
    d. competency-based pay

12. Describe the various factors relating to the employee that determine pay and benefits.

13. What is the purpose of job pricing? Discuss briefly.

14. State the basic procedure for determining pay grades.

15. What is the purpose for establishing pay ranges?

16. Define broadbanding.

17. What are some means that organizations have used to achieve workplace flexibility?

DEVELOPING HRM SKILLS

AN EXPERIENTIAL EXERCISE

In the future, one of the key issues concerning pay may be comparable worth. If comparable worth should become federal law, organizations will have to base salaries and wages on job evaluation scores. Salaries and wages will be determined by the requirements of the job itself—skills required, knowledge required, effort required, working conditions, and responsibilities—rather than the workings of the labor market. Then, equal pay for different jobs of the same value will have to be determined, not by looking at the *going rate* in the marketplace but rather at the job's difficulty, its importance, and the training required to perform it properly. This exercise has been developed to impart an understanding and appreciation of the concept of comparable worth.

Take It to the Net

We invite you to visit the Mondy home page on the Prentice Hall Web site at:

http://www.prenhall.com/mondy

for updated information, Web-based exercises, and links to other HR-related sites.

HRM SIMULATION

The wage rates for your organization are somewhat below the average for the local community. In this simulation, you will be making decisions for five levels of employees. Although decisions concerning the level of wages and benefits are not traditionally the sole responsibility of the human resource manager, the CEO has given your team the responsibility for making compensation decisions, within certain constraints.

Incident G in the *Simulation Players Manual* involves compensation plans. Your team has been concerned for quite some time about the turnover rate in your organization. The rate has improved somewhat, but your team believes the cost of turnover is too high, especially for experienced employees. What type of compensation plan will your team recommend?

HRM INCIDENT

1

It's Just Not Fair!

During a Saturday afternoon golf game with his friend Randy Dean, Harry Neil discovered that his department had hired a recent university grad as a systems analyst—at a starting salary almost as high as Harry's. Although Harry was good-natured, he was bewildered and upset. It had taken him five years to become a senior systems analyst and attain his current salary level at Trimark Data Systems. He had been generally pleased with the company and thoroughly enjoyed his job.

The following Monday morning, Harry confronted Dave Edwards, the human resource director, and asked if what he had heard was true. Dave apologetically admitted that it was and attempted to explain the company's situation: "Harry, the market for systems analysts is very tight, and for the company to attract qualified prospects, we have to offer a premium starting salary. We desperately needed another analyst, and this was the only way we could get one."

Harry asked Dave if his salary would be adjusted accordingly. Dave answered, "Your salary will be reevaluated at the regular time. You're doing a great job, though, and I'm sure the boss will recommend a raise." Harry thanked Dave for his time but left the office shaking his head and wondering about his future.

Questions

1. Do you think Dave's explanation was satisfactory? Discuss.
2. What action do you believe the company should have taken with regard to Harry?

HRM INCIDENT

2

Flextime

Kathy Collier is a supervisor of a government office in Washington, D.C. Morale in her office has been quite low recently. The workers have gone back to an 8:00 A.M. to 4:30 P.M. work schedule after having been on flextime for nearly two years.

When the directive came down allowing Kathy to place her office on flextime, she spelled out the rules carefully to her people. Each person was to work during the core period from 10:00 A.M. to 2:30 P.M.; however, they could work the rest of the eight-hour day at any time between 6:00 A.M. and 6:00 P.M. Kathy felt her workers were honest and well motivated, so she did not bother to set up any system of control.

Everything went along well for a long time. Morale improved, and all the work seemed to get done. In November, however, an auditor from the General Accounting Office investigated and found that Kathy's workers were averaging seven hours a day. Two employees had been working only during the core period for more than two months. When Kathy's department manager reviewed the auditor's report, Kathy was told to return the office to regular working hours. Kathy was upset and disappointed with her people. She had trusted them and felt they had let her down.

Questions

1. What type of controls should Kathy have used to prevent the problem? Explain your answer.
2. Should Kathy be disappointed with her people? Why or why not?

Notes

1. Vicki Fuehrer, "Total Reward Strategy: A Prescription for Organizational Survival," *Compensation & Benefits Review* 26 (January/February 1994): 45.
2. Steven E. Gross, *Compensation for Teams* (New York: American Management Association, 1995): 3.
3. Nina Gupta and G. Douglas Jenkins, Jr., "The Politics of Pay," *Compensation & Benefits Review* 28 (March/April 1996): 23–30.
4. John H. Davis, "The Future of Salary Surveys When Jobs Disappear," *Compensation & Benefits Review* 29 (January/February 1997): 18–26.
5. Robert E. Sibson, *Compensation*, 5th ed. (New York: American Management Association, 1990): 105.
6. Edward G. Vogeley and Louise J. Schaeffer, "Link Employee Pay to Competencies and Objectives," *HRMagazine* 40 (October 1995): 75.

7. Donald G. McDermott, "Case Studies: Gathering Information for the New Age of Compensation," *Compensation & Benefits Review* 29 (March/April 1997): 57–63.

8. Joseph J. Martocchio, *Strategic Compensation* (Upper Saddle River, NJ: Prentice Hall, 1998): 202–203.

9. The Small Business Protection Act of 1996, an amendment to the FLSA, raised the minimum wage to $5.15 effective September 1, 1997.

10. Fay Hansen, "FLSA Compliance and Enforcement," *Compensation & Benefits Review* 28 (July/August 1996): 8–13.

11. Larry Reynolds, "Business Calls for an Update of the FLSA," *HR Focus* 73 (May 1996): 8.

12. Robert J. Nobile, "How Discrimination Laws Affect Compensation," *Compensation & Benefits Review* 28 (July/August 1996): 38–42.

13. Sibson, *Compensation*, 104–105.

14. George T. Milkovich and Jerry M. Newman, Compensation, 5th ed. (Chicago, IL: Richard D. Irwin, 1996): 134.

15. William J. Liccione, "Evaluate the Strategic Value of Jobs," *HR Focus* 72 (April 1995): 10.

16. Martocchio, *Strategic Compensation*.

17. Clifford M. Koen, Jr., and Stephen M. Crow, "HR Know-How: Technical and Managerial Skills," *HR Focus* 72 (November 1995): 13–15.

18. Marlene L. Morgenstern, "Currents in Compensation and Benefits," *Compensation & Benefits Review* 28 (May/June 1996): 7.

19. Joanne M. Sammer, "Merit Pay Remains One Step Ahead of Inflation," *Compensation & Benefits Review* 28 (November/December 1996): 14–17.

20. Carrie Mason-Draffen, "Companies Find New Ways to Pay," *Newsday* (January 5, 1997): F8.

21. R. Bradley Hill, "The Advantages of a Two-Component Approach to Compensation," *Personnel Journal* 72 (May 1993): 154–161.

22. Mary S. Case, "Case Study: How Owens Corning Uses Cash-Equivalent Benefits to Tie Compensation to Performance," *Compensation & Benefits Review* 28 (May/June 1996): 69–74.

23. Marlene L. Morgenstern, "Currents in Compensation and Benefits," *Compensation & Benefits Review* 28 (May/June 1996): 7.

24. John A. Parnell, "Five Reasons Why Pay Must Be Based on Performance," *Supervision* 52 (February 1991): 7.

25. John L. Morris, "Lessons Learned in Skill-Based Pay," *HRMagazine* 41 (June 1996): 137.

26. Bradford A. Johnson and Harry H. Ray, "Employee-Developed Pay System Increases Productivity," *Personnel Journal* 72 (November 1993): 112–118.

27. Shari Caudron, "Master the Compensation Maze," *Personnel Journal* 72 (June 1993): 64G–64I.

28. Steven E. Gross, *Compensation for Teams* (New York: American Management Association) 1995: 47.

29. Steven E. Gross, "When Jobs Become Team Roles, What Do You Pay For?" *Compensation & Benefits Review* 29 (January/February 1997): 48–51.

30. Kenan S. Abosch, "The Promise of Broadbanding," *Compensation & Benefits Review* 27 (January/February 1995): 54–58.

31. Ibid., 55–56.

32. Susan Haslett, "Broadbanding: A Strategic Tool for Organizational Change," *Compensation & Benefits Review* 27 (November/December 1995): 40–46.

33. Gross, *Compensation for Teams*.

34. Adapted from Craig J. Cantoni, "Learn to Manage Pay and Performance Like an Entrepreneur," *Compensation & Benefits Review* 29 (January/February 1997): 52–58.

35. Howard Risher, "The End of Jobs: Planning and Managing Rewards in the New Work Paradigm," *Compensation & Benefits Review* 29 (January/February 1997): 13–17.

36. Martocchio, *Strategic Compensation*.

37. Karen Edelman, "Workplace Flexibility Boosts Profits," *Across the Board* 30 (October 1996): 56–57.

38. Marcia Brumit Kropf, "From Policy to Practice," *HRMagazine* 41 (April 1996): 88.

39. Sandra Sullivan and Robert Lussier, "Flesible Work Arrangements as a Management Tool," *Supervision* 56 (August 1995): 16.

40. Larry Reynolds, "Business Calls for an Update of the FLSA," *HR Focus* 73 (May 1996): 8.

41. Fay Hansen, "Introduction: Experts Debate the Future of the FLSA and the NLRA," *Compensation & Benefits Review* 28 (July/August 1996): 6.

42. Elizabeth Sheley, "Job Sharing Offers Unique Challenges," *HRMagazine* 41 (January 1996): 46.

43. Martocchio, *Strategic Compensation*.

44. Ibid., 299.

45. Linda Micco, "Telecommuting Increase Found," *HR News* 16 (August 1997): 23.

46. Maureen Minehan, "Consider All Possibilities for Telecommuters," *HRMagazine* 41 (November 1996): 160.

47. Mary Molina Fitzer, "Managing from Afar: Performance and Rewards in a Telecommuting Environment," *Compensation & Benefits Review* 29 (January/February 1997): 65–73.

48. Linda Bennett, "The CBR Advisory Board Comments On: Compensation Fads, Custom Pay Plans, and Team Play," *Compensation & Benefits Review* 28 (March/April 1996): 58–65.

49. Ibid., 70–71.

50. Michael A. Verespej, "The Anytime, Anyplace Workplace," *Industry Week* 243 (July 1994): 37–38.

51. Wayne F. Cascio and Manuel G. Serapio, Jr., "HR Systems In an International Alliance: The Undoing of a Done Deal?" *Organizational Dynamics* 19 (Winter 1991): 65.

52. Daniel B. Moskowitz, "How to Cut It Overseas," *International Business* 5 (October 1992): 76–78.

53. Donald J. McNerney, "Global Staffing: Some Common Problems—and Solutions," *HR Focus* 72 (June 1996): 1–4.

54. Ibid.

12
Benefits and Other Compensation Issues

CHAPTER OBJECTIVES

1. Define *benefits.*
2. Describe legally required benefits.
3. Identify the basic categories of voluntary benefits.
4. Explain premium pay.
5. Describe the Consolidated Omnibus Budget Reconciliation Act (COBRA), the Health Insurance Portability and Accountability Act, the Employee Retirement Income Security Act (ERISA), and the Older Workers Benefit Protection Act (OWBPA).
6. Explain the various incentive compensation plans.
7. Describe various companywide incentive plans.
8. Describe how compensation for executives is determined.
9. Identify the elements of executive compensation.
10. Explain how compensation for professionals is determined.
11. Describe how compensation for sales representatives is determined.
12. Explain when severance pay is used.
13. Describe the concepts of comparable worth, pay secrecy, and pay compression.

ohn Hicks, a college dropout, is a senior credit clerk at Ajax Manufacturing Company. A bright young man, John has been with Ajax for four years. He has received excellent performance ratings in each of the several positions he has held with the firm. However, during his last appraisal interview, John's supervisor implied that promotion to a higher level job would require additional formal education. Because John appeared to be receptive to the idea, his supervisor suggested that he check with human resources to learn the details of Ajax's educational assistance policy. When John checked the specifics of the educational assistance program it was excellent, covering 90 percent of tuition and the cost of required textbooks. Ajax's educational program and their other benefit programs were top notch, which is very important to John and his family.

Arnold Anderson, Bob Minnis, and Mason Kearby are all employed as shipping clerks for Mainstreet Furniture Company. Arnold and Bob are ener-getic young people who consistently work hard each day. Mason is a "good ole boy" who spends most of his time flipping quarters with dock workers and talking with anyone who will listen. They all earn about $10.50 per hour, plus benefits. Yesterday, work was piling up in the department, and Arnold and Bob were working furiously to keep up. Mason was nowhere to be found. "Arnold," Bob said dis-gustedly, "the pay here just isn't fair. We do twice as much work as Mason, yet he makes as much as we do."

"I know," Arnold acknowledged, "but we all punch in and out at the same time. Besides, I under-stand that management is looking into an incentive plan that will have us sign each shipment we are re-sponsible for bringing to the loading area. We'll be given a bonus, over our hourly wage, for the number of shipments we handle above an established norm."

"Good," said Bob. "Now they'll find out how lit-tle Mason does."

*A*lthough these anecdotes may seem to have little in common, each relates to the broad area of compensation. John is investigating the possibility of continuing his education through his company's educational assistance program. Arnold and Bob are angry because a less productive worker makes as much money as they do.

We begin the chapter with a discussion of benefits, both mandated and voluntary, other legislation related to benefits, and the proper communication of information about benefit packages. Next, we present various types of incentive compensation systems, followed by a discussion of special pay considerations provided to executives, professionals, and sales representatives. Then we describe severance pay and other compensation issues such as comparable worth, pay secrecy, and pay compression.

HR Web Wisdom

http://www.prenhall.com/mondy

BENEFITS PLUS
Various benefit issues are addressed from *A* to *Z*.

Benefits (Indirect Financial Compensation)

Benefits: All financial rewards that generally are not paid directly to an employee.

Most organizations recognize their responsibility to their employees and provide them with insurance and other programs for their health, safety, security, and general welfare (see Figure 12-1). These programs are called **benefits** and include all financial rewards that generally are not paid directly to the employee. Benefits cost the firm money, but employees usually receive them indirectly. For example, an organization may spend $3,200 a year as a contribution to the health insurance premiums for each nonexempt employee. The employee does not receive money but does obtain the benefit of health insurance coverage. This type of compensation has two distinct advantages: (1) it is generally nontaxable to the employee, and (2) the cost of some benefits may be much less for large groups of employees than for individuals.

Generally speaking, benefits are provided to employees because of their membership in the organization. John and his family received benefits as did all other Ajax employees and their families. Benefits are typically not related to employee productivity; therefore, they do not serve as motivation for improved performance. Some benefits are required by law and others are provided at the organization's discretion. Arnold, Bob, and Mason of Mainstreet Furniture Company all receive equal pay even though Arnold and Bob work much harder and contribute much more than Mason. An equitable and effective incentive plan should help the firm attract and retain qualified employees.

The cost of benefits is high and is growing rapidly. In a recent year, employers spent on average $3,079 to $4,784 for each full-time employee for legally required benefits. The average cost for discretionary benefits was $11,506 per employee.[1] A typical worker who earns $30,000 per year will receive approximately $11,700 (almost 40 percent) indirectly in the form

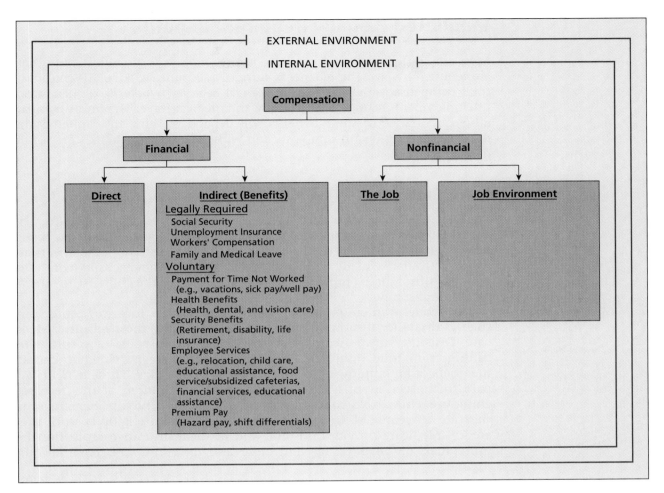

EXTERNAL ENVIRONMENT

INTERNAL ENVIRONMENT

Compensation

Financial

Nonfinancial

Direct

Indirect (Benefits)

Legally Required
  Social Security
  Unemployment Insurance
  Workers' Compensation
  Family and Medical Leave

Voluntary
  Payment for Time Not Worked
    (e.g., vacations, sick pay/well pay)
  Health Benefits
    (Health, dental, and vision care)
  Security Benefits
    (Retirement, disability, life
    insurance)
  Employee Services
    (e.g., relocation, child care,
    educational assistance, food
    service/subsidized cafeterias,
    financial services, educational
    assistance)
  Premium Pay
    (Hazard pay, shift differentials)

The Job

Job Environment

Figure 12-1
Benefits in a Total Compensation Program

of benefits. The magnitude of this expenditure no doubt accounts for the declining use of the term *fringe benefits*. In fact, the benefits that employees receive today are significantly different from those of just a few years ago. As benefit dollars compete with financial compensation, employers continue to move away from paternalistic benefits programs. They shift more responsibilities to employees as with 401(k) retirement plans discussed later.[2]

HR Web Wisdom

http://www.prenhall.com/mondy
SHRM—HR LINKS
Various compensation and benefit issues including compensation and retirement planning are addressed.

Mandated (Legally Required) Benefits

Most employee benefits are provided at the employer's discretion, but others are required by law. These benefits currently account for about 10 percent of total compensation costs. They are Social Security, workers' compensation, unemployment insurance, and family and medical leave. The future comparative importance of these benefits will depend on how the United States deals with rising health-care costs and with long-term custodial care for elderly citizens.

SOCIAL SECURITY

The Social Security Act of 1935 created a system of retirement benefits. The act established a federal payroll tax to fund unemployment and retirement benefits. It also established the Social Security Administration. Employers are required to share equally with employees the cost of old age, survivors', and disability insurance. Employers are required to pay the full cost of unemployment insurance.

Subsequent amendments to the act added other forms of protection, such as disability insurance, survivors' benefits, and, most recently, Medicare. Disability insurance protects employees against loss of earnings resulting from total disability. Survivors' benefits are provided to certain members of an employee's family when he or she dies. These benefits are paid to the widow or widower and unmarried children of the deceased employee. Unmarried children may be eligible for survivors' benefits until they are 18 years old. In some cases, students retain eligibility until they are 19. Medicare provides hospital and medical insurance protection for individuals 65 years of age and older and for those who have become disabled.

Employees must pay a portion of the cost of Social Security coverage; the employer makes an equal contribution. It is the employer's part that is considered a benefit. The 1997 tax rate was 6.2 percent for cash benefits and 1.45 percent for Medicare. The total tax rate of 7.65 percent applied to a maximum taxable wage of $65,400. The rate for Medicare, 1.45 percent, applied to earnings exceeding $65,400. Today, approximately 95 percent of the workers in this country pay into and may draw Social Security benefits.

The normal retirement age under Social Security will be increased after the turn of the century. Beginning with employees who reach age 62 in the year 2000, the retirement age will be increased gradually until 2009, when it reaches age 66. After stabilizing at this age for a period of time, it will again increase in 2027 when it reaches age 67. These changes will not affect Medicare, with full eligibility under this program holding at age 65.

UNEMPLOYMENT COMPENSATION

An individual laid off by an organization covered by the Social Security Act may receive unemployment compensation for up to 26 weeks. Although the federal government provides certain guidelines, unemployment compensation programs are administered by the states, and the benefits vary by state. A payroll tax paid solely by employers funds the unemployment compensation program. The tax burden may approximate 6.2 percent of the first $7,000 earned by each employee. However, each company's actual rate is dependent on its experience with unemployment.

Workers' Compensation

Workers' compensation benefits provide a degree of financial protection for employees who incur expenses resulting from job-related accidents or illnesses. As with unemployment compensation, the various states administer individual programs, which are subject to federal regulations. Employers pay the entire cost of workers' compensation insurance and their premium expense is directly tied to their past experience with job-related accidents and illnesses. This situation should encourage employers to pursue health and safety programs actively; these topics are discussed in chapter 13.

Family and Medical Leave Act of 1993 (FMLA)

The Family and Medical Leave Act applies to private employers with 50 or more employees and to all governmental employers regardless of the number of employees. The act provides for up to 12 work weeks of unpaid leave per year for absences due to the employee's own serious health condition or the need to care for a newborn or newly adopted child or a seriously ill child, parent, or spouse.[3] FMLA rights apply only to employees who have worked for the employer for at least 12 months and who have at least 1,250 hours of service during the 12 months immediately preceding the start of the leave. Generally, the employee must be returned to the same or equivalent position at the end of the leave and health insurance coverage must be maintained during the leave.

The FMLA prohibits employers from taking any adverse or discriminatory action against employees who exercise their rights under the FMLA. Absence on FMLA leave cannot be used as a negative factor in any employment action, including performance appraisals, promotions, or bonuses unrelated to individual production.[4]

The Department of Labor recently issued a report that suggests the cost and inconvenience of the FMLA have been insignificant. However, a study by Business and Legal Reports, Inc., revealed significant problems for businesses associated with complying with the law. Nearly half the employers responding to the survey reported incurring additional administrative expenses as a result of FMLA compliance. A few firms even indicated the need to hire additional personnel to meet the increased administrative load. In addition, FMLA reportedly makes maintaining attendance standards more difficult for employers. One-fourth of the respondents to the survey reported increased absenteeism as a serious problem; for example, employees with poor attendance habits have learned that the FMLA can shield them from discipline. According to these sources, this behavior frustrates and demoralizes the rest of the workforce.[5]

Voluntary Benefits

Organizations voluntarily provide numerous benefits. These benefits may be categorized as (1) payment for time not worked, (2) health benefits, (3) security benefits, (4) employee services, and (5) premium pay. Generally, such benefits are not legally required. They may result from unilateral management decisions in some firms and from union-management negotiations in others.

PAYMENT FOR TIME NOT WORKED

In providing payment for time not worked, employers recognize that employees need time away from the job for many purposes. Included in this category are paid vacations, payment for holidays not worked, sick pay/well pay, jury duty, national guard or other military reserve duty, voting time, and bereavement time. It is also common for organizations to provide payments to assist employees in performing civic duties.

Some payments for time not worked are provided for time off routinely taken during work hours. Common benefits in this area include rest periods, coffee breaks, lunch periods, cleanup time, and travel time.

Paid Vacations.

Payment for time not worked serves important compensation goals. For instance, paid vacations provide workers with an opportunity to rest, become rejuvenated, and—one hopes—become more productive. Vacations may also encourage employees to remain with the firm. Paid vacation time typically increases with seniority. For example, employees with six months' service might receive one week of vacation; employees with one year of service, two weeks; 10 years might earn three weeks of vacation; and 15 years could earn four weeks.

Vacation time may also vary with organizational rank. For instance, a senior-level executive, regardless of time with the firm, may be given a month of vacation. With an annual salary of $120,000, this manager would receive a benefit of approximately $10,000 each year while not working. A junior accountant earning $36,000 a year might receive two weeks of vacation time worth about $1,500.

Sick Pay/Well Pay.

Each year many firms allocate a certain number of days of sick leave to each employee; workers can use these days when they are ill. Employees who are too sick to report to work continue to receive their pay up to the maximum number of days accumulated. As with vacation pay, the number of *sick leave* days often depends on seniority.

Some sick leave programs have been severely criticized. At times they have been abused by individuals calling in sick when all they really wanted was additional paid vacation. To counter the negative aspects of sick pay, *Forbes* magazine implemented a *well pay* program. It rewarded those employees who stayed healthy and did not file medical claims by paying them the difference between $500 and their medical claims, then doubling the amount. If an employee submitted no claims in a given year, he or she would receive $1,000 ($500 × 2). By rewarding employees for good health, *Forbes* cut its major medical and dental claims by over 30 percent.[6]

HEALTH BENEFITS

Health benefits are often included as part of an employee's indirect financial compensation. Specific areas include health care, dental care, and vision care.

Health maintenance organizations (HMOs): Insurance programs provided by companies that cover all services for a fixed fee with control being exercised over which doctors and health facilities may be used.

Preferred provider organizations (PPOs): A flexible managed care system in which incentives are provided to members to use services within the system; out-of-network providers may be utilized at greater cost.

Point-of-service (POS): A managed care option that permits a member to select a healthcare provider within the network, or, for a lower level of benefits, choose one outside the network.

Exclusive provider organization (EPO): A managed care option that offers a smaller preferred provider network and usually provides few, if any, benefits when an out-of-network provider is used.

Capitation: An approach to health care in which providers negotiate a rate for health care for a covered life over a period of time.

Health Care. Benefits for health care represent the most expensive cost in the area of indirect financial compensation. A number of factors have combined to create this situation: an aging population, a growing demand for medical care, increasingly expensive medical technology, a lack of price controls, and inefficient administrative processes. Reversal of a long-term trend in rising health care costs has been attributed to a surge in the use of managed care systems.[7] These networks are made up of doctors and hospitals who agree to accept negotiated prices for treating patients. Employees are given financial incentives to use the facilities within the network. Today, a majority of all insured employees in the United States participate in some kind of managed care plan, and the growth of these plans continues.

In addition to *self-insurance* (in which firms provide benefits directly from their own assets), and *traditional commercial insurers* (which supply indemnity insurance covering bills from any health care provider), employers may utilize one of several managed care options. **Health maintenance organizations (HMOs)** cover all services for a fixed fee. However, control is exercised over which doctors and health facilities a member may use. **Preferred provider organizations (PPOs)** are a more flexible managed care system. Incentives are provided to members to use services within the system, but out-of-network providers may be utilized at greater cost. An SHRM benefits survey indicated that 74 percent of the respondents use PPOs and 62 percent have HMOs.[8] **Point-of-service (POS)** permits a member to select a provider within the network or, for a lower level of benefits, go outside the network. **Exclusive provider organizations (EPO)** offer a smaller PPO provider network and usually provide little, if any, benefits when an out-of-network provider is used. Each of these forms of managed care systems appears to be losing its uniqueness. For example, HMOs are developing more flexible products and many offer POS and PPOs. Large independent PPO companies are providing programs that resemble HMOs. Regardless of the precise form, managed care systems are achieving effective medical cost control. According to a recent national survey by KPMG Peat Marwick, health insurance premiums for HMOs advanced only 0.5 percent in 1996.[9]

Capitation, typically the reimbursement method used by primary care physicians,[10] is an approach to health care in which providers negotiate a rate for health care for a covered life over a period of time. It presumes that doctors have an incentive to keep patients healthy and avoid costly procedures when they are paid for each patient rather than for each service. This approach, long the domain of HMOs, is moving into other managed care systems. Capitation appears to control costs, reduce paperwork, and require providers to operate within a budget. It also shifts some of the financial risk to the doctors. If providers' costs exceed the cost of providing care, doctors suffer a loss. This system shifts the incentive for physicians away from providing care and toward limiting care. This change has prompted some critics to fear that the plans compromise the quality of health care.

In addition to doctor office visits, health insurance typically includes hospital room and board costs, service charges, and surgical fees. Coverage for these benefits may be paid in part or totally by the employer. Medical flexible spending accounts and prescription programs are also frequently provided benefits.

Many plans provide for major medical benefits to cover extraordinary expenses that result from long-term or serious health problems. The use of *deductibles* is a common feature of medical benefits. For example, the employee may have to pay the first $300 of medical bills before the insurance takes over payment. To control health-care costs, a number of firms have increased the amount of deductibles and/or reduced the scope of insurance coverage.

Utilization review: A process that scrutinizes medical diagnoses, hospitalization, surgery, and other medical treatment and care prescribed by doctors.

Health insurance premiums alone amount to a sizable portion of an employer's total payroll. In a further attempt to curb medical costs, many firms use some type of utilization review service. **Utilization review** is a process that scrutinizes medical diagnoses, hospitalization, surgery, and other medical treatment and care prescribed by doctors. The reviewer, often a registered nurse, explores alternatives to the treatment provided, such as outpatient treatment or admission on the day of surgery. The objective of this process is, of course, to hold down costs.

With the high cost of medical care, an individual without health care insurance is quite vulnerable. The Consolidated Omnibus Budget Reconciliation Act of 1985 (COBRA) was enacted to give employees the opportunity to temporarily continue their coverage if they would otherwise lose it because of termination, layoff, or other change in employment status. The act applies to employers with 20 or more employees. Under COBRA, individuals may keep their coverage for themselves as well as for their spouses and dependents for up to 18 months after their employment ceases. Certain qualifying events can extend this coverage for up to 36 months. The individual, however, must pay for this health insurance.

The Health Insurance Portability and Accountability Act of 1996 provides new protections for approximately 25 million Americans who move from one job to another, who are self-employed, or who have preexisting medical conditions. The law focuses on limiting exclusions for preexisting medical conditions, prohibiting discrimination against employees and dependents based on their health status, guaranteeing availability of health insurance to small employers, and guaranteeing renewability of insurance to all employers regardless of size.[11] Among other provisions, the act allows employers with 50 or fewer employees as well as self-employed individuals to establish tax-favored medical savings accounts (MSAs). This portion of the act is limited to a four-year demonstration period.[12]

Dental and Vision Care.
Dental and vision care are popular benefits in the health-care area. The 1997 SHRM Benefits Survey indicated that 91 percent of the respondents' firms provide dental insurance and 54 percent furnish vision insurance.[13] Both types of plans are typically paid for en-

tirely by the employer except for a deductible, which may amount to $25 to $50 per year.

Dental plans may cover, for example, 70 to 100 percent of the cost of preventive procedures (including semiannual examinations) and 50 to 80 percent of restorative procedures (including crowns, bridgework, etc.). Some plans also include orthodontic care. Vision care plans may cover all or part of the cost of eye examinations and glasses.

Other company programs that provide health benefits for employees include employee assistance programs (EAPs), wellness programs, and physical fitness programs. These topics are discussed in the next chapter.

SECURITY BENEFITS

Security benefits include retirement plans, disability insurance, life insurance, and supplemental unemployment benefits. These important benefits are discussed next.

Retirement Plans. Private retirement plans provide income for employees who retire after reaching a certain age or having served the firm for a specific period of time.[14] Pension plans are vitally important to employees because Social Security was not designed to provide complete retirement income. Over the next 30 years, the U.S. population will be dominated by older people who are either retired or approaching retirement. Therefore, retirement financing will become a primary issue for individuals, employers, and governments.

Defined benefit plan: A retirement plan in which an employer agrees to provide a specific level of retirement income that is either a fixed dollar amount or a percentage of earnings.

Retirement plans are generally either defined benefit plans or defined contributory plans. In a **defined benefit plan**, the employer agrees to provide a specific level of retirement income that is either a fixed dollar amount or a percentage of earnings. An employee's seniority or rank in the firm may determine the specific figure. Plans that are considered generous typically provide pensions equivalent to 50 percent to 80 percent of an employee's final earnings. Use of this type of retirement plan is declining. However, almost 50 percent of firms responding to a recent survey indicated that a defined benefit retirement plan was still in use.[15] Even so, the same survey reported that 68 percent of the companies utilized a newer approach—a defined contribution plan.

Defined contribution plan: A retirement plan that requires specific contributions by an employer.

A **defined contribution plan** is a retirement plan that requires specific contributions by an employer to a retirement or savings fund established for the employee. Employees will know in advance how much of their retirement income will be under a defined benefit plan, but the amount of retirement income from a defined contribution plan will depend on the investment success of the pension fund.

401(k) plan: A defined contribution retirement plan in which employees may defer income up to a certain maximum amount.

A **401(k) plan** is a defined contribution plan in which employees may defer income up to a maximum amount allowed. Employers typically match employee contributions 50 cents for each dollar deferred. As 401(k) plans become the primary retirement income design,[16] sponsoring firms are making them more flexible by permitting more frequent transfers between investment accounts. They are also providing more choices in which employees can invest their money. According to a study conducted by the Profit

Sharing/401(k) Council of America, three-fourths of participating firms offered five or more options in 1995, up from 16 percent of the firms only five years earlier. As an indication of their acceptance by employees, almost 90 percent of those who are eligible to participate in 401(k) plans are doing so.[17]

More firms are beginning to provide financial planning for all their employees, not just their top executives. The explosion of 401(k) retirement plans has required 23 million employees to become *investment managers* and they look to their employers for help. Federal law requires employers to give guidance on these plans but forbids their recommending specific investments. Of course, this is just what employees want and need. The role of the employer is then to get financial planners from firms such as Merrill Lynch and Price Waterhouse to provide this advice but also to protect them from lawsuits if workers lose money.[18] This protection is critically important as poor investment decisions could force individuals to delay retirement or require those already retired to go back into the workforce.

TRENDS & INNOVATIONS

EASY 401(K) ACCESS

Compaq Computer Corporation, in conjunction with the Vanguard Group, developed a system using a World Wide Web browser to access 401(k) account information. The customized system runs on 30 computer kiosks at Compaq offices around the country. All 10,300 eligible employees are able to access the intranet from office or home PCs in addition to the kiosks. The system allows employees to dial in to check their balances, take a quiz to determine their risk tolerance, review fund performance, even analyze the impact on their nest egg of changing contributions. An upcoming addition will allow employees to shift between funds or reallocate contributions on-line.

In the first 10 months of operation, Compaq's system has raised its employee participation rate from 78 percent of eligible employees to 82 percent. According to Ron Eller, vice president of compensation and benefits, "We have people accessing it all hours of the day or night."[19]

Employee stock ownership plan (ESOP): A companywide incentive plan in which the company provides its employees with common stock.

An **employee stock ownership plan (ESOP)** is a defined contribution plan in which a firm makes a tax deductible contribution of stock shares or cash to a trust. The trust then allocates the stock to participating employee accounts on the basis of employee earnings. When used as a retirement plan, employees receive income at retirement based on the value of the stock at that time. If the firm's stock performance has fared well, this type of plan will be satisfactory. However, because stock may decline in value as well, the results may be poor. More about employee stock ownership plans is provided later in this chapter.

Profit sharing, if the distribution of funds is deferred until retirement, is another form of defined contribution plan. It is also discussed later in the chapter.

Disability Protection. Workers' compensation protects employees from job-related accidents and illnesses. Some firms, however, provide additional protection that is more comprehensive. A firm's sick leave policy may provide full salary for short-term health problems; when these benefits expire, a short-term disability plan may become operative and provide pay that is equivalent to 50 percent to 100 percent of regular pay.[20] Short-term disability plans may cover periods for up to six months.

When the short-term plan runs out, a firm's long-term plan may become active; such a plan may provide 50 percent to 70 percent of an employee's wages.[21] Almost 60 percent of American businesses provide this type of insurance, and the plans that exist pay for periods from two years to the life of the employee.[22]

Supplemental Unemployment Benefits (SUB). Supplemental unemployment benefits first appeared in auto industry labor agreements in 1955. They are designed to provide additional income for employees receiving unemployment insurance benefits. These plans have spread to many industries and are usually financed by the company. They tend to benefit newer employees, as layoffs are normally determined by seniority. For this reason, employees with considerable seniority are often not enthusiastic about these benefits.

Life Insurance. Group life insurance is a benefit commonly provided to protect the employee's family in the event of his or her death. Although the cost of group life insurance is relatively low, some plans call for the employee to pay part of the premium. Coverage may be a flat amount (for instance, $50,000) or based on the employee's annual earnings. For example, a worker earning $30,000 per year may have $60,000 worth of group life coverage.

EMPLOYEE SERVICES

Organizations offer a variety of benefits that can be termed *employee services.* These benefits encompass a number of areas including relocation benefits, child care, educational assistance, food services/subsidized cafeterias, and financial services.

Relocation. Almost 60 percent of firms included in the SHRM benefits survey provide *relocation benefits.*[23] In addition to paying for moving an employee's personal goods, some firms provide assistance in buying a new home and in selling the previously occupied home. Technology has made work more efficient for relocation professionals. They can now automatically register their shipments with a van line, track the shipment status, check on delivery dates, and more through the use of on-line computer programs.[24]

In addition to providing assistance with the move itself, about 50 percent of corporations currently provide some type of *spouse employment assistance.*[25] Relocation benefits are popular because nearly one in five Americans moves each year.[26] This benefit may be necessary for firms to remain competitive in enticing individuals possessing critical skills.

Some firms such as Pacific Gas & Electric provide an on-site child care center.

Child Care.
Another benefit offered by some firms is subsidized *child care*. Here, the firm may provide an on-site child care center, support an off-site center, or subsidize the costs of child care. This benefit is an effective recruitment aid and helps to reduce absenteeism. The need for such programs is emphasized by the reality that about 70 percent of working parents missed at least one day of work in the past year because of child-related problems, and U.S. businesses lose $3 billion a year because of child care-related absences.[27]

Educational Assistance.
According to a recent benefits survey, 81 percent of businesses have *educational* benefits that reimburse employees for college tuition and books.[28] NYNEX, the $13 billion telecommunications company, has a plan that is hard to top. The firm pays employees to attend college one work day a week with a guaranteed raise on graduation. In addition to paying for tuition and books, NYNEX gives each participant a laptop computer. This program provides employees with enhanced telecommunications and communications skills that will provide them with job security. The firm believes its investment will strengthen its workforce and provide a bottom line payoff.[29]

Food Services/Subsidized Cafeterias.
There is generally no such thing as a free lunch. However, the exception to this rule is provided by firms that provide *food services* or *subsidized cafeterias*. What they hope to gain in return is increased productivity, less wasted time, increased employee morale, and, in some instances, a healthier workforce. Most firms that offer free or subsidized lunches feel that they get a high payback in terms of employee relations. Hewitt Associates, Northwestern Mutual Life, and Alliance Capital Management Corporation are among the firms that provide this benefit. Keeping the lunch hour to a minimum is an obvious advantage, but employees also appreciate the opportunity to meet and mix with people they work with. Making one entree a *heart healthy* choice and listing the calories, fat, cholesterol, and sodium content in food is also appealing to a large number of employees. Healthy meals may also result in a payoff. At Alliance, for ex-

ample, lunch costs $5 to $6 per employee per day. However, the firm has seen about a 20 percent reduction in medical claims, and its insurance premiums have not increased since it began the subsidized lunch program.[30]

Financial Services. Various types of financial services are offered by some firms, but one financial benefit that is growing in popularity permits employees to purchase various types of insurance policies through payroll deduction. Using this approach, the employer can provide a benefit at almost no cost and employees can save money by receiving a deeply discounted rate. Firms can offer discounts to employers because the plans usually eliminate the middlemen. Administrative costs are also drastically reduced. For example, the insurance company sends one statement and receives one premium check to the business. Otherwise, these transactions might involve dozens or even hundreds of individual transactions. It is also possible for employers to offer employees discounted policies on automobile or homeowner's insurance. In fact, many other benefits may be offered through payroll deduction plans.[31]

Another unique financial services benefit is provided by Xerox Corporation. This firm offers employees with at least five years of service $2,000 or 2 percent of the purchase price, whichever is less, toward first-time *home purchases*.[32]

PREMIUM PAY

Premium pay: Compensation paid to employees for working long periods of time or working under dangerous or undesirable conditions.

Premium pay is compensation paid to employees for working long periods of time or working under dangerous or undesirable conditions. As mentioned in chapter 11, payment for overtime is required for nonexempt employees who work more than 40 hours in a given week. However, some firms pay overtime for hours worked beyond eight in a given day and pay double time—or even more—for work on Sundays and holidays. Bonuses are also sometimes given for performing at a level above an estimated norm. Arnold Anderson and Bob Minnis are excited about the possibility of a bonus plan to reward them beyond their hourly wage, and beyond the amount paid to Mason Kearby who does very little work.

Hazard pay: Additional pay provided to employees who work under extremely dangerous conditions.

Hazard Pay. Additional pay provided to employees who work under extremely dangerous conditions is called **hazard pay**. A window washer for skyscrapers in New York City might well be given extra compensation because of dangerous working conditions. Military pilots receive extra money in the form of flight pay because of the hazards involved in their work.

Shift differentials: Additional money paid to reward employees for the inconvenience of working undesirable hours.

Shift Differentials. A **shift differential** is paid to employees for the inconvenience of working undesirable hours. This type of pay may be provided on the basis of additional cents per hour. For example, employees who work the second shift (*swing shift*), from 4:00 P.M. until midnight, might receive $0.75 per hour above the base rate for that job. The third shift (*graveyard shift*) often warrants an even greater differential; for example, an extra $0.90 per hour may be paid for the same job. Shift differentials are sometimes based on a percentage of the employee's base rate.

Other Benefit-Related Legislation

The Employee Retirement Income Security Act of 1974 (ERISA) was passed to strengthen existing and future retirement programs. Mismanagement of retirement funds was the primary spur for this legislation. Many employees were entering retirement only to find that the retirement income they anticipated was not available. The intent of the act was to ensure that when employees retire, they receive deserved pensions. The purpose of the act is described here:

> It is hereby declared to be the policy of this Act to protect . . . the interests of participants in employee benefit plans and their beneficiaries . . . by establishing standards of conduct, responsibility and obligations for fiduciaries of employee benefit plans, and by providing for appropriate remedies, sanctions, and ready access to the federal courts.[33]

Note that the word *protect* is used here because the act does not force employers to create employee benefit plans. It does set standards in the areas of participation, vesting of benefits, and funding for existing and new plans. Numerous existing retirement plans have been altered to conform to this legislation.

The Older Workers Benefit Protection Act (OWBPA) is a 1990 amendment to the ADEA and extends its coverage to all employee benefits. The act has an *equal benefit* or *equal cost* principle. For example, assume the firm pays $500 for life insurance for each of two employees, one 25 years of age and the other 40 (covered by ADEA). For the younger employee, $500 will buy $200,000 worth of insurance; for the older employee, it will buy only $50,000. The employer has the option of either spending the same amount of money on each or providing the same level of benefit.[34]

Communicating Information about the Benefits Package

Employee benefits can help a firm recruit and retain a quality workforce. Management depends on an upward flow of information from employees to know when benefit changes are needed. In addition, because employee awareness of benefits is often severely limited, the program information must be communicated downward. Regardless of the technical soundness of a benefits program, a firm simply cannot get its money's worth if its employees do not know what they are receiving. Workers may even become resentful if they are not frequently reminded of the value of the company's benefits.

The Employee Retirement Income Security Act provides still another reason for communicating information about a firm's benefits program. This act requires organizations with a pension or profit-sharing plan to provide employees with specific data at specified times. The act further mandates that the information be presented in an understandable manner.

Naturally, organizations can go beyond what is legally required. A corporation's benefit program that is in tune with the needs of its workers might provide a broad range of employee benefits such as those shown in Figure 12-2.

There seems to be no end to the types of benefits firms offer. This trend accelerates during periods of tight employment as firms develop strategies designed to attract and retain high-quality employees.

Personal Benefits:

Medical Plans: Two options as well as various HMOs are available.

Dental Plans: Two options as well as various Dental Maintenance Alternatives (DMAs) and the MetLife Preferred Dentist Program (PDP) are available.

Work and Personal Life Balancing:

Vacation: 1 to 4 years service—10 days per year
  5 to 9 years service (or age 50–59)—15 days
  10 to 19 years service or age 60+—20 days
  20 years or more—25 days
Holidays: 12 days per year (6 observed nationally; other 6 vary with at least one personal choice).

Life Planning Account: $250 of taxable financial assistance each year, with certain conditions.

Flexible Work Schedules, Telecommuting and Work Week Balancing: (with local management approval).

Capital Accumulation, Stock Purchase, and Retirement:

401(K) Plan: Employees may contribute up to 12 percent of eligible compensation, which is matched 50 percent on the first 6 percent.

Stock Purchase Plan: Employees may contribute up to 10 percent of eligible compensation each pay period for the purchase of company stock (pay 85 percent of average market price per share on date of purchase).

Retirement Plan: Competitive, company-paid retirement benefit plan with vesting after 5 years of continuous service.

Income and Asset Protection: Some of the plans offered include:
Sickness and Accident Income Plans

Long-Term Disability Plan

Group Life Insurance

Travel Accident Insurance

Long-Term Care Insurance

Skills Development:

Tuition Refund: If aligned with business needs and approved.

Educational Leaves of Absence: Under appropriate circumstance and approved by management.

Additional Employee Programs:

Site Offerings: Many sites offer programs including

  Fitness Centers

  Educational Courses

  Award Programs

  Career Planning Centers

Clubs: These clubs organize recreational leagues, company-sponsored trips, and a variety of classes and programs.

Figure 12-2
Corporation's Benefit Program

Incentive Compensation

To survive and prosper in a global economy, firms have placed increased attention on productivity and how to improve it. Although compensation is often determined by how much time an employee spends at work, compensation programs that relate pay to productivity are referred to as **incentive compensation**. The basic purpose of all incentive plans is to improve employee productivity in order to gain a competitive advantage. To do this, the firm must utilize various rewards and focus on the needs of employees as well as the firm's business goals. Productive workers, such as Arnold Anderson and Bob Minnis (mentioned at the beginning of the chapter), probably would prefer to be paid on the basis of their output. In fact, they may not maintain their high performance level for long if they are not paid in this way. Money can serve as an important motivator for those who value it—and many individuals do. However, a clear relationship must exist between performance and pay if money is to serve as an effective motivator.

Incentive compensation: A payment program that relates pay to productivity.

INDIVIDUAL INCENTIVE PLANS

Pay for performance was discussed briefly in the preceding chapter. The incentive plan that Mainstreet Furniture Company may institute will be well received by Arnold Anderson and Bob Minnis, but it may cause problems for Mason Kearby who is a socializer and not much of a worker. A specific form of performance-based pay is an individual incentive plan called **piecework**. Through the years, many forms of incentive pay plans have been used. However, the piecework plan is simplest and most commonly used. In such a plan, employees are paid for each unit they produce. Requirements for the plan include developing output standards for the job and being able to determine the output of a single employee. These requirements would not be feasible for many jobs. In fact, this type of plan is usually found in production work.

Piecework: An incentive pay plan in which employees are paid for each unit produced.

A basic question that should precede the introduction of any incentive plan is this: "What effect will it have on productivity and quality?" Although success can't be guaranteed, results are mostly positive, as indicated by the following account.

Safelite Glass Corporation, the nation's largest installer of automobile glass, implemented a system for determining the exact rate of installations done by each worker as well as a piecework system that would allow a productivity bonus on top of the worker's guaranteed hourly pay rate. The workers performed individual tasks that could be counted and rewarded and the firm had hard numbers of the output both before and after the new system went into effect.

The results of the piecework system:
- Productivity jumped 36 percent.
- The average worker's pay increased from $25,000 a year to $27,000 but the very able workers may make $40,000.
- Absenteeism dropped and paid sick-hours fell by 61 percent.

- Turnover among the most efficient workers decreased.
- While pay for the average worker rose by 10 percent, productivity rose by 20 percent.
- Customer satisfaction increased from a 90 percent rate to 95 percent.[35]

Safelite's production operation lends itself almost perfectly to a piece-work plan. Obviously, many other job types do not. However, Safelite's experience does give credibility to the notion that financial incentives have the potential to motivate performance in a positive way.

TEAM-BASED COMPENSATION PLANS

Team performance consists of individual efforts. Therefore, individual employees should be recognized and rewarded for their contributions. However, if the team is to function effectively, a reward based on the overall team performance should be provided as well.

Nucor, a high-performing steel company, divides its production workers into work groups of 25 to 35 people and pays work group members a bonus based on their group's production over a certain predetermined standard. If they produce 50 percent above the standard, they receive a 50 percent bonus; if they produce 100 percent above the standard, they receive a 100 percent bonus. During the past decade, Nucor's sales grew 850 percent and its profits grew 1,250 percent. When most of the U.S. steel industry was laying off workers, Nucor laid off none.[36]

Team incentives have both advantages and disadvantages. On the positive side, firms find it easier to develop performance standards for groups than for individuals. For one thing, there are fewer standards to determine. Also, the output of a team is more likely to reflect a complete product or service. Another advantage is that employees may be more inclined to assist others and work collaboratively if the reward is based on the team's output.

A potential disadvantage for team incentives relates to exemplary performers. If individuals in this category consistently do more than others in the group, they may become disgruntled and leave. A solution to this situation might be to base part of the employees' compensation on individual performance and part on the overall team's results. Aid Association for Lutherans (AAL), a fraternal benefits society, tries to cover all bases in compensating its insurance service teams. Its plan allows the firm to do the following:[37]

- *Recognize individual accomplishments.* Outstanding individual achievement is recognized through a lump-sum payment once a year. It may be worth as much as 6 percent of the individual's compensation.
- *Reward team productivity.* The entire team is awarded an annual bonus based on productivity, customer satisfaction, and quality of work.
- *Compensate employees for the acquisition of new skills.* A skill-based pay system compensates individuals for each additional skill they acquire in an effort to help the team.
- *Remain competitive with its salary structure.* The company uses market data to ensure that employees are paid a competitive wage.

Before implementing the team structure, AAL was organized on a functional basis, according to type of product. The rationale for moving to teams was the desire to have employees see the whole job, not just a part of it. The company also wanted its employees to learn additional jobs that would help the team as a whole and to boost overall performance. Does this plan work? After five years, productivity increased by 40 percent and surveys indicate that 90 percent of the firm's customers are satisfied with the service provided.

COMPANYWIDE PLANS

In baseball, an outstanding pitcher or a great outfield is not the standard by which a team is judged. The standard is the team's overall win-loss record. The criterion for success focuses on the team's performance, not the achievements of individuals. In business, companywide plans offer an additional possibility to the incentive plans previously discussed. Companywide plans may be based on the organization's productivity, cost savings, or profitability. To illustrate the concept of companywide plans, we discuss profit sharing, employee stock ownership, and the Scanlon Plan.

Profit sharing: A compensation plan that distributes a predetermined percentage of a firm's profits to its employees.

Profit Sharing. **Profit sharing** is a compensation plan that results in the distribution of a predetermined percentage of the firm's profits to employees. Many firms use this type of plan to integrate the employee's interests with those of the company. Profit sharing plans can aid in recruiting, motivating, and retaining employees, and these actions usually enhance productivity.

There are several variations of profit sharing plans, but two basic kinds are widely used today: current profit sharing and deferred profit sharing.[38]

- ■ *Current plans* provide payment to employees in cash or stock as soon as profits have been determined.
- ■ *Deferred plans* involve placing company contributions in an irrevocable trust to be credited to the account of individual employees. The funds are normally invested in securities and become available to the employee (or his or her survivors) at retirement, termination, or death.

These two plans are not mutually exclusive. *Combination plans* permit employees to receive payment of part of their share of profits on a current basis while payment of part of their share is deferred.

Normally, most full-time employees are included in a company's profit sharing plan after a specified waiting period. Vesting determines the amount of *profit* an employee actually owns in his or her account and is often established on a graduated basis. For example, an employee may become 25 percent vested after being in the plan for two years, 50 percent vested after three years, 75 percent vested after four years, and 100 percent vested after five years. This approach to vesting may reduce turnover by encouraging employees to remain with the company.

Profit sharing tends to tie employees to the economic success of the firm. Reported results include increased efficiency and lower costs. In recent years, however, increased popularity of employee thrift plans have slowed the growth of profit sharing plans. Also, variations in profits may present a spe-

HRM IN ACTION
UPPING THE STANDARDS?

"Did you realize that we spent over $70,000 on our incentive program last year?" asked Pat Shelton, production manager. She was talking to the human resource manager, Jerry Kemp. Pat continued, "For a company our size, we sure spend a lot of money for what we get. Frankly, I think our employees are paid too much. What do you think about upping the standards a bit for receiving incentive pay? It could save the company a lot of money."

If you were Jerry, how would you respond?

cial problem. When employees have become accustomed to receiving added compensation from profit sharing and then there is no profit to share, they may become disgruntled.

Problems with a profit sharing plan arise because the recipients seldom know precisely how they helped generate the profits, beyond just doing their jobs. If employees continue to receive a payment, they will come to expect it and depend on it. If they do not know what they have done to deserve it, they may view it as an entitlement program. The results may be just the opposite of what is desired. The intended *ownership* attitude may not materialize.[39]

Employee Stock Ownership Plan (ESOP).
As previously mentioned, an ESOP is a defined contribution plan in which a firm makes a tax deductible contribution of stock shares or cash to a trust. Research indicates that when employees become owners, they increase their dedication to the firm, improve their work effort, reduce turnover, and generally bring a more harmonious atmosphere to the company. These behaviors and attitudes translate into an improved bottom line.[40]

Many of the benefits that come with profit sharing plans also accrue with ESOPs. Specifically, ESOP advocates have suggested that employees obtain a stake in the business and become more closely identified with the firm—a relationship that theoretically increases their motivation. Although the potential advantages of ESOPs are impressive, critics point out the dangers of employees having *all their eggs in one basket*. Employees would be in a vulnerable position should their company fail.

Gain-Sharing.
Gain-sharing plans are designed to bind employees to the firm's performance by providing an incentive payment based on improved company performance. Improved performance can take the form of increased productivity, increased customer satisfaction, lower costs, or better safety records.[41] Gain-sharing plans (also known as productivity incentives, team incentives, and performance sharing incentives) generally refer to incentive plans that involve many or all employees in a common effort to achieve a firm's performance objectives.

The first gain-sharing plan was developed by Joseph Scanlon during the Great Depression and it continues to be a successful approach to group

Scanlon plan: A gain-sharing plan designed to bind employees to their firm's performance.

incentive, especially in smaller firms. The **Scanlon plan** provides a financial reward to employees for savings in labor costs that result from their suggestions. These suggestions are evaluated by employee-management committees. Savings are calculated as a ratio of payroll costs to the sales value of what that payroll produces. If the company is able to reduce payroll costs through increased operating efficiency, it shares the savings with its employees.

The Scanlon Plan differs from other gain-sharing programs by emphasizing the empowerment of employees. Adoption of the plan necessitates a commitment to a particular value system and management philosophy. There are four basic Scanlon Plan principles:[42]

1. *Identity.* To focus on employee involvement, the firm's mission or purpose must be clearly articulated.
2. *Competence.* The plan requires the highest standards of work behavior and continual commitment to excellence.
3. *Participation.* The plan provides a mechanism for using the ideas of knowledgeable employees and translating these into productivity improvements.
4. *Equity.* Equity is achieved when three primary stakeholders—employees, customers, and investors—share financially in the productivity increases resulting from the program.

Such firms as Herman Miller, Ameritech, Martin Marietta, Donnelly Mirrors, Motorola, and Boston's Beth Israel Hospital are realizing benefits from the Scanlon Plan. They have created formal participative means for soliciting suggestions and are sharing the revenue resulting from increases in productivity. Studies on gain-sharing indicate that firms using such plans increase their productivity from 10 to 12 percent a year.[43]

Executive Compensation

Executive skill largely determines whether a firm will prosper, survive, or fail. Therefore, providing adequate compensation for this group of managers is vital. A critical factor in attracting and retaining the best managers is a company's program for compensating executives.

DETERMINING EXECUTIVE COMPENSATION

In determining executive compensation, firms typically prefer to relate salary growth for the highest level managers to overall corporate performance. For the next management tier, they tend to integrate overall corporate performance with market rates and internal considerations to come up with compensation factors. For lower level managers, salaries are often determined on the basis of market rates, internal pay relationships, and individual performance.

In general, the higher the managerial position, the greater the flexibility managers have in designing their jobs. Management jobs are often difficult to define because of their diversity. When they are defined, they are often described in terms of anticipated results rather than tasks or how the work is accomplished. Thus, market pricing may be the best approach to use in determining executive pay for several reasons. For one, such jobs are critically important to the organization, and the people involved are highly skilled and difficult to replace. In addition, the firm often has a considerable investment in developing managers. Even though the market may support a high salary for a manager, the amount may seem extremely large. However, managers represent a relatively small percentage of the total workforce, and the overall impact of this high salary on total labor costs will be small. Finally, because of their numerous outside contacts, managers at the executive level are likely to know the current market rates.

In using market pricing, organizations utilize compensation survey data to determine pay levels for a representative group of jobs. These data may be obtained from such sources as William M. Mercer, the American Compensation Association, and Towers and Perrin.

TYPES OF EXECUTIVE COMPENSATION

Executive compensation often has five basic elements: (1) base salary, (2) short-term incentives or bonuses, (3) long-term incentives and capital appreciation plans, (4) executive benefits, and (5) perquisites.[44] The way an executive compensation package is designed is partially dependent on the ever-changing tax legislation.

Base Salary. Although it may not represent the largest portion of the executive's compensation package, salary is obviously important. It is a factor in determining the executive's standard of living. Salary also provides the basis for other forms of compensation. For example, the amount of bonuses and certain benefits may be based on annual salary.

Short-Term Incentives or Bonuses. Payment of bonuses reflects a managerial belief in their incentive value. Today, virtually all top executives receive bonuses that are tied to base salary. The popularity of this compensation component has risen rapidly in recent years.

Long-Term Incentives and Capital Appreciation. The stock option is a long-term incentive designed to integrate further the interests of management with those of the organization. The sentiments of some boards of directors may be revealed in results from a recent survey of large industrial and service corporations. Of the firms surveyed, one in six require top executives to hold some of the company's stock. Most commonly, CEOs are required to hold shares worth four to five times their base salary.[45] Although the motivational value of stock ownership seems logical, research on the subject has not been conclusive.

There are various types of plans, but the typical **stock option plan** gives the manager the option to buy a specified amount of stock in the future at or below the current market price. This form of compensation is advantageous when stock prices are rising. However, there are potential disadvantages to

Stock option plan: An incentive plan in which managers can buy a specified amount of stock in their company in the future at or below the current market price.

stock option plans. A manager may feel uncomfortable investing money in the same organization in which he or she is building a career. As with profit sharing, this method of compensation is popular when a firm is successful, but during periods of decline when stock prices fall, the participants may become disenchanted. Nevertheless, there are several bona fide reasons for including stock ownership in executive compensation plans. These include recruiting and retaining top performers, aligning employee's interests with those of shareholders, raising capital, and preventing a takeover attempt.[46]

Executive Benefits.   Executive benefits are similar to but usually more generous than those received by other employees because the benefits are tied to managers' higher salaries. However, current legislation (ERISA) does restrict the value of executive benefits to a certain level above those of other workers.

Perquisites (perks):
Special benefits provided by a firm to key executives to give them something extra.

Perquisites.   **Perquisites (perks)** are any special benefits provided by a firm to a small group of key executives and are designed to give the executives something extra. In addition to status, these rewards either are not considered as earned income or are taxed at a lower level than ordinary income.[47] An executive's perks may include some of the following:

- A company-provided car
- Accessible, no cost, parking
- Limousine service—the chauffeur may also serve as a bodyguard
- Kidnap and ransom protection
- Counseling service—including financial and legal services
- Professional meetings and conferences
- Spouse travel
- Use of company plane and yacht
- Home entertainment allowance
- Special living accommodations away from home
- Club memberships
- Special dining privileges
- Season tickets to entertainment events
- Special relocation allowances
- Use of company credit cards
- Medical expense reimbursement—coverage for all medical costs
- Reimbursement for children's college expenses
- No- and low-interest loans[48]

"Golden parachute" contract: A perquisite provided for the purpose of protecting executives in the event their firm is acquired by another.

A **"golden parachute" contract** is a perquisite that protects executives in the event their company is acquired by another firm. Usually, these contracts apply regardless of whether the new owners continue the executive's employment.[49] To retain a key executive until a buyout takes place, a firm may agree to guarantee four times the executive's salary. The company will have no problem funding this compensation because the sale will generate a large amount of cash.[50] Perquisites extend a firm's benefit program on an individual basis. Among publicly traded U.S. firms, few high-level executives go unprotected in the event of a change in business ownership. During the 1980s, these perks were often so lucrative that Congress imposed penalties on *excess* payments in the form of a nondeductible excise tax on individuals and a cap on a company's tax deductibility.[51]

The high level of compensation for top executives has received increased attention in recent years. For example, Lawrence Coss, CEO and chairman of Green Tree Financial Corporation in St. Paul, Minnesota, made $102.4 million in 1996 in salary and bonus. This was a 56 percent increase over the $65.6 million he earned in 1995. Does this amount seem obscene? Not according to Mr. Coss, who states, "I'd rather talk about the success of the company." Between 1991 and 1996, Green Tree's shares had compounded annual returns of 53 percent as the company became the largest lender to the manufactured-home sector. Although Mr. Coss's income does seem extremely high, most of the stockholders are apparently satisfied. One very large shareholder of 2.7 million shares was quoted as stating: "In no way would I consider him overpaid."[52]

Not everyone is thrilled with the high pay of executives. Especially criticized are those managers who collect megabucks when their companies are either performing poorly or are downsizing. For example, Stephen Case, CEO of America Online, Inc., earned $33.5 million in 1996 while his firm's return on investment was negative 413 percent.[53]

Compensation for Professionals

Professionals are initially paid for the knowledge they bring to the organization. Therefore, compensation programs for professionals are administered somewhat differently from those for managers. Many professional employees eventually become managers. However, for those who do not aspire to a management career, some organizations have created a dual compensation track. This approach provides a separate pay structure for professionals that overlaps the managerial pay structure. With this system, high-performing professionals are not required to enter management to obtain greater pay. Some firms face serious organizational problems when a highly competent and effective professional feels compelled to become a manager for more pay and is unable to perform well in this capacity.

Sales Compensation

Because designing compensation programs for sales employees involves unique considerations, some executives assign this task to the sales staff rather than to human resources. However, many general compensation practices apply to sales jobs. For example, job content, relative job worth, and job market value should be determined.

The straight salary approach is at one extreme in sales compensation. In this method, salespeople receive a fixed salary regardless of their sales levels. Organizations use straight salary primarily to stress continued product service after the sale. For instance, sales representatives who deal largely with the federal government are often compensated in this manner.

At the other extreme, the person whose pay is totally determined as a percentage of sales is on straight commission. If no sales are made, the person working on straight commission receives no pay. On the other hand, highly productive sales representatives can earn a great deal of money.

Between these extremes is the endless variety of part-salary, part-commission combinations. The possibilities increase when various types of bonuses are added to the basic compensation package. The emphasis given to either commission or salary depends on several factors, including the organization's philosophy toward service, the nature of the product, and the amount of time required to close a sale.

In addition to salary, commissions, and bonuses, salespeople often receive other forms of compensation that are intended to serve as added incentives. Sales contests that offer television sets, refrigerators, or expense-paid vacations to exotic locations are common.

If any one feature sets sales compensation apart from other programs, it is the emphasis on incentives. The nature of sales work often simplifies the problem of determining individual output. Sales volume can usually be related to specific individuals, a situation that encourages payment of incentive compensation. Also, experience in sales compensation practices over the years has supported the concept of directly relating rewards to performance.

Computer software has made it possible to measure sales performance much more precisely. Now, many firms have the ability to measure things like gross profits per line of billing, profitability per customer, profitability per product and sales costs as a percentage of gross profit per territory. Technology has made it feasible to align the sales compensation system more closely with corporate strategy and reward the behaviors that impact the bottom line.[54]

Severance Pay

Although the extent of downsizing in U.S. firms has subsided, it continues to occur. Compensation professionals are regularly called on to design severance packages for laid-off employees.

Although some firms are trimming the amount of severance pay offered, typically, one to two weeks of severance pay is given for every year of service, up to some predetermined maximum. Severance pay is generally shaped according to the organizational level of the employee. For example, nonmanagers may get eight or nine weeks of pay even if their length of service is greater than eight or nine years. Middle managers may receive payment for 12 to 16 weeks, and top executives could receive payment to cover nine months to a year of employment. The rationale for enhanced severance for executives is that it takes longer for an executive to secure another position.[55]

Other Compensation Issues

Several issues that relate to compensation deserve mention. These issues include comparable worth, pay secrecy, and pay compression. These issues are examined next.

HR Web Wisdom

http://www.prenhall.com/mondy

COMPARABLE WORTH
The economics of comparable worth is summarized.

COMPARABLE WORTH

Comparable worth: A determination of the values of dissimilar jobs (such as company nurse and welder) by comparing them under some form of job evaluation, and the assignment of pay rates according to their evaluated worth.

The comparable worth, or pay equity, theory extends the concept of the Equal Pay Act. Whereas the act requires equal pay for equal work, comparable worth advocates prefer a broader interpretation: requiring equal pay for comparable worth even if market rates and job duties differ. **Comparable worth** requires the value for dissimilar jobs, such as company nurse and welder, to be compared under some form of job evaluation, and pay rates for both jobs to be assigned according to their evaluated worth. Although the Supreme Court has ruled that comparable worth is not required by law, a number of state and local governments, along with some jurisdictions in Canada, have passed legislation that mandates pay equity.

The basic premise of comparable worth is that jobs traditionally held by women are paid less than those traditionally held by men, even though both types may make equal contributions to the organization's goals. Jobs that have historically been filled by women pay less, and when employers use market data for establishing pay rates, the pay differentials are perpetuated.

Opponents of comparable worth contend that the earnings gap reflects an overall statistic and does not compare the earnings of two people performing the same job. They believe that the gender difference is explainable by such variables as education and job experience.

Comparable worth detractors note that existing law prohibits employers from paying a woman less money than a man for doing the same work. A more effective solution, they suggest, would be vigorous enforcement of equal opportunity and equal pay laws. In addition, women should be encouraged to enter nontraditional occupations and be provided with equal access to education, training programs, and employment. Also, efforts should be continued to promote a nondiscriminatory socialization process for children. This view holds that these alternatives, rather than artificially raising the price of labor for special groups, will address the problem of gender discrimination.[56]

Perhaps the greatest fear of implementing comparable worth standards is the cost of replacing market forces of supply and demand with a government-imposed system of job evaluation. Estimates of costs vary, but they range into the billions of dollars per year. Proponents of comparable worth reject market pricing of jobs because they believe that markets reflect bias against occupations traditionally held by women.

The goal of nondiscriminatory pay practices is one that every organization should seek to achieve for ethical and legal reasons. Whether comparable worth is an appropriate solution remains to be seen. It seems clear that although comparable worth was tabbed as the issue of the 1980s, it will be debated as long as there is a disparity between the compensation of men and women.[57]

PAY SECRECY

Organizations tend to keep their pay rates secret for various reasons. If a firm's compensation plan is illogical, secrecy may indeed be appropriate because only a well-designed system can stand careful scrutiny. An open system would almost certainly require managers to explain the rationale for pay decisions to subordinates.

Secrecy, however, can have some negative side effects including a distortion of the actual rewards people receive. Secrecy also spawns a low trust environment in which people have trouble understanding the relationship between pay and performance. It may, therefore, cause an otherwise sound compensation system to be ineffective.[58]

PAY COMPRESSION

Organizations normally strive for both internal and external pay equity. In practice, however, this state is often difficult or even impossible to accomplish. For example, to attract an engineer to a firm, an unusually high salary may have to be paid. Individuals possessing the skills needed to perform this job are in short supply relative to the demand for their services. Therefore, these workers, and others in similar situations, are able to command high salaries.

But how does the hiring of this type of employee affect internal equity? Other jobs within the firm may have greater value to the firm—as determined by job evaluation—but are now paid less than some engineers. In this instance, the firm sacrificed internal equity because it had little choice in the matter, assuming that it had to fill the engineer's job.

Situations of this type may also result in a troublesome problem called pay compression. **Pay compression** occurs when workers perceive that the pay differential between their pay and that of employees in jobs above or below them is too small. It can be created in several ways, including the hiring of new employees at pay rates comparable to, or higher than, those of current employees who have been with the firm for several years. Making pay adjustments at the lower end of the job hierarchy without commensurate adjustments at the top is also a common cause of pay compression. Pay compression is a serious problem in many areas of our economy including nursing, engineering, and higher education.[59]

Pay compression: A situation that occurs when workers perceive that the pay differential between their pay and that of employees in jobs above or below them is too small.

A GLOBAL PERSPECTIVE

Do Not Let Global Employees "Cherry Pick"

Employee benefits often vary drastically from country to country and from industry to industry. In Europe, for instance, it is common for employees to receive added compensation in proportion to the number of their family members or the degree of their unpleasant working conditions. In Japan, a supervisor whose weekly salary is only $500 may also receive benefits that include family income allowances, housing or housing loans, subsidized vacations, year-end bonuses that can equal three months' pay, and profit sharing.[60]

Just as salaries are rising in emerging markets such as China, Eastern Europe, Southeast Asia, the Middle East, and Africa, so are accompanying benefits. Because individuals with the necessary talents are in short supply, compensation packages must be sweetened, well beyond competitive salaries. For example, in Turkey, the bidding war for talent is so intense that a new local venture offered one experienced U.S. employee double his base salary. To further sweeten the offer, the new company included a house on the Bosporus, a Mercedes, and a driver. These types of shortages have resulted in rising benefits packages, which escalate for Western companies as they try to match the offerings of local companies and outflank their Western competitors. In Indonesia, for instance, where employers commonly subsidize mortgages for valued employees, Western companies have been forced to do the same thing. Citibank carried a portfolio of employee loans in Indonesia of $25 million U.S. dollars. Even though the street rate for housing loans is about 13 percent, Citibank subsidized rates by 8 percent, so the employee pays about 5 percent and Citibank pays 8 percent.[61] In addition to containing the expansion of benefit packages, some companies are trying to reduce employee turnover in foreign markets by offering stock options with long maturities to top performers and offering job-rotation programs to talented local personnel.[62]

To get the best compensation and benefits package, local workers in foreign countries may *cherry pick* the offerings of various employers, trying to convince one company to match the individual pieces of the others' packages. "You often hear people saying, 'Chase Manhattan is giving a Cadillac and you're only giving us a Honda Civic.'" If a company falls for this—and increases its package piece by piece at the request of locals—its payroll and benefits costs will certainly spiral out of control.[63]   ■

SUMMARY

1. *Define* **benefits.**

Most organizations recognize their responsibility to provide their employees with insurance and other programs for their health, safety, security, and general welfare. These benefits include all financial rewards that generally are not paid directly to the employee.

2. *Describe legally required benefits.*

The Social Security Act of 1935 created a system that provided retirement benefits only. Subsequent amendments to the act added other forms of protection such as disability insurance, survivors' benefits, and most recently, Medicare. If an individual is laid off by an organization covered by the Social Security Act, he or she may receive unemployment compensation for up to 26 weeks. Workers' compensation benefits provide a degree of financial protection for employees who incur expenses resulting from job-related accidents or illnesses. The Family and Medical Leave Act of 1993 (FMLA) requires employers to provide eligible employees with a total of 12 weeks' leave during any 12-month period for several family and medical situations.

3. *Identify the basic categories of voluntary benefits.*
Voluntary benefits include payment for time not worked, health benefits, security benefits, employee services, and premium pay.

4. *Explain premium pay.*
Premium pay is compensation paid to employees for working long periods of time or working under dangerous or undesirable conditions. Additional pay provided to employees who work under extremely dangerous conditions is called hazard pay. A shift differential is paid to employees for the inconvenience of working undesirable hours.

5. *Describe the Consolidated Omnibus Budget Reconciliation Act (COBRA), the Health Insurance Portability and Accountability Act, the Employee Retirement Income Security Act (ERISA), and the Older Workers Benefit Protection Act (OWBPA).*
The Consolidated Omnibus Budget Reconciliation Act of 1985 (COBRA) was enacted to give employees the opportunity to continue their health coverage temporarily if they would otherwise lose it because of termination, layoff, or other change in employment status. The Health Insurance Portability and Accountability Act of 1996 provides new protections for approximately 25 million Americans who move from one job to another, who are self-employed, or who have preexisting medical conditions. The Employee Retirement Income Security Act of 1974 (ERISA) was passed to strengthen existing and future retirement programs. The Older Workers Benefit Protection Act (OWBPA) is a 1990 amendment to the ADEA and extends its coverage to all employee benefits.

6. *Explain the various incentive compensation plans.*
A specific form of performance-based pay is an individual incentive plan called piecework. Team performance consists of individual efforts. Therefore, individual employees should be recognized and rewarded for their contributions. However, if the team is to function effectively, a reward based on the overall team performance should be provided as well. Companywide plans offer a feasible alternative to the incentive plans previously discussed. They may be based on the organization's productivity, cost savings, or profitability.

7. *Describe various companywide incentive plans.*
Profit sharing is a compensation plan that results in the distribution of a predetermined percentage of the firm's profits to employees. A firm makes a tax deductible contribution of stock shares or cash to a trust under the employee stock ownership plan (ESOP). Gain-sharing plans are designed to bind employees to the firm's performance by providing an incentive payment based on improved company performance.

8. *Describe how compensation for executives is determined.*
In determining executive compensation, firms typically prefer to relate salary growth for the highest level managers to overall corporate performance. In general, the higher the managerial position, the greater will be the flexibility managers have in designing their jobs.

9. *Identify the elements of executive compensation.*

Executive compensation often has five basic elements: (1) base salary, (2) short-term incentives or bonuses, (3) long-term incentives and capital appreciation plans, (4) executive benefits, and (5) perquisites.

10. *Explain how compensation for professionals is determined.*

People in professional jobs are initially compensated primarily for the knowledge they bring to the organization. Because of this, the compensation programs for professionals is somewhat different from those for managers. Many professional employees eventually become managers. For those who do not desire this form of career progression, some organizations have created a dual track of compensation. The dual track provides a separate pay structure for professionals, which may overlap a portion of the managerial pay structure.

11. *Describe how compensation for sales representatives is determined.*

Designing compensation programs for sales employees involves unique considerations. The straight salary approach is at one extreme in sales compensation. In this method, salespeople receive a fixed salary regardless of their sales levels. At the other extreme, the person whose pay is totally determined as a percentage of sales is on straight commission. Between these extremes, there are endless part salary-part commission combinations.

12. *Explain when severance pay is used.*

Although some firms are trimming the amount of severance pay offered when an employee is downsized, typically, one to two weeks of severance pay is given for every year the person has worked for the company, up to some predetermined maximum. Severance pay is generally shaped according to the organizational level of the employee.

13. *Describe the concepts of comparable worth, pay secrecy, and pay compression.*

Comparable worth requires the value for dissimilar jobs, such as company nurse and welder, to be compared under some form of job evaluation, and pay rates for both jobs to be assigned according to their evaluated worth. With pay secrecy, organizations tend to keep their pay rates secret for various reasons. Pay compression occurs when workers perceive that the pay differential between their pay and that of employees in jobs above or below them is too small.

QUESTIONS FOR REVIEW

1. Define *benefits*.
2. Explain the legally required benefits.
3. What are the basic categories of voluntary benefits? Describe each.
4. Describe the Consolidated Omnibus Budget Reconciliation Act of 1985 (COBRA), the Health Insurance Portability and Accountability Act of 1996, the Employee Retirement Income Security Act of 1974 (ERISA), and the Older Workers Benefit Protection Act (OWBPA).
5. Distinguish among premium pay, hazard pay, and shift differential pay.

6. What is meant by the term *incentive compensation*? What are the basic forms of incentive compensation?

7. Define the following terms:
   a. *Straight piecework plan*
   b. *Profit sharing*
   c. *Employee stock ownership plan (ESOP)*
   d. *Gain-sharing*
   e. *Scanlon Plan*

8. What are major determinants of compensation for executives? List and define the primary types of executive compensation.

9. Distinguish between compensation for professionals and sales compensation.

10. What is the rationale for severance pay?

11. Describe each of the following:
    a. comparable worth
    b. pay secrecy
    c. pay compression

DEVELOPING HRM SKILLS

AN EXPERIENTIAL EXERCISE

Because of a downward trend in business and the resulting financial constraints over the last two years, Straight Manufacturing Company has been able to grant only cost-of-living increases to its employees. However, the firm has just signed a lucrative three-year contract with a major defense contractor. As a result, management has formed a salary review committee to award merit increases to deserving employees. Members of the salary review committee have only $13,500 of merit money; deciding who will receive merit increases will be difficult. Louis Convoy, Sharon Kubiak, J. Ward Archer, Ed Wilson, C. J. Sass, and John Passante have been recommended for raises.

Six students will serve on the salary review committee. While the committee would like to award significant merit increases to all those who have been recommended, there are limited funds available for raises. The committee must make a decision on how the merit funds will be distributed. Your instructor will provide the participants with additional information necessary to complete the exercise.

 Take It to the Net

We invite you to visit the Mondy home page on the Prentice Hall Web site at:

http://www.prenhall.com/mondy

for updated information, Web-based exercises, and links to other HR-related sites.

HRM SIMULATION

*Y*our organization offers very meager benefits to its employees. These benefits are currently 11 percent of wages and include Social Security tax (FICA); unemployment insurance; a low-benefit, high-deductible health care plan; and workers' compensation insurance. Some possible new benefits include life insurance, dental care, pension plans, cafeteria plans, and sick leave. Your team will need to analyze your firm's benefits and decide what, if any, new benefits are needed.

HRM INCIDENT

1

A Double-Edged Sword

*T*he decline in oil prices during the mid-1980s and early 1990s adversely affected many industries. Profits were down for all major oil companies and many of their suppliers. Few new orders were received by the producers of drilling fluids, for example, and many existing orders were canceled or scaled back. As a supplier of drilling fluids, Beta Chemical Company's sales plummeted. Beta, located in Lafayette, Louisiana, supplies companies such as Texaco, Shell, and Pennzoil as well as independent oil drillers, often called *wildcatters*.

Beta had implemented a comprehensive profit-sharing plan after several years of rapidly increasing sales and profits. The decision was based largely on an attitude survey of the employees at Beta, which showed that they strongly preferred profit sharing over other benefits.

In the early 1990s, the compensation plan at Beta provided for base wages about 20 percent below wage levels for similar jobs in Lafayette, but half of company profits were paid out each quarter as a fixed percentage of employee wages. Distributed profits averaged more than 50 percent of base wages. This caused average total compensation at Beta to be 20 percent above that of the area. Because of the high pay, Beta remained a popular employer, able to take its pick from a long waiting list of applicants.

Benefits were kept to a minimum at Beta. There was no retirement plan and a very limited medical plan designed to cover catastrophic illnesses only. Employees considered this a good bargain, though, in light of their above-average compensation.

Profits were down markedly in 1992, and the profit-sharing bonus was less than half the historical average. Earnings declined further for the first two quarters of 1994. By midyear, it was clear that the company would be in the red for the entire second half. A board meeting was called in late August to discuss the profit sharing program. One director made it known that he felt the company should drop profit sharing. The human resource director, Vince Harwood, was asked to sit in on the board meeting and to make a presentation suggesting what the company should do about compensation.

Questions
1. Evaluate the compensation plan at Beta.
2. If you were Mr. Harwood, what would you recommend for the short term? For the long term?

HRM INCIDENT

2

A Birthday Present for Kathy

*B*ob Rosen could hardly wait to get back to work Monday morning. He was excited about his chance of getting a large bonus. Bob is a machine operator with Ram Manufacturing Company, a Wichita, Kansas, maker of electric motors. He operates an armature winding machine. The machine winds copper wire onto metal cores to make the rotating elements for electric motors.

Ram pays machine operators on a graduated piece-rate basis. Operators are paid a certain amount for each part made, plus a bonus. A worker who produces 10 percent above standard for a certain month receives a 10-percent additional bonus. For 20 percent above standard, the bonus is 20 percent. Bob realized that he had a good chance of earning a 20 percent bonus that month. That would amount to $587.

Bob had a special use for the extra money. His wife's birthday was just three weeks away. He was hoping to get her a new Chevrolet Citation. He had already saved $1,000, but the down payment on the Citation was $1,500. The bonus would enable him to buy the car.

Bob arrived at work at seven o'clock that morning, although his shift did not begin until eight. He went to his workstation and checked the supply of blank cores and copper wire. Finding that only one spool of wire was on hand, he asked the fork truck driver to bring another. Then he asked the operator who was working the graveyard shift, "Sam, do you mind if I grease the machine while you work?"

"No," Sam said, "that won't bother me a bit."

After greasing the machine, Bob stood and watched Sam work. He thought of ways to simplify the motions involved in loading, winding, and unloading the armatures. As Bob took over the machine after the 8 o'clock whistle, he thought, "I hope I can pull this off. I know the car will make Kathy happy. She won't be stuck at home while I'm at work."

Question

1. Explain the advantages and disadvantages of a piecework pay system such as that at Ram.

Notes

1. Joseph J. Martocchio, *Strategic Compensation* (Upper Saddle River, NJ: Prentice Hall, 1998): 254, 274.

2. Linda Bennett, "The CBR Advisory Board Comments On: CEO Pay, Global Chaos, and a Possible Retreat from Benefits," *Compensation & Benefits Review* 28 (May/June 1996): 58–65.

3. Kim Ebert, "Employers Errors Common in Family Leave Act," *Indianapolis Business Journal* 17 (December 16, 1996): 15.

4. Ibid., 8.

5. Ronald J. Andrykovitch and Jeffrey A. VanDoren, "Legal Update: Family and Medical Leave Act's Real Impact," *Getting Results . . . For the Hands-On Manager* 42 (January 1, 1997): 7.

6. Malcolm S. Forbes, Jr., "There's a Better Way," *Forbes* 147 (April 26, 1993): 23.

7. Ron Winslow, "Employers' Costs Slip as Workers Shift to HMOs," *The Wall Street Journal* (February 14, 1995): A3, A5.

8. *1997 SHRM Benefits Survey*, Society for Human Resource Management, 22.

9. Manfred J. Nowacki, Douglas A. Collet, Shellie A. Stoddard and Elizabeth A. Runge, "Prognosis: Guarded," Best's Review—Life/Health Insurance Edition (January 1997): 68–70.

10. Ibid.

11. HCFA Issues Regulations Under Health Insurance Portability and Accountability Act: Fact Sheet. *US Newswire* (1997). http://www3.elibrary.com/getdoc.cgi?id=76 . . . D002&Form=RL&pubname=US_Newswire&puburl=0 (August 1, 1997).

12. Health Insurance Portability and Accountability Act of 1996. Washington, DC: Health and Human Services, Press Office. http://www.os.dhhs.gov/news/press/1996pres/960821.html (August 1, 1997).

13. *1997 SHRM Benefits Survey*, 22.

14. Except for certain exempt executives, the ADEA prohibits mandatory retirement at any specific age.

15. *1997 SHRM Benefits Survey*, 32.

16. The *1997 SHRM Benefits Survey* reports that almost 70 percent of responding firms have defined contribution plans.

17. Jenny C. McCune, "HR News Capsules: Downsizing on the Downswing," *HR Focus* 74 (January 1997): 6–7.

18. Anne Willette, "Firms Adding Financial Planning to List of All Workers' Benefits," *USA Today* (March 24, 1997): 1A.

19. Gary McWilliams, "Logging on to Your 401(k)," *Business Week* (May 19, 1997): 110.

20. Martocchio, *Strategic Compensation*, 278.

21. Ibid.

22. George T. Milkovich and Jerry M. Newman, *Compensation*, 5th ed. (Chicago, IL: Richard D. Irwin, 1996): 469.

23. *1997 SHRM Benefits Survey*, 18.

24. J. Stephen Mumma, "New Technologies Speed Relocation Process," *HRMagazine* 41 (October 1996): 55–56.

25. Gillian Flynn, "Relocation Has a New Look," *Personnel Journal* 74 (February 1995): 48–62.

26. Jill Vitiello, "Make Your Move," *Computerworld* 30 (December 2, 1996): 112.

27. Hillary Chura, "Careers/Fresh Starts; Companies Lend Parents a Hand," *Los Angeles Times* Home Edition (January 27, 1997): D2.

28. *1997 SHRM Benefits Survey*, 26.

29. David Fischer and Kevin Whitelaw, "A New Way to Shine Up Corporate Profits," *U.S. News & World Report* 120 (April 15, 1996): 54.

30. Julie Cohen Mason, "Whoever Said There Was No Such Thing as a Free Lunch?" *Management Review* 83 (April 1994): 60–62.

31. Bill Leonard, "Perks Give Way to Life-cycle Benefits Plans," *HRMagazine* 40 (March 1995): 46–47.

32. "Singles and Childless Couples Become More Common," *Workplace Visions, Society for Human Resource Management* (September/October 1996): 6.

33. *U.S. Statutes at Large* 88, Part I, 93rd Congress, 2nd Session, 1974: 833.

34. Milkovich and Newman, *Compensation*, 471.

35. Geoffrey Loftus, "Ultimate Pay for Performance," *Across the Board* 31 (January 1997). 9–10.

36. James Martin, "HR in the Cybercorp," *HR Focus* 74 (April 1997): 3–4.

37. Shari Caudron, "Master the Compensation Maze," *Personnel Journal* 72 (June 1993): 64a–64o.

38. Martocchio, *Strategic Compensation*, 121.

39. Jack Stack, "The Problem with Profit Sharing," *Inc* (November 1996): 67.

40. John E. Hempstead, "When Employees Want to Buy the Company," *Folio* 25 (October 15, 1996): 132.

41. Martocchio, *Strategic Compensation*, 115.

42. Steven E. Markham, K. Dow Scott, and Walter G. Cox, Jr., "The Evolutionary Development of a Scanlon Plan," *Compensation & Benefits Review* 24 (March/April 1992): 50–56.

43. Carrie Mason-Draffen, "Companies Find New Ways to Pay/Worker's Performance Tied to Stock Options, Bonuses, Raises," *Newsday* (January 5, 1997): F08.

44. Milkovich and Newman, *Compensation*, 590.

45. Jennifer Files, "More Firms Require Execs to Own Stock," *The Dallas Morning News* (June 24, 1994): 1D–13D.

46. Katherine Zoe Andrews, "Equity Compensation: A Guide for the Entrepreneur," *Harvard Business Review* 74 (March/April 1996): 14.

47. Since the late 1970s, the IRS has required firms to place a value on more perks and has recognized them as imputed income.

48. Richard I. Henderson, *Compensation Management in a Knowledge-Based World*, 7th ed. (Upper Saddle River, NJ: Prentice Hall, 1997): 508–509.

49. George B. Paulin, "Executive Compensation and Changes in Control: A Search for Fairness," *Compensation & Benefits Review* 29 (March/April 1997): 30–40.

50. Albert B. Ellentuck, "Retaining Key Executives by Using a Parachute Payment Agreement," *The Tax Advisor* (January 1997): 50.

51. Paulin, "Executive Compensation and Changes in Control: A Search for Fairness."

52. Jennifer Reingold, "Executive Pay," *Business Week* (April 21, 1997): 60.

53. Ibid., 61.

54. Dave Kahle, "Is It Time to Revise Your Sales Compensation Plan?" *Supervision* 57 (August 1996): 6–8.

55. Joan Szabo, "Severance Plans Shift Away from Cash," *HRMagazine* 41 (July 1996): 104.

56. Julie M. Buchanan, "Comparable Worth: Where Is It Headed?" *Human Resources: Journal of the International Association for Personnel Women* 2 (Summer 1985): 12.

57. Mary V. Moore and Yohannan T. Abraham, "Comparable Worth: Is It a Moot Issue?" *Public Personnel Management* 29 (September 1995): 291–313.

58. Edward E. Lawler, "The New Pay: A Strategic Approach," *Compensation & Benefits Review* 27 (July/August 1995): 14–22.

59. Richard Huseman, Warren W. McHone, and Brian Rungeling, "Academic Salary Compression: A Productivity Model as a Remedy," *Public Personnel Management* 25 (December 1996): 453.

60. Wayne F. Cascio and Manuel G. Serapio, Jr., "HR Systems in an International Alliance: The Undoing of a Done Deal?" *Organizational Dynamics* 19 (Winter 1991): 65.

61. Donald J. McNerney, "Global Staffing: Some Common Problems—and Solutions," *HR Focus* 72 (June 1996): 1–4.

62. Ibid.

63. Ibid.

ABCNEWS | VIDEO CASE

Retirement Funding: The Burden Is Now on the Individual

Today, people are living longer than ever due to advances in medical science. People may expect to enjoy retirement for much longer now than previous generations. The question is, Are we saving enough money to see us through these additional retirement years? For many, the answer is no.

Historically, a company pension could be counted on to supply a major portion of retirement income for employees in many organizations. This income was subsidized by Social Security benefits. Two factors have altered this arrangement. First, many individuals don't stay with a firm long enough to be eligible for the company's pension. Second, firms are abandoning defined benefits programs, which guaranteed a certain retirement payment, in favor of defined contribution plans. Responsibility has shifted to employees who must now make investment decisions for the money they and their firm contribute to plans such as a 401(k) plan. There is also increasing concern about the future of Social Security including fears that the system will go bankrupt.

It is extremely difficult for employees with small incomes to save and invest for retirement. Life may become even more troublesome during retirement years, however, if an income is not available that will cover their needs.

To deal with this problem, some firms have started educating their employees about investing for retirement, helping them understand the importance of retirement planning and making them aware of their investment options. Although many small businesses simply avoid the retirement issue, assistance in developing plans is available to them from U.S. Labor Department.

DISCUSSION QUESTIONS

1. Do you believe that most people are saving and investing adequately for their retirement years? Why or why not?
2. Responsibility for retirement planning is increasingly being shifted from employers to individual employees. What would you do to implement a retirement planning education program in your firm?
3. To what extent should organizations be responsible for employee education and choices regarding retirement planning?
4. Do you think an organization should take steps other than education in assisting with the retirement issue? If so, describe the steps.

Source: "Will There Be Enough Money for Your Old Age?" *Nightline*, ABC News; aired September 18, 1995.

PART SIX

SAFETY AND HEALTH

13
A Safe and Healthy Work Environment

CHAPTER OBJECTIVES

1. Define *safety* and *health.*
2. Explain the purpose of the Occupational Safety and Health Act.
3. Describe the focus of safety programs in business operations.
4. Explain how safety programs are evaluated.
5. Describe cumulative trauma disorders.
6. Explain the effect on businesses of workplace violence.
7. Describe the purposes of health and wellness programs.
8. Define *stress.*
9. Explain the importance of stress management in business today.
10. Define *burnout* and describe the warning signs of burnout.
11. Identify the sources of stress.
12. Explain means of coping with stress.
13. Describe the importance of physical fitness programs.
14. Explain alcohol abuse and drug abuse programs.
15. Describe employee assistance programs.
16. Describe the possible impact of smoking in the workplace.
17. Explain the possible impact of AIDS in the workplace.

ionne Moore, safety engineer for Sather Manufacturing, was walking through the plant when she spotted a situation that immediately caught her attention. Several employees had backed out of a room where a number of chemicals were used in a critical manufacturing process. Dionne inspected the room but couldn't determine that anything was wrong or even different from any other day. She was puzzled as to why the workers were reluctant to resume their tasks. As it turned out, the employees were not only hesitant to return to work; they were adamant in maintaining that conditions in the room were unhealthy. Dionne and the group's supervisor discussed the situation and wondered whether they should order the people to resume work as the department was already behind schedule.

Bob Byrom, CEO for Aztec Enterprises, is concerned about his vice president for marketing, thirty-eight-year-old Cecil Pierce. The two had just returned from a short walk to the corporate attorney's office to discuss plans for an overseas joint venture. As they returned to Bob's office, Cecil's face was flushed, he was breathing hard, and he had to sit down and rest. This behavior really alarmed Bob because he didn't think that such a brief bit of exercise should tire anyone, especially someone as apparently healthy as Cecil. Bob knew that the firm couldn't afford to do without Cecil's expertise even for a short time during its expansion plans.

*D*ionne and Bob are each involved with only a few of the many critical areas related to employee safety and health. Dionne realizes that safety is a major concern in her organization and that she must constantly strive to maintain a safe and healthy work environment. Bob's experience has caused him to confront the serious ramifications of losing a key executive from illness or even death.

We begin this chapter with definitions of safety and health and an overview of the Occupational Safety and Health Act. Then we discuss the following issues: safety, safety programs, ergonomics, cumulative trauma disorders, workplace and domestic violence, wellness programs, stress management, programs for physical fitness, alcohol and drug abuse programs. Employee assistance programs are examined next, and the chapter ends with discussions of smoking in the workplace, and AIDS.

HR Web Wisdom

http://www.prenhall.com/mondy

SHRM—HR LINKS
Various safety and health issues including employee assistance programs, ergonomics, and workplace violence are addressed at this site.

The Nature and Role of Safety and Health

Safety: The protection of employees from injuries caused by work-related accidents.

In our discussion, **safety** involves protecting employees from injuries caused by work-related accidents. Obviously, several employees who work for Sather Manufacturing view as unsafe the use of several chemicals in one phase of a critical manufacturing process. Dionne Moore and the group's supervisor now have a dilemma: If they ignore the workers' concerns, the group will continue to balk at working in what the group members consider an unsafe environment. If they address the employees' safety concerns, the company will probably have to modify the existing manufacturing process or reengineer the work environment for this phase. Either path will lead to further delays in the production schedule.

Health: An employee's freedom from physical or emotional illness.

Health refers to employees' freedom from physical or emotional illness. Cecil Pierce, marketing vice president for Aztec Enterprises, is obviously not as well as one might expect a 38-year-old to be. After only a short walk, Cecil is breathing hard, has a flushed face, and needs to rest. Bob Byrom, CEO of Aztec, is worried that something is wrong with Cecil's health—and his worry is justified. Managers, such as Dionne Moore and Bob Byrom, are vitally concerned with both aspects of employment: safety and health. Problems in these areas seriously affect productivity and quality of work life. They can dramatically lower a firm's effectiveness and employee morale. In fact, job-related injuries and illnesses are more common than most people realize. They cost the nation far more than AIDS or Alzheimer's disease. Job-related injuries and illnesses are grossly underestimated as a contributor to health-care costs in the United States.[1]

Although line managers are primarily responsible for maintaining a safe and healthy work environment, human resource professionals provide staff expertise to help them deal with these issues. In addition, the human resource manager is frequently responsible for coordinating and monitoring specific safety and health programs.

The Occupational Safety and Health Act

The most important federal legislation in the safety and health area is the Occupational Safety and Health Act of 1970. The purpose of this act is to assure a safe and healthful workplace for every American worker. There is little doubt that the act's intent is justified. Individual organizations must make giant strides toward achieving this goal if they are to reach their full productive potential.

The act's enforcement by the Occupational Safety and Health Administration (OSHA) dramatically altered management's role in the area of safety and health. Financial penalties serve as pointed reminders to industry of the benefits of maintaining safe and healthy working conditions. Skyrocketing costs for workers' compensation insurance, the expense of training new workers, and the reality that risky jobs command higher pay also keep safety and health issues on managers' minds.

OSHA has historically concentrated on high-risk industries in which there is greater potential for reducing injuries and illnesses. As Table 13-1 illustrates, some industries—those that deal with finance, insurance, and real estate, for example—clearly provide safer conditions than others, such as the ones that produce fabricated metal products.

Six to seven million businesses are covered by OSHA, but the agency has about 1,000 compliance officers. Therefore, the average employer will not likely see an OSHA inspector unless an employee instigates an inspection. However, a new reporting system will provide data enabling OSHA to determine an individual firm's injuries and illnesses. This information will enable the agency to make better use of its limited resources.[2]

Roughly 70 percent of OSHA inspections have resulted from employee complaints. As you recall from the incident at the beginning of this chapter, employees at Sather Manufacturing Company refused to work in an environment they considered hazardous. Under the Occupational Safety and Health Act, an employee can legally refuse to work when all the following conditions exist:[3]

- The employee reasonably fears death, disease, or serious physical harm.
- The harm is imminent.
- There is too little time to file an OSHA complaint and get the problem corrected.
- The worker has notified the employer about the condition and asked that it be corrected but the employer has not taken action.

TABLE 13-1

Occupational Injury and Illness Rates by Industry[a]

Industry (Total Cases)[b]	Incidence Rates per 100 Full-time Workers[c]		
	1985	1990	1995
Private Sector	7.9	8.8	8.1
Agriculture, Forestry, and Fishing	11.4	11.6	9.7
Mining	8.4	8.3	6.2
Construction	15.2	14.2	10.6
General Building Contractors	15.2	13.4	9.8
Heavy Construction, except Building	14.5	13.8	9.9
Special Trades Contractors	15.4	14.7	11.1
Manufacturing	10.4	13.2	11.6
Durable Goods	10.9	14.2	12.8
Lumber and Wood Products	18.5	18.1	14.9
Furniture and Fixtures	15.0	16.9	13.9
Stone, Clay, and Glass Products	13.9	15.4	12.3
Primary Metal Industries	12.6	19.0	16.5
Fabricated Metal Products	16.3	18.7	15.8
Industrial Machinery and Equipment	10.8	12.0	11.2
Electronic and Other Electrical Equipment	6.4	9.1	7.6
Transportation Equipment	9.0	17.8	18.6
Instruments and Related Products	5.2	5.9	5.3
Miscellaneous Manufacturing Industries	9.7	11.3	9.1
Nondurable Goods	9.6	11.7	9.7
Food and Kindred Products	16.7	20.0	16.3
Tobacco Products	7.3	7.7	5.6
Textile Mill	7.5	9.6	8.2
Apparel and Other Textile Products	6.7	8.8	8.2
Paper and Allied Products	10.2	12.1	8.5

Since its inception, OSHA has revised its mission. The current thrust is to give employers a choice between partnership and traditional enforcement—to inject common sense into regulation and enforcement and to eliminate red tape. The overall purpose, of course, is to reduce injuries, illnesses, and fatality rates. To help small businesses, OSHA is expanding its assistance, reducing penalties, and putting more of its informational materials in electronic formats, including CD-ROMs and Internet sites.[4] Although many of the firms covered by OSHA are small businesses, OSHA's director has emphasized that these firms will not be punished for violations if they seek OSHA's assistance in correcting problems.[5]

TABLE 13-1

Occupational Injury and Illness Rates by Industry[a] *(Continued)*

Industry (Total Cases)[b]	Incidence Rates per 100 Full-time Workers[c]		
	1985	1990	1995
Printing and Publishing	6.3	6.9	6.4
Chemicals and Allied Products	5.1	6.5	5.5
Petroleum and Coal Products	5.1	6.6	4.8
Rubber and Miscellaneous Plastic Products	13.4	16.2	12.9
Leather and Leather Products	10.3	12.1	11.4
Transportation and Public Utilities	8.6	9.6	9.1
Wholesale and Retail Trade	7.4	7.9	7.5
Wholesale Trade	7.2	7.4	7.5
Retail Trade	7.5	8.1	7.5
Finance, Insurance, and Real Estate	2.0	2.4	2.6
Services	5.4	6.0	6.4

[a]Data for 1989 and subsequent years are based on the *Standard Industrial Classification Manual,* 1987 edition. For this reason, they are not strictly comparable with data for the years 1985–1988, which were based on the *Standard Industrial Classification Manual,* 1972 edition, 1977 supplement.
[b]Beginning with the 1992 survey, the annual survey measures only nonfatal injuries and illnesses, whereas past surveys covered both fatal and nonfatal incidents. To better address fatalities, a basic element of workplace safety, BLS (Bureau of Labor Statistics) implemented the *Census of Fatal Occupational Injuries.*
[c]The incident rates represent the number of injuries and illnesses per 100 full-time workers and were calculated at (N/EH) × 200,000, where
N = number of injuries and illnesses
EH = total hours worked by all employees during the calendar year
200,000 = base for 100 full-time equivalent workers (working 40 hours per week, 50 weeks per year)
Source: *Monthly Labor Review* (May 1997): 90–91.

Safety

Job-related deaths and injuries of all types extract a high toll in human misery. The significant financial costs are often passed along to the consumer in the form of higher prices. Thus, everyone is affected (directly or indirectly) by job-related deaths and injuries. The National Safety Council estimated the total costs of job-related injuries in 1995 to be over $119 billion[6] (see Table 13-2). Some managers may be surprised to discover that motor vehicle accidents are the number one cause of death on the job. A Bureau of Labor Statistics study found that of the deaths from workplace injuries in 1992, one-third occurred as the result of either automobile accidents or homicides.[7]

TABLE 13-2

Job-Related Injury Costs

Work Injury Costs

The true cost to the nation, to employers, and to individuals of work-related deaths and injuries is much greater than the cost of workers' compensation insurance alone. The figures presented below show the National Safety Council's estimates of the total costs of occupational deaths and injuries. Cost-estimating procedures were revised for the 1993 edition of *Accident Facts*. In general, cost estimates are not comparable from year to year. As additional or more precise data become available, they are used from that year forward. Previously estimated figures are not revised.

Total cost in 1995...**$119.4 billion**

This figure includes wage and productivity losses of $59.8 billion, medical costs of $19.2 billion, and administrative expenses of $25.5 billion. It also includes employer costs of $11.0 billion, such as the money value of time lost by workers other than those with disabling injuries who are directly or indirectly involved in injuries, and the cost of time required to investigate injuries, write up injury reports, and so on. Also included is damage to motor vehicles in work injuries of $1.4 billion and fire losses of $2.5 billion.

Cost per worker...**$960**

This figure indicates the value of goods or services each worker must produce to offset the cost of work injuries. It is not the average cost of a work injury.

Cost per death...**$790,000**

Cost per disabling injury...**$28,000**

These figures include estimates of wage losses, medical expenses, administrative expenses, and employer costs; they exclude property damage costs except to motor vehicles.

Source: Accident Facts (Chicago, IL: National Safety Council, 1996): 51.

The Focus of Safety Programs

Safety programs may be designed to accomplish their purposes in two primary ways. The *first approach* is to create a psychological environment and attitudes that promote safety. Accidents can be reduced when workers consciously or subconsciously think about safety. This attitude must permeate the firm's operations, and a strong company policy emphasizing safety and health is crucial. For example, a major chemical firm's policy states, "It is the policy of the company that every employee be assigned to a safe and healthful place to work. We strongly desire accident prevention in all phases of our operations. Toward this end, the full cooperation of all employees will be required." As the policy infers, no one person is assigned the task of making the workplace safe. It is everyone's job, from top management to the lowest level employee, and everyone should be encouraged to find solutions to

HRM IN ACTION
SAFE OR NOT

Ward is a *good ol' boy* who works hard and is very productive. Last week, in accordance with company policy, you gave a three-day suspension to the man who works beside him. The man was not wearing safety gear, although he had recently received a written notice for the same violation. As you come around the corner, you see Ward working without his safety glasses. He notices you and quickly puts them on. When you return to your desk, you check your records. You find that Ward was issued a notice for safety violation two weeks ago by another supervisor.

What action would you take?

safety problems. Sather Manufacturing obviously has a real safety dilemma. Employees are adamant in declaring that they are not safe, whereas Dionne Moore, the safety engineer, and the employees' supervisor are both unsure of the safety ramifications. Accident prevention requires a sustained effort by everyone, but unfortunately, the following adage often applies: "Everyone's responsibility becomes no one's responsibility." Therefore, the firm's managers, who can authorize implementation of the safety effort, must take the lead. The unique role of management is made clear by OSHA's position— that responsibility for employee safety rests primarily on the employer.

The *second approach* to safety program design is to develop and maintain a safe physical working environment. Here, the environment is altered to prevent accidents. Even if Joe, a machine operator, has been awake all night with a sick child and can barely keep his eyes open, the safety devices on his machine will help protect him. Attempts are made to create a physical environment in which accidents cannot occur. It is in this area that OSHA has had its greatest influence.

DEVELOPING SAFETY PROGRAMS

Organizational safety programs require planning for prevention of workplace accidents. Plans may be relatively simple, as for a small retail store, or more complex and highly sophisticated, as for a large automobile assembly plant. Regardless of the organization's size, the support of top management is essential if safety programs are to be effective. The top executives in a firm should be aware of the tremendous economic losses that can result from accidents.

Some of the reasons for top management to support a safety program are listed in Table 13-3. These data show that the lost productivity of a single injured worker is not the only factor to consider. Every phase of human resource management is involved. For instance, the firm may have difficulty in recruitment if it gains a reputation for having hazardous working conditions. Employee relations may be seriously eroded if workers believe that management does not care enough about them to make their workplace safe. Compensation may also be affected if the firm must pay a premium to attract

TABLE 13-3

Reasons for Management Support of a Safety Program

- **Personal loss.** The physical pain and mental anguish associated with injuries is always unpleasant and may even be traumatic for an injured worker. Of still greater concern is the possibility of permanent disability or even death.
- **Financial loss to injured employees.** Most employees are covered by company insurance plans or personal accident insurance. However, an injury may result in financial losses not covered by insurance.
- **Lost productivity.** When an employee is injured, there will be a loss of productivity for the firm. In addition to obvious losses, there are often hidden costs. For example, a substitute worker may need additional training to replace the injured employee. Even when another worker is available to move into the injured employee's position, efficiency may suffer.
- **Higher insurance premiums.** Workers' compensation insurance premiums are based on the employer's history of insurance claims. The potential for savings related to employee safety provides a degree of incentive to establish formal programs.
- **Possibility of fines and imprisonment.** Since the enactment of the Occupational Safety and Health Act, a willful and repeated violation of its provisions may result in serious penalties for the employer.
- **Social responsibility.** Many executives feel responsible for the safety and health of their employees. A number of firms had excellent safety programs years before OSHA existed. They understand that a safe work environment is not only in the best interests of the firm; providing one is the right thing to do.

qualified applicants and retain valued employees. Maintaining a stable workforce may become very difficult if the workplace is perceived as hazardous, as was the case with Sather Manufacturing.

The Superfund Amendments Reauthorization Act, Title III (SARA—the hazard communication standard), requires businesses to communicate more openly to their workers and the public about the hazards associated with the materials they use and produce and the wastes they generate. Although SARA has been around for several years, many firms do not yet have a satisfactory program for it in place. The hazard communication standard often leads the list of OSHA violations. Dealing with this standard appears to be relatively simple and inexpensive except when its provisions are ignored.

One way to strengthen a safety program is to include employee input, a move that provides workers with a sense of accomplishment. To prevent accidents, each worker must make a personal commitment to safe work practices. A team concept, wherein employees watch out for each other as a moral obligation, is a worthy goal. Participation in such teams helps form positive attitudes, and employees develop a sense of ownership of the program. The committee may become involved not only with safety issues but also with ways to improve productivity. Employee feedback is essential for an effective program, and good safety performance must be rewarded.

Companies with effective safety programs strive to involve virtually everyone in the firm. Line managers are normally responsible for controlling conditions that cause accidents. As part of this responsibility, they must set the proper safety example for other employees. If a supervisor fails to use safety devices when demonstrating use of the equipment, subordinates may feel that the devices are not really necessary. The line manager's attitude can also affect a worker's attitude toward safety training. Supervisors can show support for the safety program by conscientiously enforcing safety rules and by closely conforming to the rules themselves.

In many companies, one staff member coordinates the overall safety program. Some major corporations have risk management departments that anticipate losses associated with safety factors and prepare legal defenses in the event of lawsuits. Such titles as safety director and safety engineer are common. One of the safety director's primary tasks is to provide safety training for company employees. This involves educating line managers about the merits of safety and recognizing and eliminating unsafe situations. Although the safety director operates essentially in an advisory capacity, a well-informed and assertive director may have considerable power in the organization.

ACCIDENT INVESTIGATION

Accidents can happen, even in the most safety conscious firms. Each accident, regardless of whether it results in an injury, should be carefully evaluated to determine its cause and to ensure that it does not recur. The safety engineer and the line manager jointly investigate accidents. One of the responsibilities of any supervisor is to prevent accidents. To do so, the supervisor must learn—through active participation in the safety program—why accidents occur, how they occur, where they occur, and who is involved. Supervisors gain a great deal of knowledge about accident prevention by helping prepare accident reports.

Safety should also be emphasized during the training and orientation of new employees. The early months of employment are often critical because work injuries traditionally decrease with an employee's length of service.

EVALUATION OF SAFETY PROGRAMS

Perhaps the best indicator that a safety program is succeeding is a reduction in the number and severity of accidents. Thus, program evaluation involves more than counting the number of accidents; it must also consider their severity. Statistics such as frequency and severity rates are often used in program evaluation. The frequency rate is expressed by the following formula, which yields the number of lost-time accidents per million person-hours worked:

$$\text{Frequency rate} = \frac{\text{Number of lost-time accidents}}{\text{Number of person-hours worked during the period}} \times 1,000,000$$

Although this formula is used, OSHA has developed one that is conceptually different:

$$\text{Incident rate} = \frac{\text{Number of injuries and/or illnesses}}{\text{Total hours worked by all employees during reference year}} \times 200{,}000$$

In this formula, the constant (200,000) represents the base for 100 full-time equivalent workers at 40 hours per week, 50 weeks per year. The major differences between the formulas are that OSHA considers both injuries and illnesses, and as a base for reporting injury frequency rates, it uses 100 full-time employees (as opposed to 1 million person-hours).

The **severity rate** indicates the number of days lost because of accidents per million person-hours worked. It is expressed by the following formula:

Severity rate: A formula that is used to calculate the number of days lost because of accidents per million person-hours worked.

$$\text{Severity rate} = \frac{\text{Number of person-days lost}}{\text{Number of person-hours worked during the period}} \times 1{,}000{,}000$$

In addition to program evaluation criteria, an effective reporting system is needed to ensure that accidents are recorded. When a new safety program is initiated, the number of accidents may decline significantly. However, some supervisors may be failing to report certain accidents to make the statistics for their units look better. Proper evaluation of a safety program depends on the accurate reporting and recording of data.

To be of value, the conclusions derived from an evaluation must be used to improve the safety program. Gathering data and permitting this information to collect dust on the safety director's desk will not solve problems or prevent accidents. The results of the evaluation must be transmitted upward to top management and downward to line managers in order to generate improvements. Most employers will also mail or electronically transmit records of occupational injuries and illnesses directly to OSHA.

RATIONALE FOR SAFETY AND HEALTH TRENDS

Organizations are giving increased attention to safety. In addition to legal requirements, the reasons for this concern include the following:

- *Profitability.* Employees can produce only while they are on the job. In addition to payouts related to medical costs, other factors, such as lost production, increased recruiting, and training requirements, add to a firm's expense when an employee is injured or becomes ill.

- *Employee and Public Relations.* A good safety record may well provide companies with a competitive edge. Firms with good records have an effective vehicle for recruiting and retaining good employees.

- *Reduced Liability.* An effective safety program can reduce corporate and executive liability for charges when employees are injured.

- *Marketing.* A positive safety record can help firms win contracts.

■ *Productivity.* An effective safety program may boost morale and productivity while simultaneously reducing rising costs.

ERGONOMICS

Ergonomics: The study of human interaction with tasks, equipment, tools, and the physical work environment.

One specific safety and health approach that seems destined to become more common is the increased use of ergonomics. **Ergonomics** is the study of human interaction with tasks, equipment, tools, and the physical environment. Through ergonomics, an attempt is made to fit the machine and work environment to the person, rather than require the person to make the adjustment. Ergonomics includes all attempts to structure work conditions so they maximize energy conservation, promote good posture, and allow workers to function without pain or impairment. The costs of failing to achieve these purposes are excessive. Back injuries alone make up 23 percent of all disabling injuries. They cost employers an estimated $6.5 billion a year nationwide and probably could have been prevented through better ergonomic practices.[8] Another major problem relates to repetitive trauma, which may result in cumulative trauma disorders. In dealing with this problem, OSHA has targeted cumulative trauma disorders and *electronic sweatshops* in proposed ergonomic standards.[9] Although federal standards have not been implemented, California has issued the nation's first ergonomics regulation. This standard is quite controversial and some trade associations contend that it will drive up the cost of producing goods and services without protecting employees' health. Nevertheless, the document may have nationwide repercussions for employers.[10]

Cumulative Trauma Disorders (CDT)

Cumulative trauma disorders: A series of disorders, often associated with using computers, that include injuries to the back and upper extremities.

Carpal tunnel syndrome: A condition caused by repetitive flexing and extension of the wrist.

More than 60 percent of all work-related injuries are cumulative trauma disorders. **Cumulative trauma disorders** include injuries to the back and upper extremities. As such, they are a primary target of ergonomics. **Carpal tunnel syndrome**, a specific CDT, is caused by repetitive flexing and extension of the wrist. A nerve in the wrist may be pinched, resulting in the person's inability to differentiate hot and cold by touch and loss of muscle strength. A recent study indicated that carpal tunnel syndrome had the second highest incidence of workers' compensation claims. Carpal tunnel syndrome injuries—described as the "plague of the information age"—are also among the most expensive workers' compensation claims. They exceed the cost of claims from injuries due to sprains, strains, and fractures. The typical cost of carpal tunnel surgery today is approximately $18,000.[11]

The growing frequency of repetitive motion problems is attributed to the increased use of computers and an aging population that is more vulnerable to such injuries. Also related to increased workers' compensation claims is the increased recognition that such injuries are compensable.[12] You can see the tremendous growth of cumulative trauma disorders compared with all other occupational illnesses in Table 13-4.

One additional area of concern occurs when a company has little control of the work environment. Employees are increasingly working at home

TABLE 13-4

Cumulative Trauma Disorders Compared with All Other Occupational Illnesses, 1985–1994

Year	Cumulative Trauma	All Other Occupational Illnesses
1985	37,000	88,600
1986	45,500	91,400
1987	72,900	117,500
1988	115,700	125,200
1989	146,900	136,800
1990	185,400	146,200
1991	223,600	144,700
1992	281,800	175,600
1993	302,400	179,700
1994	332,000	183,000

Source: U.S. Bureau of Labor Statistics, 1996.

offices and using transient office worker space, yet the company remains responsible for workers' compensation claims.[13]

As great as the risk of carpal tunnel syndrome has become, it can be prevented or at least reduced. Managers can provide ergonomic furniture, especially chairs, and assure that computer monitors are set at eye level and keyboards at elbow level. Employees can also cooperate by taking these actions:

- Keep wrists straight
- Take exercise breaks
- Alternate tasks
- Shift positions periodically
- Adjust chair height
- Work with feet flat on the floor
- Be conscious of posture
- Use padded wrist supports[14]

Wrist, hand, elbow, shoulder, and back injuries continue to be an almost unavoidable plague for workers using computers in manufacturing, service, and office businesses. However, the Bureau of National Affairs, Inc. (BNA), a Washington D.C. publishing company, has found that the combination of proper equipment, training, and education about potential injuries can significantly cut costs. According to the firm's assistant treasurer, Gilbert S. Lavine, "education is the key." In fiscal year 1991, BNA had more than 1,000 employees and a dozen claims that cost $132,000. By fiscal year 1995, 10 claims among the company's 1,600 employees cost less than $30,000. A change in medical treatment has been one element but another important factor is that informed employees report injuries sooner, "when they first feel a twinge, as opposed to waiting years and years." In studies conducted by OSHA, companies implementing ergonomics programs eliminated injuries for about 60 percent of employees.[15]

Workplace and Domestic Violence

Workplace violence in various forms continues to extract a heavy toll in many areas of business. Automobile accidents are the leading cause of death, but homicides have moved up to second place.[16] The Workplace Violence Institute estimates the cost of violence to U.S. companies at $36 billion annually. The Bureau of Labor Statistics reports that 1,000 people were murdered and a million assaulted on the job in 1995. Terminations are a growing reason that workers act out against managers, and it is important for managers to decrease the adversarial nature of the employment situation.[17] Violence results in lost business, lost productivity from injured workers, and increases in lawsuits stemming from negligent security claims. If an employee can prove, for example, that the possibility an assault could occur was foreseeable (for example, inadequate parking lot lighting in a historically high-crime area), an assaulted employee might be able to sue successfully. Employers can also be cited by OSHA if violence is a recognized hazard in their establishments and they do nothing to prevent it.[18] Workers' compensation insurance premiums are also typically increased in companies that have experienced violence.

Few firms, even today, are adequately prepared to deal with the threat of workplace violence. A typical approach has been to use the selection process to screen out applicants who had violent tendencies. However, the profile developed for a typical attacker is not helpful: "A middle-age white man who has worked for several years at his company and was dissatisfied with his career status." Firms trying to dig deeper into personality traits can run into difficulty with the Americans with Disabilities Act, which makes it difficult to reject applicants on the basis of psychological tests.

An alternative approach is being tried by some firms that have had extensive experience with workplace violence. Instead of trying to screen out violent people, they are instead attempting to detect employees who commit minor aggressive acts. These individuals often go on to engage in more serious behaviors. These people, once identified, are required to meet with trained members of the human resources staff for counseling as long as needed. This approach may require more commitment on the part of the firm, but the alternative cost of violence may make this expenditure reasonable in the long run.[19]

A study of 395 human resource managers and security managers, conducted by the University of Southern California's Center for Crisis Management, found that violence was linked to an uncertain economy or a prolonged recession. Workplace violence was attributed to such organizational deficiencies as inadequate training programs to handle stress and substance abuse; insufficient background screening checks of employees; poor communications; and general organizational instability.[20]

There is no way an employer can avoid risk when it comes to violence. However, firms might consider the following actions both to minimize violent acts and to avoid law suits:

- Implement policies that ban weapons on company property including parking lots.
- Under suspicious circumstances, require employees to submit to searches for weapons or examinations to determine their mental fitness for work.
- Have a policy stating that the organization will not tolerate any incidents of violence or even threats of violence.
- Have a policy that encourages employees to report all suspicious or violent activity to management.
- Develop relationships with mental health experts who may be contacted for recommendations in dealing with emergency situations.
- Train managers and receptionists to recognize the warning signs of violence and means to diffuse violent situations.
- Equip receptionists with panic buttons to permit instant alerting of security.[21]

Domestic violence: Violence within a family that generally occurs away from the workplace but has a negative impact on the organization.

Domestic violence generally occurs away from the workplace. However, a survey of human resource professionals revealed that a full 78 percent of them believe domestic violence is a workplace issue. In another survey, 57 percent of corporate leaders reported that they believe domestic violence is a major problem in society and 33 percent said it affects their balance sheet.[22]

The Office of Criminal Justice calculates that three to four million women are battered each year. The U.S. Surgeon General's office reports that domestic violence is the most widespread cause of injury for women between 15 to 44 years of age. Although women in traditional relationships are the most common victims by far, children and men are also affected. The most tragic aspects of domestic violence affect the home, but a shocking toll is also exacted from the workplace in terms of lost productivity, increased health-care costs, absenteeism, and sometimes even workplace violence. The Bureau of National Affairs estimates the price of domestic violence to corporate America to be $3 billion to $5 billion a year.[23]

Business organizations have a huge stake in the problem of violence. The courts apparently agree, as they have ruled that employers have a duty of care for their employees, customers, and business associates that includes taking reasonable steps to prevent violence on their premises.

Wellness Programs

The traditional view of health is changing. Health is no longer thought to be dependent on medical care and simply the absence of disease. Today, the prevailing opinion is that optimal health can generally be achieved through environmental safety, organizational changes, and healthful lifestyles. Infectious diseases, over which a person has little control, are not the problem they once were. For example, from 1900 to 1970, the death rate from major infectious diseases dropped dramatically. However, the death rate from major chronic diseases, such as heart disease, cancer, and stroke, has significantly increased. It is quite possible that Cecil Pierce, the marketing vice president for Aztec Enterprises, is a candidate for a heart attack or stroke. When a 38-year-old cannot walk a short distance without getting flushed, breathing hard, and needing to rest, he has a problem. Today, heart disease and stroke are the top two killers worldwide. Chronic obstructive pulmonary disease and lung cancer are expected to move up to numbers 3 and 4, respectively, by the year 2000. All these causes of death may be partly prevented by lifestyle measures such as not smoking, eating a healthful diet, and exercising more.[24]

Although chronic lifestyle diseases are much more prevalent than they were 100 years ago, people have a great deal of control over many of them. These are the diseases related to smoking, excessive stress, lack of exercise, obesity, and substance abuse including alcohol and drugs. Increased recognition of this link has prompted employers to become actively involved with their employees' health and to establish wellness programs. A 1997 benefits survey conducted by SHRM showed that 43 percent of responding firms have wellness programs.[25] Quite possibly, Cecil would benefit greatly from participating in such a program. Physical fitness continues to be an important component of most programs. However, the movement is now toward a more holistic approach to improving health, and wellness programs often expand their focus to include other health issues. One of these important elements is stress management.

HR Web Wisdom

http://www.prenhall.com/mondy

STRESS BUSTERS
This site offers thoughts for reducing work stress as well as stress-building concepts.

Stress Management

Stress: The body's nonspecific reaction to any demand made on it.

Stress is the body's nonspecific reaction to any demand made on it. It affects people in different ways and is, therefore, a highly individual condition. Certain events may be quite stressful to one person but not to another. Moreover, the effect of stress is not always negative. For example, mild stress actually improves productivity and can be helpful in developing creative ideas. Although everyone lives under a certain amount of stress, if it is severe enough and persists long enough, it can be harmful. In fact, stress can be as disruptive to an individual as any accident. It can result in poor attendance, excessive use of alcohol or other drugs, poor job performance, or even overall poor health. There is increasing evidence indicating that severe, prolonged stress is related to the diseases that are leading causes of death—coronary heart disease, stroke, hypertension, cancer, emphysema, diabetes, and cirrhosis; stress may even lead to suicide. Stress costs U.S. industry billions of dollars each year in lost wages and treatment of related disorders.

TRENDS & INNOVATIONS

SABBATICAL LEAVES[26]

What was once considered useful for teachers is increasingly being used by business firms to deal with employee burnout and stress. Workplace sabbatical leaves, often with full pay and benefits, give workers a break from job stress and provide the means for becoming rejuvenated. Many firms with familiar names have sabbatical leaves such as Apple Computer Inc., McDonald's Corp., Time, Inc., Wells Fargo & Co., Xerox Corp., and AT&T. This expensive benefit is particularly popular among the high-tech firms of the Silicon Valley where the dominant need is to be creative. Betsy Lamb, director of compensation and benefits for Tandem Computers Inc. states, "The intent behind our sabbatical program was to recognize that employees are more productive if they're given a chance to periodically recharge their batteries while focusing on personal priorities. They actually come back refreshed and ready to go."

Tandem employees are eligible for sabbaticals after four years of continuous service. The policy allows employees six weeks' leave with full pay and benefits during which they may engage in non-job-related activities such as writing a book and exploring family history, or pursue other personal challenges. Even part-timers, who work 20 hour weeks, are eligible for a sabbatical and receive their normal part-time pay, while they are away from the job.

Does all this sound a bit expensive? It is. However, consider that disability resulting from stress costs an estimated $75 billion annually. Paying for a chunk of this causes firms to seek some solutions, such as sabbaticals.

The National Institute for Occupational Safety and Health (NIOSH) has studied stress as it relates to work. This organization's research indicates that some jobs are generally perceived as being more stressful than others. The 12 most stressful jobs are listed in Table 13-5. The common factor among these jobs is lack of employee control over work. Workers in such jobs may feel that they are trapped, treated more like machines than people. Some of the less stressful jobs are held by workers who have more control over their jobs, such as college professors and master craftspersons.

The fact that certain jobs are being identified as more stressful than others has important managerial implications. Managers are responsible for recognizing significantly deviant behavior in employees and referring them to health professionals for diagnosis and treatment. Some signs that may indicate problems include impaired judgment and effectiveness, rigid behavior, medical problems, increased irritability, excessive absences, emerging addictive behaviors, lowered self-esteem, and apathetic behavior. In addition, managers should monitor their employees' progress and provide them with the incentive to succeed. They should inform employees that there are rewards for lifestyle changes and that the advantages of such changes are greater than the costs involved. Stress may result in many complex problems, but it can generally be handled successfully. In the following section,

TABLE 13-5
Stressful Jobs

The 12 Jobs with the Most Stress

1. Laborer	7. Manager/administrator
2. Secretary	8. Waitress/waiter
3. Inspector	9. Machine operator
4. Clinical lab technician	10. Farm owner
5. Office manager	11. Miner
6. Supervisor	12. Painter

Other High-Stress Jobs (in Alphabetical Order)

Bank teller	Nurse's aide
Clergy member	Plumber
Computer programmer	Policeperson
Dental assistant	Practical nurse
Electrician	Public relations worker
Firefighter	Railroad switchperson
Guard	Registered nurse
Hairdresser	Sales manager
Health aide	Sales representative
Health technician	Social worker
Machinist	Structural-metal worker
Meat cutter	Teacher's aide
Mechanic	Telephone operator
Musician	Warehouse worker

Source: From a ranking of 130 occupations by the federal government's National Institute for Occupational Safety and Health.

we describe burnout, a condition that often results from organizational and individual failure to deal with stress effectively.

BURNOUT

Burnout: A gradual wearing down, a depletion of one's physical and mental resources that results from stress that is not necessarily job-related.

According to a New York City psychologist, Herbert Frelindenberger, **burnout** is a gradual wearing down, a depletion of one's physical and mental resources that results from stress that is not necessarily job related. Quite often, burnout victims have been worn down by striving to reach unrealistic expectations, many of them self-imposed.[27]

Burnout is often associated with a midlife or mid-career crisis, but it can happen at different times to different people. When this occurs, they may lose their motivation to perform. Although some employees try to hide their problems, certain shifts in their behavior indicate dissatisfaction. They may start procrastinating or go to the opposite extreme of taking on too many assignments. They may lose things and become increasingly scatterbrained. Individuals who are normally amiable may turn irritable. They may become cynical, disagreeable, or even pompous, or may develop paranoia.

Individuals in the helping professions, such as teachers and counselors, seem to be susceptible to burnout because of their jobs; others may be vulnerable because of their upbringing, expectations, or personalities. Burnout is frequently associated with people whose jobs require them to work closely with others under stressful and tension-filled conditions.

Any employee may experience burnout, and no one is exempt. The dangerous part of burnout is that it is contagious. A highly cynical and pessimistic burnout victim can quickly transform an entire group. Therefore, dealing with the problem quickly is very important. Once it has begun, it is difficult to stop.

Ideally, burnout should be dealt with before it occurs. To do this, managers must be aware of potential sources of stress. These sources exist both within and outside the organization.

SOURCES OF STRESS

Regardless of its origin, stress can become devastating. Although work-related factors are controllable to varying degrees, others may not be. Three frequently cited sources of stress that reside in the job or the job environment are role ambiguity, role conflict, and workload variance.[28] Other work-related sources include managerial work, working conditions, and corporate culture. These factors are discussed next.

Role ambiguity: A condition that exists when employees lack clear information about the content of their jobs.

Role Ambiguity.   **Role ambiguity** exists when an employee does not understand the content of the job. The employee may feel stress when he or she does not perform certain duties expected by the supervisor, or when he or she attempts to perform tasks that are a part of someone else's job. Role ambiguity is a condition that can be quite threatening to an employee and produce feelings of insecurity.

Role conflict: A condition that occurs when an individual is placed in the position of having to pursue opposing goals.

Role Conflict.   **Role conflict** occurs when an individual is placed in the position of having to pursue opposing goals. For example, a manager may be expected to increase production while under pressure to decrease the size of the workforce. Attaining both goals may be impossible, and stress is likely to result.

Workload Variance.   Workload variance involves dealing with both job overload and underload. When employees are given more work than they can reasonably handle, they become victims of **job overload**. A critical aspect of this problem is that the best performers in the firm are often the ones most affected. These individuals have proven that they can perform more, so they are often given more to do. At its extreme, work overload results in burnout.

Job overload: A condition that exists when employees are given more work than they can reasonably handle.

Job underload can also be a source of job stress. This condition most likely affects highly competent employees who constantly seek challenge in their jobs. When given menial, boring tasks to perform, this type of individual is stressed.

Managerial Work.

The nature of managerial work may itself be a source of stress. Responsibility for people, conducting performance appraisals, coordinating and communicating layoffs, and conducting outplacement counseling can create a great deal of stress for some people.

Working Conditions.

The physical characteristics of the workplace, including the machines and tools used, can create stress. Overcrowding, excessive noise, poor lighting, and poorly maintained workstations and equipment can all adversely affect employee morale and increase stress.

Corporate Culture.

Corporate culture, introduced in chapter 2, has a lot to do with stress. The CEO's leadership style often sets the tone. An autocratic CEO who permits little input from subordinates may create a stressful environment. A weak CEO may encourage subordinates to compete for power, resulting in internal conflicts.

Even in the healthiest corporate culture, stressful relationships among employees can occur. Employee personality types vary; when these are combined with differing values and belief systems, communication may be so impaired that stress is inevitable. Competition encouraged by the organization's reward system for promotion, pay increases, and status may add to the problem.

Stress factors outside the job and job environment also may affect job performance. Although these are usually less controllable by management, managers should recognize that they do exist and may have implications for job performance. Factors in this category include the family, financial problems, and living conditions.

The Family.

Although a frequent source of happiness and security, the family can also be a significant stressor. As a result, over one-half of all marriages end in divorce, a procedure that in itself is generally quite stressful. When divorce leads to single parenthood, the difficulties may be compounded.

Contrary to conventional wisdom, women feel no more anxiety on the job because they are mothers than men do because they are fathers. However, concern about their children can cause either parent to suffer stress-related health problems. When trouble exists both at home and at work, a double dose of stress exists. On the positive side, a healthy home life provides a protective buffer against work-related stressors, such as an overbearing boss.[29]

An increasingly common circumstance involving a change in traditional roles is the **dual-career family**, discussed in chapter 2, in which both husband and wife have jobs and family responsibilities. What happens when one partner is completely content with a job and the other is offered a desired promotion requiring transfer to a distant city? At best, these circumstances are beset with difficulties.

Dual-career family: A family in which both husband and wife have jobs and family responsibilities.

Financial Problems.

Problems with finances may place an unbearable strain on the employee. For some, these problems are persistent and never quite resolved. Unpaid bills and bill collectors can create great tension and play a role in divorce or poor work performance.

Living Conditions. Stress levels may be higher for people who live in densely populated areas. These people face longer lines, endure more hectic traffic jams, and contend with higher levels of air and noise pollution. Urban life has many advantages, but the benefits are not without costs—often in the form of stress.

COPING WITH STRESS

It is important for managers to be aware of sources of stress as it affects their employees and themselves. Equally important is that they implement plans to deal with stress. A number of programs and techniques are available which may prevent or relieve excessive stress. General organizational programs, although not specifically designed to cope with stress, may nevertheless play a major role. The programs and techniques listed in Table 13-6 are discussed in the chapters of this text as indicated. Their effective implementation will achieve these results:

- A corporate culture that holds anxiety and tension to an acceptable level is created. Employee inputs are sought and valued, employees are given greater control over their work, and communication is emphasized.

TABLE 13-6

Organizational Programs and Techniques That Can Be Helpful in Coping with Stress

General Organizational Programs Addressed in This Book	Chapter
Corporate Culture (Effective communication, motivation, and leadership styles)	2
Job Analysis	4
Training and Development	8
Organization Development	8
Career Planning and Development	9
Performance Appraisal	10
Compensation and Benefits	11, 12
Specific Techniques	
Hypnosis	13
Transcendental Meditation	13
Biofeedback	13
Specific Organizational Programs	
Physical Fitness	13
Alcohol and Drug Abuse	13
Employee Assistance Programs	13

- Each person's role is defined, yet care is taken not to discourage risk takers and those who want to assume greater responsibility.

- Individuals are given the training and development they need to successfully perform current and future jobs. Equal consideration is given to achieving personal and organizational goals. Individuals are trained to work as effective team members and to develop an awareness of how they and their work relate to others.

- Employees are assisted in planning for career progression.

- Employees participate in making decisions that affect them. They know what is going on in the firm, what their particular roles are, and how well they are performing their jobs.

- Employee needs, financial and nonfinancial, are met through an equitable reward system.

Table 13-6 also identifies several specific techniques that individuals can use to deal with stress. These methods include hypnosis, biofeedback, and transcendental meditation.

Hypnosis: An altered state of consciousness that is artificially induced and characterized by increased receptiveness to suggestions.

Hypnosis is an altered state of consciousness that is artificially induced and characterized by increased receptiveness to suggestions. A person in a hypnotic state may, therefore, respond to the hypnotist's suggestion to relax. Hypnosis can help many people cope with stress. The serenity achieved through dissipation of anxieties and fears can restore an individual's confidence. A principal benefit of hypnotherapy is that peace of mind continues after the person awakens from a hypnotic state. This tranquillity continues to grow, especially when the person has been trained in self-hypnosis.

Biofeedback: A method of learning to control involuntary bodily processes, such as blood pressure or heart rate.

Biofeedback is a method that can be used to control involuntary bodily processes, such as blood pressure or heart rate. For example, using equipment to provide a visual display of blood pressure, individuals may learn to lower their systolic blood pressure levels.

Transcendental meditation (TM): A stress-reduction technique in which an individual, comfortably seated, mentally repeats a secret word or phrase (mantra) provided by a trained instructor.

Transcendental meditation (TM) is a stress-reduction technique in which an individual, comfortably seated, repeats silently a secret word or phrase (mantra) provided by a trained instructor. Repeating the mantra over and over helps prevent distracting thoughts. Transcendental meditation has produced the following physiologic changes: decreased oxygen consumption, decreased carbon dioxide elimination, and decreased breathing rate. The technique results in a decreased metabolic rate and a restful state.

Table 13-6 also lists organizational programs that are designed specifically to deal with stress and related problems. These include physical fitness, alcohol and drug abuse, and employee assistance programs, discussed next.

Physical Fitness Programs

According to an SHRM study, 16 percent of responding firms have on-site physical fitness centers and 21 percent provide fitness center/gym subsidies.[30] In addition, thousands of U.S. business firms have exercise programs designed to help keep their workers physically fit. Cecil Pierce, the vice president introduced earlier, obviously needs medical attention and probably

Thousands of U.S. business firms provide exercise programs designed to help keep their workers physically fit.

would benefit greatly from a physician-supervised fitness program. From management's viewpoint, this effort makes a lot of sense. Loss of productivity resulting from coronary heart disease alone costs U.S. businesses billions of dollars annually. Company-sponsored fitness programs often reduce absenteeism, accidents, and sick pay. There is increasing evidence that if employees stick to company fitness programs, they will experience better health and the firm will have lower costs. A study at Steelcase, an office equipment manufacturer, found that participants in a corporate fitness program had medical claims costs that were 55 percent lower over a six-year period than did nonparticipants.[31] Table 13-7 lists some positive effects that have resulted from physical fitness and wellness programs.

TABLE 13-7

Examples of the Benefits of Physical Fitness and Wellness Programs

- In San Diego, the health care expenses for school employees and firefighters average $548 less for fitness program participants.
- The fitness program at SpeedCall Corporation resulted in a 65 percent decline in smoking and a 50 percent drop in the number of insurance claims filed by those who quit smoking.
- Weyerhaeuser Company claimed savings of about $8 million in two years through a program designed to enhance employee health.
- Dallas school teachers involved in a fitness program took an average of three fewer sick days per year. This saved almost $500,000 a year in substitute teacher pay alone.
- At Tenneco, the average insurance claim for exercising women was less than half that for nonexercising women. Similar statistics exist for men.
- Absenteeism at Lockheed was 60 percent lower for exercisers than for nonexercisers. The turnover rate is 13 percent lower among regular exercisers.

Source: Otto H. Chang and Cynthia Boyle, "Fitness Programs: Hefty Expense or Wise Investment?" *Management Accounting* 20 (January 1989): 47. Reprinted by permission. Published by Institute of Management Accountants (formerly National Association of Accountants), 10 Paragon Drive, Montvale, NJ 07645.

The Fitness Program of Northwestern Mutual Life Insurance Company

As a life insurance company, Northwestern Mutual Life Insurance Company (NML) has long focused on the health and well-being of its employees as well as its policy owners. The firm has long had a commitment to employee health, and in 1990, it moved into a new building that included an updated fitness center. The fitness center is open to NML's 3,300 employees 24 hours a day. The center offers aerobic exercise as well as weight training and the expertise of a part-time fitness consultant. The center is used by almost half the employee population. For those who want a little variety, the company will reimburse their YMCA memberships.

Medical screening programs are an important part of the services offered. Not only does NML provide testing for blood pressure and cholesterol; it also offers ergonomic assessments, weight-reduction programs, smoking cessation, and stress management. To demonstrate its commitment, flextime arrangements are offered to employees if they choose to attend wellness seminars.

NML's planning has focused on three major health care issues:

- Practicing prevention: Informing employees about a broad range of topics that range from smart eating habits to maintaining healthy relationships to getting regular examinations.

- Medical benefits: Providing education on the health-care system and insurance benefits, including the firm's employee assistance program.

- Becoming a partner with a medical provider: Informing employees on obtaining cost-effective medical care, choosing a physician, and working actively toward health with that physician.

Renee Dziekan, administrator of health services, states that "people who are trying to make healthy lifestyle choices need a lot of support, and we provide support with a very warm, caring environment at NML. It really is a hallmark of our corporate culture."[32]

Alcohol and Drug Abuse Programs

Alcoholism: A treatable disease characterized by uncontrolled and compulsive drinking that interferes with normal living patterns.

Alcoholism is a disease characterized by uncontrolled and compulsive drinking that interferes with normal living patterns. It is a significant problem that affects people at every level of society and it can both result from and cause excessive stress. As a person starts to drink excessively, the drinking itself results in greater stress. This increased stress is dealt with by more drinking, creating a vicious cycle. Early signs of alcohol abuse are especially difficult to identify. Often the symptoms are nothing more than an increasing number of absences from work. Although our society attaches a stigma to alcoholism, in 1956 the American Medical Association described it as a treatable disease.

TABLE 13-8

Signs Suggesting Employee Impairment Because of Substance Abuse

- Tardiness, poor attendance, or problems performing the job.
- Accident proneness and multiple workers' compensation claims.
- Physical appearance, e.g., dilated or constricted pupils.
- Lack of coordination.
- Mood swings.
- Psychomotor agitation or retardation. Alcohol, marijuana, and opioids can all cause fatigue. Cocaine, amphetamines, and hallucinogens can cause anxiety.
- Thought disturbances. Cocaine, alcohol, PCP, amphetamines, and inhalants often cause grandiosity or a subject sense of profound thoughts.
- Other indicators. Cocaine, PCP, and inhalants can all cause aggressive or violent behavior. Alcohol and other sedatives reduce inhibition. Marijuana increases appetite, whereas stimulants decrease it. Both drugs cause excessive thirst.

Source: Deanna Kelemen, "How to Recognize Substance Abuse in the Workplace," *Supervision* 56 (September 1995): 4.

As with alcohol, drug abuse has also impacted the workplace. According to the National Institute on Drug Abuse (NIDA), almost 70 percent of the nation's illicit drug users are employed. In some instances, problems associated with drug abusers may consume as much as 35 percent of a firm's profits.[33] In certain industries—transportation, for example—drug use on the job is especially hazardous and potentially devastating to the firm. Think of the damage that can be done by a 40-ton truck careening out of control. Under ideal conditions, a fully loaded truck in daylight on a dry road cannot stop in a space shorter than 300 feet: the length of a football field.

All illegal drugs have some adverse effects. Although marijuana is touted as innocuous by some, a Stanford University study confirms that even occasional marijuana use can impair eye-hand coordination up to 24 hours after ingestion.[34]

Chemically dependent employees exhibit behaviors that distinguish them from drug-free workers. In one study, employees who had a positive drug test, but were hired anyway, missed 50 percent more time from work than other employees. They also had a 47 percent higher chance of being fired. According to NIDA, one Utah power company found that drug-positive employees were five times more likely than other employees to cause an on-the-job accident. Substance abuse, involving either alcohol or drugs, increases employee theft, lowers morale, and reduces productivity.[35]

The Drug-free Workplace Act of 1988 requires firms with large government contracts or grants to make a good faith effort to maintain a *drug-free workplace*. Because substance abuse is so expensive, all firms should have the same goal. Drug testing as a component in an organization's selection process is one means of achieving this goal. However, as a large percentage of substance abusers are already employed, this is obviously not the solution to the problem. For one thing, managers must learn to recognize impaired or intoxicated employees and those who may be addicted. Signs that suggest an employee may be impaired are shown in Table 13-8. Remember that none of the signs alone necessarily means that an employee is impaired. Also, the behavior must be observed over a long period of time.

Numerous firms have recognized the pervasiveness of drug problems in our society and have taken positive action to deal with them. A major goal of many firms is to ensure that drug abusers are not hired. However, if a person becomes an abuser after employment, a supervisor may be forced to resort to discipline for work-related irregularities, such as absenteeism and low productivity. All supervisors should be trained to look for signs of substance abuse. If evidence is found that it does exist, the employee should be required to report to the medical department or to the firm's employee assistance program—if the company has these units—where an attempt will be made to salvage the person. The consequences of a positive test will depend on the firm's policy. For example, Texas Instrument's policy is simple: "There will be no use of any illegal drug. There will be no illicit use of a legal drug." The difficult part is not formulating the policy but rather implementing it. Also, remember that an employee in a substance abuse rehabilitation program is protected by the Americans with Disabilities Act.

HR Web Wisdom

http://www.prenhall.com/mondy
EMPLOYEE ASSISTANCE PROGRAMS (EAPs)
Information on program design, implementation, counseling, and evaluation is included.

Employee Assistance Programs (EAPs)

Employee assistance program (EAP): A comprehensive approach that many organizations have taken to deal with burnout, alcohol and drug abuse, and other emotional disturbances.

An **employee assistance program (EAP)** is a comprehensive approach that many organizations have taken to deal with numerous problem areas, including marital or family difficulties, job performance problems, stress, emotional or mental health issues, financial troubles, alcohol and drug abuse, and grief. Most programs are created to control substance abuse or mental health costs, according to Timothy E. Glaros, marketing manager for Ceridian Corporation.[36] Some have also become concerned with HIV and AIDS, eldercare, workplace violence, and natural disasters, such as earthquakes, floods, and tornadoes.[37]

In an employee assistance program, a firm either provides in-house professional counselors or refers employees to an appropriate community social service agency. Typically, most or all of the costs—up to a predetermined amount—are borne by the employer. The EAP concept includes a response to personal psychological problems that interfere with both an employee's well-being and overall productivity. The purpose of assistance programs is to provide emotionally troubled employees with the same consideration and assistance given employees with physical illnesses.

The Drug Free Workplace Act of 1988 requires federal employees and employees of firms under government contract to have access to employee assistance program services. As you would imagine, EAPs grew rapidly in number following that act. However, many firms have determined that such programs offer many advantages and have implemented them voluntarily. In 1958, employee assistance counseling was offered by fewer than 50 American firms. In 1997, a study by SHRM indicated that 58 percent of responding firms had an employee assistance program.[38] These programs are being set up primarily to increase worker productivity and reduce costs. Utah Power and Light's program receives a $3.73 return of every dollar invested. This return stems from less time off required by employees and reduced medical costs for the EAP users. R.R. Donnelley & Sons found a return of $1.61 for each dollar invested in the first year its employee assistance program was in operation.[39] Returns on investment will vary, but one executive estimates that a mature, well-run program will return a minimum of three dollars for every dollar spent on it. This level of return will not happen, however, unless the employer is committed to promoting the program, educating employees and managers about its purpose, and eliminating the stigma from the environment. Advantages claimed for EAPs include lower absenteeism, decreases in workers' compensation claims, and fewer accidents.

A primary concern is getting employees to use the program. Some employees perceive a stigma attached to *needing help*. Supervisors must receive training to help them acquire the specialized interpersonal skills needed for recognizing troubled employees and encouraging them to utilize the firm's employee assistance program. Addicted employees are often experts at denial and deception and they can fool even experienced counselors.

Two additional health issues of concern to management include smoking and AIDS. These topics are dealt with in the next section of the chapter.

Smoking in the Workplace

An important health issue facing employers today is environmental tobacco smoke (ETS). Although some smokers and advocates remain adamant that passive smoking is not harmful, the Environmental Protection Agency has determined that ETS is a class A carcinogen. This classification puts it in the same cancer-causing category as asbestos and benzene. A study conducted by the Centers for Disease Control and Prevention (CDC) reinforces past studies showing that secondhand smoke is a significant public health risk.[40] The study will likely strengthen efforts to ban smoking. Smoking bans have already been enacted in businesses and public buildings nationwide. OSHA has proposed banning smoking or limiting it to separately ventilated areas in 6 million U.S. businesses. According to Dr. James Pirkle of the CDC's National Center for Environmental Health, secondhand or environmental tobacco smoke causes 3,000 lung cancers a year.[41] The American Heart Association estimates that secondhand, or passive, smoke kills 53,000 nonsmokers each year by causing cancer, heart disease, and other smoke-related illnesses. In fact, smoking is the leading cause of preventable death, resulting in more deaths than the combined toll from AIDS, cocaine, heroin, alcohol, fire, automobile accidents, homicide, and suicide.

Numerous studies have concluded that workplace smoking not only is hazardous to employees' health but is also detrimental to the firm's financial health. Increased costs of insurance premiums, higher absenteeism, and lost productivity cost the U.S. economy $65 billion a year. These factors, along with rising opposition from nonsmokers and widespread local and state laws, have spurred many firms into action, and the trend continues. For example, one recent survey indicated that in 1991, 32 percent of all companies banned smoking at work. By 1993, 56 percent had eliminated workplace smoking, and on August 11, 1997, President Clinton banned smoking in federal buildings. A separate study indicated that by the year 2002, no less than 96 percent of the companies surveyed had a goal of being smoke free.[42]

When tough smoking policies prove ineffective, some employers think it is time to quit battering morale by booting smokers out into blizzards or heat waves. Companies are also concerned about lost productivity. Smoke breaks taken some distance away from the work place eat up a lot of time. To deal with this, State Farm Insurance will soon have a covered smoking area near the main building. For this step, a two-year-old edict prohibiting smoking anywhere on company property was reversed. At the other end of a continuum, Motorola is making smoking even tougher. This firm has started enforcing a policy at four plants that prohibits employees from smoking anywhere on company property, including in their own cars parked in the Motorola parking lot.[43] Another approach is being taken by an increasing number of firms. Nearly 25 percent of large companies charge smokers higher premiums than nonsmoking co-workers for health insurance. U-Haul and Texas Instruments add an extra $10 to $50 a month and a group of more aggressive firms are charging double.[44]

Regardless of the twist a firm's smoking policy takes, the company will have to maintain fresh indoor air for its employees. The alternative will be a backlash from nonsmokers and lawsuits from survivors of those who may one day die from secondhand smoke.

AIDS in the Workplace

AIDS (acquired immune deficiency syndrome): A disease that undermines the body's immune system, leaving the person susceptible to a wide range of fatal diseases.

AIDS (acquired immune deficiency syndrome) is a disease that undermines the body's immune system, leaving the person susceptible to a wide range of fatal diseases. AIDS is definitely a workplace issue and one that impacts productivity. Employees fearful of associating with those infected with the virus create an atmosphere that is not conducive to productivity. A challenge to management is to educate all employees about the disease and how to deal with it and understanding medical expert assurance that the disease cannot be transmitted through casual contact. Outside of health care, workplace exposure to blood is rare. Therefore, there is no rational reason for employees to fear working with someone who has AIDS or who has been exposed to the virus. Unfortunately, the vast majority of employers have not provided workplace AIDS education for their employees.[45]

Today, approximately one million people in North America are estimated to be infected with the human immunodeficiency virus (HIV)—the virus that causes AIDS.[46] If a firm has a workforce of 300 people, at least one is probably HIV positive or has AIDS. As of 1995, there have been approximately half a million cases of AIDS in the United States. The cause is a bloodborne virus with very limited avenues of transmission. Humans acquire HIV infection by having unprotected sex with an infected partner, by sharing contaminated needles, by being born to an infected mother, or by receiving a contaminated blood product.[47]

Medical researchers have determined that some individuals who are HIV positive are long-term nonprogressors; that is, they may never develop AIDS. Approximately 6 percent to 9 percent of people infected with HIV for more than 10 years are symptom free. They show no signs of progressing to symptomatic infection and have a normal anticipated life span in the workplace. The main point here is that management cannot automatically assume that the infected individual will have anything other than a normal life span in the workplace.[48] This situation is different from the assumption only a few years ago when an individual with AIDS was presumed to have a short work life.

OSHA's Bloodborne Pathogen Standards are apparently clear for healthcare providers who are at higher risk for exposure to blood and other body fluids. However, for other industries, the guidelines are somewhat ambiguous. Nevertheless, compliance is mandatory and OSHA made over 1,000 citations against non-health-care organizations for violations of its standard during a two-year period. The standards require organizations to determine which individuals or job classes might be reasonably anticipated to contact blood or body fluids in the course of employment and to make the appropriate provisions for their protection.[49] For the infected employee, the Americans with Disabilities Act requires that reasonable accommodations be made. They may include, for example, equipment changes, workstation modifications, adjustments to work schedules, or assistance accessing the facility.[50]

A GLOBAL PERSPECTIVE
Global Health and Safety: Be Prepared

Specific issues impacting the health and safety of expatriates are of concern to employers. The international movement of employees can be a major stressor for these expatriates. A vitally important service of human resource professionals is to prepare employees and their families to cope with the stress they will encounter because of global assignments. Expatriates often experience stress from the moment they learn of global assignments until well after returning home.

Stress and its health implications are evident in almost any work environment, but they are usually quite high in the global arena. A firm that inappropriately addresses global stressors can experience failure and disinterested employees. Also, because the cost of a failed expatriate assignment can carry a price tag of a million dollars, recruiting the right local talent, at the right price, can set international expansion plans back by months or years.[51] Human resource management practices that prepare expatriates to deal with the norms, values, goals, and objectives of the host country will help ensure the health and effectiveness of these employees.[52]

Global assignments for unprepared employees are costly to the individual involved and quite expensive for the organization. Basically, to ensure a healthy and effective expatriate the right person must be selected, the employee and the employee's family must be properly prepared, and everyone transferred must understand and be ready to cope with differences in culture, communication, and language. A repatriation plan must be developed to ease the reentry of the employee and the family back to the United States, and companies must follow through with an employee career development plan.

Concern with international occupational health and safety issues is expanding even beyond concern over expatriate matters. A worldwide concern for worker health and safety is emerging. Unfortunately, laws and standards regulating working conditions vary greatly among countries, as does the ability to enforce these laws, but concerns are increasing and are getting more global recognition through attention by the news media and from concern of governments throughout the world. Workers in many countries operate unsafe equipment, are exposed to hazardous chemicals or materials, and work without appropriate protective equipment. Other significant international health and safety concerns include AIDS in the workplace, smoking, and a variety of environmental considerations. Global human resource professionals need to be involved with more than just understanding and complying with the various health and safety standards. They should also consider the ethical implications of merely complying with substandard regulations or perpetuating unsafe conditions in countries that lack legal standards or effective means of enforcement.[53]

SUMMARY

1. *Define* safety *and* health.

   Safety involves protecting employees from injuries resulting from work-related accidents. Health refers to the employees' freedom from physical or emotional illness.

2. *Explain the purpose of the Occupational Safety and Health Act.*

   OSHA has dramatically altered management's role in the area of safety and health. Under a new policy, OSHA focuses on work sites that are most exposed to three risks: problems with confined space, construction materials containing lead, and tuberculosis. The organizations primarily affected are health-care facilities, nursing homes, construction companies, and manufacturers whose products or processes contain dangerous chemicals.

3. *Describe the focus of safety programs in business operations.*

   Safety programs may be designed to accomplish their purposes in two primary ways. The first is to create a psychological environment and attitudes that promote safety. A strong company policy emphasizing safety and health is crucial. The second approach to safety program design is to develop and maintain a safe physical working environment.

4. *Explain how safety programs are evaluated.*

   An indicator that a safety program is succeeding is a reduction in the number and severity of accidents. The frequency rate is expressed by a formula that yields the number of lost-time accidents per million person-hours worked. The severity rate indicates the number of days lost because of accidents per million person-hours worked.

5. *Describe cumulative trauma disorders.*
Cumulative trauma disorders, include injuries to the back and upper extremities and are a primary target of ergonomics. Carpal tunnel syndrome is a specific problem caused by repetitive flexing and extension of the wrist.

6. *Explain the effect on businesses of workplace violence.*
Violence results in lost business, lost productivity from injured workers, and increases in lawsuits stemming from negligent security claims. Workers' compensation insurance premiums are also typically increased in companies that have experienced violence.

7. *Describe the purposes of health and wellness programs.*
The traditional view is changing. No longer is health considered to be dependent on medical care and simply the absence of disease. Today, the prevailing opinion is that optimal health can generally be achieved through environmental safety, organizational adaptations, and changed lifestyles.

8. *Define* stress.
Stress is the body's nonspecific reaction to any demand made on it.

9. *Explain the importance of stress management in business today.*
Employees are increasingly holding their employers liable for emotional problems they claim are work related, and stress-related mental disorders have become the fastest growing occupational disease. There is increasing evidence that severe, prolonged stress is related to the diseases that are leading causes of death: coronary heart disease, stroke, hypertension, cancer, emphysema, diabetes, and cirrhosis. Stress may even lead to suicide.

10. *Define* burnout *and describe the warning signs of burnout.*
Burnout has been described as a state of fatigue or frustration, which stems from devotion to a cause, way of life, or relationship that did not provide the expected reward. Warning signs of burnout are (1) irritability, (2) forgetfulness, (3) frustration, (4) fatigue, (5) procrastination, (6) tension, and (7) increased alcohol or drug use.

11. *Identify the sources of stress.*
Sources of stress include role ambiguity, role conflict, financial problems, workload variance, managerial work, working conditions, corporate culture, the family, financial problems, and living conditions.

12. *Explain means of coping with stress.*
Hypnosis is an altered state of consciousness that is artificially induced and characterized by increased receptiveness to suggestions. *Biofeedback* is a method that can be used to control involuntary bodily processes, such as blood pressure or heart rate. *Transcendental meditation* (TM) is a stress-reduction technique in which a person, comfortably seated, silently repeats a secret word or phrase (mantra) provided by a trained instructor.

13. *Describe the importance of physical fitness programs.*
Many U.S. business firms have exercise programs designed to help keep their workers physically fit. These programs often reduce absenteeism, accidents, and sick pay.

14. *Explain alcohol abuse and drug abuse programs.*

Alcohol, cocaine, and other mind-altering drugs have impacted the workplace. Numerous firms have recognized the pervasiveness of these problems in our society and have taken positive action to deal with them.

15. *Describe employee assistance programs.*

An employee assistance program (EAP) is a comprehensive approach that many organizations have taken to deal with marital or family problems, job performance problems, stress, emotional or mental health issues, financial troubles, alcohol and drug abuse, and grief. More recently, some EAPs have also become concerned with HIV and AIDS, eldercare, workplace violence, and natural disasters, such as earthquakes, floods, and tornadoes. Employee assistance programs are being set up primarily to increase worker productivity and reduce costs.

16. *Describe the possible impact of smoking in the workplace.*

Numerous studies have concluded that workplace smoking is not only hazardous to employees' health but is also detrimental to the firm's financial health. Increased costs of insurance premiums, higher absenteeism, and lost productivity cost the U.S. economy billions each year. These factors along with rising opposition from nonsmokers and widespread local and state laws have spurred many firms into action—and the trend continues.

17. *Explain the possible impact of AIDS in the workplace.*

AIDS is a disease that undermines the body's immune system, leaving the person susceptible to a wide range of fatal diseases. A direct effect on business is that it drains the pool of healthy adults of working age. Although AIDS has become more feared than cancer, a relatively small percentage of firms have established formal policies to deal with it. The need for educating employees is obvious.

QUESTIONS FOR REVIEW

1. Define safety and health.
2. Describe the purpose of the Occupational Safety and Health Act.
3. What effect does workplace violence have on an organization?
4. What are the primary ways in which safety programs are designed? Discuss.
5. What are some measurements that would suggest the success of a firm's safety program?
6. Distinguish between cumulative trauma disorders and carpal tunnel syndrome.
7. What are the purposes of health and wellness programs?
8. Why should a firm attempt to identify stressful jobs? What could an organization do to reduce the stress situations associated with a job?
9. Why should a firm be concerned with employee burnout?
10. Describe the major sources of stress.

11. Explain the means of coping with stress.

12. Why should alcohol and drug abuse programs be established?

13. Explain why employee assistance programs are being established.

14. What concerns should a manager have regarding smoking and AIDS in the workplace?

DEVELOPING HRM SKILLS

AN EXPERIENTIAL EXERCISE

At times, workers have personal problems that negatively influence their work and that may make the workplace unsafe. When this occurs, both managers and human resource professionals may be required to become involved to maintain a safe and healthy work environment. Dealing with one's own personal problems is often difficult, and assisting employees in dealing with their personal problems can be even more taxing on managers. However, since a problem employee can have a negative effect on workforce productivity, such a situation must be addressed by individuals involved in human resource management. This exercise should provide a better understanding of how to handle a most difficult issue—that of resolving employee problems.

If you are a sensitive person, you may want to play a role in this exercise. Two students will actively participate. One will play Annette and one will play Walter. The rest of you should observe carefully. Your instructor will provide any additional information necessary to participate.

Take It to the Net

We invite you to visit the Mondy home page on the Prentice Hall Web site at:

http://www.prenhall.com/mondy

for updated information, Web-based exercises, and links to other HR-related sites.

HRM SIMULATION

*O*ne of the problems facing the human resources director of your firm is an accident rate higher than it should be. Some of the causes of this are a higher-than-average turnover rate, a less-than-satisfactory morale level, and a lack of any type of accident prevention or safety program. The accident rate for the organization (as measured by employee-days lost per 1 million employee-hours) is 494. The industry average accident rate is also 494. However, both of these rates are above local accident rates and those of many other industries. Your team has the option of implementing a program and budget to deal with this problem. As always, there is an associated cost.

In Incident I, several proposals have been submitted concerning health, assistance, and wellness issues. Your team will have the task of studying these proposals and making a recommendation.

HRM INCIDENT

1

Here Comes OSHA!

*W*anda Zackery was extremely excited a year ago when she joined Landon Electronics as its first safety engineer. She had graduated from Florida State University with a degree in electrical engineering and a strong desire to enter business. Wanda had selected her job at Landon Electronics over several other offers. She believed that it would provide her with a broad range of experiences, which she could not receive in a strictly engineering job. Also, when she was interviewed by the company president, Mark Lincoln, he promised her that the firm's resources would be at her disposal to correct any safety-related problems.

Her first few months at Landon were hectic but exciting. She immediately identified numerous safety problems. One of the most dangerous involved a failure to install safety guards on all exposed equipment. Wanda carefully prepared her proposal, including expected costs, to make needed minimum changes. She estimated that it would take approximately $50,000 to complete the necessary conversions. Wanda then presented the entire package to Mr. Lincoln. She explained the need for the changes to him and Mr. Lincoln cordially received her presentation. He said he would like to think it over and would get back to her.

That was six months ago! Every time Wanda attempted to get some action on her proposal, Mr. Lincoln was friendly but still wanted some more time to consider it. In the meantime, Wanda had become increasingly anxious. Recently, a worker had barely avoided a serious injury. Some workers had also become concerned. She heard through the grapevine that someone had telephoned the regional office of OSHA.

Her suspicions were confirmed the very next week when an OSHA inspector appeared at the plant. No previous visits had ever been made to the company. Although Mr. Lincoln was not overjoyed, he permitted the inspector access to the company. Later he might have wished he had not been so cooperative. Before the inspector left, he wrote violations for each piece of equipment that did not have the necessary safety guards. The fines would total $5,000 if the problems were not corrected right away. The inspector cautioned that repeat violations could cost $50,000 and possible imprisonment.

As the inspector was leaving, Wanda received a phone call. "Wanda, this is Mark. Get up to my office right now. We need to get your project under way."

Questions

1. Discuss Mr. Lincoln's level of commitment to occupational safety.
2. Is there a necessary tradeoff between Landon's need for low expenses and the workers' need for safe working conditions? Explain.

HRM INCIDENT

2

A Star Is Falling

"*J*ust leave me alone and let me do my job," said Manuel Gomez.

Dumbfounded, Bill Brown, Manuel's supervisor, decided to count to 10 and not respond to Manuel's comment. As he walked back to his office, Bill thought about how Manuel had changed over the past few months. He had been a hard worker and extremely cooperative when he came to work for Bill two years earlier. The company had sent Manuel to two training schools and had received glowing reports about his performance in each of them.

Until about a year ago, Manuel had a perfect attendance record and was an ideal employee. At about that time, however, he began to have personal problems, which resulted in a divorce six months later. Manuel had requested a day off several times to take care of personal business. Bill had attempted to help in every way he could without getting directly involved in Manuel's personal affairs, but he was aware of the strain Manuel must have experienced as his marriage broke up and he and his wife engaged in the inevitable disputes over child custody, alimony payments, and property.

During the same period, top management initiated a push for improving productivity. Bill found it necessary to put additional pressure on all his workers, including Manuel. He tried to be considerate, but he had to become much more performance oriented, insisting on increased output from every worker. As time went on, Manuel began to show up late for work and actually missed two days without calling Bill in advance. Bill attributed Manuel's behavior to extreme stress. Because Manuel had been such a good worker for so long, Bill excused the tardiness and absences, only gently suggesting that Manuel should try to do better.

Sitting at his desk, Bill thought about what might have caused Manuel's outburst a few minutes earlier. Bill had simply suggested to Manuel that he shut down the machine he was operating and clean up the surrounding area. This was a normal part of Manuel's job and something he had been careful to do in the past. Bill felt the disorder around Manuel's machine might account for the increasing number of defects in the parts he was making. "This is a tough one. I think I'll talk to the boss about it," thought Bill.

Questions
1. What do you think is likely to be Manuel's problem? Discuss.
2. If you were Bill's boss, what would you recommend that he do?

Notes

1. "Job Related Injuries, Illness Take Heavy Toll," *Houston Chronicle* (July 28, 1997): A1.
2. "New OSHA Rule Clarifies Injury, Illness Data Collection Requirements," *US Newswire* (via Comtex) http://www3elibrary.com/getdoc.cgi?id=76...m=RL&pubname=US_Newswire&puburl (11August 1997).

3. Lynn Atkinson, "Avoiding 'Safety Walkouts,'" *HR Focus* 73 (October 1996): 20.

4. Linda Micco, "OSHA Reform Legislation Premature, Official Says," *HR News* 16 (August 1997): 11.

5. "OSHA to Mix a Little Mercy with Latest Crackdown," *The Wall Street Journal* (February 1, 1994): B2.

6. "Job Related Injury Costs," *Accident Facts* (Chicago, IL: National Safety Council, 1996): 51.

7. Stephenie Overman, "Driving the Safety Message Home," *HRMagazine* 39 (March 1994): 58.

8. Robert D. Ramsey, "What Supervisors Should Know about Ergonomics," *Supervision* 56 (August 1995): 10.

9. Dominic Bencivenga, "Economics of Ergonomics: Finding the Right Fit," *HRMagazine* 41 (August 1996): 70.

10. Robert W. Thompson, "Ergonomics Is Subject of Federal Report, California Rule," *HR News* 16 (August 1997): 4.

11. Ramsey, "What Supervisors Should Know about Ergonomics."

12. Stephanie D. Esters, "Safeco Offers Ergonomics Program for PC Operators," *National Underwriter* (Property and Casualty/Risk and Benefits Management Edition) (November 11, 1996): 61–62.

13. "Performance of Mobile Worker Tied to Flexible Office Design," *Supervision* 57 (June 1996): 12.

14. Ramsey, "What Supervisors Should Know about Ergonomics," 12.

15. Bencivenga, "Economics of Ergonomics: Finding the Right Fit."

16. Ron Panko, "Workplace Violence Guidelines Create New Risks," *Best's Review* (Property/Casualty Insurance Edition) (July 1996): 55.

17. Tom Lowry, "Executives Warned to Curb Workplace Violence," *USA Today* (November 20, 1996): 02B.

18. Panko, "Workplace Violence Guidelines Create New Risks."

19. John T. Landry, "Workplace Violence: Preventing the Unthinkable," *Harvard Business Review* 75 (January/February 1997): 11–12.

20. "Workplace Violence Linked to WC Claims, EAP Usage," *National Underwriters*, Property & Casualty Risk & Benefits Management Edition (January 8, 1996): 15.

21. Patrick Mirza, "Tips Offered on Minimizing Workplace Violence," *HR News* 16 (July 1997): 15.

22. Charlene Marmer Solomon, "Talking Frankly about Domestic Violence," *Personnel Journal* 74 (April 1995).

23. Ibid., 64.

24. "Longevity Facts," *The Johns Hopkins Medical Letter: Health After 50* 9 (September 1997): 1.

25. "1997 SHRM Benefits Survey," *Society for Human Resource Management* (1997): 22.

26. Christopher J. Bachler, "Workers Take Leave of Job Stress," *Personnel Journal* 74 (January 1995): 38–42.

27. Tom Robotham, "How to Beat Job Burnout," *Cosmopolitan* 220 (June 1996): 190.

28. Max E. Douglas, "Creating Eustress in the Workplace: A Supervisor's Role," *Supervision* 57 (October 1996): 6.

29. Deborah Erickson, "Are Women and Men That Different?" *Harvard Business Review* 73 (September/October 1995): 12–13.

30. "1997 SHRM Benefits Survey," Society for Human Resource Management (1997): 22.

31. Michael Barrier, "How Exercise Can Pay Off," *Nation's Business* 85 (February 1997): 41.

32. Gillian Flynn, "Companies Make Wellness Work," *Personnel Journal* 74 (February 1995): 65–66.

33. Bill Oliver, "How to Prevent Drug Abuse in Your Workplace," *HRMagazine* 38 (December 1993): 79–80.

34. Paul Farrell, "Pass or Fail: Managing a Drug and Alcohol Testing Program," *Risk Management* 43 (May 1996): 34.

35. Deanna Kelemen, "How to Recognize Substance Abuse in the Workplace," *Supervision* 56 (September 1995): 3.

36. Peggy Stuart, "Investments in EAPs Pay Off," *Personnel Journal* 72 (February 1993): 42.

37. Sharon A. Haskins and Brian H. Kleiner, "Employee Assistance Programs Take New Directions," *HR Focus* 71 (January 1994): 16.

38. "1997 SHRM Benefits Survey," *Society for Human Resource Management* (1997): 22.

39. Gillian Flynn, "Nice Companies Don't Finish Last: A Look at Assistance That Works," *Personnel Journal* 74 (October 1995): 176.

40. Jennifer J. Laabs, "Companies Kick the Smoking Habit," *Personnel Journal* 73 (January 1994): 38–43.

41. Anne Rochell, "Secondhand Smoke Hits 9 of 10, CDC Says," *The Atlanta Journal* (April 24, 1996): A1.

42. Ibid., 38.

43. Del Jones, "Breathing Room for Smokers: Employers Are Bringing Them in from the Cold," *USA Today* (July 10, 1996): 1B.

44. "More Employers Charge Smokers Higher Premiums," *USA Today* (July 28, 1997): PG1.

45. Nancy L. Breuer, Emerging Trends for Managing AIDS in the Workplace," *Personnel Journal* 74 (June 1995): 126.

46. Eileen Marie Oswald, "No Employer is Immune: AIDS in the Workplace," *Risk Management* 43 (February 1996): 18.

47. Breuer, "Emerging Trends for Managing AIDS in the Workplace."

48. Ibid.

49. Oswald, "No Employer Is Immune: AIDS in the Workplace."

50. Ibid.

51. Donald J. McNerney, "Global Staffing: Some Common Problems—and Solutions," *HR Focus* 43 (June 1996): 1–4.

52. Mark C. Butler and Mary B. Teagarden, "Strategic Management of Worker Health, Safety, and Environmental Issues In Mexico's Maquiladora Industry," *HR Management* 32 (Winter 1993): 479–503.

53. David Cherrington and Laura Middleton, "An Introduction to Global Business Issues," *HR Magazine* 40 (June 1995): 124.

ABCNEWS   ## VIDEO CASE

Has Managed Health Care Replaced Quality Health Care?

Health Maintenance Organizations (HMOs) are giant firms that sell health care. They, or similar forms such as PPOs (Preferred Provider Organizations), appear to be the wave of the future. These systems have initiated a debate over profits and patients, however, and whether the two are in conflict. For example, what if your medical plan rewarded your physician for denying you emergency care or referring you to a specialist when perhaps one was needed or cut short your hospital stay? These are the primary concerns of those who are opposed to this form of managed care.

One physician in this video provided evidence that his HMO contract specifies incentives to restrict hospital stays, referrals to specialists, and trips to the emergency room. In other words, the less money spent on the patient, the more the doctor makes; the doctor is paid for everything that isn't done. An interesting point is that most HMOs prohibit doctors from telling their patients what their financial arrangements with the HMO are. As one doctor put it, "American medicine has gone from a caring profession to a corporate enterprise."

Advocates for HMOs point out the advantages of such a system. They focus on preventive measures that provide better care for patients such as immunization levels in children, flu vaccines in the elderly, and similar practices. The goal is to provide the right care at the right time and in the right place. HMO proponents criticize the old fee for service system when excessive tests could be ordered, unnecessary surgeries could be performed, and where there was no accountability for physicians.

HMOs and similar systems such as PPOs are growing rapidly and at the same time changing the way they do business. Perhaps the cost advantages of these systems can somehow be merged with the advantages of the more personal medical care once generally available through fee for services.

DISCUSSION QUESTIONS

1. Compare the advantages of HMOs with fee for services.
2. Should HMOs be required to spell out exactly how doctors are paid? Why?
3. Explain why you would prefer your physician to participate in an HMO or be in private practice.
4. Has the quality of health care declined since the emergence of HMOs? Explain your answer.

Source: "For Profit HMOs: Money vs. Quality," *Nightline*, ABC News; aired on December 26, 1995.

PART SEVEN

EMPLOYEE AND LABOR RELATIONS

14
The Evolution of Labor Unions

CHAPTER OBJECTIVES

1. Describe the labor movement prior to 1930.
2. Explain the major labor legislation that was passed after 1930.
3. Describe the labor movement into the year 2000.
4. Describe the relationship between teams and organized labor.
5. Explain unionization in the public sector.
6. Identify the reasons that employees join unions.
7. Describe the basic structure of the union.
8. Identify the steps involved in establishing the collective bargaining relationship.
9. Explain union decertification.
10. List and describe union-free strategies and tactics.

Robert Bandy, president of United Technologies, was disturbed and disappointed. He had just been informed by the National Labor Relations Board that a majority of his employees had voted to have the union represent them. The past months had been difficult ones, with charges and countercharges being made by both management and labor. The vote had been close, with only a few votes tipping the scales in favor of labor instead of maintaining a union-free environment.

He looked at the human resource manager, Marthanne Bello, and said, "I don't know what to do. The union will demand so much we can't possibly be competitive. One of their main demands will be for more full-time employees. I know they don't understand that we can't make our part-timers full-time employees. We don't fire people, but when we need to reduce the size of our workforce, part-timers give us the flexibility we need."

Marthanne replied, "Just because the union has won the right to be represented doesn't mean that we have to accept all their terms. I believe that a reasonable contract can be negotiated. I know many of those guys, and I am sure that we can work out a contract that will be fair to both sides."

*R*obert Bandy is not only troubled but he is also misinformed as to the necessary impact of unionization—specifically regarding collective bargaining. Employees have decided to move from a union-free workplace to a unionized one, but that in no way mandates management acceptance of contractual terms that would adversely impact the health and profitability of the company.

We begin this chapter with a history of the U.S. labor movement and resulting legislation, followed by a discussion of the labor movement into the year 2000, and legislation relating to the labor movement. Then we discuss teams and organized labor and unionism in the public sector. Next, we discuss the objectives of unions, the reasons employees join unions, and the multilevel organizational structure of unions. We then address the steps used to establish a collective bargaining relationship. Finally, we review decertification and union-free strategies and tactics.

The Labor Movement before 1930

Unions are not a recent development in American history. The earliest unions originated toward the end of the eighteenth century, about the time of the American Revolution. Although these early associations had few characteristics of present-day labor unions, they did bring workers in craft or guild-related occupations together to consider problems of mutual concern. These early unions were local in nature and usually existed for only a short time.[1]

Development of the labor movement has been neither simple nor straightforward. Instead, unionism has experienced as much failure as success. Employer opposition, the impact of the business cycle, the growth of American industry, court rulings, and legislation have exerted their influence in varying degrees at different times. As a result, the history of the labor movement has somewhat resembled the swinging of a pendulum. At times, the pendulum has moved in favor of labor; at other times, it has swung toward the advantage of management.

Prior to the 1930s, the trend definitely favored management. The courts strongly supported employers in their attempts to thwart the organized labor movement. This climate was first evidenced by the use of criminal and civil conspiracy doctrines derived from English common law. A **conspiracy**, generally defined, is the combination of two or more persons who band together to prejudice the rights of others or of society (e.g., by refusing to work or demanding higher wages). An important feature of the conspiracy doctrine is that an action by one person, though legal, may become illegal when carried out by a group. In 1806, the year in which the conspiracy doctrine was first applied to labor unions, the courts began to influence the field of labor relations.[2] From 1806 to 1842, the courts heard 17 cases charging labor unions with conspiracies. These cases resulted in the demise of several unions and they certainly discouraged other union activities. The conspiracy doctrine was softened considerably by the decision in the landmark case *Commonwealth v Hunt* in 1842. In that case, Chief Justice Shaw of the Supreme Judi-

Conspiracy: The combination of two or more persons who band together to prejudice the rights of others or of society (such as by refusing to work or demanding higher wages).

Injunction: A prohibiting legal procedure used by employers to prevent certain union activities, such as strikes and unionization attempts.

Yellow-dog contract: A written agreement between an employee and a company made at the time of employment, prohibiting a worker from joining a union or engaging in union activities.

cial Court of Massachusetts contended that labor organizations were legal. Thus, for a union to be convicted under the conspiracy doctrine, the union's objectives had to be shown as unlawful, or the means employed to gain a legal end needed to be proved unlawful. To this day, the courts continue to exert a profound influence on both the direction and character of labor relations.

Other tactics used by employers to stifle union growth were injunctions and yellow-dog contracts. An **injunction** is a prohibiting legal procedure used by employers to prevent certain union activities, such as strikes and unionization attempts. A **yellow-dog contract** was a written agreement between the employee and the company made at the time of employment, prohibiting a worker from joining a union or engaging in union activities. Each of these defensive tactics, used by management and supported by the courts, severely limited union growth.

In the latter half of the nineteenth century, the American industrial system started to grow and prosper. Factory production began to displace handicraft forms of manufacturing. The Civil War gave the factory system a great boost. Goods were demanded in quantities that only mass production methods could supply. The railroads developed new networks of routes spanning the continent and knitting the country into an economic whole. Employment was high, and unions sought to organize workers in both new and expanding enterprises. Most unions during this time were small and rather weak, and many did not survive the economic recession of the 1870s. Union membership rose to 300,000 by 1872 and then dropped to 50,000 by 1878.[3] This period also marked the rise of radical labor activity and increased industrial strife as unions struggled for recognition and survival.[4]

Out of the turbulence of the 1870s emerged the most substantial labor organization that had yet appeared in the United States. The Noble Order of the Knights of Labor was founded in 1869 as a secret society of the Philadelphia garment workers. After its secrecy was abandoned and workers in other areas were invited to join, the union grew rapidly, reaching a membership of more than 700,000 by the mid-1880s. Internal conflict among the Knights' leadership in 1881 gave rise to the nucleus of a new organization that would soon replace it on the labor scene.[5] That organization was the American Federation of Labor (AFL).

Devoted to what is referred to as either *pure and simple unionism*, or *business unionism*, Samuel Gompers of the Cigarmakers Union led some 25 labor groups representing skilled trades to found the AFL in 1886. Gompers was elected the first president of the AFL, a position he held until his death in 1924 (except for one year, 1894–1895, when he adamantly opposed tangible support for the strikers of the Pullman group). He is probably the single most important individual in American trade union history. The AFL began with a membership of some 138,000 and doubled that number during the next 12 years.[6]

In 1890, Congress passed the Sherman Anti-Trust Act, which marked the entrance of the federal government into the statutory regulation of labor organizations. Although the primary stimulus for this act came from public concern over the monopoly power of business, court interpretations soon applied its provisions to organized labor. Later, in 1914, Congress passed the

Clayton Act (an amendment to the Sherman Act), which, according to Samuel Gompers, was the Magna Carta of Labor. The intent of this act was to remove labor from the purview of the Sherman Act. Again, judicial interpretation nullified that intent and left labor even more exposed to lawsuits.[7] Nonetheless, as a result of industrial activity related to World War I, the AFL grew to almost 5 million members by 1920.[8]

During the 1920s, labor faced legal restrictions on union activity and unfavorable court decisions. The one exception to such repressive policies was the passage and approval of the Railway Labor Act of 1926. Passage of this legislation marked the first time that the government declared without qualification the right of private employees to join unions and bargain collectively through representatives of their own choosing without interference from their employers. The act also set up special machinery for settling labor disputes. Although the act covered only employees in the railroad industry (a later amendment extended coverage to the airline industry), it foreshadowed the extension of similar rights to other classes of employees in the 1930s.

HR Web Wisdom

http://www.prenhall.com/mondy

SHRM–HR LINKS
Various labor issues are addressed at this site, including union information.

The Labor Movement after 1930

The 1930s found the United States in the midst of the worst depression in its history. The unemployment rate rose as high as 25 percent.[9] The sentiment of the country began to favor organized labor as many people blamed business for the agony that accompanied the Great Depression. The pendulum began to swing away from management and toward labor. This swing was assisted by several acts and actions that supported the cause of unionism.

ANTI-INJUNCTION ACT (NORRIS-LAGUARDIA ACT)—1932

The Great Depression caused a substantial change in the public's thinking about the role of unions in society. Congress reflected this thinking in 1932 with the passage of the Norris-LaGuardia Act. It affirms the sanction of collective bargaining by U.S. public policy and approves the formation and effective operation of labor unions. This act did not outlaw the use of injunctions, but it severely restricted the federal courts' authority to issue them in labor disputes. It also made yellow-dog contracts unenforceable in the federal courts.[10]

NATIONAL LABOR RELATIONS ACT (WAGNER ACT)—1935

In 1933, Congress made an abortive attempt to stimulate economic recovery by passing the National Industry Recovery Act (NIRA). Declared unconstitutional by the U.S. Supreme Court in 1935, the NIRA did provide the nucleus for legislation that followed it. Section 7a of the NIRA proclaimed the right of workers to organize and bargain collectively. Congress did not, however, provide procedures to enforce these rights.[11]

Undeterred by the Supreme Court decision and strongly supported by organized labor, Congress speedily enacted a comprehensive labor law, the National Labor Relations Act (Wagner Act). This act, approved by President Roosevelt on July 5, 1935, is one of the most significant labor-management relations statutes ever enacted. Drawing heavily on the experience of the Railway Labor Act of 1926 and Section 7a of the NIRA, the act declared legislative support, on a broad scale, for the right of employees to organize and engage in collective bargaining. The spirit of the Wagner Act is stated in Section 7, which defines the substantive rights of employees:

> Employees shall have the right to self-organization, to form, join, or assist labor organizations, to bargain collectively through representatives of their own choosing, and to engage in other concerted activities, for the purpose of collective bargaining or other mutual aid or protection.

The rights defined in Section 7 were protected against employer interference by section 8, which detailed and prohibited five management practices deemed to be unfair to labor:

1. Interfering with or restraining or coercing employees in the exercise of their right to self-organization
2. Dominating or interfering in the affairs of a union
3. Discriminating in regard to hire or tenure or any condition of employment for the purpose of encouraging or discouraging union membership
4. Discriminating against or discharging an employee who has filed charges or given testimony under the act
5. Refusing to bargain with chosen representatives of employees

The National Labor Relations Board (NLRB) was created by the National Labor Relations Act to administer and enforce the provisions of the act. The NLRB was given two principal functions: (1) to establish procedures for holding bargaining-unit elections and to monitor the election procedures, and (2) to investigate complaints and prevent unlawful acts involving unfair labor practices. Much of the NLRB's work is delegated to 33 regional offices throughout the country.

Following passage of the Wagner Act, union membership increased from approximately 3 million to 15 million between 1935 and 1947.[12] The increase was most conspicuous in industries utilizing mass production methods. New unions in these industries were organized on an industrial basis rather than a craft basis, and members were primarily unskilled or semi-skilled workers. An internal struggle developed within the AFL over whether unions should be organized to include all workers in an industry or strictly on a craft or occupational basis. In 1935, a new group was formed by 10 AFL-affiliated unions and the officers of two other AFL unions. Called the Committee for Industrial Organization, its purpose was to promote the organization of workers in mass production and unorganized industries. The controversy grew to the point that in 1938 the AFL expelled all but one of the Committee for Industrial Organization unions. In November 1938, the expelled unions held their first convention in Pittsburgh, Pennsylvania, and reorganized as a federation of unions under the name of Congress of Industrial Organizations (CIO). The new federation included the nine unions expelled from the AFL and 32 other groups established to recruit workers in various industries. John L. Lewis, president of the United Mine Workers, was elected the first president of the CIO.

The rivalry generated by the two large federations stimulated union organizing efforts in both groups. With the ensuing growth, the labor movement gained considerable influence in the United States. However, many individuals and groups began to feel that the Wagner Act favored labor too much. This shift in public sentiment was in part related to a rash of costly strikes following World War II. Whether justified or not, much of the blame for these disruptions fell on the unions.

LABOR-MANAGEMENT RELATIONS ACT (TAFT-HARTLEY ACT)—1947

In 1947, with public pressure mounting, Congress overrode President Truman's veto and passed the Labor Management Relations Act (Taft-Hartley Act). The Taft-Hartley Act extensively revised the National Labor Relations Act and became Title I of that law. A new period began in the evolution of public policy regarding labor. The pendulum had begun to swing toward a more balanced position between labor and management.

Some of the important changes introduced by the Taft-Hartley Act included the following:

1. Modifying Section 7 to include the right of employees to refrain from union activity as well as engage in it
2. Prohibiting the closed shop (the arrangement requiring that all workers be union members at the time they are hired) and narrowing the freedom of the parties to authorize the union shop (the situation in which the employer may hire anyone he or she chooses, but all new workers must join the union after a stipulated period of time)
3. Broadening the employer's right of free speech
4. Providing that employers need not recognize or bargain with unions formed by supervisory employees
5. Giving employees the right to initiate decertification petitions
6. Providing for government intervention in "national emergency strikes"

Another significant change extended the concept of unfair labor practices to unions. Labor organizations were to refrain from the following:

1. Restraining or coercing employees in the exercise of their guaranteed collective bargaining rights
2. Causing an employer to discriminate in any way against an employee in order to encourage or discourage union membership

3. Refusing to bargain in good faith with an employer regarding wages, hours, and other terms and conditions of employment

4. Engaging in certain types of strikes and boycotts

5. Requiring employees covered by union-shop contracts to pay initiation fees or dues "in an amount which the Board finds excessive or discriminatory under all circumstances"

6. "Featherbedding," or requiring that an employer pay for services not performed

Right-to-work laws:
Laws that prohibit management and unions from entering into agreements requiring union membership as a condition of employment.

One of the most controversial elements of the Taft-Hartley Act is its Section 14b, which permits states to enact right-to-work legislation. **Right-to-work laws** are laws that prohibit management and unions from entering into agreements requiring union membership as a condition of employment. Twenty-one states, located primarily in the South and West, have adopted such laws, which are a continuing source of irritation between labor and management.[13] Much of the impetus behind the right-to-work movement is provided by the National Right to Work Committee, based in Springfield, Virginia.

For about 10 years after the passage of the Taft-Hartley Act, union membership expanded at about the same rate as nonagricultural employment, but all was not well within the organized labor movement. Since the creation of the CIO, the two federations had engaged in a bitter and costly rivalry. Both the CIO and the AFL recognized the increasing need for cooperation and reunification. In 1955, following two years of intensive negotiations between the two organizations, a merger agreement was ratified, the AFL-CIO became a reality, and George Meany was elected president. In the years following the merger, the labor movement faced some of its greatest challenges.

LABOR-MANAGEMENT REPORTING AND DISCLOSURE ACT (LANDRUM-GRIFFIN ACT)—1959

Corruption had plagued organized labor since the early 1900s. Periodic revelations of graft, violence, extortion, racketeering, and other improper activities aroused public indignation and invited government investigation. Even though the number of unions involved was small, every disclosure undermined the public image of organized labor as a whole.[14] Corruption had been noted in the construction trades and Laborers, Hotel and Restaurant, Carpenters, Painters, East Coast Longshoremen, and Boilermakers unions.

Scrutiny of union activities is a focal point in today's labor environment, but it began to intensify immediately after World War II. Ultimately, inappropriate union activities led to the creation in 1957 of the Senate Select Committee on Improper Activities in the Labor or Management Field, headed by Senator McClellan of Arkansas. Between 1957 and 1959, the McClellan Committee held a series of nationally televised public hearings that shocked and alarmed the entire country. As evidence of improper activities mounted—primarily against the Teamsters and Longshoremen/Maritime unions—the AFL-CIO took action. In 1957, the AFL-CIO expelled three unions (representing approximately 1.6 million members) for their practices. One of them, the Teamsters, was the largest union in the country.

In 1959, largely as a result of the recommendations of the McClellan Committee, Congress enacted the Labor-Management Reporting and Disclosure Act (Landrum-Griffin Act). This act marked a significant turning point in the involvement of the federal government in internal union affairs. The Landrum-Griffin Act spelled out a Bill of Rights for Members of Labor Organizations designed to protect certain rights of individuals in their relationships with unions. The act requires extensive reporting on numerous internal union activities and contains severe penalties for violations. Employers are also required to file reports when they engage in activities or make expenditures that might undermine the collective bargaining process or interfere with protected employee rights. In addition, the act amended the Taft-Hartley Act by adding additional restrictions on picketing and secondary boycotts.[15]

In 1974, Congress extended coverage of the Taft-Hartley Act to private, not-for-profit hospitals. This amendment brought within the jurisdiction of the National Labor Relations Board some two million employees. Proprietary (profit-making) health-care organizations were already under NLRB jurisdiction. The amendment does not cover government-operated hospitals; it applies only to the private sector.

Even though the AFL-CIO merger was completed in 1955, internal conflict remained. Expulsion of the Teamsters was followed in 1968 by the disaffiliation of the second largest union in the country, the United Automobile Workers (UAW). This split was caused primarily by personality and philosophical clashes between Walter Reuther, president of the UAW, and Meany. Shortly thereafter, the UAW and the Teamsters formed the Alliance of Labor Action (ALA) with the possible aim of developing a rival federation.[16] The ALA lasted only until the untimely death of Walter Reuther in a plane crash

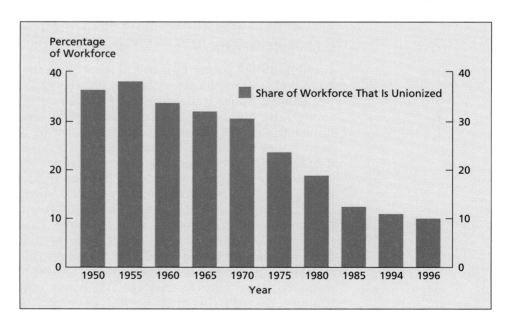

Figure 14-1
Percentage of the Private Workforce That Is Unionized

Source: Labor Department.

in 1970. The UAW reaffiliated with the AFL-CIO in July, 1981. The Teamsters Union was allowed to reaffiliate in October 1987, when it brought its 1.6 million members back into the AFL-CIO.[17] Currently, the AFL-CIO leads 78 unions with 13 million members.[18] The fastest growing segment of the AFL-CIO is the service workers union, which has doubled its size to 1.02 million workers since 1980.[19]

Overall, the fall of Big Labor has been dramatic since the 1970s. Despite the reaffiliation of the Teamsters with the AFL-CIO, union membership dropped from about one-third of the nonfarm workforce in 1950 to 14.5 percent in 1996.[20] As shown in Figure 14-1, the unionized share of the private workforce has currently shrunk to about 10 percent.[21] Unions have also won fewer representation elections as collective bargaining agents in recent years.[22] In addition, labor's gains have lagged behind the increase in the number of wage and salary workers, and this widening gap has caused the share of unionized jobs to continue to decline.[23]

The Labor Movement into the Year 2000

As always, the labor movement involves a series of measures and counter-measures by management and labor that are impacted by, among other things, politics and global economic factors. According to John J. Sweeney, the recently elected president of the AFL-CIO, "You will see a much stronger labor movement in the year 2000." The key to this stronger movement is a union that is "stronger in voice, stronger in membership, [and] stronger in perception."[24]

Organized labor's new strategies for a stronger movement involve practices such as greater political involvement, union salting, flooding the community, and corporate labor campaigns.

Enthusiastic supporters hold signs bearing the slogan "A New Voice for American Workers" at a rally.

■ Political involvement means that unions endorse candidates at all levels of politics, then attempt to deliver the vote of their membership. Unions are giving money to candidates who pledge to help pass pro-labor legislation. AFL-CIO's Sweeney made political action a top priority in 1996, pumping $35 million into political activities that include the training of political organizers and politicians in labor issues. At a special convention, AFL-CIO delegates approved a 15 cents per member per month assessment for the next 12 months to fund political efforts. Also, the AFL-CIO is taking its political efforts on the road, holding town meetings in 27 communities throughout the country to promote its *America Needs a Raise* campaign. Specifically, the union wants to change the perception that it has historically supported only the efforts of white employees.[25]

■ Union salting involves trained union organizers applying for jobs at a company and, once hired, working to unionize employees. Construction companies and health-care facilities have been the most common targets of union salting. The U.S. Supreme Court recently ruled that employers cannot discriminate against union salts (*NLRB v Town & Electric Inc.*). Therefore, a company cannot terminate these employees solely because they also work for a union.[26]

■ Flooding the community requires unions to *flood* communities with organizers to target a particular business. With their flooding campaigns, unions typically choose companies in which nonunionized employees have asked for help in organizing. Generally, organizers have been recruited and trained by the national union. They are young, ambitious, college-educated people with a passion for the American labor movement. Organizers meet with employees in small groups and even visit them at home. They know every nuance of a company's operations and target weak managers' departments as a way to appeal to dissatisfied employees who may be willing to organize.[27]

■ Corporate labor campaigns involve labor maneuvers that do not coincide with a strike or organizing campaign to pressure an employer for better wages, benefits, and the like. Increasingly, these campaigns are used as an alternative to strikes because more employers are willing to replace their striking employees.

Strikes have become a less potent weapon, with strikes involving 1,000 or more workers declining sharply since 1970. In 1970 there were 381 strikes involving 1,000 or more workers; in 1975, 235; in 1980, 187; in 1985, 54; in 1990, 44; and in 1996, there were only 37 strikes that involved 1,000 or more workers.[28] Employers have less recourse against labor campaigns in which members join political and community groups that support union goals, picket the homes of a company's board of directors, initiate proxy challenges to actions negative to labor, write letters to the editor of the local newspaper, and file charges with administrative agencies, such as OSHA, the Department of Labor, and the NLRB. This type of public awareness campaign, which is not tied directly to labor gains, is often an effective method of developing union leverage. Also, fighting such campaigns is often time-consuming and costly for companies.[29]

Even with the rosy prediction of labor's future by AFL-CIO's Sweeney and these new union tactics, the road to recovery will be very difficult for the labor movement. The American workplace and workers have changed, with traditional assembly-line jobs being replaced by jobs that require trained professionals who are usually unsympathetic to adversarial labor-management relationships. These individuals are more receptive to teams, employee involvement, and employee empowerment. Also, unions have been weakened by corporate downsizing, technological advancements that have displaced less skilled workers, and the rise of small, service-oriented firms. Additionally, the U.S. economy has become highly integrated into the global economy, and many manufacturing and low-skilled jobs have gone overseas. Also, to temper union demands, companies sometimes threaten to send more jobs overseas to cut costs.[30] Finally, organizations are intent on employing individuals who can work in teams, who will work for competitive wages, and who are willing to work with global competition in mind. Some of these efforts are prohibited by the National Labor Relations Act of 1935.

Many American firms appear unwilling to accept unions. For instance, Robert Bandy, president of United Technologies (UT), is quite disturbed that a majority of UT employees voted to unionize. He worried that the union may even threaten UT's competitiveness. In fact, about two-thirds of all American companies that face union organizing drives hire anti-union consultants to plan and execute counterorganizing drives. A counterorganizing drive often uses daily company meetings, leaflets, and newsletters to depict the union as an outside business that enriches itself by collecting dues, fees, and fines from thousands of hapless employees. A counterorganizing drive deliberately delays a certification election for months by raising legal issues before the NLRB while management threatens utter disaster if any employee so much as thinks of joining a union.[31] The key to union survival and growth may well be union-management collaboration, utilizing teams and other cooperative measures to maximize global competitiveness.

Teams and Organized Labor

Modern business managers try to forge cooperative workplace cultures in which employees work together and with management to solve problems, increase productivity, and improve quality. The old top-down mentality in which the boss issues orders and subordinates snap to attention is obsolete. To be globally competitive, most organizations must use cohesive teams that take maximum advantage of the physical and mental capacities of each employee. Unfortunately, the 1935 National Labor Relations Act prohibits such arrangements because some companies could establish management-labor teams as *sham* unions to avert union organizing. In 1992, the National Labor Relations Board (NLRB) ruled that a system of teams or committees by a company is analogous to a company-dominated-union, which is prohibited by law.

The Teamwork for Employees and Management Act (TEAM Act) would amend the 1935 National Labor Relations Act's ban on company or sham unions by allowing nonunion companies to set up worker-management groups that could "address matters of mutual interest" but not negotiate contracts. In 1996, both houses of Congress enacted identical versions of the TEAM Act. This proposed legislation encountered criticism and resistance from organized labor, and was vetoed by President Clinton, even though the legislation expressly excludes unionized companies from coverage. Congress will likely revive the TEAM Act and attempt once again to bring the nation's labor laws into the modern age. There will probably be amendments to the legislation designed to appease union concerns and hence improve the prospect that the act will be signed into law.

Organized labor believes that the legislation, which gives legal status to an already widespread practice, would make it far more difficult to persuade employees to vote for union representation. The TEAM Act would allow selected workers and managers to discuss wages, hours, and working conditions in a nonunion setting, a practice now illegal under the National Labor Relations Act.[32]

Unfortunately, union resistance to management-labor teams is undermining the best efforts of corporations to become more competitive globally and more progressive in terms of dealing with employee needs. This prohibition even forbids managers and employees from discussing safety and quality of life issues.

Employers believe the TEAM Act is necessary to allow employers and employees to work together as a team to assure a mutually better future.[33] Under the current law, nonunion, management-controlled committees can discuss only certain issues, such as product quality and sales. Currently, worker group involvement in determining terms and conditions of employment must be free of employer control.[34]

T R E N D S   &   I N N O V A T I O N S

SUPPORT FOR THE TEAM ACT

Although unions are against the TEAM Act, certain union leaders apparently realize that union-management cooperation is essential for corporate competitiveness and union survival. In fact, after years of skepticism, some unions are now advocating partnerships with management. For instance, the AFL-CIO started a Center for Workplace Democracy to help unions develop expertise to become more involved in managerial decisions. The Laborers union set up a foundation with contractors to train construction workers in specialized skills. The Machinists union runs courses for plant managers and local union leaders on high-performance work systems and even sends union consultants to help set up teams to lift productivity. The Needle Trades formed an extensive partnership with Levi Strauss to cut costs and keep production in the United States.

The Steelworkers union persuaded major steelmakers to appoint union-designated board members and even trains union leaders in business skills so they can be effective on union/management councils.[35] However, such initiatives are not far-reaching enough to make a significant impact on corporate competitiveness. Although opponents believe the TEAM Act would let businesses sap labor's strength, companies believe that they must be allowed to create their own worker-management teams to foster global competitiveness.

The Public Sector

Government (public sector) employees are generally considered a class apart from private-sector workers. This is reflected in their exclusion from coverage of general labor legislation.[36] However, like their counterparts in private industry, government employees have demonstrated a persistence in organizing in order to gain an effective voice in the terms and conditions of their employment. The unionized share of government workers is now approximately 40 percent—almost four times that of the private sector.[37] Employee involvement and participation in decision making is much more accepted in the public sector than in the private sector. Quality management programs are on the rise in the public sector because a true union-management partnership is much closer to being a reality than it is in the private sector. In the public sector, employee involvement and participation are accepted as critical factors in achieving quality improvements and enhancing organizational effectiveness. The U.S. Department of Labor's "Employee-Involvement/Quality Improvement" is a quality improvement program that is actually working. This program—a true partnership between management and labor—has improved the productivity of the departments involved and the working lives of participating employees. In this program, employees and managers work in teams and together make recommendations and decisions to best benefit everyone concerned.[38]

For many years the federal government had no well-defined policy on labor-management relations regarding its own employees. To address this situation, President Kennedy issued Executive Order 10988 in 1962. Section 1(a) of the Order stated:

> Employees of the federal government shall have, and shall be protected in the exercise of, the right, freely and without fear of penalty or reprisal, to form, join and assist any employee organization or to refrain from any such activity.

For the first time in the history of the federal civil service, a uniform, comprehensive policy of cooperation between employee organizations and management in the executive branch of government was established. Employees were permitted to organize and negotiate human resource policies and practices and matters affecting working conditions that were within the administrative discretion of the agency officials concerned. However, Public Law 84-330, passed in 1955 made it a felony for federal employees to strike against the U.S. government.[39] In 1995, President Clinton issued Executive Order 12954, which bans the hiring of permanent strike replacements by certain federal contractors and subcontractors. This Executive Order is now caught up in a series of legal challenges; but if it is implemented, unions will have an easier time getting unionized federal contractors and subcontractors to agree to more favorable contract terms, because employers would not be able to bring in a new workforce during a strike.[40]

Executive Order 10988 established the basic framework for collective bargaining in federal government agencies. Subsequent executive orders revised and improved this framework and brought about a new era of labor relations in the public sector.[41] In fact, the federal government codified the provisions of those orders and transferred them to Title VII of the Civil Service Reform Act of 1978. This act regulates most of the labor-management relations in the federal service. It establishes the Federal Labor Relations Authority (FLRA), which is modeled on the National Labor Relations Board. The intent of the FLRA is to bring the public sector model in line with that of the private sector. Requirements and mechanisms for recognition and elections, dealing with impasses, and handling grievances are covered in the act.

The U.S. Postal Service is not subject to Title VII of the Civil Service Reform Act of 1978. It was given independent government agency status by the Postal Reorganization Act of 1970. Postal employees were given collective bargaining rights comparable to those governing private industry. National Labor Relations Board rules and regulations controlling representation issues and elections are applicable to the postal service. Unfair labor practice provisions are also enforced by the NLRB. However, the right to strike is prohibited, and union-shop arrangements are not permitted.

LABOR RELATIONS AND BARGAINING PATTERNS

There is no uniform pattern to state and local labor relations and bargaining rights. Some states have no policy at all, whereas a haphazard mixture of statutes, resolutions, ordinances, and civil service procedures exists in others. However, public-employer legislation passed by state and local governments accelerated noticeably after the issuance of EO 10988 in 1962.[42] By 1984, the District of Columbia and 41 states had collective bargaining statutes covering all or some categories of public employees. By 1980, some form of legislation that obligates state agencies and local governments to permit their public employees to join unions and to recognize bona fide labor organizations had been passed in 38 states. Prior to 1960, just a handful of states had such legislation. The diversity of state labor laws makes it difficult to generalize about the legal aspects of collective bargaining at the state and local levels.

EMPLOYEE ASSOCIATIONS

In the past, employee associations were concerned primarily with the professional aspects of employment and avoided any semblance of unionism. In recent years, this approach has changed as public- and private-sector unions have actively organized both professional and government employees. Many employee associations now enthusiastically pursue collective bargaining relationships. The National Education Association (NEA) has become the largest in the United States, with 2.2 million teachers and educational administrators.[43]

The greater public-sector penetration of unions in recent years indicates that the process of unionization in the public sector differs from that in the private labor market. One factor that accounts for membership gains is clearly the role played by government employee associations, particularly at the state and local level. Challenged by established unions, the associations either merged with unions or transformed themselves into collective bargaining organizations. Many are becoming de facto unions, such as the NEA. Another reason that membership gains were made so quickly was the encouragement union organizations received from public-sector management.[44]

Union Objectives

The labor movement has a long history in the United States. Although each union is a unique organization seeking its own objectives, several broad objectives characterize the labor movement as a whole:

1. To secure and, if possible, improve the living standards and economic status of its members
2. To enhance and, if possible, guarantee individual security against threats and contingencies that might result from market fluctuations, technological change, or management decisions
3. To influence power relations in the social system in ways that favor and do not threaten union gains and goals
4. To advance the welfare of all who work for a living, whether union members or not[45]
5. To create mechanisms to guard against the use of arbitrary and capricious policies and practices in the workplace

The underlying philosophy of the labor movement is that of organizational democracy and an atmosphere of social dignity for working men and women. To accomplish these objectives, most unions realize that they must strive for continued growth and power. Although growth and power are related, we discuss them separately to identify the impact of both factors on unionization.

GROWTH

To maximize its effectiveness, a union must strive for continual growth. Members pay dues, which are vital to promoting and achieving union objectives. Obviously, the more members the union enlists, the more dues they pay to support the union and the labor movement. Thus, an overall goal of most unions is continued growth. However, the percentage of union members in the workforce is declining. Most union leaders are concerned about this trend. Much of a union's ability to accomplish its objectives is derived from strength in numbers. For this reason, unions must continue to explore new sources of potential members. Unions are now directing much of their attention to organizing the service industries, professional employees, and government employees.

New-collar workers:
Younger, well-educated, independent workers, who appear to be particularly sensitive to issues related to job security.

There is a glimmer of hope for unions, but the *mild* resurgence of unionism, predicted in the 1990s, has failed to materialize, possibly partially because of the new-collar worker class. **New-collar workers** are younger, better educated, and more independent; they appear to be particularly sensitive to issues related to job security. If unions are to grow appreciably in the private sector, acceptance by this new worker segment is necessary. However, these workers are well under 50 years of age, while the average union member is over 50. In addition, these new-collar workers believe that seniority rules protect older workers at their expense. While new-collar workers are concerned with job security issues, many in this group believe such security can be provided only by cooperative employers.[46]

POWER

Every indication is that management continues to improve its power base in relation to organized labor.[47] Most observes agree that the power base of organized labor will continue to erode. We define *power* here as the amount of external control an organization is able to exert. A union's power is influenced to a large extent by the size of its membership and the possibility of future growth. However, we also have to consider other factors when assessing the future power base of unions.

The importance of the jobs held by union members significantly affects union power. For instance, an entire plant may have to be shut down if unionized machinists performing critical jobs decide to strike. Thus, a few strategically located union members may exert a disproportionate amount of power. A union's power can also be determined by the type of firm that is unionized. Unionization of truckers, steel workers, or farm workers can affect the entire country and, subsequently, enhance the union's power base. Through control of key industries, a union's power may extend to firms that are not unionized.

By achieving power, a union is capable of exerting its force in the political arena. The political arm of the AFL-CIO is the Committee on Political Education (COPE). Founded in 1955, its purpose is to support politicians who are friendly to the cause of organized labor. The union recommends and assists candidates who will best serve its interests. Union members also encourage their friends to support those candidates. The larger the voting membership, the greater will be the union's influence with politicians. With friends in government, the union is in a stronger position to maneuver against management.

As reduced union strength contributes to weaker unions at the bargaining table, labor leaders will continually strive to increase their political clout. The slowdown in union gains, coupled with declining union membership and organizing activities, caused unions to compensate by attempting to increase their political activity.[48] The AFL-CIO has been particularly aggressive lately, targeting vulnerable Republican congressional freshman in 75 systematically chosen races across the United States.[49] Even though unions have taken their political knocks over the past decade, they remain a fairly potent political force. The AFL-CIO imposed an extraordinary surcharge of $35 million on union locals to spend on political activities.[50] Unions also provide many members to staff phone banks and organize campaigns. The unions' long association with such narrow issues as picketing rules and organizing regulations have given way to more popular campaigns for plant-closing legislation, child care, and family leave.[51] The political activity of unions will continue to parallel their changing philosophy toward a desire for more government intervention in the U.S. economy and society.[52]

Why Employees Join Unions

Individuals join unions for many different reasons, which tend to change over time. The reasons may involve job, personal, social, or political considerations. It would be impossible to discuss them all, but some of the major ones are dissatisfaction with management, compensation, job security, management's attitude, the need for a social outlet, the opportunity for leadership, forced unionization, and peer pressure.

DISSATISFACTION WITH MANAGEMENT

Every job holds the potential for real dissatisfactions. Each individual has a boiling point that can trigger him or her to consider a union as a solution to real or perceived problems. Unions look for problems in organizations and then emphasize the advantages of union membership as a means of solving them. Some of the other more common reasons for employee dissatisfaction are described in the following paragraphs.

Compensation. Employees want their compensation to be fair and equitable. Wages are important to them because they provide both the necessities and pleasures of life. If employees are dissatisfied with their wages, they may look to a union for assistance in improving their standard of living. However, the ability of unions to make satisfactory gains in income has been severely hampered in the past few years.

An important psychological aspect of compensation involves the amount of pay an individual receives in relation to that of other employees performing similar work. If an employee perceives that management has shown favoritism by paying someone else more to perform the same or a lower level job, the employee will likely become dissatisfied. Union members know precisely the basis of their pay and how it compares with others. In the past, pay inequities, with seniority as the accepted criterion for fairness, was generally accepted by union members, but with the growth of the new-collar worker class, this position may be perceived as grossly unfair, further decreasing union membership.[53]

Job Security. Historically, young employees have been less concerned with job security than older workers. The young employee seemed to think, "If I lose this job, I can always get another." In recent years, however, young employees have witnessed management consistently terminating older workers to make room for even younger, more aggressive employees, and now the younger ones may have begun to think about job security. If the firm does not provide its employees with a sense of job security, workers may turn to a union. Robert Bandy of United Technologies believes that the main reason the union barely won in their organizing attempt is UT's refusal to allow part-timers to achieve full-time employment status under normal circumstances. Generally, employees are more concerned than ever about job security, largely because of a decline in employment in such key industries as automobiles, rubber, and steel. Unfortunately for union organizing attempts, whereas new-collar workers appear to be particularly sensitive to job security issues, many in this group believe that security can be provided only by cooperative employers—not unions.[54] Even the United Farm Workers (UFW) did not vote to strike in an attempt to hold onto their $8,500-a-year jobs.[55]

The Attitude of Management. People like to feel that they are important. They do not like to be considered a commodity that can be bought and sold. Thus employees do not like to be subjected to arbitrary and capricious actions by management. In some firms, management is insensitive to the needs of its employees. In such situations, employees may perceive that they have little or no influence in job-related matters. Workers who feel that they are not really part of an organization are prime targets for unionization.

Management's attitude may be reflected in such small actions as how bulletin board notices are written. Memos addressed "To All Employees" instead of "To *Our* Employees" may indicate managers that are indifferent to employee needs. Such attitudes likely stem from top management, but they are noticed initially by employees in the actions of first-line supervisors. Workers may notice that supervisors are judging people entirely on what they can do, how much they can do, and when they can do it. Employees may begin to feel they are being treated more as machines than people. Supervisors may fail to give reasons for unusual assignments and may expect employees to dedicate their lives to the firm without receiving adequate rewards. The prevailing philosophy may be: "If you don't like it here, leave." A management philosophy such as this, which does not consider the needs of employees as individuals, makes the firm ripe for unionization. Management must keep in mind that unions would never have gained a foothold if management had not abused its power.[56]

A Social Outlet

By nature, many people have strong social needs. They generally enjoy being around others who have similar interests and desires. Some employees join a union for no other reason than to take advantage of union-sponsored recreational and social activities that members and their families find fulfilling. Some unions now offer day care centers and other services that appeal to working men and women and increase their sense of solidarity with other union members. People who develop close personal relationships, in either a unionized or union-free organization, will likely stand together in difficult times.

OPPORTUNITY FOR LEADERSHIP

Some individuals aspire to leadership roles, but it is not always easy for an operative employee to progress into management. However, employees with leadership aspirations can often satisfy them through union membership. As with the firm, the union also has a hierarchy of leadership, and individual members have the opportunity to work their way up through its various levels. Employers often notice employees who are leaders in the union, and it is not uncommon for them to promote such employees into managerial ranks as supervisors.

FORCED UNIONIZATION

Requiring an individual to join a union prior to employment is generally illegal. However, in the 29 states without right-to-work laws, it is legal for an employer to agree with the union that a new employee must join the union after a certain period of time (generally 30 days) or be terminated. This is referred to as a *union-shop agreement*.

PEER PRESSURE

Some individuals will join a union simply because they are urged to do so by other members of the work group. Friends and associates may constantly remind an employee that he or she is not a member of the union. In the past, this social pressure from peers was difficult to resist, but as the age gap between workers increases and the educational gap broadens, peer pressure becomes less and less of an issue. Quite possibly, rejection of these employees by current union members has less influence than in the past. In extreme cases, union members threaten nonmembers with physical violence and sometimes carry out these threats.

Union Structure

The labor movement has developed a multilevel organizational structure over time. This complex of organizations ranges from local unions to the principal federation, the AFL-CIO. Each level has its own officers and ways of managing its affairs. Many national unions have intermediate levels between the national and the local levels. In this section, however, we describe only the three basic elements of union organization: (1) the local union, (2) the national union, and (3) the federation, or AFL-CIO.

THE LOCAL UNION

Local union: The basic element in the structure of the U.S. labor movement.

The basic element in the structure of the American labor movement is the **local union** (or simply, the local). To the individual union member, it is the most important level in the structure of organized labor. Through the local, the individual deals with the employer on a day-to-day basis. There are approximately 65,000 locals in the United States, most of which are affiliated with one of the 170 or so national or international unions. The latter are generally organized along industry or craft lines.

Craft union: A bargaining unit, such as the Carpenters and Joiners union, that is typically composed of members of a particular trade or skill in a specific locality.

There are two basic kinds of local unions: craft and industrial. A **craft union**, such as the Carpenters and Joiners union, is typically composed of members of a particular trade or skill in a specific locality. Members usually acquire their job skills through an apprenticeship training program. An **industrial union** generally consists of all the workers in a particular plant or group of plants. The type of work they do and the level of skill they possess are not a condition for membership in the union. An example of an industrial union is the United Auto Workers.

Industrial union: A bargaining unit that generally consist of all the workers in a particular plant or group of plants.

The local union's functions are many and varied. Administering the collective bargaining agreement and representing workers in handling grievances are two quite important activities. Other functions include keeping the membership informed about labor issues, promoting increased membership, maintaining effective contact with the national union, and, when appropriate, negotiating with management at the local level.

HR Web Wisdom

http://www.prenhall.com/mondy

LABOR QUOTES

Quotes related to various aspects of labor are included, with easy access via hot links.

THE NATIONAL (OR INTERNATIONAL) UNION

The most powerful level in the union structure is the national union. Most locals are affiliated with national unions. Some national unions are called *international unions* because they have affiliated locals in Canada.

National union: An organization composed of local unions, which it charters.

A **national union** is composed of local unions, which it charters. As such, it is the parent organization to local unions. The local union—not the individual worker—holds membership in the national union. The national union is supported financially by each local union, whose contribution is based on its membership size.

The national union is governed by a national constitution and a national convention of local unions, which usually meets every two to five years. The day-to-day operation of the national union is conducted by elected officers, aided by an administrative staff. The national union is active in organizing workers within its jurisdiction, engaging in collective bargaining at the national level, and assisting its locals in their negotiations. In addition, the national union may provide numerous educational and research services for its locals, dispense strike funds, publish the union newspaper, provide legal counsel, and actively lobby at national and state levels.

AFL-CIO

The American Federation of Labor and Congress of Industrial Organizations (AFL-CIO) is the central trade union federation in the United States. It represents the interests of labor and its member national unions at the highest level. The federation does not engage in collective bargaining; however, it provides the means by which member unions can cooperate to pursue common objectives and attempt to resolve internal problems faced by organized labor. The federation is financed by its member national unions and is governed by a national convention, which meets every two years.

As shown in Figure 14-2, the structure of the AFL-CIO is complex. The federation has state bodies in all 50 states and Puerto Rico. In addition, national unions can affiliate with one or more of the trade and industrial departments. These departments seek to promote the interests of specific groups of workers who are in different unions but who have common interests. The federation's major activities include the following:

1. Improving the image of organized labor
2. Lobbying extensively on behalf of labor interests
3. Politically educating constituencies and others through the Committee on Political Education
4. Resolving disputes between national unions
5. Policing internal affairs of member unions

The AFL-CIO is a loosely knit organization of more than 90 national unions. It has little formal power or control. The member national unions remain completely autonomous and decide their own policies and programs. Not all national unions are members of the federation. Currently, the AFL-CIO represents approximately 13 million members in 78 unions, down 1 million since 1992.

HR Web Wisdom

http://www.prenhall.com/mondy

COLLECTIVE BARGAINING
This site offers various quotations related to negotiations and collective bargaining during labor's history.

Establishing the Collective Bargaining Relationship: Union Certification

Collective bargaining:
The performance of the mutual obligation of the employer and the representative of the employees to meet at reasonable times and confer in good faith with respect to wages, hours, and other terms and conditions of employment, or the negotiation of an agreement, or any question arising thereunder, and the execution of a written contract incorporating any agreement reached if requested by either party; such obligation does not compel either party to agree to a proposal or require the making of a concession.

The primary law governing the relationship of companies and unions is the National Labor Relations Act, as amended. Collective bargaining is one of the key parts of the act. Section 8(d) of the act defines **collective bargaining** as follows:

> The performance of the mutual obligation of the employer and the representative of the employees to meet at reasonable times and confer in good faith with respect to wages, hours, and other terms and conditions of employment, or the negotiation of an agreement, or any question arising thereunder, and the execution of a written contract incorporating any agreement reached if requested by either party, but such obligation does not compel either party to agree to a proposal or require the making of a concession.

The act further provides that the designated representative of the employees shall be the exclusive representative for all the employees in the unit

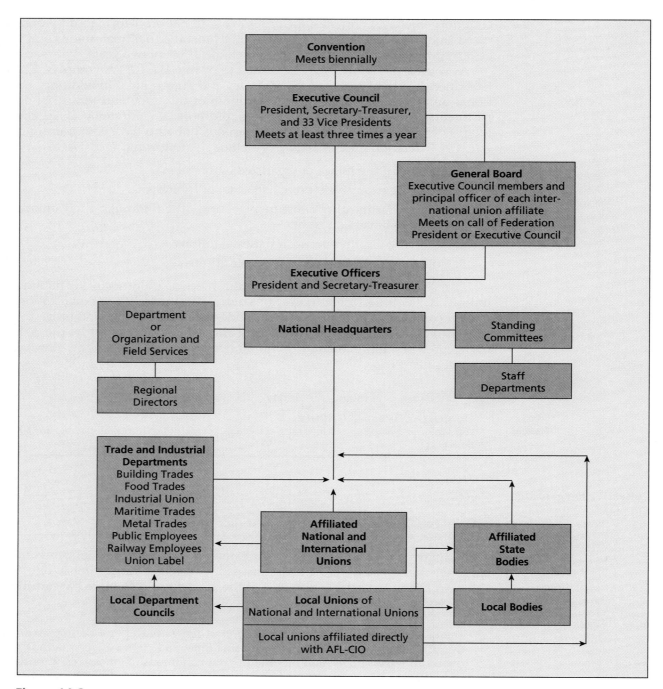

Figure 14-2
The Structure of the AFL-CIO
Source: Bureau of Labor Statistics, *Directory of National Unions and Employee Associations*.

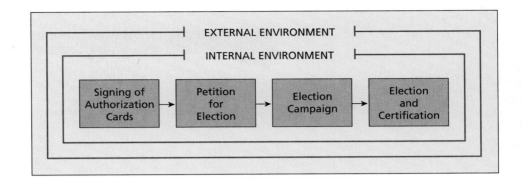

Figure 14-3
The Steps That Lead to
Forming a Bargaining
Unit

Bargaining unit: A
group of employees, not
necessarily union mem-
bers, recognized by an employer or certified by an
administrative agency as
appropriate for representation by a labor organiza-
tion for purposes of collective bargaining.

for purposes of collective bargaining. A **bargaining unit** consists of a group
of employees, not necessarily union members, recognized by an employer or
certified by an administrative agency as appropriate for representation by a
labor organization for purposes of collective bargaining. A unit may cover
the employees in one plant of an employer, or it may cover employees in
two or more plants of the same employer. Although the act requires the representative to be selected by the employees, it does not require any particular
procedure to be used as long as the choice clearly reflects the desire of the
majority of the employees in the bargaining unit. The employee representative is normally chosen in a secret ballot election conducted by the NLRB.
When a union desires to become the bargaining representative for a group
of employees, several steps leading to certification have to be taken (see
Figure 14-3).

SIGNING OF AUTHORIZATION CARDS

A prerequisite to forming a recognized bargaining unit is determining
whether there is sufficient interest on the part of employees to justify the
unit. Evidence of this interest is expressed when at least 30 percent of the
employees in a work group sign an authorization card. The **authorization
card** is a document indicating that an employee wants to be represented by
a labor organization in collective bargaining. Most union organizers will not
proceed unless at least 50 percent of the workers in the group sign cards. An
authorization card used by the International Association of Machinists and
Aerospace Workers is shown in Figure 14-4.

Authorization card: A
document indicating that
an employee wants to be
represented by a labor organization in collective
bargaining.

PETITION FOR ELECTION

After the authorization cards have been signed, a petition for an election
may be made to the appropriate regional office of the NLRB. When the petition is filed, the NLRB will conduct an investigation. The purpose of the investigation is to determine, among other things, the following:

1. Whether the Board has jurisdiction to conduct an election
2. Whether there is a sufficient showing of employee interest to justify
   an election

YES, I WANT THE IAM

I, the undersigned, an employee of

(Company) _____

hereby authorize the International Association of Machinists and
Aerospace Workers (IAM) to act as my collective bargaining
agent with the company for wages, hours, and working
conditions.

NAME (print) _____ DATE _____

ADDRESS (print) _____

CITY _____ STATE _____ ZIP _____

DEPT. _____ SHIFT _____ PHONE _____

Classification _____

SIGN HERE ✗_____

NOTE: THIS AUTHORIZATION IS TO BE SIGNED AND DATED IN
EMPLOYEE'S OWN HANDWRITING. YOUR RIGHT TO SIGN THIS CARD
IS PROTECTED BY FEDERAL LAW.

Figure 14-4
An Authorization Card
Source: The International
Association of Machinists
and Aerospace Workers.

3. Whether a question of representation exists (for example, the employee representative has demanded recognition, which has been denied by the employer)

4. Whether the election will include appropriate employees in the bargaining unit (for instance, the Board is prohibited from including plant guards in the same unit with the other employees)

5. Whether the representative named in the petition is qualified (for example, a supervisor or any other management representative may not be an employee representative)

6. Whether there are any barriers to an election in the form of existing contracts or prior elections held within the past 12 months.[57]

If these conditions have been met, the NLRB will ordinarily direct that an election be held within 30 days. Election details are left largely to the agency's regional director. Management is prohibited from making unusual concessions or promises that would encourage workers to vote against union recognition.

ELECTION CAMPAIGN

Workers at nonunion companies are requesting fewer elections to form unions. In 1970, the greatest number of certification elections were held, numbering 7,773; in 1980, the number was 7,296; in 1990, it had dropped to 3,623. In 1996, the number of elections fell to 2,792, the lowest level since 1940. Also, when elections are held, unions are winning less often. They had 56 percent victories in 1970, 48 percent in 1980, 50 percent in 1990, and 47 percent in 1996.[58] When an election has been ordered, both union and management usually promote their causes actively. Unions will continue to encourage workers to join the union, and management may begin a campaign to tell workers the benefits of remaining union free. The supervisor's role during the campaign is crucial. Supervisors need to conduct themselves in a manner that avoids violating the law and committing unfair labor practices. Specifically, they should be aware of what can and cannot be done in the preelection campaign period. In many cases, it is not so much what is said by the supervisor as how it is said.[59] Throughout the campaign, supervisors should keep upper management informed about employee attitudes.

Theoretically, both union and management are permitted to tell their stories without interference from the other side. At times, the campaign becomes quite intense. Election results will be declared invalid if the campaign was marked by conduct that the NLRB considers to have interfered with the employee's freedom of choice. Examples of such conduct are these:

- An employer or a union threatens loss of jobs or benefits to influence employees' votes or union activities.
- An employer or a union misstates important facts in the election campaign when the other party does not have a chance to reply.
- Either an employer or a union incites racial or religious prejudice by inflammatory campaign appeals.
- An employer fires employees to discourage or encourage their union activities, or a union causes an employer to take such an action.
- An employer or a union makes campaign speeches to assembled groups of employees on company time within 24 hours of an election.

ELECTION AND CERTIFICATION

The NLRB monitors the secret-ballot election on the date set. Its representatives are responsible for making sure that only eligible employees vote and for counting the votes. Following a valid election, the board will issue a certification of the results to the participants. If a union has been chosen by a majority of the employees voting in the bargaining unit, it will receive a certificate showing that it is now the official bargaining representative of the employees in the unit. However, the right to represent employees does not mean the right to dictate terms to management that would adversely affect the organization. The bargaining process does not require either party to make concessions; it only compels them to bargain in good faith. Robert Bandy of United Technologies is misinformed in his belief that the company had to accept all the terms outlined by the union. In fact, the only obligation UT has is to bargain in good faith.

UNION STRATEGIES IN OBTAINING BARGAINING UNIT RECOGNITION

Unions may use various strategies to obtain recognition by management. Unions generally try to make the first move because this places management in the position of having to react to union maneuvers. The search for groups of employees to organize involves a continuous effort by union leaders. To begin a drive, unions often look for areas of dissatisfaction. Union organizers are aware that an overall positive attitude toward management among employees generally indicates that organizing employees will be extremely difficult.

Some situations indicate that employees are ripe for organizing:

- A history of management's unjustified and arbitrary treatment of employees
- Compensation below the industry average
- Management's lack of concern for employee welfare

A union does not normally look at isolated conditions of employee unrest. Rather, it attempts to locate general patterns of employee dissatisfaction. Whatever the case, the union will probably not make a major attempt at organizing unless it believes it has a good chance of success.

The union may take numerous approaches in getting authorization cards signed. One effective technique is first to identify workers who are not only dissatisfied but also influential in the firm's informal organization. These individuals can assist in developing an effective organizing campaign. Information is obtained through the grapevine regarding who was hired, who was fired, and management mistakes in general. Such information is beneficial to union organizers as they approach company employees. Statements such as this are common: "I hear Bill Adams was fired today. I also understand that he is well liked. There is no way that would have happened if you had a union."

Ultimately, the union must abandon its secret activities. Sooner or later management will discover the organizing attempt. At this point, union organizers may station themselves and other supporters at company entrances and pass out *throwsheets* or campaign literature proclaiming the benefits of joining the union and emphasizing management weaknesses. They will talk to anyone who will listen in their attempt to identify union sympathizers. Employees who sign an authorization card are then encouraged to convince their friends to sign also. The effort often mushrooms, yielding a sufficient number of signed authorization cards before management has time to react.

Union efforts continue even after the election petition has been approved by the NLRB. Every attempt is made by the organizers to involve as many workers from the firm as possible. The outside organizers would prefer to take a back seat and let company employees convince their peers to join the union. Peer pressure typically has a much greater effect on convincing a person to join a union than outside influence does. Whenever possible, unions utilize peer pressure to encourage and expand unionization.

Union Decertification: Reestablishing the Individual Bargaining Relationship

Until 1947, once a union was certified, it was certified forever. However, the Taft-Hartley Act made it possible for employees to decertify a union. In such an action, a union loses its right to act as the exclusive bargaining

Decertification: Election by a group of employees to withdraw a union's right to act as their exclusive bargaining representative.

representative of a group of employees. **Decertification** is essentially the reverse of the process that employees must follow to be recognized as an official bargaining unit. In recent years, many decertification elections have been held.

The 1980s and 1990s were not good times for America's labor unions. Currently, organized labor's share of the workforce is only 14.5 percent. In addition, this decline occurred while the nation's workforce increased. As a percent of the workforce, union membership is at the lowest level in at least 50 years.[60] The outcome of certification and decertification elections are of increasing concern to unions.

DECERTIFICATION PROCEDURE

The rules established by the NLRB spell out the conditions for filing a decertification petition. At least 30 percent of the bargaining unit members must petition for an election. As might be expected, this task by itself may be difficult because union supporters are likely to oppose the move strongly. Although the petitioners' names are supposed to remain confidential, many union members are fearful that their signatures on the petition will be discovered. Timing of the NLRB's receipt of the decertification petition is also critical. The petition must be submitted between 60 and 90 days before the expiration of the current contract. When all these conditions have been met, the NLRB regional director will schedule a decertification election by secret ballot.

The NLRB carefully monitors the events leading up to the election. Current employees must initiate the request for the election. If the NLRB determines that management initiated the action, it will not certify the election. After a petition has been accepted, however, management can support the decertification attempt. If a majority of the votes cast are against the union, the employees will be free of the union. Strong union supporters are all likely to vote. Thus, if a substantial number of employees are indifferent to the union and choose not to vote, decertification may not occur.

MANAGEMENT AND DECERTIFICATION

When management senses employee discontent with the union, it often does not know how to react. Many times, management decides to do nothing, reasoning that the best course is not to get involved or that doing so may even be illegal. But if it does want to get involved, management can use a variety of legal tactics. If management really wants the union decertified, it must learn how to be active rather than passive.

Meetings with union members to discuss the benefits of becoming union free have proven beneficial. In fact, such discussions are often cited as being the most effective campaign tactic. These meetings may be with individual employees, small groups, or even entire units. Management explains the benefits and answers employees' questions.

Management may also provide workers with legal assistance in preparing for decertification. Because the workers probably have never been through a decertification election, this type of assistance may prove invaluable. For example, the NLRB may not permit an election if the paperwork has not been properly completed. Management must always remember that it cannot initiate the decertification action; that is the workers' responsibility.

The most effective means of accomplishing decertification is to improve the corporate culture so that workers no longer feel the need to have a union. This cannot be done overnight, as mutual trust and confidence must be developed between workers and the employer.

If decertification is to succeed, management must eliminate the problems that initially led to unionization. Although many executives believe that pay and benefits are the primary reasons for union membership, these factors are probably not the real cause.[61] Failure to treat employees as individuals is often the primary reason for unionization. The real problems often stem from practices such as failing to listen to employees' opinions, dealing with workers unfairly and dishonestly, and treating employees as numbers and not as people. Employers who desire to remain or become union free can employ certain strategies and tactics that benefit both employers and employees, but not unions.

Union-Free Strategies and Tactics

Employers who adhere to certain union-free strategies and tactics can remain or become union free. Some managers believe that the presence of a union is evidence of management's failure to treat employees fairly.[62] This is true in certain cases, but the factors that the AFL-CIO believes will significantly reduce the chances of unionizing are notable, and are therefore listed in Table 14-1. According to a report published in *Unions in Transition*, certain similar

TABLE 14-1

AFL-CIO: Factors That Reduce the Chances for Union Organizing

1. A conviction by employees that the boss is not taking advantage of them.
2. Employees who have pride in their work.
3. Good performance records kept by the company. Employees feel more secure on their jobs when they know their efforts are recognized and appreciated.
4. No claims of high-handed treatment. Employees respect firm but fair discipline.
5. No claim of favoritism that's not earned through work performance.
6. Supervisors who have good relationships with subordinates. The AFL-CIO maintains that this relationship of supervisors with people under them—above all—stifles organizing attempts.

Source: "What to Do When the Union Knocks," *Nation's Business* 54 (November 1966): 107. Copyright 1977 by Nation's Business. Reprinted by permission.

characteristics help organizations remain union free: competitive pay and strong benefits, a team environment, open communication, a pleasant work environment, and the avoidance of layoffs.[63] Currently, both organized labor and progressive management realize that these positive characteristics will be a part of future work environments regardless of the union status of a company.

If a firm's goal is to remain union free, it should establish its strategy long before a union-organizing attempt begins. The development of long-term strategies and effective tactics for the purpose of remaining union free is crucial because the employees' decision to consider forming a union is usually not made overnight. Negative attitudes regarding the company are typically formed over a period of time and well in advance of any attempt at unionization.[64]

If a firm desires to remain union free, it must borrow some of the union's philosophy. Basically, management must be able and willing to offer workers equal or better conditions than they could expect with a union; this is becoming easier and easier to do. Weakness in any critical area may be an open invitation to a union.[65] As shown in Figure 14-5, all aspects of an organization's operations are involved in maintaining its union-free status.

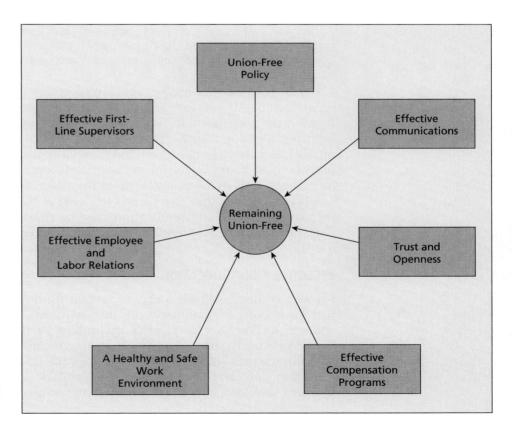

Figure 14-5
Factors Involved in Maintaining a Union-Free Status

EFFECTIVE FIRST-LINE SUPERVISORS

Extremely important to an organization's ability to remain union free is the overall effectiveness of its management, particularly its first-line supervisors. These supervisors represent the first line of defense against unionization. Their supervisory ability often determines whether unionization will be successful. The supervisor assigns work, evaluates each individual's performance, and provides praise and punishment. The manner in which he or she communicates with the employee in these and other matters can affect the individual's attitude toward the firm. Even though the first-line supervisor is the lowest level of management in the workplace, this person usually has more influence over employees than any other manager.

UNION-FREE POLICY

When the organization has a goal of remaining union free, this should be clearly and forcefully communicated to all its members. Such a policy statement might read this way:

> Our success as a company is founded on the skill and efforts of our employees. Our policy is to deal with employees as effectively as possible, respecting and recognizing each of them as individuals.
>
> In our opinion, unionization would interfere with the individual treatment, respect, and recognition the company offers. Consequently, we believe a union-free environment is in the employees' best interest, the company's best interest, and the interest of the people served by the corporation.[66]

This type of policy evolves into a philosophy that affects everyone in the organization. All employees, from the lowest paid worker to top management, must understand it. No major human resource-related decision should be made without asking, "How will this affect our union-free status?" The union-free policy should be communicated repeatedly to every worker. Employees must be told why the company advocates the policy and how it affects them. This involves much more than sending a memo each year to all employees stating that the company's goal is to remain union free. Every means of effective communication may be needed to convince employees that the organization intends to remain union free.

EFFECTIVE COMMUNICATION

For an organization that wants to remain union free, one of the most important actions the company can take is to establish credible and effective communication. A very positive by-product of the movement toward participative management, cooperation, and teamwork is open and effective communication. Employees must be given the information they need to perform their jobs and then be provided feedback on their performance. Management should openly share information with workers concerning activities taking place within the organization.

One approach that encourages open communication is the open-door
policy. The **open-door policy** gives employees the right to take any grievance to the person next in the chain of command if the problem cannot be
resolved by the immediate supervisor. Delta Air Lines is well known for its
open-door policy, which enables employees to express their grievances. An
effective open-door policy represents an attitude of openness and trust
among people within the organization. It is counterproductive to state that
an open-door policy exists and then punish an employee for bypassing his
or her immediate supervisor. The employee must not fear that talking to the
manager next in line will be detrimental to his or her career. Although it
might seem that an open-door policy would result in wasted time for upper
and middle managers, in most instances this has not proven to be the case.
The mere knowledge that an employee can move up the chain of command
with a complaint without fear of retribution often encourages the immediate
supervisor and the employee to work out their differences.

TRUST AND OPENNESS

Openness and trust on the part of managers and employees alike are important for a company to remain union free. The old expression, "Actions
speak louder than words," is certainly valid for such an organization.
Credibility, based on trust, must exist between labor and management,
and this trust develops only over time. If employees perceive that the
manager is being open and receptive to ideas, feedback is likely to be encouraged. Managers need this feedback to do their jobs effectively. However, if managers give the impression that their directives should never be
questioned, communication will be stifled and credibility lost. Here again,
the participative style that is becoming more pervasive will enhance trust,
openness, and employee involvement, helping management to maintain a
union-free organization.

EFFECTIVE COMPENSATION PROGRAMS

The financial compensation that employees receive is the most tangible
measure they have of their worth to the organization. If an individual's
pay is substantially below that provided for similar work in the area, the
employee will soon become dissatisfied. Compensation must be relatively
competitive if the organization expects to remain union free.[67] Pay equity
is becoming less of a problem now than in the past because of the slow
rate of compensation growth for unionized employees, not only in salary
but also in bonuses, cost-of-living allowances, and contributions to pension plans.

A HEALTHY AND SAFE WORK ENVIRONMENT

An organization that gains a reputation for failing to maintain a safe and
healthy work environment leaves itself wide open for unionization. For
years, unions have campaigned successfully by convincing workers that the

▼ HRM IN ACTION
WHY DON'T THEY WANT A UNION?

Wayne Boudreaux recently joined Royal Airlines as a reservation agent in Dallas. Prior to this job, he had been employed by Muse Airline of New York. When Muse went out of business recently, Wayne was offered a job with Royal. The pay wasn't as good, and he seemed to be working harder, but he needed the job.

During his first week on the job, Wayne was talking with several workers on his shift. "I don't see why we don't have a union here. Who's going to represent us when management puts the screws on?" Wayne's conversation was quickly cut off by one of the other workers, who replied, "We don't believe in unions at Royal. Management has done a good job. If you believe you need a union to represent you, maybe you don't need to work here." Wayne nodded his head to indicate his understanding and decided not to mention his feelings about wanting a union again.

➤ *What situations could have caused the workers to not want a union?*

union will provide them with a safer work environment. In fact, labor organizations were leading advocates of the Occupational Safety and Health Act, and they continue to support this type of legislation.

EFFECTIVE EMPLOYEE AND LABOR RELATIONS

Grievance procedure: A formal, systematic process that permits employees to complain about matters affecting them and their work.

No organization is free from employee disagreements and dissatisfaction. Therefore, a way to resolve employee complaints, whether actual or perceived, should be available. The **grievance procedure** is a formal process that permits employees to complain about matters affecting them. Most labor-management agreements contain formal grievance procedures, and union members regard handling grievances as one of the most important functions of a labor union. Until the early 1980s, grievance procedures were not so common in union-free organizations. However, since that time many nonunion firms have started grievance procedure programs. When employees do not have ways to voice their complaints and have them resolved, even small gripes may grow into major problems.

One way to resolve grievances in union-free organizations is through the use of ombudspersons. This approach has been used for some time in Europe, and the practice is becoming more popular in the United States. An **ombudsperson** is a complaint officer with access to top management; he or she hears employees' complaints, investigates them, and sometimes recommends appropriate action. Because of their access to top management, ombudspersons can often resolve problems swiftly.

Ombudsperson: A complaint officer with access to top management who hears employees' complaints, investigates them, and sometimes recommends appropriate action.

In recent years, the ombudsperson has assumed the additional duties of helping uncover scandals within organizations. Large defense contractors, such as McDonnell Douglas and General Electric, have used ombudspersons to respond to questions raised regarding product design safety or defense contract billings. Workers who believe that a problem exists can now bypass the supervisor and talk to the ombudsperson.[68]

A GLOBAL PERSPECTIVE

The Plight of Global Unionism: Not as Bad as in the United States, at Least Not Yet!

Although the future of unionism abroad seems much brighter than domestic unionism, the future is not as bright as it was even in the early 1990s. According to economist Richard Freeman, union membership fell in some countries in the 1980s, but no country had the same consistent abrupt drop experienced by U.S. unions. Whereas unionism has waned in the United States, it has maintained much of its strength abroad. Even though unions in all countries have been under increasing pressure in recent decades because of slowing productivity, lower economic growth, rapid technological changes, and a shift toward a free market system, unionism in the United States has suffered the most.[69]

Reflecting the spread of free market systems throughout the world, Mercedes-Benz chose to locate production facilities outside Germany and in the United States, China, and India to escape Germany's strict work rules and extremely high union wage rates. Mercedes-Benz is reinventing itself, outside Germany, because the labor situation in Germany is not conducive to competitiveness. This turn of events surprised many people, especially in Germany. The United States is the recipient of such jobs, which is a reversal of recent history. According to Daimler Chairman Jurgen Schrempp, Mercedes-Benz quality is most important and will not be compromised; this is one of the main reasons that Mercedes is restructuring. To compete globally, new products must be competitively priced and of uncompromising quality. This condition is accomplished through applying cost-cutting, using competitive global wage rates, and adopting the best practices of German, U.S., and Japanese manufacturers. Doing this required Mercedes-Benz to move production out of Germany. *Quality at competitive prices* is the watch phrase of global competitiveness, and in this case the United States is the beneficiary of such a move.[70] Although foreign unions are generally less adversarial with management and less focused on wage gains, globalization is a major threat to wage gains worldwide. The tide of union membership overseas may well be on a downturn.[71]

SUMMARY

1. *Describe the labor movement prior to 1930.*

   Prior to the 1930s, the trend definitely favored management. The courts strongly supported employers in their attempts to thwart the organized labor movement. This favoritism was first evidenced by the use of criminal and civil conspiracy doctrines derived from English common law.

2. *Explain the major labor legislation that was passed after 1930.*

The Anti-Injunction Act (Norris-Laguardia Act) of 1932 affirms that U.S. public policy sanctions collective bargaining and approves the formation and effective operation of labor unions. The National Labor Relations Act (Wagner Act) of 1935 created the National Labor Relations Board. The Labor Management Relations Act (Taft-Hartley Act) of 1947 revised the National Labor Relations Act and made significant changes in the act, extending the concept of unfair labor practices to unions. The Labor-Management Reporting and Disclosure Act (Landrum-Griffin Act) of 1959 requires extensive reporting on numerous internal union activities and contains severe penalties for violations.

3. *Describe the labor movement into the year 2000.*

The labor movement involves a series of measures and countermeasures by management and labor; these are impacted by, among other things, politics and global economic factors. Organized labor's new strategies for a stronger movement involve practices such as greater political involvement, union salting, flooding the community, and corporate labor campaigns.

4. *Describe the relationship between teams and organized labor.*

To be globally competitive, most organizations must utilize cohesive teams that take maximum advantage of the physical and mental capacities of each employee. However, the 1935 National Labor Relations Act prohibits such arrangements because some companies could establish management-labor teams as *sham* unions to avert union organizing.

5. *Explain unionization in the public sector.*

For many years, the federal government had no well-defined policy on labor-management relations regarding its own employees. To address this situation, President Kennedy issued Executive Order 10988 in 1962. Employees were permitted to organize and negotiate human resource policies and practices and matters affecting working conditions that were within the administrative discretion of the agency officials concerned. However, Public Law 84-330, passed in 1955, made it a felony for federal employees to strike against the U.S. government.

6. *Identify the reasons employees join unions.*

The reasons individuals join unions are many and varied, and they tend to change over time. They may involve job, personal, social, or political considerations. Some of the major reasons are these: dissatisfaction with management, need for a social outlet, need for avenues of leadership, forced unionization, and social pressure from peers.

7. *Describe the basic structure of the union.*

The basic element in the structure of the American labor movement is the local union. Basically, local unions are either craft or industrial. A craft union is typically composed of members of a particular trade or skill in a specific locality. An industrial union generally consists of all the workers in a particular plant or group of plants. The most powerful level in the union structure is the national union. A national union is composed of local union charters that supports it financially. The American Federation of Labor and Congress of Industrial Organizations (AFL-CIO) is the central trade union federation in the United States. It represents the interests of labor and its member national unions at the highest level.

8. *Identify the steps involved in establishing the collective bargaining relationship.*
The steps involved include signing authorization cards, petitioning for election, campaigning, winning the election and being certified.

9. *Explain union decertification.*
Decertification is essentially the reverse of the process that employees must follow to be recognized as an official bargaining unit. The rules established by the NLRB spell out the conditions for filing a decertification petition. At least 30 percent of the bargaining unit members must petition for an election. Timing of the NLRB's receipt of the decertification petition is also critical. The petition must be submitted between 60 and 90 days prior to the expiration of the current contract. When all these conditions have been met, the NLRB regional director will schedule a decertification election by secret ballot. If a majority of the votes cast are against the union, the union will be decertified.

10. *List and describe union-free strategies and tactics.*
Tactics employers can use to remain union free include effective first-line supervision, union-free policy, effective communication, trust and openness, effective compensation programs, a healthy and safe work environment, and effective employee and labor relations.

QUESTIONS FOR REVIEW

1. Describe the development of the labor movement in the United States before 1930.

2. What major labor legislation was passed after 1930?

3. List the unfair labor practices by management that were prohibited by the Wagner Act.

4. What union actions were prohibited by the Taft-Hartley Act?

5. In what way does unionization of the public sector differ from unionization of the private sector?

6. Why would unions strive for continued growth and power? Discuss.

7. What are the primary reasons for employees to join labor unions?

8. Describe the union structure in the United States.

9. What steps must a union take in attempting to form a bargaining unit? Briefly describe each step.

10. Describe the ways unions might go about gaining bargaining unit recognition.

11. Discuss the process of decertification.

12. Briefly describe union-free strategies and tactics.

DEVELOPING HRM SKILLS

AN EXPERIENTIAL EXERCISE

Unionization is often met with mixed feelings by all concerned. Management is usually opposed to such efforts. Beth Morrison, the production manager of the heavy motors division of MNP Corporation, knows that upper management does not care much for unions. Senior officials believe the unionizing effort is not good for anybody involved with the company and that the union wants to turn the employees against them. Upper management also feels that a union will destroy the company's competitive edge—something that has happened to many other firms. The firm must do everything possible to circumvent this union-organizing effort, but it must do so in line with NLRB guidelines.

If you are either in favor of or opposed to unions, there is a role for you here. One of you will play the production manager and another will play the supervisor. The rest of you should observe carefully. Your instructor will provide the participants with additional information.

Take It to the Net

We invite you to visit the Mondy home page on the Prentice Hall Web site at:

http://www.prenhall.com/mondy

for updated information, Web-based exercises, and links to other HR-related sites.

HRM SIMULATION

*I*ncident L in the *Human Resources Management Simulation Players Manual* deals with unionization. Three weeks ago the Amalgamated Workers Union began organizing efforts with the workers in your organization. The CEO has given your team the responsibility of combating this perceived threat. Numerous options are available, so your team needs to study them carefully and make its recommendation.

HRM INCIDENT

1

A Bad Situation

The attitude on the production floor at Ajax Manufacturing was a somber one. On the surface, there appeared to be little communication between the workers, but the untrained eye can often be deceptive. As Joe Morgan passed Bob Williams, he whispered, "We're meeting at the bowling alley tonight at 10:00. We need you there!" When Alice Stephens met Sharon Prewett in the wash room, essentially the same words were said. All during the day, the same procedure was followed while the supervisor kept wondering why things were going so smoothly.

That night at the bowling alley, the level and intensity of the conversation increased. Although the meeting was informal, Joe Morgan started it off by saying, "I took the opportunity to invite Harry Sims, a union representative, down here to visit us tonight. He'd like to hear your gripes."

Alice started: "Last year a new plant manager took over and things just haven't been the same since."

Bob interrupted, saying, "Yeah, it really burns me up. Since he came in, even the supervisors' attitudes have changed. They won't even make a decision on their own. It's a major concession to even let us go to the bathroom."

"And not only that," Sharon said, "If you even try to express your opinion, you might get fired. Remember what happened to Joanne last month. She argued about the new standard she'd been given, and the next week she was gone."

The dialogue continued in much the same manner through much of the evening. Finally, after several hours of patient listening, Harry Sims asked to say a few words. He began, "I understand your problem. I see situations like this all the time. But if you want it to stop, you must be prepared to do something about it. It will take some work on your part, but you don't have to be treated like that. Here is what I would suggest."

Questions
1. What do you believe that Harry Sims is going to say to the Group? Discuss.
2. Identify some of the major mistakes that management had made to create this situation.

HRM INCIDENT

2

Union Appeal

In late 1998, a vigorous union-organizing campaign was under way at Dodge Tube Company in Rochester, North Carolina. The management at Dodge was strongly anti-union and made no secret of it. Roger Verdon was a general supervisor at Dodge, with the responsibility for four supervisors and about 80 machine operators and helpers. Roger had become increasingly incensed as the union's organizing attempts became more apparent.

At first, flyers and other promotional literature had been handed out at the plant gates. There had been an increasing number of complaints, many of which Roger felt were caused by the union-organizing activity. The workers in general had become more belligerent, Roger thought, and he saw indications of more and more secret communication. Workers who had previously been his friends seemed to have pulled away. Although they were not unfriendly, they typically limited their conversation with him to office matters.

Roger felt that Dodge was a good employer and treated its people fairly. Discipline was administered by supervisors on the spot. Helpers were paid minimum wage, but few stayed in that position very long. Most helpers were either fired or promoted to machine operator within about six months. The machine operators were placed in pay grades 1, 2, or 3 at the discretion of the supervisor. Supervisors were encouraged to base pay grade assignments only on job proficiency. Most of the supervisors were required to participate in the company's management training program. The ones who were not college graduates were required to complete a correspondence course in management from the University of Maryland during their first six months as supervisors.

The company had an aggressive health and safety program. Workers in noisy areas were required to wear earplugs, and a worker who failed to do so was immediately fired. The same was true of safety glasses in areas involving grinding, drilling, or chipping. The workers in and around the tube-cleaning area were required to wear respirators because an OSHA inspector had cited the company for the amount of particulate matter in the air.

One day in early December, Roger observed what he considered the last straw. He saw a worker from another part of the plant walking through his area handing out cards to the workers. Bob asked to see one of the cards and realized that it was a union authorization card. He decided to have a meeting with his supervisors.

Questions
1. What factors could have produced union-organizing activity?
2. What can Roger do about it?

Notes

1. *Brief History of the American Labor Movement*, Bulletin 1000 (Washington, DC: U.S. Department of Labor Statistics, 1970): 1.

2. Benjamin J. Taylor and Fred Witney, *Labor Relations Law*, 5th ed. (Englewood Cliffs, NJ: Prentice Hall, 1987): 12–13.

3. *Brief History of the American Labor Movement*, 9.

4. Foster Rhea Dulles, *Labor in America*, 3rd ed. (New York: Crowell, 1966): 114–125.

5. Ibid., 126–149.

6. *Brief History of the American Labor Movement*, 15–16.

7. E. Edward Herman, Alfred Kuhn, and Ronald L. Seeber, *Collective Bargaining and Labor Relations* (Englewood Cliffs, NJ: Prentice Hall, 1987): 32–34.

8. *Brief History of the American Labor Movement*, 27.

9. *Historical Statistics of the United States, Colonial Times to 1970*, Bicentennial Edition, Part I (Washington, DC: U.S. Bureau of the Census, 1975): 126.

10. Benjamin J. Taylor and Fred Witney, *Labor Relations Law*, 78–81.

11. Ibid., 150–151.

12. *Brief History of the American Labor Movement*, 65.

13. Right-to-work states include Alabama, Arizona, Arkansas, Florida, Georgia, Idaho, Iowa, Kansas, Louisiana, Mississippi, Nebraska, Nevada, North Carolina, North Dakota, South Carolina, South Dakota, Tennessee, Texas, Utah, Virginia, and Wyoming.

14. Foster Rhea Dulles, *Labor in America*, 382–383.

15. *Brief History of the American Labor Movement*, 58–61.

16. Ibid., 139.

17. Aaron Bernstein and Susan B. Garland, "The AFL-CIO: A Tougher Team with the Teamsters," *Business Week* (November 9, 1987): 110.

18. James Worsham, "Labor Comes Alive," *Nation's Business* 84 (February 1996): 16.

19. John Greenwald, "Labor: The Battle to Revive U.S. Unions," *Time* (October 30, 1995): 64.

20. Aaron Bernstein, "Workplace: Unions: Sweeney's Blitz," *Business Week* (February 2, 1997): 56.

21. John E. Lyncheski and Joseph M. McDermott, "Unions Employ New Growth Strategies," *HR Focus* 73 (September 1996): 22.

22. Bill Leonard, "1996 Contract Negotiations Will Affect 1.7 Million Workers," *HR Magazine* 31 (October 1995): 4.

23. Greenwald, "Labor: The Battle to Revive U.S. Unions," 64.

24. Worsham, "Labor Comes Alive," 16.

25. Lyncheski and McDermott, "Unions Employ New Growth Strategies."

26. Ibid.

27. Ibid.

28. National Labor Relations Board.

29. Ibid.

30. Worsham, "Labor Comes Alive," 16.

31. M. E. Sharpe, "Labor's Future," *Challenge* 39 (March/April 1996): 65.

32. Faye Fiore and Martha Groves, "Bill to Curb Union Power Passes Senate; Veto Likely," *Los Angeles Times* (July 11, 1996): A-1.

33. Richard Lesher, "Management and Labor Work Best as Cohesive Teams," *Human Events* (March 7, 1997): 27.

34. Peter Szekely, "TEAM Act: New Political Hot Potato," *Reuters* (May 8, 1996): 1.

35. Aaron Bernstein, "Look Who's Pushing Productivity," *Business Week* (April 7, 1997): 72–75.

36. Examples include the Social Security Act, the Fair Labor Standards Act, and the National Labor Relations Act, as amended.

37. Sharpe, "Labor's Future," 65.

38. Jim Armshaw, David Carnevale, and Bruce Waltuck, "Union-Management Partnership in the U.S. Department of Labor," *Review of Public Personnel Administration* 13 (Summer 1993): 94–101.

39. Section 305 of the Labor Management Relations Act of 1947 also makes it unlawful for government employees to participate in any strike.

40. Lyncheski and McDermott, "Unions Employ New Growth Strategies," 22.

41. They are Executive Order 11491 (effective January 1, 1970); EO 11616 (effective November 1971); EO 11636 (effective December 1971); and EO 11828 (effective May 1975).

42. Herman, Kuhn, and Seeber, *Collective Bargaining and Labor Relations*, 407.

43. Amity Shales, "Labor's Return," *Commentary* 1 (October 1996): 49.

44. Leo Troy, "The Rise and Fall of American Trade Unions," 85.

45. Edwin F. Beal and James P. Begin, *The Practice of Collective Bargaining*, 5th ed. (Homewood, IL: Richard D. Irwin, 1982): 91.

46. Sam F. Parigi, Frank J. Cavaliere, and Joel L. Allen, "Improving Labor Relations in an Era of Declining Union Power," *Review of Business* 14 (Winter 1992): 31–35.

47. Greenwald, "Labor: The Battle to Revive U.S. Unions," 64.

48. Troy, "The Rise and Fall of American Trade Unions," 104.

49. Shales, "Labor's Return."

50. Ibid.

51. Susan B. Garland, "Why Democrats Still Want to Wear the Union Label," *Business Week* (March 5, 1990): 37.

52. Stan Crock, "The Duke Is Still Playing Hard-to-Get with Labor," *Business Week* (August 29, 1988): 39.

53. Parigi, Cavaliere, and Allen, "Improving Labor Relations in an Era of Declining Union Power."

54. Ibid.

55. Aaron Bernstein, "Big Labor Invites a Few Friends Over," *Business Week* (April 21, 1997): 44.

56. Ibid., 14.

57. *A Guide to Basic Law and Procedures under the National Labor Relations Act* (Washington, DC: U.S. Government Printing Office, October 1978): 11–13.

58. National Labor Relations Board.

59. Art Bethke, R. Wayne Mondy, and Shane R. Premeaux, "Decertification: The Role of the First-Line Supervisor," *Supervisory Management* 31 (February 1986): 21–23.

60. Bernstein, "Workplace: Unions: Sweeney's Blitz."

61. Ibid.

62. Wiley L. Beavers, "Employee Relations without a Union," in Dale Yoder and Herbert S. Heneman, Jr., eds., *ASPA Handbook of Personnel and Industrial Relations: Employee and Labor Relations*, vol. III (Washington, DC: The Bureau of National Affairs, 1976): 7–83.

63. Alexander B. Trowbridge, "A Management Look at Labor Relations, in *Unions in Transition* (San Francisco: ICS Press, 1988): 415–416.

64. Kevin Kelly, "Cat Is Purring, but They're Hissing on the Floor," *Business Week* (May 16, 1994): 33.

65. Trowbridge, "A Management Look at Labor Relations," 417.

66. James F. Rand, "Preventive Maintenance Techniques for Staying Union Free," *Personnel Journal* 59 (June 1980): 497.

67. Ibid., 498.

68. Michael Brody, "Listen to Your Whistleblower," *Fortune* 124 (November 1986): 77–78.

69. Worsham, "Labor Comes Alive," 16.

70. Donald W. Nauss, "It's Fun, It's Useful, It's a Mercedes?" *Los Angeles Times* (May 18, 1997): A-1.

71. Ibid.

15
Labor Management Relations

CHAPTER OBJECTIVES

1. Explain labor management relations and individual bargaining.
2. Describe the collective bargaining process.
3. Explain the psychological aspects of collective bargaining.
4. Explain typical bargaining issues.
5. Identify the topics included in virtually all labor agreements.
6. Identify ways to overcome breakdowns in negotiations.
7. Describe what is involved in administering the agreement.
8. Explain the future of collective bargaining.

Labor management relations have changed significantly since MBI, Inc. became unionized. Individual bargaining was replaced by a collective bargaining relationship. Barbara Washington, the chief union negotiator, was meeting with company representatives on a new contract. Both the union team and management had been preparing for this encounter for a long time. Barbara's deep concern was whether union members would support a strike vote if one were called. Sales for the industry were generally down because of imports. In fact, there had even been some layoffs at competing firms. The union members' attitude could be described as "Get what you can for us, but don't rock the boat." She hoped, however, that skillful negotiating could win concessions from management.

In the first session, Barbara's team presented its demands to management. The team had determined that pay was the main issue, and they demanded a 20 percent increase spread over three years. Management countered by saying that because sales were down, the company could not afford to provide any pay raises. After much heated discussion, both sides agreed to reevaluate their positions and meet again

in two days. Barbara met with her negotiating team in private, and it decided to decrease the salary demand slightly. The team felt that the least they could accept was a 15 percent raise.

At the next meeting, Barbara presented the revised demands to management. They were not well received. Bill Thompson, the director of industrial relations, began by saying, "We cannot afford a pay increase in this contract, but we will make every attempt to ensure that no layoffs occur. Increasing wages at this time will virtually guarantee a reduction in the workforce."

Barbara's confidence collapsed. She knew there was no way the general membership was willing to accept layoffs and that a strike vote would be virtually impossible to obtain. She asked for a recess to review the new proposal.

Barbara is experiencing the negotiating crunch that has existed for several years in the United States. The power pendulum has swung in favor of management, making it very difficult for union negotiators to bargain effectively with management on certain issues, including pay increases.

*W*e devote the first portion of the chapter to labor management relations involving both individual and collective bargaining. Then we describe the psychological aspects of collective bargaining and preparing for negotiations. Next, we address bargaining issues, negotiating the agreement, and overcoming breakdowns in negotiations. We conclude the chapter with a discussion of the ratification and administration of the agreement and the future of collective bargaining.

HR Web Wisdom

http://www.prenhall.com/mondy

SHRM–HR LINKS
Various labor relations issues are addressed here.

Labor Management Relations and Individual Bargaining

We stated in chapter 14 that approximately 10 percent of the private workforce is unionized. Therefore, about 90 percent of the private workforce bases their labor management relations on individual bargaining. We also mentioned in chapter 14 that one of the goals of a union is to gain power, and this is largely dependent on the size of union membership. In individual negotiations, however, the worker is alone in negotiating with company representatives. Even so, negotiations can still be on a power basis, depending on the value of the individual to the company. An employee who continuously adds value to himself or herself and the company is in a position of power. Should an individual desire job security, a raise, or other tangible evidence of value, negotiations will likely receive positive results if the worker is valued by the company. Seniority means little in this environment. Remember a section in chapter 9 entitled Adding Value to Retain Present Job. Negotiations are ineffective unless the worker has a positive value component.

Another factor influencing individual negotiations is the concept of supply and demand. In the 1980s and early 1990s, certain business disciplines were in *great* demand. In universities, business faculty members could demand and receive promotions and raises; if these were not forthcoming, they could move easily to another university. Thus, negotiations on an individual basis are more effective when demand is high and supply is down.

Employment at will:
An unwritten contract that is created when an employee agrees to work for an employer but includes no agreement as to how long the parties expect the employment to last.

An individual negotiator usually falls under the concept of employment at will. **Employment at will** is an unwritten contract created when an employee agrees to work for an employer, but no agreement exists as to how long the parties expect the employment to last. Historically, because of a century-old common law precedent in the United States, employment of indefinite duration could, in general, be terminated at the whim of either party. Remember from chapter 7 that Conoco had this statement on their employment application: "I understand that any employment which may be offered to me will not be for any definite period of time and that such employment is subject to termination by me or by Conoco Inc. at any time, with or without cause." Employment at will is discussed in greater detail in chapter 16.

One might think that an individual employee would be extremely vulnerable when dealing with individual negotiations. As our society becomes more legalistic, more and more individual rights are protected. Think back to chapter 3 regarding the many laws and court decisions that have been developed to protect individual rights. In the past, many of these protections were based on union representation. Individual negotiators now possess many of these rights. As you will see in the next chapter, even the concept of employment at will has eroded somewhat in recent years.

Even though most workers in the U.S. economy are not unionized, if a firm desires to remain union free, its management must sustain an environment that discourages unionizing attempts. The old saying, "Management gets what it deserves," is never more true than when a union successfully organizes a group of employees. After the union arrives and successfully organizes, management usually recognizes the avoidable mistakes that led to unionization. However, a well-conceived and implemented employee relations system, in which every manager is sensitive to employee needs, could substantially reduce the likelihood of unionization.[1] On the other hand, firms believing that "environmental changes will forever conspire against the survival and growth of unions" will probably contribute to the survival of unions, most probably in firms that dismiss the concept of equity and employee involvement.[2] When unionization occurs, collective bargaining follows, as the union becomes the third party within the corporate setting.

Labor Management Relations and the Collective Bargaining Process

Even though collective bargaining is widely practiced, there is no precise format of what to do or how to do it. In fact, diversity is probably the most prominent characteristic of collective bargaining in the United States. The collective bargaining process, in general, is shown in Figure 15-1.

As you can see, both external and internal environmental factors can influence the process. For instance, the form of the bargaining structure can affect the conduct of collective bargaining. The four major types of structure are (1) one company dealing with a single union, (2) several companies dealing with a single union, (3) several unions dealing with a single company, and (4) several companies dealing with several unions. Most contract bargaining is carried out under the first type of structure, as was the case with MBI, Inc. The United Automobile Workers (UAW) has been employing a unique approach to gain additional bargaining power. When General Motors (GM) would not meet union demands at one of their automobile assembly plants, the union called a strike at GM's Warren, Michigan, transmission and parts plant, effectively shutting down six GM car assembly plants. This action increased union leverage and brought GM back to the bargaining table, resulting in settlements.[3]

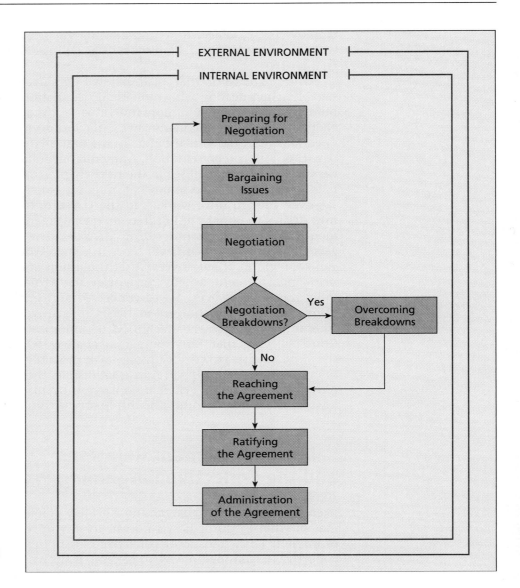

Figure 15-1
The Collective Bargaining
Process

The process can become quite complicated when several companies and unions are involved in the same negotiations. However, even when there is only one industry involved and one group of workers with similar skills, collective bargaining can be quite problematic. Another environmental factor influencing collective bargaining is the type of union-management relationship that exists. When a group of workers decide they want union representation, changes occur in the organization. In the absence of a union, management exercises virtually unlimited authority, except for the limitations imposed by the growing web of employee legal rights protection. Although legal protections could essentially replace collective bargaining in the future, for the present, when a union becomes the bargaining representative, management must change its style of decision making to include union bargaining agents. When employees take collective action, such as slow-downs and strikes, an adversarial relationship can be created, with varying degrees of conflict. Sloane and Witney list six types of union-management relations that may exist in an organization:

1. *Conflict.* Each side challenges the other's actions and motivation; co-operation is nonexistent, and uncompromising attitudes and union militancy are present.[4]

2. *Armed truce.* Each side views the other as antagonistic but tries to avoid head-on conflict; bargaining obligations and contract provisions are strictly interpreted.

3. *Power bargaining.* Management accepts the union; each side tries to gain advantage from the other.

4. *Accommodation.* Each tolerates the other in a *live and let live* atmosphere and attempts to reduce conflict without eliminating it.

5. *Cooperation.* Each side accepts the other, and both work together to resolve human resource and production problems as they occur. Although the National Labor Relations Act of 1935 prohibits management domination of unions, cooperation is allowed if prescribed in the collective bargaining agreement. It appears that this type relationship best describes the future of collective bargaining agreements in the private sector.[5]

6. *Collusion.* Both *cooperate* to the point of adversely affecting the legitimate interests of employees, other businesses in the industry, and the consuming public; this involves conniving to control markets, supplies, and prices illegally and/or unethically.[6]

The nature and quality of union-management relations vary over time. The first three types of relationships mentioned are generally unsatisfactory; collusion is unacceptable, and cooperation, although rare in the past, may be the nature of future collective bargaining agreements. Typically, U.S. union-management relations appear to be some form of accommodation. According to Xerox CEO Paul A. Allaire, "If we have a cooperative model, the union movement will be sustained and the industries it's in will be more competitive." The bottom line in effective bargaining arrangements is the overwhelming issue of joint economic survival. Furthermore, the lessening of adversarial relationships and the increased cooperation in areas never possible in the past offer real prospects for both management and labor in the future.[7]

The acceptance of cooperative relationships between management and labor is spreading among the few dozen major companies that are developing real partnerships with labor. According to David H. Hoag, CEO of LTV Corporation, the union agreed to team methods and other efficiency measures in exchange for a union nominee on the board. Ford's head of cooperative labor programs goes beyond this sentiment and declares, "If unions were to disappear, the country would be in serious trouble." On the other hand, most employers could not agree less; they have never accepted unions, and they appear unwilling to accept them at this time. Basically, during the past

12 years, U.S. industry has conducted one of their most successful anti-union wars ever, and many managers appear eager to continue their assault on labor.[8]

Cooperative practices empower employees, foster pride in them, and help assure joint economic survival. As both groups agree, now more than ever, that joint economic survival is most important, it is quite possible that past adversarial relationships will be replaced with cooperation. When both groups cooperate, everyone involved benefits, particularly the unions. This reality could explain why unions are embracing cooperation with unprecedented enthusiasm. Unions are currently accepting the notion that they must reinvent themselves to practice cooperation and balance better wages with efforts to help employers win competitive battles. This attitude will, no doubt, be an integral part of collective bargaining in the future.[9] In the case of MBI, union negotiator Barbara Washington came to the realization that pay raises were out of the question, and layoffs were a real possibility. Barbara also realized that union members were aware of competitive pressures impacting MBI, and therefore a strike vote was unlikely. She had virtually no power in the collective bargaining situation.

Depending on the type of relationship encountered, the collective bargaining process may be relatively simple, or it may be a long, tense struggle for both parties, as was the case with major league baseball. In the case of MBI, the process will be relatively simple even though both sides are far apart. Management must reduce costs and union members are probably unwilling to strike; management has virtually all the power, so they will win. Veteran labor negotiator Robert J. Harding, a consulting firm executive, offers the following seven tips for successful collective bargaining:

1. Don't underestimate the importance of the first preparatory, nonadversarial meeting between labor and management representatives; use this opportunity to set the ground rules for future sessions.

2. Carefully document each meeting because accurate, well-organized notes can be quite useful in initial, and subsequent, contract negotiations.

3. If the CEO is well regarded by employees, consider including him or her in the sessions.

4. Within the bounds of law and propriety, develop a personal profile of each member of the committee who will take part in the collective bargaining process.

5. Accept negotiators as peers; never underestimate them.

6. Maintain strong communications with those individuals who best know the people most affected by the contract and the issues being discussed.

7. If negotiations break down, consider federal mediation.[10]

Regardless of the complexity of the bargaining issues, the ability to reach agreement is the key to any successful negotiation. Success requires good communication skills and an understanding of these seven negotiation tips.

The first step in the collective bargaining process, you recall, is preparing for negotiations. This step is often extensive and ongoing for both union and management. After the issues to be negotiated have been determined, the two sides confer to reach a mutually acceptable contract. Although breakdowns in negotiations can occur, both labor and management have at their disposal tools and arguments that can be used to convince the other side to accept their views. It is interesting to note that successful unions—those that are growing—are unions that embrace cooperation and are more likely to avoid bargaining breakdowns. Basically, unions are giving up more ground than ever before in collective bargaining agreements because many union officials have accepted the notion that increased wages and benefits result from cooperative work efforts, team management, and overall productivity gains. Wage increases are at their lowest levels in years, having fallen in 1995 and 1996. In addition, benefits are dropping, as are other costly rewards such as pension plan contributions.[11] In an effort to stem this tide, WHX steelworkers went out on strike over pensions, a strike that may destroy the company. Chairman Ronald LaBow has seen the strike reduce stock value from 19 3/4 three years ago to 6 1/2 today. Currently, he is considering a liquidation of the company and thus far has stockholder support.[12] Eventually, however, management and the union usually reach an agreement that defines the rules of the game for the duration of the contract. The next step is for the union membership to ratify the agreement.

Note the feedback loop from "Administration of the Agreement" to "Preparing for Negotiation" in Figure 15-1. Collective bargaining is a continuous and dynamic process, and preparing for the next round of negotiations often begins the moment a contract is ratified.

Psychological Aspects of Collective Bargaining

Prior to collective bargaining, both the management team and the union team have to prepare positions and accomplish certain tasks. Vitally important for those involved are the psychological aspects of collective bargaining. Psychologically, the collective bargaining process may be difficult when an adversarial situation exists, and it must be approached as such. It is "a situation that is fundamental to law, politics, business, and government, because out of the clash of ideas, points of view, and interests come agreement, consensus and justice."[13]

In effect, those involved in the collective bargaining process will be matching wits with the competition, will experience victory as well as defeat, and will usually resolve problems, resulting in a contract. The role of those who meet at the bargaining table essentially involves the "mobilization and management of aggression" in a manner that allows them to hammer out a collective bargaining agreement.[14] Because those involved must "mobilize and manage aggression," their personalities have a major impact on the negotiation process. The attitudes of the people who will be negotiating have a direct effect on what can be accomplished and how quickly a mutually agreed-on contract can be finalized. Problems are compounded by differences in the experience and educational backgrounds of those involved in the negotiation process. Finally, the longer, more involved, and intense the bargaining sessions are, the greater will be the psychological strain on all concerned.

Scare tactics have intensified the psychological pressures of collective bargaining. In fact, estimates are that nearly half the managers facing a union election threaten to close plants. Also, half the time labor loses when threats are made versus one-third of the time when no warnings are issued.[15] Management at MBI was very straightforward, stating upfront that no pay increases will result from the bargaining effort and all management can do is try to avoid layoffs. With no real possibility of a strike, Barbara has no power over management. In order to break unions in the 1980s, management permanently replaced striking workers, a trend that continued throughout the 1990s. Certain companies have placed advertisements and even hired permanent replacements during contract talks. This dramatically tipped the scales toward management because employees knew that a decision to strike could cost them their jobs. However, a recent NLRB ruling presumes that replacement workers support the union.[16] In the past, employers replaced striking workers without taking a vote because the assumption was made that newly hired workers opposed the union. If employers use a permanent replacement threat and it does not work, it may become even harder for management to ease the tensions between them and labor.[17] Some unions, such as the UAW, are reaching the bargaining table in a combative mood, all but stating that union members are quite willing to strike, particularly at essential parts plants. One UAW negotiator viewed this approach as bringing all the ingredients for disaster together.[18] As psychological pressures intensify, the gap between labor and management can easily widen, further compounding the problems of achieving mutual accommodation. Even in Britain, where unions have flourished for decades, union-management adversary positions are increasing. The current role of unions is to step in when workers resent the employers' insistence on their absolute and unqualified right to manage in whatever way they see fit. Thus, these psychological pressures are intensifying even overseas.[19]

Preparing for Negotiations

Because of the complex issues facing labor and management today, the negotiating teams must carefully prepare for the bargaining sessions. Prior to meeting at the bargaining table, the negotiators should thoroughly know the culture, climate, history, present economic state, and wage and benefits structure of both the organization and similar organizations.[20] Because the length of a typical labor agreement is three years, negotiators should develop a contract that is successful both now and in the future. This consideration should prevail for both management and labor, although it rarely does. During the term of an agreement, the two sides usually discover contract provisions that need to be added, deleted, or modified. These items become proposals to be addressed in the next round of negotiations.

Bargaining issues can be divided into three categories: mandatory, permissive, and prohibited. **Mandatory bargaining issues** fall within the defin-

Mandatory bargaining issues: Bargaining issues that fall within the definition of wages, hours, and other terms and conditions of employment; refusal to bargain in these areas is grounds for an unfair labor practice charge.

Permissive bargaining issues: Issues that may be raised by management or a union; neither side may insist that they be bargained over.

ition of wages, hours, and other terms and conditions of employment (see Table 15-1 on page 550). These issues generally have an immediate and direct effect on workers' jobs. A refusal to bargain in these areas is grounds for an unfair labor practice charge. **Permissive bargaining issues** may be raised, but neither side may insist that they be bargained over. For example, the union may want to bargain over health benefits for retired workers or union participation in establishing company pricing policies, but management may choose not to bargain over either issue. One issue on which the AFL-CIO has vowed to increase their bargaining is work-family issues, particularly child care. According to Karen Nassbaum, head of the AFL-CIO's newly created Department of Working Women, "Despite the fact that over half the women with young children work outside the home, as a country, we still cling to the 'every woman for herself attitude' and dare to call it a solution to the country's child care crisis." Basically, this is a critical issue because fewer than 10 percent of Americans feel that the country's child care system meets the essential child care criteria.[21] **Prohibited bargaining issues**, such as the issue of the closed shop, are statutorily outlawed.

Prohibited bargaining issues: Issues that are statutorily outlawed from collective bargaining.

The union must continuously gather information regarding membership needs to isolate areas of dissatisfaction. The union steward is normally in the best position to collect such data. Because stewards are usually elected by their peers, they should be well informed regarding union members' attitudes. The union steward constantly funnels information up through the union's chain of command, where the data are compiled and analyzed. Union leadership attempts to uncover any areas of dissatisfaction because the general union membership must approve any agreement before it becomes final. Union leaders must be elected, and they will lose their positions if the demands they make of management do not represent the desires of the general membership.

Management also spends long hours preparing for negotiations. The many interrelated tasks that management must accomplish are presented in Figure 15-2 on page 551. In this example, the firm allows approximately six months to prepare for negotiations. All aspects of the current contracts are considered, including flaws that should be corrected. When preparing for negotiations, management should listen carefully to first-line managers. These individuals administer the labor agreement on a day-to-day basis and must live with errors made in negotiating the contract. An alert line manager is also able to inform upper management of the demands unions may plan to make during negotiations.

Management also attempts periodically to obtain information regarding employee attitudes. Surveys are often administered to workers to determine their feelings toward their jobs and job environment. When union and management representatives sit down at the bargaining table, both sides like to know as much as possible about employee attitudes.

Another part of preparation for negotiations involves identifying various positions that both union and management will take as the negotiations progress. Each usually takes an initial extreme position, representing the conditions union or management would prefer. The two sides will likely determine absolute limits to their offers or demands before a breakdown in negotiations occurs. They also usually prepare fallback positions based on

TABLE 15-1

Mandatory Bargaining Issues

Wages	Plant closedown and relocation
Hours	Change in operations resulting in reclassifying workers from incentive to straight time, or a cut in the workforce, or installation of cost-saving machinery
Discharge	
Arbitration	
Paid holidays	
Paid vacations	Price of meals provided by company
Duration of agreement	Group insurance—health, accident, life
Grievance procedure	Promotions
Layoff plan	Seniority
Reinstatement of economic strikers	Layoffs
Change of payment from hourly base to salary base	Transfers
	Work assignments and transfers
Union security and checkoff of dues	No-strike clause
Work rules	Piece rates
Merit wage increase	Stock purchase plan
Work schedule	Workloads
Lunch periods	Change of employee status to independent contractors
Rest periods	
Pension plan	Motor carrier-union agreement providing that carriers use own equipment before leasing outside equipment
Retirement age	
Bonus payments	
Cancellation of seniority upon relocation of plant	Overtime pay
	Agency shop
Discounts on company products	Sick leave
Shift differentials	Employer's insistence on clause giving an arbitrator the right to enforce an award
Contract clause providing for supervisors keeping seniority in unit	
	Management rights clause
Procedures for income tax withholding	Plant closing
Severance pay	Job posting procedures
Nondiscriminatory hiring hall	Plant reopening
Plant rules	Employee physical examination
Safety	Arrangement for negotiation
Prohibition against supervisor doing unit work	Change in insurance carrier and benefits
Superseniority for union stewards	Profit-sharing plan
Partial plant closing	Company houses
Hunting on employer's forest reserve where previously granted	Subcontracting
	Production ceiling imposed by union

Source: Reed Richardson, "Positive Collective Bargaining," Chapter 7.5 of ASPA *Handbook of Personnel and Industrial Relations,* 7–121. Copyright 1979 by The Bureau of National Affairs, Inc., Washington, DC. Reprinted by permission.

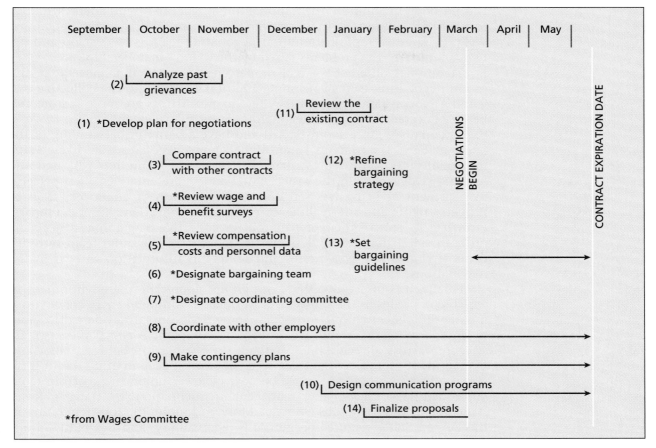

| September | October | November | December | January | February | March | April | May |

(2) Analyze past grievances

(1) *Develop plan for negotiations

(11) Review the existing contract

(3) Compare contract with other contracts

(12) *Refine bargaining strategy

(4) *Review wage and benefit surveys

(5) *Review compensation costs and personnel data

(13) *Set bargaining guidelines

(6) *Designate bargaining team

(7) *Designate coordinating committee

(8) Coordinate with other employers

(9) Make contingency plans

(10) Design communication programs

(14) Finalize proposals

*from Wages Committee

NEGOTIATIONS BEGIN

CONTRACT EXPIRATION DATE

Figure 15-2
An Example of Company Preparations for Negotiations
Source: Adapted from Ronald L. Miller, "Preparations for Negotiations," *Personnel Journal,* Vol. 57, 38. Copyright January 1978. Reprinted with permission.

combinations of issues. Preparations should be detailed because clear minds often do not prevail during the heat of negotiations.

A major consideration in preparing for negotiations is selection of the bargaining teams. The makeup of the management team usually depends on the type of organization and its size. Normally, bargaining is conducted by labor relations specialists, with the advice and assistance of operating managers. Sometimes, top executives are directly involved, particularly in smaller firms. Larger companies utilize staff specialists (a human resource manager or industrial relations executive), managers of principal operating divisions, and in some cases an outside consultant, such as a labor attorney. However, it is essential that the human resource manager become actively involved in the collective bargaining process whenever possible.

The responsibility for conducting negotiations for the union is usually entrusted to union officers. At the local level, the bargaining committee will normally be supplemented by rank-and-file members elected specifically for this purpose. In addition, the national union will often send a representative to act in an advisory capacity or even participate directly in the bargaining sessions. The real task of the union negotiating team is to develop and obtain solutions to the problems raised by the union's membership.

Traditional differences—real or perceived—between management and union negotiating teams contribute additional friction to the collective bargaining process. Management may feel its negotiators are more mature and better educated than labor negotiators. From management's point of view, their people are more sophisticated and have a better understanding of the issues at hand than labor's team. Management negotiators are likely to be impatient with union representatives they view as being less educated and less knowledgeable. On the other hand, labor representatives often perceive management as being less sensitive to the feelings of employees than to property rights and the realities of economic survival and future company growth.[22] As part of their preparation for collective bargaining, negotiators on both sides should fully appraise the makeup of the other team in terms of its strengths and weaknesses and bring this information to bear in the negotiations.

Finally, it is imperative that both groups appreciate the environment in which companies in the industry must operate. Although there are environmental differences among industries, some basic similarities do exist. Rapid technological changes and ever-increasing competitive global pressures are sweeping across all economies, making the partnership between labor and management more essential than ever. Labor must keep in mind that it is often at a bargaining disadvantage because of lower union membership rates, outmoded labor laws, and management inclination to transfer lower skilled/labor intensive jobs overseas. More and more, the jobs remaining in the United States require specific skills, adaptability, and flexibility—traits that many traditional core union members have historically lacked. Last, worker involvement is a reality and not an option for larger corporations. The *Journal of Commerce* noted that 80 percent of Fortune 500 companies, both union and nonunion, have established worker involvement programs, a necessity for the future of both global business and unions.[23]

Bargaining Issues

The document that emerges from the collective bargaining process is known as a *labor agreement* or *contract*. It regulates the relationship between employer and employees for a specified period of time. Collective bargaining basically determines the relationship between labor and management. Even some individuals who have been long-term foes of organized labor believe that the existence of organized labor and the collective bargaining process is essential. Senator Orrin G. Hatch (R-Utah), labor's arch rival on Capitol Hill for nearly two decades, believes that labor unions have value. Hatch still opposes many actions of organized labor, but according to him, "There are always going to be people who take advantage of workers. Unions even that out, to their credit. We need them to level the field between labor and management. If you didn't have unions, it would be very difficult for even enlightened employers not to take advantage of workers on wages and working conditions, because of (competition from) rivals."[24] Collective bargaining is an essential, but difficult task because each agreement is unique, and there is no standard or universal model. Despite many dissimilarities, certain topics are included in virtually all labor agreements. These include recognition, management rights, union security, compensation and benefits, grievance procedure, employee security, and job-related factors.

RECOGNITION

A section on recognition usually appears at the beginning of the labor agreement. Its purpose is to identify the union that is recognized as the bargaining representative and to describe the bargaining unit—that is, the employees for whom the union speaks. A typical recognition section might read as follows:

> The XYZ Company recognizes the ABC Union as the sole and exclusive representative of the bargaining unit employees for the purpose of collective bargaining with regard to wages, hours, and other conditions of employment.

MANAGEMENT RIGHTS

A section that is often, but not always, written into the labor agreement spells out the rights of management. If no such section is included, management may reason that it retains control of all topics not described as bargainable in the contract. The precise content of the management rights section will vary by industry, company, and union. When included, management rights generally involve three areas:

1. Freedom to select the business objectives of the company
2. Freedom to determine the uses to which the material assets of the enterprise will be devoted
3. Power to discipline for cause[25]

In a brochure the company publishes for all its first-line managers, AT&T describes management's rights when dealing with the union, including the following:

> You should remember that management has all such rights except those restricted by law or by contract with the union. You either make these decisions or carry them out through contact with your people. Some examples of these decisions and actions are:
>
> - To determine what work is to be done and where, when, and how it is to be done.
> - To determine the number of employees who will do the work.
> - To supervise and instruct employees in doing the work.
> - To correct employees whose work performance or personal conduct fails to meet reasonable standards. This includes administering discipline.
> - To recommend hiring, dismissing, upgrading, or downgrading of employees.
> - To recommend employees for promotion to management.[26]

Management rights in collective bargaining could be somewhat restricted by a ruling from the NLRB stating that companies must bargain with workers prior to relocating their business operations. The current standard directs employers to bargain over proposed relocations unless they can prove (1) that labor costs were not a factor in the relocation decision or (2) that if labor costs were a consideration, other costs of staying were greater than any wage concessions the union could offer. If the union offered concessions that equaled the size of the financial gains of moving, employers have a bargaining obligation. However, if the relocation involves "a basic change in the nature of the employer's operation," employers do not have to bargain over relocation.[27]

UNION SECURITY

Union security is typically one of the first items negotiated in a collective bargaining agreement. The objective of union security provisions is to ensure that the union continues to exist and perform its functions. A strong union security provision makes it easier for the union to enroll and retain members. Some basic forms of union security clauses are discussed in the following paragraphs.

Closed shop: An arrangement making union membership a prerequisite to employment.

Closed Shop.
A **closed shop** is an arrangement making union membership a prerequisite to employment. Such provisions are generally illegal in the United States.

HR Web Wisdom

http://www.prenhall.com/mondy

UNION SHOP VERSUS NONUNION SHOP

At this site, the advantages and disadvantages of both the union and nonunion shop are explored.

Union shop: A requirement that all employees become members of the union after a specified period of employment (the legal minimum is 30 days) or after a union shop provision has been negotiated.

Union Shop.
As mentioned in chapter 14, a **union shop** arrangement requires that all employees become members of the union after a specified period of employment (the legal minimum is 30 days) or after a union shop provision has been negotiated. Employees must remain members of the union as a condition of employment. The union shop is generally legal in the United States, except in states that have right-to-work laws.

Maintenance of Membership.
Employees who are members of the union at the time the labor agreement is signed or who later voluntarily join must continue their memberships until the termination of the agreement, as a condition of employment. This form of security is prohibited in most states that have right-to-work laws.

Agency shop: A labor agreement provision requiring, as a condition of employment, that each nonunion member of a bargaining unit pay the union the equivalent of membership dues as a service charge in return for the union's acting as the bargaining agent.

Open shop: Employment that is open on equal terms to union members and nonmembers alike.

Checkoff of dues: An agreement by which a company agrees to withhold union dues from members' paychecks and to forward the money directly to the union.

Agency Shop.
An **agency shop** provision does not require employees to join the union; however, the labor agreement may require, as a condition of employment, that each nonunion member of the bargaining unit pay the union the equivalent of membership dues as a kind of tax, or service charge, in return for the union acting as the bargaining agent. Remember that the National Labor Relations Act requires the union to bargain for all members of the bargaining unit, including nonunion employees. The agency shop is outlawed in most states that have right-to-work laws.

Exclusive Bargaining Shop.
Thirteen of the 21 states having right-to-work laws allow only exclusive bargaining shop provisions. Under this form of recognition, the company is legally bound to deal with the union that has achieved recognition, but employees are not obligated to join or maintain membership in the union or to contribute to it financially.

Open Shop.
An open shop describes the absence of union security rather than its presence. The **open shop**, strictly defined, is employment that has equal terms for union members and nonmembers alike. Under this arrangement, no employee is required to join or contribute to the union financially.

Dues Checkoff.
Another type of security that unions attempt to achieve is the checkoff of dues. A checkoff agreement may be used in addition to any of the previously mentioned shop agreements. Under the **checkoff of dues** provision, the company agrees to withhold union dues from members' paychecks and to forward the money directly to the union. Because of provisions in the Taft-Hartley Act, each union member must voluntarily sign a statement authorizing this deduction. Dues checkoff is important to the union because it eliminates much of the expense, time, and hassle of collecting dues from each member every pay period or once a month.

COMPENSATION AND BENEFITS

A section on compensation and benefits typically constitutes a large portion of most labor agreements. Virtually any item that can affect compensation and benefits may be included in labor agreements. Some of the items frequently covered include the following:

Wage Rate Schedule.
The base rates to be paid each year of the contract for each job are included in the wage rate schedule. At times, unions are able to obtain a cost-of-living allowance (COLA) or escalator clause in the contract to protect the purchasing power of employees' earnings. These clauses are generally related to the Consumer Price Index (CPI) prepared by the Bureau of Labor Statistics. However, the average COLA has increased at a smaller percentage in recent years. Currently, increases in pay remain scarce in key sectors of the economy because employers cannot simply raise prices to compensate for higher wages. Predictions of an average increase of 4.1 percent in total hourly nonfarm compensation is up from 3.5 percent in 1996, but unions are not doing as well.[28]

Overtime and Premium Pay. Another section of the agreement may cover hours of work, overtime pay, and premium pay, such as shift differentials.

Jury Pay. Some firms pay an employee's entire salary when he or she is serving jury duty. Others pay the difference between jury pay and the compensation that would have been earned. The procedure covering jury pay is typically stated in the contract.

Layoff or Severance Pay. The amount that employees in various jobs and/or seniority levels will be paid if they are laid off or terminated is a frequently included item.

Holidays. The holidays to be recognized and the amount of pay that a worker will receive if he or she has to work on a holiday are specified. In addition, the pay procedure for times when a holiday falls on a worker's nominal day off may be provided.

Vacation. The amount of vacation a person may take is set, based on seniority. Any restrictions as to when the vacation may be taken are also stated.

Family Care. Family care is a benefit that has been included in recent collective bargaining agreements, with child care expected to be a hot bargaining issue in the near future.

GRIEVANCE PROCEDURE

A portion of most labor agreements is devoted to a grievance procedure. It contains the means whereby employees can voice dissatisfaction with and appeal specific management actions. Also included in this section are procedures for disciplinary action by management and the termination procedure that must be followed.

EMPLOYEE SECURITY

Another section of the labor agreement establishes the procedures that cover job security for individual employees. Security continues to be a major concern for employees. Recent labor negotiations have dramatically focused on the security issue. Since 1990, labor agreements with the "Big Three" automakers have included provisions to protect employee security. Settlements with the Big Three provided lower wage rate changes than those negotiated in the contracts they replaced, but the firms did fully restore funding for job security and supplemental unemployment benefits provided in previous agreements.[29]

Seniority and grievance handling procedures are the key topics related to employee security. Seniority is determined by the amount of time an employee has worked in various capacities with the firm. Seniority may be companywide, by division, by department, or by job. Agreement on seniority is important because the person with the most seniority, as defined in the labor agreement, is typically the last to be laid off and the first to be recalled. The seniority system also provides a basis for promotion decisions. When qualifications are met, employees with the greatest seniority will likely be considered first for promotion to higher level jobs. However, many new-collar workers, who are younger and better educated, see seniority as putting them at an unfair advantage; therefore, they are possibly less likely to join unions.

Negotiating the Agreement

There is no way to ensure speedy and mutually acceptable results from negotiations. At best, the parties can attempt to create an atmosphere that will lend itself to steady progress and productive results. For example, the two negotiating teams usually meet at an agreed-on neutral site, such as a hotel. When a favorable relationship can be established early, eleventh-hour bargaining can often be avoided.[30] Equally important is for union and management negotiators to strive to develop and maintain clear and open lines of communication. Collective bargaining is a problem-solving activity; consequently, good communication is essential to its success. Negotiations should be conducted in the privacy of the conference room, not in the news media. If the negotiators feel that publicity is necessary, joint releases to the media may avoid unnecessary conflict.

The negotiating phase of collective bargaining begins with each side presenting its initial demands. Because a collective bargaining settlement can be expensive for a firm, the cost of various proposals should be estimated as accurately as possible. Some changes can be quite expensive; others may cost little or nothing; but the cost of the various proposals being considered must always be carefully deliberated. The term *negotiating* suggests a certain amount of give-and-take, the purpose of which is to lower the other side's expectations. In the initial encounter, Barbara Washington, the union negotiator, got into a heated debate with management representatives in an attempt to force them into reevaluating their position. However, MBI

Negotiations should be conducted in the privacy of the conference room, not in the news media.

management had a company position that was not negotiable: MBI would give no pay increases but would try to avoid layoffs. After their second meeting, Barbara knew that probably the best she could do would be to try to avoid layoffs. The union will bargain to upgrade its members' economic and working conditions. The company will negotiate to maintain or enhance its profitability. One of the most costly components of any collective bargaining agreement is a wage increase provision. An example of the negotiation of a wage increase is shown in Figure 15-3. In this example, labor initially demands a $0.40 per hour increase. Management counters with an offer of only $0.10 per hour. Both labor and management—as expected—reject the other's demand. Plan B calls for labor to lower its demand to a $0.30 per hour increase. Management counters with an offer of $0.20. The positions in plan B are feasible to both sides, as both groups are in the bargaining zone. Wages within the bargaining zone are those that management and labor can both accept—in this case, an increase between $0.20 and $0.30 per hour. The exact amount will be determined by the power of the bargaining unit and the skills of the negotiators.

The realities of negotiations are not for the weak of heart and at times are similar to a high-stakes poker game. A certain amount of bluffing and raising of the ante takes place in many negotiations. The ultimate bluff for the union would be when a negotiator says, "If our demands are not met, we are prepared to strike." Management's version of this bluff would be to threaten a lockout. We discuss each of these tactics later as a form of power politics. The party with the greater leverage can expect to extract the most concessions.

Even though one party in the negotiating process may appear to possess the greater power, negotiators often take care to keep the other side from losing face. They recognize that the balance of power may switch rapidly. By the time the next round of negotiations occurs, the pendulum may be swinging back in favor of the other side. Even when management appears to

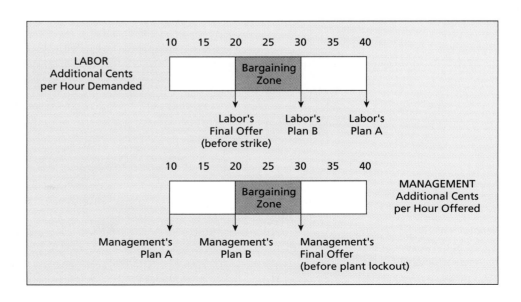

Figure 15-3
An Example of Negotiating a Wage Increase

have the upper hand, it may make minor concessions that will allow the labor leader to claim gains for the union. Management may demand that workers pay for grease rags that are lost (assuming that the loss of these rags has become excessive). In order to obtain labor's agreement to this demand, management may agree to provide new uniforms for the workers if the cost of these uniforms would be less than the cost of lost rags. Thus, labor leaders, although forced to concede to management's demand, could show the workers that they have obtained a concession from management.

Each side usually does not expect to obtain all the demands presented in its first proposal. Management must remember that a concession may be difficult to reverse in future negotiations. For instance, if management agreed to provide dental benefits, withdrawing these benefits in the next round of negotiations would be difficult. Labor, on the other hand, can lose a demand and continue to bring it up in the future. Demands that the union does not expect to receive when they are first made are known as **beachhead demands**.

Beachhead demands: Demands that the union does not expect management to meet when they are first made.

Breakdowns in Negotiations

At times negotiations break down, even though both labor and management may sincerely want to arrive at an equitable contract settlement. Several means of removing roadblocks may be used to get negotiations moving again. Breakdowns in negotiations can be overcome through third-party intervention, union strategies, and management strategies. Even with the success of traditional collective bargaining, the caseload for third-party neutrals, such as arbitrators, has increased. It appears that there is no relationship between the number of collective bargaining agreements or the percentage of workers unionized and the number of cases submitted to third-party neutrals.[31]

THIRD-PARTY INTERVENTION

Often an outside person can intervene to provide assistance when an agreement cannot be reached and the two sides reach an impasse. The reasons behind each party's position may be quite rational, or the breakdown may be related to emotional disputes that tend to become distorted during the heat of negotiations. Regardless of the cause, something must be done to continue the negotiations. The two basic types of third-party intervention are mediation and arbitration.

Mediation: A process in which a neutral third party enters and attempts to resolve a labor dispute when a bargaining impasse has occurred.

Mediation. In **mediation**, a neutral third party enters a labor dispute when a bargaining impasse has occurred. A mediator basically acts like a facilitator with an objective to persuade the parties to resume negotiations and reach a settlement. A mediator has no power to force a settlement but can help in the search for solutions, make recommendations, and work to open blocked channels of communication. Successful mediation depends to a substantial degree on the tact, diplomacy, patience, and perseverance of the mediator. The mediator's fresh insights are used to get discussions going again.

Mediation skills are becoming more important in labor relations and other management areas. Executives are now spending 18 percent of their time on various types of mediation activities.[32]

Arbitration: A process in which a dispute is submitted to an impartial third party for a binding decision.

Arbitration.

In **arbitration**, a dispute is submitted to an impartial third party for a binding decision by an arbitrator who basically acts as a judge. There are two principal types of union-management disputes: rights disputes and interests disputes. Those that involve disputes over the interpretation and application of the various provisions of an existing contract are referred to as *rights arbitration*. This type of arbitration is used in settling grievances. Grievance arbitration is common in the United States. The other type of arbitration, *interest arbitration*, involves disputes over the terms of proposed collective bargaining agreements. In the private sector, the use of interest arbitration as an alternative procedure for impasse resolution is not a common practice. Unions and employers rarely agree to submit the basic terms of a contract (such as wages, hours, and working conditions) to a neutral party for disposition. They prefer to rely on collective bargaining and the threat of economic pressure (such as strikes and lockouts) to decide these issues.

In the public sector, most governmental jurisdictions prohibit their employees from striking. As a result, interest arbitration is used to a greater extent than in the private sector. Although there is no uniform application of this method, 14 states have legislation permitting the use of interest arbitration to settle unresolved issues for public employees. In a number of states, compulsory arbitration of interest items is required at various jurisdictional levels.[33] A procedure used in the public sector is *final-offer arbitration*, which has two basic forms: package selection and issue-by-issue selection. In package selection, the arbitrator must select one party's entire offer on all issues in dispute. In issue-by-issue selection, the arbitrator examines each issue separately and chooses the final offer of one side or the other on each issue.[34]

SOURCES OF MEDIATORS AND ARBITRATORS

The principal organization involved in mediation efforts, other than some state and local agency, is the Federal Mediation and Conciliation Service (FMCS). The FMCS was established as an independent agency by the Taft-Hartley Act in 1947. Either one or both parties involved in negotiations can seek the assistance of the FMCS, or the agency can offer its help if it feels that the situation warrants this. Federal law requires that the party wishing to change a contract must give notice of this intention to the other party 60 days prior to the expiration of a contract. If no agreement has been reached 30 days prior to the expiration date, the FMCS must be notified.

In arbitration, the disputants are free to select any person as their arbitrator, as long as they agree on the selection. Most commonly, however, the two sides make a request for an arbitrator to either the American Arbitration Association (AAA) or the FMCS. The AAA is a nonprofit organization with offices in many cities. Both the AAA and the FMCS maintain lists of arbitrators. Only people who can show, through references, experience in labor-management relations and acceptance by both labor and management as neutrals are selected for inclusion on these lists.[35]

UNION STRATEGIES FOR OVERCOMING NEGOTIATION BREAKDOWNS

There are times when a union believes it must exert extreme pressure to get management to agree to its bargaining demands. Strikes, boycotts, and activism are the primary means that the union may use to overcome breakdowns in negotiations.

HR Web Wisdom

http://www.prenhall.com/mondy

STRIKES
Strikes and certain acts of civil disobedience are addressed at this site.

Strike: An action by union members who refuse to work in order to exert pressure on management in negotiations.

Unions' Use of Strikes.
When union members refuse to work as a way to exert pressure on management in negotiations, their action is referred to as a **strike**. A strike halts production, resulting in lost customers and revenue, consequences the union hopes will force management to submit to its terms.

The timing of a strike is important in determining its effectiveness. An excellent time is when business is thriving and the demand for the firm's goods or services is expanding. However, the union might be hard pressed to obtain major concessions from a strike if the firm's sales are down and it has built up a large inventory. In this instance, the company would not be severely damaged.

Contrary to many opinions, unions prefer to use the strike only as a last resort. In recent years, many union members have been even more reluctant to strike because of the fear of being replaced. The Supreme Court ruled in 1989 that when a union goes on strike and the company hires replacements, the company does not have to lay off these individuals at the end of the strike. With the threat of replacement looming and union membership declining, organized labor is quite cautious about striking. Even companies like General Motors, which for years have backed down to organized labor, are beginning to draw the line against striking employees. General Motors held fast during a 17-day strike in Ohio and in Canada and won the right to slash up to one-fifth of its 26,000 Canadian jobs.[36]

A union's treasury is often depleted by payment of strike benefits to its members. In addition, members suffer because they are not receiving their normal pay. Although strike benefits help, union members certainly cannot maintain a normal standard of living from these relatively minimal amounts. Sometimes during negotiations (especially at the beginning), the union may want to strengthen its negotiating position by taking a strike vote. Members often give overwhelming approval to a strike. This vote does not necessarily mean that there will be a strike, only that the union leaders now have the authority to call one if negotiations reach an impasse. A favorable strike vote can add a sense of urgency to efforts to reach an agreement.

Successful passage of a strike vote has additional implications for union members. Virtually every national union's constitution contains a clause requiring the members to support and participate in a strike if one is called. If a union member fails to comply with this requirement, he or she can be fined. Therefore, union members place themselves in jeopardy if they cross a picket line without the consent of the union. Fines may be as high as 100 percent of wages for as long as union pickets remain outside the company. However, the Supreme Court has ruled that an employee on strike may resign from the union during a strike and avoid being punished by the union. More subtle measures, such as sickouts and work slowdowns, have been used successfully by union members to avoid the impact of a strike on the membership and still bring pressure on the company to meet union demands.

Boycotts. The boycott is another of labor's weapons to get management to agree to its demands. A **boycott** involves an agreement by union members to refuse to use or buy the firm's products. A boycott exerts economic pressure on management, and the effect often lasts much longer than that of a strike. Once shoppers change their buying habits, their behavior will likely continue long after the boycott has ended. At times, significant pressures can be exerted on a business when union members, their families, and friends refuse to purchase the firm's products. This approach is especially effective when the products are sold at retail outlets and are easily identifiable by brand name. For instance, the decade-old boycott against Adolph Coors Company was effective because the product, beer, was directly associated with the company.[37] The practice of a union attempting to encourage third parties (such as suppliers and customers) to stop doing business with the company is known as a **secondary boycott**. This type of boycott was declared illegal by the Taft-Hartley Act.

Boycott: Refusal by union members to use or buy the firm's products.

Secondary boycott: A union's attempt to encourage third parties (such as suppliers and customers) to stop doing business with a firm.

TRENDS & INNOVATIONS

UNION ACTIVISM AND FOCUS

Activism and focus are some of the weapons of choice of recently elected AFL-CIO president John J. Sweeney. Activism is the union practice of vigorous action and involvement as a means of achieving recruitment goals by activities such as demonstrations and protests. Under certain circumstances, activism and focus may be more effective than strikes or boycotts. Activism and focus have resulted in the recruiting of 2,700 new members at the Las Vegas MGM Grand, the world's largest hotel. It took focus to wage a three-year activism campaign of street demonstrations, mass arrests, and attacks on the company's business record to help oust the stridently anti-labor CEO. In late 1995, MGM Grand recognized the union without an election. Another group was victorious at New York New York, a new Las Vegas hotel that acceded to the unionization of 900 workers without a certification election.

Such victories have turned Local 226 of the Hotel Employees & Restaurant Employees into one of the country's fastest-growing local unions. The local's ranks have doubled in the past decade to 40,000 members, and it now represents virtually every major Las Vegas hotel. Much of this success lies with the "spirited rank and file." When meetings end, crowds, which are largely black and Hispanic women, jump to their feet, clap, and shout "Unions, yes." Some members even gather the following morning—on their day off—to sign up recruits outside the New York New York hiring office. According to Edelisa Wolf, an $11.25-an-hour waitress at the MGM Grand: "I spend a day a week volunteering for the union because otherwise, we would earn $7.50 an hour and no benefits." A combination of "in-your-face activism and a single minded-focus on recruitment" apparently has been quite successful. Use of this approach has doubled the membership of the Service Employees International Union (SEIU) to 1.1 million members.

MANAGEMENT'S STRATEGIES FOR OVERCOMING NEGOTIATION BREAKDOWNS

Lockout: A management decision to keep employees out of the workplace and to operate with management personnel and/or temporary replacements.

Management may also use various strategies to encourage unions to come back to the bargaining table. One form of action that is somewhat analogous to a strike is called a **lockout**. In a lockout, management keeps employees out of the workplace and may run the operation with management personnel and/or temporary replacements. Unable to work, the employees do not get paid. Although the lockout is used rather infrequently, the fear of a lockout may bring labor back to the bargaining table. A lockout is particularly effective when management is dealing with a weak union, when the union treasury is depleted, or when the business has excessive inventories.

Another course of action that a company can take if the union goes on strike is to operate the firm by placing management and nonunion workers in the striking workers' jobs. The type of industry involved has considerable effect on the impact of this maneuver. If the firm is not labor intensive and if maintenance demands are not high, such as at a petroleum refinery or a chemical plant, this practice may be quite effective. When it is utilized, management will likely attempt to show how production actually increases with the use of nonunion employees. For example, unionized employees at Southwestern Bell Telephone Company went on strike, and the company continued to provide virtually uninterrupted service to consumers. At times, management personnel will actually live in the plant and have food and other necessities delivered to them.

Another way management can continue operating a firm during a strike is to hire replacements for the strikers. Hiring replacements on either a temporary or a permanent basis is legal when the employees are engaged in an economic strike—that is, one that is a part of a collective bargaining dispute. However, a company that takes these courses of action risks inviting violence and creating bitterness among its employees, a result that may adversely affect the firm's performance long after the strike has ended.

Ratifying the Agreement

Most collective bargaining leads to an agreement without a breakdown in negotiations or disruptive actions. Typically, agreement is reached before the current contract expires. After the negotiators have reached a tentative agreement on all contract terms, they prepare a written agreement covering those terms, complete with the effective and termination dates. The approval

HRM IN ACTION
WHAT DID I DO?

Mat Dehay eagerly drove his new company pickup truck onto the construction site. He had just been assigned by his employer, Lurgi-Knost Construction Company, to supervise a crew of 16 equipment operators, oilers, and mechanics. This was the first unionized crew Mat had supervised and he was unaware of the labor agreement in effect that carefully defined and limited the role of supervisors. As he approached his work area, he noticed one of the cherry pickers (a type of mobile crane with an extendable boom) standing idle with the operator beside it. Mat pulled up beside the operator and asked, "What's going on here?"

"Out of gas," the operator said.

"Well, go and get some," Mat said.

The operator reached to get his thermos jug out of the toolbox on the side of the crane and said, "The oiler's on break right now. He'll be back in a few minutes."

Mat remembered that he had a five-gallon can of gasoline in the back of his pickup. So he quickly got the gasoline, climbed on the cherry picker, and started to pour it into the gas tank. As he did so, he heard the other machines shutting down in unison. He looked around and saw all the other operators climbing down from their equipment and standing to watch him pour the gasoline. A moment later, he saw the union steward approaching.

If you were Mat, what would you do now?

process for management is often easier than for labor. The president or CEO has usually been briefed regularly on the progress of negotiations. Any difficulty that might have stood in the way of obtaining approval has probably already been resolved with top management by the negotiators.

However, the approval process is more complex for the union. Until a majority of members voting in a ratification election approve it, the proposed agreement is not final. At times, union members reject the proposal and a new round of negotiations must begin. In recent years, approximately 10 percent of all tentative agreements have been rejected when presented to the union membership. Many of these rejections might not have occurred if union negotiators had been better informed of the desires of the membership.

Administration of the Agreement

Negotiating, as it relates to the total collective bargaining process, may be likened to the tip of an iceberg. It is the visible phase, the part that makes the news. The larger and perhaps more important part of collective bargaining is administration of the agreement, which the public seldom sees.[38] The agreement establishes the union-management relationship for the duration of the contract. Usually, neither party can change the contract's language until the expiration date, except by mutual consent. However, the main problem encountered in contract administration is uniform interpretation and application of the contract's terms. Administering the contract is a day-to-day activity. Ideally, the aim of both management and the union is to make the agreement work to the benefit of all concerned. Often, this is not an easy task.

Management is primarily responsible for explaining and implementing the agreement. This process should begin with meetings or training sessions not only to point out significant features but also to provide a clause-by-clause analysis of the contract. First-line supervisors, in particular, need to know their responsibilities and what to do when disagreements arise. Additionally, supervisors and middle managers should be encouraged to notify top management of any contract modifications or new provisions required for the next round of negotiations.

The human resource manager or industrial relations manager plays a key role in the day-to-day administration of the contract. He or she gives advice on matters of discipline, works to resolve grievances, and helps first-line supervisors establish good working relationships within the terms of the agreement. When a firm becomes unionized, the human resource manager's function tends to change rather significantly and may even be divided into separate human resource and industrial relations departments. The Bendix Corporation provides an excellent example of this separation of activities. The company has both a vice president of human resources and a vice president of industrial relations (see Figures 15-4 and 15-5). In situations such as

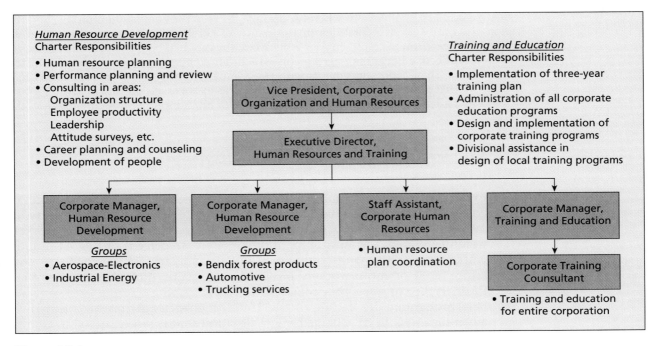

Figure 15-4
The Organization of the Human Resource Department at Bendix Corporation
Source: Bendix Corporation.

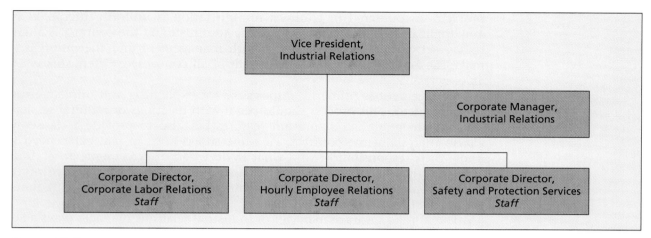

Figure 15-5
The Corporate Industrial Relations Department of Bendix Corporation by Functional Responsibility
Source: Bendix Corporation.

this, the vice president of human resources may perform all human resource management tasks with the exception of industrial relations. The vice president of industrial relations would likely deal with all union-related matters. As one vice president of industrial relations stated:

> My first challenge is, wherever possible, to keep the company union free and the control of its operations in the hands of corporate management at all levels. Where unions represent our employees, the problem becomes one of negotiating collective bargaining agreements which our company can live with, administering these labor agreements with the company's interests paramount (consistent with good employee relations), and trying to solve all grievances arising under the labor agreement short of their going to arbitration, without giving away the store.

The Future of Collective Bargaining

Extensive collective bargaining activity occurs each year, but the outcomes of collective bargaining have been disappointing to unions in recent years. In 1996, major collective bargaining agreements for about 1.7 million workers were negotiated, accounting for approximately 32 percent of the 5.4 million workers under all major contracts in private industry. Such agreements covering 1,000 or more workers provided wage gains that were smaller than those in the contracts they replaced.[39]

Throughout the decade of the 1990s, management has had the power advantage in collective bargaining, a situation that is not expected to change in the foreseeable future. From the early 1980s throughout the 1990s, management has achieved their collective bargaining goals. Among the unusual features of collective bargaining settlements in the 1990s, which indicate increased management clout, were the large proportion of workers receiving very slight wage increases, the increasing number of performance-based contracts negotiated, the increasing importance of lump-sum payments, the large proportion of workers who were not covered by cost-of-living adjustments, and the increased acceptance of outsourcing.[40] The number of strikes has also sharply declined, with major strikes involving 1,000 or more employees falling dramatically.[41] Some workers, particularly younger, better educated workers, believe that if harm is done to the employer, their job opportunities will be reduced. Other employees are avoiding strikes because they do not want to lose wages. Some workers fear that management will replace them with nonstriking employees or even close the plant.[42]

A GLOBAL PERSPECTIVE

NAFTA: A New Union-Busting Weapon?

Unions often point to multinational corporations as an important cause of U.S. economic problems, especially unemployment. Obviously, both NAFTA (North American Free Trade Agreement) and GATT (General Agreement on Tariffs and Trade) will be singled out by unions as the main cause of the loss of additional manufacturing jobs. Many companies have located part or all of their operations outside the United States to take advantage of lower labor and material costs and favorable tax laws. Investment funds have also been diverted to foreign operations, costing the U.S. economy jobs. However, proponents of NAFTA and GATT believe that the increased exports that result from these agreements will increase the number of higher paying jobs in the United States.[43] Japanese and European firms have invested significantly in U.S. marketing and manufacturing, a move that has created new jobs here in the United States. As these firms hire American workers, some interesting collective bargaining situations are created. The key to global success, and the best way to deal with global competition, is through a real partnership between management and labor. Unions throughout the world must contribute with greater productivity and increased flexibility or their numbers will decline.[44]

Early predictions claimed that NAFTA would dramatically alter the nature of business in North America. This may yet become a reality, but currently NAFTA may be being used as a new union-busting weapon. According to the NAFTA Cornell commission study, since the North American Free Trade Agreement (NAFTA) took effect, U.S. employers have routinely threatened during union elections to close plants and move production to Mexico or elsewhere. The report, based on union elections from 1993 to 1995, indicates that half the employers threaten to close plants when facing a union vote. Labor loses nearly half the time when that happens, versus nearly one-third when no warnings are issued. When employers lose, 7.5% do close the plant—triple the level in the pre-NAFTA 1980s. According to Kate Bronfenbrenner, the researcher who headed up the study, "NAFTA created a climate that has emboldened employers."[45]

SUMMARY

1. *Explain labor management relations and individual bargaining.*

   In individual negotiations, the worker is negotiating with company representatives. However, negotiations can still be on a power basis, depending on how valuable the individual is to the company. Individuals who continuously add value to themselves and the company are in a position of power. Should an individual desire job security, a raise, or other tangible evidence of value, negotiations will likely receive positive results if the worker is valued by the company. Seniority means little in this environment.

2. *Describe the collective bargaining process.*

   The first step in the collective bargaining process is preparing for negotiations. Once issues to be negotiated are determined, the two sides confer to reach a mutually acceptable contract. If breakdowns in negotiations occur, both labor and management have at their disposal tools and arguments that can be used to convince the other side to accept their views. Eventually, management and the union reach an agreement that defines the rules of employment for the duration of the contract. The next step is for the union membership to ratify the agreement.

3. *Explain the psychological aspects of collective bargaining.*

   Prior to collective bargaining, both the management team and the union team have to prepare positions and accomplish certain tasks. Vitally important for those involved are the psychological aspects of collective bargaining. Psychologically, the collective bargaining process is often difficult because an adversarial situation may exist.

4. *Explain typical bargaining issues.*

   Mandatory bargaining issues are those issues that fall within the definition of wages, hours, and other terms and conditions of employment. Permissive bargaining issues are those issues that may be raised, but neither side may insist that they be bargained over.

5. *Identify the topics included in virtually all labor agreements.*

   Topics typically included are recognition, management rights, union security, compensation and benefits, and employee security.

6. *Identify ways to overcome breakdowns in negotiations.*

   Breakdowns in negotiations can be overcome through third-party intervention, union tactics, and management recourse. The basic types of third-party intervention are mediation and arbitration. Strikes and boycotts are the primary means the union may use to overcome breakdowns in negotiations. Management recourse includes a lockout and keeping the firm operating by utilizing management and nonunion employees in the striking workers' jobs.

7. *Describe what is involved in administering the agreement.*

   Administering the contract is a day-to-day activity. Ideally, the aim of both management and the union is to make the agreement work to the mutual benefit of all concerned. This is not easy. In the daily stress of the work environment, terms of the contract are not always uniformly interpreted and applied.

8. *Explain the future of collective bargaining.*
Throughout the 1990s, management had the power advantage in collective bargaining, a situation that is not expected to change in the foreseeable future.

<table>
<tr><td>

QUESTIONS FOR REVIEW

</td><td>

1. Describe the negotiation process for a worker in a nonunion environment.
2. Describe the basic steps involved in the collective bargaining process.
3. Distinguish among mandatory, permissive, and prohibited bargaining issues.
4. What are the topics included in virtually all labor agreements?
5. Define each of the following:
   a. Closed shop
   b. Union shop
   c. Agency shop
   d. Maintenance of membership
   e. Checkoff of dues
6. What are the primary means by which breakdowns in negotiations may be overcome? Briefly describe each.
7. What is involved in the administration of a labor agreement?
8. What appears to be the future of collective bargaining?

</td></tr>
</table>

<table>
<tr><td>

DEVELOPING HRM SKILLS

</td><td>

AN EXPERIENTIAL EXERCISE
A major part of the human resource manager's job is to advise managers at all levels regarding human resource matters. The human resource manager's knowledge and experience are often required in dealing with union matters, especially in handling situations that have an impact on future unionization. This exercise provides additional insight into the importance of properly handling employee problems in a unionized environment.

Three individuals will participate in this exercise: one to serve as the human resource manager, one to serve as the supervisor, and another to play the role of union steward. Your instructor will provide the participants with additional information necessary to complete the exercise.

</td></tr>
</table>

 *Take It to the Net*

We invite you to visit the Mondy home page on the Prentice Hall Web site at:

http://www.prenhall.com/mondy

for updated information, Web-based exercises, and links to other HR-related sites.

HRM SIMULATION

*T*he grievance procedure is usually determined in collective bargaining. This simulation offers an option for your firm to establish a formal grievance program—something it currently does not have. The grievance panel consists of an even number of employees and supervisors. Such programs increase morale by helping employees feel they have a *court of last resort*. As with any decision, costs are involved.

HRM INCIDENT

1

Maybe I Will, and Maybe I Won't

*Y*esterday Bill Brown was offered a job as an operator trainee with GEM Manufacturing. He had recently graduated from Milford High School in a small town in the Midwest. Bill had no college aspirations, so upon graduation, he moved to Chicago to look for a job.

Bill's immediate supervisor spent only a short time with him before assigning him to Gaylord Rader, an experienced operator, for training. After they had talked for a short time, Gaylord asked, "Have you given any thought to joining our union? You'll like all our members."

Bill had not considered this. Moreover, he had never associated with union members and his parents had never been members either. At Milford High, his teachers had never really talked about unions. The fact that this union operated as an open shop meant nothing to him. Bill replied, "I don't know. Maybe. Maybe not."

The day progressed much the same way, with several people asking Bill the same question. They were all friendly, but there seemed to be a barrier that separated Bill from the other workers. One worker looked Bill right in the eyes and said, "You're going to join aren't you?" Bill still did not know, but he was beginning to lean in that direction.

After the buzzer rang to end the shift, Bill went to the washroom. Just as he entered, David Clements, the union steward, also walked in. After they exchanged greetings, David said, "I hear that you're not sure about wanting to join our union. You and everyone else reaps the benefits of the work we've done in the past. It doesn't seem fair for you to be rewarded for what others have done. Tell you what, why don't you join us down at the union hall tonight for our beer bust? We'll discuss it more then."

Bill nodded yes and finished cleaning up. "That might be fun," he thought.

Questions
1. Why does Bill have the option of joining or not joining the union?
2. How are the other workers likely to react toward Bill if he chooses not to join? Discuss.

HRM INCIDENT

2

So, Strike!

*B*inky Wilkes, the chief union negotiator, was meeting with management on a new contract. The union team had been preparing for this encounter for a long time, Binky felt that she was on top of the situation. Her only worry was whether the union members would support a strike vote if one were called. Because of the recession, there was high unemployment in the area. The members' attitude was "We are generally pleased, but get what you can for us." She believed, however, that skillful negotiating could keep the union team from being placed in a position where the threat of a strike would be needed.

In the first session, Binky's team presented its demands to management. Pay was the main issue, and a 30 percent increase spread over three years was demanded. Management countered with an offer of a 10 percent raise over three years. After some discussion, both sides agreed to reevaluate their positions and meet again in two days.

Binky met with her negotiating team in private, and it was the consensus that they would decrease the salary demand slightly. They felt that the least they could accept was a 25 percent increase.

At the next meeting, Binky presented the revised demands to management. They were not well received. Sam Waterson, the director of industrial relations, began by saying: "Our final offer is a 15 percent increase over three years. Business has been down and we have a large backlog of inventory. If you feel that it is in your best interest to strike, go ahead."

Binky was confident that there was no way a strike vote could be obtained. Management accurately read the mood of the workers, and Binky quickly asked for additional time to consider the new information.

Questions

1. How important is the threat of a strike to successful union negotiations?
2. What do you recommend that Binky do when she next confronts management?

Notes

1. Paul S. McDonough, "Maintaining a Union-Free Status," *Personnel Journal* 69 (April 1990): 108.
2. Dave Weil, *Turning the Tide: Strategic Planning for Labor Unions* (New York: Lexington Books, 1994): 255–256.
3. Micheline Maynard, "Back to Work: GM, Workers Settle Strike," *USA Today* (July 28, 1997): 1A.
4. Keith L. Alexander and Stephen Baker, "The Steelworkers vs. the Smiling Barracuda," *Business Week* (May 23, 1994): 26.
5. M. E. Sharpe, "Labor's Future," *Challenge* 39 (March 1996): 65.
6. Arthur A. Sloane and Fred Witney, *Labor Relations*, 4th ed. (Englewood Cliffs, NJ: Prentice Hall, 1981): 28–35.

7. Aaron Bernstein, "Why America Needs Unions but Not the Kind It Has Now," *Business Week* (May 23, 1994): 70; "The Workplace: Unions: Look Who's Pushing Productivity," *Business Week* (April 7, 1997): 56.

8. Bill Vlasic and Aaron Bernstein, "Workplace: Unions: Why Ford Is Riding Shotgun for the UAW," *Business Week* (March 17, 1997): 11.

9. Ibid.

10. Abby Brown, "Labor Contract Negotiations: Behind the Scenes," *Labor Relations: Reports from the Firing Line* (Plano, TX: Business Publications, 1988): 305–308.

11. Joel Rogers and Richard Freeman, "Why Labor Keeps Losing," *Fortune* 130 (July 11, 1994): 54.

12. Stephen Baker, "Workplace: Unions: Why This Steel Chief Has Such an Iron Will," *Business Week* (May 19, 1997): 90.

13. Harry Levinson, "Stress at the Bargaining Table," *Labor Relations: Reports from the Firing Line* (Plano, TX: Business Publications, 1988): 310.

14. Ibid.

15. Aaron Bernstein, "Up Front: Labor Pains: NAFTA: A New Union-Busting Weapon?" *Business Week* (January 27, 1997): 4.

16. "HR Focus: Labor Relations: Court Sides with Unions," *Personnel* 67 (June 1990): 6–7.

17. Aaron Bernstein and Jim Bartimo, "Wrong Time for Scare Tactics?" *Business Week* (April 16, 1990): 28.

18. Wendy Zellner, "All the Ingredients for Disaster Are There," *Business Week* (April 16, 1990): 28.

19. Sid Kessler, "Is There Still a Future for Unions?" *Personnel Management* 25 (July 1993): 24–30.

20. Abby Brown, "Labor Contract Negotiations: Behind the Scenes," *Labor Relations: Reports from the Firing Line* (Plano, TX: Business Publications, 1988): 305–308.

21. Larry Reynolds, "Washington Update: A Crisis in Childcare?" *HR Focus* 74 (May 1997): 2.

22. Harry Levinson, "Stress at the Bargaining Table," 312.

23. Editorial, *Journal of Commerce* (March 26, 1993); Henry P. Guzda, "Workplace Partnerships in the United States and Europe," *Monthly Labor Review* 117 (October 1993): 67–72.

24. Bernstein, "Why America Needs Unions but Not the Kind It Has Now."

25. Edwin F. Beal and James P. Begin, *The Practice of Collective Bargaining*, 6th ed. (Homewood, IL: Richard D. Irwin, 1982): 295–298.

26. Management/Employee/Union Relations (Dallas, TX: Southwestern Bell Telephone Company, December 1971): 3.

27. "NLRB Requires Firms to Bargain before Relocating," *The Wall Street Journal* (June 17, 1991): A12.

28. Aaron Bernstein, "The Workplace: Unions: Andy Stern's Mission Impossible," *Business Week* (June 10, 1996): 7.

29. Vlasic and Bernstein, "Workplace: Unions:" 11; William Symonds and Kathleen Kerwin, "Labor: So Much for Hardball," *Business Week* (November 4, 1996): 48.

30. "Eleventh-hour bargaining" refers to last-minute settlement attempts just prior to the expiration date of an existing agreement. Failure to reach agreement in this manner frequently results in a strike.

31. David A. Dilts, "The Future of Labor Arbitrators," *Arbitration Journal* 48 (June 1993): 24–31.

32. Elaine McShulskis, "Managing Employee Conflicts," *HRMagazine* 41 (September 1996): 16.

33. Benjamin J. Taylor and Fred Witney, *Labor Relations Law*, 4th ed. (Englewood Cliffs, NJ: Prentice Hall, 1983): 652–653.

34. Robert E. Allen and Timothy J. Keaveny, *Contemporary Labor Relations* (Reading, MA: Addison-Wesley, 1983): 558–559.

35. Donald Austin Woolf, "Arbitration in One Easy Lesson: A Review of Criteria Used in Arbitration Awards," *Personnel* 55 (September/October 1978): 76; Bill Leonard, "Groups Adopt New Arbitration Procedural Rules," *HRMagazine* 41 (July 1996): 8.

36. Symonds and Kerwin, "Labor: So Much for Hardball," 48.

37. Sandra Atchison and Aaron Bernstein, "A Silver Bullet for the Union Drive at Coors?" *Business Week* (July 11, 1988): 61.

38. Harold W. Davey, *Collective Bargaining*, 3rd ed. (Englewood Cliffs, NJ: Prentice Hall, 1972): 141.

39. Bill Leonard, "1996 Contract Negotiations Will Affect 1.7 Million Workers," *HRMagazine* 40 (October 1995): 4.

40. Ibid.

41. Bernstein, "Why America Needs Unions but Not The Kind It Has Now."

42. Edward J. Wasilewski, Jr., "Collective Bargaining in 1992: Contract Talks and Other Activity," *Monthly Labor Review* 115 (January 1992): 5.

43. Laurence I. Barrett, Michael Duffy, Laura Lopez, and Joseph R. Szczesny, "Time Daily News Summary-America Online," *Time, Inc.* (November 11, 1993): 1–5.

44. Guzda, "Workplace Partnerships in the United States and Europe," 67–72.

45. Bernstein, "Up Front: Labor Pains: NAFTA: A New Union-Busting Weapon?" 4.

16
Internal Employee Relations

1. Describe internal employee relations.
2. Define *discipline* and *disciplinary action.*
3. Identify the steps involved in the disciplinary process.
4. Describe the approaches to discipline.
5. Describe the steps involved in progressive disciplinary action.
6. Explain how grievance handling is typically conducted under a collective bargaining agreement.
7. Explain how grievance handling is typically conducted in union-free firms.
8. Define *alternative dispute resolution.*
9. Describe how termination conditions may differ with regard to nonmanagerial/nonprofessional employees, executives, managers, and professionals.
10. Explain the concept of employment at will.
11. Describe the purpose of the exit interview.
12. Explain demotions, transfers, and promotions.
13. Describe the legal implications of internal employee relations.
14. Explain the importance of evaluating the human resource management functions.

*B*ob Halmes, the production supervisor for American Manufacturing, was mad at the world when he arrived at work. The automobile mechanic had not repaired his car on time the day before, so Bob had been forced to take a taxi to work this morning. Because no one was safe around Bob today, it was not the time for Phillip Martin, a member of Local 264, to report for work late. Without hesitation, Bob said, "You know our company can't tolerate this type of behavior. I don't want to see you around here any more. You're fired." Just as quickly, Phillip replied, "You're way off base. Our contract calls for three warnings for tardiness. My steward will hear about this."

Bill Morton, a 10-year employee at Ketro Productions, arrived at the office of the human resource manager to turn in his letter of resignation. Bill was very upset with his supervisor, John Higgins. When the human resource manager, Robert Noll, asked what was wrong, Bill replied, "Yesterday, I made a mistake and set my machine up wrong. It was the first time in years that I'd done that. My boss chewed me out in front of my friends. I wouldn't take that from the president, much less a two-bit supervisor!"

*T*hese scenarios represent only two of the many situations that managers confront when dealing with internal employee relations. Bob Halmes has just been reminded that his power to fire Phillip Martin has limits. The resignation of Bill Morton might have been avoided if his supervisor had not shown poor judgment and disciplined him in front of his friends.

In this chapter, we first define *internal employee relations*. Next, we discuss the reasons for disciplinary action, the disciplinary action process, approaches to disciplinary action, and the administration of disciplinary action. We then describe grievance handling under a collective bargaining agreement and for nonunion employees. This is followed by a review of termination, employment at will, demotion as an alternative to termination, layoffs, transfers, promotion, resignation, and retirement. Finally, the last portion of the chapter is devoted to the legal implications of internal employee relations and evaluating the human resource management functions.

HR Web Wisdom

http://www.prenhall.com/mondy

SHRM–HR LINKS
Various issues including arbitration, mediation, handbooks, and policies are addressed here.

Internal Employee Relations Defined

Internal employee relations: Those human resource management activities associated with promotion, transfer, demotion, resignation, discharge, layoffs, and retirement.

The status of most workers is not permanently fixed in an organization. Employees constantly move upward, laterally, downward, and out of the organization. To ensure that workers with the proper skills and experience are available at all levels, constant and concerted efforts are required to maintain good internal employee relations. A well-conceived and implemented employee relations program is very beneficial to both the organization and its employees. **Internal employee relations** comprises the human resource management activities associated with the movement of employees within the organization. These activities include promotion, transfer, demotion, resignation, discharge, layoff, and retirement. Discipline and disciplinary action are also crucial aspects of internal employee relations.

Disciplinary Action

Discipline: The state of employee self-control and orderly conduct.

Disciplinary action: The invoking of a penalty against an employee who fails to meet organizational standards or comply with organizational rules.

Discipline is the state of employee self-control and orderly conduct and indicates the extent of genuine teamwork within an organization. **Disciplinary action** invokes a penalty against an employee who fails to meet established standards. Effective disciplinary action addresses the employee's wrongful behavior, not the employee as a person. Incorrectly administered disciplinary action is destructive to both the employee and the organization. Thus, disciplinary action should not be applied haphazardly. Both Bob Halmes and John Higgins were haphazard in their application of discipline, with the result that two problematic employee relations situations developed.

A necessary but often trying aspect of internal employee relations is the application of disciplinary action.

A necessary but often trying aspect of internal employee relations is the application of disciplinary action. Disciplinary action is not usually management's initial response to a problem. Normally, there are more positive ways of convincing employees to adhere to company policies that are necessary to accomplish organizational goals. However, managers must administer disciplinary action when company rules are violated. Disciplinary policies afford the organization the greatest opportunity to accomplish organizational goals, thereby benefiting both employees and the corporation. Not only is there a need for such policies, but a process should also exist to assist employees in appealing disciplinary actions. Because disciplinary action involves interaction between human beings, the process is sometimes biased and emotional; therefore, such actions are not always justified. There is little doubt that Bob Halmes of American Manufacturing acted emotionally when he inappropriately fired Phillip Martin for being late for work. Unjustified action is unfair to the employee involved and is counterproductive. John Higgins's overt disciplinary action was so unfair to Bill Morton, a 10-year employee, that Bill is intent on quitting. Even if employees do not react overtly to unjustified disciplinary actions, their morale will likely decline, and this can negatively affect the firm.

Despite management's desire to solve employee problems in a positive manner, at times this is not possible. A major purpose of disciplinary action is to ensure that employee behavior is consistent with the firm's rules. Rules are established to further the organization's objectives. When a rule is violated, the effectiveness of the organization is diminished to some degree, depending on the severity of the infraction. For instance, if a worker is late to work once, the effect on the firm may be minimal. Recall that Bob Halmes attempted to fire Phillip Martin for being late one time when policy stated that three warnings are required for tardiness before a worker can be dismissed. Consistently being late is another matter because it negatively affects both the productivity of the worker and the morale of other employees. Supervisors must realize that disciplinary action can be a positive force for the company when it is applied responsibly and equitably. The firm benefits from developing and implementing effective disciplinary policies. Without a healthy state of discipline or the potential for disciplinary action, the firm's effectiveness may be severely limited.

Disciplinary action can also help the employee become more productive, thereby benefiting him or her in the long-run. For example, if a worker is disciplined because of failure to monitor the quality of his or her output and quality improves after the disciplinary action, the action has been useful in the worker's development. Because of improved performance, the individual may receive a promotion or pay increase. The employee is reminded of what is expected and fulfills these requirements better. Effective disciplinary action can therefore encourage the individual to improve his or her performance, ultimately resulting in gain for that individual.

The Disciplinary Action Process

The disciplinary action process is dynamic and ongoing. Because one person's actions can affect others in a work group, the proper application of disciplinary action fosters acceptable behavior by other group members. Conversely, unjustified or improperly administered disciplinary action can have a detrimental effect on other group members.

The disciplinary action process is shown in Figure 16-1. The external environment affects every area of human resource management, including disciplinary policies and actions. Changes in the external environment, such as technological innovations, may render a rule inappropriate and may even necessitate new rules. Laws and government regulations that affect company policies and rules are also constantly changing. For instance, the Occupational Safety and Health Act has caused many firms to establish safety rules.

Unions are another external factor. Specific punishment for rule violations is subject to negotiation and inclusion in the agreement. For example, the union may negotiate for three written warnings for tardiness before a worker is suspended instead of the two warnings a present contract might require. This was the case with American Manufacturing; the labor-management agreement in force there required three warnings for tardiness before termination.

Changes in the internal environment of the firm can also alter the disciplinary process. Through organizational development, the firm may change its culture. As a result of this shift, first-line supervisors may begin handling disciplinary action more positively. Organization policies can also have an impact on the disciplinary action process. For instance, a policy of treating employees as mature human beings would significantly affect the process.

The disciplinary action process deals largely with infractions of rules. Rules are specific guides to behavior on the job. The do's and don'ts associated with accomplishing tasks may be highly inflexible. For example, a company rule may require that hard hats be worn in hazardous areas for safety reasons; a rule that no personal programs be loaded on the company personal computers may stem from an incident in which a personal program introduced an undetected virus that once wiped out the company database. Failure to abide by these rules will result in immediate termination.

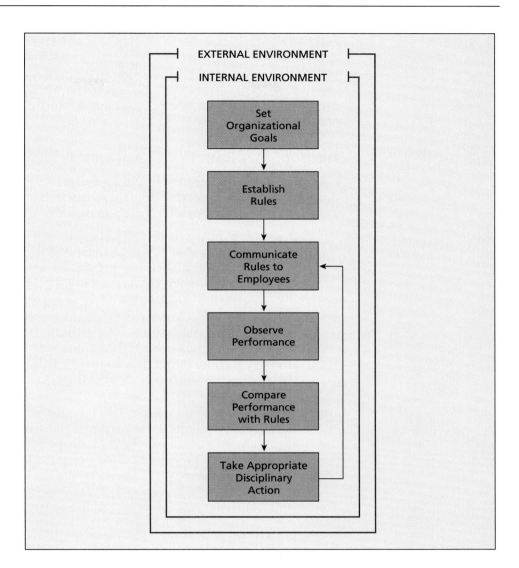

Figure 16-1
The Disciplinary Action
Process

After management has established rules, it must communicate these rules to employees.[1] Individuals cannot obey a rule if they do not know it exists. As long as employee behavior does not vary from acceptable practices, there is no need for disciplinary action, but when an employee's behavior violates a rule, corrective action may be necessary. The purpose of this action is to alter the types of behavior that can have a negative impact on achievement of organizational objectives—not merely to chastise the violator.

Note that the process shown in Figure 16-1 includes feedback from the point of taking appropriate disciplinary action to communicating rules to employees. When appropriate disciplinary action is taken, employees should realize that certain behaviors are unacceptable and should not be repeated. However, if appropriate disciplinary action is not taken, employees may view the behavior as acceptable and repeat it.

Approaches to Disciplinary Action

Several concepts regarding the administration of disciplinary action have been developed. Three of the most important concepts are the hot stove rule, progressive disciplinary action, and disciplinary action without punishment.

THE HOT STOVE RULE

One approach to administering disciplinary action is referred to as the *hot stove rule*. According to this approach, disciplinary action should have the following consequences, which are analogous to touching a hot stove:

1. *Burns immediately*. If disciplinary action is to be taken, it must occur immediately so that the individual will understand the reason for it. With the passage of time, people have the tendency to convince themselves that they are not at fault, and this behavior tends to nullify later disciplinary effects.

2. *Provides warning*. Another extremely important element of the Hot Stove Rule is providing advance warning that punishment will follow unacceptable behavior. As individuals move closer to a hot stove, they are warned by its heat that they will be burned if they touch it; therefore, they have the opportunity to avoid the burn if they so choose.

3. *Gives consistent punishment*. Disciplinary action should also be consistent in that everyone who performs the same act will be punished accordingly. As with a hot stove, each person who touches it with the same degree of pressure and for the same period of time is burned to the same extent.

4. *Burns impersonally*. Disciplinary action should be impersonal. The hot stove burns anyone who touches it—without favoritism.

Although the hot stove approach has some merit, it also has weaknesses. If the circumstances surrounding all disciplinary situations were the same, there would be no problem with this approach. However, situations are often quite different, and many variables may be present in each individual disciplinary case. For instance, does the organization penalize a loyal 20-year employee the same as an individual who has been with the firm less than six weeks? A supervisor often finds that he or she cannot be completely consistent and impersonal in taking disciplinary action. Because situations do vary, progressive disciplinary action may be more realistic—and more beneficial to both the employee and the organization.

PROGRESSIVE DISCIPLINARY ACTION

Progressive disciplinary action is intended to ensure that the minimum penalty appropriate to the offense is imposed. Its use involves answering a series of questions about the severity of the offense. The manager must

Progressive disciplinary action: An approach to disciplinary action designed to ensure that the minimum penalty appropriate to the offense is imposed.

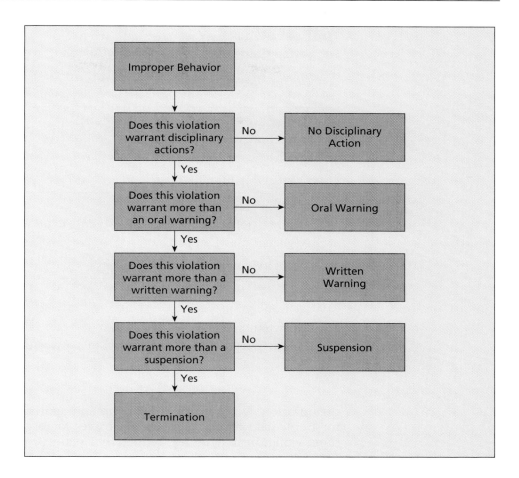

Figure 16-2
The Progressive
Disciplinary Approach

ask these questions—in sequence—to determine the proper disciplinary action, as illustrated in Figure 16-2. After the manager has determined that disciplinary action is appropriate, the proper question is this: "Does this violation warrant more than an oral warning?"[2] If the improper behavior is minor and has not previously occurred, perhaps an oral warning will be sufficient. Also, an individual may receive several oral warnings before a *yes* answer applies. The manager follows the same procedure for each level of offense in the progressive disciplinary process. The manager does not consider termination until each lower level question is answered *yes*. However, major violations, such as assaulting a supervisor or another worker, may justify immediate termination of the employee.[3]

To assist managers in recognizing the proper level of disciplinary action, some firms have formalized the procedure. One approach is to establish progressive disciplinary action guidelines, as shown in Table 16-1. In this example, a worker who is absent without authorization will receive an oral warning the first time it happens and a written warning the second time; the third time, the employee will be terminated. Fighting on the job is an offense that normally results in immediate termination. However, specific guidelines for various offenses should be developed to meet the needs of the

---

TABLE 16-1

Suggested Guidelines for Disciplinary Action

Offenses Requiring First, an Oral Warning;
Second, a Written Warning; and Third, Termination

Negligence in the performance of duties
Unauthorized absence from job
Inefficiency in the performance of job

Offenses Requiring a Written Warning and Then Termination

Sleeping on the job
Failure to report to work one or two days in a row without notification
Negligent use of property

Offenses Requiring Immediate Discharge

Theft
Fighting on the job
Falsifying time cards
Failure to report to work three days in a row without notification

---

organization. For example, smoking in an unauthorized area may be grounds for immediate dismissal in an explosives factory. On the other hand, the same violation may be less serious in a plant producing concrete products. Basically, the penalty should be appropriate to address the severity of the violation, and no greater.[4]

DISCIPLINARY ACTION WITHOUT PUNISHMENT

Disciplinary action without punishment: A process in which a worker is given time off with pay to think about whether he or she wants to follow the rules and continue working for a company.

Disciplinary action without punishment gives a worker time off with pay to think about whether he or she wants to follow the rules and continue working for the company. When an employee violates a rule, the manager issues an *oral* reminder. Repetition brings a written reminder. The third violation results in the worker's having to take one, two, or three days off (with pay) to think about the situation. During the first two steps, the manager tries to encourage the employee to solve the problem.[5] If the third step is taken, on the worker's return, he or she and the supervisor meet to agree that the employee will not violate the rule again or that the employee will leave the firm. When disciplinary action without punishment is used, it is especially important that all rules be explicitly stated in writing. At the time of orientation, new workers should be told that repeated violations of different rules will be viewed in the same way as several violations of the same rule. This approach keeps workers from taking undue advantage of the process.

Administration of Disciplinary Action

As you might expect, disciplinary actions are not pleasant supervisory tasks. Although the manager is in the best position to recommend disciplinary action, many managers find them to be quite difficult to implement.[6] The reasons that managers want to avoid disciplinary action include the following:

1. *Lack of training.* The manager may not have the knowledge and skill necessary to handle disciplinary problems.

2. *Fear.* The manager may be concerned that top management will not support a disciplinary action.

3. *The only one.* The manager may think, "No one else is disciplining employees, so why should I?"

4. *Guilt.* The manager may think, "How can I discipline someone if I've done the same thing?"

5. *Loss of friendship.* The manager may believe that disciplinary action will damage friendship with an employee or the employee's associates.

6. *Time loss.* The manager may begrudge the valuable time that is required to administer and explain disciplinary action.

7. *Loss of temper.* The manager may be afraid of losing his or her temper when talking to an employee about a rule violation.

8. *Rationalization.* The manager may think, "The employee knows it was a wrong thing to do, so why do we need to talk about it?"[7]

These reasons apply to all forms of disciplinary action—from an oral warning to termination. Managers often avoid disciplinary action, even when it is in the company's best interest. Such reluctance often stems from breakdowns in other areas of the human resource management function. For instance, if a manager has consistently rated an employee high on annual performance appraisals, the supervisor's rationale for terminating a worker for poor performance would be weak. It is embarrassing to decide to fire a worker and then be asked why you rated this individual so high on the previous evaluation. It could be that the employee's productivity has actually dropped substantially. It could also be that the employee's productivity has always been low but that the supervisor may have trouble justifying to upper-level management that a person should be terminated. Rather than run the risk of having a decision overturned, the supervisor retains the ineffective worker.

Finally, some managers believe that even attempting to terminate women and minorities is useless. However, the statutes and subsequent court decisions associated with women and minorities in the workplace were not intended to protect nonproductive workers. Anyone whose performance is consistently below standard can, and should, be terminated after the supervisor has made reasonable attempts to salvage the employee.

A supervisor may be perfectly justified in administering disciplinary action, but there is usually a proper time and place for doing so. For example,

HRM IN ACTION
SHOULD HE BE FIRED?

Dwayne Berdit is the Washington, D.C.-area supervisor for Quik-Stop, a chain of convenience stores. He has full responsibility for managing the seven Quik-Stop stores in Washington. Each store operates with only one person on duty at a time. Although several of the stores stay open all night, every night, the Center Street store is open all night Monday through Thursday but open only from 6:00 A.M. to 10:00 P.M. Friday through Sunday. Because the store is open fewer hours during the weekend, money from sales is kept in the store safe until Monday. Therefore, the time it takes to complete a money count on Monday is greater than normal. The company has a policy that when the safe is being emptied, the manager has to be with the employee on duty, and the employee has to place each $1,000 in a brown bag, mark the bag, and leave the bag on the floor next to the safe until the manager verifies the amount in each bag.

Bill Catron worked the Sunday night shift at the Center Street store and was trying to save his manager time by counting the money prior to his arrival. The store got very busy, and, while bagging a customer's groceries, Bill mistook one of the money bags for a bag containing three sandwiches and put the money bag in with the groceries. Twenty minutes later, Dwayne arrived, and both men began to search for the money. While they were searching, a customer came back with the bag of money. Quik-Stop has a policy that anyone violating the money counting procedure must be fired immediately.

Bill was very upset. "I really need this job," Bill exclaimed. "With the new baby and all the medical expenses we've had, I sure can't stand to be out of a job."

"You knew about the policy, Bill," said Dwayne.

"Yes, I did, Dwayne," said Bill, "and I really don't have any excuse. If you don't fire me, though, I promise you that I'll be the best store manager you've got."

While Bill waited on a customer, Dwayne called his boss at the home office in Houston. With the boss's approval, Dwayne decided not to fire Bill.

Do you agree with Dwayne's decision in view of the discussion on progressive discipline?

disciplining a worker in the presence of others may embarrass the individual and actually defeat the purpose of the action. Even when they are wrong, employees resent disciplinary action administered in public. The scenario at the beginning of the chapter, in which Bill Morton quit his job because he was disciplined in front of his peers, provides an excellent illustration. By disciplining employees in private, supervisors prevent them from losing face with their peers.

In addition, many supervisors may be too lenient early in the disciplinary action process and too strict later. This lack of consistency does not give the worker a clear understanding of the penalty associated with the

TABLE 16-2

Recommended Disciplinary Procedures

- All employees should be given a copy of the employers' rules on disciplinary procedures. The procedures should specify which employees they cover and what disciplinary actions may be taken, and should allow matters to be dealt with quickly.

- Employees should be told of complaints against them and given an opportunity to state their case. They should have the right to be accompanied by a trade union representative or fellow employee of their choice.

- Disciplinary action should not be taken until the case has been fully investigated. Immediate superiors should not have the power to dismiss without reference to senior management, and, except for gross misconduct, no employee should be dismissed for a first breach of discipline.

- Employees should be given an explanation for any penalty imposed, and they should have a right of appeal, with specified procedures to be followed.

- When disciplinary action other than summary dismissal is needed, supervisors should give a formal oral warning in the case of minor offenses or a written warning in more serious cases.

Source: "Code on Discipline Procedure," *Industrial Management* 7 (August 1977): 7. Used with permission.

inappropriate action. As a manager of labor relations for Georgia-Pacific Corporation once stated, "A supervisor will often endure an unacceptable situation for an extended period of time. Then, when the supervisor finally does take action, he or she is apt to overreact and come down excessively hard." However, consistency does not necessarily mean that the same penalty must be applied to two different workers for the same offense. For instance, employers would be consistent if they always considered the worker's past record and length of service. For a serious violation, a long-term employee might receive only a suspension whereas a worker with only a few months' service might be terminated for the same act. This type of action could reasonably be viewed as being consistent.

To assist management in administering discipline properly, a guideline document, *Code on Discipline Procedure*, has been prepared by the Advisory, Conciliation and Arbitration Service. The purpose of the code is to give practical guidance on how to formulate disciplinary rules and procedures and to use them effectively. The code recommends the actions shown in Table 16-2. As you can see, it stresses communication of rules, telling the employee of the complaint, conducting a full investigation, and giving the employee an opportunity to tell his or her side of the story. Some schools are now specifying what disciplinary action should be taken for each violation. Possible penalties range from an oral warning, detention, parent notification, revocation of parking permit, and in-school and out-of-school suspension.[8]

Grievance Handling under a Collective Bargaining Agreement

If employees in an organization are represented by a union, workers who believe they have been disciplined or dealt with unjustly can appeal through the grievance and arbitration procedures of the collective bargaining agreement. Obviously, Phillip Martin knew that the collective bargaining agreement negotiated by the union required three warnings for tardiness, and therefore he could not be fired for being late one time. Bob Halmes, the production supervisor, was wrong for not following the collective bargaining agreement and Phillip let him know it. The grievance procedure has been described as "one of the truly great accomplishments of the American industrial relations movement. For all its defects . . . it constitutes a social invention of great importance."[9] The grievance system encourages and facilitates the settlement of disputes between labor and management. A grievance procedure permits employees to express complaints without jeopardizing their jobs. It also assists management in seeking out the underlying causes and solutions to employee complaints.

THE GRIEVANCE PROCEDURE

Grievance: An employee's dissatisfaction or feeling of personal injustice relating to his or her employment.

Virtually all labor agreements include some form of grievance procedure. A **grievance** can be broadly defined as an employee's dissatisfaction or feeling of personal injustice relating to his or her employment. A grievance under a collective bargaining agreement is normally well defined. It is usually restricted to violations of the terms and conditions of the agreement. There are other conditions that may give rise to a grievance:

- A violation of law
- A violation of the intent of the parties as stipulated during contract negotiations
- A violation of company rules
- A change in working conditions or past company practices
- A violation of health and/or safety standards

Grievance procedures have many common features. However, variations may reflect differences in organizational or decision-making structures or the size of a plant or company. Some general principles based on widespread practice can serve as useful guidelines for effective grievance administration:

- Grievances should be adjusted promptly.
- Procedures and forms used for airing grievances must be easy to utilize and well understood by employees and their supervisors.
- Direct and timely avenues of appeal from rulings of line supervision must exist.

The multiple-step grievance procedure shown in Figure 16-3 is the most common type. In the first step, the employee usually presents the grievance orally and informally to the immediate supervisor in the presence of the

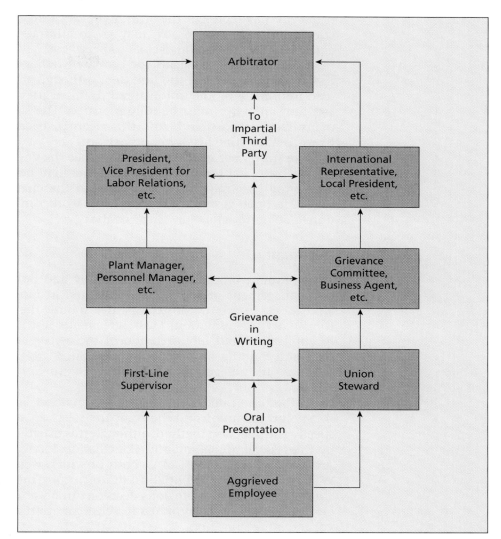

Figure 16-3
A Multiple-Step
Grievance Procedure

Source: Robert W. Eckles et al., *Essentials of Management for First-Line Supervision* (New York: John Wiley & Sons, 1974): 529. Reprinted by permission of John Wiley & Sons, Inc.

union steward. This step offers the greatest potential for improved labor relations and a large majority of grievances are settled here. The procedure ends if the grievance can be resolved at this initial step. If the grievance remains unresolved, the next step involves a meeting between the plant manager or human resource manager and higher union officials, such as the grievance committee or the business agent or manager. Prior to this meeting, the grievance is written out, dated, and signed by the employee and the union steward. The written grievance states the events as the employee perceives them, cites the contract provision that allegedly has been violated, and indicates the settlement desired. If the grievance is not settled at this meeting, it is appealed to the third step, which typically involves the firm's top labor representative (such as the vice president of industrial relations) and high-level union officials. At times, depending on the severity of the grievance, the president may represent the firm. A grievance that remains unresolved at the conclusion of the third step may go to arbitration, if provided for in the agreement and the union decides to persevere.

Labor-relations problems can escalate when a supervisor is not equipped to handle grievances at the first step. Although the first step is usually handled informally by the union steward, the aggrieved party, and the supervisor, the supervisor must be fully prepared. The supervisor should obtain as many facts as possible before the meeting, because the union steward is likely to have done his or her homework.

The supervisor needs to recognize that the grievance may not reflect the real problem. For instance, the employee might be angry at the company for modifying its pay policies, even though the change was agreed to by the union. In order to voice discontent, the worker might file a grievance for an unrelated minor violation of the contract.

ARBITRATION

The grievance procedure has successfully and peacefully resolved many labor-management problems. The final step in most grievance procedures is arbitration. In arbitration, the parties submit their dispute to an impartial third party for resolution. Most agreements restrict the arbitrator's decision to application and interpretation of the agreement and make the decision final and binding on the parties. Although arbitration at times is used to settle contract negotiation conflicts, its primary use has been in settling grievances.

If the union decides in favor of arbitration, it notifies management. At this point, the union and the company select an arbitrator. Most agreements specify the selection method, although it is usually made from a list supplied by the Federal Mediation and Conciliation Service (FMCS) or the American Arbitration Association (AAA), both of which were discussed in chapter 15. When considering potential arbitrators, both management and labor will study the candidates' previous decisions in an attempt to detect any biases. Obviously, neither party wants to select an arbitrator who might tend to favor the other's position.

When arbitration is used to settle a grievance, a variety of factors may be used to evaluate the fairness of the management actions that caused the grievance. These factors include the following:

- Nature of the offense
- Due process and procedural correctness
- Double jeopardy
- Grievant's past record
- Length of service with the company
- Knowledge of rules
- Warnings
- Lax enforcement of rules
- Discriminatory treatment

The large number of interacting variables in each case makes the arbitration process difficult. The arbitrator must possess exceptional patience and judgment in rendering a fair and impartial decision.

After the arbitrator has been selected—and has agreed to serve—a time and place for a hearing will be determined. The issue to be resolved will be presented to the arbitrator in a document that summarizes the question(s) to be decided. It will also point out any contract restrictions that prohibit the arbitrator from making an award that would change the terms of the contract.

At the hearing, each side presents its case. Arbitration is an adversarial proceeding, so a case may be lost because of poor preparation and presentation. The arbitrator may conduct the hearing much like a courtroom proceeding. Witnesses, cross-examination, transcripts, and legal counsel may all be used. The parties may also submit, or be asked by the arbitrator to submit, formal written statements. After the hearing, the arbitrator studies the material submitted and testimony given and is expected to reach a decision within 30 to 60 days. The decision is usually accompanied by a written opinion giving reasons for the decision.

The courts will generally enforce an arbitrator's decision unless (1) the arbitrator's decision is shown to be unreasonable or capricious in that it did not address the issues; (2) the arbitrator exceeded his or her authority; or (3) the award or decision violated a federal or state law.

PROOF THAT DISCIPLINARY ACTION WAS NEEDED

Any disciplinary action administered may ultimately be taken to arbitration, when such a remedy is specified in the labor agreement. Employers have learned that they must prepare records that will constitute proof of disciplinary action and the reasons for it. Although the formats of written warning may vary, all should include the following information:

1. Statement of facts concerning the offense
2. Identification of the rule that was violated
3. Statement of what resulted or could have resulted because of the violation
4. Identification of any previous similar violations by the same individual
5. Statement of possible future consequences should the violation occur again
6. Signature and date

An example of a written warning is shown in Figure 16-4. In this instance, the worker has already received an oral reprimand. The individual is also warned that continued tardiness could lead to termination. It is important to document oral reprimands because they may be the first step in disciplinary action leading ultimately to arbitration.

> **Date:**   August 1, 1998
>
> **To:**   Shane Boudreaux
>
> **From:**   Wayne Sanders
>
> **Subject:**   Written Warning
>
>   We are quite concerned because today you were thirty minutes late to work and offered no justification for this. According to our records, a similar offense occurred on July 25, 1998. At that time, you were informed that failure to report to work on time is unacceptable. I am, therefore, notifying you in writing that you must report to work on time. It will be necessary to terminate your employment if this happens again.
>
>   Please sign this form to indicate that you have read and understand this warning. Signing is not an indication of agreement.
>
> _____
> Name
>
> _____
> Date

Figure 16-4
An Example of a Written
Warning

WEAKNESSES OF ARBITRATION

Arbitration has achieved a certain degree of success in resolving grievances. However, it is not without weaknesses. Some practitioners claim that arbitration is losing its effectiveness because of the length of time between the first step of the grievance procedure and final settlement. Often, 100 to 250 days may elapse before a decision is made. The reason for the initial filing of the grievance may actually be forgotten before it is finally settled. Some people object to the cost of arbitration, which has been rising at an alarming rate. The cost of settling even a simple arbitration case can be quite high, even though it is typically shared by labor and management. Forcing every grievance to arbitration could be used as a tactic to place either management or the union in a difficult financial position.

Grievance Handling in Union-Free Organizations

In the past, few union-free firms had formalized grievance procedures. Today, this is not the case, as more and more firms have established formal grievance procedures and encouraged their use.[10]

Although the step-by step procedure for handling union grievances is common practice, the means of resolving complaints in union-free firms varies. A well-designed grievance procedure ensures that the worker has ample opportunity to make complaints without fear of reprisal. If the system is to work, employees must be well informed about the program and convinced that management wants them to use it. Most employees are hesitant to formalize their complaints and must be constantly urged to avail themselves of the process.[11] Simply because a manager says "Our workers must be happy because I have received no complaints" does not necessarily mean that employees have no grievances. In a closed, threatening corporate culture, workers may be reluctant to voice their dissatisfaction to management.

Typically, an employee initiates a complaint with his or her immediate supervisor. However, if the complaint involves the supervisor, the individual is permitted to bypass the immediate supervisor and proceed to the employee-relations specialist or the manager at the next higher level. The grievance ultimately may be taken to the organization's top executive for a final decision. Brown & Root, a Houston-based engineering, construction, and maintenance company, has a unique dispute resolution program. Whenever workers feel they need to resolve a dispute, the program allows them to choose one or all four options: open-door policy, conference, mediation, or arbitration. "We wanted to give our employees several ports of entry to lodge a complaint if they wanted to," says Ralph Morales, manager of employee relations and administrator of the program."[12]

HR Web Wisdom

http://www.prenhall.com/mondy

DISPUTE RESOLUTION
At this site you can review the resources offered by the CPR Institute for Dispute Resolution.

TRENDS & INNOVATIONS

ALTERNATIVE DISPUTE RESOLUTION

Alternative dispute resolution (ADR): A procedure agreed to ahead of time by the employee and the company for resolving any problems that may arise.

As the number of employment-related lawsuits has exploded, companies have looked for ways to protect themselves against the costs and uncertainties of the judicial system. **Alternative dispute resolution (ADR)** is a procedure in which the employee and the company agree that any problems will be addressed by an agreed-on means ahead of time. Some of these means include arbitration, mediation, or mini-trials. ADR might be used to settle such complaints as being fired without cause, sexual harassment, or discrimination. Alcoa, Brown & Root, Fairchild Aircraft, Levi Strauss, and McGraw-Hill are some of the companies that have implemented an ADR program.[13] When ADR is used there is typically a stepped procedure. The steps might first call for a facilitated interaction between the complaining employee and the supervisor involved, followed by a review with a senior manager or a review board. Then mediation would be attempted followed by arbitration at the end.[14]

Critics of ADR say that it forces employees to sign away their right to be heard in the judicial system, even when they claim to have been discriminated against for such things as age, sex, or race. The key to this problem is whether the employee entered into the agreement voluntarily. For example, in one dispute, brokers on Wall Street were required to sign a form to get their licenses in which they agreed to take employee-related disputes to an arbitration panel run by the industry.[15] Evidently, however, if agreed-on voluntarily, ADR is acceptable.

Termination

Termination is the most severe penalty an organization can impose on an employee; therefore, it should be the most carefully considered form of disciplinary action. Bob Halmes, who tried to fire Phillip Martin for being late one time, did not carefully consider this decision. The experience of being terminated is traumatic for employees, regardless of their position in the organization. They can experience feelings of failure, fear, disappointment, and anger. It is also a difficult time for the person making the termination decision. Knowing that termination may affect not only the employee but an entire family increases the trauma. Not knowing how the terminated employee will react also may create considerable anxiety for the manager who must do the firing. Recall from chapter 13 that an individual who is terminated may respond with violence in the workplace. Regardless of the similarities in the termination of employees at various levels, distinct differences exist with regard to nonmanagerial/nonprofessional employees, executives, managers, and professionals. Termination is an extremely serious form of discipline and must, therefore, always be carefully considered and appropriate. Furthermore, in today's business environment, companies need to be as concerned with the termination process as with the hiring process.[16] Just as it is important to train recruiters to be effective, managers should also receive training in how to terminate an employee.[17]

TERMINATION OF NONMANAGERIAL/NONPROFESSIONAL EMPLOYEES

Individuals in this category are neither managers nor professionally trained individuals, such as engineers or accountants. They generally include such employees as steel workers, truck drivers, and waiters. If the firm is unionized, the termination procedure is typically well defined in the labor-management agreement. For example, drinking on the job might be identified as a reason for immediate termination. Excessive absences, on the other hand, may require three written warnings by the supervisor before termination action can be taken.

When the firm is union free, these workers can generally be terminated more easily. A history of unjustified terminations within a firm, however, may provide an opportunity for unionization. In many union-free organizations, violations justifying termination are included in the firm's employee handbook. At times, especially in smaller organizations, the termination process is informal, with the first-line supervisor advising employees as to what actions warrant termination. Regardless of the size of the organization, employees should be informed by a representative of management of the actions that warrant termination.

TERMINATION OF EXECUTIVES

Unlike individuals in most organization positions, CEOs normally do not have to worry about their positions being eliminated. Their main concern is whether they themselves will become excess baggage. Turnover at the top occurs quite often. For example, from 1992 through the first half of 1996, 163 Fortune-500 CEOs, or 32.6 percent, lost their jobs.[18]

Executive termination must be viewed from a different perspective. Executives usually have no formal appeal procedure. The decision to terminate an executive is normally made by the board of directors of the organization. In addition, the reasons for termination may not be as clear as those for lower level employees. Some of the reasons include the following:

1. *Economic.* At times, business conditions may force a reduction in the number of executives.

2. *Reorganization/downsize.* In order to improve efficiency or as a result of merging with another company, a firm may reorganize or downsize, resulting in the elimination of some executive positions.

3. *Philosophical differences.* A difference in philosophy of conducting business may develop between an executive and other key company officials. To maintain consistency in management philosophy, the executive may be replaced.

4. *Decline in productivity.* The executive may have been capable of performing satisfactorily in the past, but, for various reasons, he or she can no longer perform the job as required.

This list does not include factors related to illegal activities or actions taken that are not in the best interests of the firm. Under those circumstances, the firm has no moral obligation to the terminated executive.

An organization may derive positive benefits from terminating executives, but these actions also present a potentially hazardous situation for the company. Many corporations are concerned about developing a negative public image that reflects insensitivity to the needs of their employees. They fear that such a reputation would impede their efforts to recruit high-quality managers. Also, terminated executives have, at times, made public statements detrimental to the reputation of the firm.

TERMINATION OF MIDDLE AND LOWER LEVEL MANAGERS AND PROFESSIONALS

In the past, the most vulnerable and perhaps the most neglected group of employees with regard to termination has been middle and lower level managers and professionals, who are generally not union members and, thus, not protected by a labor-management agreement. One study estimates that between 1985 and 1995, almost 14 million white-collar jobs disappeared.[19]

Employees in these jobs also may not have the political clout that a terminated executive has. Termination may have been based on something as simple as the attitude or feelings of an immediate superior on a given day.

Employment at Will

In approximately two of every three U.S. jobs, the worker's continued employment depends almost entirely on the continued goodwill of his or her employer. Individuals falling into this category are known as *at-will employees*. Generally, the U.S. legal system has held that the jobs of such employees may be terminated at the will of the employer and that these employees have a similar right to leave their jobs at any time. As mentioned in chapter 15, employment at will is an unwritten contract created when an employee agrees to work for an employer but with no agreement as to how long the parties expect the employment to last. Historically, because of a century-old common law precedent in the United States, employment of indefinite duration could, in general, be terminated at the whim of either party.

The concept of employment at will has eroded somewhat in recent years. A current research study showed that 41 states had state court decisions recognizing implied contracts.[20] Some courts have decided that terminations of at-will employees are unlawful if they are contrary to general notions of acceptable "public policy" or if they are done in "bad faith." Judges, legislators, and employees are increasingly willing to challenge rigid notions of unlimited employer discretion. In Montana, for instance, the practice of at-will employment effectively ended when the state adopted a law prohibiting the termination of employment except for *good cause*.

Employers can do certain things to help protect themselves against litigation for wrongful discharge based on a breach of implied employment contract. In fact, in one survey, 60 percent of the companies responding said that they included an employment at will statement on the application blank that applicants are required to sign.[21] Statements in such documents as employment applications and policy manuals that suggest job security or permanent employment should be avoided if employers want to minimize charges of wrongful discharge.[22] Other guidelines that may assist organizations in avoiding wrongful termination suits include clearly defining the worker's duties, providing good feedback on a regular basis, and conducting realistic performance appraisals on a regular basis.[23] However, recent statements in employment contracts aimed at preserving employers' control over at-will decisions do not guarantee employers protection from employment at will liability.[24] For example, in *Criado v ITT (SDNY 1993)*, ITT had disclaimers in its handbook regarding the at-will status of employment. The handbook, however, also contained a corporate code of conduct and an accompanying letter from the president urging all employees who suspect illegal or unethical conduct to come forward without penalty for making a report. Criado, an employee, came forward with suspicions of illegal activity by a vice president and was subsequently fired. The court found that although Criado was an at-will employee, ITT had created an expressed limitation on its right to fire any employee who followed the code of conduct.[25]

Demotion as an Alternative to Termination

Termination frequently is the solution when a person is not able to perform his or her job satisfactorily. At times, however, demotions are used as an alternative to discharge, especially when a long-term employee is involved. The worker may have performed satisfactorily for many years, but his or her productivity may then begin to decline for a variety of reasons. Perhaps the worker is just not physically capable of performing the job any longer, or the individual may no longer be willing to work the long hours the job requires. **Demotion** is the process of moving a worker to a lower level of duties and responsibilities, a move that typically involves a reduction in pay. Emotions often run high when an individual is demoted. The demoted person may suffer loss of respect from peers and feel betrayed, embarrassed, angry, and disappointed. The employee's productivity may also decrease further. For these reasons, demotion should be used very cautiously.

Demotion: The process of moving a worker to a lower level of duties and responsibilities; typically involves a pay cut.

If demotion is chosen over termination, efforts must be made to preserve the self-esteem of the individual. The person may be asked how he or she would like to handle the demotion announcement. A positive image of the worker's value to the company should be projected.

The handling of demotions of bargaining unit employees in a unionized organization is usually spelled out clearly in the labor-management agreement. Should a decision be made to demote a worker for unsatisfactory performance, the union should be notified of this intent and given the specific reasons for the demotion. Often the demotion will be challenged and carried through the formal grievance procedure. Documentation is necessary for the demotion to be upheld. Even with the problems associated with demotion for cause, it is often easier to demote than to terminate an employee. In addition, demotion is often less devastating to the employee. For the organization, however, the opposite may be true if the demotion creates lingering ill will and an embittered employee.

As firms downsize and reduce the number of layers in the organizational structure, positions that may have been held by highly qualified employees may be eliminated. Rather than lose a valued employee, firms, at times, offer this employee a lower level position, often at the same salary.

Layoffs

Historically, the economic well-being of many companies rises and falls in cycles. At times, a firm's goods or services may be in great demand; at other times, demand falls. Often when demand is low, the firm has no choice but to lay off workers. Although being laid off is not the same thing as being fired, it has the same effect: The worker is unemployed. In today's work environment, there may be little chance for a worker being rehired. Examples of massive layoffs have become commonplace as firms downsize to position themselves in the highly competitive global environment. For example, IBM has cut 170,000 jobs worldwide, and Chevron reduced its workforce by nearly half, to about 50,000 people, after its merger with Gulf Oil Company.

Then Chevron cut its staff by another 6,500.[26,27] AT&T has eliminated more than 100,000 jobs in the last 10 years.[28] Today, only 15 percent of laid-off workers expect their jobs back, compared to 44 percent in past recoveries.[29]

Being laid off can often have extreme psychological consequences. Says an electrical engineer who was laid off after nearly 30 years with Xerox, "Losing my job was the most shocking experience I've ever had in my life. I almost think it's worse than the death of a loved one, because at least we learn about death as we grow up. No one in my age group ever learned about being laid off."[30]

LAYOFF/RECALL PROCEDURES

Even in this rapidly changing environment, at times workers are called back to work. Whether the firm is union free or unionized, carefully constructed layoff/recall procedures should be developed.[31,32] Workers should understand when they are hired how the system will work in the event of a layoff. When the firm is unionized, the layoff procedures are usually stated clearly in the labor-management agreement. Seniority is usually the basis for layoffs, with the least senior employees laid off first. The agreement may also have a clearly spelled out *bumping procedure*. When senior-level positions are eliminated, the people occupying them have the right to bump workers from lower level positions, assuming that they have the proper qualifications for the lower level job. When bumping occurs, the composition of the workforce is altered.

Procedures for recalling laid-off employees are also usually spelled out in labor-management agreements. Again, seniority is typically the basis for worker recall, with the most senior employees being recalled first.

Regardless of a union-free firm's current stand on the issue of layoffs, it should establish procedures for a layoff prior to facing one. In union-free firms, seniority should also be an integral part of any layoff procedure. Frequently, however, other factors should be considered. Productivity of the employee is typically the most important consideration. When productivity is a factor, management must be careful to ensure that productivity, not favoritism, is the actual basis. Workers may have an accurate perception of their own productivity level and that of their fellow employees. Therefore, it is important to define accurately both seniority and productivity considerations well in advance of any layoffs.

HR Web Wisdom

http://www.prenhall.com/mondy

OUTPLACEMENT
The transition team's potential role in outplacement and downsizing is briefly addressed at this site.

OUTPLACEMENT PROCEDURES

Many organizations have established a systematic way to assist laid-off or terminated employees in locating jobs.[33] The use of outplacement began at the executive level but has recently been used at other organizational levels.

Outplacement: A company procedure that assists a laid-off employee in finding employment elsewhere.

In **outplacement**, laid-off employees are given assistance in finding employment elsewhere. In today's environment, mass layoffs have often necessitated group outplacement. Through outplacement, the firm tries to soften the impact of displacement. Some of the services provided by group outplacement are use of a transition center, individual counseling, job fairs, complete access to office equipment (such as computers, fax machines, copy machines), and free postage for mailing application letters and resumes.[34]

Outplacement may not be used as much as in the past. When the concept was first introduced 25 years ago, it dealt with specific individuals, usually executives. When it was introduced to address the needs of larger groups, it was still perceived to be in response to a one-time event. Today's college students are likely to have eight to ten jobs and as many as three careers. The outplacement system was designed to guide people from one job to a similar job, and not for the environment workers face today.[35]

Transfers

Transfer: The lateral movement of a worker within an organization.

The lateral movement of a worker within an organization is called a **transfer**. A transfer may be initiated by the firm or by an employee. The process does not, and should not, imply that a person is either being promoted or demoted.

Transfers serve several purposes. First, firms often find it necessary to reorganize. Offices and departments are created and abolished in response to the company's needs. To fill positions created by reorganization, a company may have to move employees without promoting them. A similar situation may exist when an office or department is closed. Rather than terminate valued employees, management may transfer them to other areas within the organization. These transfers may entail moving an employee to another desk in the same office or to a location halfway around the world.

A second reason for transfers is to make positions available in the primary promotion channels. Firms are typically organized into a hierarchical structure resembling a pyramid. Each succeeding promotion is more difficult to obtain because fewer positions exist. At times, very productive but unpromotable workers may clog promotion channels. Other qualified workers in the organization may find their opportunities for promotion blocked. When this happens, a firm's most capable future managers may seek employment elsewhere. To keep promotion channels open, the firm may decide to transfer employees who are unpromotable but productive in their present positions.

Another reason for transfers is to satisfy employees' personal desires. The reasons for wanting a transfer are numerous. An individual may need to accompany a transferred spouse to a new location, work closer to home to care for aging parents, or the worker may dislike the long commuting trips to and from work. Factors such as these may be of sufficient importance that employees may resign if a requested transfer is not approved. Rather than risk losing a valued employee, the firm may agree to the transfer.

Transfers may also be an effective means of dealing with personality clashes. Some people just cannot get along with one another. Because each individual may be a valued employee, transfer may be an appropriate solution to the problem. But managers must be cautious regarding the "grass is always greener on the other side of the fence" syndrome. When some workers encounter a temporary setback, they immediately ask for a transfer—before they even attempt to work through the problem.

Finally, because of the downsizing of management levels, it is becoming necessary for managers to have a wide variety of experiences before achieving a promotion. According to some estimates, by the year 2000, the typical *large* corporation will have half the management levels and one-third the managers that it had in 1990.[36] Individuals who desire upward mobility often explore possible lateral moves so they can learn new skills.[37]

Before any worker's request for transfer is approved, it should be analyzed in terms of the best interests of both the firm and the individual. Disruptions may occur when the worker is transferred—for example, a qualified worker might not be available to step into the position being vacated.

Management should establish clear policies regarding transfers. Such policies let workers know in advance when a transfer request is likely to be approved and what its ramifications will be. For instance, if the transfer is for personal reasons, some firms do not pay moving costs. Whether the organization will or will not pay transfer costs should be clearly spelled out.

Promotion

Promotion: The movement of a person to a higher level position in an organization.

A **promotion** is the movement of a person to a higher level position in the organization. The term *promotion* is one of the most emotionally charged words in the field of human resource management. An individual who receives a promotion normally receives additional financial rewards and the ego boost associated with achievement and accomplishment. Most employees feel positively about being promoted; but for every individual who gains a promotion, there are probably others who were not selected. If these individuals wanted the promotion badly enough, or their favorite candidate was overlooked, they may slack off or even resign. If the consensus of employees directly involved is that the wrong person was promoted, considerable resentment may result.

In the future, promotions will not be as available as in the past.[38] For one thing, many firms are reducing the number of levels in their hierarchies. As the number of middle-management positions declines, fewer promotional opportunities will be available. The effect of these changes is that more people will be striving for fewer promotion opportunities. Consequently, organizations must look for ways other than promotion to reward employees. One alternative is the dual track system that we described in chapter 9, whereby highly technical individuals can continue to receive financial rewards without progressing into management. Another option, discussed in chapter 11, is skill-based pay, a system that compensates employees on the basis of job-related skills they acquire.

Resignation

Even when an organization is totally committed to making its environment a good place to work, workers will still resign. Some employees cannot see promotional opportunities—or at least not enough—for themselves and will move on. A certain amount of turnover is healthy for an organization and is often necessary for employees to have the opportunity to fulfill their career objectives. When turnover becomes excessive, however, the firm must do something to slow it. The most qualified employees are often the ones who resign because they are more mobile.[39] On the other hand, marginally qualified workers seem never to leave. If excessive numbers of a firm's highly qualified and competent workers are leaving, a way must be found to reverse the trend. It is probably not in the best interest of the company for Bill Morton, a 10-year employee, to resign. Apparently, he is a good employee who makes very infrequent mistakes.

THE EXIT INTERVIEW—ANALYZING VOLUNTARY RESIGNATIONS

The reasons individuals leave an organization have been of interest to practitioners for many years.[40] A frequently given explanation for resignation is to obtain a better salary and/or benefits. However, most firms either conduct salary surveys or keep in touch with what competitors are paying. Research has shown that when workers mention pay as a reason for resigning, they often have other, deeper reasons for deciding to leave. The cause may be a department manager who is impossible to work with or the company's failure to provide developmental opportunities needed to compete in today's rapidly changing work environment. Management should identify the causes and correct them as quickly as possible. One way to do this is through an exit interview. The exit interview is not just for individuals lower in the organization. It is also used to determine why key executives leave the organization.[41]

When a firm wants to determine the real reasons that individuals decide to leave, it can use the exit interview and/or the postexit questionnaire.[42] In a survey conducted by HR News and the Bureau of National Affairs, Inc., 96 percent of respondents indicated that their companies have some form of exit interview program.[43] Often the exit interview is conducted by a third party because many former employees will not air their problems in the organization.[44] The typical exit interview involves the following:

- Establishing rapport
- Stating the purpose of the interview
- Exploring the employee's attitudes regarding the old job
- Exploring the worker's reasons for leaving
- Comparing the old and new jobs
- Recording the changes recommended by the employee
- Concluding the interview[45]

Figure 16-5
Questions Related to General Job Factors

Source: Wanda R. Embrey, R. Wayne Mondy, and Robert M. Noe, "Exit Interview: A Tool for Personnel Development." Reprinted from the May 1979 issue of *Personnel Administrator,* copyright 1979. Reprinted with permission from *HRMagazine* (formerly *Personnel Administrator*), published by the Society for Human Resource Management, Alexandria, Virginia.

1. Let's begin by your outlining briefly some of the duties of your job.
2. Of the duties you just outlined, tell me three or four that are crucial to the performance of your job.
3. Tell me about some of the duties you liked the most and what you liked about performing those duties.
4. Now, tell me about some of the duties you liked least and what you did not like about performing those duties.
5. Suppose you describe the amount of variety in your job.
6. Let's talk a little bit now about the amount of work assigned to you. For example, was the amount assigned not enough at times, perhaps too much at times, or was it fairly stable and even overall?
7. Suppose you give me an example of an incident that occurred on your job that was especially satisfying to you. What about an incident that was a little less satisfying?
8. Let's talk now about the extent to which you feel you were given the opportunity to use your educational background, skills, and abilities on your job.
9. Tell me how you would assess the quality of training on your job.
10. Suppose you describe the promotional opportunities open to you in your job.

Specific topics that might be covered by the interviewer during the exit interview are listed in Figure 16-5. Note that the interviewer is focusing on job-related factors and probing for the real reasons the person is leaving. Over a period of time, properly conducted exit interviews can provide considerable insight into why employees are leaving. Patterns are often identified that uncover weaknesses in the firm's human resource management system. Knowledge of the problem permits the company to take corrective action. Also, the exit interview helps to identify training and development needs, create strategic planning objectives, and identify areas in which changes need to be made.[46]

When a postexit questionnaire is used, it is sent to former employees several weeks after they leave the organization. Usually, they have already started work at their new companies. The questionnaire is structured to draw out the real reason the employee left. Ample blank space is also provided so that a former employee can express his or her feelings about and perceptions of the job and the organization. One strength of this approach is that the individuals are no longer with the firm and may respond more freely to the questions. A weakness is that the interviewer is not present to interpret and probe for the real reasons the person left.

ADVANCE NOTICE OF RESIGNATION

Most firms would like to have at least two weeks' notice of resignation from departing workers. However, a month's notice may be desired from professional and managerial employees who are leaving. When notice is desired by the firm, the policy should be clearly communicated to all employees. If they want departing employees to give advance notice, companies have certain obligations. For instance, suppose that a worker gives notice—then is terminated immediately. Word of this action will spread rapidly to other employees. Later, should they decide to resign, they will likely not give any advance notice.

However, permitting a worker to remain on the job once he or she has submitted a resignation may create some problems. If bad feelings exist between the employee and the supervisor or the company, the departing worker may be a disruptive force. On a selective basis, the firm may wish to pay the employee for the notice time and ask him or her to leave immediately. However, this action should not often be necessary.

Retirement

Many long-term employees leave an organization by retiring. While the Age Discrimination in Employment Act generally makes it illegal to mandate a specific retirement age, retirement plans are often based on a certain age or working a certain number of years with the firm, or both. On retirement, former employees usually receive compensation either from a defined benefits plan or a defined contributions plan, both of which were discussed in chapter 12.

In the past, there were far too many instances of retirement plan failure. Many workers who retired believing that they would receive lifelong pensions were devastated to find that retirement programs had been insufficiently funded by their employers. You may recall from chapter 12 that the Employee Retirement Income Security Act (ERISA) was passed in 1974 for the purpose of protecting employees participating in company-sponsored retirement plans.

EARLY RETIREMENT

Sometimes employees will be offered early retirement before reaching the organization's normal length-of-service requirement.[47] In fact, the traditional approach to downsizing has been to use early retirement.[48] Often retirement pay is reduced for each year the retirement date is advanced. From an organization's viewpoint, early employee retirement has both positive and negative aspects.

Because of the large number of staff reductions many firms are now encountering, early retirement is often viewed as an attractive solution.[49] If an extended layoff is expected, a product line is being discontinued, or a plant is being closed, early retirement may be a responsible solution to the problem of surplus employees.

From a negative viewpoint, valued employees may take advantage of the early retirement option and leave the organization. In addition, early retirement is often more expensive to the company than normal retirement. Also, early retirement decisions are often made on short notice, resulting in some disruption of a company's operations.

RETIREMENT PLANNING

Strong emotions often accompany anticipation of retirement. As retirement approaches, the individual may be haunted by these and other questions: Do I have enough money? What will I do? Will I be able to adjust? Just as a well-planned orientation program eases the transition of a new hire into the organization, a company-sponsored retirement planning program eases the transition of long-term employees from work to leisure. To eliminate the shock of thinking about retirement, some firms such as Polaroid allows their employees to *test* retirement for six months of unpaid leave. About half of them decide to resume working full time.[50]

Often a firm devotes time, staff, and money to provide useful information to workers approaching retirement. Typically, such information relates to finances, housing, relocation, family relations, attitude adjustment, and legal affairs.

Some firms have taken retirement planning a step further. At times, firms consider both the social and psychological implications of the retirement process. Adaptation to retirement living is the focus of this form of planning. Individuals who have already retired are brought to meetings to speak and answer questions regarding life after retirement. Managing the change in lifestyle is often a topic for discussion, a useful topic for all those considering retirement. Retirement is a major event in an individual's life, and employers can often help to smooth the transition from work to leisure.

Legal Implications of Internal Employee Relations

In chapter 3, we listed several employment standards to avoid. Many people believe that equal employment opportunity legislation primarily affects individuals entering the company for the first time. Nothing could be further from the truth. Remember the Employment Standards to Avoid that were discussed in chapter 3. Every aspect of internal employee relations is covered by these standards—promotions, demotions, transfers, discipline, and termination. The Household Finance Corporation (HFC) was required to pay more than $125,000 to white-collar women employees who charged that they were denied promotion because of their gender. Under terms of a consent decree, the company also agreed to hire women for 20 percent of the branch representative openings (subject to availability). HFC was also required to hire 20 percent of its new employees from specified minority groups for clerical, credit, and branch representative jobs until the total of such employees reached 65 percent of their population proportion in the labor area. In addition, HFC agreed to train women and minority employees to help them qualify for better jobs in areas where they were underrepresented.[51]

One of the largest payments ever made was under an agreement signed by AT&T with the Equal Employment Opportunity Commission and the Department of Labor. It provided for payment of approximately $15 million to employees allegedly discriminated against. The agreement also called for additional affirmative action and for an estimated $50 million in yearly payments for promotion and wage adjustment to minority and women employees.[52]

As described in chapter 3, termination of workers who have reached a certain age is a major concern in enforcement of the Age Discrimination Act. In *EEOC v Liggett and Myers*, the Equal Employment Opportunity Commission alleged that age was a factor in the discharge of approximately 10 percent of Liggett and Myers' employees during a reduction in force. The court ruled against the company, and back-pay recovery was estimated at $20 million. In *EEOC v Home Insurance Company*, an age discrimination case was won on behalf of 143 employees at Home Insurance Company who had been forced to retire at age 62; back-pay recovery was estimated at $6 to 8 million.

The Age Discrimination in Employment Act now has no upper-age ceiling for mandatory retirement. Employers who attempt to retire workers systematically for factors other than performance are coming under scrutiny by the EEOC. The problem in many cases is that for appraisal periods prior to termination, high-performance evaluations had often been given to the employees involved. These evaluations provided the terminated employees with the data they needed to develop valid cases contending that the reason for their termination was age, not declining performance.

Some firms have tried to open avenues for promotion of younger workers by offering older workers early voluntary retirement. A potential problem with this option is whether the retirement is truly voluntary. Exerting pressure on employees to retire when they really do not want to is beginning to receive considerable EEOC attention.

The thrust of equal employment opportunity legislation is that women and minorities should receive equal treatment, and internal employee relations must reflect this principle. For instance, are blacks being fired at a higher rate than whites? Are women not receiving promotional opportunities? The same kinds of questions may be asked about demotions and layoffs. As more women and minorities enter the workforce, administration of equal employment opportunities will likely focus increasingly on internal employee relations.

Evaluating the Human Resource Management Function[53]

Throughout the book, we have stressed that the human resource function is now being measured just like any other department.[54] The success of any organization depends not only on the formulation and execution of superb plans but also on the continuous evaluation of progress toward the accomplishment of specified objectives. For an organization as a whole, evaluation may be performed in terms of profitability ratios, sales increases, market penetration, and a host of other factors. Today, it is important for human resources to receive the same degree of cost evaluation as do other operations.[55]

How should an organization go about evaluating its human resource management function? An HR self-audit of the functional areas is a good first step.[56] In this audit, it would be well to determine how well a function is

TABLE 16-3

Typical Human Resource Checklist Questions

- Are all legally mandated reports submitted to requiring agencies on time?
- Have formalized procedures and methods been developed for conducting job analysis?
- Are forecasts for human resource requirements made at least annually?
- Is the recruiting process effectively integrated with human resource planning?
- Does the application form conform to applicable legal and affirmative action standards?
- Are all employees appraised at least annually?
- Are skills inventories maintained on all employees?
- Are career opportunities communicated clearly to all employees?

being managed for value added.[57] Are there particular measures or indicators that reveal how well this function is meeting its responsibilities and supporting the organization's efforts to reach its objectives? Two basic methods may be used to evaluate human resource management activities: checklists and quantitative measures.

The checklist approach poses a number of questions that can be answered either *yes* or *no*. This method is concerned with determining whether important activities have been recognized and, if so, whether they are being performed. Essentially, the checklist is an evaluation of what should be done and the extent to which it is being done. Some typical human resource checklist questions are shown in Table 16-3. The more *yes* answers there are, the better the evaluation; *no* answers indicate areas or activities where follow-up or additional work is needed to increase the effectiveness of human resource management. Organizations deciding to use this evaluation approach will undoubtedly come up with many other questions to ask. The checklist method is purely an internal evaluation device and might be considered a first step in the audit.

The other method for evaluating the performance of human resource activities is a quantitative one. It relies on the accumulation of various types of numerical data and the calculation of certain ratios from them. Numerical data are useful primarily as an indicator of activity levels and trends. Ratios show results that are important in themselves but that also reveal (when maintained over a period of time) trends that may be even more important. Possible human resource areas to track include recruitment, turnover, absenteeism, salary levels, temporary help, overtime, unemployment, insurance, and workers' compensation. For instance, what is the cost for recruiting a particular skill? Is one recruitment method superior to another? Employment agencies are commonly used but they are expensive. Could other methods be more cost effective?[58] Some examples of quantitative measures for human resource management are listed in Table 16-4.

TABLE 16-4

Examples of Quantitative Human Resource Management Measures

- Women and minorities selection ratio
- Women and minorities promotion ratio
- Women and minorities termination ratio
- Minority and women hiring percentage
- Minority and women workforce percentage
- Requirements forecast compared to actual human resource needs
- Availability forecast compared to actual availability of human resources
- Average recruiting cost per applicant
- Average recruiting cost per employee hired
- Percentage of positions filled internally
- Average testing cost per applicant
- Percentage of required appraisals actually completed
- Percentage of employees rated in highest performance category
- Percentage of appraisals appealed
- Turnover percentage
- New hire retention percentage
- Percentage of new hires lost

A GLOBAL PERSPECTIVE

Don't Make a Move without an Expatriate Transfer Policy

Global transfers involve the movement of employees within an international organization. A transfer may be initiated by the firm or by an employee, but most international transfers are initiated by the firm. Global transfers are used to take advantage of domestic talent in global business operations and to maintain ties with the home country. Such transfers are often necessary to manage global operations effectively, but inappropriately handled transfers may do personal and career damage to those involved. Also, instead of benefiting the company, ill-advised transfers can cost as much as a million dollars per expatriate failure. The failure to attract the right local talent, at the right price, can set back global expansion plans for months or even years.[59]

A well-thought-out expatriate transfer policy can help a company avoid many of the frustrations and pitfalls of sending the wrong people abroad while achieving cost savings. When developing an expatriate policy, the first thing the company needs to consider is why it is sending people abroad. The policy should be directed at achieving the company's business objectives while considering the needs of expatriates. The decision to go overseas should be mutually acceptable to both parties because people moving for the first time will probably have real fears and concerns. It is essential that expatriate candidates have the necessary skills and be adaptable to overseas assignments. According to Bill Sheridan, director of international compensation services at NFTC, "line of sight [selection]" must be avoided. This is where "we look up and down the hallway and we send Sheridan off to Japan—because we see him."[60] Such haphazard selection is inappropriate. However, once appropriate expatriates are selected, they and their families must be properly prepared for the global move. Then, a well-designed repatriation plan, which enhances the expatriate's domestic career, must be developed and implemented.

Finally, the importance of so-called soft issues cannot be ignored. Many companies focus on the "hard" issues surrounding expatriate assignments such as taxes, cost-of-living allowances, and premiums, while overlooking the "soft" issues. These issues include employment for the expatriate's spouse, schooling for his or her children, and the family's adjustment to a new culture. Paul Patt, director of business development at Runzheimer International, a relocation consulting firm based in Rochester, Wisconsin, believes these questions should be addressed: "Will the trailing spouse be able to work?" "How are you going to keep that spouse happy?" "What can the company do to help the family be more accepting of the assignment?"[61] Only by utilizing a well-thought-out expatriate transfer policy can companies limit the problems of sending people abroad and best utilize their talents.

SUMMARY

1. **Describe internal employee relations.**

Internal employee relations consists of the human resource management activities associated with the movement of employees within the firm after they have become organizational members. It includes the actions of promotion, transfer, demotion, resignation, discharge, layoff, and retirement. Discipline and disciplinary action are included within the bounds of internal employee relations because of the possible impact of disciplinary measures on employee relations.

2. **Define** discipline **and** disciplinary action.

Discipline is the state of employee self-control and orderly conduct present within an organization. It indicates the extent of genuine teamwork that exists. *Disciplinary action* occurs when standards are maintained by invoking a penalty against an employee who fails to meet them. Effective disciplinary action addresses the employee's wrongful behavior, not the employee as a person.

3. **Identify the steps involved in the disciplinary process.**

The steps include establishing organizational goals, establishing rules, communicating rules to employees, observing performance, comparing performance with rules, and taking appropriate disciplinary action.

4. **Describe the approaches to discipline.**

According to the hot stove rule, disciplinary action should have the consequences that are similar to touching a hot stove. Progressive disciplinary action is intended to ensure that the minimum penalty appropriate to the offense is imposed. Disciplinary action without punishment gives a worker time off with pay to think about whether he or she really wants to follow the rules and continue working for the company.

5. *Describe the steps involved in progressive disciplinary action.*

After the disciplinary action has been determined appropriate, this question is asked: "Does the violation warrant more than an oral warning?" If the improper behavior is minor and has not previously occurred, perhaps only an oral warning will be sufficient. An individual may receive several oral warnings before a "yes" answer might apply to the question, "Does this violation warrant more than an oral warning?" The same procedure would be used for each level in the progressive disciplinary process. The manager does not consider termination until each lower level question is answered "yes."

6. *Explain how grievance handling is typically conducted under a collective bargaining agreement.*

The first step involves an informal oral presentation of the employee's grievance to the immediate supervisor in the presence of the union steward. If unresolved, the next step involves the plant manager or human resource manager meeting with higher level union officials such as the grievance committee or the business agent or manager. If the grievance is not adjusted at this meeting, it is appealed to the third step. This step typically involves the firm's top labor representative (such as the vice president of industrial relations) and high-level union officials. A grievance that still remains unresolved at the conclusion of the third step may go to arbitration.

7. *Explain how grievance handling is typically conducted in union-free firms.*

A well-designed union-free grievance procedure ensures that the worker has ample opportunity to make complaints without fear of reprisal. If the system is to work, employees must be well informed about the program and be convinced that management wants them to use it. Typically, an employee initiates a complaint with his or her immediate supervisor. If the complaint involves the supervisor, the individual is permitted to bypass that supervisor and proceed to the employee-relations specialist or the manager at the next level. The grievance ultimately may be taken to the organization's top executive for a final decision.

8. *Define* alternative dispute resolution.

Alternative dispute resolution (ADR) is a procedure in which the employee and the company agree that any problems will be addressed by an agreed-on means ahead of time.

9. *Describe how termination conditions may differ with regard to nonmanagerial/nonprofessional employees, executives, managers, and professionals.*

The procedure used to terminate unionized employees is typically well defined in the labor-management agreement. When the firm is union free, these individuals are employment-at-will workers and can be terminated at any time for any reason. There is likely no formal appeal procedure with regard to executives, and the decision to terminate them has probably been approved by the top-level officer in the organization. The reasons for termination may not be clear. Middle- and lower-level managers and professionals are generally neither members of a union nor protected by a labor agreement. They may not have the political clout that a terminated executive may have. The reasons for their termination may be based solely on the attitude of their immediate superior on a given day.

10. *Explain the concept of employment at will.*
Employment at will is an unwritten contract that is created when an employee agrees to work for an employer, but there is no agreement as to how long the parties expect the employment to last. Because of a century-old common law rule in the United States, employment of indefinite duration can, in general, be terminated at the whim of either party.

11. *Describe the purpose of the exit interview.*
When a firm wants to determine the real reasons that individuals decide to leave the organization, it can use the exit interview. The exit interview encourages the employee to tell his or her resignation story openly and freely.

12. *Explain demotions, transfers, and promotions.*
The process of moving a worker to a lower level of duties and responsibilities, and typically a pay decrease, is a demotion. Transfers are lateral movement of workers within the organization. The movement of a person to a higher level position in the company is a promotion.

13. *Describe the legal implications of internal employee relations.*
The thrust of equal employment opportunity legislation is that members of protected groups should not receive unequal treatment, and internal employee relations should reflect this principle. As more and more members of protected groups enter the workforce, the focus of equal employment opportunity administration will likely continue to shift to internal employee relations.

14. *Explain the importance of evaluating the human resource management functions.*
The success of any organization depends not only on the formulation and execution of superb plans but also on the continuous evaluation of progress toward the accomplishment of specified objectives. For an organization as a whole, evaluation may be performed in terms of profitability ratios, sales increases, market penetration, and a host of other factors. Today, it is important for human resources to receive the same degree of cost evaluation as does operations.

QUESTIONS FOR REVIEW

1. Define *internal employee relations*.
2. Distinguish between discipline and disciplinary action.
3. Describe the following approaches to disciplinary action:
   a. hot stove rule
   b. progressive disciplinary action
   c. disciplinary action without punishment

4. In progressive disciplinary action, what steps are involved before employee termination?

5. What are the steps that should typically be followed in handling a grievance under a collective bargaining agreement?

6. Why is arbitration often used in the settlement of grievances in a unionized firm?

7. How would grievances typically be handled in a union-free firm? Describe briefly.

8. Define alternative dispute resolution (ADR). What is the purpose of ADR?

9. How does termination often differ among nonmanagerial/nonprofessional employees, executives, managers, and professionals?

10. What is meant by the phrase *employment at will*?

11. Briefly describe the techniques available to determine the real reasons an individual decides to leave the organization.

12. Distinguish between demotions, transfers, and promotions.

13. What are some legal implications of internal employee relations?

14. Why is it important to evaluate the human resource management function?

15. How should an organization go about evaluating its human resource management function?

DEVELOPING HRM SKILLS

AN EXPERIENTIAL EXERCISE

Isadore Lamansky is the manager of the machine tooling operations at Lone Star Industries and has five supervisors who report to him. One of his employees is Susie Canton, a supervisor in maintenance. As Isadore comes to work this morning, his thoughts focus on Susie, "Today is the day that I must talk to Susie. I sure hate to do it. I know she is going to take it the wrong way. Ever since Susie was promoted to unit supervisor, she has had trouble maintaining discipline. She tries too hard to keep the men in line because she thinks they are continually trying to push her, and she lets the women get away with murder. Well, I guess I'll get this over with; that's what I get paid for."

One person will play Susie, and another person will play Isadore. All others should observe carefully. The instructor will provide additional information to participants.

Take It to the Net

We invite you to visit the Mondy home page on the Prentice Hall Web site at:

http://www.prenhall.com/mondy

for updated information, Web-based exercises, and links to other HR-related sites.

HRM SIMULATION

*I*ncident K in the *Simulation Players Manual* deals with outplacement. Your team has been given the responsibility of formulating a policy on termination and the possibility of using an outplacement service provided by a national consulting firm. Your team has the responsibility of assessing whether to offer outplacement services to terminated employees.

Incident N in the *Simulation Players Manual* deals with a promotion decision. Your team will study and make a recommendation about whom to promote.

HRM INCIDENT

1

Too Much Absenteeism

*Q*uality Business Forms, Inc., has a policy stating that employee absenteeism should not exceed four days during a 90-day work period without medical verification. If an employee does not have medical reasons for excessive absences, he or she may be subject to disciplinary action.

Ed Thompson has been employed by Quality for over 21 years. In the past three years he has had an abnormal number of absences, which his supervisor chose to ignore because of Ed's long tenure with the company. When Ed's supervisor was transferred and another individual in the department, Alice Randall, assumed the supervisory position, she immediately advised Ed that his absenteeism was excessive and that it would have to cease or disciplinary action would be taken. Ed claimed that he had been injured five years earlier on his job and that his absences were a result of that injury. A review of Ed's health records was made; no such injury had ever been reported.

Ed's attendance improved during the first six months of Randall's supervision but began to deteriorate during the latter part of the year. Ed, warned again about the absenteeism, came back with his previous excuse. At this point, Randall contacted the personnel manager for assistance in dealing with Ed. She was told that further disciplinary steps should be taken along with a complete physical evaluation by the corporate medical doctor. The physical exam was conducted immediately and no physical abnormalities were found.

This information was given to Ed verbally by the doctor, but Ed did not accept the findings. He was then counseled by the personnel manager, his supervisor, and his department manager. Ed listened very intently to what was being said and took notes. Ed was told that the next step in the disciplinary procedure would be dismissal if his absenteeism continued. He said he understood and he would work when he felt good and would not work when he did not feel good.

Thirty days later Ed and his supervisor were called in to the personnel office at 7:00 A.M., and Ed was terminated. Ed was shocked at actually being fired, as it was necessary for the president of the company to approve the termination of an employee with a long service record. Ed filed a discrimination charge, but it was dropped when no grounds for it could be established. He also filed a workers' compensation claim, but this claim also could not be substantiated. Finally, he submitted an unemployment claim, but it too was dismissed.

Questions
1. Do you agree with the standards developed by the firm with regard to absenteeism?
2. What responsibilities rest with an employer regarding when a long-term employee should be terminated?
3. How much documentation is really needed to be fair?

HRM INCIDENT

2

Something Is Not Right

As Norman Blankenship came to the office at Consolidated Coal Company's Rowland mine, near Clear Creek, West Virginia, he told the mine dispatcher not to tell anyone of his presence. Norman was the general superintendent of the Rowland operation. He had been with Consolidated for more than 23 years, having started out as a coal digger.

Norman had heard that one of his section bosses, Tom Serinsky, had been sleeping on the job. Tom had been hired two months earlier and assigned to the Rowland mine by the regional human resource office. He went to work as section boss, working the midnight to 8:00 A.M. shift. Because of his age and experience, Tom was the senior person in the mine on his shift.

Norman took one of the battery-operated jeeps used to transport workers and supplies in and out of the mine and proceeded to the area where Tom was assigned. Upon arriving, he saw Tom lying on an emergency stretcher. Norman stopped his jeep a few yards away from where Tom was sleeping and approached him. "Hey, you asleep?" Norman asked.

Tom awoke with a start and said, "No, I wasn't sleeping."

Norman waited a moment for Tom to collect his senses and then said, "I could tell that you were sleeping. But that's beside the point. You weren't at your workstation. You know that I have no choice but to fire you."

After Tom had left, Norman called his mine supervisor, who had accompanied him to the dispatcher's office and asked him to complete the remainder of Tom's shift.

The next morning, Norman instructed the mine human resource officer to terminate Tom officially. As part of the standard procedure, the mine human resource officer notified the regional human resource director that Tom had been fired and gave the reasons for firing him. The regional director asked the human resource officer to put Norman on the line. When he did so, Norman was told, "Did you know that Tom is the brother-in-law of our regional vice president, Bill Frederick?"

"No, I didn't know that," replied Norman, "but it doesn't matter. The rules are clear, and I wouldn't care if he was the regional vice president's son."

The next day the regional director showed up at the mine just as Norman was getting ready to make a routine tour of the mine. "I guess you know what I'm here for," said the regional director.

"Yeah, you're here to take away my authority," replied Norman.

"No, I'm just here to investigate," said the regional director.

When Norman returned to the mine office after his tour, the regional director had finished his interviews. He told Norman, "I think we're going to have to put Tom back to work. If we decided to do that, can you let him work for you?"

"No, absolutely not," replied Norman. "In fact, if he works here, I go."

A week later Norman learned that Tom had gone back to work as section boss at another Consolidated coal mine in the region.

Questions

1. What would you do now if you were Norman?
2. Do you believe the regional director handled the matter in an ethical manner? Explain.

Notes

1. Brian W. Gill, "Successfully Implementing Discipline," *American Printer* 218 (November 1996): 70.
2. Lauren M. Bernardi, "Progressive Discipline: Effective Management Tool or Legal Trap?" *Canadian Manager* 21 (January 1996): 9.
3. Gill, "Successfully Implementing Discipline."
4. Robert N. Lussier, "16 Guidelines for Effective Discipline," *Supervisory Management* 35 (March 1990): 10.
5. David N. Campbell, R. L. Fleming, and Richard C. Grote, "Discipline without Punishment—At Last," *Harvard Business Review* 63 (July/August 1985): 168.
6. Edward Seidler, "Discipline and Deselection in the TQM Environment," *Public Personnel Management* 25 (December 1996): 530.
7. Wallace Wohlking, "Effective Discipline in Employee Relations," *Personnel Journal* 54 (September 1975): 489.
8. Julie K. Miller, "Officials Say New Conduct Code Promotes Uniformity," *The Atlanta Journal and Constitution* (July 26, 1997): M14.
9. Neil W. Chamberlain, *The Labor Sector* (New York: McGraw-Hill, 1985): 240.
10. Paula Eubanks, "Employee Grievance Policy: Don't Discourage Complaints," *Hospitals* 64 (December 20, 1990): 36.
11. James P. Swann, Jr., "Formal Grievance Procedures in Non-Union Plants," *Personnel Administrator* 26 (August 1991): 67.
12. Jennifer Laabs, "Remedies for HR's Legal Headache," *Personnel Journal* 73 (December 1994): 69.
13. Edward Baig, "Careers: When It's Time to Do Battle with Your Company," *Business Week* (February 10, 1997): 130.

14. Robert V. Kuenzel, "Alternative Dispute Resolution: Why All the Fuss?" *Compensation & Benefits Review* 28 (July/August 1996): 43.

15. Susan Benkelman, "A Blow against Arbitration—Seeking a Ban on Signing Away Workplace Rights," *Newsday* (April 6, 1997): A32.

16. Elliot H. Shaller, "Avoid Pitfalls in Hiring, Firing," *Nation's Business* 79 (February 1991): 53.

17. Therese Fitz Maurice, "Training the Terminators," *Fairfield County Business Journal* 34 (May 22, 1995): 15.

18. Donald J. McNerney, "News Capsules," *HR Focus* 74 (April 1997): 6–9.

19. N. Fredric Crandall and Marc J. Wallace, Jr., "Inside the Virtual Workplace: Forging a New Deal for Work and Rewards," *Compensation & Benefits Review* 29 (January/February 1997): 27–36.

20. Richard Edwards, *Rights at Work: Employment Relations in the Post Union Era* (Washington: The Brookings Institution, 1993): Appendix.

21. Raymond L. Hilgert, "Employers Protected by At-Will Statement," *HRMagazine* 36 (March 1991): 60.

22. Catherine Corfee, "Take Steps to Maintain At-Will Employment," *Business Journal Serving Greater Sacramento* 13 (June 1996): 16.

23. Clinton O. Longnecker and Frederick R. Post, "The Management Termination Trap," *Business Horizons* 37 (May/June 1994): 71.

24. Lisa Jenner, "Employment-at-Will Liability: How Protected Are You?" *HR Focus* 71 (March 1994): 11.

25. Ibid.

26. Stratford Sherman, "Is He too Cautious to Save IBM?" *Fortune* 130 (October 3, 1994): 82.

27. Brian O'Reilly, "The New Deal: What Companies and Employees Owe One Another," *Fortune* 129 (June 13, 1994): 45.

28. Ibid., 46.

29. Kenneth Labich, "The New Unemployed," *Fortune* 127 (March 8, 1993): 40.

30. Susan Caminiti, "What Happens to Laid-Off Managers," *Fortune* 129 (June 13, 1994): 69.

31. Michael Smith, "Help in Making Those Tough Layoff Decisions," *Supervisory Management* 35 (January 1990): 3.

32. Robert W. Keidel, "Layoffs Take Advance Preparation," *Management Review* 80 (May 1991): 6.

33. Loretta D. Foxman and Walter L. Polsky, "Outplacement Results in Success," *Personnel Journal* 69 (February 1990): 30.

34. Virginia M. Gibson, "In the Outplacement Door," *Personnel* 68 (October 1991): 3–4.

35. William J. Morin, "Smart Managing/You Inc.: You Are Absolutely Positively on Your Own, Outplacement Is Dead, and Truth about Your Future Is Hard to Come By at Many Companies," *Fortune* 134 (December 9, 1996): 222.

36. David Kirkpatrick, "Is Your Career on Track?" *Fortune* 122 (July 2, 1990): 39.

37. Harvey Mackay, "A Career Roadmap: Getting Started," *Modern Office Technology* 35 (June 1990): 12.

38. Joseph R. Rich and Beth C. Florin-Thuma, "Rewarding Employees in an Environment of Fewer Promotions," *Pension World* 26 (November 1990): 16.

39. Marilyn Moats Kennedy, "What Managers Can Find Out from Exit Interviews," *Physician Executive* 22 (October 1996): 45.

40. Stephen B. Knouse, Jon W. Beard, Hinda Greyser Pollard, and Robert A. Giacalone, "Willingness to Discuss Exit Interview Topics: The Impact of Attitudes toward Supervisor and Authority," *The Journal of Psychology* 130 (May 1996): 249.

41. Sherwood Ross, "Key Executive's Defection Requires Prompt Response," *Reuters Business Report* (January 1997).

42. Lin Grensing, "Don't Let Them Out the Door without an Exit Interview," *Management World* 19 (March/April 1990): 11.

43. Robert Wolfe, "Most Employers Offer Exit Interviews," *HRNews* 10 (June 1990): 2.

44. Barbara Ettorre, "The Unvarnished Truth," *Management Review* 86 (June 1997): 54.

45. Wanda R. Embrey, R. Wayne Mondy, and Robert M. Noe, "Exit Interview: A Tool for Personnel Development," *Personnel Administrator* 24 (May 1979): 46.

46. Knouse, Beard, Pollard, and Giacalone, "Willingness to Discuss Exit Interview Topics."

47. Beverly G. Landstrom and Thomas B. Bainbridge, "What's New in Pensions: Defined Lump Sum Plans," *Compensation & Benefits Review* 28 (January/February 1996): 40.

48. Suzanne Crampton, John Hodge, and Jitendra Mishra, "Transition-Ready or Not: The Aging of American's Work Force," *Public Personnel Management* 25 (July 1996): 247.

49. Jeffrey S. Hoffman, "Sweetening Early-Retirement Programs," *Personnel* 67 (March 1990): 18.

50. Crampton, Hodge, and Mishra, "Transition-Ready or Not: The Aging of American's Work Force."

51. *U.S. v Household Finance Corporation*, 4 EPD para. 7680 (N.D. Ill., 1972) — Consent decree.

52. U.S. Equal Employment Opportunity Commission, *Affirmative Action and Equal Employment: A Guidebook for Employers*, vol. 1 (Washington, DC: U.S. Government Printing Office, January 1974): 10.

53. Portions of this section are adapted from Donald L. Caruth, Robert M. Noe, III, and R. Wayne Mondy, *Staffing the Contemporary Organization* (Westport, CT: Greenwood Press, 1988): 283–299.

54. Melody Jones, "Four Trends to Recond With," *HR Focus* 73 (July 1996): 23.

55. Nancy Sorensen, "Measuring HR for Success," *Training & Development* 49 (November 1995): 49.

56. Sacha Cohen, "Manuals That Reenergize HRD," *Training & Development* 50 (December 1996): 63.

57. James S. Pepitone, "Strategy: Four Ways to Measure HR's Value," *HR Focus* 74 (July 1997): 13–14.

58. Sorensen, "Measuring HR for Success."

59. Donald J. McNerney, "Global Staffing: Some Common Problems — and Solutions," *HR Focus* 73 (June 1996): 1–4.

60. Ibid.

61. McNerney, "Global Staffing: Some Common Problems — and Solutions."

ABCNEWS | VIDEO CASE

The Changing Face of Labor

Labor unions were once a dominant force in our society. Strikes and the threat of strikes were weapons used by unions to gain concessions from management. The workplace has changed, however. With union membership representing only about 10 percent of the private workforce, the labor union has lost much of its clout. Global competition and technology have played a large role in the changes that have taken place including downsizing, outsourcing, and the exporting of manufacturing facilities. Many organizations are much flatter than before and there is less distinction between management and operative employees, who often make decisions previously reserved for managers. Cooperation and teamwork have replaced confrontation and collective bargaining in many organizations. Another change has been the need for increased worker flexibility. Employees must continuously learn new skills to remain important contributors to the bottom line. American workers are now more educated but less secure in their jobs than ever before.

For many individuals today, especially those with a limited education, there is little or no job security; their wages are generally flat, and most of the potential employment is in the lower-paid service sector. When unions do strike, their members might lose their jobs to replacement workers. These are the general conditions that exist in today's labor market.

Circumstances are more positive in some organizations, however. In one firm, United Airlines, the employees have a controlling interest. The interests of management and labor in such an organization should be closely aligned. As owners, employees would not want to take any action that would reduce the firm's effectiveness. Cooperation rather than an adversarial relationship should be achieved more easily, benefiting both parties.

Discussion Questions

1. Are labor-management relations better or worse today than one or two decades ago? Explain.
2. The history of the relationship between labor and management in the United States has resembled the swinging of a pendulum, at times moving in favor of labor and at other times swinging toward management's advantage. Has it swung so far toward management that labor has lost the power struggle?
3. Should organizations be responsible for educating and retraining workers? If not, who should be responsible?
4. Is it possible for labor unions to abandon their traditional adversarial role, emphasize cooperation, and at the same time remain viable?

Source: "The Changing Face of Labor," *This Week with David Brinkley*, ABC News; aired on September 4, 1994.

PART EIGHT

OPERATING IN A GLOBAL ENVIRONMENT

17
Global Human Resource Management

CHAPTER OBJECTIVES

1. Describe the evolution of global business.
2. Explain the goal of global human resource management.
3. Identify the global human resource management functions.
4. Differentiate among expatriates, host-country nationals, and third-country nationals.
5. Identify possible barriers to effective global human resource management.
6. Explain Equal Employment Opportunity (EEO) and global human resource management.

In 1989, the vice president of human resources for Boundless Technologies, headquartered in Hauppauge, Long Island, rose to leave the executive meeting. She realized that her job would be even busier and much more complex for an extended period because Boundless management had decided to move their operations to Hong Kong. Boundless Technologies produces network computers (NCs), which some predict will eventually replace personal computers. The decision to move production to Hong Kong means that the company must deal with a new workforce, a new work environment, new pay structures, and a multitude of other global human resource issues. High wage rates were the driving force behind the relocation decision, with Hong Kong wages being considerably less than those in Long Island. The vice president of human resources was somewhat uncomfortable with the relocation decision because the move was made primarily to escape high wage pressures, without regard to other human resource issues. Unfortunately, the overall strategic mission appeared to be secondary to wage pressure concerns. Even though the human resources vice president was only marginally involved with the relocation decision, she must now develop and execute a major human resources plan to help Boundless Technologies make its global operation a success.

Surprisingly, only a few years after the move to Hong Kong, the organization returned to the United States, creating even more human resource problems and requiring another massive human resource effort. Failure to consider problems that could result in a global relocation caused major disruptions in Boundless Technologies' operations. As it turned out, Boundless Technologies returned to the United States to be closer to their consumer base and because the company could achieve productivity rates in the United States that were high enough to nearly offset the higher wage expense. In preparation for the move back to the United States, the human resources area was again quite busy. A new, trained, and motivated workforce was required, as was a switch to a Japanese-style "just-in-time" system to reduce inventories.[1]

A strategic vision, influenced by human resource considerations, possibly could have prevented the decision to move to Hong Kong. The company's focus on wage pressures rather than on its strategic mission was expensive and unfortunate. In the future, the firm's managers should ensure that their global management decisions clearly emphasize accomplishing the corporate mission and that they involve human resources as a strategic partner.

This case is unusual because companies that move production to low-wage countries rarely return. However, it does show that companies should not simply move production to the country with the lowest wage rates. Human resource problems abound when operations are moved overseas, and in some cases advanced countries still have certain human resource advantages. Regardless of the global location, input from human resources is essential to corporate success.

Boundless Technologies is a real company that actually did return to the United States and is attempting to compete, even with higher U.S. wage rates. If human resource issues had been carefully considered prior to the move, managers might have realized that factors other than wage rates have equal or even greater importance. Although an American-type factory can be constructed overseas, it will not necessarily operate as an American factory. The reasons often revolve around human resource management issues. Global managers must constantly function in a human resources environment that is often more volatile and unpredictable than its domestic counterpart. Managing people in global organizations is more complex than ever, not only because of the rapidly changing and increasingly complicated global work environments but also because global environments are often so different.

In the first part of this chapter, we discuss the evolution of global business and global human resource management as well as global productivity. Next, we review the global aspects of various human resource management functions. Then we present possible barriers to effective global human resource management and discuss equal employment opportunity and global human resource management. Finally, global human resource management of expatriates is discussed.

The Evolution of Global Business

IBM did it, and Ford and General Motors have both done it. Coca-Cola did it a very long time ago, and more companies will do it in the future. What did they do? These American business firms evolved into global corporations. In today's domestic economic environment, companies are realizing that to grow, they must expand overseas. Global expansion is necessary for the continued existence of many firms, regardless of their size or the products and services they offer. Given the mature markets that exist in the United States and other countries, business growth depends on building new markets in developing countries.[2] Twenty years ago, many U.S. multinational corporations had operations in Canada but not in many other countries. Today, most international corporations are becoming truly global.

American companies still regularly do business in Canada, but increasingly they have operations in Hong Kong, Singapore, Japan, the United Kingdom, France, and Germany, to name a few. More and more U.S. global corporations are even showing interest in doing business in former Eastern Bloc countries. This interdependence of national economies has created a global marketplace in which worldwide products and services are bought and sold. The globalization of the marketplace has created special human resource challenges that will endure well into the next century.[3] Realizing that globalization is inevitable for many firms, a group of international human resource professionals, led by AT&T, Xerox, Allied Signal, and Mobil, organized a think tank to determine the best global human resource practices.[4] Results have yet to be published.

Normally, companies evolve to the point of being truly global over an extended period of time. Most companies initially become global without making substantial investments in foreign countries, by either exporting, licensing, or franchising. Exporting is a common choice when manufacturers go global. **Exporting** means selling abroad, either directly or indirectly by retaining foreign agents and distributors. **Licensing**, another global alternative, is an arrangement through which an organization grants a foreign firm the right to use intellectual properties such as patents, copyrights, manufacturing processes, or trade names for a specific period of time. **Franchising** is a similar option; here the parent company grants another firm the right to do business in a prescribed manner. Franchisees must follow stricter operational guidelines than do licensees. Licensing is usually limited to manufacturers, whereas franchising is popular with service firms such as restaurants and hotels.

Although exporting, licensing, and franchising are good initial entry options, to take full advantage of global opportunities, companies must make a substantial investment of their own funds in another country. Generally, global investment refers to operations in one country that are controlled by entities in another country. For example, Mercedes-Benz built their new sport utility production facility outside of Germany, in Vance, Alabama. Normally, a foreign investment means acquiring control of more than 50 percent of a global operation.

Basically, companies can vary greatly in their degree of global involvement, but an international business is any firm that engages in global trade and/or investment. The multinational corporation is one type of global business enterprise. A **multinational corporation (MNC)** is a firm that is based in one country (the parent or home country) and produces goods or provides services in one or more foreign countries (host countries). A multinational corporation directs manufacturing and marketing operations in several countries and these operations are coordinated by a parent company, usually based in the firm's home country. General Motors and Ford are multinational corporations that have evolved to the point of being truly global. As previously defined in chapter 2, a *global corporation* (GC) has corporate units in a number of countries that are integrated to operate as one organization worldwide. Whereas the multinational corporation operates in a number of countries and adapts its products and practices to each, the global corporation operates as if the entire world were one entity. Global

Exporting: Selling abroad, either directly or indirectly, by retaining foreign agents and distributors.

Licensing: A global arrangement whereby an organization grants a foreign firm the right to use intellectual properties such as patents, copyrights, manufacturing processes, or trade names for a specific period of time.

Franchising: A multinational option whereby the parent company grants another firm the right to do business in a prescribed manner.

Multinational corporation (MNC): An organization that conducts a large part of its business outside the country in which it is headquartered and has a significant percentage of its physical facilities and employees in other countries.

Today, most international corporations are becoming truly global.

corporations sell essentially the same products in the same manner through-out the world with components that may be made and/or designed in different countries. Expectations are that as the world becomes more globally open, global corporations will become much more commonplace.

HR Web Wisdom

http://www.prenhall.com/mondy
SHRM–HR LINKS
Various global issues including associations in various countries are presented at this site.

The Evolution of Global Human Resource Management

Globally, human resource executives are strategic partners with line managers and actively participate in top-level business decisions. They bring human resource perspectives to the global management of a company.[5] According to Ronny Vansteenkiste, Seagram's director of European training and development, "HR people . . . [must] lift themselves out of the administrative role to become strategic HR thinkers. But, despite title changes and all the hype about [the strategic importance of] HR, many people in HR have missed this trend or have not fully understood what it means."[6] Basically, the role of the global human resource executive is focused on being a strategic business partner and decision maker. Any human resource initiative must be based on maximizing productivity to best benefit the bottom line; therefore, a solid understanding of the total global system is essential.[7]

Just as global business enterprises evolve, so do the human resources that support them. According to the Council on Competitiveness, Washington, D.C., human resources are the key to global competitiveness.[8] Human resource management involves formulating and implementing HR policies, practices, and activities in global companies like Coca-Cola and McDonald's. Such activities include selecting, training, and transferring parent-company personnel abroad, and formulating policies and practices for the entire firm and for its foreign operations. However, most companies merely adapt their domestic HR policies and practices to the host country. This practice no doubt stems from a lack of global experience in HR managers. Melissa DeCrane of the Corporate Resources Group believes that international expertise is an essential asset for human resources people because every company is challenged by the global marketplace.[9] Effectively dealing with global human resource issues is essential for success in the global marketplace and in order to maximize profitability.[10]

Regardless of the nature of the global enterprise or the HR policies and practices in place, the basic goal of all global corporations is profitability, which is tied directly to productivity. The key to success and profitability is cost-effective productivity, and the key to ensuring cost-effective productivity is effective human resource management. Globally, productivity involves much more than reducing wage pressures; it often requires overcoming other limitations resulting from abandoning a high-wage, highly trained workforce. Lower wages may be accompanied by a multitude of human resource problems that must be effectively dealt with to achieve acceptable global productivity. Apparently Boundless Technologies could not overcome the problems it encountered and made a rare retreat to the United States. However, in most cases, once the global move is made, HR must rise to the occasion and provide the support required for acceptable productivity levels. Human resources must ensure that the company has a smart, adaptable workforce so that it will remain globally competitive.[11] The bottom line, according to David Wimpress of Peritus in the United Kingdom, is that "the indispensable HR professional will be the person who adopts a strategic view and delivers measurable results."[12]

HR Web Wisdom

http://www.prenhall.com/mondy

GLOBAL HR POLICY
The nature of an international human resources policy is briefly addressed here.

Global Human Resource Management Functions

Global human resource management (GHRM):
The use of global human resources to achieve organizational objectives without regard to geographic boundaries.

Global human resource management (GHRM) is the utilization of global human resources to achieve organizational objectives without regard to geographic boundaries. Consequently, global managers are no longer able simply to strategize from the standpoint of domestic considerations; they must think globally.

Global human resource problems and opportunities are enormous and are expanding at a much greater rate than domestic problems and opportunities. Individuals dealing with global human resource matters face a multitude of challenges that their domestic counterparts have probably never imagined. These considerations range from cultural barriers to political barriers, to international aspects such as compensation. Before upper management decides on a global move, it is vitally important that they consider the critical nature of human resource issues. Failure to do so could result in problems as well as lost opportunities, as was the case with Boundless Technologies.

Those engaged in the management of global human resources develop and work through an integrated global human resource management system similar to the one they experience domestically. As Figure 17-1 shows, the five functional areas associated with effective global human resource management are the same as those experienced domestically. These five areas are global human resource planning, recruitment, and selection; global training and development; global compensation and benefits; global safety and health; and global employee and labor relations. Although the five areas are the same globally and domestically, they differ with regard to many specifics. Sound global human resource management practices are required for successful performance in each area. As with domestic human resources, the functional areas of global human resource management are not separate and distinct, but are highly interrelated. Global human resource managers must recognize that decisions in one area will affect other areas. Global human resource management is so complex that certain components must be automated. Nestlé USA, the food conglomerate, automated human resource administration for its 22,000 employees.[13]

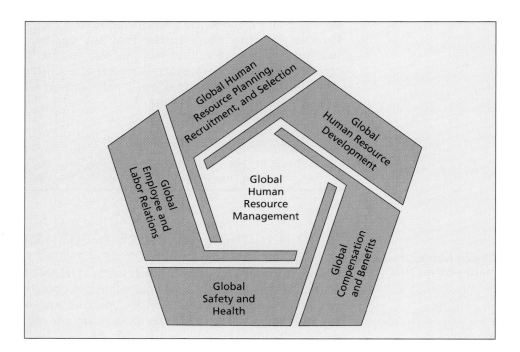

Figure 17-1
The Global Human Resource Management System

GLOBAL HUMAN RESOURCE PLANNING, RECRUITMENT, AND SELECTION

A global organization must have qualified individuals in specific jobs at specific places and times to accomplish its goals. This process involves obtaining such people globally through human resource planning, recruitment, and selection. According to Bill Fontana, a veteran of many foreign assignments for Citibank and the vice president of the National Foreign Trade Council (NFTC), "There's no shortage of brain power [overseas]." This would seem to make global human resource planning, recruitment, and selection easier. Unfortunately, Fontana believes there is "a shortage of people with the right mix of technical skills and a willingness to accept the Western style of business."[14] This lack could make global planning, recruitment, and selection quite difficult.

When developing a global staff, managers and other professionals are normally selected first, followed by operative employees. These individuals can be from the home-country, the host-country, the operational region, or from anywhere in the globe. Unfortunately, it is quite difficult to locate managers with sufficient international experience, and over 70 percent of recruiters expect the problem to continue in the future.[15] Other problems include the high cost of establishing a manager or professional in another country, the extreme cost of placing a key manager outside the United States, and the reality that failure rates for managers sent to other countries is approaching 50 percent.[16] Because of such problems and the potential for losses, global human resource management practices focus heavily on planning, recruitment, and selection.

Once the leadership core is in place, other global employees must be found. Global employees can be selected from three different areas including expatriates, host-country nationals, and third-country nationals. An **expatriate** is an employee working in a firm who is not a citizen of the country in which the firm is located but is a citizen of the country in which the organization is headquartered. A **host-country national (HCN)** is an employee working in a firm who is a citizen of the country in which the firm is located, but the firm is operated by an organization headquartered in another country. Normally the bulk of employees in international offices will be host-country nationals. According to Roberta Davis, expatriate services manager at Chubb & Son, Inc., "As a company develops its presence in a foreign market, . . . it's a wise strategy to be seen as a local company with a local staff."[17] That means hiring local people and operating the company like local companies whenever possible. A **third-country national (TCN)** is a citizen of one country, working in a second country, and employed by an organization headquartered in a third country. Each of these individuals presents some unique human resource management challenges and advantages. Boundless brought some of their own people to Hong Kong as managers (expatriates), but the majority of their labor force was made up of workers from Hong Kong (host-country nationals).

Generally, expatriates are used to ensure that foreign operations are linked effectively with parent corporations. However, the use of expatriate employees must be carefully considered because the cost of an international assignment in Europe is usually two to three times the employee's annual

Expatriate: An employee working in a firm who is not a citizen of the country in which the firm is located but is a citizen of the country in which the organization is headquartered.

Host-country national (HCN): An employee working in a firm who is a citizen of the country in which the firm is located whereas the firm is operated by an organization headquartered in another country.

Third-country national (TCN): A citizen of one country, working in a second country, and employed by an organization headquartered in a third country.

salary. An Asian assignment can cost three to five times the employee's annual salary.[18] Most global employees are usually host-country nationals because employing local individuals helps to establish that the company is making a commitment to the host country and not just setting up a foreign operation. Compared to an outsider, host-country nationals often know much more thoroughly the culture, the politics, and the laws of the locale as well as how business is done.[19] The use of third-country nationals is common when a truly global approach is followed, and these individuals are used to handle responsibilities throughout a continent or region.

Once the decision is made of whether to use an expatriate, a host-country national, a third-country national, or some combination, the selection process begins. The selection process for an international assignment should begin with a comprehensive description of the job to be done. This description should be used as a guide in the selection process. If the decision is made to employ expatriates, certain selection criteria should be carefully considered. Ideally, expatriate selection criteria include cultural adaptability, strong communication skills, technical competence, professional or operational expertise, global experience, country-specific experience, interpersonal skills, language skills, family flexibility, and other country- or region-specific considerations.[20] One can only imagine the culture shock of the managers from Long Island who moved to Hong Kong. Boundless probably had had few managers who had ever visited, much less worked in, Hong Kong.

Mercedes-Benz thoroughly planned every aspect of relocation including the human resources aspects of their move to the United States. The U.S. operation in Vance, Alabama, is being used as the test bed to determine whether the company should extend its globalization to Brazil, China, and India. Through effective planning, every desirable attribute of a Mercedes-Benz employee was isolated, with the most desirable trait, beyond general aptitude, being the ability to work in teams.[21] Mercedes-Benz was able to attract a pool of 45,000 applicants to select from. Finally, the Mercedes-Benz selection process involved over 80 hours of applicant testing to help ensure the selection of the most qualified and appropriate applicants. Successful accomplishment of these three tasks is vital if the global organization is to achieve its mission effectively. Accomplishing these three tasks resulted in the selection of the most qualified 900 employees from the 45,000-applicant pool.[22]

GLOBAL TRAINING AND DEVELOPMENT (GT&D)

Global training and development is needed because people, jobs, and organizations are often quite different globally from the way they are domestically. To address such problems, Bill Fontana of NFTC suggests developing a *farm team* of foreign nationals from sources outside local markets, such as U.S. and Western business schools. These individuals will be partially developed by already being immersed in Western business practices and therefore capable of filling high-skill jobs in their home country.[23]

With less-skilled workforces, training and development must be emphasized and will often require more time and resources than they would domestically. Continually upgrading workforce knowledge and skills has become increasingly important to global competitiveness, but unfortunately, the United States lags behind other countries in developmental activities.[24] According to David Wimpress, executive chairman of the United Kingdom's Peritas, "We need to ensure that the skills of our people are kept up-to-date." If people are not properly developed they probably will be laid off.[25] Mary McCain, vice president at the American Society for Training & Development, noted, "Because new technology and new products can easily be copied within three to six months . . . the only ongoing competitive edge any company in any country has is its workforce."[26] And its workforce will not be competitive unless it is adequately trained. Unfortunately, American business firms' failure to measure up in terms of global training and development is damaging our status as a competitor in the world arena."[27]

The development process should start as soon as the workforce is selected, even before beginning global operations if possible. Mercedes-Benz sent 165 early hires to Germany for their training. After receiving this training, these individuals, along with 70 Germans, conducted employee training in the United States.[28] Large-scale training and development programs, like that of Mercedes-Benz, are essential for most global relocations. The purpose of these development programs is to alter the environment within the firm to help global employees perform more productively in the host country. The development program at Boundless was evidently not sufficient to overcome the advantages of a significantly lower wage level. Such a program would probably require a very sophisticated approach, taking into account factors that are not inherent in domestic development programs, such as political, legal, economic, and cultural differences. Global expansion for McDonald's into China has been particularly problematic because of the aftermath of the Cultural Revolution of the 1960s and 1970s, which closed most schools in China. As a result, an entire generation did not receive much education. McDonald's must personally develop these individuals. Bob Wilner, McDonald's director of international human resources, says that McDonald's tries to develop local people in Asia, finding them more effective than expatriates because they better understand the Asian marketplace and customers.[29] David Hoff of Anheuser-Busch in Asia is developing host-country nationals in a rather unique way. Hoff hires host-country nationals, develops their talents in the United States, and reassigns them abroad as local managers.[30]

Other aspects of global training and development include career planning and performance appraisal, which will also require changes if they are to be appropriate for overseas operations. Performance appraisal affords employees the opportunity to capitalize on their strengths and overcome identified deficiencies, thereby becoming more satisfied and productive employees. Properly structured performance appraisals could be quite useful for tracking strengths and weaknesses in a global workforce, thereby enhancing productivity levels more quickly.[31]

It is very important that operative employees be developed properly because this is the level at which significant productivity gaps can result. Those in leadership positions must also be as fully trained and as prepared as possible because they must develop operational employees to achieve acceptable productivity levels.

TRENDS & INNOVATIONS

EXPATRIATE DEVELOPMENT

There is a growing trend for global training and development of expatriates—and in certain cases their families—to go beyond the aforementioned developmental process. Organizations are recognizing that expatriate employees and their families face special situations and pressures and that training and development activities must prepare them to deal with these.[32] Employees, and sometimes their families, must have an effective orientation program, continual development, and a readjustment training program. Figure 17-2 illustrates the expatriate preparation and development program that includes pre-move orientation and training, continual development, and repatriation orientation and training.

Pre-move orientation and training of expatriate employees and their families is essential before the global assignment begins. The pre-move orientation involves training and familiarization in language, culture, history, living conditions, and local customs and peculiarities.[33] Continuing employee development in which the employee's global skills are fitted into career planning and corporate development programs makes the eventual transition to the home country less disruptive. Continual development involves skill expansion, at both the professional and operational levels when appropriate, comprehensive career planning, and involvement in home-country development programs. Finally, repatriation orientation and training is necessary prior to **repatriation,** which is the process of bringing expatriates home. Repatriation orientation and training is needed to prepare the employee, and the family, for a return to the home-country culture and to prepare the expatriate's new subordinates and supervisor for the return. Adjustments involve helping the individual—and the family, when appropriate—get ready to return to the U.S. lifestyle. This preparation is particularly necessary if the assignment was in a third-world country. Training and orientation must also ready the employee, the supervisor, and the subordinates for the expatriate's return. This process is much easier if the ongoing employee development program is well structured and implemented.

Repatriation: The process of bringing expatriates home.

GLOBAL COMPENSATION AND BENEFITS

The main reason that organizations relocate to other areas of the world is probably the high wage pressures that threaten their ability to compete on a global basis. Wage pressures and union inflexibility in Germany were the primary reasons that Mercedes-Benz located its sport utility plant in the United States.[34] Once wage pressures become so high they cannot be offset by increased productivity, a company will often make a global move. When the price of Mercedes-Benz luxury cars rose $15,000 above the competition, a global move was eminent.[35] On the other hand, Boundless returned to the United States—its home country—even though salaries here were substantially higher than those in Hong Kong. Globally, the question of what

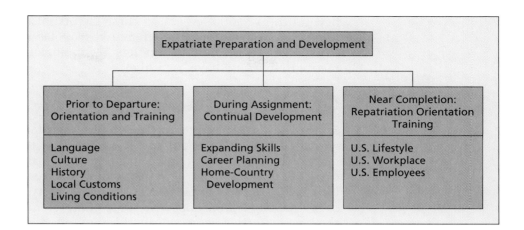

Figure 17-2
The Expatriate
Preparation and
Development Program

constitutes a fair day's pay is not as complicated as it is in the United States; normally, it is slightly above the prevailing wage rates in the area. Mercedes-Benz went global to avoid paying $30 an hour in Germany. Although prevailing manufacturing wages in Alabama were $8 to $10, Mercedes-Benz paid about $13 an hour and within two years $18 an hour, only slightly below union wages for the Big Three.[36] The same pattern is often true of benefits and nonfinancial rewards. Basically, compensation levels are usually much lower globally. However, variations in laws, living costs, tax policies, and other factors all must be considered when a company is establishing global compensation packages.

EXPATRIATE COMPENSATION PACKAGES

According to Roberta Davis of Chubb & Sons, Inc., overcompensating expatriates is common. Companies must have well-thought-out global compensation policies. "Don't simply give whatever the expatriate ask for, but rather provide what they need." Trying to preserve the expatriate's home-country standard of living in a foreign country may not be practical.[37] Paul Patt, director of business development at Runzheimer International, believes that companies should "try not to start out overly generous, because it is very, very difficult to scale back packages once they're in place."[38] For expatriate managers and professionals, the situation is more complex than simply paying at or slightly above local host-country compensation rates. Even minor changes in the value of the U.S. dollar may result in compensation adjustments for expatriates. Also, expatriate compensation packages must cover the extra costs of housing, education for children, and yearly transportation home for the employees and their family members. Additionally, compensation packages may include foreign service and hardship premiums, relocation and moving allowances, cost-of-living adjustments, and tax equalization payments. With regard to tax equalization payments, under Internal Revenue Service rules, U.S. citizens living overseas can exclude from taxes up to $70,000 of income earned abroad. Also, credits against U.S. income taxes are given for a portion of the foreign income taxes paid by U.S. expatriates beyond the $70,000 level.[39] All these factors make global compensation extremely complex. Even though the cost of labor was substantially less in Hong Kong, the cost to Boundless Technologies to support their management group would have been high.

GLOBAL SAFETY AND HEALTH

Safety and health aspects of the job are important because employees who work in a safe environment and enjoy good health are more likely to be productive and yield long-term benefits to the organization than those in less desirable circumstances. For this reason, progressive global managers have long advocated and implemented adequate safety and health programs. Basically, U.S.-based global operations are often safer and healthier than those of the host country, but frequently they are not as safe as similar operations in the United States.[40]

Safety and health laws and regulations vary greatly from country to country. Such laws can range from virtually nonexistent to more stringent than those in the United States. In fact, the importance of workplace safety varies significantly among different countries.[41] Also, health care facilities across the globe show wide diversity in their state of modernization.

Other considerations specific to global assignments are emergency evacuation services and global security protection. Often, the means of evacuating and caring for injured employees is done through private companies. Also, employees and their families living abroad must constantly be aware of security issues. Many firms even provide bodyguards who escort executives everywhere. Some firms have disaster plans for evacuating expatriates if natural disasters, civil conflicts, or wars occur.

GLOBAL EMPLOYEE AND LABOR RELATIONS

Although unionism abroad seems to have a much brighter future than domestic unionism, it is not as positive as it was even in the mid-1990s. According to economist Richard Freeman, unionism has declined in some countries, but no country had the same consistently abrupt drop experienced by U.S. unions. Whereas unionism has waned in the United States, it has maintained much of its strength abroad. Even though unions in all countries have been under increasing pressure in recent decades because of slowing productivity, lower economic growth, rapid technological changes, and a shift toward a free market system, unionism in the United States has suffered the most.[42]

In the United States, the rate of unionism is 14.5 percent; in Sweden, the rate is 96 percent; it is 50 percent in the United Kingdom, 43 percent in Germany, 36 percent in Canada, and 28 percent in Japan and France.[43] Although the overseas rates appear impressive, as free market systems spread throughout the world the strength of unions overseas will likely continue to decline. Although foreign unions are generally less adversarial with management, and less focused on wage gains, globalization is a major threat to wage gains worldwide. This was definitely the situation when Mercedes-Benz dealt with Germany union inflexibility. When Mercedes-Benz decided to reinvent itself, the company decided to do it without union restrictions and subsequently went global.[44] The tide of union membership overseas may well be on a downturn, but unions are still quite influential around the globe. For this reason, human resource policies and practices must be geared to deal with the global differences in collective bargaining.

Obviously, the strength and nature of unions differ from country to country, with unions being nonexistent to relatively strong. Some countries, like Germany, even require firms to have union or worker representatives on their boards of directors. This practice is very common in European countries, where it is called co-determination. As a result, many European firms, like Mercedes-Benz, move operations to the United States, which provides certain advantages, or to other countries that have less restrictive employment practices, higher productivity rates, or lower wage rates. Even facing global competition, unions in several European countries have resisted changing their laws and removing government protections.

The creation of the North American Free Trade Agreement (NAFTA) among Canada, Mexico, and the United States facilitated the movement of goods across boundaries within North America. Labor relations took a major step forward with a *side agreement* on labor designed to protect workers in all three countries from the effects of competitive economic pressures. NAFTA established a Commission for Labor Cooperation with offices in each country; it is governed by a council made up of labor ministers of Canada, Mexico, and the United States. Each country is accountable for complying with its *own* labor laws dealing with occupational safety and health; child labor; migrant workers; human resource development; labor statistics; work benefits; social programs for workers; productivity improvements; labor-management relations; employment standards; the equality of men and women in the workplace; and forms of cooperation among workers, management, and government. A country that consistently fails to enforce its own labor laws could be fined up to $20 million per violation; if the offending nation is either the United States or Mexico, trade sanctions could be imposed between those two countries. There are also a number of principles identifying broad areas of common agreement to protect the rights and interest of each workforce.[45]

Possible Barriers to Effective Global Human Resource Management

Regardless of the organization's location, effectively performing the five functions of global human resource management is necessary if the company is to overcome certain global barriers. These blocks must be hurdled if the firm is to maximize global productivity.

To a great extent, domestic companies deal with a relatively known set of political, cultural, economic, legal, and labor-management relations variables. U.S. politics basically ranges from liberal to conservative within a capitalist society. Although cultural and ethnic differences exist in the United States, various accepted values mediate the impact of otherwise keen cultural differences in the workplace. Basically, labor-management relations are also guided by federal laws. This legislation provides a basic legal framework and a fairly predictable set of legal guidelines regarding areas such as employment discrimination, labor relations, safety, health, and other workplace issues.

Unfortunately, a global organization must cope with a multitude of unknowns. The management of HR functions globally is enormously complicated by the need to adapt HR policies and practices to different host countries. HR management must consider the potential impact of global differences on human resources. Differences in politics, law, culture, economics, labor-management relations systems, and other factors complicate the task of global human resource management. Figure 17-3 illustrates some of the possible barriers to effective global management.

POLITICAL AND LEGAL FACTORS

The nature and stability of political and legal systems vary throughout the globe. U.S. firms enjoy a relatively stable political and legal system. The same is true in many of the other developed countries, particularly in Europe. In other nations, however, the political and legal systems are much more unstable. Some governments are subject to coups, dictatorial rule, and corruption, and these can substantially alter the business as well as the legal environment. Legal systems can also become unstable, with contracts suddenly being unenforceable because of internal politics. Also, because of restrictions imposed on U.S.-based firms by the Foreign Corrupt Practices Act, a gray area exists between paying legal agency fees and bribery, which is illegal.

Additionally, HR regulations and laws vary greatly among countries. In many western European countries, laws addressing labor unions and employment make it difficult for a company to reduce the number of its

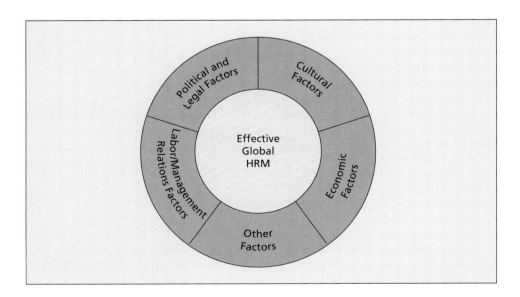

Figure 17-3
Barriers to Effective
Global Human Resource
Management

workers. Equal employment legislation and sexual harassment laws exist to varying degrees, but they often differ significantly from U.S. laws and regulations. In other countries, religious or ethical differences make employment discrimination an acceptable practice. Because of political and legal differences, it is essential that a comprehensive review of the political and legal environment of the host country be conducted prior to beginning global operations.

Americans may encounter laws that are routinely ignored, creating a dilemma. As *60 Minutes* and *Dateline NBC* discovered, the laws in some countries that require a minimum age for factory workers are not enforced. Such practices are fairly common in countries such as Bangladesh, China, Pakistan, Brazil, India, Indonesia, Kenya, and the Philippines. According to a United Nations agency, the International Labor Organization (ILO), the number of children performing jobs instead of attending school is increasing throughout the world, both in absolute terms and as a proportion of the world's children. Basically, competitive pressures led individual countries to ignore their own laws on the minimum working age, even in hazardous industries, such as the manufacture of fireworks and glassware. Regardless of local laws, some countries in the global economy are clearly promoting child labor.[46]

Cultural Factors

Cultural influences vary from country to country, with corresponding differences in human resource practices. For example, the cultural norms of Asia promote loyalty and teamwork in typical Japanese workers and influence how these people work. Japanese workers often expect lifetime employment in return for unquestioned loyalty. In Japan, the focus is on the work group; in the United States the focus is still on the individual. Obviously, such cultural differences have specific human resource implications. Employment practices must be adapted to local cultural norms, and therefore most human resource staff members in a foreign subsidiary should be drawn from host-country nationals. Think of the many cultural differences that would exist in moving from Long Island to Hong Kong.

However, just because certain cultural norms are restrictive does not mean that an attempt at change should not be made. In Japan, women rarely rise above the secretarial ranks, but that practice did not deter David Hoff, director of international resources for Anheuser-Busch. According to Hoff, Anheuser-Busch recruited women in Asia for its joint venture and discovered that Asian women are particularly effective in sales.[47] Also, Bank of America discovered that Japanese male employees opened up and shared their problems more readily with women, even expatriate women.[48] It is extremely important to preserve the desired corporate culture. Companies must bring in a critical mass of expatriates who carry the culture with them, and always leave one or two behind to oversee locals and ensure that they are following corporate policies. The key is to accommodate local cultures while maintaining the critical nature of the corporate culture.[49]

ECONOMIC FACTORS

Differences in economic systems must also be thoroughly investigated. In a capitalist system, the overwhelming need for efficiency encourages human resource policies and practices that emphasize productivity. In a socialist system, human resource practices favor the prevention of unemployment, often at the expense of productivity and efficiency. In a competitive global economy, the results of this approach are ultimately unacceptable. Perhaps this reality explains why the countries in the world that embrace socialism are declining in number.

The impact of economic factors on pending global operations must be fully understood and accounted for before human resource policies and practices can be developed. Probably one of the greatest economic factors is the difference in labor costs between the host country and the home country. Such variations could produce real differences in human resource policies and practices. Higher labor costs would likely encourage a firm to recruit and select more highly skilled employees and emphasize efficiency. Lower wage rates might result in a workforce that required more extensive training and development activities simply to ensure acceptable productivity levels. Evidently, the latter course did not work for Boundless when they moved from Long Island to Hong Kong. Lower wages did not offset the result of lower productivity in their case. The same result has been experienced in other countries. Even though wages may be much lower than in the home country, some companies have discovered that performance is 40 percent or even 30 percent of the U.S. norm.[50]

LABOR-MANAGEMENT RELATIONS FACTORS

The relationship among workers, unions, and employers varies dramatically from country to country and obviously has an enormous impact on human resource management practices. In Germany, for instance, co-determination is the rule, with employees having a legal right to influence company policies. In that country, worker representatives serve on the employer's supervisory board, and there is also a vice president representing labor. In other countries, the relations between employers and unions are not interfered with. In the United States, HR policies on most matters involving compensation and benefits are determined by the employer—at times with the intervention of labor unions. Various laws basically determine the nature of HR policies in many German firms.[51] A recent trend has companies like General Electric (GE), Volkswagen, and Volvo attempting international bargaining that would require companies to adopt a global code of conduct. This global code of conduct would protect the rights of all employees globally and lay the groundwork for global collective bargaining and global organizing.[52]

OTHER BARRIERS

Other factors that could be barriers to developing the most effective HR system include language barriers, the preference for individualism or collectivism, power distance variations, masculinity versus femininity, long-term versus short-term orientations and other country-to-country differences.

Equal Employment Opportunity and Global Human Resources

The global assignment of women and members of racial/ethnic minorities can involve legal issues, as these individuals may be protected by Equal Employment Opportunity (EEO) regulations. Many U.S. firms operating internationally have limited assignments of women and other members of protected groups because of cultural concerns. In a case brought by a Lebanese-American working in Saudi Arabia who was fired by Aramco Oil Company, the U.S. Supreme Court ruled that the EEO regulations of Title VII did not cover U.S. employees working for U.S. firms globally.[53]

The Civil Rights Act of 1991, however, overturned this decision and extended coverage of EEO laws and regulations to U.S. citizens working internationally for U.S. controlled companies. However, the act also states that if laws in a foreign country require actions that conflict with U.S. equal employment opportunity laws, the foreign laws will apply. If no laws exist—only customs or cultural considerations—then the U.S. EEO laws apply. Note also that most equal employment opportunity regulations and laws apply to foreign-owned firms operating in the United States. In most cases regarding equal employment opportunity, the courts have treated foreign-owned firms just as they would firms owned by U.S. citizens.

If a universal model existed for equal employment opportunity (EEO), it would probably be the Swedish model. In Sweden, equal employment opportunity is fundamentally concerned with the ability of each individual to achieve economic independence through gainful employment. This means that it must be possible for everybody, regardless of gender, to develop and participate in work according to his or her own abilities. The high demand for labor in the 1960s and 1970s resulted in substantial job gains for women. Political action gave separate taxation for husbands and wives, and amendments to matrimonial legislation clearly uphold the economic independence of all adults. Finally, with the expansion of child care facilities and parental benefits, gainful employment and parenthood are fully possible, greatly benefiting women. All these conditions were formalized with the creation of the Equal Opportunities Committee, to implement the Equal Opportunities Act that guarantees equality of the sexes. Additionally, the Office of Equal Opportunities Ombudsman is an independent agency that can order an employer to take measures to promote equality between the sexes.[54] Swedish equal employment opportunity may truly be the global model to be emulated elsewhere.

Eight Keys to Global Human Resource Management of Expatriates

The decision to enter foreign markets has profound implications on human resources, particularly when expatriates are used. Assigning and managing U.S. employees outside the United States is a complex and sometimes

HRM IN ACTION
WOMEN IN THE MIDDLE EAST!

"Stan, I know you are concerned with the ramifications we could suffer if women aren't fast-tracked into management positions overseas, but I would like you to reconsider your decision to put three women on the six-person management review team that will oversee our Middle Eastern production facility. As most of our Mideast employees are male host-country nationals sending women there could cause unnecessary problems. Instead, we could assign these women to the review team going to Britain next month, OK?"

How should Stan respond?

overwhelming task. Global human resource management of expatriates can be made simpler and more manageable by following eight steps, which are general guidelines for developing an expatriate workforce.

First, everyone involved must completely understand the global business plan. This knowledge will make it easier to determine how existing human resources policies can be adapted to accomplish global objectives.

Second, the company's foreign service policy should be a set of guidelines, not rigid rules, for relocating employees and their families around the world while maintaining the domestic corporate culture.

Third, a global budget process should be developed so the overall cost of each expatriate global assignment can be estimated. This cost represents enormous investments and should be carefully considered to determine whether expatriates or host-country or third-country nationals should be used.

Fourth, the candidate and his or her family should be profiled to determine whether he or she might be an effective selection for a global assignment. Often, an entire family, not just an employee, must be considered in this determination.

Fifth, the terms and conditions of the global assignment should be clearly stated up front. Expatriates should be given both a verbal and written presentation of the terms and conditions of the assignment to ensure that they completely understand both the benefits and responsibilities of the assignment.

Sixth, expatriates and their families must be prepared for relocation with departure orientation and training. This should include language training, cultural training, and a general orientation to everyday living and local customs.

Seventh, a continual development process must be designed and implemented to take advantage of the employee's global experiences. This will include career planning as well as home-country development during the global assignment period.

Eighth, returning expatriates and their families must receive repatriation orientation training, as discussed earlier in the chapter.

Unfortunately, according to David Hoff, Anheuser-Busch's director of international resources, "The cost of expatriates is enormous." Hoff recommends that as a long-term strategy, companies need alternatives, such as hiring foreign nationals, developing their talents in the United States, and reassigning them abroad as local managers.[55] This may be an effective long-term solution, but expatriates will probably always be used to some degree overseas, if for no other reason than to maintain ties with the home country.

Maintaining Corporate Identity through Corporate Culture

Maintaining an effective corporate culture that reflects the culture of the home country is essential for continuity worldwide; achieving this often requires innovative insight. When a U.S. company hires too many local people in its foreign offices, it risks losing the unique set of values and operating procedures that define its corporate culture. According to Bill Fontana, a veteran of many foreign assignments for Citibank and now vice president of NFTC, "If you rely too heavily on locals, you're going to have a local culture, not the corporate culture you want. . . . And the local culture may be totally foreign to the way you operate." To ensure a parallel corporate culture, firms should bring in a critical mass of expatriates who carry the culture with them at the beginning of the start-up. Also critical is for global corporations to leave at least one or two expatriates behind to oversee the locals and ensure that they are following corporate policies."[56]

Often, a global U.S. corporation forms an alliance with a company in the host country. In such situations, the corporate cultures and management styles of the partners must be blended together as quickly as possible.[57] Long-term success means having a corporate culture that supports the goals of the global organization and effectively deals with the international business environment. As a firm becomes more and more global in nature, having a supportive corporate culture becomes more difficult. Alliances are useful for all partners because collaboration makes possible sharing the costs and risks of doing business. It enables companies to share financial resources, technology, production facilities, marketing expertise, and, of course, human resources. However, problems may occur in international alliances when people from different organizations and national cultures work together.[58]

Regardless of whether an alliance exists, the corporate culture must focus on making a profit. Global firms must strive to achieve a corporate culture that effectively copes with the global environment and at the same time is profitable. Although it may be impossible to achieve, the ideal corporate culture of global corporations will closely parallel that of the home country.

Keeping Up Globally with Human Resources

Human resource managers must follow trends toward globalization while still accommodating local needs. Global human resource demands will be greater than domestic demands alone. For instance, global human resources may require paychecks to be cut in different currencies and often requires the adherence to regulations of multiple taxing agencies. Also, certain practices must be consistent across the company whereas others must change to accommodate local customs and norms. Human resource departments must often redesign their operations to keep up with globalization. As globalization becomes a reality, human resources must adapt domestic methods and procedures to accommodate global operations. Realistically, successfully managing human resources on a global level must be done with new technology, such as client/server computing, supernetworks, and groupware as well as a comprehensive awareness by human resource professionals of the new human resource demands of globalization.[59]

A GLOBAL PERSPECTIVE

The Battle Cry: Preparation, Preparation, Preparation, and Watch the Dog

Most managers and employees think domestically in that they are guided mostly by their domestic environment, understanding their own cultures and certain aspects of the cultures of others they work with. Additionally, U.S. laws are fairly well defined and understood by most, and employees are cognizant of the nature of prejudices and problems that occur in the domestic workplace. Even the nature of right and wrong is usually fairly straightforward, not that everyone follows the ethical outline. However, ethics is often fairly well defined in most companies and understood by most managers and employees. Further enhancing domestic effectiveness is that, for the most part, the English language is understood and embraced by most U.S. employees. Such things are fairly well understood by most U.S. managers and employees, which allows them to focus on enhancing productivity and adding value to organizations. However, when going global, all these things that come so naturally can no longer be taken for granted. Preparation, preparation, preparation is the battle cry for those who intend to go overseas and perform well. Also, not only the individual but also the employee's family must be prepared to cope with a global assignment.

Preparation is essential for the employee and his or her family. Expatriates and their families must be prepared to have their personal rights curtailed due to cultural differences. Global orientations must consider international differences and prepare everyone involved for a stressful situation. Expatriates and their families must be prepared to deal with the norms, values, goals, and objectives of the host country. For instance, an American expatriate and his family went to a restaurant in Indonesia with their pet dog. "The restaurant manager politely greeted them at the door, took their dog and, 30 minutes later—much to the family's horror—served it to them."[60]

This example might seem outrageous, but the failure to prepare expatriates and their families properly make such occurrences all too commonplace overseas. Companies should also give overseas employees and their families language training, cultural training, and a general orientation to everyday living in the host country, such as information about schools, banks, and shopping. For the expatriate, an introduction should include an overview of the history, traditions, and corporate values of partners, if any. Then it should include a description of the new venture, its organization, and its management structure, followed by an introduction of the employee to the manager, department, and co-workers.

Professional skills and job qualifications are important, but without adequate preparation, failure or less success is likely overseas. International success requires preparing employees to deal with the social context of their jobs and cope with the insecurities and frustrations of a new global work situation. To ensure an effective expatriate, the right person must be selected, the employee and the employee's family must be properly prepared, and everyone transferred must understand and be ready to cope with differences in culture, communication, and language. A repatriation plan must be developed to ease the reentry of the employee and the family back to the United States. ■

SUMMARY

1. *Describe the evolution of global business.*

   Most companies initially become global without making substantial investments in foreign countries, by either exporting, licensing, or franchising. A multinational corporation (MNC) is a firm that is based in one country (the parent or home country) and produces goods or provides services in one or more foreign countries (host countries). A global corporation (GC) has corporate units in a number of countries; these units are integrated to operate as one organization worldwide.

2. *Explain the goal of global human resource management.*

   The role of the global human resource executive is focused on being a strategic business partner and decision maker. Any human resource initiative must be based on maximizing productivity to best benefit the company's bottom line; therefore, a solid understanding of the total global system is essential for these executives.

3. *Identify the global human resource management functions.*

   The functions are global human resource planning, recruitment, and selection; global human resource development; global compensation and benefits; global safety and health; and global employee and labor relations.

4. *Differentiate among expatriates, host-country nationals, and third-country nationals.*

   An expatriate is an employee working in a firm who is not a citizen of the country in which the firm is located but is a citizen of the country in which the organization is headquartered. A host-country national (HCN) is an employee working in a firm who is a citizen of the country in which the firm is located, but the firm is operated by an organization headquartered in another country. A third-country national (TCN) is a citizen of one country, working in a second country, and employed by an organization headquartered in a third country.

5. *Identify possible barriers to effective global human resource management.*
   Possible barriers include political and legal factors, cultural factors, economic factors, and labor/management relations factors.

6. *Explain Equal Employment Opportunity (EEO) and global human resource management.*
   The global assignment of women and members of racial/ethnic minorities can involve legal issues, as these individuals may be protected by Equal Employment Opportunity (EEO) regulations. The Civil Rights Act of 1991 extended coverage of equal employment opportunity laws and regulations to U.S. citizens working internationally for U.S.-controlled companies. The act also states that if laws in a foreign country require actions that conflict with U.S. equal employment opportunity laws, the foreign laws will apply. If no laws exist—only customs or cultural considerations—then U.S. equal employment opportunity laws apply.

QUESTIONS FOR REVIEW

1. Describe the evolution of global business.
2. Describe the evolution of global human resource management.
3. What is global productivity?
4. What are the five functional areas associated with effective global human resource management? Discuss each.
5. Explain the expatriate development program.
6. Explain the general makeup of an expatriate compensation package.
7. What are the possible barriers to effective global human resource management?
8. Describe equal employment opportunity (EEO) and global human resource management.
9. What are the keys to global human resource management of expatriates?

DEVELOPING HRM SKILLS

AN EXPERIENTIAL EXERCISE
After studying this textbook, students should have a much better appreciation of the type of work human resource managers are involved in. In this exercise, participants will attempt to develop a profile of the attributes a human resource manager should possess. Knowledge gained throughout the course should be used in identifying necessary attributes. The result of this exercise should be a realistic profile of what attributes an effective human resource manager should have.

Take It to the Net

We invite you to visit the Mondy home page on the Prentice Hall Web site at:

http://www.prenhall.com/mondy

for updated information, Web-based exercises, and links to other HR-related sites.

HRM SIMULATION

*E*stablishing successful strategies is important for all firms, but doing so is especially crucial for global organizations. You have been informed by your CEO that your company is going global. You will determine how your strategies change as you move into a global environment.

HRM INCIDENT 1

Preparation for an Expatriate Assignment

"*H*i Sam, how are the preparations going for your assignment in Japan?"

"Well, Elvis, I really feel prepared for the assignment, and the high level of apprehension I first experienced is gone."

"What exactly did the preparation program involve, Sam?"

"The experience was really exhaustive. First, I spent a good deal of time in a comprehensive orientation and training program. The program covered familiarization with the language, culture, history, living conditions, and local customs of Japan. Then, to make the transition home easier and better for my career, I have developed a plan with my boss that includes several trips back here to remain a key part of this operation. Also, my career development training will include the same training as the other managers in the home office. Finally, I was completely briefed on repatriation orientation and training that I would experience when I returned. I was fully briefed on the compensation package, which appears to be fairly generous."

"That's great, Sam; have you found a place to live?"

"Not yet, Elvis, but my wife and children are leaving in three days to meet with the company's relocation person to consider the various possibilities."

"How did the family like the orientation training, Sam?"

"Well, my wife ordered some Japanese language tapes and I think she read all the information that was covered in the class. She and the children will be fine because they have time to adapt; they don't have to hit the ground running like I do."

Questions

1. Do you believe that Sam's family is adequately prepared for the move to Japan?

2. Should the company's orientation program have included training for Sam's family?
3. Is repatriation orientation and training necessary for Sam's family upon their return to the United States?

HRM INCIDENT 2

No Host-Country Nations in This Russian Subsidiary

"*B*ob, I just reviewed the global staffing plan and there must be a mistake; the plan requires a 100 percent expatriate workforce, including the staff, legal, and marketing areas. The technical people are also all expatriates, but that did not surprise me as much."

"I know, Robert; I was also surprised when I first reviewed the plan, but when I inquired, I was told that because we would be involved in the creation of a wireless communication system in Russia, based on our super-secret technology, no outsiders are allowed."

"Well, Bob, I understand that the pirating of intellectual property is fairly common overseas, but we can protect our technical secrets and still have a support staff of host-country nationals in our Russian subsidiary."

"I understand your apprehension, Robert, but the decision has been made; let's get ready to go global."

As Robert walked back to his office, he thought, "This is a big mistake."

Questions
1. Why does Robert believe that excluding host-country nationals from the staff in Russia is a big mistake?
2. Do you believe that secrecy could have been maintained even with a staff of Russian nationals?

Notes

1. This is an adaptation of the actual experiences of Boundless Technologies. Paul Krugman, "Lower Wages Weren't Enough to Keep U.S. Company Abroad," *USA Today* (June 16, 1997): 19A.
2. David E. Molnar, "Global Assignments: Seven Keys to International HR Management," *HR Focus* 74 (May 1997): 9.
3. Mike Fergus, "Employees on the Move," *HRMagazine* 36 (May 1990): 44.
4. Max Messmer, "How to Keep Competition from Backfiring," *HR Focus* 71 (June 1994): 23–24.
5. James W. Down, "HR Research: A Strategic Model Emerges," *HR Focus* 74 (June 1997): 11.
6. Mike Johnson, "The 'New Europe' Redefines HR," *HR Focus* 72 (August 1995): 12–14.
7. John F. Hohnson, "HR Career: The 21st-Century HR Executive," *HR Focus* 74 (April 1997): 5.

8. Elizabeth Connor, "Will Our Human Resources Measure Up?" *HR Focus* 72 (October 1995): 22.

9. Stephenie Overman, "Is HR a Weak Link in the Global Chain?" *HRMagazine* 38 (June, 1994): 67–68.

10. Michael J. Lotito, "A Call to Action for U.S. Business and Education," *Employment Relations Today* (Winter 1992/1993): 379–387.

11. Karen Mailliard, "Case Study: Linking Performance to the Bottom Line," *HR Focus* 74 (June 1997): 8.

12. Ibid.

13. Row Henson, "HRIMS for Dummies: A Practical Guide to Technology Implementation," *HR Focus* 73 (November 1996): 3–6.

14. Donald J. McNerney, "Global Staffing: Some Common Problems—And Solutions," *HR Focus* 73 (June 1996): 1–5.

15. "The Shortage of Global Managers," *Issues in HR* (March/April 1995): 3.

16. "Study of Global Sourcing and Selection Finds Troubling Rate of Assignment Failure," *International HR Update* (March 1996): 6.

17. McNerney, "Global Staffing: Some Common Problems—And Solutions."

18. Molnar, "Global Assignments: Seven Keys to International HR Management."

19. Charlene M. Soloman, "Learning to Manage Host-Country Nationals," *Personnel Journal* 74 (March 1995): 60–67.

20. Charlene M. Soloman, "Success Abroad Depends on More than Job Skills," *Personnel Journal* 73 (April 1994): 51–59.

21. David Lawder, "Mercedes Mulls Expansion of U.S. Assembly Plant," *Reuters Business Report* (May 22, 1997): 1.

22. Ibid.

23. McNerney, "Global Staffing: Some Common Problems—And Solutions."

24. Connor, "Will Our Human Resources Measure Up?"

25. Johnson, "The 'New Europe' Redefines HR."

26. Connor, "Will Our Human Resources Measure Up?"

27. Ibid.

28. Donald W. Nauss, "It's Fun, It's Useful, It's a Mercedes?" *Los Angeles Times* (May 18, 1997): A-1.

29. Clifford C. Hebard, "Managing Effectively in Asia," *Training & Development* (April 1996): 34.

30. Ibid.

31. Maddy Janssens, "Evaluating International Managers' Performance: Parent Company Standards as Control Mechanism," *The International Journal of Human Resource Management* (December 1994): 853–873; Diane Arthur, "Performance Appraisals: Face-to-Face with the Employee," *HR Focus* 73 (March 1996): 17–19.

32. Shirley Fishman, "Developing a Global Workforce," *Canadian Business Review* 23 (April 1996): 18.

33. Mark E. Mendelhall and Carolyn Wiley, "Strangers in a Strange Land: The Relationship between Expatriate Adjustment and Impression Management," *American Behavioral Scientist* (March/April 1994): 605–621.

34. Nauss, "It's Fun, It's Useful, It's a Mercedes."

35. Lawder, "Mercedes Mulls Expansion of U.S. Assembly Plant."

36. Ibid.

37. McNerney, "Global Staffing: Some Common Problems—And Solutions."

38. Ibid.

39. Bent M. Longnecker and Wendy Powell, "Executive Compensation in a Global Market," *Benefits & Compensation Solutions* (April 1996): 40–43.

40. M. Janssens, J. M. Brett, and F. J. Smith, "Confirmatory Cross-Cultural Research Testing the Viability of a Corporation-Wide Safety Policy," *Academy of Management Journal* 38 (June 1995): 364–380.

41. R. B. Palchak and R. T. Schmidt, "Protecting the Health of Employees Abroad," *Occupational Health & Safety* (February 1996): 53–56.

42. James Worsham, "Labor Comes Alive," *Nation's Business* 84 (February 1996): 16.

43. M. E. Sharpe, "Labor's Future," *Challenge* 39 (March 1996): 65.

44. Lawder, "Mercedes Mulls Expansion of U.S. Assembly Plant."

45. NAFTA Supplemental Agreements, Annex 1 (Washington, DC: U.S. Government Printing Office, 1993).

46. Robert A. Senser, "Danger! Children at Work," *Commonwealth* (August 19, 1994): 12–15.

47. Hebard, "Managing Effectively in Asia."

48. Ibid.

49. McNerney, "Global Staffing: Some Common Problems—And Solutions."

50. Paul Krugman, "Lower Wages Weren't Enough to Keep U.S. Company Abroad," *USA Today* (June 16, 1997): 19A.

51. Christopher-Friedland Erickson, "Book Reviews: Labor Management Relations," *Industrial & Labor Relations* (January 1996): 356.

52. David Moberg, "Labor: GE Workers' Union Tests International Bargaining," *International Press Service English News Wire* (June 28, 1997).

53. *EEOC and Boureslan v Aramco*, 111 Section 1227 (1991).

54. Swedish Institute, Sweden: "Equality between Men and Women in Sweden," *Countries of the World* (January 1991).

55. Hebard, "Managing Effectively in Asia," 34.

56. McNerney, "Global Staffing: Some Common Problems—and Solutions."

57. Wayne F. Cascio and Manuel G. Serapio, Jr., "HR Systems in an International Alliance: The Undoing of a Done Deal?" *Organizational Dynamics* 19 (Winter 1991): 65.

58. Ibid.

59. Row Henson, "Globalization: A Human Resources Mandate," *SoftBase* (March 3, 1996): 62–64.

60. David Cherrington and Laura Middleton, "An Introduction to Global Business Issues," *HRMagazine* 40 (June 1995): 124.

ABCNEWS | VIDEO CASE

Images of Japan

Some individuals think of Japan as an economic monster that plans to take over American manufacturing and relegate our country to second-class status. This feeling has intensified since the collapse of the Soviet Union. Without a major global military threat, attention has focused on Japanese economic power. In the late 1980s and early 1990s, American industry got sloppy while their Japanese counterparts improved. The fairness of Japan's fair trade practices were, and remain, a concern. These factors further increased the tension felt by the American public.

In more recent years, as the quality and productivity of American businesses improved and as the Japanese suffered through an economic recession, fears of Japanese supremacy have subsided. Polls of American attitudes reveal a significant shift in a relatively short period of time. For example, an ABC poll revealed that a majority of participants did not view Japan as a threat to our country. One expert stated flatly, "The idea of Japan as a threat is gone, is finished."

One interesting view of Japanese-American relations is that the competitiveness of Japanese industry has really done our business organizations a favor. It has stimulated our own competitiveness and increased the quality of many of our products; especially those in the auto and electronic industries.

Rather than view Japan as an opponent, it has been suggested that it would be wise to realize that we are partners in world activity. Our countries are too interdependent economically and otherwise to be continuously combative. This approach gains credibility as China increases its stature as a world power.

DISCUSSION QUESTIONS

1. Does Japan continue to threaten the health of American industry? Explain your answer.
2. Explain why you think Japanese industry is more productive (or less productive) than our own?
3. What Japanese attributes do Americans admire most?
4. Describe the impact that Japanese business successes have had on American firms. How has this affected the practice of human resource management in our country?

Source: "Images of Japan," *Nightline*, ABC News; aired on April 15, 1996.

INTEGRATIVE VIDEO CASE

This is the first of eight cases in this book. These cases explore a variety of management-related issues at Showtime Networks Inc., a premium television network company. This installment is designed to be a general introduction. You may want to refer to it when you are studying the cases that follow.

Part One—Introduction

WELCOME TO SHOWTIME NETWORKS

In the high-stakes world of cable television, the stars behind the scenes are the managers and employees whose work and dedication are essential ingredients in any successful business strategy. Consider the corporate cast at Showtime Networks Inc. (SNI), the second largest premium television network company in the United States. SNI is a wholly-owned subsidiary of Viacom, a $13 billion media giant that also owns MTV, Nickelodeon, VH1, and Paramount Pictures.

Matt Blank, chairman and chief executive officer, joined SNI in 1988 after 12 years at rival HBO; he was named to the top position in 1995. Working with a talented team of top managers, Blank is responsible for SNI's broad array of program services.

Among SNI's offerings are the premium television networks Showtime, The Movie Channel (TMC), Flix, and Showtime en Español, an audio feed of Showtime for Spanish-speaking audiences. The company also operates Sundance Channel, a joint venture with Robert Redford and PolyGram Filmed Entertainment. In addition, the company has a distinct pay-per-view distribution service that creates, markets, and distributes sports and entertainment events.

COMPANY AND INDUSTRY BACKGROUND

SNI packages and distributes entertainment programs through its premium networks, which are offered to viewers on a subscription basis. Programs include theatrical movies, original pictures and series, championship boxing, and family entertainment. In addition to exhibiting theatrical releases from its sister division, Paramount Pictures, the company obtains exclusive premium television rights to theatrical movies from several leading motion picture studios and producers.

Together, Showtime and TMC account for almost 99 percent of SNI's premium-service revenues. Showtime, SNI's flagship brand, is an award-winning network. TMC, a supplementary movie service to Showtime, is typically sold to subscribers who already have at least two other premium networks.

The main distribution method for premium networks is through the cable industry, which delivers basic cable services to 64.9 million subscribers. Cable operators sell premium networks such as Showtime as an additional purchase over and above the cost of basic cable service. In total,

SNI's cable networks are purchased by about 18 million subscribers; in contrast, HBO's cable networks are purchased by about 40 million subscribers.

In the 1960s, television viewers had few choices. Cable was in its infancy, and three television networks ruled the airwaves. These days, viewers enjoy dozens of television-viewing choices as well as many other entertainment options. Consumers are spending more than ever on media and entertainment, but the increase in spending is much lower than in the past. At the same time, networks have been feeling the pinch of higher costs since a third premium network, Starz, joined the premium category, competing with HBO and SNI for the rights to first-run movies and movies in film libraries.

HUMAN RESOURCES AT SNI

Human resource management plays a critical role in SNI's overall strategy. By applying HRM techniques, SNI has assembled an excellent workforce led by skilled top managers including: Jerry Offsay, President, SNI Programming; Gwen Marcus, Executive Vice President, General Counsel and Administration; Jerry Cooper, Executive Vice President, Finance and Operations; Len Fogge, Executive Vice President, Creative/Marketing Services; Jeff Wade, Executive Vice President, Sales and Affiliate Marketing; and Mark Greenberg, Executive Vice President, Corporate Marketing and Communications.

The SNI continuing video case showcases a multitude of human resource considerations, including corporate culture, workforce diversity, HR's role in strategic planning, team building, compensation and benefits, safety and health, employee and labor relations, and global expansion.

Source: This case was prepared by Prof. dt ogilvie, Rutgers University, for purposes of class discussion, based on interviews and materials provided by Showtime Networks Inc.

INTEGRATIVE VIDEO CASE

This is the second case in this book that explores a variety of management-related issues at Showtime Networks Inc., a premium television network company. You may want to refer to the Introduction when studying the case that follows.

Part Two—The Environment of HRM, Legal Aspects of HRM, and Job Analysis

THE HR ENVIRONMENT AT SNI

Showtime Networks, like all organizations, operates within two complex and ever-changing environments that exert pressure on human resource management. In SNI's external environment, key factors include competition and workforce diversity. In SNI's internal environment, key factors include the corporate culture. The interaction of these environmental factors complicates the management of human resources—and, ultimately, affects SNI's overall organizational productivity and performance.

SNI'S COMPETITIVE SITUATION

Competition is fierce among the premium networks. HBO, the first premium cable network, remains the industry leader with the largest share of the premium category. Future growth in the cable industry is projected at a minimal one percent per year, even though 25 percent of all households with television sets do not subscribe to cable. Therefore, the networks can gain share only at the expense of rivals.

SNI and other premium networks are sold through cable operators, who have considerable bargaining power because they are typically the only distributors of wired cable television service in certain communities. Cable operators control marketing, pricing, and distribution in their franchise areas, so they can pit the premium networks against each other. In this competitive situation, SNI would be at a disadvantage, for example, if a cable operator priced HBO lower than Showtime or offered Showtime only to customers who also purchase HBO.

SNI'S CORPORATE CULTURE

As SNI's top executives describe the corporate culture, a picture emerges of a hard-driving, multi-faceted organization. Nat Fuchs, Vice President of Human Resources Development, says, "Our culture is dynamic, aggressive, and changing. People are extremely proud of what they're doing; we have an edgy humor and we value flexibility."

Cultural fit is very important at SNI, observes Ray Gutierrez, Senior Vice President of Human Resources and Administration. "Our people have a sense of ownership and a responsibility to 'make it work,'" he says. "If you can't, you shouldn't be here. There's no time to waste, but if some people flounder, others offer help."

SNI's culture definitely encourages individuality, says Mark Greenberg, Executive Vice President, Corporate Marketing and Communications. Yet collaboration and teamwork are also highly prized, stresses Gwen Marcus, Executive Vice President, General Counsel and Administration. "We are a family," she says. "This is a home-away-from-home, and we hire people who are fun, informal, and funny—people who work hard and play hard."

Chairman and CEO Matt Blank sets the tone for SNI's corporate culture by encouraging creativity and rational risk-taking. As he notes, "We reward creativity when we see it, but in a competitive industry in which every mistake can be said to affect the bottom line, there is little room for failure."

WORKFORCE DIVERSITY

Workforce diversity is one of SNI's top strategic priorities. Top management believes in diversity because it is consistent with SNI's ethical values; it supports the firm's business objectives; it adds new viewpoints; and it is a strong defense against groupthink.

A committee of SNI executives worked with an outside expert to design an internal study covering diversity, management style, and other elements. Building on this research, the committee developed a diversity initiative encompassing differences in race, age, gender, sexual orientation, physical and mental capabilities, and family situation.

Gwen Marcus, Executive Vice President, General Counsel and Administration, recalls that at first, diversity in staffing raised red flags among people who thought it meant nothing more than "hiring people of color." Over time, however, that misperception was erased as people realized that SNI's commitment to diversity is not intended to promote preferential hiring on the basis of such factors of race, but rather that it addresses broader issues such as offering employee benefits programs like telecommuting, flexible work schedules, and similar work and family initiatives to accommodate the needs of a workforce with diverse backgrounds and lifestyles.

Over time, the organization learned to perceive diversity in terms of visible and invisible differences, and SNI emerged as a leader in workforce diversity. "We were the first in Viacom and in the industry to promote acceptance of alternate work arrangements and same-sex domestic arrangements," notes Nat Fuchs.

QUESTIONS

1. Describe SNI's corporate culture.

2. How did the corporate culture affect SNI's diversity initiative? Discuss.

Source: This case was prepared by Prof. dt ogilvie, Rutgers University, for purposes of class discussion, based on interviews and materials provided by Showtime Networks Inc.

INTEGRATIVE VIDEO CASE

This is the third case in this book that explores a variety of management-related issues at Showtime Networks Inc., a premium television network company. The first installment is a general introduction. You may want to refer to it when you are studying the case that follows.

Part Three—Human Resource Planning, Recruitment, and Selection

STRATEGIC PLANNING AT SNI

One of the first tasks Matt Blank undertook as Chairman and CEO of SNI was to set up a comprehensive strategic planning process to reevaluate the company's goals, direction, and structure. "We're in a highly competitive environment," he notes. "We can't dramatically increase prices or share. So I instituted a new set of goals and restructured Showtime organizationally, strategically, and in the executive area, essentially reengineered the company."

Mark Greenberg, Executive Vice President of Corporate Marketing and Communications, was in charge of the strategic planning process. He and all the top managers who directly report to the CEO participated by collecting and analyzing mountains of data about SNI's current situation, including pricing, ratings, packaging and so on. Rather than focusing exclusively on internal issues, the group broadened the inquiry to include the many external elements that could potentially affect SNI's future performance, including new entrants in the industry and innovative distribution alternatives.

After the executives came to agreement on SNI's overriding goals, they identified several areas for improvement, such as programming, branding, and sales force management. No area of the organization escaped scrutiny. The executive area was reengineered, overhead was reduced, marginal businesses were jettisoned, and a new strategic review process was put in place to reexamine strategy every 1 1/2 to 2 years.

For example, in the course of the strategic planning process, Blank realized that SNI's branding needed more work. "We get hurt when customers don't know where they saw a movie," Blank explains. "We found we were undefined as a product—we were nothing special. One critical strategic shift we made was to produce more original movies than any other premium network." This shift means that SNI now makes up to 40 original movies per year. As a result, SNI has been able to reduce its reliance on theatrical movies, which are more widely available (through pay-per-view TV and video rental) than ever before.

Another shift that occurred as a result of the strategic planning process was a decision to "grow as part of a category," says Blank. That's why SNI's goal is now to encourage subscribers to buy the entire Showtime package, not just one of SNI's branded channels.

INTEGRATING HUMAN RESOURCE PLANNING AT SNI

Human resources was an integral part of this two-year strategic planning process. Commenting on HRM's pivotal role, Ray Gutierrez, Senior Vice President of Human Resources and Administration, says: "We are partners with other line managers in developing strategic plans. Our goal in HR is to make sure we make optimum use of human resources. Everything is tied to the bottom line."

Linking human resource planning to the overall strategic planning process enables SNI to fill key positions with qualified managers. For example, the strategic review revealed that "our branding didn't look good," remembers Matt Blank. "I hired Len Fogge as creative director for advertising and on-air promotion. Prior to Len, there was no passion or feeling in our ads and test spots; Len gave us a whole new look for our product and services and for the company."

To support SNI's new strategic direction, Blank wants to "give employees license to believe in the company and product." He takes his message to the entire workforce by visiting every SNI office at least once a year and hosting company-wide videoconferences during the year. During these events, the CEO and his senior management team are on hand to answer employee questions and to honor the outstanding achievements of SNI employees and managers. In this way, the entire workforce is kept up-to-date on company news—and can feel pride in the contributions of those whose actions are recognized.

QUESTIONS

1. What role does human resource management play in the strategic planning process at SNI?
2. How can managers in human resources management use recruitment and selection to support the implementation of SNI's strategic goals?

Source: This case was prepared by Prof. dt ogilvie, Rutgers University, for purposes of class discussion, based on interviews and materials provided by Showtime Networks Inc.

INTEGRATIVE VIDEO CASE

This is the fourth case in this book that explores a variety of management-related issues at Showtime Networks Inc., a premium television network company. The first installment is a general introduction. You may want to refer to it when you are studying the case that follows.

Part Four—Human Resource Development

FIRST STEPS IN TEAMWORK AT SNI

In the race to become the leading premium network, one ongoing goal for SNI is to increase revenues. Jerry Cooper, Executive Vice President of Finance and Operations for SNI, was pursuing this goal when he implemented a new team structure for the finance and technology-oriented groups in the company. Using job analysis, he had found that no two employees were doing exactly the same job—and none were authorized to deal directly with SNI's customers, the cable operators.

In devising a new structure, Cooper created teams of employees (known as *rings*) responsible for both revenue and customers. Implementing the team structure meant changing internal processes, information systems, job descriptions, skill requirements, incentive compensation, corporate culture, and management systems. Cooper also developed performance measures backed by quarterly incentive programs and other rewards. These changes were designed to streamline and automate SNI's billing procedures so cable operators could easily calculate the amount to be paid every month, speeding payments.

To make the new team structure work, Cooper had to establish a higher level of competency. To earn a place on a team, employees would have to meet the new stricter criteria. Only about 25 percent actually met the criteria—but those who qualified were better positioned for new career paths.

Each team was empowered to select, hire, and evaluate its own members, with members subject to 360-degree feedback from peers and management. Team members exerted peer pressure to maintain performance levels, so the teams achieved higher productivity as well as higher satisfaction.

Cooper arranged for the teams to report up through the finance department, working simultaneously with SNI's regional sales operations. Forging closer relationships with sales cemented the department's new structure and supported the value-added dimension that Cooper was seeking to boost revenues.

COMPLETING THE MOVE TO TEAMS

Two years after most of the finance department was restructured into teams, Jerry Scro, the new Chief Financial Officer, restructured the remainder of the department into teams. He consolidated two arms of the organization—financial planning/budgeting and accounting—into one planning, budgeting, and accounting group.

He also created the position of financial business analyst and organized FBAs into self-directed work teams. These teams created their own work initiatives and used 360-degree feedback for performance appraisals. Clerical staff was eliminated in the new team structure as Scro (like Cooper) raised the competency requirements for team members.

During the transition to teams, SNI provided employees with appropriate training. For example, team members received training in conflict management so they could learn to resolve team problems. They also received cross-functional training in accounting and budgeting so they would have the skills to work on both accounting and financial planning projects.

Scro also set deadlines by which employees had to demonstrate that they had attained the new skill levels needed for teamwork. Employees received continuous feedback on their progress during the transition, and managers were careful to share information with the teams. In the end, more than half of the employees demonstrated the required skills.

The last group to be reorganized into teams was the accounts payable group, because most of the employees lacked the educational background and skills to become financial business analysts. In fact, only a handful of employees were able to meet the stricter team standards. So Scro filled out the teams with MBAs and CPAs who could work on a variety of projects for SNI's various business units. Because the teams were versatile and highly skilled, they achieved higher productivity and simultaneously reduced backlogs and errors—which, in turn, led to higher customer satisfaction.

Commenting on the effect of the new structure, Scro says: "We now have a finance department that is in partnership with the rest of company. They are part of the business decision-making process and an integral part of the programming department's financial decisions."

QUESTIONS

1. Why did SNI's financial business analysts need training to become effective team members?
2. What characteristics do you think are necessary for a team-based management system to work?

Source: This case was prepared by Prof. dt ogilvie, Rutgers University, for purposes of class discussion, based on interviews and materials provided by Showtime Networks Inc.

INTEGRATIVE VIDEO CASE

This is the fifth case in this book that explores a variety of management-related issues at Showtime Networks Inc., a premium television network company. The first installment is a general introduction. You may want to refer to it when you are studying the case that follows.

Part Five—Compensation and Benefits

THE ROLE OF NONFINANCIAL COMPENSATION AT SNI

The need for talented employees who could add new viewpoints and help SNI achieve its business objectives has prompted top management to institute a workforce diversity process. Ray Gutierrez, Senior Vice President of Human Resources and Administration, notes, "We keep expanding diversity as it plays into our business needs." For example, SNI was the first in the industry to offer same-sex life partner insurance programs, a commitment that earned the company the GLAAD (Gay Lesbian Alliance Against Defamation) Fairness Award in 1997.

Because SNI recruits people from all kinds of backgrounds and family situations, SNI managers had to consider a broad variety of employee needs when designing both nonfinancial and financial compensation. One of the first changes SNI's management considered was an alternative work arrangement (AWA) such as flextime or a compressed workweek. This approach would, for example, accommodate working parents who wanted a more flexible schedule because of child care responsibilities.

The idea of offering AWA to employees initially caused internal controversy. As a result, the company chose to experiment with a three-month AWA trial—which was judged a success. "We made AWA subject to business needs, therefore it worked," says Gwen Marcus, Executive Vice President, General Counsel and Administration.

Laurie Fett, SNI's Vice President of Compensation and Benefits, recognizes that AWA effectively allows employees to address a variety of needs, including child care, care of aging parents, and multiple career, education, or family obligations. Reinforcing Fett's views, Gwen Marcus observes that "one of my most talented staff members is our paralegal by day and a novelist by night. He came to a point where he needed either to work a compressed workweek or to quit SNI entirely. To retain the talents of a person like this, we accepted the change in hours, and it works great."

THE ROLE OF FINANCIAL COMPENSATION AT SNI

SNI also looked carefully at the role of financial compensation in attracting, retaining, and motivating a diverse workforce. Top executives determined that management skills should be weighed more heavily among the elements used to evaluate, promote, and compensate managers. "In the past," says Ray Gutierrez, "people were promoted to manager or vice president without management skills or experience." Changing this situation, SNI began to actively seek out and reward job candidates who demonstrated effective management skills. Now "managers' management skills are viewed as critical to the bottom-line performance of the company, as well as their business skills," says Gwen Marcus.

To determine pay levels, SNI uses what it calls a market-driven approach, leading to different compensation opportunities for different jobs. The company also analyzes the compensation offered by competing firms when considering where to set pay levels for new hires and current employees.

Under its formal appraisal system, SNI evaluates performance, in part, based on the results of upward feedback and, in some cases, 360-degree feedback. In addition, the company conducts climate surveys asking employees how they prefer to be managed, using this input to shape management decisions and policies.

All SNI employees receive annual merit reviews. Some employees are also eligible for a short-term incentive program for achieving specific goals; spot bonuses for particular achievements; team-oriented process rewards; and long-term incentives such as stock options. The parent company, Viacom, presents the Chairman's Award, which recognizes outstanding employees who have been nominated by their managers. Other SNI awards include the "Unsung Hero" award; tenure awards; and team-based merit performance awards, in which the level of the raise (not the amount) is determined by the employee's own team.

This combination of financial and nonfinancial compensation has allowed SNI to support diversity, and in turn, its business goals. Concludes Nat Fuchs, VP of Human Resource Development: "Diversity has filtered down through the company. We now talk about diversity of styles, of sales ability, customers, etc. We don't have a lock-step process, but one driven by business imperatives."

QUESTIONS

1. Should SNI substitute nonfinancial compensation programs such as AWA for financial compensation programs such as pay for performance? Discuss.

2. Would SNI want to penalize managers whose management skills were less developed than their business skills—and if so, why? Explain your answer.

Source: This case was prepared by Prof. dt ogilvie, Rutgers University, for purposes of class discussion, based on interviews and materials provided by Showtime Networks Inc.

INTEGRATIVE VIDEO CASE

This is the sixth case in this book that explores a variety of management-related issues at Showtime Networks Inc., a premium television network company. The first installment is a general introduction. You may want to refer to it when you are studying the case that follows.

Part Six—Safety and Health

HELPING SNI EMPLOYEES HELP THEMSELVES

SNI's success in the cable television industry depends on the best efforts of its workforce. However, employees who are injured or struggling with severe personal problems will not be able to concentrate on job performance. This is why managers at all levels within SNI take a proactive approach to creating a safe and healthy work environment. In particular, stress management has become a critical issue for organizations and individuals. More than ever before, employees are feeling the pressure of work and family obligations—and they need help in restoring a healthy balance to their lives.

The employee assistance program (EAP) at SNI provides resources for employees dealing with a wide range of problems. In addition to stress management, EAP personnel can help with marital or family difficulties, job performance problems, emotional or mental health issues, financial troubles, alcohol and drug abuse, and bereavement.

"Our employee assistance program is designed to help our employees deal with problems they believe cannot be handled on their own," explains Ray Gutierrez, Senior Vice President of Human Resources and Administration. "A worker with a problem cannot be as effective as he or she would normally be. If we can offer assistance with personal difficulties, we are not only helping the individual, we are also ensuring that productivity at Showtime is maintained."

AVOIDING COMPUTER-RELATED INJURIES AT SNI

SNI executives are always alert for the early warning signals of potential problems. For example, computer technology is indispensable in today's workplace. However, employees who work almost constantly at their computer keyboards may risk developing carpal tunnel syndrome, a condition caused by repetitive flexing and extension of the wrist. This condition pinches a nerve in the wrist, resulting in the inability to differentiate hot and cold by touch and the loss of muscle strength.

Ray Gutierrez began looking into carpal tunnel syndrome before he joined SNI, after reading a study suggesting that this condition was the second most common injury leading to workers' compensation claims. He discovered that carpal tunnel syndrome injuries—described as the "plague of the information age"—were among the most expensive workers' compensation claims, even more costly than job-related claims from injuries due to sprains, strains and fractures. His research revealed that the typical cost of carpal tunnel surgery was approximately $18,000.

Gutierrez checked with SNI employees about the incidence of carpal tunnel syndrome among company employees. He learned that there were some problems, although the number of complaints was low. To help reduce the possibility of carpal tunnel syndrome injuries at SNI, he consulted experts about ergonomically-correct work stations for data entry specialists and other employees whose job duties kept them at the keyboard for lengthy periods.

Learning that ergonomic keyboards were readily available for installation, Gutierrez quickly offered to provide one for any employee who was interested in switching from the traditional keyboard. However, rather than mandate the use of the new keyboards, he offered them as an option; in the end, most employees chose to keep their current equipment.

Even before the new keyboards were installed, one employee began complaining of the type of pain typically associated with carpal tunnel syndrome. Gutierrez immediately arranged for the employee to receive treatment, stressing that the company was willing to make any needed accommodations to facilitate her care and recovery. This kind of response is a powerful demonstration of how much employees are valued at SNI. Gutierrez sums up the company's commitment this way: "We will do whatever we can to make Showtime a good and safe place to work."

QUESTIONS

1. Do you agree that companies such as Showtime should have an employee assistance program to help employees deal with their personal problems? Why or why not?

2. Is Ray Gutierrez's concern over carpal tunnel syndrome really justified? Do you think he should have mandated the use of ergonomic keyboards to help employees avoid carpal tunnel syndrome? Defend your answers.

Source: This case was prepared by Prof. dt ogilvie, Rutgers University, for purposes of class discussion, based on interviews and materials provided by Showtime Networks Inc.

INTEGRATIVE VIDEO CASE

This is the seventh case in this book that explores a variety of management-related issues at Showtime Networks Inc., a premium television network company. The first installment is a general introduction. You may want to refer to it when you are studying the case that follows.

Part Seven—Employee and Labor Relations

EMPLOYEE-MANAGEMENT RELATIONS AT SNI

Relations between employees and management at SNI have traditionally been good. Even so, company officials remain alert to internal and external events that might signal a change. Ray Gutierrez, Senior Vice President of Human Resources and Administration, recently considered the company's situation and listed many of the reasons that make SNI a good place for employees to work, including:

Open-door policy. SNI is known for its open, employee-friendly attitude. "If employees have a problem, they can usually resolve it by working with their supervisors," explains Gutierrez. "If this doesn't work, employees are free to take their concerns to a higher management level. Sometimes supervisors do not like the idea that their employees can go to a higher level in the organization with a problem, but the system works well at Showtime. Overall, I believe most managers are comfortable with our open-door policy."

Employee trust. "Our employees believe that we are looking out for the best interests of everyone at Showtime," Gutierrez says. "When trust exists, employees do not go about trying to discover the *real* reason for a decision. They believe that management is doing the proper thing to help Showtime accomplish its objectives. You do not develop such trust overnight." And one bad incident can virtually destroy a bond of trust that has taken years to develop.

Family attitude. Despite continued growth, SNI maintains a corporate environment in which each person is treated with respect and seen as an individual rather than as a number. Managers and employees alike feel they are an integral part of the SNI family. Still, no family is perfect. Gutierrez points out that the family attitude "does not mean that we won't have problems; at times, every family does. However, we believe in treating employees fairly because that is the right thing to do."

Effective, equitable compensation programs. Compensation can significantly affect employee-management relations. "Our goal is to pay above the market rate and to ensure that compensation is fair," Gutierrez says. "We pay for performance, and we also have merit pay. One of the worst situations that can exist is for an outstanding worker to be paid the same amount as a marginal employee."

Upward feedback. Employees have the opportunity to evaluate their managers at SNI. With this system, "any problems can be resolved before they are blown out of proportion," observes Gutierrez. "It makes managers work a little harder to be fair to all employees."

Communications advisory board. Employees from all levels and all departments are represented on this board, which meets regularly to discuss matters of concern. Through this board, SNI allows direct access to the chairman and promotes open discussion of key issues. Moreover, the operation of this board also "sets an example for all managers," says Gutierrez. "The management group takes their lead from the chairman."

Alternative work arrangements. "We attempt to accommodate the needs of our employees so that they can achieve their greatest productivity," the SNI executive says. "Without flexible work arrangements, I am confident that we would not have been able to keep some of our most productive employees. Alternative work arrangements let our employees know that we are truly interested in them as individuals."

Employee Assistance Program (EAP). The EAP has helped any number of SNI employees through some extremely difficult periods. Whether employees are dealing with stress, family crises, job performance problems, or bereavement, having an EAP is tangible proof "that we really care about them," says Gutierrez.

Looking over his list, Gutierrez saw many positive features that help keep SNI's workforce satisfied. Yet he also knew that maintaining a good relationship between management and the workforce is an ongoing process that must be constantly monitored and refined.

QUESTIONS

1. How do SNI's open-door policy and communications advisory board encourage more effective communication between managers and employees?
2. How could SNI use its exit interviews to identify additional issues of concern to be addressed through appropriate employee relations programs?

Source: This case was prepared by Prof. dt ogilvie, Rutgers University, for purposes of class discussion, based on interviews and materials provided by Showtime Networks Inc.

INTEGRATIVE VIDEO CASE

This is the eighth case in this book that explores a variety of management-related issues at Showtime Networks Inc., a premium television network company. The first installment is a general introduction. You may want to refer to it when you are studying the case that follows.

Part Eight—Operating in a Global Environment

SNI'S GLOBAL DILEMMA

The battle for success in the premium television business is not confined to the United States. SNI is also going after subscribers and revenue from the international marketplace, including Europe and Asia. However, because size is constrained overseas, and there are considerable political risks associated with entering many overseas markets, SNI does not expect to have an extremely significant global presence.

In light of these concerns, SNI has chosen to expand globally by forging partnerships with other companies. For example, Viacom holds a 25 percent stake in HBO Asia, and SNI works through MTV (owned by Viacom, SNI's parent company) in certain markets. Another way that SNI achieves global distribution for selected events—such as boxing matches—is by selling the rights to other companies.

To spearhead SNI's global strategy, Matt Blank brought in Judy Pless as Vice President of International Business Development in 1995. Pless came to SNI from Viacom Worldwide, where she was Vice President of Marketing and New Media Development in the international arena. She had served as National Accounts Manager for HBO earlier in her career, so she was very familiar with the environment and the competitive situation within the premium cable industry. After Pless's promotion to SNI's Senior Vice President of Business Development in 1997, she became responsible for enhancing the company's U.S. and global business opportunities as well as negotiating alliances between SNI and its international partners.

One of the business issues confronting Pless is the complexity of arranging programming for a global audience. "Rights [to programs] are bought separately for each country, even in Europe," she explains. This prevents SNI from offering programming suited to a broad multinational audience; instead, it must handle programming differently for each country. Given these market differences, Pless carefully analyzes potential revenues and profits before making a decision about SNI's international activities.

GLOBAL HUMAN RESOURCE MANAGEMENT AT SNI

How does SNI's international strategy affect its human resource management planning and processes? Ray Gutierrez, Senior Vice President of Human Resources and Administration says:

> To date, SNI's forays into international channel development remain fairly limited. However, should SNI elect to pursue a more active global strategy in

the future, it would look to parent company Viacom to assist with its human resource management development. Already a global powerhouse with its MTV and Nickelodeon brands, Viacom has well-developed international HR policies, procedures, and expertise, upon which SNI could draw. Taking the lead from Viacom's experience would be a great help to SNI in the global marketplace.

Bill Roskin, Senior Vice President for Human Resources at Viacom, suggests that the MTV and Nickelodeon experiences have indeed been educational as well as very successful. His advice to SNI, as it builds relationships abroad and ventures into the global market, would be to identify and address these five critical factors:

Diverse political and legal systems. "The nature and stability of political and legal systems vary throughout the globe," he states. "Also, HR regulations and laws vary greatly from country to country." This is clearly an important factor for SNI management to consider in the course of entering new international markets.

Cultural differences. Differences in culture often lead to differences in HR practices, even among countries that are close-knit economically, such as those in the European Community. To be effective, SNI personnel who are stationed in other countries must understand and respect the cultural differences.

Economic differences. Before entering a new market, SNI thoroughly investigates the impact of that country's economic factors on HR policies and practices. For example, says Roskin, "We must ensure that those who are sent on global assignments maintain a satisfactory standard of living."

Employee relations. The nature of the relationship between employees and employers can vary dramatically from country to country, says the SNI executive. In turn, these differences can have an enormous impact on the development and implementation of HR management policies and practices.

Language differences. Even countries that share a common border often have a different primary language. "We have to ensure that anyone who is sent to any country has a basic understanding of the language," stresses Roskin.

These five factors can complicate the global expansion strategies of even the most experienced multinational firms—which is why SNI plans carefully for each factor, step by step, as it moves forward in exploring an international market for subscription television.

QUESTIONS

1. Can SNI use exactly the same HR policy manual in every country where English is the primary language? Explain your answer.

2. Do you agree with Roskin's assessment of the factors affecting global HRM? Are there additional factors that should be considered? Discuss.

Source: This case was prepared by Prof. dt ogilvie, Rutgers University, for purposes of class discussion, based on interviews and materials provided by Showtime Networks Inc.

Glossary

Adverse impact: A concept established by the *Uniform Guidelines;* it occurs if women and minorities are not hired at the rate of at least 80 percent of the best-achieving group.

Advertising: A way of communicating the firm's employment needs to the public through media such as radio, newspaper, or industry publications.

Affirmative action: Stipulated by Executive Order 11246, it requires employers to take positive steps to ensure employment of applicants and treatment of employees during employment without regard to race, creed, color, or national origin.

Affirmative action program (AAP): A program that an organization develops to employ women and minorities in proportion to their representation in the firm's relevant labor market.

Agency shop: A labor agreement provision requiring, as a condition of employment, that each nonunion member of a bargaining unit pay the union the equivalent of membership dues as a service charge in return for the union acting as the bargaining agent.

AIDS (acquired immune deficiency syndrome): A disease that undermines the body's immune system, leaving the person susceptible to a wide range of fatal diseases.

Alcoholism: A treatable disease characterized by uncontrolled and compulsive drinking that interferes with normal living patterns.

Alternative dispute resolution (ADR): A procedure agreed to ahead of time by the employee and the company for resolving any problems that may arise.

Apprenticeship training: A combination of classroom instruction and on-the-job training.

Arbitration: A process in which a dispute is submitted to an impartial third party for a binding decision.

Assessment center: An employee selection or appraisal approach that requires individuals to perform activities similar to those they might encounter in an actual job.

Authorization card: A document indicating that an employee wants to be represented by a labor organization in collective bargaining.

Availability forecast: A process of determining whether a firm will be able to secure employees with the necessary skills from within the company, from outside the organization, or from a combination of the two sources.

Bargaining unit: A group of employees, not necessarily union members, recognized by an employer or certified by an administrative agency as appropriate for representation by a labor organization for purposes of collective bargaining.

Beachhead demands: Demands that the union does not expect management to meet when they are first made.

Behavior description interview: A structured interview that uses questions designed to probe an applicant's past behavior in specific situations.

Behavior modeling: A training method that utilizes videotapes to illustrate effective interpersonal skills and the ways managers function in various situations.

Behaviorally anchored rating scale (BARS) method: A performance appraisal method that combines elements of the traditional rating scale and critical incidents methods.

Benchmark job: A well-known job, in which a large percentage of a company's workforce is employed, that represents the entire job structure.

Benefits: All financial rewards that generally are not paid directly to an employee.

Biofeedback: A method of learning to control involuntary bodily processes, such as blood pressure or heart rate.

Board interview: A meeting in which one candidate is interviewed by several representatives of a company.

Bonus (lump-sum payment): A one-time award that is not added to employees' base pay.

Bottom-up approach: A forecasting method beginning with the lowest organizational units and progressing upward through an organization ultimately to provide an aggregate forecast of employment needs.

Boycott: Refusal by union members to use or buy their firm's products.

Broadbanding: A compensation technique that collapses many pay grades (salary grades) into a few wide bands in order to improve organizational effectiveness.

Burnout: A gradual wearing down, a depletion of one's physical and mental resources that results from stress that is not necessarily job-related.

Business games: Simulations that represent actual business situations.

Business-level strategic planning: The planning process concerned primarily with how to manage the interests and operations of a particular business.

Capitation: An approach to health care in which providers negotiate a rate for health care for a covered life over a period of time.

Career: A general course of action a person chooses to pursue throughout his or her working life.

Career development: A formal approach taken by an organization to ensure that people with the proper qualifications and experience are available when needed.

Career developmental tools: Consist of skills, education, experiences as well as behavioral modification and refinement techniques that allow individuals to work better and add value.

Career path: A flexible line of progression through which an employee may move during his or her employment with a company.

Career planning: An ongoing process through which an individual sets career goals and identifies the means to achieve them.

Career security: The development of marketable skills and expertise that helps ensure employment within a range of careers.

Carpal tunnel syndrome: A condition caused by repetitive flexing and extension of the wrist.

Case study: A training method that presents simulated business problems for trainees to solve.

Central tendency: A common error in performance appraisal that occurs when employees are incorrectly rated near the average or middle of a scale.

Checkoff of dues: An agreement by which a company agrees to withhold union dues from members' paychecks and to forward the money directly to the union.

Classification method: A job evaluation method in which classes or grades are defined to describe a group of jobs.

Closed shop: An arrangement making union membership a prerequisite to employment.

Coaching: An on-the-job approach in which a manager has the opportunity to teach an employee on a one-to-one basis.

Cognitive aptitude tests: Tests that measure an individual's ability to learn as well as to perform a job.

Collective bargaining: The performance of the mutual obligation of the employer and the representative of the employees to meet at reasonable times and confer in good faith with respect to wages, hours, and other terms and conditions of employment, or the negotiation of an agreement, or any question arising thereunder, and the execution of a written contract incorporating any agreement reached if requested by either party; such obligation does not compel either party to agree to a proposal or require the making of a concession.

Comparable worth: A determination of the values of dissimilar jobs (such as company nurse and welder) by comparing them under some form of job evaluation, and the assignment of pay rates according to their evaluated worth.

Compensation: The total of all rewards provided employees in return for their labor.

Compensation survey: A means of obtaining data regarding what other firms are paying for specific jobs or job classes within a given labor market.

Competency-based pay: A compensation plan that rewards employees for their demonstrated expertise.

Compressed work week: Any arrangement of work hours that permits employees to fulfill their work obligation in fewer days than the typical five-day work week.

Computer-based training: A teaching method that takes advantage of the speed, memory, and data manipulation capabilities of the computer for greater flexibility of instruction.

Concurrent validity: A validation method in which test scores and criterion data are obtained at essentially the same time.

Conspiracy: The combination of two or more persons who band together to prejudice the rights of others or of society (such as by refusing to work or demanding higher wages).

Construct validity: A test validation method to determine whether a selection test measures certain traits or qualities that have been identified as important in performing a particular job.

Content validity: A test validation method in which a person performs certain tasks that are actual samples of the kind of work a job requires or completes a paper-and-pencil test that measures relevant job knowledge.

Corporate culture: The system of shared values, beliefs, and habits within an organization that interacts with the formal structure to produce behavioral norms.

Corporate-level strategic planning: The process of defining the overall character and purpose of the organization, the businesses it will enter and leave, and the way resources will be distributed among those businesses.

Cost-of-living allowance (COLA): An escalator clause in a labor agreement that automatically increases wages as the U.S. Bureau of Labor Statistics' cost-of-living index rises.

Craft union: A bargaining unit, such as the Carpenters and Joiners union, that is typically composed of members of a particular trade or skill in a specific locality.

Criterion-related validity: A test validation method that compares the scores on selection tests to some aspect of job performance as determined—for example, by performance appraisal.

Critical incident method: A performance appraisal technique that requires a written record of highly favorable and highly unfavorable employee work behavior.

Cumulative trauma disorders: A series of disorders, often associated with using computers, that include injuries to the back and upper extremities.

Cutoff score: The score below which an applicant will not be considered further for employment.

Decertification: Election by a group of employees to withdraw a union's right to act as their exclusive bargaining representative.

Defined benefit plan: A retirement plan in which an employer agrees to provide a specific level of retirement income that is either a fixed dollar amount or a percentage of earnings.

Defined contribution plan: A retirement plan that requires specific contributions by an employer.

Demotion: The process of moving a worker to a lower level of duties and responsibilities; typically involves a pay cut.

Development: Learning that looks beyond the knowledge and skill needed for a present job.

Direct financial compensation: Pay that a person receives in the form of wages, salary, bonuses, and commissions.

Disciplinary action: The invoking of a penalty against an employee who fails to meet organizational standards or comply with organizational rules.

Disciplinary action without punishment: A process in which a worker is given time off with pay to think about whether he or she wants to follow the rules and continue working for a company.

Discipline: The state of employee self-control and orderly conduct.

Diversity: Any perceived difference among people: age, functional specialty, profession, sexual orientation, geographic origin, lifestyle, tenure with the organization, or position.

Domestic violence: Violence within a family that generally occurs away from the workplace but has a negative impact on the organization.

Downsizing: A reduction in the number of people employed by a firm (also known as *restructuring* and *rightsizing*).

Dual-career family: A family in which both husband and wife have jobs and family responsibilities.

Dual career path: A method of rewarding technical specialists and professionals who can, and should be allowed to, continue to contribute significantly to a company without having to become managers.

Employee assistance program (EAP): A comprehensive approach that many organizations have taken to deal with burnout, alcohol and drug abuse, and other emotional disturbances.

Employee equity: A condition that exists when individuals performing similar jobs for the same firm are paid according to factors unique to the employee, such as performance level or seniority.

Employee requisition: A document that specifies a particular job title, the appropriate department, and the date by which an open job should be filled.

Employee stock ownership plan (ESOP): A companywide incentive plan in which the company provides its employees with common stock.

Employment agency: An organization that assists firms in recruiting employees and also aids individuals in their attempts to locate jobs.

Employment at will: An unwritten contract that is created when an employee agrees to work for an employer but includes no agreement as to how long the parties expect the employment to last.

Employment interview: A goal-oriented conversation in which an interviewer and an applicant exchange information.

Equity: The perception by workers that they are being treated fairly.

Ergonomics: The study of human interaction with tasks, equipment, tools, and the physical work environment.

Essay method: A performance appraisal method in which the rater writes a brief narrative describing an employee's performance.

Ethics: The discipline dealing with what is good and bad, or right and wrong, or with moral duty and obligation.

Exclusive provider organization (EPO): A managed care option that offers a smaller preferred provider network and usually provides few, if any, benefits when an out-of-network provider is used.

Executive: A top-level manager who reports directly to a corporation's chief executive officer or the head of a major division.

Executive orders (EO): Directives issued by the president that have the force and effect of laws enacted by the Congress.

Executive search firms: Organizations retained by a company to search for the most qualified executive available for a specific position.

Exempt employees: Those categorized as executive, administrative, or professional employees and outside salespersons.

Expatriate: An employee working in a firm who is not a citizen of the country in which the firm is located but is a citizen of the country in which the organization is headquartered.

Experiment: A method of inquiry that involves the manipulation of certain variables while others are held constant.

Expert system: A system that uses knowledge about a narrowly defined, complex area to act as a consultant to a human.

Exporting: Selling abroad, either directly or indirectly, by retaining foreign agents and distributors.

External environment: The factors that affect a firm's human resources from outside the organization's boundaries.

External equity: Payment of employees at rates comparable to those paid for similar jobs elsewhere.

Factor comparison method: A job evaluation method in which raters (1) need not keep an entire job in mind as they evaluate it and (2) make decisions based on the assumption that there are five universal job factors.

Flexible compensation plans: A method that permits employees to choose from among many alternatives in deciding how their financial compensation will be allocated.

Flextime: The practice of permitting employees to choose, with certain limitations, their own working hours.

Forced-choice performance report: A performance appraisal technique in which the rater is given a series of statements about an individual and indicates which items are most or least descriptive of the employee.

Forced distribution method: An appraisal approach in which the rater is required to assign individuals in a work group to a limited number of categories similar to a normal frequency distribution.

401(k) plan: A defined contribution retirement plan in which employees may defer income up to a certain maximum amount.

Franchising: A multinational option whereby the parent company grants another firm the right to do business in a prescribed manner.

Functional Job Analysis (FJA): A comprehensive approach to formulating job descriptions that concentrates on the interactions among the work, the worker, and the work organization.

Functional-level strategic planning: The process of determining policies and procedures for relatively narrow areas of activity that are critical to the success of the organization.

Generalist: A person who perform tasks in a wide variety of human resource-related areas.

Genetic testing: An approach that can show whether a person carries the gene mutation for certain diseases.

Glass ceiling: The invisible barrier in organizations that prevents many women and minorities from achieving top-level management positions.

Global corporation: An organization that has corporate units in a number of countries; the units are integrated to operate as one organization worldwide.

Global human resource management (GHRM): The use of global human resources to achieve organizational objectives without regard to geographic boundaries.

"Golden parachute" contract: A perquisite provided for the purpose of protecting executives in the event their firm is acquired by another.

Grievance: An employee's dissatisfaction or feeling of personal injustice relating to his or her employment.

Grievance procedure: A formal, systematic process that permits employees to complain about matters affecting them and their work.

Group interview: A meeting in which several job applicants interact in the presence of one or more company representatives.

Guidelines-Oriented Job Analysis (GOJA): A method that responds to the growing amount of legislation affecting employment decisions by utilizing a step-by-step procedure to describe the work of a particular job classification.

Halo error: The perception by an evaluator that one factor is of paramount importance and then gives a good or bad overall rating to an employee based on this particular factor.

Hay Guide Chart-Profile Method (Hay Plan): A highly refined version of the point method of job evaluation that uses the factors of know-how, problem solving, accountability, and additional compensable elements.

Hazard pay: Additional pay provided to employees who work under extremely dangerous conditions.

Health: An employee's freedom from physical or emotional illness.

Health maintenance organizations (HMOs): Insurance programs provided by companies that cover all services for a fixed fee with control being exercised over which doctors and health facilities may be used.

Host-country national (HCN): An employee working in a firm who is a citizen of the country in which the firm is located whereas the firm is operated by an organization headquartered in another country.

Human resource information system (HRIS): Any organized approach to obtaining relevant and timely information on which to base human resource decisions.

Human resource management (HRM): The utilization of a firm's human resources to achieve organizational objectives.

Human resource managers: Individuals who normally act in an advisory (or staff) capacity when working with other (line) managers regarding human resource matters.

Human resource planning (HRP): The process of systematically reviewing human resource requirements to ensure that the required number of employees, with the required skills, are available when they are needed.

Hypnosis: An altered state of consciousness that is artificially induced and characterized by increased receptiveness to suggestions.

In-basket training: A simulation in which the participant is asked to establish priorities for and then handle a number of business papers, such as memoranda, reports, and telephone messages, that would typically cross a manager's desk.

Incentive compensation: A payment program that relates pay to productivity.

Indirect financial compensation: All financial rewards that are not included in direct compensation.

Industrial union: A bargaining unit that generally consist of all the workers in a particular plant or group of plants.

Injunction: A prohibiting legal procedure used by employers to prevent certain union activities, such as strikes and unionization attempts.

Internal employee relations: Those human resource management activities associated with promotion, transfer, demotion, resignation, discharge, layoffs, and retirement.

Internal equity: Payment of employees according to the relative values of their jobs within an organization.

Internship: A special form of recruitment that involves placing students in temporary jobs with no obligation either by the company to hire the student permanently or by the student to accept a permanent position with the firm following graduation.

Intranets: Proprietary electronic networks that permit delivery of programs that have been developed specifically for an organization's particular learning needs.

Job: A group of tasks that must be performed if an organization is to achieve its goals.

Job analysis: The systematic process of determining the skills, duties, and knowledge required for performing specific jobs in an organization.

Job Analysis Schedule (JAS): A systematic method of studying jobs and occupations; developed by the U.S. Department of Labor.

Job bidding: A technique that permits individuals in an organization who believe that they possess the required qualifications to apply for a posted job.

Job description: A document that provides information regarding the tasks, duties, and responsibilities of a job.

Job design: A process of determining the specific tasks to be performed, the methods used in performing these tasks, and how the job relates to other work in an organization.

Job enlargement: A change in the scope of a job so as to provide greater variety to a worker.

Job enrichment: The restructuring of the content and level of responsibility of a job to make it more challenging, meaningful, and interesting to a worker.

Job evaluation: That part of a compensation system in which a company determines the relative value of one job in relation to another.

Job knowledge questions: Questions that probe the knowledge a person possesses for performing a particular job.

Job knowledge tests: Tests designed to measure a candidate's knowledge of the duties of a job for which he or she is applying.

Job overload: A condition that exists when employees are given more work than they can reasonably handle.

Job posting: A procedure for communicating to company employees the fact that a job opening exists.

Job pricing: Placing a dollar value on the worth of a job.

Job rotation: A training method that involves moving employees from one job to another to broaden their experience.

Job-sample simulation questions: Situations in which an applicant may be required to actually perform a sample task from a particular job.

Job sharing: The filling of a job by two part-time people who split the duties of one full-time job in some agreed-on manner and are paid according to their contributions.

Job specification: A document that outlines the minimum acceptable qualifications a person should possess to perform a particular job.

Job Training Partnership Act (JTPA): A federal law that provides job training and employment services for economically disadvantaged adults and youth, dislocated workers, and other persons who face exceptional employment hurdles.

Labor market: The geographical area from which employees are recruited for a particular job.

Lateral skill path: A career path that allows for lateral moves within the firm; these permit an employee to become revitalized and find new challenges.

Learning organizations: Firms that recognize the critical importance of continuous performance-related training and development and take appropriate action.

Leniency: Giving undeserved high performance appraisal rating to an employee.

Licensing: A global arrangement whereby an organization grants a foreign firm the right to use intellectual properties such as patents, copyrights, manufacturing processes, or trade names for a specific period of time.

Likes and dislikes survey: A procedure that helps individuals recognize restrictions they place on themselves.

Local union: The basic element in the structure of the U.S. labor movement.

Lockout: A management decision to keep employees out of the workplace and to operate with management personnel and/or temporary replacements.

Management by objectives (MBO): A philosophy of management that emphasizes the setting of agreed-on objectives by superior and subordinate managers and the use of these objectives as the primary basis of motivation, evaluation, and self-control.

Management development: Learning experiences provided by an organization for the purpose of upgrading skills and knowledge required in current and future managerial positions.

Management inventory: Detailed data regarding each manager in an organization; used in identifying individuals possessing the potential to move into higher level positions.

Management Position Description Questionnaire (MPDQ): A form of job analysis designed for management positions that uses a checklist method to analyze jobs.

Mandatory bargaining issues: Bargaining issues that fall within the definition of wages, hours, and other terms and conditions of employment; refusal to bargain in these areas is grounds for an unfair labor practice charge.

Market (going) rate: The average pay that most employers provide for the same job in a particular area or industry.

Mediation: A process in which a neutral third party enters and attempts to resolve a labor dispute when a bargaining impasse has occurred.

Mentoring: An on-the-job approach to training and development in which the trainee is given an opportunity to learn on a one-to-one basis from more experienced organizational members.

Merit pay: Pay increase given to employees based on their level of performance as indicated in the appraisal.

Modified retirement: An option that permits older employees to work fewer than regular hours for a certain period of time preceding retirement.

Multimedia: A computer application that enhances learning through presentations combining automation, stereo sound, full-motion video, and graphics.

Multinational corporation (MNC): An organization that conducts a large part of its business outside the country in which it is headquartered and has a significant percentage of its physical facilities and employees in other countries.

National union: An organization composed of local unions, which it charters.

Network career path: A method of job progression that contains both vertical and horizontal opportunities.

New-collar workers: Younger, well-educated, independent workers, who appear to be particularly sensitive to issues related to job security.

Nonfinancial compensation: The satisfaction that a person receives from the job itself or from the psychological and/or physical environment in which the job is performed.

Norm: A distribution that provides a frame of reference for comparing an applicant's performance with that of others.

Objectivity: The condition that is achieved when all

individuals scoring a given test obtain the same results.

Ombudsperson: A complaint officer with access to top management who hears employees' complaints, investigates them, and sometimes recommends appropriate action.

On-the-job training (OJT): An informal approach to training in which an employee learns job tasks by actually performing them.

Open-door policy: A company policy allowing employees the right to take any grievance to the person next in the chain of command if a satisfactory solution cannot be obtained from their immediate supervisor.

Open shop: Employment that is open on equal terms to union members and nonmembers alike.

Operative employees: All workers in a firm except managers and professionals such as engineers, accountants, or professional secretaries.

Organization development (OD): An organization-wide application of behavioral science knowledge to the planned development and reinforcement of a firm's strategies, structures, and processes for improving its effectiveness.

Organizational career planning: The process of establishing career paths within a firm.

Orientation: The guided adjustment of new employees to the company, the job, and the work group.

Outplacement: A company procedure that assists a laid-off employee in finding employment elsewhere.

Outsourcing: The process of transferring responsibility for an area of service and its objectives to an external provider.

Paired comparison: A variation of the ranking method of performance appraisal in which the performance of each employee is compared with that of every other employee in the particular group.

Pay compression: A situation that occurs when workers perceive that the pay differential between their pay and that of employees in jobs above or below them is too small.

Pay followers: Companies that choose to pay below the going rate because of a poor financial condition or a belief that they simply do not require highly capable employees.

Pay grade: Similar jobs grouped to simplify the job-pricing process.

Pay leaders: Organizations that pay higher wages and salaries than competing firms.

Pay range: A minimum and maximum pay rate for a job, with enough variance between the two to allow for some significant pay difference.

Performance appraisal (PA): A formal system of periodic review and evaluation of an individual's job performance.

Performance management: A process which significantly affects organizational success by having managers and employees work together to set expectations, review results, and reward performance.

Permissive bargaining issues: Issues that may be raised by management or a union; neither side may insist that they be bargained over.

Perquisites (perks): Special benefits provided by a firm to key executives to give them something extra.

Piecework: An incentive pay plan in which employees are paid for each unit produced.

Plateauing: A career condition that occurs when an employee's job functions and work content remain the same because of a lack of promotional opportunities within a company.

Point-of-service (POS): A managed care option that permits a member to select a health care provider within the network, or, for a lower level of benefits, choose one outside the network.

Point method: An approach to job evaluation in which numerical values are assigned to specific job components and the sum of these values provides a quantitative assessment of a job's relative worth.

Position: The tasks and responsibilities performed by one person; there is a position for every individual in an organization.

Position Analysis Questionnaire (PAQ): A structured job analysis questionnaire that uses a checklist approach to identify job elements.

Predictive validity: A validation method that involves administering a selection test and later obtaining the criterion information.

Predictor variables: Factors known to have an impact on a company's employment levels.

Preferred provider organizations (PPOs): A flexible managed care system in which incentives are provided to members to use services within the system; out-of-network providers may be utilized at greater cost.

Premium pay: Compensation paid to employees for working long periods of time or working under dangerous or undesirable conditions.

Private employment agencies: Agencies utilized by firms for virtually every type of position; best known for recruiting white-collar employees.

Proactive response: Taking action in anticipation of environmental changes.

Profession: A vocation whose practitioners share and use a common body of knowledge and recognize a procedure for certifying the practitioners.

Profit sharing: A compensation plan that distributes a predetermined percentage of a firm's profits to its employees.

Programmed instruction (PI): A teaching method that provides instruction without the intervention of an instructor.

Progressive disciplinary action: An approach to disciplinary action designed to ensure that the minimum penalty appropriate to the offense is imposed.

Prohibited bargaining issues: Issues that are statutorily outlawed from collective bargaining.

Promotion: The movement of a person to a higher level position in an organization.

Promotion from within (PFW): The policy of filling vacancies above entry-level positions with employees presently employed by a company.

Psychomotor abilities tests: Aptitude tests that measure strength, coordination, and dexterity.

Public employment agencies: Employment agencies that are operated by each state but receive overall policy direction from the U.S. Employment Service; best known for recruiting and placing individuals in operative jobs.

Quality circles: Groups of employees who meet regularly with their supervisors to identify production problems and recommend solutions.

Ranking method: A job evaluation method in which the rater examines the description of each job being evaluated and arranges the jobs in order according to their value to the company; also a performance appraisal method in which the rater places all employees in a given group in rank order on the basis of their overall performance.

Rating-scales method: A widely used performance appraisal method that rates employees according to defined factors.

Reactive response: Simply reacting to environmental changes after they occur.

Realistic job preview (RJP): A method of conveying job information to an applicant in an unbiased manner, including both positive and negative factors.

Recruitment: The process of attracting individuals on a timely basis, in sufficient numbers and with appropriate qualifications, and encouraging them to apply for jobs with an organization.

Recruitment methods: The specific means by which potential employees are attracted to an organization.

Recruitment sources: Various locales in which qualified individuals are sought as potential employees.

Reengineering: The fundamental rethinking and radical redesign of business processes to achieve dramatic improvements in critical, contemporary measures of performance, such as cost, quality, service, and speed.

Reference checks: A way to gain additional insight into the information provided by an applicant and a way to verify the accuracy of the information provided.

Reliability: The extent to which a selection test provides consistent results.

Repatriation: The process of bringing expatriates home.

Requirements forecast: An estimate of the numbers and kinds of employees an organization will need at future dates to realize its stated objectives.

Resumé: A common method used by job seekers to present their qualifications.

Right-to-work laws: Laws that prohibit management and unions from entering into agreements requiring union membership as a condition of employment.

Role ambiguity: A condition that exists when employees lack clear information about the content of their jobs.

Role conflict: A condition that occurs when an individual is placed in the position of having to pursue opposing goals.

Role playing: A training method in which participants are required to respond to specific problems they may actually encounter in their jobs.

Safety: The protection of employees from injuries caused by work-related accidents.

Scanlon plan: A gain-sharing plan designed to bind employees to their firm's performance.

Secondary boycott: A union's attempt to encourage third parties (such as suppliers and customers) to stop doing business with a firm.

Selection: The process of choosing from a group of applicants those individuals best suited for a particular position and an organization.

Selection ratio: The number of people hired for a particular job compared to the total number of individuals in the applicant pool.

Self-assessment: The process of learning about oneself.

Sensitivity training: An organizational development technique that is designed to make people aware of themselves and their impact on others.

Severity rate: A formula that is used to calculate the number of days lost because of accidents per million person-hours worked.

Shareholders: The owners of a corporation.

Shared service centers (SSC): A central place where routine, transaction-based activities that are dispersed throughout the organization are consolidated.

Shift differentials: Additional money paid to reward employees for the inconvenience of working undesirable hours.

Simulation: A technique for experimenting with a real-world situation by means of a mathematical model that represents the actual situation.

Simulators: Training devices of varying degrees of complexity that duplicate the real world.

Situational questions: Questions that pose a hypothetical job situation to determine what the applicant would do in such a situation.

Skill-based pay: A system that compensates employees on the basis of job-related skills and the knowledge they possess.

Skills inventory: Information maintained on nonmanagerial employees in a company regarding their availability and preparedness to move either laterally or into higher level positions.

Social responsibility: The implied, enforced, or felt obligation of managers, acting in their official capacities, to serve or protect the interests of groups other than themselves.

Special events: A recruitment method that involves an effort on the part of a single employer or group of employers to attract a larger number of applicants for interviews.

Specialist: An individual who may be a human resource executive, a human resource manager, or a nonmanager, and who is typically concerned with only one of the five functional areas of human resource management.

Standardization: The degree of uniformity of the procedures and conditions related to administering tests.

Status symbols: Organizational rewards that take many forms such as office size and location, desk size and quality, private secretaries, floor covering, and title.

Stock option plan: An incentive plan in which managers can buy a specified amount of stock in their company in the future at or below the current market price.

Strategic business unit (SBU): Any part of a business organization that is treated separately for strategic planning purposes.

Strategic planning: The determination of overall organizational purposes and goals and how they are to be achieved.

Strength/weakness balance sheet: A self-evaluation procedure, developed originally by Benjamin Franklin, that helps people to become aware of their strengths and weaknesses.

Stress: The body's nonspecific reaction to any demand made on it.

Stress interview: A form of interview that intentionally creates anxiety to determine how a job applicant will react in certain types of situations.

Strictness: Being unduly critical of an employee's work performance.

Strike: An action by union members who refuse to work in order to exert pressure on management in negotiations.

Structured interview: A process in which an interviewer consistently presents the same series of job-related questions to each applicant for a particular job.

Succession development: The process of determining a comprehensive job profile of the key positions and then ensuring that key prospects are properly developed to match these qualifications.

Succession planning: The process of ensuring that a qualified person is available to assume a managerial position once the position is vacant.

Survey feedback: A survey method and research technique that systematically collects information about organizations and employee attitudes and makes the data available in aggregate form to employees and management so that problems can be diagnosed and plans developed to solve them.

Team building: A conscious effort to develop effective work groups throughout an organization.

Team equity: Paying more productive teams in an organization at a higher rate than less productive teams.

Telecommuting: A procedure allowing workers to remain at home or otherwise away from the office and perform their work over data lines tied to a computer.

Third-country national (TCN): A citizen of one country, working in a second country, and employed by an organization headquartered in a third country.

360-degree feedback: An increasingly popular appraisal method that involves input from multiple levels within the firm and external sources as well.

Total Quality Management (TQM): A top management philosophy that emphasizes the continuous improvement of the processes that result in goods or services.

Traditional career path: A vertical line of career progression from one specific job to the next.

Training: Activities designed to provide learners with the knowledge and skill needed for their present jobs.

Training and development: A planned, continuous effort by management to improve employee competency levels and organizational performance.

Transcendental meditation (TM): A stress-reduction technique in which an individual, comfortably seated, mentally repeats a secret word or phrase (mantra) provided by a trained instructor.

Transfer: The lateral movement of a worker within an organization.

Union: A group of employees who have joined together for the purpose of dealing collectively with their employer.

Union shop: A requirement that all employees become members of the union after a specified period of employment (the legal minimum is 30 days) or after a union shop provision has been negotiated.

Unstructured interview: A meeting with a job applicant during which the interviewer asks probing, open-ended questions.

Utilization review: A process that scrutinizes medical diagnoses, hospitalization, surgery, and other medical treatment and care prescribed by doctors.

Validity: The extent to which a test measures what it purports to measure.

Variable pay: Compensation based on performance.

Vestibule training: Training that takes place away from the production area on equipment that closely resembles the actual equipment used on the job.

Virtual job fair: A recruitment method in which students meet recruiters face-to-face in interviews conducted over special computers that have lenses that transmit head-and-shoulder images of both parties.

Vocational interest tests: A method of determining the occupation in which a person has the greatest interest and from which the person is most likely to receive satisfaction.

Wage curve: The fitting of plotted points on a curve to create a smooth progression between pay grades (also known as the *pay curve*).

Weighted checklist performance report: A performance appraisal technique in which the rater completes a form similar to a forced-choice performance report except that the various responses have been assigned different weights.

Work-sample tests: Tests requiring the identification of a task or set of tasks that are representative of a particular job.

Work standards method: A performance appraisal method that compares each employee's performance to a predetermined standard or expected level of output.

Worker requirements questions: Questions that seek to determine the applicant's willingness to conform to the requirements of a job.

Yellow-dog contract: A written agreement between an employee and a company made at the time of employment, prohibiting a worker from joining a union or engaging in union activities.

Zero-base forecasting: A method for estimating future employment needs using the organization's current level of employment as the starting point.

Name Index

Company Index

Subject Index

PHOTO CREDITS

Chapter 1 José L. Pelaez/The Stock Market

Chapter 2 Bruce Ayres/Tony Stone Images

Chapter 3 Bruce Ayres/Tony Stone Images

Chapter 4 Charles Thatcher/Tony Stone Images

Chapter 5 Frank Herholdt/Tony Stone Images

Chapter 6 Robert E. Daemmrich/Tony Stone Images

Chapter 7 Joseph Pobereskin/Tony Stone Images

Chapter 8 Michael Rosenfeld/Tony Stone Images

Chapter 9 Howard Grey/Tony Stone Images

Chapter 10 Bruce Ayres/Tony Stone Images

Chapter 11 Bruce Ayres/Tony Stone Images

Chapter 12 Courtesy of Pacific Gas & Electric Company

Chapter 13 Michael Newman/PhotoEdit

Chapter 14 Chris Pizzello/AP/Wide World Photos

Chapter 15 David H. Wells/The Image Works

Chapter 16 Bruce Ayres/Tony Stone Images

Chapter 17 Greg Davis/The Stock Market

Cover Barton Stabler/Stock Illustration Source

Companies highlighted in this edition include:

Adolph Coors Company • ALCOA Alliance Capital Management • Allied Signal, Inc. Allstate Corporation • America Online, Inc. AT&T Corporation • Ameritech Corporation Amoco Corporation • Andersen Consulting Anheuser-Busch Companies, Inc. • AT&T Global Business Communications Systems (GBCS) Avon Engineering • Bank of America • Bendix Corporation • Benji Electronics, Inc. • Boston's Beth Israel Hospital • Boundless Technologies BP Oil Company • Brown & Root, Inc. • Ceridian Corporation • The Chase Manhattan Corporation The Chemical Bank Corporation • Chevron Corporation • Chubb & Son • Citibank • Compaq Computer Corporation • Corning Incorporated Corporate Resources Group • Delta Air Lines, Inc. Detroit Edison Company •DFS Group Limited R.R. Donnelley & Sons Company • Donnelly Corporate Products • Dow Corning • Drake Beam Morin, Inc. • Eastman Chemical Company Fairchild Aircraft • Federal Express Corporation _Forbes_ Magazine • Ford Motor Company • Forklift Systems, Inc. • General Electric • General Motors Corporation • General Motors Corporation, Saturn Division • Georgia-Pacific Corporation Golden West Financial Corporation • W.L. Gore & Associates • Green Tree Financial Corporation Greyhound Lines, Inc. • Harley-Davidson Herman Miller, Inc. • Hewitt Associates

DATE DUE

APR 04 2006			

Demco, Inc. 38-293

DEMCO